Review Text in American History

(REVISED)

IRVING L. GORDON

When ordering this book, please specify:
either **R 47 P** or REVIEW TEXT IN AMERICAN HISTORY

AMSCO SCHOOL PUBLICATIONS, INC.
315 Hudson Street / New York, N.Y. 10013

Books by Irving L. Gordon

American History, Second Edition
Review Text in American History
World History, Second Edition

ISBN 0-87720-606-6

Revised 1996

PREFACE

In every generation, Americans have encountered and solved problems besetting the nation. Today, Americans must contend with both domestic and foreign problems of great urgency. They must determine our national goals and the appropriate means for moving toward these goals. Americans can gain perspective and guidance for this task through an understanding of our past and our national heritage.

High school students delve into these topics in their course in American history. There, they now face new interpretations, shifts in emphasis, and growing amounts of historical information. Consequently, they need a concise text that can be used by itself, as a supplement to a more elaborate text, or as a review book for examinations.

To meet this need, *Review Text in American History* offers the following features:

1. In addition to traditional topics, it deals with recent economic and social developments. It places considerable emphasis upon current problems, including urbanization, senior citizens, education, civil rights, poverty, and world leadership. It omits irrelevant data so as to focus attention upon significant developments and concepts.

2. The text draws upon the latest historical scholarship. It does not, however, neglect the traditional scholarship but seeks to present differing points of view fairly. This approach is meant to enrich the subject matter and to stimulate interest among students.

3. To facilitate understanding, every effort has been made to provide crisp and clear language. Nevertheless, the text conveys the complexity of our historical development. It is mature, not simplistic, and it is geared to the high school level.

4. The text contains much illustrative material. Maps relate geographic factors to historical events. Cartoons illuminate and comment upon current problems. Charts provide data for analyzing recent economic and social trends.

5. The book includes ample test material, consisting of a variety of short-answer and essay questions, arranged by topic and placed after the appropriate chapters. The questions probe significant information and measure the student's mastery of the content. Many questions require logical reasoning and mature understanding—major objectives of social studies teaching.

—I. L. G.

CONTENTS

UNIT I. A NEW WORLD IS FOUND AND A NEW NATION BORN

UNIT II. THE CONSTITUTION IS THE BASIS OF AMERICAN GOVERNMENT

UNIT III. THE YOUNG NATION TACKLES ITS MANY PROBLEMS

UNIT IV. THE NATION IS TORN BETWEEN NATIONALISM AND SECTIONALISM

UNIT V. THE UNITED STATES CHANGES FROM AN AGRICULTURAL TO AN INDUSTRIAL SOCIETY

UNIT VI. THE AMERICAN PEOPLE DEVELOP A DISTINCTIVE WAY OF LIFE

UNIT VII. POLITICAL DEVELOPMENTS MIRROR A CHANGING AND COMPLEX AMERICA

UNIT I. A NEW WORLD IS FOUND AND A NEW NATION BORN

Part 1. Developments in the Old World Lead to the Discovery of America

The discovery of America was the result of a series of Old World developments, namely the Crusades, the Renaissance, and the rise of absolute monarchs ruling national states.

CRUSADES (1095–1291)

1. Brief History. In 1095 Pope Urban II summoned western Christendom to wrest the Holy Land, Palestine, from the Moslem Turks by undertaking a military expedition, the first *Crusade*. Over a period of almost 200 years, western Europe launched seven major Crusades, during which thousands of Crusaders reached the Middle East and came in contact with the advanced Moslem and Byzantine civilizations. Despite some temporary successes, the Crusades failed to establish permanent Christian rule in Palestine.

2. Results of the Crusades. The significance of the Crusades lies in the great changes they wrought in western European life, notably the revival of trade. The Crusades aroused European demand for Eastern products: spices, sugar, silk, rugs, paper, glassware, steel, and precious stones. This profitable trade became the monopoly of (*a*) Asian middlemen, who brought Eastern goods by overland caravan to eastern Mediterranean ports, especially Alexandria and Constantinople, and (*b*) Italian merchants from such city-states as Genoa and Venice, who shipped the products from the eastern Mediterranean to western Europe. Because of the many middlemen, each tacking on the cost of his services, Eastern goods remained high-priced luxuries. Meanwhile, the Italian city-states grew prosperous.

The Crusades also helped, in a limited way, to bring about the Renaissance and to strengthen royal power.

RENAISSANCE (14TH THROUGH 17TH CENTURIES)

1. Meaning and Distinctive Features. *Renaissance* means "rebirth or revival." The Renaissance was a period of growing intellectual interest by

1

western Europeans in worldly, or nonreligious, aspects of civilization. Renaissance scholars emphasized reason, questioned authority, and pursued free inquiry. They showed (a) interest in the Byzantine and Moslem civilizations, and (b) curiosity about the ancient Greco-Roman civilization. The Renaissance arose in the Italian city-states because (a) Italy had been a center of Greco-Roman culture, (b) Italians were in close contact with the advanced Byzantine and Moslem worlds, and (c) Italy had wealthy merchants and rulers who supported literature, art, and science.

2. **The Renaissance Stimulates Interest in Geography and Navigation.** During the Middle Ages, western Europeans traveled little, and such travel was mainly overland by foot or horse, or along the Atlantic and Mediterranean coasts in small ships. The geographic knowledge of western Europeans was limited to Europe, northern Africa, and western Asia. When the Renaissance directed man's attention to scientific matters, Europeans wanted to know more about the world's size, shape, and people. In order to reach distant lands by water, they drew precise maps, built faster and safer ships, and achieved greater accuracy in using the compass to determine direction and in using the astrolabe to determine latitude. By the 15th century, educated Europeans accepted the belief, held by the ancient Greeks, that the world is not flat but round.

RISE OF ABSOLUTE MONARCHS RULING NATIONAL STATES

1. **Brief History.** During the Middle Ages most kings exercised little power. They ruled only their royal domains and had little control over their feudal lords, who held most of the land. Near the end of the Middle Ages, the kings began to extend their authority over the lords and eventually became absolute monarchs. Royal power was strengthened by (a) the Crusades and other wars, which killed many feudal lords, (b) the rising merchant or middle class, which supported the king to assure protection of property and trade, and (c) the awakening spirit of nationalism, according to which the king was considered the symbol of national unity. In western Europe, monarchs united peoples of a common nationality and molded unified national states. Among the national states established by the end of the 15th century were England, France, Portugal, and Spain.

2. **Encouragement of Overseas Voyages.** The rise of national states in western Europe led to the undertaking of voyages of discovery because (a) national states possessed sufficient wealth to finance such voyages, (b) their absolute monarchs sought colonial empires, and (c) their middle classes wanted increased trade. Portugal and Spain, desiring to smash the monopoly of Italian city-states, sought an all-water route to the Far East and took the lead in sponsoring voyages of discovery.

PORTUGAL REACHES THE EAST

Inspired by Prince *Henry the Navigator*, Portugal began to search for an all-water route around Africa and on to the East. Gradually, Portuguese sea captains pushed southward along the Atlantic coast of Africa. In 1488 *Bartholomew Diaz* reached the southern tip of Africa, the Cape of Good Hope. In 1498 *Vasco da Gama* rounded the Cape and sailed on to India. Because he returned with a cargo of spices worth 60 times the cost of the voyage, his trip excited western Europe.

SPAIN FINANCES AN EXPEDITION BY COLUMBUS

In 1492 *Christopher Columbus*, an Italian navigator, led an expedition for Spain's King Ferdinand and Queen Isabella. Convinced that the earth is round, Columbus planned to reach the Far East by sailing westward across the Atlantic Ocean. After a two-month voyage he came upon several islands in the Caribbean. Columbus thought he was in the Indies off the coast of Asia, and consequently he named the natives Indians. Actually, Columbus had discovered the New World. Because *Amerigo Vespucci*, an Italian explorer, after reaching the mainland, was the first to declare it a new continent, the New World was named *America*.

COMMERCIAL REVOLUTION

By the late 15th century, western Europe stood at the threshold of a new era to be marked by (1) overseas exploration and colonization, (2) expansion of world trade, and (3) the shift of major trade routes from the Mediterranean to the Atlantic. These developments have been termed the *Commercial Revolution*.

Part 2. Europeans Explore and Settle in the New World

PERIOD OF EXPLORATION
(Late 15th to Early 17th Centuries)

REASONS FOR VOYAGES OF EXPLORATION

Spurred by Columbus' trip, the leading western European nations sent explorers to the New World to (1) seek a passage through or around the Americas to the Far East, (2) secure gold, silver, precious gems, and other valuable products, (3) establish claims to new lands, (4) convert the Indians to Christianity, (5) satisfy the spirit of adventure and intellectual curiosity, and (6) pave the way for trading posts and settlements.

IMPORTANT EXPLORERS AND THEIR ACHIEVEMENTS

EXPLORERS AND DATES	ACHIEVEMENTS
1. For Portugal	
Cabral (1500)	While en route around Africa to the Indies, Cabral was blown westward off his course and accidentally discovered Brazil.
2. For Spain	
Balboa (1513)	Having heard rumors of gold and "another sea," Balboa crossed the Isthmus of Panama and discovered the Pacific Ocean.
Ponce de Leon (1513)	In search of a legendary "Fountain of Youth," Ponce de Leon discovered Florida.
Cortez (1519–1521)	An adventurer and fortune hunter, Cortez conquered the Aztec Indians in Mexico.
Magellan (1519–1522)	The expedition that Magellan headed was the first to circumnavigate the world, although he had died en route, in the Philippines.
Coronado (1540–1542)	Lured by rumors of cities of gold, Coronado explored the American Southwest.
De Soto (1541)	While searching for gold from Florida westward, de Soto discovered the Mississippi River.

3. For France

Verrazano (1524)	Commissioned to find a route to Asia, Verrazano explored the Atlantic coast of North America and sailed into New York Harbor.
Cartier (1535)	In search of riches and a northwest passage to Asia, Cartier discovered and sailed up the St. Lawrence River.
Champlain (1603–1608)	Interested in discovery and empire-building, Champlain explored northern New England, northern New York, and eastern Canada. He founded a settlement at Quebec.

4. For Holland

Hudson (1609)	Instructed to locate a northwest passage to Asia, Hudson entered New York Harbor and sailed up the Hudson River.

5. For England

Cabot (1497–1498)	Authorized to claim new lands, Cabot discovered Labrador and other parts of the northeastern coast of North America.
Drake (1577–1580)	An explorer and adventurer, Drake led the second expedition to circumnavigate the world.
Davis (1585–1587)	Though unable to find a passage around North America, Davis helped chart the Arctic waters bordering northeastern Canada.

PERIOD OF COLONIZATION
(Early 16th to Mid-18th Centuries)

PORTUGUESE COLONIZATION

In 1493–1494, by a *Line of Demarcation*, drawn by the Pope, and by a subsequent Portuguese-Spanish treaty, Portugal received title to eastern South America, or Brazil. To assure control of the territory and to cultivate the sugar crop, the Portuguese soon afterwards established settlements.

SPANISH COLONIZATION

1. Motives. Spain encouraged settlements in the New World to strengthen her claims to territory; to secure gold, silver, and valuable agricultural produce, such as sugar and indigo (a blue dye); and to convert the Indians to Catholicism. Spanish settlers were chiefly government officials, soldiers, noblemen, merchants, and missionaries.

2. Extent. The Papal decision and the subsequent treaty assigned the New World, except for Brazil, to Spain. The Spanish first settled in the islands of the West Indies: Cuba, Puerto Rico, and Hispaniola (Santo Domingo). From these bases, Spain proceeded to colonize Mexico, Central America, and most of South America.

Spain also established colonies in territory that today is part of the United States. In 1565, in Florida, the Spanish founded St. Augustine, the oldest city in the United States. In 1605, in New Mexico, they founded Santa Fe, the second oldest city in the United States. Other settlements were made throughout Florida, New Mexico, Arizona, Texas, and California.

In 1600, before the English had made their first settlement, Spanish colonists in the New World numbered about 200,000.

3. Life in the Spanish Colonies

a. Culture. Spain gave the New World her culture, notably her language and religion. She permitted only Catholics to settle in her colonies. In the major cities, Spain built impressive cathedrals and church-conducted universities.

Missionaries labored, with considerable success, to convert the native Indians to Christianity. Also, Spanish settlers and Indians intermarried, and their offspring, called *mestizos,* were raised within the Spanish culture.

b. Economy. The Spanish introduced wheat, barley, domestic animals such as horses and cattle, and trees bearing fruits and nuts. They also introduced the feudal European system of landholding, in accordance with which the king granted large estates to Spanish noblemen. These estates were first worked by the Indians, who were practically enslaved and were often cruelly treated. Later, plantation owners also used Negro slaves imported from Africa, as well as mestizos, who were virtual slaves.

Colonial merchants were permitted to trade only with the mother country, Spain. This restriction accorded with the prevailing idea that colonies exist to enrich the mother country, an idea expounded in the economic doctrine of *mercantilism.* From her colonies, Spain obtained a treasure of gold and silver that helped maintain her, during the 16th and most of the 17th century, as a leading world power.

c. Government. The king of Spain permitted no self-government at home and none in the colonies. He exercised strict control over the colonies by giving absolute powers to the officials whom he sent from Spain to serve as royal governors, or *viceroys.*

4. Decline of the Spanish Empire. After the defeat of the Spanish Armada in 1588 by the English, Spain slowly declined as a world power. In the 19th century, Spain lost all her American colonies, most of them by revolution during the Napoleonic Era and the rest as a result of the Spanish-American War. Although Spanish political control ended, Spain left a heritage of wide social distinctions, concentrated land ownership, Roman Catholicism, and the Spanish language.

FRENCH COLONIZATION

1. Motives. When the king of France heard the news that the New World had been apportioned between Spain and Portugal by Papal decision, he demanded to see "the clause in Adam's will" that excluded his country. The French wanted to acquire an empire in the New World, to fish for cod on the Newfoundland banks, to trade with the Indians for furs, and to convert the Indians to Catholicism.

2. Extent. The French utilized the vast inland waterways to explore and settle in North America. In 1608 *Samuel de Champlain* established the first permanent French settlement, at Quebec on the St. Lawrence River. In 1673 the missionary *Jacques Marquette* and the fur trader *Louis Joliet* paddled across Lake Michigan and down most of the Mississippi River. In 1681–1682 the explorer *Sieur de La Salle* descended the entire length of the Mississippi. Along the St. Lawrence, the Great Lakes, and the Mississippi, the French established many fur-trading posts and settlements, notably Montreal, Detroit, St. Louis, and New Orleans.

3. Few White Settlers. In 1750 *New France*, as the extensive French colonial territories in North America were called, held only **80,000** white settlers. The reasons for this small number were: (*a*) New France contained no treasure of gold and silver to lure fortune seekers. (*b*) France restricted immigration to Catholics, thereby excluding French Protestants. (*c*) Frenchmen engaged primarily in the fur trade and were little interested in farming. (*d*) Like France, the colonies were under the strict rule of the king, who opposed the growth of self-government.

4. Decline. France lost her possessions in North America as a result of the French and Indian War (1754–1763). However, French influence in the New World has remained strong in the province of Quebec, with its predominantly French-Canadian population, and in the state of Louisiana.

DUTCH COLONIZATION

1. Motive and Extent. Interested in the fur trade, the Dutch West India Company in 1621 founded the colony of *New Netherland*. It included trading posts and settlements along the Hudson River, especially at Albany and New Amsterdam, now New York City. In 1626 *Peter Minuit*, the Dutch governor, gave the Indians goods reputedly worth $24 for Manhattan Island.

The Dutch also expanded into Long Island and New Jersey. In 1655 they annexed New Sweden, a Swedish settlement in Delaware.

2. Small White Population. Since Holland was prosperous and few Hollanders were willing to migrate, the Dutch West India Company tried to attract settlers by offering a *patroonship*, a huge tract of land, to any of its members who would transport 50 tenants to the colony. Also, the Company raised little objection to non-Dutch immigrants. By the 1660's the colony contained settlers speaking some 18 different languages. Nevertheless, the total population did not exceed 10,000.

3. Decline. Holland and England were commercial and colonial rivals, and England considered the Dutch colony an obstacle to her ambition to colonize the Atlantic seaboard of North America. In 1664 an English naval force appeared before New Amsterdam and compelled the Dutch governor, *Peter Stuyvesant,* to surrender the colony.

Dutch influence remains in New York State, as evidenced by place-names and by a number of old homes and churches.

ENGLISH COLONIZATION

1. Extent. England founded ten colonies along the northern Atlantic seaboard and formed three colonies out of New Netherland, which she had seized from the Dutch. These thirteen English colonies formed the basis of our country, the United States of America.

2. Motives of the English Settlers

a. Religious. King Henry VIII broke with the Papacy and in 1534 established the independent Anglican Church, or Church of England. During the reign of Henry's daughter, Queen Elizabeth I (ruled 1558–1603), Anglicanism became firmly entrenched as the English religion. Catholics as well as dissenting Protestants, such as Puritans and Quakers, suffered discrimination and sometimes persecution. To gain religious freedom, many Englishmen migrated to the New World.

b. Political. In the 17th century, England was torn by political strife between Parliament and the absolutist Stuart kings. In succession, England experienced civil war (1642–1645), the beheading of King Charles I (1649), a Puritan military dictatorship under Oliver Cromwell (1649–1658), the restoration of the Stuarts (1660), and the final overthrow of Stuart rule by the Glorious Revolution (1688–1689). To escape governmental tyranny and political unrest, many Englishmen migrated to the colonies.

c. Economic. In the 16th and 17th centuries, many English lords fenced in their lands for use as sheep pastures, thus driving out their tenant farmers.

The landless peasants moved to the cities, where many experienced unemployment and fell into debt. Under England's severe criminal code, debtors faced imprisonment. To start life anew, with the possibility of acquiring their own farms, many impoverished Englishmen looked to the New World.

3. Motives of the English Government

a. World Power. In striving for world leadership, England came into conflict with Spain, as shown by raids of the English sea captains Sir John Hawkins and Sir Francis Drake upon Spain's colonies in the New World and upon Spanish treasure ships. In 1588, when war broke out between England and Spain, Drake and the other sea captains annihilated the "invincible" Spanish Armada. This event marked the emergence of England as a world power and as the "mistress of the seas." Equating a colonial empire with world power, the English government generally encouraged colonial settlement.

b. Economic Benefits. The English government, like other European governments, accepted the mercantilist doctrine that colonies serve to enrich the mother country. If regulated along mercantilist lines, colonies would assure raw materials and markets for English manufacturers, trade for English merchants, and revenues for the English treasury.

THE THIRTEEN ENGLISH COLONIES

1. Virginia

a. Founding of Jamestown (1607). The first permanent English settlement in the New World was undertaken as a business venture by a group of merchants organized into a joint-stock company, the *Virginia Company of London,* also called the *London Company.* In 1607, after the company secured a charter from King James I, a group of more than 100 settlers founded Jamestown.

b. Early Mistakes. The original settlers included too few farmers and artisans and too many "gentlemen" unaccustomed to work. They located the colony on a low marshy area, infested by malaria-carrying mosquitoes. They began to search for gold instead of undertaking the tasks necessary for survival. Thereupon, *John Smith,* a practical-minded soldier, forced his way into control. He secured food from the Indians and compelled the settlers to build fortifications, plant food crops, and stock firewood. Nevertheless, fewer than half the settlers survived the early years. In 1610 the colony was saved from abandonment only by the arrival of new settlers and supplies from England.

c. Tobacco Cultivation. In 1612 *John Rolfe* began cultivating a West Indian species of tobacco in Virginia. At last, the colony had a crop that was suitable to its soil and that commanded a good price in Europe. The raising of tobacco was further encouraged when, in 1619, the Virginia Company permitted each settler to claim his own farm of 50 or more acres.

d. Survival Assured. In 1624 Virginia became a *royal colony*. As a business venture, Virginia had proved unprofitable, and the Virginia Company went bankrupt. As a colony, however, Virginia had proved successful. It had overcome inexperienced leadership, starvation, disease, and Indian attacks; and in 1624 the colony contained more than 1200 settlers, most of them engaged in the flourishing tobacco culture. Virginia thus faced the future with confidence.

2. Massachusetts

a. Plymouth (1620). The Pilgrims, a small group of Protestant dissenters who had been persecuted by the Anglicans, sailed for the New World on their ship, the *Mayflower*. They had received permission from the London Company to settle in its territory, but they were blown northward off their course and instead landed at *Plymouth*. Beset by cold, hunger, and disease, only half the group lived through the first winter. However, under the leadership of *William Bradford* and with the help of friendly Indians, the colony farmed, fished, and survived. In the fall of 1621, the Pilgrims held a celebration to give thanks to God for His bounty and blessings—the origin of our Thanksgiving Day. Plymouth did not attract many settlers and finally was absorbed by the Massachusetts Bay Colony.

b. Massachusetts Bay (1630). The Puritans, so named because they wished to "purify" the Anglican Church of practices remindful of Roman Catholicism, suffered discrimination at the hands of Anglican churchmen and King Charles I. Nevertheless, a Puritan group, organized as the Massachusetts Bay Company, managed to secure a charter from the King. In 1630, led by *John Winthrop*, 1000 Puritans settled in the Massachusetts Bay area, most of them at *Salem, Cambridge,* and *Boston.* The settlers were well equipped with food, tools, and valuable skills, and the colony prospered almost immediately. During the 1630's, as Puritans in England suffered greater persecution and as England moved toward civil war, additional Puritans migrated. By 1640 the Massachusetts Bay Colony had grown to 20,000 inhabitants. The colonial government strongly supported the Puritan church and did not tolerate disagreement with Puritan beliefs and practices.

3. Rhode Island (1636). *Roger Williams*, minister of the church in Salem, challenged Puritan rule. He condemned the seizure of land without payment to the Indians and denied the right of the Massachusetts government to interfere in religious matters. Expelled in 1635, Roger Williams and his followers went to Rhode Island, where they founded *Providence*. Another Massachusetts rebel, *Anne Hutchinson*, also went to Rhode Island.

In 1644 Williams secured from the English Parliament a charter for Rhode Island Colony and set up a government which permitted religious freedom for all people and provided for the separation of church and state. Rhode Island's enlightened religious policy attracted many settlers.

4. Connecticut (1636). *Thomas Hooker*, pastor of the church at Cambridge, led his congregation to Connecticut to settle at *Hartford*. These

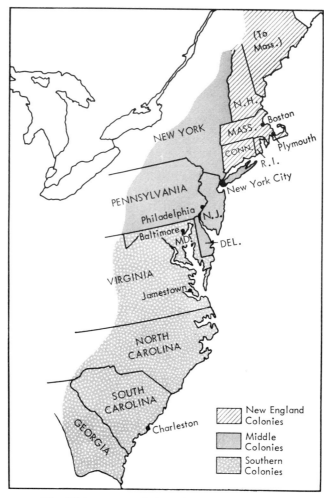

The Thirteen English Colonies, About 1750

settlers were not religious reformers but desired better farmlands and a government less restrictive than that of Massachusetts. In 1662 Connecticut received a royal charter confirming the settlers' right to self-government.

5. New Hampshire (1638). This area was settled chiefly by colonists who left Massachusetts for political, religious, and economic reasons. For a while New Hampshire was under the control of Massachusetts, but in 1679 it received its own charter as a royal colony.

6. Maryland (1634). *George Calvert,* the first *Lord Baltimore,* a convert to Catholicism, secured a royal grant of land around Chesapeake Bay for the colony of Maryland. It was the first *proprietary colony,* so called because it belonged to a proprietor, or owner. Lord Baltimore hoped that the colony would improve his family fortune by providing him with land rents and would also afford a place of refuge for English Catholics. His son, the second Lord Baltimore, in 1634 sent the first group of settlers to the colony. They were capably led and well equipped, and they treated the Indians fairly. Turning quickly to growing tobacco, the settlers prospered from the start. Maryland attracted Protestants as well as Catholics and soon granted freedom of religion to all Christians.

7 and 8. North and South Carolina (1663). A group of proprietors received a royal grant to the Carolinas. The northern portion was settled chiefly by pioneers from Virginia; the southern portion, including Charles Town (later Charleston), was settled by colonists from the British Isles and other European nations. The settlers earned a living by raising rice and tobacco, producing naval stores (pitch and tar) from the pine forests, and trading for furs with the Indians.

The Carolina settlers long opposed proprietary rule chiefly because the proprietors rebuffed demands for greater self-government. Finally, when the proprietors surrendered their charter to the crown, North Carolina and South Carolina each became a royal colony.

9. New York (1664). Shortly before the English navy seized New Netherland from the Dutch in 1664, King Charles II had assigned the region to his brother James, then Duke of York. Renaming the colony *New York,* James confirmed the rights of the Dutch settlers to retain their lands, observe their religion, and speak the Dutch tongue. He also continued the Dutch practice of governing the colony without a legislative assembly. When James became king in 1685, New York became a royal colony. After James was deposed by the Glorious Revolution of 1688–1689, New York gained a representative assembly.

10. New Jersey (1664). Immediately after acquiring New Netherland, James granted the area between the Hudson and Delaware Rivers to two of his friends, *Lord John Berkeley* and *Sir George Carteret*. This area, named New Jersey, already had some Dutch and Swedish settlements. The new proprietors, eager for income from land rents, encouraged the coming of additional settlers but had difficulty governing them and collecting rents. Eventually, Berkeley and Carteret sold their proprietary interests to Quaker groups who hoped to use the colony as a religious haven. In 1702 New Jersey became a royal colony.

11. Pennsylvania (1681). *William Penn* received a charter to Pennsylvania as payment for a sum of money owed him by King Charles II. Penn envisioned the colony not only as a business venture, but mainly as a place of refuge for his persecuted co-religionists, the *Quakers*, or *Society of Friends*. The Quakers had no formal church organization. They believed in humility, hard work, help for unfortunates, and brotherly love. They opposed violence, rank, and pride. In 1682 Penn came to the New World and for two years personally supervised the colony, which he called a "Holy Experiment." Penn himself planned the "city of brotherly love," *Philadelphia*.

Pennsylvania became renowned for religious freedom, a popularly elected legislature, fertile land, and fair treatment of the Indians. It attracted many settlers from the British Isles and also from the continent, especially German and Swiss Quakers, Mennonites, and Amish—the ancestors of today's Pennsylvania Dutch. Pennsylvania soon became a most prosperous colony.

12. Delaware (1682). William Penn also received a grant to Delaware, already containing Swedish and Dutch settlers. These people did not want to be ruled by the Pennsylvania legislature, and so in 1701 Penn granted them their own representative assembly.

13. Georgia (1732). *James Oglethorpe,* heading a group of philanthropists, secured a charter from King George II for this last and southernmost English colony, Georgia. It was designed as a military outpost against Spanish Florida and also as a haven for honest but impoverished debtors. Although the trustees at first forbade the importing of slaves and assigned each settler a small farm, Georgia rapidly developed into a colony of large plantations employing slave labor. In 1752 Georgia became a royal colony.

MULTIPLE-CHOICE QUESTIONS

Select the *number* preceding the choice that best completes the statement or answers the question.

1. By the Crusades, western Europeans sought to (1) seize control of an all-water route to the East (2) drive the Turks from Constantinople (3) establish Christian rule over the Holy Land (4) further trade between East and West.

2. An important result of the Crusades was the (1) increase in importance of the middle class (2) decline of the Italian city-states (3) establishment of European colonies in India (4) spread of the Moslem religion into Spain.

3. The Crusades helped to bring about the discovery of America by (1) stimulating European demand for goods of the East (2) encouraging the movement for a united Europe (3) reviving the power of the Catholic Church (4) encouraging Europeans to settle in the Middle East.

4. Which is most typical of the spirit of the Renaissance? (1) rejection of religion (2) lack of interest in man's past (3) questioning of authority (4) revolt against absolutism.

5. The Renaissance began in Italy because (1) the Italian city-states had conquered the nations of the East (2) Italian merchants and rulers became wealthy from trade with the East (3) the Roman Empire was at the height of its power (4) the Italians are the most scientific of all peoples.

6. Which was a direct result of the European Renaissance? (1) defeat of the Spanish Armada (2) spirit of inquiry as exhibited in the period of exploration (3) exclusion of non-Catholics from French colonies in North America (4) idea of separation of church and state as expressed by Roger Williams.

7. An important cause for the rise of national states in Europe was the (1) development of the middle class (2) collapse of the Roman Empire (3) growth of democracy (4) aid given by the Roman Catholic Church.

8. In the 14th and 15th centuries, western Europeans sought an all-water route to Asia in order to (1) break the Italian trade monopoly (2) stimulate progress in agriculture (3) add new territory to their empires (4) transport surplus population to colonies in Asia.

9. An immediate result of the Commercial Revolution was the rise in importance of (1) Venice and Genoa (2) Constantinople and Baghdad (3) Lisbon and London (4) Hamburg and Bremen.

10. Spanish colonies in the New World were typified by (1) the prohibition of trade with any country but Spain (2) self-government (3) fair treatment of Indians (4) admission of peoples of all religions.

11. According to mercantilism, a world power should (1) not seek colonies (2) seek only colonies rich in gold (3) permit colonial self-government (4) regulate colonies so as to enrich the mother country.

12. The French did *not* establish a settlement in North America at (1) Detroit (2) New Orleans (3) St. Louis (4) St. Augustine.

13. The Puritan settlement in the Massachusetts Bay Colony resulted most directly from the (1) political and religious policies of King Charles I (2) ambitions of Dutch merchants (3) flight of Huguenot families from France (4) European demand for furs.

14. Which three colonies were offshoots of the Massachusetts Bay Colony? (1) New Jersey, Vermont, Maine (2) New York, New Jersey, Delaware (3) Virginia, Connecticut, Pennsylvania (4) Connecticut, Rhode Island, New Hampshire.

15. Early English settlements in the New World were largely financed by (1) the royal family (2) military leaders (3) private corporations and individuals (4) the Anglican Church.

16. Prince Henry the Navigator directed his sailors to (1) round Africa (2) go westward across the Atlantic (3) gain control of the Mediterranean (4) seize Constantinople.

17. What was the attitude of merchants and kings toward overseas voyages? (1) Both groups supported them. (2) Both groups opposed them. (3) Merchants supported them; kings opposed them. (4) Kings supported them; merchants opposed them.

18. The American Indian was so named because (1) the Indians had migrated to the Americas from India (2) American Indians followed Hindu religious practices (3) Columbus believed he had reached the East Indies (4) Columbus believed he had discovered a new world.

MATCHING QUESTIONS

Select the *letter* of the item in column *B* that matches each item in column *A*.

Column A—Achievements

1. Was first to reach India by sailing around Africa
2. Discovered New York Harbor
3. Was first to identify the New World as a continent
4. Discovered the Pacific Ocean
5. Conquered the Aztec Indians of Mexico
6. Headed the expedition that first circumnavigated the world
7. Founded the city of Quebec
8. Led the second expedition to circumnavigate the world
9. Discovered Brazil
10. Explored eastern North America, where a major river was named after him

Column B—Explorers

a. Balboa
b. Cabral
c. Cartier
d. Champlain
e. Drake
f. Cortez
g. Da Gama
h. Hudson
i. Magellan
j. Ponce de Leon
k. Verrazano
l. Vespucci

IDENTIFICATION QUESTIONS: WHO AM I?

For each description below, write the name of the person to whom the description best applies, making your selection from the following list:

William Bradford   James Oglethorpe   Peter Stuyvesant
George Calvert   William Penn   Roger Williams
Thomas Hooker   John Smith   John Winthrop

1. A practical-minded soldier, I compelled the first Jamestown settlers to undertake tasks necessary for their survival.
2. One of the "Pilgrim Fathers" and governor of the colony, I made provision for a day of thanksgiving.
3. Expelled from Massachusetts, I founded a colony famed for separation of church and state.
4. As first Lord Baltimore, I planned a colony partly as a refuge for Catholics.
5. I founded a colony mainly to provide a place of refuge for Quakers.
6. As governor of New Netherland, I was compelled to surrender the colony to an English naval force.
7. I founded a colony in the South mainly to enable debtors to start life anew.

ESSAY QUESTIONS

1. The discovery of America resulted from developments in Europe, most notably (a) the Crusades, (b) the Renaissance, and (c) the rise of absolute monarchs ruling national states. Select *two* of these developments and for each show how it (1) affected Europe, and (2) related directly to the discovery of America.

2. In the late 1400's, western Europe entered upon the Age of Discovery and Exploration. Today, the world has entered upon the Space Age. Explain how these two periods are similar *or* different in regard to (a) leading nations, (b) motives for exploration, (c) financing of trips, (d) vehicles and other necessary equipment, (e) recruiting of explorers, (f) actual and potential results.

3. (a) Name *four* west European countries that explored the New World and name *one* explorer who sailed for each country. (b) Of the four explorers named, state the one you would most have liked to accompany. Discuss *two* reasons for your choice.

4. By the 18th century, the white population in the New World colonies of England far exceeded the white population of the colonies of any other European power. Comparing the English colonies with either the Spanish *or* the French colonies, discuss *two* reasons why the English colonies attracted the greater number of settlers.

5. In discussing the English colonies, we must distinguish between the motives of the settlers and the motives of the government. (a) Discuss *two* motives that led Englishmen to settle in the New World. (b) Discuss *two* motives that led the English government to encourage such settlement.

6. For *each* of the following pairs of colonies, show that their early histories were (a) in *one* way similar, and (b) in *one* way different: (1) Virginia and New York, (2) Rhode Island and New Hampshire, (3) Maryland and Georgia, (4) Pennsylvania and Massachusetts Bay.

Part 3. The Colonists Develop Distinctive American Practices

Life in the colonies was quite different from that in England and in Continental Europe. Settlers who came to the New World had to adjust to new conditions. They had to discard many of their old customs and gradually develop new ones. Soon their way of life was no longer European, but American.

COLONIAL POLITICAL PRACTICES

COLONISTS AND THE "RIGHTS OF ENGLISHMEN"

In a number of royal charters authorizing the establishment of colonies, starting with the charter for Virginia, the colonists were assured their rights and privileges as Englishmen. These rights and privileges rested upon four major landmarks in English history:

1. Magna Carta (1215). King John was compelled by the feudal nobles to sign the *Great Charter*, or *Magna Carta*. In time Magna Carta came to mean that (*a*) the king is not an absolute ruler but is subject to the laws, (*b*) all persons are guaranteed trial by jury, and (*c*) Parliament alone may levy taxes.

2. Evolution of Parliament. By the 14th century, Parliament had split into two houses: representatives of the higher clergy and nobility constituted the hereditary *House of Lords;* representatives of the wealthy middle class constituted the elected *House of Commons.* Also, by threatening to withhold tax laws, Parliament compelled English kings to accept its legislation, not only on taxes, but also on all other matters.

3. English Common Law. By the 14th century, English courts had established the practice of referring to similar past cases and following the previous decisions of judges. These legal precedents collectively formed a body of judge-made law, called the *common law.* Its principles, some of which in time became English *statute law* (enacted by a legislature), helped protect the individual against governmental tyranny. By the end of the 17th century, common law, as supplemented by statute law, had given every Englishman certain basic rights: (*a*) His life, liberty, and property could not be taken away arbitrarily. (*b*) If arrested, he was entitled to a writ of habeas corpus (providing for a statement of charges and a speedy trial) and to a trial by jury. (*c*) His home was considered his "castle." Government officials could not search a private home without first securing from a court a search warrant specifically stating the goods being sought.

4. English Bill of Rights (1689). As part of the Glorious Revolution in England, Parliament passed the Bill of Rights. It provided that (*a*) the king may not make or suspend laws, levy taxes, or maintain an army without the consent of Parliament, (*b*) the king may not interfere with Parliamentary elections and debates, and (*c*) the people are guaranteed the right to petition the government; the right to an impartial and speedy jury trial; and the right to protection against excessive fines and bails, and against cruel and unusual punishments.

THE COLONISTS ESTABLISH DEMOCRATIC INSTITUTIONS

Although the colonies were far from being democratic, as we understand the term today, they were significantly more democratic than Continental Europe and, in some ways, even England. The American colonists introduced the following institutions:

1. Virginia House of Burgesses (1619). The Virginia Company gave the colonists of Virginia the right to elect representatives to a colonial legislature, the *House of Burgesses.* This was the first elected legislature and the first institution of representative government in the New World. Other colonies followed its pattern in establishing similar lawmaking bodies.

2. Mayflower Compact (1620). Before disembarking from their ship, the *Mayflower*, the Pilgrims had made plans for self-government in their new home at Plymouth. In a compact to further the general good of the colony, they pledged to enact and obey just and equal laws. The Mayflower Compact was an example of (a) *direct democracy*, wherein the citizens themselves, not their representatives, were the lawmakers, (b) acceptance of majority rule, and (c) the principle that laws should treat all persons fairly.

3. New England Town Meetings. The Pilgrims began the practice, which became typical of colonial New England, of building towns with farms at the outskirts and a church meetinghouse at the center. Town life concentrated around the church. The freemen, originally only men who owned property and belonged to the town church, conducted town affairs and enacted local ordinances in *town meetings*. They also elected town representatives to serve in the colonial assembly. The town meeting, an example of direct democracy and possible only in a small community, provided the colonists with training in self-government.

4. Fundamental Orders of Connecticut (1639). Led by Thomas Hooker, the settlers of Connecticut drew up the first successful written constitution of modern times. It permitted all loyal citizens to elect a legislative assembly, which in turn would choose a governor. The Fundamental Orders implied that government rests upon the consent of the governed and that it should express the will of the majority.

COLONIAL GOVERNMENT IN THE 1750's

1. Types. (a) *Two Self-Governing Colonies.* In Connecticut and Rhode Island, the colonists directly or indirectly elected the governor and members of both houses of the legislature. (b) *Three Proprietary Colonies.* In Delaware, Maryland, and Pennsylvania, the proprietor selected the governor; the eligible voters elected the colonial assembly. (c) *Eight Royal Colonies.* In the other colonies the king selected the governor. Except for Massachusetts, the king also appointed the members of the governor's council, which was the upper house of the colonial legislature. The qualified voters elected the lower house.

2. Undemocratic Aspects. In the royal and proprietary colonies the colonists had little voice in the selection of a governor. The royal or proprietary governor retained the power to veto laws passed by the colonial legislature and to appoint lesser colonial officials. In the Southern colonies, the governor appointed county agents and other local officials. Furthermore, the English crown claimed the power to review and reject any law passed in the colonies.

In many colonies, voters had to meet religious qualifications. In all colonies, landless urban dwellers could not satisfy property qualifications for voting. Frontier settlers, living in danger and isolation, found it difficult to vote and were under-represented in the colonial assemblies. Finally, membership in the assembly was restricted to the well-to-do by the high property qualifications for officeholding.

3. Democratic Features. The legal rights of the colonists were protected by colonial judges, who followed English common law. The colonists were also protected against tyranny by the separation of governmental powers. With power divided between a royal governor representing the crown and a colonial assembly representing the settlers, neither branch of government could become all-powerful.

The colonial assembly was elected by the qualified voters, and its consent was necessary to enact laws, such as to levy taxes and dispense funds. Often, the assembly was able to bend the governor to its will by withholding funds for his salary or for running the government. Such use of a legislature's financial power has been named the *power of the purse*.

COLONIAL RELIGIOUS PRACTICES

EARLY INTOLERANCE IN COLONIAL AMERICA

Following Old World practices, most colonies set up an *official* or *established church*. These colonies supported the official church with government funds and, especially in the 17th century, required church membership for voting. In the Southern colonies and in New York, the official church was the *Anglican Church*. In the New England colonies, except for Rhode Island, the official church was the *Puritan* or *Congregational Church*.

In Massachusetts, the early Puritan leaders were intolerant of dissent. They punished and exiled any religious nonconformists. In time, however, even Massachusetts conceded that other religious sects were entitled to the same rights as Puritans.

FACTORS PROMOTING RELIGIOUS TOLERANCE

1. Number of Religious Groups. Because England had permitted members of all religions to come to the New World, the settlers in the thirteen colonies represented a great number of religions. They were chiefly Protestants (Puritan, Anglican, Quaker, Presbyterian, Dutch Reformed, Baptist, and Lutheran), but there were also some Catholics and a small number of Jews. The settlers realized that, if their own religion was to survive, all the other religions had to be tolerated.

2. Splits Within Existing Churches. Many religious groups were shaken by a religious movement, called the *Great Awakening*. This movement, under the intellectual leadership of *Jonathan Edwards*, brought out the emotional aspects of religion. Itinerant (traveling) ministers conducted mass revival meetings, emphasizing fear of Hell and love of God. By causing schisms (splits) in the existing churches, the Great Awakening promoted religious diversity and therefore tolerance.

3. Frontier Conditions. Faced with the difficulties of securing a living and withstanding Indian attack, frontier settlers had little time for theological disputes. Nor were they disposed to question the religion of their neighbors, who helped them in taming the wilderness and safeguarding the settlement.

STEPS TOWARD RELIGIOUS TOLERANCE

1. Rhode Island. In 1636 Roger Williams and his followers, fleeing from religious intolerance in Massachusetts, founded Rhode Island. Williams provided complete religious freedom for all people and did not set up an established church. The government of Rhode Island did not use public funds for religious purposes, did not require anyone to join a church, and did not establish any religious qualifications for voting. This idea of *separation of church and state* was later incorporated in the First Amendment to the United States Constitution.

2. Maryland. Although Lord Baltimore founded Maryland as a haven for Catholics, the colony soon attracted a majority of Protestants. To protect the Catholic minority and to prevent religious strife, Lord Baltimore in 1649 secured from the colonial assembly the *Maryland Toleration Act*. It granted religious freedom to all Christians.

3. Pennsylvania. William Penn founded Pennsylvania as a haven for Quakers. However, he opposed setting up any established church. In 1682 he granted religious freedom to all colonists, no matter what their religion, as long as they believed in God.

COLONIAL ECONOMIC PRACTICES

GEOGRAPHIC CONDITIONS INFLUENCE COLONIAL OCCUPATIONS

1. New England Colonies. The rocky, inhospitable soil and the cold climate discouraged agriculture. Farms were small and produced little beyond the needs of the farmer and his family. On the other hand, the abundant forests, swift-flowing streams, and fine natural harbors—such as at Portsmouth, Boston, and Providence—turned New Englanders to lumbering, shipbuilding, whaling, fishing for cod and mackerel, and trade.

New England merchants developed various trade routes, several involving a *triangular trade*. One profitable route took fish, grain, and lumber from the colonies to the West Indies for sugar and molasses, which, in turn, were exchanged in England for manufactured goods needed in the colonies. On another profitable trade route, New Englanders took rum to Africa and exchanged it for Negro slaves. The slaves were sold in the West Indies for sugar and molasses, and these products were shipped back to New England and distilled into rum.

New England's merchants made substantial profits, but they also faced great obstacles: the hazards of the sea, the dangers of pirate attack, and the mercantilist laws of England. These laws, known as the *Navigation Acts,* were designed to keep colonial ships trading with England and the British West Indies rather than with the European Continent or the French and Spanish West Indies. For example, the *Sugar and Molasses Act* of 1733 required the colonists to pay a high duty on these products if they were secured from any place but the British West Indies.

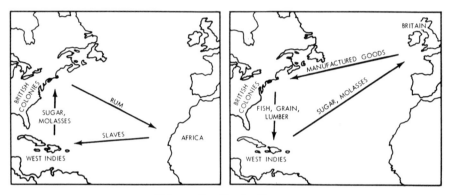

Triangular Trade Routes

2. Middle Colonies. Fertile, level land and a favorable climate encouraged family-size farms, which produced surplus grain (wheat, corn, and oats) for export to the other colonies and to England. The Middle Colonies soon became known as the *bread colonies.* Long, navigable rivers—such as the Hudson, Susquehanna, and Delaware—promoted trade with the Indians for furs. First-class harbors, such as at New York and Philadelphia, stimulated trade with other colonies, England, and the European Continent.

3. Southern Colonies. Forests yielded pitch and tar—naval stores that were vital to English and colonial shipping.

Fertile soil and a warm climate resulted in a plantation economy that raised indigo, rice, and tobacco. These products were shipped mainly to England in return for manufactured goods.

As the planters became wealthy, they steadily added new lands to their plantations, in part because tobacco-raising quickly exhausted the soil. They dominated Southern colonial society and sought to imitate the ways of the English aristocracy. The planters' lives contrasted sharply with those of the small Southern farmers and of the frontiersmen struggling in the back country.

(For colonies included in each geographic division, see map, page 11.)

COLONIAL SHORTAGE OF LABOR

Planters and farmers had difficulty in securing enough workers. Settlers were unwilling to work for others when they could easily acquire land and become independent farmers themselves. To overcome the labor shortage, colonists turned to Negro slaves and indentured servants.

1. Negro Slaves. In 1619 a Dutch sailing ship brought 20 Negroes to Jamestown, Virginia. This first cargo of Negroes led to the institution of slavery in the English colonies. Within 100 years slavery spread to all the colonies. It remained strongest in the South, where tobacco and rice planters came to depend upon these quickly trained workers. In 1750 the colonies contained 400,000 Negro slaves, of whom three-fourths were in the South.

2. Indentured Servants. These impoverished persons from Britain and Continental Europe totaled over one-half of all white immigrants to colonial America. They agreed, usually by signing contracts called *indentures,* to work for four to seven years in exchange for passage money to the New World. They worked hard as household help, artisans, and farmhands. After their period of indenture, they became free and sometimes received a parting wage of land or tools.

COLONIAL INDUSTRIES

1. Beginnings of Colonial Manufacturing. The colonists were overwhelmingly engaged in obtaining furs, fish, and lumber, and in raising farm produce. They also engaged in certain basic manufactures: weaving cloth and sewing clothes, tanning leather and making shoes, trimming lumber and making furniture, forging iron and shaping implements. These activities were at first performed on the farm or plantation as household industries.

As the colonial population grew and as manufactured goods came into greater demand, craftsmen began founding small local shops. In time textiles, iron implements, and beaver hats became somewhat larger industries, and manufacturers sought to expand beyond local markets. The most important manufacturing activity, centered in New England, was shipbuilding.

2. Obstacles to Industrialization in the Colonies. Colonial manufacturing remained limited because of (a) the lack of capital, (b) the lack of skilled workmen, (c) the lack of adequate inland transportation facilities for the distribution of goods, and (d) opposition from England.

England passed laws in accordance with the mercantile theory: that colonies should produce raw materials and exchange them for manufactured goods from the mother country. The *Woolen Act* (1699) and the *Hat Act* (1732) prohibited any colony from exporting these manufactured goods to any other colony or overseas. The *Iron Act* (1750) encouraged the shipment of crude iron to England but prohibited the colonists from making finished iron products.

COLONIAL SOCIAL AND CULTURAL PRACTICES

COLONIAL POPULATION

1. Rapid Growth. In 1700 the English colonies contained 250,000 people. By 1750, only 50 years later, the population had increased sixfold to 1,500,000. This rapid growth was due both to a considerable immigration and to a high native birth rate.

2. Variety of Peoples. The English colonies admitted persons of many diverse nationalities and cultures. Thus began the American tradition of the *melting pot*. From the British Isles came the English, Welsh, Scotch, Scotch-Irish (of Ulster in northern Ireland), and the Irish. Since the colonies accepted non-British immigrants too, many settlers came from Continental Europe, especially from France and Germany. In Delaware and New York, both formerly part of New Netherland, the original settlers were Swedish and Dutch.

3. Social Classes and Mobility. The colonial peoples were divided into three broad classes: (a) the aristocracy of wealth (planters and merchants) and of education (clergymen and lawyers), (b) the middle class of small farmers and skilled workers, and (c) the bottom group of indentured servants and slaves. However, colonial classes were not hereditary except for the slaves, and colonists moved easily up and down the social ladder.

COLONIAL EDUCATION

1. Elementary Education. The colonists were better educated than the people of England and Continental Europe. Nevertheless, colonial schooling varied, depending upon colony and social status. In general, upper-class children were educated by costly private tutors or in private schools. They learned both practical and classical subjects. Children of frontiersmen had the least formal education but were often taught the three R's—reading, 'riting, and 'rithmetic—by their parents at home.

Especially in New England, parents were motivated to educate their children by the Protestant emphasis upon personal Bible reading. Massachusetts, in 1647, and later other New England colonies passed laws requiring towns to provide schools for the teaching of reading. These first public education laws were poorly enforced.

2. Higher Education. To prepare young people for the ministry, the colonists established several colleges and universities: Harvard (1636), William and Mary (1693), Yale (1701), Princeton (1746), and Columbia (1754). *Benjamin Franklin* founded the University of Pennsylvania (1751), which from the outset offered a broad practical and liberal arts education. By the late 18th century most schools of higher learning were training students for medicine, law, and other secular professions.

PRINTED MATERIALS

1. Books and Newspapers. Although books were expensive, a number of planters and merchants possessed sizable personal libraries. In Philadelphia, in 1731, Benjamin Franklin founded the first subscription library. Each member contributed funds for the purchase of books and could borrow from the collection. Other colonial cities soon established their own library societies.

Most colonists, however, relied heavily upon only two books: the *Bible* for religious guidance and an *almanac* containing a calendar and various articles on agriculture, health, cooking, science, and politics. A popular almanac was Benjamin Franklin's *Poor Richard's Almanac.*

The colonists also published newspapers. The *Boston Weekly News-Letter*, the first colonial newspaper, was started in 1704. Within 50 years, 27 newspapers were being published in 11 of the colonies. Printing presses were also used to turn out pamphlets, especially on political matters.

2. Zenger Trial (1735). *John Peter Zenger*, a New York newspaper publisher, was tried for libel because he had written articles criticizing the royal governor of New York. Zenger was acquitted by the jury on the ground that he had published the truth. Henceforth, writers were free to criticize the government. The principle of *freedom of the press*, thus proclaimed, was later reaffirmed in the First Amendment to the United States Constitution.

SUPERSTITION AND SCIENCE

1. Salem Witch Trials. In 1692 the townspeople of Salem, Massachusetts, panicked in their fear of witchcraft. The authorities arrested several hundred persons, and 20 were formally tried and hanged as witches. As the

24. In the New England Colonies, elementary schools were generally maintained by the (1) towns (2) English government (3) Anglican Church (4) colonial legislatures.

25. The first colleges in New England were organized primarily to (1) teach medicine and law (2) teach the practical arts and sciences (3) prepare persons for the ministry (4) train gentlemen-farmers.

26. An important cultural achievement during the colonial period was the (1) development of a distinctive American music (2) printing of newspapers to influence public opinion (3) advance in medical science that eliminated colonial superstitions (4) establishment of schools for the children of factory workers.

27. Which principle was promoted as a result of the Zenger trial? (1) A newspaper must publish the replies of its critics. (2) A provable statement may be published without fear of punishment. (3) A newspaper may print the testimony given in criminal trials. (4) Newspapers may be operated under private ownership.

28. Which reinforced the principle established in the Zenger case? (1) Mayflower Compact (2) Fundamental Orders of Connecticut (3) Salem witch trials (4) First Amendment to the United States Constitution.

29. Benjamin Franklin, an outstanding colonist, did *not* win fame as (1) a frontiersman and explorer (2) an educator (3) a writer (4) a scientist.

30. A pledge to "frame such just and equal laws . . . as shall be thought most meet and convenient for the general good" is contained in (1) the Mayflower Compact (2) the Maryland Toleration Act (3) the royal charter for Pennsylvania (4) Benjamin Franklin's *Poor Richard's Almanac.*

ESSAY QUESTIONS

1. Show in *one* way how the thirteen colonies were influenced by their English heritage with respect to *each* of the following: (*a*) law and court procedures, (*b*) individual rights, (*c*) structure of government, (*d*) religious beliefs.

2. Democratic government in the United States had its beginnings during our colonial period. Show how *each* of the following was an important step in the development of our democracy: (*a*) Mayflower Compact, (*b*) House of Burgesses, (*c*) New England town meetings, (*d*) Fundamental Orders of Connecticut, (*e*) General School Act of 1647 in Massachusetts, (*f*) Maryland Toleration Act of 1649, (*g*) Zenger trial.

3. Choose *one* of the thirteen English colonies in America. Compare life about 1750 in that colony with life today in the same area with reference to *three* of the following topics: (*a*) education, (*b*) religion, (*c*) means of earning a living, (*d*) amusements and recreation, (*e*) methods of communication.

4. The colonial period in United States history (1607–1776) provided new opportunities for developing (1) political democracy, and (2) social democracy. (*a*) Explain why the colonial period offered new opportunities to the colonists. (*b*) Describe *two* developments in political democracy and *two* developments in social democracy that resulted from the colonists' taking advantage of these new opportunities.

5. Although the English colonies developed certain democratic institutions, they also displayed undemocratic practices. (*a*) Discuss *one* political, *one* economic, and *one* social development that illustrate colonial democracy. (*b*) Discuss *one* political, *one* economic, and *one* social practice that illustrate colonial lack of democracy.

6. The thirteen English colonies usually are considered as three groups—(*a*) New England, (*b*) Middle, (*c*) Southern—chiefly because each group had its own distinctive geographic features. For *each* group of colonies (1) describe *two* of its distinctive geographic features, and (2) show how these features influenced the way its colonists earned a living.

Part 4. The Colonists Fight the American Revolution and Gain Independence

WORLDWIDE STRUGGLE BETWEEN FRANCE AND ENGLAND

Starting in 1689 England and France engaged in a series of wars for mastery in Europe, and for commercial and colonial supremacy throughout the world. The first three of these wars were indecisive, but the fourth—the Seven Years' War in Europe and its American counterpart, the French and Indian War—brought victory to England.

FRENCH AND INDIAN WAR (1754–1763)

In 1754 hostilities began when colonial Virginia militiamen clashed with French forces for control of the Ohio Valley. Initially, the French won many victories, the most important being their ambush of General Edward Braddock as he marched against the French Fort Duquesne (located at the present-day site of Pittsburgh). Braddock's forces might have been completely destroyed had it not been for the skill of one of his colonial officers, George Washington.

In 1757, when William Pitt became Prime Minister, Great Britain redoubled her war efforts in North America. Additional British troops, together with additional colonial militia, began to turn the tide of battle. In 1759 General James Wolfe captured Quebec, the French fortress on the St. Lawrence River. The following year General Jeffrey Amherst captured Montreal, ending the war in Canada. These British victories in North America were paralleled by British triumphs in India and by the success of Britain's ally, Prussia, in Europe. France was completely defeated.

The *Treaty of Paris* (1763) eliminated France as a colonial power in North America. France ceded (1) to Spain: all French territory west of the Mississippi, as well as the city of New Orleans, and (2) to Britain: Canada and all French territory east of the Mississippi, except New Orleans.

RESULTS OF THE FRENCH AND INDIAN WAR

1. On the Colonies. The American colonists were favorably affected because they (*a*) gained self-confidence and valuable military experience, (*b*) saw the need for colonial unity in order to meet common problems, and, most important, (*c*) had the danger of attack by the French and certain Indian tribes removed from their frontiers and thus became less dependent on the mother country.

2. On Britain. Concentrating on wars against France, Britain had followed a colonial policy of "salutary neglect." She had permitted her American colonies to exercise virtual self-government and evade British mercantilist restrictions on the colonial economy. Now Britain determined to change her policy. She believed that the colonies (a) had not cooperated sufficiently in the war against France, (b) had gained much from the victory over the French and the Indians, and (c) should help pay the cost of fighting the war.

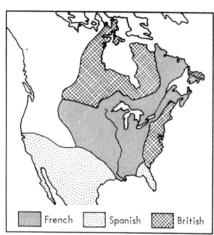

North America in 1689   North America in 1763

Growth of the British Empire in North America

BRITAIN'S NEW POLICY FOR COLONIAL AMERICA

Starting in 1763 the British government adopted a new colonial policy with three basic objectives: (1) to place the colonies under strict British political and economic control, (2) to compel the colonists to demonstrate respect for and obedience to English laws, and (3) to make the colonies bear their part of the cost of maintaining the British Empire.

1. Strict Enforcement of Existing Laws

a. Navigation Acts. Reflecting mercantilist doctrine, these laws required the colonists to (1) transport their goods only in British (and colonial) ships (although Dutch freighters offered lower rates), (2) export certain *enumerated articles,* such as tobacco, sugar, indigo, and furs, only to Britain (although Continental European markets offered higher prices), and (3) purchase their imports from Britain or, when colonial ships secured goods from the European Continent, to stop at a British port and pay duties. These laws sought to benefit British (and also colonial) shipbuilders, British merchants, and British manufacturers. Beginning in 1763, *George Grenville*, British Prime Minister, sent·to the colonies an increasing number of customs collectors, royal inspectors, and naval patrols to enforce the laws.

b. Writs of Assistance. These general search warrants were court orders authorizing British officials to search colonial homes, buildings, and ships for smuggled goods. Unlike a search warrant in the United States today, which authorizes an officer to search only a particular place for specified goods, a writ of assistance permitted a colonial official to search any place and seize any smuggled goods.

2. New Taxes

a. Sugar Act (1764). This act reduced the existing duties on colonial imports of sugar and molasses from the Spanish and French West Indies, but called for strict enforcement.

b. Stamp Act (1765). This was the first *internal tax* (as contrasted with import and export duties) levied on the colonies. It required the purchase of stamps that were to be put on printed materials such as wills, mortgages, almanacs, pamphlets, and newspapers. It mostly affected influential groups such as lawyers, clergymen, and printers.

c. Townshend Acts (1767). At the suggestion of Chancellor of the Exchequer *Charles Townshend,* Parliament levied new import duties on the colonies. These acts taxed colonial imports of paper, glass, paint, and tea. Part of the fines levied against colonists who violated these tax laws was to go directly to the royal governors so as to make them financially independent of colonial assemblies.

Colonists accused of violating the British tax laws were tried in Admiralty (military) Courts, where they were denied a jury trial. The colonists very likely would have found more sympathy from a jury in a colonial court.

3. Western Land Policy: Proclamation of 1763.
This royal decree prohibited colonists from settling west of the Appalachian Mountains. By reserving this region for the Indians, George III sought to protect the fur trade and remove a cause of Indian uprisings, such as the rebellion led in 1763 by the Indian chief *Pontiac.* The Proclamation also sought to prevent colonial settlements beyond the reach of British authorities.

4. Stationing of Soldiers: Quartering Act of 1765.
This law required the colonists to provide food and living quarters for British soldiers. Supposedly, the soldiers were to protect the colonists from the Indians. However, they were mostly stationed not in frontier settlements, but in populous coastal cities, such as New York and Boston.

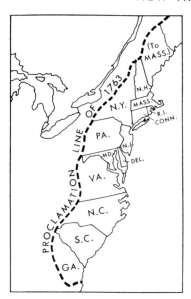

Proclamation Line of 1763

COLONIAL OPPOSITION

1. Violations of British Laws. Merchants and shipowners continued to smuggle goods into the colonies to avoid import duties. When the *Gaspee*, an English naval patrol vessel, ran aground off Rhode Island, colonists boarded the ship and set it afire. Frontiersmen and Southern planters continued to settle the fertile lands beyond the Appalachians.

2. Protests Against Writs of Assistance. Lawyers and writers protested the writs of assistance as illegal invasions of colonial property. Appearing before a Boston court, *James Otis* eloquently but unsuccessfully denounced the writs for violating the English common law principle that "a man's home is his castle."

3. Cooperation Among the Colonies

a. Albany Plan of Union: A Failure. In 1754, on the eve of the French and Indian War, delegates of seven colonies met in Albany, New York. Here Benjamin Franklin proposed the *Albany Plan of Union.* It called for an intercolonial council to handle relations with the Indians, western land settlement, and, most important, colonial defense. Franklin's plan was rejected by the various colonial assemblies, each eager to preserve its powers.

b. Stamp Act Congress of 1765. At the urging of the Massachusetts assembly, delegates from nine colonies met in New York City to plan united action against the Stamp Act. The meeting asserted that the colonists possessed all the rights of Englishmen and could be taxed by colonial legislatures, but not by Parliament. The delegates also initiated a colonial boycott of British goods.

c. Committees of Correspondence. Inaugurated in 1772 in Massachusetts by *Samuel Adams*, these committees provided an intercolonial network of information. The committees communicated with each other on mutual problems and helped organize the opposition to British policies.

4. Mass Action: Boycotts and Demonstrations. The delegates to the Stamp Act Congress urged colonial merchants to sign *nonimportation agreements*. These were pledges not to import British goods until the repeal of the Stamp Act. In addition, resistance throughout the colonies prevented distribution of the tax stamps. Parliament finally repealed the Stamp Act but passed the *Declaratory Act*, reaffirming its power to tax the colonies.

When Parliament exercised its taxing power by passing the Townshend Acts, colonial consumers again boycotted British goods. The *Sons of Liberty*, an organization of colonial patriots, helped enforce the boycott. The colonists hoped that English businessmen would pressure Parliament into repealing the hated tax laws. In 1770 Britain yielded to the colonists and repealed all the Townshend import duties except on tea.

In Boston, the colonists frequently demonstrated against the British soldiers, or *redcoats*. In 1770 soldiers fired upon a hostile but unarmed crowd and killed five men. The colonists named this event the *Boston Massacre*.

BOSTON TEA PARTY (1773)

Parliament passed the Tea Act (1773), exempting the East India Company from paying taxes in England on tea shipped to the colonies. By this act, Parliament offered the colonists the cheapest tea ever. Nevertheless, the colonists resented the Tea Act. (1) Colonial merchants, who had smuggled tea from Holland to avoid paying the import duty, would be unable to compete with the inexpensive tea of the East India Company. (2) The colonists would still have to pay a duty to England under the Townshend Act. In New York and Philadelphia, colonists turned back the English tea ships with their full cargoes of tea. In Boston, colonists disguised as Indians boarded the English ships and dumped the tea into the harbor. This action, defying English authority and destroying English property, was named the *Boston Tea Party*.

"INTOLERABLE" ACTS (1774)

Determined to punish Massachusetts and assert British authority, Parliament passed a series of acts that the colonists termed "intolerable." These acts (1) closed the harbor of Boston until the colonists paid for the destroyed tea, (2) authorized the quartering of troops in any colonial town, (3) permitted British officials accused of crimes in Massachusetts to stand trial in England, and (4) drastically curtailed self-government in Massachusetts. By their severity, these acts solidified colonial support for Massachusetts. (Also considered "intolerable" was the *Quebec Act* of 1774, which transferred to Quebec Province western lands north of the Ohio River. These lands had been claimed by several of the American colonies.)

FIRST CONTINENTAL CONGRESS (1774)

To present unified colonial resistance to the Intolerable Acts, delegates of twelve colonies met at Philadelphia as the *First Continental Congress*. They addressed a "Declaration of Rights and Grievances" to King George III, asking for a redress (correction) of wrongs, especially for repeal of the Intolerable Acts. Meanwhile, they voted to impose a boycott on British goods.

In Virginia, *Patrick Henry* acclaimed the work of the Continental Congress in a famous speech, concluding with: "Give me liberty, or give me death." Realizing that liberty might require defense, colonial patriots began training militiamen and storing military supplies.

OUTBREAK OF THE AMERICAN REVOLUTION (APRIL, 1775)

In Massachusetts the British General Thomas Gage ordered a detachment of troops to seize colonial military supplies at Concord and to arrest the colonial leaders John Hancock and Samuel Adams, believed to be at Lexington. Forewarned by Paul Revere, *Minutemen*, who were Massachusetts militiamen pledged to be ready at a minute's notice, were waiting to resist the British troops. Fighting broke out. As the poet Ralph Waldo Emerson later said, "Here once the embattled farmers stood and fired the shot heard round the world." Thus started the American Revolution.

BASIC CAUSES OF THE AMERICAN REVOLUTION

1. **Economic Causes.** The colonists resented British mercantilist laws, claiming that they hampered colonial trade and industry, and raised the cost of many consumer articles. The colonists were determined to free themselves from such restrictions and from exploitation by the mother country. These feelings were strongly held by the merchants, shipowners, and manufacturers who led colonial public opinion. Moreover, frontiersmen and Southern planters resented British efforts to halt westward migration.

The British argued that Britain's mercantilist laws assigned the colonies their proper role in the economy of the British Empire as producers of raw materials. They further pointed out that mercantilist laws encouraged colonial shipbuilding, provided bounties for colonial producers of such essential products as naval stores, and helped colonial planters by requiring British merchants to buy tobacco only from the British colonies. Finally, Britain claimed that her armed might protected colonial shipping and frontier settlements.

2. Political Causes. The colonists maintained that they were entitled to self-government, and that they could be taxed only by their own elected colonial legislatures. They felt that the taxes imposed upon them by the British Parliament constituted "taxation without representation." Furthermore, the colonists were incensed by the writs of assistance and the denial of trial by jury. They argued that these measures deprived them of their "rights as Englishmen."

The British asserted that the Parliament at London had the unquestionable right to legislate for all parts of the Empire. Each member of Parliament, they argued, represented not only the people who elected him, but all Britishers in the Empire. The British pointed out that the taxes levied in the colonies were being used for the defense and government of the colonies. Finally, the British claimed that colonial defiance of authority made harsher laws necessary.

3. Misunderstandings. Separated by 3000 miles of ocean, the American colonies and England did not understand each other. Although a majority of the colonists were of English origin, they had been transformed by their environment into Americans. They proved unwilling or unable to understand the viewpoints of the English. Furthermore, many non-English colonists had come from countries traditionally hostile to Great Britain. Finally, a small but active minority resented the British monarchy and desired independence.

Likewise, the English authorities failed to comprehend the colonial position. King George III, who was seeking to revive royal executive power in Britain, considered the colonists ungrateful and disloyal, rejected efforts at compromise, and pursued a policy of suppressing the colonies by force.

REASONS FOR THE DECLARATION OF INDEPENDENCE

During the first year of active warfare, the colonists were not certain whether they were fighting for their rights as Englishmen within the Empire or for complete freedom. By the summer of 1776, the colonists had decided that this was a war for independence.

1. The colonists were outraged by British military conduct and by the British use of German mercenaries, the *Hessians.*

2. The colonists believed that a declaration of independence would entitle captured American soldiers to the status of prisoners of war rather than traitors to the crown.

3. *Thomas Paine*, a recent immigrant from England, published a simply written, persuasive, and widely read pamphlet, called *Common Sense*. He declared that common sense forbade a continent to remain subservient to an island and forbade a people to remain loyal to a king who was spilling their blood. Paine convinced many colonists that independence was the only sensible goal.

4. American forces had fared well against British troops. The Americans had retreated from their position near Bunker Hill only after having inflicted heavy casualties on the British, and they had subsequently forced the British to evacuate Boston. These achievements gave the colonists the confidence to declare their independence. Colonial leaders further thought that such a declaration would inspire the American armies to continue the war.

5. Colonial leaders believed that independence would help the colonies to secure assistance from foreign nations, especially from France, which wanted revenge for her defeat by Britain in the French and Indian War.

BASIC IDEAS OF THE DECLARATION OF INDEPENDENCE

On July 4, 1776, the Second Continental Congress formally adopted the Declaration of Independence. Although Benjamin Franklin and John Adams made some contributions, the Declaration was written chiefly by *Thomas Jefferson*. He based his ideas on those of the English philosopher *John Locke*, who, nearly a century before, had defended the right of the English people to revolt against their king.

1. **Philosophy of Government.** In simple yet eloquent language, Jefferson declared: (*a*) "All men are created equal" and "are endowed by their Creator with certain unalienable rights," including "life, liberty, and the pursuit of happiness." (*b*) "To secure these rights, governments are instituted [started] among men, deriving their just powers from the consent of the governed." (*c*) "Whenever any form of government becomes destructive of these ends, it is the right of the people to alter or to abolish it, and to institute new government."

2. **List of Grievances.** The Declaration enumerated the many "injuries and usurpations" committed by King George III against the colonists.

3. **Conclusion.** Jefferson concluded that "these united colonies are, and of right ought to be, free and independent states."

SIGNIFICANCE OF THE DECLARATION OF INDEPENDENCE

1. **Effects Upon the American Revolution.** The Declaration elevated the struggle against the English armies into a war for independence. It encouraged France and Spain to assist the colonists, and it made possible the alliance in 1778 between the Americans and France.

2. **Long-Term Effects Throughout the World.** To peoples throughout the world, the Declaration became a source of inspiration. It inspired the French revolutionaries, who in 1789 rebelled against their old regime and adopted the *Declaration of the Rights of Man*. It encouraged Latin American leaders, in the early 19th century, to fight for independence from Spain. It inspired Asian and African nationalists, in the 20th century, to oppose imperialist control and to achieve national independence.

3. **Long-Term Effects Within the United States.** The Declaration has inspired Americans to undertake movements for social and democratic reforms, such as for the abolition of slavery, for equal rights for women, and recently for the extension of full civil rights to the American Negro.

BRIEF SURVEY OF THE REVOLUTIONARY WAR

1. **British Successes in the Middle States (1776–1777).** Britain, a major military power, expected to subdue her rebellious subjects with little difficulty. Under Sir William Howe, a sizable British army sailed into New York Harbor, defeated George Washington's poorly trained forces, and occupied New York City. Washington retreated into New Jersey, where he gained morale-boosting triumphs at Trenton and Princeton. Thereafter, the British redcoats defeated the colonial forces in several engagements near Philadelphia and occupied that city.

2. **American Victory at Saratoga (1777).** In upstate New York, at Saratoga, the Americans defeated and captured General John Burgoyne and his entire army, which had come southward from Canada. The Battle of Saratoga was the turning point of the war. It convinced the French government that the Americans had a chance of winning the war. Until then, France had been providing the colonists with loans and munitions secretly. Now the French government, heeding our minister, Benjamin Franklin, recognized American independence and in 1778 signed a treaty of alliance with the new nation.

3. **American Suffering at Valley Forge (1777–1778).** Meanwhile, having lost Philadelphia to the British, Washington and his men retreated some 20 miles away to Valley Forge. Inadequately fed and clothed, they suffered through an especially harsh winter. Washington held his army together only with great difficulty.

4. American Victory in the Northwest Territory (1778–1779). George Rogers Clark led a force of less than 200 frontiersmen down the Ohio River and into the western lands. Clark won a series of victories against British garrison forces, climaxed by the recapture of Vincennes. Clark's exploits ended British control of the Northwest Territory and established American claims to the area.

5. War in the South (1778–1781). The British left Philadelphia in 1778 and returned to New York City. Part of the British forces next moved southward. The British won several battles and occupied the major seaport cities of Savannah and Charleston. However, they could not crush the American forces. By early 1781 in the interior of the Carolinas, the British had suffered a series of reverses. British General Charles Cornwallis eventually withdrew northward to Yorktown, Virginia.

6. Yorktown: The Final American Victory (1781). By 1781 Washington's forces in the New York area had been augmented by a French army. Also, a French navy was moving northward from the West Indies. With Cornwallis sitting at Yorktown, Washington quickly moved his forces southward to overwhelm the British on land while the French navy cut off any possible British escape by sea. Cornwallis surrendered, and the war practically ended. The peace treaty was signed two years later.

REASONS FOR THE AMERICAN VICTORY

1. The Americans were fighting on their own soil, for their own homes, and for their own freedom. The British forces, consisting of British soldiers and Hessian mercenaries, were in enemy territory, some 3000 miles from home. They did not match the Americans in their determination and persistence for victory.

2. The Americans were superior wilderness fighters. (They used their frontier experience to defeat the British at Saratoga in upstate New York and at Vincennes in the Northwest Territory.)

3. The American forces were led by men of courage, determination, and ability. Outstanding, of course, was *George Washington.* A leader with military experience and good judgment, Washington set an example of devotion, integrity, and steadfastness. By strength of personality, he instilled confidence in his men and held his army together during its darkest days.

Other outstanding American military leaders were: (*a*) Colonel *George Rogers Clark*, who drove the British out of much of the Northwest Territory, (*b*) General *Nathanael Greene*, who exhausted the British army in the Carolinas by his hit-and-run tactics, and (*c*) Captains *John Paul Jones* and *John Barry*, who upheld the American cause on the sea.

The British forces, although superior in manpower and equipment, were led by generals who were often overconfident and incompetent. For example, the British General William Howe moved southward from New York City to occupy Philadelphia in 1777 instead of moving northward to join Burgoyne. This blunder made possible the American victory at Saratoga.

4. Notable foreign volunteers who came to help the colonists in the struggle for freedom were: (a) *Marquis de Lafayette* of France, who joined Washington's staff, (b) *Baron de Kalb*, a soldier of fortune who had served in the French army, (c) *Baron von Steuben* of Prussia, who served as drillmaster of the colonial army, (d) *Count Pulaski*, a cavalry leader who had headed a Polish uprising against Russia, and (e) *Thaddeus Kosciusko*, a military engineer who later became one of Poland's great patriotic heroes.

5. As the American Revolution progressed, other nations—first France, then Spain and Holland—entered the struggle against Great Britain. Now facing several enemies, Britain could not concentrate her full efforts on suppressing the colonists.

6. Within England, public opinion was divided on supporting the war against the American colonists. William Pitt and Edmund Burke, influential British statesmen, publicly defended the colonial cause, asserting that the colonists were seeking only their "rights as Englishmen." Such an attitude in England did not encourage wholehearted prosecution of the war.

WARTIME PROBLEMS FACING THE COLONISTS

1. **Providing a Government.** The Second Continental Congress acted as a central government for the thirteen colonies, or states. From 1775 to 1781 it concerned itself primarily with one objective—winning the war. The Congress was handicapped in several ways because: (a) it lacked essential governmental powers and could only request men, money, and cooperation of the states; (b) it was inexperienced and followed inefficient and wasteful procedures; and (c) some members of the Congress engaged in petty political bickering.

Nevertheless, the Second Continental Congress compiled an impressive record of achievements. The Congress (a) held the thirteen states together, (b) authorized an army and appointed George Washington as commander in chief, (c) encouraged a small but useful American navy, (d) issued the Declaration of Independence, (e) arranged the military alliance with France, (f) raised funds to finance the war, and (g) proposed the Articles of Confederation, which in 1781 became the framework for the government of the new nation.

2. Raising Funds. To feed, clothe, equip, and pay the Continental Army, Congress needed large sums of money. Congress proceeded on many fronts: (a) It issued paper money, called Continentals, totaling nearly $250 million. This money was backed not by specie, such as gold, but rather by public faith and confidence in the American cause. As the British won victories in the early days of the war, this currency depreciated (fell in value) steadily until it was practically worthless. (b) Congress requested funds of the states, but these requests were scarcely heeded. (c) Congress floated loans, both domestic and foreign, especially from the Netherlands, Spain, and France. However, these amounts were far short of the money needed for the war. (d) Congress obtained some funds through the efforts of patriotic Americans. *Haym Salomon,* a Jewish refugee from Russian rule in Poland who had become a New York banker, gave his entire fortune to the American cause. *Robert Morris,* a Pennsylvania merchant and banker who served as Superintendent of Finance, guaranteed government loans with his personal credit.

3. Maintaining an Army. During most of the war, the Continental Army did not number more than several thousand men. They were volunteers who usually signed up for short-term enlistments. Because of the constant turnover, most recruits never became properly trained or disciplined. Their food, shelter, and military equipment were inadequate, and their families received no assistance while the men were in service.

When the Continental Army faced battle, it was often reinforced by local militiamen. These were civilians who dropped their daily pursuits and served as temporary soldiers.

4. Dealing With the Tories. Not all the colonists supported the war against Britain. Historians are generally agreed that, at the start of the war, the population of the thirteen colonies was divided as follows: (a) One-third, the organized *Patriots,* actively supported independence. (b) One-third was undecided while waiting to see what would develop. (c) One-third, the unorganized *Tories,* or *Loyalists,* remained completely loyal to Britain and the king. The Tories consisted chiefly of the more prosperous and conservative groups, especially wealthy landowners and officeholders. As the war progressed, most Tories fled to Canada and England to escape the wrath of the American Patriots. However, some Tories remained to fight in the British armies. With most Tories gone, the Patriots took control of the state governments and, while the war was still in progress, revised the state constitutions to provide for greater democracy. The Patriots also confiscated the Tory estates, subdividing and selling the land in small parcels. This virtual civil war between Patriots and Tories illustrates a second aspect of the American Revolution—it was not only a struggle against England for political independence but also a struggle within the country for greater democracy.

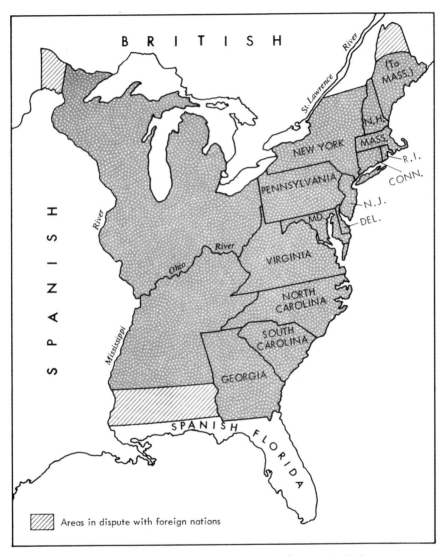

The United States After the Treaty of Paris (1783)

TREATY OF PARIS (1783)

The American negotiators—Benjamin Franklin, John Jay, and John Adams—secured a highly favorable treaty of peace with Britain.

1. Britain recognized the thirteen American states as independent. The new nation was bounded (a) on the north by Canada and the Great Lakes, (b) on the south by Spanish-owned Florida, (c) on the east by the Atlantic Ocean, and (d) on the west by the Mississippi River.

2. The Americans retained their previous rights to fish on the banks off Newfoundland.

3. The United States agreed to recommend to the various states the restoration of confiscated Loyalist properties and the payment of debts owed to British merchants. (The state governments paid little attention to this provision.)

EFFECTS OF THE AMERICAN REVOLUTION

1. In the United States

a. Political. The thirteen American colonies became thirteen independent states, loosely bound together by a central government under the Articles of Confederation. Although this government was not very powerful, it was an important step on the road to an effective national union.

Most states drafted new written constitutions containing many democratic features. "Bills of rights" guaranteed the people freedom of speech, press, and religion; assured trial by jury; and prohibited illegal search and seizure. As a result of colonial experiences with royal governors, the state constitutions granted most power to the legislatures and restricted the authority of the governors. The constitutions kept officeholders subject to the popular will by requiring short terms of office and frequent elections.

As had been the practice in colonial times, most state constitutions contained property qualifications for voting and officeholding, and some also retained religious qualifications.

b. Economic. The American Revolution resulted in (1) the end of restrictions on American trade and industry, and the growth of an American merchant marine and American manufacturing, (2) the end of restrictions on migration across the Appalachians and the movement of land-hungry settlers westward, (3) the breakup of large estates, especially those belonging to the Tories, and an increase in the number of small, independent farmers, and (4) the end of *primogeniture,* the right of the oldest son to inherit the entire estate of his deceased father. The Revolution also brought economic problems, including a large public debt and inflation (see pages 46 and 108–110).

c. Social. (1) All state constitutions, except three, guaranteed separation of church and state. In Virginia, this separation became law in 1786 by passage of Thomas Jefferson's *Statute of Religious Freedom.* (2) Criminal codes were revised and made more humane by the abolishment of severe punishments for minor infractions. (3) Negro slaves in the Northern states were gradually freed. (However, slavery remained fastened on the Southern economy.)

2. In France. The American Revolution encouraged many Frenchmen to hope that they might overthrow the absolute monarchy in France and establish a democratic government. Thus the French Revolution of 1789 was partly inspired by the American Revolution of 1775.

3. In Latin America. Throughout the Spanish colonies in the Western Hemisphere, people were thrilled by the success of the American Revolution. While Spain was involved in the Napoleonic Wars in Europe (1799–1815), the Spanish colonists followed the example of the United States and revolted for independence and democracy.

4. In the British Empire. The American Revolution (*a*) discredited King George III and his efforts to revive royal power, and (*b*) led to a gradual change in Britain's colonial policy. By the mid-19th century the British had abandoned the mercantilist idea that colonies exist solely to enrich the mother country. To prevent colonial rebellion and to encourage colonial loyalty, Britain gradually extended self-government throughout her Empire, starting in 1867 with Canada.

MATCHING QUESTIONS

Column A	Column B
1. Spoke for "liberty or death"	*a.* Haym Salomon
2. Secured new taxes on the colonists	*b.* John Burgoyne
3. Denounced the "writs of assistance" in a Boston court	*c.* Samuel Adams
4. Negotiated the American alliance with France	*d.* Charles Townshend
5. Won the Northwest Territory	*e.* Edmund Burke
6. Surrendered his army at Yorktown	*f.* Benjamin Franklin
7. Gave his fortune to the colonial cause	*g.* James Otis
8. Wrote the Declaration of Independence	*h.* John Hancock
9. Organized Committees of Correspondence	*i.* Thomas Jefferson
10. Spoke for the colonial cause in Britain	*j.* Patrick Henry
	k. George Rogers Clark
	l. George Washington
	m. Charles Cornwallis

MULTIPLE-CHOICE QUESTIONS

1. An important result of the French and Indian War was that it (1) ended the Indian menace in North America (2) caused France to cede her claims west of the Mississippi to Great Britain (3) encouraged a spirit of independence in the colonies (4) lessened English restrictions on the colonists.

2. The French and Indian War increased tension between Britain and the American colonies because the (1) colonists had not been allowed to participate in that war (2) colonists had hoped to win independence (3) British pressed the colonists to adopt the Albany Plan of Union (4) British insisted that the colonists share the expenses of the war.

3. Which statement best describes the reaction of leading American colonists toward British colonial policy following the French and Indian War? (1) They rejected Parliament's right to manage their internal affairs. (2) They petitioned Parliament for immediate independence. (3) They urged the colonial legislatures to enforce the taxation program of Parliament. (4) They demanded colonial representation in Parliament.

4. The English contended that the American colonists were represented in Parliament because (1) members of Parliament spoke for all Englishmen (2) colonial governors could communicate colonial demands to Parliament (3) colonial legislatures had the same power as Parliament (4) colonists had been given the rights of English citizens in their charters.

5. Immediately following the French and Indian War, the colonists opposed the British policy of (1) stricter enforcement of mercantilism (2) stricter adherence to "salutary neglect" (3) prohibition of emigration to the colonies (4) greater attention to new possessions in India and Canada.

6. Which legislation of the British Parliament concerning the thirteen colonies most clearly illustrates the principles of mercantilism? (1) Intolerable Acts (2) Navigation Acts (3) Stamp Act (4) Proclamation of 1763.

7. The purpose of the Navigation Acts was to protect (1) New England merchants (2) the economic interests of the British Empire (3) colonial trade with the West Indies (4) the slave trade between England and the colonies.

8. Which action of the British government most directly affected the people on the frontier? (1) Intolerable Acts (2) Stamp Act (3) Proclamation of 1763 (4) Townshend Acts.

9. The Intolerable Acts were passed as a result of the (1) Boston Massacre (2) Boston Tea Party (3) writs of assistance (4) Stamp Act Congress.

10. The colonists opposed British taxation policies most effectively by using (1) "salutary neglect" (2) petitions (3) sabotage and violence (4) economic boycotts.

11. In 1775–1776 one factor that tended to delay the separation of the colonies from Great Britain was the (1) publication of *Common Sense* (2) willingness of King George III to compromise (3) feeling of loyalty to England by many colonists (4) military aid supplied to the colonies by France.

12. The significance of Thomas Paine's *Common Sense* was that it (1) suggested a plan of reconciliation with Britain (2) pointed out the absurdity of continued loyalty to the king (3) argued that protests of the colonies should be made only to Parliament (4) outlined a "common sense" approach to commonwealth status.

13. The statement "governments are instituted among men, deriving their just powers from the consent of the governed" is from the (1) Mayflower Compact (2) Declaration of Independence (3) proclamation by Washington to his troops at Yorktown (4) treaty of alliance with France.

14. According to the Declaration of Independence, the purpose of government is to (1) secure the people in their natural rights (2) equalize opportunities for all citizens (3) provide for the common defense (4) establish a system of free public schools.

15. Which is *not* a part of the Declaration of Independence? (1) a statement of the rights of the individual (2) a listing of grievances against King George III (3) a framework for a new government (4) an assertion of the freedom of the colonies.

16. The principles of the Declaration of Independence can be described as (1) part of America's debt to European thought (2) Roger Williams' contribution to political philosophy (3) concepts of government inconsistent with accepted American ideals (4) a defense of the Articles of Confederation.

17. The chief significance of the Declaration of Independence is that it (1) expressed for the first time the right of a people to petition the government (2) attracted thousands of Loyalists to the colonial cause (3) reflected the democratic ideals of the French government of 1776 (4) furnished a body of ideals for future generations.

18. In what sense was the American Revolutionary War a civil war? (1) Colonial troops fought the Hessians. (2) State militias fought to defend only their own states. (3) French troops helped the Americans fight the British. (4) Some Americans fought on the side of the British.

19. Which statement best explains the outbreak of the American Revolution? (1) The colonists wanted free land. (2) Colonial taxes were too low to pay governmental officials. (3) Radical colonial leaders aroused colonial opinion against British policies. (4) The Articles of Confederation assured a united opposition against Britain.

20. In which pair is the second event or development a direct result of the first? (1) British surrender at Saratoga—signing of the treaty of alliance with France (2) Intolerable Acts—Boston Massacre (3) publication of Declaration of the Rights of Man—signing of the Declaration of Independence (4) George Washington appointed commander in chief of the Continental Army—battles of Lexington and Concord.

21. The primary motive behind French aid to the United States during the Revolutionary War was the French government's desire to (1) regain Canada and Florida (2) promote the principles of the French Revolution (3) force British evacuation of French islands in the West Indies (4) obtain revenge against Great Britain for previous French colonial losses.

22. As a result of the Treaty of Paris (1783), the United States was bounded by all of the following *except* the (1) Atlantic Ocean (2) Great Lakes (3) Mississippi River (4) Gulf of Mexico.

23. The American Revolution resulted in all of the following *except* the (1) breakup of large estates (2) abolition of property qualifications for voting (3) inclusion of a bill of rights in the new state constitutions (4) emancipation of Negroes in the Northern states.

24. Which event occurred *first?* (1) Boston Tea Party (2) meeting of the First Continental Congress (3) issuance of the Intolerable Acts (4) issuance of the Townshend Acts.

25. Which is the most valid generalization that can be drawn from the study of our colonial period? (1) Domination by the Church of England was unacceptable to the thirteen colonies. (2) Widespread desire on the part of ordinary people is the secret of a successful revolution. (3) Economic boycott is an effective means of expressing protest. (4) Crushing taxation breeds revolutionary discontent.

26. Which date marks the winning of independence from Britain and the end of the colonial period of American history? (1) 1754 (2) 1763 (3) 1783 (4) 1801.

27. About how many years did our colonial period last? (1) 75 (2) 125 (3) 175 (4) 225.

DISCUSSION ANALYSIS QUESTIONS

Base your answers to the questions below on the statements of Speakers *A, B, C,* and *D,* and on your knowledge of the American Revolution.

Speaker A: Americans were opposed to British restrictions on their colonial governments, and this was a major factor in bringing on the Revolution.

Speaker B: The basic cause was Great Britain's imposition of taxes on the colonists. Colonists fought in order to avoid taxation.

Speaker C: Britain's economic policies, designed to benefit British merchants, were very harmful to colonial merchants.

Speaker D: Colonial reaction to the Boston Massacre and the Battle of Bunker Hill eliminated all possibility for a peaceful settlement.

1. Which speaker considers mercantilism the most important reason for the American Revolution? (1) *A* (2) *B* (3) *C* (4) *D.*

2. If a person considers the American Revolution as primarily a movement for self-government, he would be most likely to agree with Speaker (1) *A* (2) *B* (3) *C* (4) *D.*

3. Which speaker considers emotional reasons the most important? (1) *A* (2) *B* (3) *C* (4) *D.*

4. The Stamp Act could be cited in support of Speaker (1) *A* (2) *B* (3) *C* (4) *D.*

5. The suspension of the Massachusetts Charter could be cited in support of Speaker (1) *A* (2) *B* (3) *C* (4) *D.*

6. The Navigation Acts could be cited in support of Speaker (1) *A* (2) *B* (3) *C* (4) *D.*

ESSAY QUESTIONS

1. Show *one* way in which each of the following contributed to the revolt of the American colonies against Britain: (*a*) geography, (*b*) mercantilism, (*c*) "rights of Englishmen," (*d*) Proclamation of 1763, (*e*) conflicts between royal governors and colonial legislatures, (*f*) French and Indian War.

2. "The history of the present King of Great Britain is a history of repeated injuries and usurpations. . . . To prove this, let facts be submitted to a candid world."— The Declaration of Independence
   (*a*) State *three* examples of these "injuries and usurpations" that, in the opinion of the colonists, justified their decision to declare themselves independent. (*b*) Discuss *three* basic principles that the colonists advanced in the Declaration of Independence to justify their action.

3. (*a*) State *two* principles of the Declaration of Independence. (*b*) Describe *two* ways in which the United States has tried since the adoption of the federal Constitution to carry out *each* of these principles. (*c*) Giving specific illustrations, show how *one* foreign government pursues policies contrary to the principles of the Declaration of Independence.

4. The American Revolution, with its surprising victory by the colonists, had significant domestic and worldwide effects. (*a*) Discuss *one* reason why Britain expected to subdue her rebellious colonists easily. (*b*) Discuss *three* factors that enabled the colonists to achieve victory. (*c*) Describe *two* effects of the American Revolution within the United States. (*d*) Describe *two* effects of the American Revolution upon the rest of the world.

Part 5. The Critical Period Leads to the Creation of a More Perfect Union

ONE NATION OR THIRTEEN?

With the Revolutionary War won, the American people faced the problem of whether they were to constitute one unified nation or thirteen separate states. Several factors encouraged unity: (1) Most Americans shared a common English language and culture, and had a growing sense of being one people. (2) Being located along the North Atlantic coast, the states formed a single geographic unit. (3) The states had no tradition of hostility or war against one another. (4) The states had cooperated in a common effort to win independence from England.

Other forces, however, worked against unity: (1) The people were divided by strong loyalties to their individual states. (2) The states occupied a large area and lacked close contact because of poor roads and slow means of transportation. (3) The states were not interdependent economically, having traded more with the West Indies and Europe than with one another. (4) The states no longer faced a common enemy.

CRITICAL PERIOD (1781–1789)

During the years following the Revolutionary War, many Americans wondered whether their country would survive as a unified nation. Beset by economic distress and political disunity, the United States underwent a period that has been aptly called "critical."

1. **Economic Distress.** The country was plagued by hard times. American merchants were excluded from the British West Indies and lost their favored position in English markets. As wartime demand for goods ended, farmers and planters saw agricultural prices decline, and city workers experienced unemployment. Soldiers went unpaid for wartime service.

As Congress lacked exclusive control over issuance of money, each state printed its own. Some states printed huge quantities of paper money unbacked by metal, thereby causing the value of money to fall and prices to rise. This *cheap money* pleased the debtor class of small farmers and city workers because it enabled them to repay their mortgages and other loans easily. Other states refused to cheapen the value of their money, thus pleasing the creditor class of bankers and merchants. The lack of a uniform currency made merchants reluctant to do business outside their own states. Commerce was further hampered by quarrels among the states and by the inability of Congress to control foreign trade.

2. **Weaknesses of the Articles of Confederation.** This framework for the new government, adopted in 1781, created a league of thirteen sovereign and

independent states. The new government proved extremely weak and was unable to maintain order at home, to command respect from foreign countries, or to improve economic conditions. These failings of the Confederation most dejected the propertied and business groups: merchants, shippers, bankers, manufacturers, and large landowners. Even George Washington wondered aloud whether "the Revolution must ultimately be considered as a blessing or as a curse."

The fundamental weakness in any confederation is that power resides in the individual members, not in the central government. This was true of the Articles of Confederation, which provided for a central government consisting of only a Congress. This was a one-house legislature with delegates from the thirteen states, each state casting one vote. The weaknesses of this central government were as follows:

a. Congress was practically unable to enact laws since (1) passage of a bill required a vote of nine out of the thirteen states, and (2) delegates from more than ten states were rarely present at any one time.

b. There was no provision for a chief executive, and all law enforcement was left to the states.

c. No central courts existed to handle disputes between citizens of different states.

d. An amendment to the Articles required a unanimous vote, that is, the approval of all thirteen states.

e. Congress had no power to levy taxes directly upon the people, but could only request funds from the states. Over 75 percent of these requests were ignored.

f. Although Congress could issue money, it had no power to prevent each state from issuing its own currency.

g. Congress had no power to raise an army by directly recruiting men, but could only request the states to supply troops. However, the states rarely provided men, and the central government remained militarily helpless. This was demonstrated in Massachusetts in *Shays' Rebellion. Daniel Shays* led debtors in an armed rebellion in **1786-1787** seeking to end imprisonment for debt, halt the foreclosure of farm mortgages, and compel the state to issue cheap paper money. The debtors seized a number of courthouses and tried to seize the United States arsenal at Springfield. The central government stood by helpless. Shays' Rebellion was finally suppressed by the Massachusetts state militia.

h. Congress had no power to control interstate commerce (commerce between the states). Each state established its own tariffs and regulations. New York taxed farm products from Connecticut and New Jersey, and these states retaliated by taxing goods from New York. Maryland and Virginia each claimed control of navigation on the Potomac, an interstate river. Such disputes disrupted trade between states.

i. Congress had no power to control foreign commerce, and each state maintained its own tariffs on foreign goods. Britain refused to enter into commercial treaties with the United States, realizing that Congress could not enforce such treaties.

j. Congress commanded little respect abroad and was ineffective in dealing with foreign governments. This was demonstrated by British actions in the Northwest Territory and by foreign restrictions upon American shipping.

(1) *British Posts in the Northwest Territory.* In violation of the Treaty of Paris, the British retained their military and trading posts on American soil (see map, page 49). They justified these posts by arguing that the United States was violating the Treaty of Paris by its failure to restore Loyalist estates and repay British merchants. The national government made no effort to drive the British from American territory.

(2) *British and Spanish Prohibitions Against American Shipping.* Britain closed her West Indies ports to American ships so as to protect British merchants. Spain closed the lower Mississippi to American shipping. Spain realized that the settlers on the western frontier depended upon the lower Mississippi for transporting their agricultural produce. Spain hoped that the western settlers would break away from the United States and accept Spanish rule. Both Britain and Spain were well aware that the American government lacked the power to retaliate.

ACHIEVEMENTS UNDER THE ARTICLES OF CONFEDERATION

Many small farmers, frontiersmen, and city workers, having seen their states gain independence from a strong English government, were satisfied with the weak Articles of Confederation. They held that this government was least likely to threaten their rights and liberties.

Supporters of the government also pointed to its achievements. Under the Articles of Confederation, Congress (1) brought the American Revolution to a successful conclusion, (2) negotiated and signed the advantageous Treaty of Paris of 1783, (3) kept the states united in name, if not always in fact, through a period of great difficulty, and (4) passed the Land Ordinance of 1785 and the Northwest Ordinance of 1787.

ORDINANCES FOR THE WESTERN TERRITORIES

1. **Background.** The adoption of the Articles of Confederation had been delayed because Maryland had refused to ratify the Articles until the states

with claims to western lands had ceded these lands to the central government. When Virginia agreed to do so, several other states followed this example. As a result, the government gained title to the Northwest Territory,
an area bounded by the Mississippi River, the Ohio River, and the Great
Lakes (see map below). To provide for the settling and governing of the
Northwest Territory, Congress passed two laws.

2. Land Ordinance of 1785. This ordinance provided that (a) the Western
lands be surveyed and divided into square townships of 36 sections each, a
section being a square mile (640 acres), (b) the income from one section of
every township be used to support public education, and (c) the land be sold
in 640-acre sections at no less than $1 per acre.

3. Northwest Ordinance of 1787

a. The entire Northwest Territory was to be divided into no less than
three nor more than five territories, each of which would eventually become
a state. (Five states were formed from the Northwest Territory: Ohio, Indiana, Michigan, Illinois, and Wisconsin.)

b. As soon as any territory contained 5000 male adults, it could elect a
territorial legislature. Together with a governor and judges appointed by
Congress, this body would rule the territory.

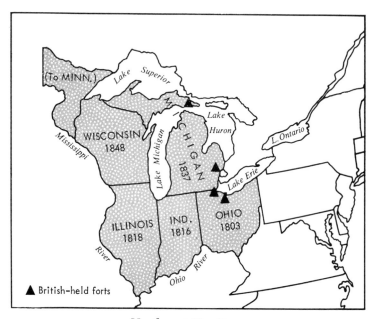

Northwest Territory

c. As soon as any territory contained 60,000 inhabitants, it could adopt a constitution and apply for statehood "on an equal footing with the original states in all respects whatever."

d. Slavery was forbidden in the Northwest Territory.

e. A "bill of rights" guaranteed basic civil liberties, including habeas corpus, trial by jury, and freedom of religion, speech, and press.

f. Public education was to be encouraged.

4. Significance. The Land Ordinance established national policy for the sale of Western lands and encouraged public education. The Northwest Ordinance served as a model for the democratic treatment of territories. It contrasted sharply with England's handling of the thirteen colonies. Also, it set a precedent for the admission of new states.

CONSTITUTIONAL CONVENTION AT PHILADELPHIA (1787)

1. Background. Five states sent delegates to a convention at Annapolis, Maryland, in 1786 to discuss commercial relations among the states. This *Annapolis Convention* petitioned Congress for a conference of all the states to remove the weaknesses of the Articles. Reluctantly yielding, Congress issued a call for a convention at Philadelphia for the "sole and express purpose of revising the Articles of Confederation."

2. Absentees. The Philadelphia Convention included scarcely any representatives of the small farmers, city workers, and frontiersmen, although these groups totaled over 90 percent of the country's population. Also, several leaders of the Revolutionary period were absent: Samuel Adams was not elected as a delegate; Patrick Henry, opposing a stronger central government, refused to attend. Other absentees were John Adams and Thomas Jefferson, our ministers at London and Paris.

3. Delegates. The Philadelphia Convention consisted of 55 delegates from all the states except Rhode Island. Since they were mainly lawyers, large landowners, bankers, and merchants, they reflected propertied and business interests. They were well-educated men who had read widely in history, government, and law. They were especially familiar with England's progress toward democracy and with the ideas of great political philosophers such as Locke and Montesquieu. Moreover, many delegates had practical experience in politics, having served as governors, judges, and legislators.

Several outstanding leaders exercised great influence over the convention: (*a*) *George Washington* presided over the convention with dignity and fairness. (*b*) *James Madison,* a scholar of government, took detailed notes of the proceedings. Since the delegates conferred in secret to facilitate agreement,

Madison's notes are our chief source of information about the convention. Madison himself played a major role in shaping our Constitution. He has been called "father of the Constitution." (*c*) **Alexander Hamilton** was an effective spokesman for the propertied interests. (*d*) **Benjamin Franklin** employed his wisdom and prestige to bring about agreement on crucial issues.

4. Points of Agreement. (*a*) Agreeing that the Articles of Confederation were entirely inadequate, the delegates at Philadelphia proceeded to draw up an entirely new Constitution, thus turning the meeting into a Constitutional Convention. Its members have become known as the *Founding Fathers*. (*b*) The delegates wanted a government strong enough to govern effectively at home and to command respect abroad, yet not so strong as to become a tyranny and threaten the liberties of the people. (*c*) The delegates believed that such a government must have a visible executive head and an independent judiciary as well as a legislature. (*d*) The delegates believed that the central government had to have the power to levy taxes, control interstate commerce, raise an army, and protect property. Furthermore, it had to be able to exercise these powers directly on the people, not indirectly through the states.

THE CONSTITUTION AS A "BUNDLE OF COMPROMISES"

1. Representation. The more populous states supported the Virginia Plan, that representation in the national legislature be based on population. The less populous states supported the New Jersey Plan, that each state have equal representation. This issue, the most serious one dividing the delegates, was settled by the *Great Compromise,* or *Connecticut Compromise.* The legislature was to consist of two houses: (*a*) a House of Representatives, where representation was to be based on population, and (*b*) a Senate, where each state was to have equal representation.

2. Slavery. The Southern states, which contained many Negro slaves, proposed that (*a*) slaves be counted as part of the population for purposes of representation, thus increasing the number of Southerners in the House of Representatives, and (*b*) slaves not be counted as part of the population for purposes of direct taxation, thus decreasing the Southern tax burden. The Northern states, in which slavery was fast dying out, supported the opposite positions. The issue was settled by the *Three-Fifths Compromise:* five slaves were to be counted as three free persons for purposes of both representation and direct taxation.

By another compromise on slavery, Congress was forbidden for 20 years (until 1808) to interfere with the importation of slaves into the country.

3. Tariffs. The Southern states opposed giving the central government the power to levy tariffs. Since they were chiefly agricultural, they feared that

Congress would pass a tariff on their exports of indigo, rice, and tobacco. The Northern states, being highly commercial, wanted the central government to have the power to establish uniform regulations on commerce with foreign nations. The issue was settled by granting Congress the power to control foreign commerce and to levy tariffs on imports but not on exports.

④ **Presidency.** The delegates disagreed over the term of office of the President and over the method of choosing him. Suggestions for his term of office ranged from three years to life. Some delegates wanted the President elected directly by the people. Others, fearing too much democracy, suggested that he be elected by Congress. The issues were settled (*a*) by authorizing a tenure of four years, and (*b*) by establishing a complex procedure for electing the President through an electoral college or, if no candidate received a majority in the electoral college, through the House of Representatives (see page 69). By this procedure, the delegates meant to allow the people only an indirect voice in choosing the President.

ADOPTION OF THE CONSTITUTION

1. Method of Ratification. The Founding Fathers provided that the new Constitution go into effect when ratified by conventions in nine of the thirteen states. Thus they disregarded the Articles of Confederation, which had specified that all changes be approved by the legislatures of all thirteen states.

2. Debate Over Ratification. The *Federalists,* supporters of the Constitution, consisted of men with business and property interests, and of others who considered the nation more important than their state. They argued that the Constitution would provide a stable government capable of maintaining law and order, furthering economic prosperity, and commanding respect abroad. The *Anti-Federalists,* opponents of the Constitution, consisted of farmers, city workers, and others who gave their chief loyalty to their state or community. They argued that the Constitution served the propertied classes, threatened the powers of the states, and left the people unprotected against federal encroachment upon their civil liberties. Acknowledging the last argument, the Federalists pledged to add a Bill of Rights to the Constitution.

3. Process of Ratification. Each state held its own Constitutional convention to consider ratification. The less populous states of Delaware, New Jersey, and Georgia quickly and overwhelmingly gave their approval. The more populous states approved ratification more slowly and by narrow margins. In Massachusetts, the sixth state to ratify, the convention voted 187 to 168. In Virginia, the tenth state, the convention vote was 89 to 79. In New York, the eleventh state, the convention voted 30 to 27.

After George Washington was inaugurated as first President of the new government, the Constitution was ratified by the last two states, North Carolina and then Rhode Island. The thirteen states were now bound together in a strong federal union.

4. Reasons for the Success of the Federalists

a. A well-organized group, the Federalists expended much energy and money toward achieving ratification. At various state ratifying conventions, the Federalists won the support of doubtful delegates and delayed the voting until they were assured a majority. The Anti-Federalists could not compare with them in funds, organization, and effectiveness. The Anti-Federalists were further handicapped by the fact that they were supporting the weak Articles of Confederation.

b. Most supporters of ratification could satisfy state property qualifications for voting and could therefore vote for convention delegates. The Anti-Federalist urban workers and poorer people, probably one-third of the population, lacked property and were denied the vote.

c. Alexander Hamilton, James Madison, and John Jay argued persuasively for the new Constitution by writing a series of articles for New York newspapers. These learned essays helped swing New York public opinion in favor of ratification. The articles were later collected and published under the title *The Federalist*. Read to this day, *The Federalist* provides insights into the political thinking of the Founding Fathers and into the principles of the Constitution.

d. The Federalists enjoyed the support of two highly respected men: Benjamin Franklin and George Washington. Their approval of the Constitution influenced many doubters.

MULTIPLE-CHOICE QUESTIONS

1. In the government provided by the Articles of Confederation (1) the states exercised most of the power (2) Congress enforced its will by its power of taxation (3) the central government exercised most of the power (4) the consent of a simple majority of the states was necessary to amend the Articles.

2. Which best explains the dissatisfaction of the merchant class with the Articles of Confederation? (1) The power of Congress to tax was unlimited. (2) Individual states lacked the power to regulate commerce. (3) The President's treaty-making power was unchecked. (4) There was no provision for a uniform currency.

3. During the period of the Articles of Confederation, there were economic difficulties because of (1) continuous cheapening of the currency (2) high taxes levied by the central government (3) a revival of the system of indentured servants (4) the refusal of Americans to trade with England.

4. Shays' Rebellion was a protest against (1) debts and lack of currency (2) the tax on whisky (3) the closing of the lower Mississippi by Spain (4) the calling of the Constitutional Convention.

5. In 1786 which person would most likely have favored Shays' Rebellion? (1) a Boston merchant (2) a New England sea captain (3) a Philadelphia banker (4) a Massachusetts farmer.

6. An important accomplishment of the government under the Articles of Confederation was (1) support of the principle of public education (2) free navigation of the entire Mississippi River (3) establishment of the domestic credit of the United States (4) recognition of the prestige of the United States by European governments.

7. The Northwest Ordinance is significant because it (1) provided for territorial government and the admission of new states (2) guaranteed the suffrage to all men (3) gave free land to settlers (4) prohibited selling arms to Indians.

8. Which provision of the Northwest Ordinance was based upon an established practice followed in Great Britain? (1) prohibition of slavery (2) admission of new states on an equal footing with the original states (3) guarantee of habeas corpus and trial by jury (4) encouragement of public schools.

9. The Philadelphia Convention (1787) was called for the purpose of (1) choosing a President for the new republic (2) revising the Articles of Confederation (3) making plans to suppress Shays' Rebellion (4) drafting a new Constitution.

10. At the Philadelphia Convention of 1787, on which issue was there the most agreement? (1) representation in a new Congress (2) importation of slaves (3) increased power for the central government (4) method of electing the President.

11. Which group was largely unrepresented at the Constitutional Convention (1787)? (1) lawyers (2) small farmers (3) large landowners (4) wealthy merchants.

12. The Great Compromise in the Constitutional Convention of 1787 dealt with the question of (1) the legality of slavery (2) election of the President (3) regulation of trade (4) Congressional representation.

13. At the Constitutional Convention, the Great Compromise was agreed upon to settle the controversy between the (1) slave states and free states (2) Southern states and Northern states (3) farm states and industrial states (4) large states and small states.

14. One basic reason for the inclusion of democratic features in the original Constitution was the (1) influence of the small landowners (2) fact that some states already had democratic constitutions (3) ideas of Alexander Hamilton (4) work of Thomas Jefferson at the Constitutional Convention.

15. The Three-Fifths Compromise, which became a part of our Constitution, related to (1) the metric system (2) slavery (3) the tariff (4) the election of the President.

16. The Constitution was an improvement over the Articles of Confederation in that the Constitution (1) provided for a federal legislature (2) delegated to Congress the power to declare war (3) gave the national government control over United States territories (4) enabled the national government to act directly on the people.

17. Which power did the federal government *lack* under the Articles of Confederation? (1) issuing money (2) regulating territories (3) regulating interstate commerce (4) selling public lands.

18. The delegates to the Constitutional Convention were strongly influenced in their decisions by their (1) faith in direct democracy (2) distrust of the states (3) fear of unchecked majorities (4) belief in compulsory education.

19. *The Federalist*, a series of political essays, was written to urge (1) ratification of the Constitution (2) rejection of the Constitution (3) the election of Washington as President (4) adoption of the Northwest Ordinance.

20. An important objection to the ratification of the Constitution was its failure to provide for (1) regulation of interstate commerce (2) a guarantee of a republican form of government (3) sufficient protection of individual rights (4) ownership of slaves.

21. Which argument against the ratification of the federal Constitution was used *least?* (1) The President would become too powerful. (2) The states would lose their power. (3) Senators would be elected by state legislatures. (4) A Bill of Rights was not included.

MODIFIED TRUE-FALSE QUESTIONS

If the statement is correct, write the word *true.* If the statement is incorrect, substitute a word or phrase for the italicized term to make the statement correct.

1. Under the Articles of Confederation, the states were *sovereign.*

2. Amendments to the Articles of Confederation required the approval of *three-quarters* of the states.

3. The issuance of huge quantities of paper money caused the value of money to *rise.*

4. The state of *Wisconsin* was formed from part of the Northwest Territory.

5. *Alexander Hamilton* was president of the Constitutional Convention.

6. In New York State, the Constitution was ratified by *an overwhelming* majority.

7. *Rhode Island* did not ratify the Constitution until after the new government was organized.

8. The Great Compromise at the Constitutional Convention was sponsored by the state of *New Jersey.*

9. The Constitutional Convention provided that the Constitution go into effect when ratified by *seven* of the thirteen states.

10. The "father of the Constitution," who kept detailed notes of the proceedings of the Constitutional Convention, was *Benjamin Franklin.*

ESSAY QUESTIONS

1. Although the government under the Articles of Confederation had many weaknesses and was soon discarded, it also compiled a record of achievement. In regard to the government under the Articles of Confederation, (a) explain *three* of its weaknesses, and (b) discuss *two* of its achievements.

2. The Northwest Ordinance has been called a model for democratic treatment of colonies. Discuss *three* provisions of the Northwest Ordinance and show how each justifies this statement.

3. The United Nations has often been compared to the American government under the Articles of Confederation. (a) Show *three* ways in which this comparison is justified. (b) Show *two* ways in which the situations are *different.*

4. (a) Show how the Constitutional Convention of 1787 settled a dispute that arose over *each* of the following: (1) control of commerce, (2) election of the President, (3) representation of the states in Congress. (b) State *two* ways in which the organization of the government under the federal Constitution differed from its organization under the Articles of Confederation.

5. The Federalists and Anti-Federalists battled vigorously over the ratification of the Constitution. (a) Explain *two* arguments advanced by the Federalists in favor of ratification. (b) Explain *two* arguments presented by the Anti-Federalists against ratification. (c) Discuss *two* factors that enabled the Federalists to secure ratification of the Constitution.

UNIT II. THE CONSTITUTION IS THE BASIS OF AMERICAN GOVERNMENT

Part 1. The Constitution Divides and Separates the Powers of Government

{ PREAMBLE: PURPOSES OF THE CONSTITUTION

The *Preamble,* or introduction, explains briefly why "we, the people of the United States" established the Constitution. The purposes of the Founding Fathers were "to form a more perfect Union, establish justice, insure domestic tranquility, provide for the common defense, promote the general welfare, and secure the blessings of liberty to ourselves and our posterity."

{ FEDERAL SYSTEM: DIVISION OF POWERS

The Constitution set up a system of *federalism,* a dual system of government whereby powers are divided between the state governments and the central (also known as the national or federal) government. The Constitution limits the federal government to *delegated,* or *enumerated,* powers. These are powers specifically listed in the Constitution as being granted to the federal government. Powers not given to the federal government and not denied to the states are reserved to the states or to the people. These are called *residual* powers. Certain powers, called *concurrent* powers, may be exercised by both the federal government and state governments.

Under the federal system each government is supreme within its own sphere. Every American is a citizen both of the United States and of the state in which he resides.

DELEGATED, OR ENUMERATED, POWERS (Article I, Section 8)

The following powers are specifically granted to Congress. They are the delegated, or enumerated, powers of the federal government.

1. **Financial.** To levy and collect taxes; borrow money; coin money and regulate its value; punish counterfeiters.

②. **Commercial.** To regulate interstate and foreign commerce; establish rules for bankruptcy; establish post offices and post roads; grant patents and copyrights.

③ **Military.** To declare war; raise, support, and make rules for an army and navy; call up the state militia to enforce federal laws; suppress insurrections and repel invasions; punish piracy.

④. **Miscellaneous.** To establish rules for the naturalization of aliens; provide for courts below the Supreme Court; control the seat of government (Washington, D.C.) and all federal property.

ELASTIC CLAUSE (Article I, Section 8, Clause 18)

1. **Statement.** Concluding the list of delegated powers, the Constitution grants Congress the power "to make all laws which shall be necessary and proper for carrying into execution the foregoing powers." Because this statement enables Congress to expand its delegated powers, it is known as the *elastic clause.*

②. **Applications: The Elastic Clause and Implied Powers.** (*a*) Congress in 1791 authorized a national bank although the Constitution nowhere specifically grants this power. Nevertheless, Congress considered the law "necessary and proper" for carrying out its delegated powers to collect taxes, coin and borrow money, and regulate its value. (*b*) Congress, beginning in 1877, passed legislation to regulate railroad fares, although, when the Constitution was written, the railroad had not been invented. Since railroads go from state to state, such federal control is based upon the elastic clause together with the delegated power "to regulate commerce among the states."

Such powers, each of which is derived from the elastic clause plus one or more of the foregoing delegated powers, are not specifically granted in the Constitution but can be inferred from it. Consequently, they are called *implied* powers.

3. **Controversy Regarding the Use of the Elastic Clause.** Throughout our history, Americans have debated the extent to which the federal government should use the elastic clause.

ⓐ *Strict Construction or Interpretation.* Some Americans have held that the Constitution should be interpreted strictly and that Congress should be limited to its specific delegated powers. These people advocate restraints on the federal government so that the states may exercise more power. This attitude is called "states' rights." Although states' righters have been found in all sections of the nation, they have been most numerous and influential in the South.

b. Loose Construction or Interpretation. Other Americans have held that the Constitution should be interpreted broadly and that Congress should exercise many powers not specifically given to it, but merely implied. These people, champions of a powerful federal government, have usually been in the majority.

4. Historic Trend Toward Loose Construction. Over the years, the central government has greatly increased the scope of its functions by using its implied powers. Today, the federal government utilizes the elastic clause: (*a*) together with the clause giving Congress control of interstate commerce, to regulate all interstate transportation and communication, and to control business practices, the sale of securities, labor unions, and working conditions, (*b*) together with the power to tax for the general welfare, to maintain Social Security and Medicare, and (*c*) together with the power to raise and support armies, to further atomic research and development for peaceful as well as military purposes.

RESERVED, OR RESIDUAL, POWERS (Amendment X)

Adopted in 1791, the Tenth Amendment to the Constitution states: "The powers not delegated to the United States by the Constitution, nor prohibited by it to the states, are reserved to the states respectively, or to the people." The states consequently have retained control over such matters as education, intrastate (within the state) commerce, most intrastate crimes, traffic laws, marriage, and divorce. Many state powers are called *police powers* —the protection of the health, welfare, safety, and morals of the people.

CONCURRENT POWERS

Concurrent powers are exercised by both the federal government and the states. Concurrent powers include levying taxes, borrowing money, building roads, and maintaining courts.

POWERS DENIED THE FEDERAL GOVERNMENT

1. Article I, Section 9. The original Constitution specifically prohibits the federal government from (*a*) passing any commerce or revenue law favoring one state at the expense of another, (b) granting any title of nobility, (c) levying any tax on exports, (d) levying any direct tax not based on population, (e) spending money without an appropriation authorized by law, and (f) encroaching upon the civil liberties of the people by suspending the right of habeas corpus (except in time of rebellion or invasion) or passing a bill of attainder or an ex post facto law (see pages 90–91).

2. Amendments I–X. These amendments, called the Bill of Rights, deny the federal government the power to interfere with various civil liberties (see pages 91–92).

3. Amendments XV, XIX, XXIV, and XXVI. These amendments prohibit the federal government from interfering with voting rights (see pages 99–101).

POWERS DENIED THE STATES

1. Article I, Section 10. The original Constitution also denies some powers to the states. The Founding Fathers thus meant to reserve certain powers exclusively for the federal government and to prevent state actions that might violate property rights and civil liberties. (a) States may not coin money, enter into foreign treaties, or impair (lessen) obligations of contract. (b) Without the consent of Congress, states may not levy import or export duties, enter into agreements with each other, maintain troops in peacetime, or engage in war. (c) Like the federal government, the states may not grant titles of nobility or pass bills of attainder or ex post facto laws.

2. Amendments XIV, XV, XIX, XXIV, and XXVI. These amendments prohibit states from interfering with voting and other rights (see pages 99–101).

RELATIONS BETWEEN THE STATES (Article IV, Sections 1 and 2)

The Constitution specifies that each state shall (1) give "full faith and credit" to the legal actions of the other states (a couple married in New York is still considered married even though they move to California), (2) extend to citizens of other states the privileges of local citizenship, such as the right to own property and engage in business, and (3) honor requests from other states for *extradition*, that is, the return of a fugitive charged with committing a crime.

FEDERAL GOVERNMENT AND THE STATES (Article IV, Sections 3 and 4)

The Constitution empowers Congress to admit new states into the Union. It also requires the federal government to assure each state (1) a republican form of government, (2) protection against invasion, and (3) upon request of the state, protection against domestic violence.

FEDERAL GOVERNMENT COMPARED WITH UNITARY GOVERNMENT

The United States (Federal)	Great Britain (Unitary)
1. Powers are divided between the federal government and the states.	1. Powers are concentrated within the national government.
2. The states are supreme in matters of local government, and each state derives its authority from and is responsible to the people of the state.	2. Local governmental bodies are subordinate agencies, deriving their authority from and owing responsibility to the national government.
3. Federalism meets the diverse needs throughout the vast territorial extent of the United States.	3. Unitary government provides competent rule over the limited area constituting Great Britain.

EVALUATION OF FEDERALISM: STRENGTHS AND WEAKNESSES

1. **Strengths.** (*a*) The federal government can best handle matters of national interest. State governments, being closer to the people, are best aware of local conditions and are best qualified to handle local problems. (*b*) By dividing powers between the federal government and a group of independent states jealously guarding their authority, federalism prevents complete centralization, which might lead to tyranny. Democracy survives best, it is argued, when powers are divided, not concentrated. (*c*) By preserving independent states, federalism prevents sole reliance upon national authority and encourages the people to exercise local initiative and civic responsibility. (*d*) A state may serve as a laboratory for reform without involving the entire nation. For example, Wyoming experimented with woman suffrage and Wisconsin with unemployment insurance before these measures were adopted by the national government.

2. **Weaknesses.** (*a*) Conflicts arise between the federal government and the states because the Constitutional provisions dividing their powers have proved vague and subject to differing interpretations. For example, advocates of states' rights consider education an area reserved for the states. Nevertheless, the federal government has legislated on education, claiming that scientific knowledge is essential for national defense. (*b*) On matters reserved to the states, laws have varied considerably from state to state. For example, Nevada permits gambling casinos; other states do not. New Jersey requires a minimum age of 17 for a driver's license; most states accept age 16, and some, age 15. (*c*) Federalism results in inefficiency, waste, and overlapping administration. For example, duplicate federal and state agencies exist in such areas as housing, agriculture, and law enforcement.

WITHIN THE FEDERAL GOVERNMENT: SEPARATION OF POWERS

The Founding Fathers provided that the powers of the federal government be separated among three distinct branches: (1) The *executive branch*, headed by the President, administers, or carries out, the laws. (2) The *legislative branch*, Congress, enacts, or makes, the laws. (3) The *judicial branch*, the court system, interprets the laws, that is, it settles disputes regarding the meaning of the laws.

To reinforce the separation of powers, the Constitution provides that no member of Congress may serve, at the same time, in another branch of the federal government. Thus, before John F. Kennedy took office as President, he was compelled to resign his position as Senator from Massachusetts. Nor, by tradition, may a person simultaneously serve in the executive and judicial branches.

CHECKS AND BALANCES

The Constitution enables each branch of the federal government to brake and counteract the powers of the other two branches through a system of checks and balances.

(1) **Executive.** (*a*) The President may check Congress by vetoing legislation. He may exert influence on Congress also by calling it into special session and by recommending legislation. (*b*) The President may check the federal courts by nominating judges, by granting pardons and reprieves (except in cases of impeachment), and by refusing to enforce court orders.

(2) **Legislative.** (*a*) Congress may check the President by refusing to pass legislation and to appropriate funds, and by overriding the President's veto by a two-thirds vote of each house. In addition, the Senate may check the President by refusing to approve his appointments and to ratify treaties. The House of Representatives may bring impeachment charges against the President, and the Senate, acting as the jury, may by a two-thirds vote find the President guilty of the charges and remove him from office. (*b*) Congress may check and balance the Supreme Court by passing a somewhat altered law to replace a law held unconstitutional, by initiating an amendment to the Constitution, by impeaching and convicting judges, and by increasing the number of judges on the Supreme Court. The Senate also has the power to refuse to approve men nominated by the President for judgeships. (*c*) The House of Representatives and the Senate may check each other, since approval of both houses is necessary to pass laws.

3. Judicial. (*a*) The Supreme Court may check the President by declaring actions of the executive branch unconstitutional. (*b*) The Supreme Court may check Congress by declaring laws unconstitutional.

SEPARATION OF POWERS COMPARED WITH PARLIAMENTARY SUPREMACY

THE UNITED STATES (Separation of Powers)	GREAT BRITAIN (Parliamentary Supremacy)
1. The President is chosen by a nation-wide vote of the people (as expressed through the electoral college). Regardless of how Congress responds to his requests for legislation, the President serves a fixed four-year term.	1. The Prime Minister secures office as leader of the majority party in Parliament. He remains in office as long as he retains the support of a Parliamentary majority. If defeated by Parliament on a significant issue, the Prime Minister either resigns or calls for new elections in an attempt to reestablish his Parliamentary majority.
2. No Cabinet member may be, at the same time, a member of Congress. The Cabinet exercises executive functions chiefly.	2. Cabinet members are also members of Parliament. The Cabinet exercises both executive and legislative functions. Its legislative duties include introducing bills into Parliament, defending them in debate, and guiding them to passage.
3. The President and his Cabinet may belong to one political party, while Congress (or either house) is controlled by another party. Thus the executive and legislative branches may be in conflict.	3. The Prime Minister and his Cabinet must come from the majority party in Parliament and are responsible to Parliament. Thus the executive and legislative branches work in harmony.
4. The Supreme Court may declare laws unconstitutional, that is, in violation of the written Constitution.	4. No formal written constitution exists, and so no court may declare laws invalid.

EVALUATION OF CHECKS AND BALANCES: STRENGTHS AND WEAKNESSES

1. Strengths

a. Checks and balances prevent any branch of government from becoming too powerful and establishing a dictatorship. The Founding Fathers greatly feared the danger of tyranny and derived the idea of checks and balances from (1) the political theory of Montesquieu in his book *The Spirit of the Laws*, and (2) their experiences before the Revolution, when the colonial legislatures had fought to check the royal governors.

b. Hasty, ill-considered action by any one branch of government is discouraged, since each branch is aware that its action is subject to checks by the other two.

c. In national emergencies, the branches temporarily and voluntarily suspend their powers of check and balance in order to work together quickly and efficiently. In 1933, to combat the depression, President Franklin D. Roosevelt requested a considerable number of major New Deal laws, which Congress passed within a 100-day period. On December 7, 1941, Japan attacked Pearl Harbor; on December 8, President Roosevelt requested a declaration of war, and Congress passed it on the same day. In these two instances, Congress suspended or abbreviated its usual procedures of debating, criticizing, and deliberating so as to accede quickly to executive requests.

2. Weaknesses

a. Checks and balances may paralyze the workings of government, especially if one party controls Congress and another the executive. For example, in 1947–1948, when President Harry S. Truman, a Democrat, and Congress, controlled by Republicans, disagreed on most domestic matters, little was accomplished toward meeting the nation's domestic needs.

b. In case of an executive-legislative deadlock, no provision exists for calling a special election so that the voters may end the deadlock. Instead, the nation must await the next regular election.

c. Checks and balances may cause delay and uncertainty. For example, a law passed by Congress and signed by the President may be declared unconstitutional by the Supreme Court after an interval of several years.

MULTIPLE-CHOICE QUESTIONS

1. The ultimate source of all political power in the United States is the (1) people of the United States (2) laws made by Congress (3) state constitutions (4) United States Constitution.

2. Which basic principle of the Constitution has been involved in the controversy between those who advocate states' rights and those who favor an increase in federal power? (1) separation of powers (2) division of powers (3) due process of law (4) concurrent powers.

3. A federal system of government is one in which (1) all the power is concentrated in the national government (2) powers are divided between the national and the state governments (3) the states are supreme (4) there is a system of Cabinet responsibility.

4. The Constitution of the United States guarantees to each state (1) an equal share of federal funds (2) federal aid for flood control (3) a republican form of government (4) the power to grant patents to inventors.

5. Which illustrates the fact that the United States has a federal system of government? (1) Congress passes laws, but the President enforces them. (2) The President appoints Cabinet members, but the Senate must approve them. (3) The Supreme Court has the power to declare laws of Congress unconstitutional. (4) The national government regulates interstate commerce, but state governments regulate commerce within the states.

6. The expansion of federal power since the end of the Civil War has (1) threatened the existence of our republican system of government (2) weakened the system of checks and balances in our Constitution (3) altered the division of powers in our nation (4) strengthened the powers of the House of Representatives at the expense of the Senate.

7. The Constitution contains "delegated powers," which are (1) found in the elastic clause (2) reserved to the states (3) the enumerated powers of Congress (4) the purposes listed in the Preamble.

8. The powers of Congress derived from the provision "to make all laws which shall be necessary and proper for carrying into execution the foregoing powers" are said to be (1) concurrent (2) implied (3) residual (4) enumerated.

9. According to the Tenth Amendment, the powers "not delegated to the United States by the Constitution, nor prohibited by it to the states," are reserved to the (1) Congress (2) Supreme Court (3) President with the advice and consent of the Senate (4) states or the people.

10. Which two functions are carried on by both the federal and state governments? (1) maintaining highways and operating a postal system (2) conserving natural resources and coining money (3) appointing ambassadors and financing schools (4) levying taxes and apprehending criminals.

11. Which is an example of a power denied both to the federal government and to the states? (1) enactment of ex post facto legislation (2) impeachment of judges (3) levying of tariffs (4) coining of money.

12. Appointments to the United States Supreme Court must be approved by the (1) House of Representatives (2) United States Senate (3) United States Supreme Court (4) state legislatures.

13. In adopting the principle of separation of powers, the framers of the Constitution were most influenced by the writings of (1) Diderot (2) Rousseau (3) Voltaire (4) Montesquieu.

14. The system of checks and balances was made part of our federal government in order to prevent (1) the federal government from obtaining too much power over the states (2) the states from seceding (3) any one branch of the federal government from becoming too powerful (4) the Supreme Court from declaring laws unconstitutional.

15. A Congressman may *not* be a member of the President's Cabinet because such a practice would violate the principle of (1) separation of powers (2) division of powers (3) the federal system (4) Cabinet responsibility.

16. A bill may become a law over the veto of the President by a (1) two-thirds vote of Congress (2) three-fourths vote of Congress (3) judicial interpretation of the Supreme Court (4) three-fourths vote of the Senate.

17. Which feature of our heritage was derived from England? (1) "direct democracy" (2) a written constitution (3) representative government (4) federal system of government.

18. Both the President of the United States and the Prime Minister of Great Britain are (1) presiding officers of the legislatures (2) persons responsible for declaring war (3) members of the legislatures of their countries (4) leaders of political parties.

APPLICATION QUESTIONS

Constitutional Powers: (A) Delegated (B) Reserved (C) Implied (D) Denied

For each of the following statements, select the *letter* of the power, chosen from the group above, that best applies to that situation.

1. New York State requires a course in American history in its high schools.
2. California issues a "Bear State Dollar" for use along the Pacific Coast area.
3. The Federal Communications Commission assigns television channels.
4. Congress decides to change the gold content of the dollar.
5. Wisconsin passes a law conferring the rank of Baron on all ex-governors of the state.
6. The Interstate Commerce Commission regulates rates of an interstate bus line.
7. Congress raises the salaries of members of the Armed Forces.
8. Congress places a tax on exports from the West Coast states.
9. In Georgia a driver seeking an auto license must be at least 16 years old.
10. Congress lowers tariff rates on goods imported through Charleston and Savannah.

ESSAY QUESTIONS

1. (a) By giving *two* examples, prove that the Constitution divided powers between the states and the national government. (b) Give *two* examples of the increase in power of the national government in the 20th century. (c) Give *one* argument for *or one* argument against the increase in power of the national government now.
2. (a) Giving *two* examples, illustrate the operation of the system of checks and balances in our federal government. (b) State *one* reason for including this system in our Constitution. (c) Explain *one* advantage and *one* disadvantage of this system. (d) Giving *one recent* example, illustrate the workings of this system.
3. Compare the English with the American system of government, illustrating (a) *two* ways in which they are similar, and (b) *two* ways in which they are different.

Part 2. Executive Power Shall Be Vested in a President

SELECTION OF PRESIDENTIAL CANDIDATES

CONSTITUTIONAL REQUIREMENTS

A candidate for the Presidency must be a "natural-born" citizen of the United States, at least 35 years of age, and for 14 years a resident within the United States. The Constitution is silent regarding the nominating of Presidential candidates. This task was assumed by political parties.

BRIEF HISTORY OF NOMINATING PROCEDURES

1. **Caucus System (To 1828).** A *caucus,* or meeting of a small group of influential party leaders, mostly Congressmen, selected the party candidate

for the Presidency. Because the rank-and-file party members had no voice in this process, "King Caucus" was condemned as undemocratic.

2. Nominating Convention (Since 1832). During the Age of Jackson, political parties began selecting Presidential candidates by a new method, the *nominating convention.* Since a large group of party members attended the convention, it was considered a democratic advance over the caucus.

NATIONAL NOMINATING CONVENTION SYSTEM TODAY

1. Selection of National Convention Delegates

   a. By District and State Conventions. In about one-quarter of the states, delegates are chosen by the political parties through district and state conventions. These procedures, operating through the party machinery, usually are controlled by local and state party leaders.

   b. By Presidential Primaries. In about three-quarters of the states, delegates are chosen by the party members in preliminary elections, called *primaries.* Usually, delegates pledge to vote for a specific candidate on at least the first ballot of the convention. In recent years, the number of Presidential primaries has increased sharply.

   Presidential primaries have been hailed as a democratic advance over state and district conventions, since primaries reflect the wishes not of a few party leaders, but of the many party members. To better represent the party members, recent primary slates have included more women, youth, and ethnic minority delegates. However, the primaries have been criticized because the expense of these contests favors the candidate with the greater campaign funds and because both the expense and the time expended in primaries discourage many qualified candidates from actively seeking the Presidency.

2. National Convention. Held some two to three months before Election Day, the convention—full of noise, motion, and color, and broadcast over radio and television—has been called a "political circus." It serves to center public attention upon the party, to enthuse rank-and-file party workers, to reconcile differing party views and unite delegates on a *party platform,* and to nominate the party candidates for President and Vice President.

3. Qualifications Considered in Selecting a Candidate. Each party seeks to nominate a candidate who can win. Such a person, party leaders generally believe, should (*a*) possess great personal popularity and have few enemies, (*b*) reflect moderate views on controversial issues, and (*c*) come from a heavily populated and "doubtful" state, that is, a state that has not consistently voted for one major party.

No major political party has ever nominated a black, a Jew, or a woman. Twice only, the Democrats have nominated a Catholic—in 1928 Alfred E. Smith, who lost the election, and in 1960 the victorious John F. Kennedy.

With these two exceptions, the candidates of the major parties have been white, Protestant, and male.

4. The Convention Selects the Party Ticket

a. Presidential Candidate. The names presented to the convention include those of (1) *active candidates,* who have previously declared their intention to seek the nomination and possibly have won the support of delegates in various states through Presidential primaries and political arrangements, and (2) *favorite sons,* who are state leaders honored by their delegations on the basis of state loyalty even though they may not be active candidates. A majority vote at the convention is necessary for nomination. If repeated balloting fails to give any candidate a majority, the convention is deadlocked and may unite behind a compromise choice, usually a person not previously considered and therefore called a *dark horse.*

If the President is seeking a second term, the convention usually loses the sense of battle and becomes "cut-and-dried" as it renominates him.

b. Vice Presidential Candidate. After the Presidential candidate is nominated, the convention selects the Vice Presidential candidate. Usually, the convention respects the wishes of the Presidential nominee as to his running mate. The Vice Presidential candidate is expected to bring strength to the ticket by attracting voters indifferent to the Presidential nominee. For example, the two candidates may come from different sections of the country and may be identified with different economic interests. The Vice Presidential candidate is said, therefore, to *balance the ticket.*

ELECTION OF THE PRESIDENT

ELECTION CAMPAIGN

1. **Appeal to the Voters.** For eight to ten weeks, the Presidential candidates "go to the people." They present their philosophies of government and views on current issues. They employ publicity staffs, travel extensively, deliver major addresses, and appear on radio and television.

2. **Campaign Finances.** Presidential campaigns are expensive. Candidates spend tens of millions of dollars to publicize their views. In the past, the major parties raised money chiefly from well-to-do contributors.

To prevent "corrupt practices" in the financing of federal elections, Congress enacted several laws—none really effective. One provision prohibits corporations or unions from contributing campaign funds. However, corporate officials may contribute as individuals; also union members may contribute voluntarily to labor's *Committee on Political Education (COPE).*

The 1972 Presidential election disclosed two major weaknesses: *(a)* A number of corporations and milk cooperatives had made large and illegal campaign contributions, mostly to the Committee to Reelect the President [Richard Nixon]. *(b)* The Justice Department lacked the manpower to handle all the reports of election law violations. To remedy such weaknesses, Congress enacted the 1974 *Federal Campaign Reform Act:*

a. The law limited spending and provided federal funds for Presidential elections. For Presidential primaries, each candidate who raises $100,000 in private contributions of $250 or less from at least 20 states is eligible for federal funds. These funds are to match all private contributions of $250 or less up to a maximum of $5 million, thereby limiting the spending of each candidate in the primaries to $10 million. For the national nominating convention, each major party is to receive federal funds of $2 million. For the Presidential general election, each major party candidate is to receive and be limited to federal funds of $20 million. (A minor party may receive election funds in proportion to its votes in the previous election.) These monetary limits, in future years, were to be increased in keeping with the Consumer Price Index. These federal funds are to come from individual income tax payers who may assign $1 of tax payment for election purposes.

b. The law provided no federal funds for Senate and House candidates, and it limited spending by these candidates.

c. The law limited contributions by individuals and political organizations. For a single federal candidate, an individual is limited to a contribution of $1000 for the primaries and $1000 for the general election. Political organizations—such as labor, business, and public interest groups—may contribute to a Presidential candidate no more than $5000. Contributions of over $100 may not be in cash. Presidential candidates may spend on their own behalf no more than $50,000.

d. The law established a *Federal Elections Commission* of six members—two named by the President and four by Congress. The Commission is to receive reports from candidates of receipts and expenditures, to investigate suspicious contributions, and to institute civil suits against suspected campaign law violators. Candidates who violate the law may be barred for a number of years from running again for federal office. All violators may be fined up to $50,000.

3. The 1976 Supreme Court Decision on the Campaign Reform Act.

(a) The Court held unconstitutional the spending limits on Presidential candidates for themselves and on Senate and House candidates. Such limits, the Court reasoned, violated the First Amendment guarantee of free speech. *(b)* The Court ordered the restructuring of the Federal Elections Commission to have all six members named by the President. The Commission, the Court held, is an executive agency and must conform to the principle of separation of powers. (By law, the Commission was so restructured.) *(c)* The Court upheld (i) limits on individual and group contributions to political candidates as only a "marginal" restraint on free speech, outweighed by

the need to insure the "integrity" of the election process; (ii) requirements that political candidates provide detailed reports of contributions and expenditures; and (iii) public financing of Presidential candidates. In upholding these provisions, the Court cited the need to avoid the "actuality and appearance of corruption" in federal elections.

(In 1985 the Supreme Court by 7 to 2 held that the $1000 limit on contributions by political action committees (P.A.C.s) to Presidential candidates in general elections was unconstitutional—a violation of free speech.)

4. Election Day. On the first Tuesday after the first Monday in November each leap year, the people go to the polls. They vote for their candidate, not directly, but through a group of persons called *electors*.

ELECTORAL SYSTEM

1. Election Procedures. The President and Vice President are chosen by the *electoral college*, which now consists of 538 electors. Each state is entitled to as many electors as the total number of its Representatives and Senators in Congress. (The District of Columbia, according to the Twenty-third Amendment, is currently entitled to three electors.) Although the names of only the Presidential and Vice Presidential candidates appear on the ballot, the voters in each state actually choose from among several slates of electors, each slate being pledged to support its party's candidates. The winning slate receives either *(a)* a *majority*—more than half the votes cast in the state, or *(b)* a *plurality*—the largest number of votes, though less than half, as may happen if more than two slates are involved.

The Presidential and Vice Presidential candidates of the winning slate in each state receive all the state's electoral votes—the *winner-take-all* principle. For election, a candidate must secure an electoral college majority, or 270 votes.

2. Appeals From an Electoral College Deadlock. If the electoral college does not give any candidate the necessary majority, the House of Representatives chooses the President from among the three candidates having the most electoral votes. In such a situation the House votes by states, with each state having one vote. To be elected President, a candidate must receive the votes of a majority of the states. For the Vice Presidency, if no candidate receives a majority in the electoral college, the Senate selects a Vice President from the top two candidates.

Twice the electoral college failed to elect a President and sent the election into the House: in 1800 (see page 118) and in 1824 (see page 136).

3. From Undemocratic Intent to "Rubber Stamp." The Founding Fathers devised the electoral system so as to reduce the voice of the people in electing the President. They intended that the electors express their own judgment. Since 1796, however, political parties have overcome this undemocratic intent by naming electors who were pledged in advance to vote for the party's Presidential candidate. Thus the people vote for the Presidential candidate they desire by voting for his group of electors, and the electoral college reflects the people's wishes. It has become a "rubber stamp."

4. Effects of the Electoral College System

a. The electoral vote distorts the popular vote. In 1980 Ronald Reagan defeated Jimmy Carter in the popular vote by 43 to 35 million (55 to 45 percent), but the electoral vote of 489 to 49 indicated a landslide Reagan victory.

b. A candidate may lose the small states overwhelmingly in the popular vote while carrying the large states by narrow margins. The electoral votes of the large states may then give the candidate a victory in the electoral college though his opponent had more popular votes. In 1888, although Grover Cleveland outdrew Benjamin Harrison by 100,000 popular votes, Harrison received a majority of the electoral votes and was elected President.

c. When more than two strong candidates are running, the electoral college may convert a popular plurality into an electoral majority and so prevent a deadlock. In 1968 Richard Nixon led in a field of three candidates and, although he lacked a popular majority, was elected President.

d. Most minor parties are discouraged by the electoral system, since they rarely poll enough popular votes to capture any electoral votes. People often feel that a vote for a minor party candidate is a "wasted" vote.

e. In most states, electors are not legally bound to honor their pledges to vote for their party's candidates. In a few recent instances, electors have broken their pledges.

f. Candidates tend to campaign little in small states and rural areas. They concentrate upon the industrial states, and upon heavily populated cities and suburbs, aiming to win the states with the most electoral votes.

g. To carry closely contested states, especially in the North, candidates seek to satisfy minority groups whose numbers could determine the electoral vote of an entire state.

5. Proposed Changes. The House of Representatives in 1969 proposed a Constitutional Amendment to (*a*) abolish the electoral college, (*b*) base the election upon the popular vote, (*c*) require the top pair of candidates for President and Vice President to secure at least 40 percent of the popular vote, and (*d*) if no pair secured this minimum, provide for a runoff election between the top two pairs. To be adopted, this proposal still requires a two-thirds vote in the Senate and ratification by 38 state legislatures.

PRESIDENTIAL INAUGURATION

On the 20th of January following the election, the President takes office. In a solemn and impressive ceremony, he takes an oath or affirmation to "preserve, protect, and defend the Constitution of the United States."

PRESIDENTIAL TENURE AND SUCCESSION

TERM OF PRESIDENTIAL OFFICE

1. Two-Term Tradition. The Constitution sets the term of office at four years. George Washington, our first President, originated the tradition of serving no more than two terms.

2. Breaking the Two-Term Tradition. In 1940 Franklin D. Roosevelt broke the two-term tradition when he was nominated for and elected to a third term. His supporters argued that the people (a) needed an experienced statesman to deal with the critical problems of World War II, and (b) had made and therefore could unmake traditions. His opponents insisted that the people (a) should not consider any one man indispensable, and (b) needed the two-term tradition as a safeguard against dictatorship.

3. Twenty-second Amendment (1951). Passed after Roosevelt's breaking of the two-term tradition, this amendment prohibits any one person from being elected President for more than two terms. A person who has served more than two years of another person's term may be elected for only one additional term.

SUCCESSION TO THE PRESIDENCY

1. Original Constitution. In case of the death, resignation, or removal of the President, the Constitution provides that the Vice President succeed him.

2. Presidential Succession Act of 1947. In the event of a vacancy in both the Presidency and the Vice Presidency, the *Presidential Succession Act of 1947* provides the following order of succession to the Presidency: the Speaker of the House of Representatives, then the President pro tempore of the Senate, and finally the Cabinet members, starting with the Secretary of State.

This act was considered democratic because it provided that elected officials be next in line for the Presidency. However, the act was criticized because (a) the will of the people, as expressed in the Presidential election, would be reversed if the Speaker of the House were of a different political party than the President, (b) the Speaker of the House, having attained his position in part through length of legislative service, is usually an elderly person with little or no executive experience.

3. Problems of Presidential Disability and Succession. Until the 1960's, Congress failed to deal with the problem of succession in case of Presidential disability. For example, in 1919–1920 President Wilson was bedridden with a stroke, and, for much of this time, the executive branch remained leaderless. Also, from 1955 to 1957 President Eisenhower suffered three serious illnesses.

Still another problem was the fact that the Vice Presidency has often been vacant. In 1963, following President Kennedy's assassination, Lyndon B. Johnson was sworn in as President, and the Vice Presidency remained vacant for over a year. This event and Eisenhower's illnesses turned the nation's attention to the problem of Presidential disability and succession.

4. Twenty-fifth Amendment (1967): Presidential Disability and Succession

   a. In case the office of Vice President is vacant, the President shall nominate a new Vice President, subject to approval by a majority vote of both houses of Congress. (For first applications of this provision, check the Index for "Amendments to Constitution, Twenty-fifth.")

   b. In case of Presidential disability, the President himself or—if he does not or cannot—the Vice President, with a majority of the Cabinet members, may so inform Congress. Thereupon, the Vice President shall serve as Acting President.

   c. When the President informs Congress that his inability no longer exists, he shall resume the duties of his office. In case the Vice President and a majority of the Cabinet officers dispute the President's ability to resume office, the President may be declared still disabled and kept from office by a two-thirds vote of Congress. The Vice President then continues as Acting President.

THE PRESIDENT IN OFFICE

POWERS OF THE PRESIDENT

The President of the United States is the most powerful democratically elected official in the world. His powers are derived from the Constitution as well as from customs and traditions.

1. Executive Powers. (*a*) The President enforces the Constitution and the laws passed by Congress. For these purposes, he may issue executive orders. (*b*) With the consent of a majority of the Senate, he appoints all important government officials, including Cabinet officers and members of administrative agencies. (*c*) He serves as ceremonial head of the government and as a symbol of national unity. (*d*) He is commander in chief of the armed forces.

2. Powers Over Foreign Affairs. (*a*) The President determines the foreign policy of the nation and is responsible for the conduct of foreign affairs. Today, he is also considered the leader of the free nations of the world. (*b*) With the consent of a majority of the Senate, he appoints officials to assist him in foreign affairs: the Secretary of State, ambassadors, consuls, and ministers. (*c*) He negotiates treaties with foreign countries, but such treaties must be ratified by a two-thirds vote of the Senate. (*d*) He receives foreign ambassadors, and he may therefore recognize or refuse to recognize foreign governments. (e) As commander in chief, he may order the armed forces to intervene in disturbances abroad. His power, however, is limited by the power of Congress to declare war and to appropriate money for the armed forces. His power is also limited by the terms of the 1973 War-Powers Resolution (check the Index).

3. **Legislative Powers.** (a) In his "State of the Union" message, required by the Constitution, and in other messages, the President may request that Congress pass specific legislation. (b) If Congress adjourns without passing the requested legislation or if an emergency arises, the President may recall Congress into special session. (c) He may veto legislation of which he disapproves. (d) As head of his political party, the President may often influence the votes of the members of his party in Congress. He may also use his power of patronage; that is, he may offer political jobs for distribution by those members of Congress who vote as he wishes. (e) Through radio, television, and press, the President may appeal for public support.

4. **Judicial Powers.** (a) The President may grant pardons and reprieves in cases involving federal crimes, except in cases of impeachment. (b) With the consent of a majority of the Senate, he appoints all federal judges. (c) He enforces or may refuse to enforce federal court decisions.

PHILOSOPHIES REGARDING THE USE OF PRESIDENTIAL POWER

Each President has had substantially the same powers, but the extent to which each has used these powers has varied greatly.

1. **Weak Presidents.** This type of President sees himself as a purely administrative officer. He follows Congressional initiative and uses Presidential powers sparingly. One exponent of this philosophy was James Buchanan.

2. **Moderately Active Presidents.** This type of President sees himself as an administrative officer, and as a defender of executive power and public welfare against Congressional encroachment. He uses Presidential powers moderately. One exponent of this philosophy was Grover Cleveland.

3. **Strong Presidents.** This type of President sees himself as a forceful political leader. He advocates a legislative program, rallies public opinion, and battles to secure Congressional enactment. He tries to anticipate the needs of the nation and uses Presidential powers to the utmost. The earliest exponents of this philosophy were Andrew Jackson and Abraham Lincoln.

PRESIDENTIAL POWERS AND EMERGENCIES

During national crises, such as war and economic depression, the people demand strong Presidential leadership. In response, certain Presidents have stretched their authority, acted with speed and decision, and exercised almost dictatorial power. Voluntarily, Congress cooperated with the President. Thus Lincoln met the crisis of the Civil War, Wilson the crisis of World War I, and Franklin D. Roosevelt the Great Depression of the 1930's and World War II. However, with the passing of each crisis, Congress has reasserted its full powers, including its power to check upon the President.

SIZE AND COMPLEXITY OF THE EXECUTIVE BRANCH

EXECUTIVE DEPARTMENTS AND THE CABINET

Each executive department enforces relevant laws and furthers governmental policies. The head of each executive department is appointed by the President with the consent of the Senate. Together, the department heads form a group of top-level Presidential advisers, the Cabinet.

The Constitution mentions executive departments, but it says nothing about a Cabinet. This institution therefore arose by tradition. The first Cabinet, established by George Washington, consisted of four members.

As the federal government grew in complexity, the number of Cabinet departments expanded. Today it totals 14 as follows: State; Treasury; Defense; Justice; Interior; Agriculture; Commerce; Labor; Health and Human Services (formerly Health, Education, and Welfare); Housing and Urban Development; Transportation; Energy; Education; Veterans Affairs.

EXECUTIVE OFFICE OF THE PRESIDENT

Since 1939 the President has been assisted by the *Executive Office of the President*. It helps the President in his day-to-day activities, keeps him informed on current developments, and advises him in planning programs. Its units, directly under the President's control, include the *White House Office* (consisting of the President's press secretary, legislative liaison official, speech writers, assistant for national security affairs, and other assistants), the *Office of Management and Budget*, the *Council of Economic Advisers*, and the *National Security Council*. (For details, see the Index.)

INDEPENDENT AGENCIES

The members of the independent agencies are appointed by the President, with the consent of the Senate, for fixed terms. Most of these agencies administer laws dealing with specialized economic or technical problems. They issue detailed rules and regulations, thereby exercising *quasi-legislative* powers. Many agencies also investigate charges of violations, hold hearings, and hand down decisions, thereby exercising *quasi-judicial* powers. (However, an individual or corporation found guilty before an independent agency may appeal the case to the federal courts.) The number of independent agencies has increased as our society has become more complex.

Among major agencies are the Interstate Commerce Commission, Federal Trade Commission, Federal Mediation and Conciliation Service, Securities and Exchange Commission, National Labor Relations Board, and National Aeronautics and Space Administration. (For details, see the Index.)

CIVIL SERVICE

Federal employees, some 2.5 million, include top decision makers as well as persons who perform the routine work of enforcing the laws.

1. **Selection by the "Spoils System."** For about 100 years the successful Presidential candidate filled even the humblest federal job with a "deserving" member of his political party. This practice, illustrating the statement, "To the victor belong the spoils," was called the *spoils system.*

In time, the spoils system revealed its disadvantages: (*a*) Incompetent men were permitted to hold office. (*b*) Capable, experienced officials were discharged for political reasons. (*c*) Federal employees were compelled to contribute funds to political parties. (*d*) Too much of the President's time and energy was consumed in making appointments.

2. **Selection by the Merit System.** After the Civil War, *Carl Schurz* led a reform movement to end the spoils system. The country became especially aroused in 1881, when a rejected office seeker assassinated President Garfield. In 1883 Congress passed the *Pendleton Act,* setting up a *Civil Service Commission.* This impartial body was to test and rate applicants for federal jobs. Although only about one-tenth of the federal employees at the time were affected, this law set the basis for the *merit system.*

Since 1883 each President has placed additional positions within the merit system so that today the proportion of federal employees so chosen nears 95 percent. To remove political influence further, Congress passed the *Hatch Act* (1939). It provided that civil service employees may not be asked for political contributions and may not actively engage in politics.

3. **Recent Changes.** In 1978 President Carter acted to improve government efficiency by shaking up the "horrible federal bureaucracy." He abolished the Civil Service Commission and transferred its functions—hiring new employees, hearing grievances and discipline cases involving existing employees, and dealing with civil service unions—to three new agencies. The President also secured from Congress the *Civil Service Reform Act of 1978.* It provided that (*a*) salary increases for top-level and middle-level bureaucrats be based, not on length of service but on quality of work, (*b*) rules be eased for disciplining and discharging lazy and incompetent workers, and (*c*) protection against reprisals be given to "whistle blowers"—persons who call attention to illegal or wasteful practices. Critics claimed that the law would open the door to political favoritism. The President held that the law would make civil service workers more responsive and efficient.

MULTIPLE-CHOICE QUESTIONS

1. Which statement concerning the national nominating conventions for the Presidency is true? (1) They are provided for in the federal Constitution. (2) They preceded the Congressional caucus as a nominating procedure. (3) They have been the basic Presidential nominating procedure since the early 1830's. (4) They are not held when a President seeks reelection.

2. The practice that Presidential electors vote for the candidate nominated by their political party is based upon (1) the Constitution (2) custom and tradition (3) a law of Congress (4) a decision of the Supreme Court.

3. A Governor of New York State is likely to be a candidate for the Presidential nomination because (1) he is a "dark horse" (2) New Yorkers are better known nationally (3) his state has a large number of electoral votes (4) New York State is the most rapidly growing state in the nation.

4. A voter in a Presidential election casts his ballot for (1) his candidate directly (2) a slate of electors (3) a candidate selected by a Congressional caucus (4) the state party committee.

5. Which is true of a Presidential election under the electoral college system? (1) The winner of a plurality of the popular votes in a state wins all the electoral votes of that state. (2) The winner of the majority of the popular vote in the country is elected President. (3) The ratio of the electoral vote usually follows closely the ratio of the popular vote. (4) The winning candidate usually does not have a majority of the popular vote.

6. The election of a President is decided by the House of Representatives when (1) the Senate is unable to decide on a candidate (2) no candidate receives a majority of the electoral vote (3) no candidate receives a majority of the popular vote (4) the President-elect dies before January 20.

7. As a result of the election of 1860, Lincoln was a "minority" President. This means that he (1) received less than 50 percent of the popular vote (2) received less than 50 percent of the electoral vote (3) was elected by running on the tickets of two parties (4) was elected by the House of Representatives.

8. In his oath of inauguration, the President of the United States swears (or affirms) to preserve, protect, and defend (1) the Constitution (2) democracy (3) the nation (4) the states.

9. According to a law of Congress, the person next to the President and the Vice President in line of succession is the (1) Secretary of State (2) Speaker of the House (3) Secretary of the Treasury (4) President pro tempore of the Senate.

10. The limitation on the number of terms a President may serve is based upon (1) a law of Congress (2) a Constitutional amendment (3) an agreement between the two major political parties (4) a decision of the Supreme Court.

11. In case the office of Vice President is vacant, the Twenty-fifth Amendment provides that a new Vice President be nominated by (1) the President (2) a special meeting of the electoral college (3) the Senate (4) the President's Cabinet.

12. Which person is an employee of the executive branch? (1) a page boy in the Senate (2) a secretary of a member of the House of Representatives (3) an Associate Justice of the Supreme Court (4) a representative of the State Department in a foreign city.

13. As commander in chief of the armed forces, the President can (1) declare war (2) lower the age for drafting men and women into the armed forces (3) establish a treaty of peace (4) order the Marines into foreign countries to protect American interests.

14. President Franklin D. Roosevelt's recognition of the Soviet Union in 1933 was based primarily on his Constitutional power to (1) sign or veto bills (2) receive ambassadors and other public ministers (3) be commander in chief of the armed forces (4) inform Congress on the "State of the Union."

15. According to the Constitution, the conduct of foreign affairs is the responsibility of (1) the Secretary of State (2) the Senate Foreign Affairs Committee (3) the President (4) Congress.

16. The President's "State of the Union" message to Congress is an example of (1) a Constitutional requirement (2) a Presidential practice of recent years (3) the carrying out of a federal law (4) custom and tradition.

17. To secure Congressional support for his legislative program, the President may make use of (1) the merit system (2) his police power (3) patronage (4) gerrymandering.

18. Which best describes a reform designed to lessen the excesses of the spoils system? (1) The President's power to appoint ambassadors was restricted. (2) Responsibility for making appointments to federal positions was given to political party leaders. (3) A commission was given authority to conduct competitive examinations. (4) Senators were empowered to make appointments to federal positions.

19. The establishment of a merit system in the federal civil service received most opposition from (1) professional politicians (2) suffragettes (3) heavy contributors to Presidential campaign funds (4) labor union members.

ESSAY QUESTIONS

1. (a) Explain fully the part played in selecting the President of the United States by (1) party conventions, (2) the electoral college. (b) Discuss one criticism that has been made of each of these procedures.

2. Discuss two facts to prove each of the following statements concerning the Presidency of the United States: (a) Amendments to the federal Constitution have affected the Presidency. (b) Political parties play a major part in the nomination of Presidential candidates. (c) The process of electing the President encourages candidates to concentrate much campaign activity in certain states. (d) To fulfill his many responsibilities, the President is assisted by a number of individuals and agencies. (e) A President may be considered as strong or weak not according to the powers available to him, but according to his use of these powers.

3. The problem of Presidential succession has received considerable attention. (a) Discuss two criticisms that have been voiced concerning the factors that at present help to determine the selection of a party's Vice Presidential nominee. (b) Discuss one argument for and one argument against the Presidential Succession Act of 1947. (c) State one provision of the Twenty-fifth Amendment and explain whether or not you approve of this provision.

4. Discuss two powers by which the President may accomplish each of the following: (a) influencing Congress, (b) enforcing laws, (c) controlling his own political party, (d) determining foreign policy. For each power discussed, indicate whether it is stated in the Constitution or derived from custom and tradition.

5. It has been said that the President of the United States has one of the most difficult executive jobs in the world. (a) Discuss briefly two major responsibilities of the President. (b) Explain two ways in which the system of checks and balances limits the power of the President. (c) Discuss briefly two different reasons for the increase in the power of the President during the 20th century.

Part 3. Legislative Power Shall Be Vested in Congress

ORGANIZATION OF CONGRESS

Congress consists of two houses: the House of Representatives and the Senate. For legislative work, each house requires the presence of a majority of its members. This number is called a *quorum*.

1. House of Representatives

a. Requirements. A candidate for the House must be at least 25 years of age, a citizen of the United States for seven years, and an inhabitant of the state from which he seeks election.

b. Membership. By law the House has 435 members. The number of Representatives for each state is calculated from the ratio of the population of the state to the population of the nation. The 1990 census showed that New York's population had reached 18 million while the national figure had increased to 250 million. New York faced a decrease in Representatives from 34 to 31. This meant one Representative for about 575,000 persons.

c. Term of Office. Each Representative serves a two-year term. Since the entire House membership is elected every two years, it may be drastically altered in a single election.

d. Presiding Officer. The *Speaker of the House* serves as its presiding officer. Elected by the Representatives voting along strict party lines, he is therefore always a member of the majority party.

e. Rules on Debate. The House maintains strict rules limiting debate. These rules enable the House to discuss bills and reach decisions without endless delay.

2. Senate

a. Requirements. A candidate for the Senate must be at least 30 years of age, a citizen of the United States for nine years, and an inhabitant of the state from which he seeks election.

b. Membership. The Senate has 100 members, two from each of the 50 states, regardless of population.

c. Term of Office. Senators are elected for a six-year term, but elections are staggered so that only one-third of the members of the Senate are chosen every two years. As a result, membership of the Senate cannot be drastically altered by any one election.

d. Presiding Officer. According to the Constitution, the Vice President serves as the presiding officer of the Senate but votes only in case of a tie. Since the Vice President frequently does not attend Senate sessions, the Senators, voting along party lines, elect a *President pro tempore* (President for the time being).

e. Rules on Debate. The Senate usually permits its members the privilege of unlimited debate. This makes possible the *filibuster.*

FILIBUSTER IN THE SENATE

1. Purpose. A filibuster is a deliberate attempt by a minority group of Senators (or a single Senator) to talk continuously in order to prevent a favorable vote on a bill. In recent years Southern Senators have used the filibuster to stall voting on civil rights legislation.

2. Cloture. A filibuster may be halted by *cloture,* a special vote to close debate. Since 1975 the Senate permits cloture—on all issues but cloture itself—by a vote of three-fifths of its total membership, or 60 Senators. Cloture has rarely been used because (*a*) Southern Senators are opposed to cloture and have often mustered enough votes to block it, and (*b*) many Senators are unwilling to employ cloture against others for fear that, at some future time, it may be used against themselves.

3. Evaluation of the Filibuster

a. Merits. A filibuster against a specific bill (1) permits thorough discussion and free expression of ideas, (2) allows time for the public to be informed and to make known its views, and (3) protects the rights and interests of the minority.

b. Criticisms. A filibuster (1) prevents meaningful discussion on a bill when filibustering Senators "talk a bill to death," as by reading such extraneous materials as telephone directories and novels, (2) frustrates the will of the majority, and (3) wastes time and prevents the Senate from functioning.

Critics of the filibuster point out that the rights of minorities are adequately safeguarded by the Constitution and that minorities have the opportunity to appeal to the voters to elect Senators favorable to their viewpoint.

SPECIAL PRIVILEGES OF MEMBERS OF CONGRESS

1. Senatorial Courtesy. A Senator of the same political party as the President expects to be heeded on important federal appointments (district attorneys, judges, revenue collectors) within his state. If the President nominates a candidate in opposition to the Senator's wishes, then the Senate will show "courtesy" to its member by not approving the appointment.

2. Immunities Granted to Congressmen

a. Freedom From Arrest. While attending sessions, Congressmen are free from arrest on civil charges and misdemeanors. Freedom from arrest (except on charges of treason or major crimes) protects Congressmen from undue interference with their legislative duties.

b. Freedom From Suits for Libel and Slander. For any speech on the floor of Congress, Congressmen "shall not be questioned in any other place," that is, they shall be immune, or exempted, from law suits for libel and slander. Immunity permits Congressmen to talk freely in Congressional debates. (Occasionally, Congressmen abuse this privilege and malign individuals by making personal attacks and unsupported charges.)

SESSIONS OF CONGRESS

Each Congress exists for a two-year term. By custom, beginning with our first Congress of 1789–1790, Congresses have been numbered consecutively.

Each Congress meets in two regular sessions, each session convening, in accordance with the Twentieth Amendment, on January 3. Congress remains in session as long as it feels that it has important work to do. With our society growing more complex, Congressional sessions have increased in length. In recent times, most sessions have run into autumn.

GENERAL POWERS OF CONGRESS

The chief duty of Congress is to enact laws for the nation's welfare. Congress may legislate on those matters specifically enumerated in the Constitution or implied by the elastic clause. Congressional committees may hold hearings and conduct investigations as necessary to the main purpose of Congress—the passage of laws.

SPECIAL POWERS OF THE HOUSE OF REPRESENTATIVES

The House has the sole power (1) to start all revenue (tax) bills (which the Senate may amend), (2) to bring charges of impeachment against federal officials, including the President, and (3) to elect the President if the electoral college fails to give any one candidate a majority.

SPECIAL POWERS OF THE SENATE

The Senate has the sole power (1) to ratify treaties negotiated by the President (requiring a two-thirds vote), (2) to approve Presidential appointments (majority vote), (3) when the House brings charges of impeachment, to sit as a jury and to convict the impeached person (two-thirds vote), and (4) to elect the Vice President if the electoral college is deadlocked (majority vote).

CONGRESSIONAL LAWMAKING: THE COMMITTEE SYSTEM

1. **Introduction of the Bill.** Except for money bills, which originate in the House, any bill may be introduced by any Congressman. The bill may re-

HOW A BILL BECOMES A LAW
(When the bill originates in the House)

Representative introduces bill by placing it in hopper. Speaker refers bill to proper committee.

Committee studies bill, holds hearings, and may change provisions. If approved, bill goes to Rules Committee.

Rules Committee places bill on calendar for discussion by entire House.

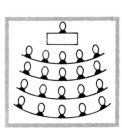

The bill is introduced in Senate, considered by committee, and debated by entire Senate. If Senate passes bill different from House version, bill goes to conference committee.

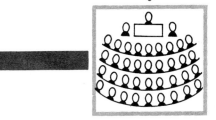

House debates bill and may pass it as is or with further change. If passed, bill goes to Senate.

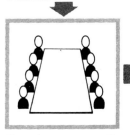

If conference committee, of House and Senate members, resolves differences, compromise bill is submitted to both House and Senate.

If both House and Senate pass compromise bill, it goes to President for signature.

If President signs, bill becomes law; if he vetoes, Congress may override veto by two-thirds vote of both House and Senate.

flect the thinking of the Congressman, of a special interest group, or of the executive branch. In the Senate the bill is announced orally; in the House of Representatives the bill is placed in a basket, called the *hopper*.

2. Referral to Committee. Thousands of bills, on many subjects, are introduced during each session of Congress. Since neither house acting as a whole can adequately consider all these bills, each house is divided into small legislative bodies, called *committees*. In each house, the presiding officer refers each bill to the appropriate committee.

3. Number and Organization of Committees. The House of Representatives and the Senate each has about 20 standing (regular) committees. Among the House committees are *Agriculture; Armed Services; Banking, Finance, and Urban Affairs; Education and Labor; Foreign Affairs; Judiciary; Rules; Science and Technology; and Ways and Means* (taxation). Among the Senate committees are *Agriculture, Nutrition, and Forestry; Armed Services; Energy and Natural Resources; Environment and Public Works; Finance;* and *Foreign Relations.*

Committee members are chosen from both political parties. On each committee, the majority of the members belong to the majority party, which thereby controls the committee. Committee members are expected to become experts in their respective fields. Committee chairmen, always of the majority party, are chosen on the basis of length of service, or *seniority.*

4. Committee Proceedings. The committee disposes of most bills speedily by pigeonholing them, that is, deferring consideration indefinitely. Over 90 percent of all bills introduced in Congress are *killed in committee.*
On a major bill the committee usually holds hearings and considers arguments for and against the measure. After fact-finding and discussion, the committee, by majority vote, may approve the bill as it was introduced, approve an amended version of the bill, or reject the bill.

5. Action in the Originating House. If approved by the committee, the bill is scheduled for consideration by the entire house by being placed on the *calendar.* (In the House of Representatives, this function is performed by the powerful *Rules Committee.*) The originating house debates the bill, possibly amends it, and finally takes a vote. The *majority leader* and *majority whip* seek votes for their party's bills. The *minority leader* and *minority whip* direct the opposition party. If a majority votes against it, the bill is dead. If a majority approves, the bill goes to the other house.

6. Action in the Second House. Here the bill follows a similar path: introduction, referral to committee; consideration in committee, referral to the entire body, and decision.

7. Conference Committee. A bill is often approved by the two houses in versions that differ from one another in various details. To adjust these differences, members designated by the presiding officer of each house meet as a temporary *conference committee.* Usually, they arrive at a compromise bill, and this bill is then submitted to each house for approval.

8. Presidential Action. After passage by Congress, the bill goes to the President for his approval. If the President signs the bill within ten days, it becomes a law. If the President holds the bill for ten days without signing it and Congress is still in session, the bill becomes a law without his signature. (However, if Congress is not in session and the President holds the bill for ten days without signing it, the bill is automatically killed. This is known as a *pocket veto.*) If the President vetoes the bill, he returns it to the originating house together with a statement of reasons for his veto. Congress may override the Presidential veto by a two-third vote in each house.

EVALUATION OF CONGRESSIONAL LAWMAKING PROCEDURES

1. Committee System. (*a*) *Merits.* The committee system provides a sensible way of handling the great number of bills proposed in Congress. It assures bills a thorough and careful consideration. Committee hearings enable interested parties to express their views. (*b*) *Criticisms.* The commitee system is time-consuming and complex. It involves needless duplication, as House and Senate committees cover essentially the same ground. The committee system prevents most bills from ever being considered by Congress. In killing over 90 percent of the bills proposed in Congress, the committees do not necessarily reflect the views of Congress or of the people.

2. Seniority and Committee Chairmen. (*a*) *Merits.* Chosen by seniority, committee chairmen are men of experience. They are capable of exercising strong control and seeing to it that their committees function smoothly. (*b*) *Criticisms.* Seniority does not necessarily mean ability. Committee chairmen usually represent "safe" districts and states, such as the Democratic South and the Republican states in the Midwest, where voters consistently support the same party. They rarely come from "doubtful" districts and states, where voters often switch support, thus making it difficult for their Congressmen to acquire sufficient seniority. Also, chairmen exercise too much power over their committees. They hire secretarial and research staffs, call (or postpone) meetings, and determine matters to be discussed.

In 1975 three veteran committee chairmen, whose thinking was out of step with the House Democratic majority, were ousted. The vacated positions went to men with less seniority. This was a one-time violation of seniority.

3. Rules Committee in the House of Representatives. (*a*) *Merits.* The Rules Committee arranges the orderly flow of bills for consideration by the entire House. It serves as a "traffic director." (*b*) *Criticisms.* If it opposes a bill passed along by a standing committee, the Rules Committee may prevent consideration by the entire House. It may serve as a "roadblock."

LOBBYING

1. Meaning. To secure the passage of laws they desire or to defeat laws unfavorable to their interests, many economic and social organizations try to "pressure" Congress. Typical pressure groups include the National Association of Manufacturers, the American Federation of Labor and Congress of Industrial Organizations, the Farm Bureau Federation, the American Medical Association, and the American Legion. Such groups employ experienced and highly trained persons called *lobbyists*.

Lobbyists seek to influence the votes of Congressmen by (*a*) drafting bills, testifying at hearings, and supplying data to support their views, (*b*) cultivating personal contacts with Congressmen—arranging parties, granting favors, and providing campaign funds, and (*c*) urging the public to deluge Congress with postcards, letters, and telegrams. Sometimes the work of one lobby, such as a businessmen's organization, is offset by the work of another lobby, such as a labor organization.

2. Arguments in Favor of Lobbies. (*a*) Lobbying is in accord with the Constitutional guarantee that the people have the right to petition the government. (*b*) Lobbying enables special groups to make known their views. (*c*) Lobbyists call attention to the need for laws and provide Congressmen with valuable information.

3. Arguments Against Lobbies. (*a*) Lobbyists sometimes utilize questionable methods, including the giving of lavish gifts and bribes. (*b*) Lobbying gives well-organized groups, such as industry and labor, an advantage over poorly organized groups, such as consumers. (*c*) Lobbying fosters laws that benefit special interest groups. (*d*) The information that lobbyists provide Congressmen is one-sided.

4. Federal Regulation. By the *Regulation of Lobbying Act* (1946), Congress defined lobbyists as persons seeking to influence legislation and required that they (*a*) register with Congress, and (*b*) file quarterly statements regarding the source of their funds and the nature of their expenditures.

5. Weaknesses of Federal Regulation. (*a*) The law defines lobbying in a limited way. Some lobbyists have claimed that their chief work is not to influence legislation but to educate the public and that they therefore need not register. (*b*) No bounds have been set on the activities and expenditures of lobbyists. (*c*) Enforcement has been inadequate.

OTHER PRACTICES RELATED TO CONGRESS

1. Logrolling. A Congressman may sometimes say to another, "If you vote for my bill, I'll vote for yours." This trading of votes, despite the shortcomings of the respective bills, is called *logrolling*.

2. Pork-Barrel Legislation. Congressmen are eager to provide their home districts with public works such as additional post offices, new highways, and river and harbor improvements—regardless of need. Public works provide employment and prove to the "folks back home" that their Congressman is looking out for their best interests. Such bills, usually passed by means of logrolling, are called *pork-barrel* legislation.

3. Gerrymandering. Members of the House of Representatives are, with few exceptions, elected by districts. Consequently, within each state the party in power often seeks to draw district boundaries so as to concentrate its opponent's strength in a few districts while spreading its own strength in order to give itself a majority in many districts. This practice, used in 1812 by Governor Elbridge Gerry of Massachusetts, is known as *gerrymandering*.

4. Rider. This is an unrelated provision that Congress adds to a vital bill. The provision may be objectionable to the President; but, since he cannot veto single items in a bill, he must approve the entire bill, including the rider.

ANALYSIS QUESTIONS: SENATORIAL ACTIVITY

Base your answers to the following questions on the activities of the United States Senators described below and on your knowledge of government.

Senator A is talking with a representative of the AFL-CIO concerning a labor bill about to be introduced.

Senator B has been speaking on the floor of the Senate for several hours in an effort to prevent a vote on a bill he opposes.

Senator C is attending committee hearings on a treaty about to be submitted to the Senate for ratification.

Senator D is drafting a bill that will provide for a federal flood control project in his home state.

1. Which Senator would be most opposed to cloture? (1) *A* (2) *B* (3) *C* (4) *D*.
2. Which Senator is most likely to be involved with pork-barrel legislation? (1) *A* (2) *B* (3) *C* (4) *D*.
3. Which Senator appears to be most directly involved with a lobbyist? (1) *A* (2) *B* (3) *C* (4) *D*.
4. Which pair of Senators is engaged in activities that might also be typical of those carried on by members of the House of Representatives? (1) *A* and *B* (2) *A* and *C* (3) *A* and *D* (4) *B* and *D*.

MULTIPLE-CHOICE QUESTIONS

1. According to the Constitution of the United States, Congress is required to meet (1) twice a year (2) annually (3) once every two years (4) only when called into session by the President.
2. The framers of the Constitution best expressed their faith in the people by the provision for choosing the (1) Justices of the Supreme Court (2) President and Vice President (3) Speaker of the House of Representatives (4) members of the House of Representatives.

3. According to the Constitution, the House of Representatives has the sole power to (1) approve appointments (2) impeach federal officials (3) override Presidential vetoes (4) filibuster.

4. In the House of Representatives, the period of debate is likely to be shorter than in the Senate because the House (1) remains in session longer (2) has rules that limit discussion (3) considers bills only after the Senate has passed them (4) is generally composed of less experienced members.

5. The Senate *differs* from the House of Representatives in that (1) the Senate is continuously in session (2) a two-thirds vote is required to pass bills in the Senate (3) one-third of the Senate is elected every two years (4) Senators must be native-born Americans.

6. Which action of the Senate requires a simple majority vote? (1) ratification of a treaty (2) approval of an appointment (3) passage of a bill vetoed by the President (4) conviction of an impeached official.

7. Filibustering is most likely to be used by a (1) lobbyist favoring a new federal law (2) majority attempting to override a Presidential veto (3) minority seeking to delay a vote (4) Congressional committee chairman attempting to kill a bill.

8. According to the Constitution, the Senate has the exclusive power to (1) declare war (2) appoint committees (3) try impeachment cases (4) select a President when no candidate receives a majority of the electoral votes.

9. By its 1975 rule on debate, the Senate (1) outlawed filibusters (2) required the vote of 60 Senators to limit debate on any measure except a Senate rules change (3) extended unlimited debate to the House of Representatives (4) required a two-thirds vote of the Senators present to end a filibuster.

10. Suppose the President filled an important federal position in State X without consulting either of the two Senators from that state. Such a procedure would be (1) illegal because of the Constitutional provision governing appointments (2) appropriate if neither Senator were of the President's party (3) commendable as an indication that the President would not engage in logrolling (4) proper because of the Corrupt Practices Act.

11. Congressional immunity prevents (1) taxation of a Congressman's salary by the federal government (2) prosecution of a Congressman for remarks made in Congress (3) expulsion of a member of Congress (4) arrest of a Congressman by a foreign power.

12. No bill may become a law without the approval of (1) the United States Supreme Court (2) the President (3) a two-thirds vote of the Senate (4) both houses of Congress.

13. The Constitutional justification for Congressional hearings on crime is that they (1) give Congress information on needed legislation (2) expose criminals to public disapproval (3) furnish information to the FBI (4) assist the Internal Revenue Service to collect income taxes from criminals.

14. Usually, after a bill has been introduced into either house of Congress, it is first (1) signed by the presiding officer of that house (2) debated by members of that house (3) referred to a committee of that house (4) considered by a joint committee representing both houses.

15. In the legislative process, a conference committee is usually appointed (1) when Congress desires to investigate corrupt practices in government (2) when the President wishes to call Congress into special session (3) after the President has vetoed an act of Congress (4) after the Senate and the House have passed different versions of the same bill.

16. The chairmen of Congressional committees get their positions by (1) a vote of committee members (2) appointment by the presiding officer (3) seniority on the committee (4) recommendation of the President.

17. If an agricultural group from Kansas sends a spokesman to Washington, D.C., to urge the passage of a flood-control bill, he is said to be engaged in (1) filibustering (2) logrolling (3) lobbying (4) gerrymandering.

18. According to federal law, all lobbyists must (1) confine their activities to the lobbies of Congress (2) refrain from influencing United States Senators (3) reside in Washington, D.C. (4) register with Congress.

19. The Rules Committee of the House of Representatives is important because it (1) acts as a liaison between the House and the President (2) functions as an independent legislative body (3) censures members who are out of order (4) determines the order in which bills are to be put before the House.

20. A Senator from the Midwest votes in favor of higher government-supported prices for cotton in return for a Southern Senator's vote in favor of higher government-supported prices for corn. The two Senators are said to be engaged in (1) Senatorial courtesy (2) patronage (3) lobbying (4) logrolling.

21. The term "gerrymandering" refers to the (1) unequal distribution of campaign contributions (2) unfair system of apportionment of districts for election purposes (3) unusual power of the Southern states in Congress (4) unjust practice of dismissing officeholders for political reasons.

22. What is the *smallest* number of members of Congress that a state, regardless of its population, may have? (1) five (2) two (3) three (4) four.

ESSAY QUESTIONS

1. President Kennedy is said to have remarked, "It is very easy to defeat a bill in Congress. It is much more difficult to pass one." (a) Discuss *two* specific features of Congressional organization and procedures to support President Kennedy's point of view. (b) Show how the roles of the President of the United States and the Prime Minister of Great Britain in the legislative process are in *one* way similar *and* in *one* way different. (c) Explain *one* way in which the legislative process is affected by (1) public opinion, and (2) special interest groups.

2. The practices of Congress have been both vigorously defended and vigorously attacked. (a) Discuss *two* Congressional practices to show why each has been defended. (b) Discuss *two* other Congressional practices to show why each has come under attack. (c) Explain *one* remedy proposed for *each* of these attacked Congressional practices.

3. Assume that you have heard these statements over the radio: "Our taxes are twice as high as they should be. The reason is clear. Congress is wastefully squandering public funds. *Logrolling*, the *pork barrel*, and selfish *lobbies* must be swept out. I call on every citizen to help in doing this long-needed job."
   (a) Define *each* of the *italicized* terms. (b) Discuss *two* ways in which a citizen can determine to what extent these statements are true. (c) Explain *two* ways by which he could help remedy such conditions if they existed.

4. Present *one* argument to support *or one* argument to oppose each of the following statements: (a) Congress remains in session too long. (b) The requirements for members of Congress should include a college education. (c) The filibuster is undemocratic. (d) A majority vote of both houses of Congress should be required to ratify treaties. (e) The committee system of Congress is a sensible way of handling legislation. (f) Congress should outlaw all lobbying in Washington, D.C.

Part 4. Judicial Power Shall Be Vested in the Courts

FEDERAL JUDGES

The Constitution sets no qualifications for federal judges. They are appointed by the President with the consent of the Senate and serve for life. Since they receive life tenure, judges can render impartial decisions free from unwarranted pressures.

Federal judges may be removed from office for "treason, bribery, or other high crimes and misdemeanors" through the process of impeachment. Of thousands of federal judges in our history, only four have been impeached by the House of Representatives and found guilty by the Senate.

JURISDICTION OF THE FEDERAL COURTS

The federal courts handle cases concerning (1) the Constitution and federal laws and treaties, (2) maritime law, (3) citizens of different states, (4) two or more states, (5) representatives of foreign countries, (6) treason, the only crime specifically defined in the Constitution: "levying war" against the United States or giving "aid and comfort" to its enemies, and (7) the constitutionality of federal and state laws and of executive actions.

FEDERAL COURT SYSTEM

The Constitution specifically provides for one Supreme Court and empowers Congress to establish "inferior," or lower, courts. Accordingly, today the federal court system consists of the following:

1. **About Ninety District Courts.** These lowest courts in the federal system have *original jurisdiction;* that is, they hold the first trials. In all criminal and most civil cases, the District Courts provide trial by jury.

2. **Eleven Circuit Courts of Appeals.** These intermediate courts have *appellate jurisdiction;* that is, they hear cases on appeal from the District Courts. The Circuit Court reviews the record to determine (a) whether there was any irregularity in the trial of the accused in the District Court, and (b) whether the law that the accused is said to have violated is constitutional. The Circuit Court may confirm or void the judgment of the lower court. Decisions are made by a panel of two or more judges.

3. **One Supreme Court.** This highest judicial authority has appellate jurisdiction over cases coming from lower federal courts and from the highest state courts. The Supreme Court is not required to hear all cases appealed to it; it hears only a small percentage of them. Usually, it considers only those cases involving new or important legal principles. If an appeal is rejected by the Supreme Court, the decision of the lower court remains in effect.

The Supreme Court also has original jurisdiction in cases involving a state and in cases involving ambassadors, foreign ministers, and consuls.

The Supreme Court today consists of one Chief Justice and eight Associate Justices, totaling nine judges. Decisions are made by a majority vote. One Justice of the majority writes an explanation of the decision, the *majority opinion* or the *opinion of the Court*. A Justice who agrees with the court's decision but disagrees with its reasoning may write a *concurring opinion*. A Justice who disagrees with the court's decision may write a *dissenting opinion*. Supreme Court decisions are final.

4. Special Courts. The Court of Claims handles claims against the government of the United States. The Customs Court handles questions of tariffs on imports. The Court of Customs and Patent Appeals handles appeals from the Customs Court and the Patent Office.

SUPREME COURT AND JUDICIAL REVIEW

Under Chief Justice *John Marshall* the Supreme Court in 1803 first declared a provision of a federal law (1) out of harmony with the Constitution, and therefore (2) unconstitutional and invalid. Arguing that the Constitution is the supreme law of the land and that the Supreme Court is its final interpreter, Marshall concluded that the Supreme Court may declare laws to be in conflict with the Constitution. This power to determine constitutionality, implied but not specifically stated in the Constitution, is called *judicial review*. (For the 1803 case of *Marbury vs. Madison,* check the Index.)

Since 1803 the Supreme Court has used judicial review to declare a number of federal and state laws and executive actions unconstitutional. Among democratic nations this power of the Supreme Court remains unique.

SUPREME COURT: CENTER OF CONTROVERSY

At various times, the Supreme Court has delivered decisions upon vital public matters. In 1935–1936 the Supreme Court declared unconsitutional major New Deal laws that President Franklin D. Roosevelt considered necessary to revive the nation's economy. From 1953 to 1969, under Chief Justice *Earl Warren,* the Supreme Court outlawed segregation in public schools, limited police powers so as to protect the rights of persons accused of crimes, and ordered reapportionment of legislative election districts. By such decisions, the Supreme Court aroused storms of controversy.

Supporters have defended the Supreme Court for upholding the Constitution, protecting the rights of the people against governmental tyranny, and furthering democracy. Opponents have condemned the Supreme Court for violating precedents, delivering politically minded rather than legally justified decisions, and usurping powers of other bodies of government.

PROPOSALS TO LIMIT THE SUPREME COURT: NONE SO FAR ADOPTED

Opponents of the Supreme Court claim that the traditional checks upon judicial powers are insufficient. They have therefore proposed other checks upon its operations.

1. The number of Supreme Court judges is not fixed by the Constitution, and court membership has varied from a low of five judges (1801–1807) to a high of ten (1863–1867). In 1937 President Roosevelt requested Congress to enlarge the Supreme Court to as many as fifteen Justices. By appointing additional judges, Roosevelt hoped to obtain a pro-New Deal majority on the court. After a bitter political struggle, Congress refused to pass legislation "packing the Supreme Court."

2. Congress is empowered by the Constitution to control the appellate jurisdiction of the Supreme Court by making "exceptions" and "regulations." (a) Opponents of the Supreme Court have urged Congress to limit the Supreme Court's appellate jurisdiction. For example, they would deny the Supreme Court the right to consider any matter involving the national security. (b) They have also urged Congress to prohibit the Supreme Court from declaring a law unconstitutional by a bare majority. They would require a vote of at least 6 to 3 or of 7 to 2.

3. Court opponents have also urged an amendment to permit Congress, by a two-thirds vote, to override a Supreme Court decision holding a federal law unconstitutional.

Part 5. The Constitution Protects Rights and Liberties

PROTECTION OF CIVIL LIBERTIES: ORIGINAL CONSTITUTION (Article I, Sections 9 and 10)

The framers of the Constitution, remembering their experiences with Britain, sought to protect the individual against governmental tyranny. Consequently, the original Constitution contains the following restrictions on the powers of government:

1. Safeguarding of Writ of Habeas Corpus. Except during rebellion or invasion, the federal government may not suspend the privilege of the *writ of habeas corpus*. This document, issued by a judge upon the request of a defense attorney, protects an arrested individual. It provides that the police must bring the prisoner before the judge and provide a statement of charges. If the judge determines that the prisoner is being held illegally, he is freed.

If he is being held legally, the prisoner is released on bail or returned to jail pending a speedy trial.

2. Prohibition of Bill of Attainder. Neither the federal legislature nor the states may pass a *bill of attainder*. This is a law that punishes an individual without granting him a trial in court.

3. Prohibition of Ex Post Facto Law. Neither the federal legislature nor the states may pass an *ex post facto law*. Such a law punishes persons for acts that were not criminal at the time committed.

PROTECTION OF CIVIL LIBERTIES: BILL OF RIGHTS

Called the *Bill of Rights,* the first ten amendments were added to the Constitution to protect the people against tyranny by the federal government. (A similar bill of rights is contained in most state constitutions to protect the people against tyranny by the states.)

The **First Amendment** prohibits Congress from interfering with freedom of speech, press, and religion, and with the right to assemble peaceably and to petition the government. It provides for the separation of church and state.

The **Second Amendment** declares that, a state militia being necessary, the right of the people to bear arms shall not be infringed.

The **Third Amendment** forbids the quartering of soldiers in private homes in peacetime except with the owner's consent.

The **Fourth Amendment** prohibits the unreasonable search and seizure of persons and property, and forbids the use of general warrants for search or arrest.

The **Fifth Amendment** provides that a person accused of a crime may not be tried twice (be put in *double jeopardy*) for the same offense and that he may not be compelled to be a witness against himself (give *self-incriminating* evidence).

The **Sixth Amendment** gives an accused person in a criminal case the right to a speedy trial, to an impartial jury, to knowledge of the charges against him, and to defense counsel. The accused also has the right to confront hostile witnesses and to obtain friendly witnesses.

The **Seventh Amendment** guarantees a jury trial in most civil cases.

The **Eighth Amendment** prohibits excessive fines and bails, and cruel punishments.

The **Ninth Amendment** states that the rights of the people are not limited to the rights enumerated in the first eight amendments.

The *Tenth Amendment* reserves to the states or to the people all powers not prohibited to the states or given to the federal government.

PROTECTION OF CIVIL LIBERTIES (Amendments XIV and XV)

The *Fourteenth Amendment* provides that no state may make any law abridging the privileges of citizens and that no state may deny any person the equal protection of the laws.

The *Fifteenth Amendment* provides that neither the United States nor any state shall deny the right of a citizen to vote on account of race, color, or previous condition of servitude.

PROTECTION OF PROPERTY RIGHTS (Article I, Section 10, and Amendment V)

The original Constitution provides that no state may pass a law impairing the obligation of contracts. This means that no state law may alter the terms of a valid business contract. The Fifth Amendment states that the federal government may take private property for public use, providing it compensates the owner. This power is called the right of *eminent domain*.

"DUE PROCESS" CLAUSE (Amendments V and XIV)

The Fifth Amendment prohibits the federal government and the Fourteenth Amendment prohibits the states from depriving any person of "life, liberty, or property without due process of law." The "due process" clause serves to protect the people's civil liberties and property rights. Many federal and state laws affecting life, liberty, or property have been challenged in the courts for denying "due process."

As interpreted by the courts, the "due process" clause of the Fourteenth Amendment makes much of the federal Bill of Rights applicable to the laws and actions of the states.

RIGHTS IMPLY DUTIES

Our rights as Americans carry with them certain duties. Freedom of speech implies the duty to speak honestly and with a full knowledge of the facts. Freedom of religion implies the duty to respect the freedom of others whose religion differs from our own. The right to vote implies the duty to know the candidates and the issues in an election. The right to trial by jury implies the duty to respond willingly when called for jury service.

INDIVIDUAL RIGHTS VERSUS THE NEEDS OF SOCIETY

Democratic peoples constantly face the problem of adjusting the rights of the individual to the needs of society. May the individual exercise freedom of speech even if his words cause a riot? May he exercise freedom of the press even if his writings obstruct the nation's war effort? Such questions arising out of specific cases have been answered by the Supreme Court.

In general, the Court has held that *individual rights are not absolute but relative,* depending upon specific circumstances: what, where, when, and how.

SELECTED CASES INVOLVING CIVIL LIBERTIES

1. **Schenck vs. United States (1919)—Issue: Freedom of the Press.** Schenck, a pacifist, published pamphlets urging World War I draftees to resist conscription. Convicted of violating the Federal Espionage Act, Schenck appealed the case, claiming that the law violated freedom of the press. Justice *Oliver Wendell Holmes,* speaking for a unanimous Supreme Court, held that "free speech would not protect a man falsely shouting fire in a theater" and that Schenck's writings created a "clear and present danger" to the American government and people. Schenck's conviction was upheld.

The "clear and present danger" doctrine, first stated in this case, became the yardstick for subsequent cases involving the freedoms protected by the First Amendment.

2. **West Virginia State Board of Education vs. Barnette (1943)—Issue: Freedom of Religion.** The Jehovah's Witnesses, a religious sect, consider saluting the flag a form of idolatry. Their children therefore refuse to give the flag salute in the public schools. Since such refusal violated a West Virginia statute, the children were threatened with expulsion and their parents with prosecution. The Jehovah's Witnesses brought suit to restrain enforcement of this statute as a violation of freedom of religion. By a 6-to-3 decision, the Supreme Court pointed out that refusal to salute the flag does not infringe upon the rights of others and does not constitute a "clear and present danger." Consequently, the West Virginia flag-salute statute was declared in violation of the First Amendment and unconstitutional.

3. **Feiner vs. New York (1951)—Issue: Freedom of Speech.** Feiner, a university student speaking to a crowd from a box on the sidewalk, urged Negroes to "rise up in arms and fight for their rights." His speech made the crowd restless and belligerent. Requested by the police to stop speaking, Feiner refused and was arrested. Feiner appealed his conviction for disorderly conduct as a violation of his freedom of speech. By a 6-to-3 decision, the Supreme Court held that Feiner had attempted "incitement to riot" and had created a clear danger of public disorder. The conviction was upheld.

4. **Rochin vs. California (1952)—Issue: Due Process of Law and Self-Incrimination.** Rochin, a narcotics suspect facing arrest by state police, swallowed two morphine capsules. Forcibly subjected to a stomach pump, he

vomited the capsules, which were later used as evidence to convict him. Rochin appealed his conviction. The Supreme Court unanimously held that the police methods had denied Rochin his due process of law. The Justices further held that forcibly taking evidence from the defendant had compelled him to be a witness against himself. The conviction was overturned.

5. Gideon vs. Wainwright (1963)—Issue: Due Process of Law and Right to Counsel. Clarence Gideon, charged with burglary, was tried in a Florida state court. Too poor to afford a lawyer, Gideon requested free legal counsel of the state court, but his request was refused. Found guilty and imprisoned, Gideon appealed to the Supreme Court, which unanimously overturned his conviction. The Supreme Court held that Florida had denied Gideon his "due process" under the Fourteenth Amendment, which, the Court reasoned, requires that the state fulfill the Sixth Amendment guarantee of "assistance of counsel," even for the indigent. Subsequently assisted by a lawyer in a new trial in Florida, Gideon was acquitted of the original burglary charge.

6. Escobedo vs. Illinois (1964)—Issue: Self-Incrimination and Right to Counsel. Escobedo was arrested as a murder suspect. The police told him that they had a "pretty tight" case and subjected him to a continuous barrage of questioning. The police refused Escobedo's repeated demands to see his lawyer and failed to inform him that he had a right to remain silent. Escobedo eventually made incriminating statements that were used against him in court to secure a verdict of "guilty." Escobedo appealed the case, and the Supreme Court, by a 5-to-4 decision, reversed the conviction. The majority opinion held that the police had denied the accused his Constitutional rights: to speak to his counsel and to be informed of his privilege against self-incrimination. The dissenting opinion held that the ruling was "wholly unworkable" and claimed that it would cripple law enforcement.

7. Miranda vs. Arizona (1966)—Issue: Self-Incrimination and Right to Counsel. Ernesto Miranda was picked up by the police for questioning about kidnapping and assaulting a young woman. Placed in a police lineup, Miranda was identified by the victim, whereupon he confessed his guilt. His confession was used in court and helped to convict him. This case was appealed on the ground that the police had denied the suspect his Constitutional protection against self-incrimination. In a 5-to-4 decision overturning the conviction, the Supreme Court expanded the Escobedo case doctrine. The majority opinion held that, before questioning, the police must inform the suspect of his rights to remain silent and to legal counsel, and must warn him that his remarks may be used against him. The dissenting judges attacked the opinion for enabling criminals to gain freedom on technicalities. In a second trial Miranda was found guilty upon testimony of his common-law wife.

MULTIPLE-CHOICE QUESTIONS

1. The framers of the Constitution provided long terms for judges of the Supreme Court in order to (1) save expenses incurred by frequent changes in office (2) enable judges to acquire skill in trying cases (3) reward political followers with secure jobs (4) make it easier for judges to render decisions without political interference.

2. The number of Justices on the Supreme Court is determined by (1) its own membership (2) a law of Congress (3) a Constitutional provision (4) the President.

3. Supreme Court judges are (1) elected by the people (2) chosen by Congress in a joint session (3) nominated by the President (4) chosen by the electoral college.

4. A Supreme Court decision to declare an act of Congress unconstitutional requires (1) at least a simple majority vote (2) at least a two-thirds vote (3) at least a three-fourth vote (4) a unanimous vote.

5. According to the Constitution, which of these constitutes treason? (1) selling one's vote for money (2) giving aid and comfort to the enemy (3) refusing to bear arms in defense of one's country (4) working for an international organization.

6. In which instance would the Supreme Court have original jurisdiction? (1) New York State suing New Jersey over navigation on the Hudson River (2) the robbing of a national bank (3) violation by a citizen of the federal income-tax law (4) violation of a citizen's civil rights.

7. What is the role of the Supreme Court in the legislative process? (1) Congress must receive an advisory opinion from the Court before it passes a bill (2) A citizen does not have to obey a law until the Court pronounces it constitutional (3) The Court deals with legislation only when acting on a case (4) The Court may act on the constitutionality only of laws affecting states.

8. The power of the Supreme Court to declare acts of Congress unconstitutional was (1) assumed by the Court itself (2) granted by President Washington (3) granted by Congress in 1789 (4) secured by a Constitutional amendment.

9. A writ of habeas corpus would probably be sought by a person who has been (1) charged with a crime and who cannot afford bail (2) imprisoned without being charged with a crime (3) tried and convicted (4) tried twice for the same crime.

10. In 1920 a man committed a murder in State X. In 1921 the penalty for murder in State X was changed from life imprisonment to death. In 1922 this man was convicted of this crime in a state court and sentenced to death. On what Constitutional grounds might he appeal to a federal court? (1) "due process of law"—Fourteenth Amendment (2) double jeopardy (3) bill of attainder (4) ex post facto.

11. The Constitution of the United States prohibits the passage of a bill of attainder. The effect of this provision is that a citizen is guaranteed (1) a trial (2) the right to vote (3) the right to bear arms (4) freedom of religion.

12. Which part of the Constitution has been the basis of controversies over federal censorship and federal aid to religious schools? (1) Preamble (2) First Amendment (3) Thirteenth Amendment (4) powers denied to Congress.

13. The "clear and present danger" rule for cases involving freedom of speech was first stated in (1) the original Constitution (2) the Bill of Rights (3) an opinion written by John Marshall (4) an opinion written by Oliver Wendell Holmes.

14. ". . . nor shall any state deprive any person of life, liberty, or property, without due process of law . . ." is quoted from the (1) Northwest Ordinance (2) Preamble to the United States Constitution (3) First Amendment (4) Fourteenth Amendment.

15. The Constitutional provision ". . . nor shall [any person] be compelled in any criminal case to be a witness against himself . . ." protects against (1) a bill of attainder (2) cruel and unusual punishment (3) double jeopardy (4) self-incrimination.

16. The right of the government to take private property for public use, providing just compensation is made, is known as (1) bill of attainder (2) eminent domain (3) habeas corpus (4) ex post facto.

17. The federal Bill of Rights provides that (1) Congress shall not prohibit the free exercise of religion (2) the writ of habeas corpus shall not be suspended (3) Congress must guarantee each state a republican form of government (4) no citizen may be deprived of the right to vote.
18. A decision of the Supreme Court declaring a law unconstitutional can be reversed by (1) a Presidential veto (2) a vote of the legislatures of three-fourths of the states (3) an amendment to the Constitution (4) a two-thirds vote of Congress.

ESSAY QUESTIONS

1. (a) Describe the issues involved in an imaginary or real case involving freedom of speech. (b) Trace the case through the federal court system to explain the roles of the District Court, the Circuit Court, and the Supreme Court.
2. (a) Explain how the power of judicial review was established by the Supreme Court. (b) Discuss one reason for limiting the power of the Supreme Court and one reason against limiting the power of the Supreme Court. (c) Evaluate one proposal for limiting the power of the Supreme Court.
3. (a) Describe the historical circumstances under which the Bill of Rights became a part of the Constitution. (b) Several amendments in the federal Bill of Rights safeguard the rights of individuals before the courts. Give three provisions of these amendments relating to court procedures and show how each provision protects the individual against an unjust practice followed in totalitarian countries.

Part 6. The Constitution Is a Living Document

THE LIVING CONSTITUTION

In 1787, when the Constitution was written, the United States consisted of thirteen states with a total population of 4 million people, over 90 percent occupied in agriculture. As yet unknown were the large factories, the giant machines, the huge cities, and the rapid means of transportation and communication that are commonplace today. How has it been possible for this Constitution, drawn up in a small and simple agricultural society, to function in today's huge and complex industrial civilization?

Ours is a living Constitution, able to grow and adjust to new situations and problems. The flexibility of the Constitution has been based upon (1) the use of the elastic clause and a loose interpretation of the Constitution, (2) the adoption of amendments, and (3) the growth of a body of traditions and practices, called the *unwritten Constitution*.

ELASTIC CLAUSE AND LOOSE INTERPRETATION

The powers of Congress, enumerated in the Constitution, are generally stated as broad principles. By using its implied powers derived from the elastic clause and by adopting a loose interpretation of the Constitution, Congress has been able to pass laws satisfying the needs of the changing times. (For examples, see pages 57–58.)

LAW COMPARED WITH AMENDMENT

A federal law must be based upon a power granted or implied in the Constitution. For example, acting on a granted power, Congress authorized District and Circuit Courts; acting on an implied power, Congress established the National Bank. An amendment may add a new power to those granted by the Constitution. For example, the Sixteenth Amendment gave Congress the added power to levy income taxes. An amendment may also remove or change an existing power of the federal government or of state governments. For example, the Seventeenth Amendment transferred the power to elect United States Senators from the state legislatures to the people.

PROCESS OF AMENDMENT

An amendment to the Constitution must be proposed and ratified as follows:

Proposed by	Ratified by
1. A two-thirds vote of each house of Congress.	1. The legislatures of three-fourths of the states.
or	*or*
2. A national convention called by Congress upon the request of two-thirds of the states. (This method has never been used.)	2. Special conventions called by three-fourths of the states. (This method has been used only once—for the Twenty-first Amendment.)

EVALUATION OF THE PROCESS OF AMENDMENT

1. Merits. (*a*) By requiring the approval of many legislatures, the amending process prevents hasty and ill-considered changes in the Constitution. (*b*) By requiring an "extraordinary" majority, the amending process prevents any "temporary" majority, arising out of momentary excitement, from tampering with our governmental system or revoking basic civil liberties. A difficult amending process seeks to place our Constitution beyond the reach of any "ordinary" majority. (*c*) Members of special state conventions, which may be called to ratify a proposed amendment, are elected by the voters on that single issue. The state convention, a method used only once, reflects public opinion.

2. Criticisms. (*a*) The amending process, necessitating action by many legislative bodies, is cumbersome and time-consuming. (*b*) Since the amending process requires far more than a simple majority, few amendments are passed, and the process may thwart the will of the people. Of thousands of amendments introduced in Congress, very few have become part of the Constitution. (c) State legislators, who are empowered to ratify proposed amendments, may have been elected on other issues. Lacking a formal expression of the public will, they may vote their personal preference.

BRIEF SUMMARY OF AMENDMENTS

First Ten Amendments (1791). The first ten amendments list the basic civil liberties of the people and are known as the Bill of Rights (see pages 91–92).

Background. The supporters of the original Constitution promised these amendments to secure votes for ratification.

Eleventh Amendment (1798). A state shall not be sued in a federal court by a citizen of another state or by a citizen of a foreign country.

Background. In *Chisholm vs. Georgia* (1793), the Supreme Court had affirmed the right of a citizen of South Carolina to sue Georgia. Georgia denied the authority of the federal courts in this matter and rejected the decision. To protect state sovereignty, the states secured adoption of the Eleventh Amendment.

Twelfth Amendment (1804). Electors (members of the electoral college) shall cast separate ballots for President and Vice President.

Background. According to the original Constitution each elector voted for two persons. The candidate with the most votes became President, provided that he had the votes of a majority of the electors. The runner-up became Vice President. In 1800 the Democratic-Republican party nominated Thomas Jefferson for President and Aaron Burr for Vice President, and the party won a majority in the electoral college. The Democratic-Republican electors cast an equal number of votes for Jefferson and Burr, thereby creating a tie and throwing the election into the House of Representatives. On the 36th ballot Jefferson was chosen President. The Twelfth Amendment prevents a repetition of such a tie between a Presidential and a Vice Presidential candidate.

Thirteenth Amendment (1865). No slavery shall exist within the United States.

Background. In 1863, during the Civil War, President Lincoln's Emancipation Proclamation declared free the slaves in the states still in rebellion. The Proclamation did not apply to slaves in Confederate territories occupied by Union armies and in border states loyal to the Union. The Thirteenth Amendment, the first Civil War amendment, prohibited slavery in the entire country.

Fourteenth Amendment (1868). (*a*) All persons born or naturalized in the United States are citizens. (*b*) No state shall abridge the privileges of · citizens, or deprive "any person of life, liberty, or property without due process of law," or deny to any person "equal protection of the laws." (*c*) Any state unfairly denying citizens the right to vote shall have its representation in the House proportionately reduced. (*d*) Leading Confederate officials shall be disqualified from holding public office. (*e*) The Confederate debt shall be void.

Background. This second Civil War amendment, passed during the Reconstruction Era, was intended to protect the rights of blacks and to punish leaders of the Confederacy.

Fifteenth Amendment (1870). The right of citizens to vote "shall not be abridged by the United States or any state on account of race, color, or previous condition of servitude."

Background. This third Civil War amendment was intended to assure the voting rights of blacks.

Sixteenth Amendment (1913). Congress shall have the power to levy a tax on incomes.

Background. To supplement federal revenue from tariffs, Congress in 1894 authorized a 2-percent tax on certain incomes. In *Pollock vs. the Farmers' Loan and Trust Company* (1895), the Supreme Court held the income tax to be a direct tax not levied among the states in proportion to population and therefore in violation of the Constitution. The Sixteenth Amendment, vigorously supported by the progressive movement, overcame this Supreme Court ruling. The income tax, on individuals and corporations, has become the main source of federal revenue.

Seventeenth Amendment (1913). Senators shall be elected directly by the people.

Background. The Seventeenth Amendment ended the election of Senators by state legislatures. It was a reform urged by the progressive movement.

Eighteenth Amendment (1919). The manufacture, sale, or transportation of intoxicating beverages was prohibited.

Background. For years, temperance groups—most notably the Anti-Saloon League and the Woman's Christian Temperance Union—had agitated for prohibition so as to protect the people against the evils of intoxicating beverages. Starting in Maine in the mid-19th century, some form of prohibition was adopted in about half the states. During World War I, to conserve grain, which is used in manufacturing liquor, Congress authorized prohibition as a wartime measure and submitted the Eighteenth Amendment to the states.

Nineteenth Amendment (1920). The right to vote shall not be denied by the United States or any state on account of sex.

Background. For years, women known as suffragettes had demanded that women be given the right to vote. Some states, chiefly in the West, gradually permitted woman suffrage. In recognition of women's services during World War I, the nation adopted the Nineteenth Amendment.

Twentieth Amendment (1933). Congress shall meet annually on January 3, and a new President shall take office on January 20 following his election.

Background. The Twentieth Amendment recognized advances in communication and transportation by moving up the dates for taking office. Previously, the new Congress, elected in November, did not meet until 13 months later. The old Congress, which met in December immediately following the election, contained some defeated Congressmen, called *lame ducks*. The "lame duck" Congress rarely proved to be a productive legislative session. Also, before this amendment, a new President waited an additional six weeks before taking office on March 4.

Twenty-first Amendment (1933). The Eighteenth (Prohibition) Amendment was repealed.

Background. The Eighteenth Amendment, attempting to legislate moral standards and change personal habits, aroused widespread opposition. It gave rise to an era of gangsters, bootleggers, speakeasies, and public disrespect for the law. Its repeal, quickly ratified by special state conventions, returned liquor control primarily to the states.

Twenty-second Amendment (1951). No person shall be elected President for more than two terms.

Background. The two-term tradition, established by George Washington, had been broken in 1940 by Franklin D. Roosevelt. The Twenty-second Amendment transformed a tradition into a Constitutional provision.

Twenty-third Amendment (1961). Residents of the District of Columbia shall have the right to vote for the President. The District's electoral vote shall be no greater than that of the least populous state (currently Alaska with three electoral votes).

Background. Since the District of Columbia is not a state and has no representation in Congress, its residents previously had no vote in Presidential elections.

Twenty-fourth Amendment (1964). The right to vote in primaries and general elections for federal officials—President, Vice President, Senators, and Representatives—shall not be denied because of failure to pay a poll tax.

Background. The poll tax had been used chiefly to keep poor whites and blacks from voting. The amendment affected five Southern states.

Twenty-fifth Amendment (1967). In case the office of Vice President is vacant, the President shall select a new Vice President subject to Congressional approval. In case of Presidential disability, the Vice President may serve as Acting President until the President is able to resume his duties.

Background. The public worried over (1) Presidential disability—President Eisenhower suffered three major illnesses, and (2) Presidential succession—the Vice Presidency was vacant for 14 months after Kennedy was assassinated and Vice President Johnson became President.

Twenty-sixth Amendment (1971). The right of citizens, 18 years old or older, to vote shall not be denied on account of age.

Background. The Supreme Court ruled that a 1970 federal law granting the vote to 18-year-olds was valid for federal, but not state and local, elections. The amendment gave 18-year-olds the vote in all elections.

Twenty-seventh Amendment (1992). Salary raises for members of Congress—Senators and Representatives—shall not take effect until after the next election of Representatives.

Background. First proposed in 1789 by James Madison, this amendment was not ratified until the 38th state, Michigan, approved it more than 200 years later. (Normally, Congress has put a seven-year time limit for ratification of an amendment.) The amendment prevents Congress from voting itself an immediate pay raise.

THE UNWRITTEN CONSTITUTION

The "unwritten Constitution" consists of the American governmental practices and institutions not specifically set down in the Constitution but based upon custom and tradition. Examples are (1) judicial review by the Supreme Court, (2) the committee system in Congress, (3) the President's Cabinet, (4) pledges by Presidential electors to vote for specific candidates, and (5) political parties.

POLITICAL PARTIES

1. Purpose. Although not mentioned in the Constitution, political parties appeared as early as George Washington's first administration. In a democracy a political party arises when people with similar interests and ideas band together to advance their program by peacefully gaining control of the government.

2. Two-Party System. Traditionally, the United States has had a *two-party system*. The two major parties today are the Democrats and the Republicans. Although both parties have supporters from all social, ethnic, and economic backgrounds, each party has traditionally been identified with certain segments of our population. The Democratic party has drawn support from among laborers, poor farmers, and minority groups. The Republican party has drawn support from among businessmen and well-to-do farmers.

Since control of the government depends upon gaining the support of a majority of the American electorate, our major parties today usually avoid narrow regional or class appeals. Each party contains spokesmen of divergent political views—liberal, moderate, and conservative. Each party, however, usually adopts moderate positions so as to gain the widest possible public support. Nevertheless, the parties do differ, sometimes slightly and sometimes considerably, on major issues.

3. Role of Minor Parties. Minor political parties usually have sought limited objectives and have had limited appeal. (*a*) The Free Soil party opposed the extension of slavery. (*b*) The Greenback-Labor party favored cheap money. (*c*) The Populist party appealed to farmers with a program of cheap money and such other reforms as government control of railroads. (*d*) The Progressive, or "Bull Moose," party was organized in 1912 in an unsuccessful effort to win the Presidential election for Theodore Roosevelt on a broad program of reform. (*e*) The Socialist party advocated many economic reforms but appealed only to a relatively small number of workers. Such "third" parties usually have been short-lived.

The Republican party, which started in 1854, has been the only minor party to become a major party. Its initial success was due, in part, to its broad appeal—not only to antislavery groups, but also to businessmen, farmers, Western settlers, and supporters of a strong national government.

Minor parties have made contributions to our government chiefly by presenting the people with new ideas, such as the income tax, direct election of Senators, and Social Security. In time the major parties have adopted and enacted into law such new ideas as are in keeping with American tradition.

4. Political Parties Further Democracy. Political parties hold conventions, draw up political platforms, nominate candidates for public office, and conduct campaigns. Thus they crystallize campaign issues, educate the public, and offer the voters a choice of ideas and candidates. Parties also keep check on each other, since each party is eager to uncover and publicize the other's mistakes.

5. Dangers of Political Parties

a. Party Machines. Especially on the local level, political parties may be controlled undemocratically by a small group of insiders, called a *party machine*. These insiders are professional politicians who devote their lives to politics, usually as a means of earning a living. They are generally led by a *party boss*. The political machine remains in power as long as it is able to crush opposition, control votes, and win elections. Many party machines have become infamous for graft, corruption, and disregard of public welfare. These have included the *Pendergast Machine* in Missouri, the *Vare Machine* in Pennsylvania, and the *Tweed Ring*, which controlled Tammany Hall in New York City.

b. Public Apathy. Although the average citizen has little contact with or knowledge of political parties, he is usually content to permit them to control his government. The average citizen generally restricts his political activities to reading the newspaper and to voting in general elections. The "man in the street" remains indifferent, even for long periods, to rule by party machine. Only when machine rule becomes flagrant and a fighting reform leader appears, does the average citizen become aroused. He may join a political club, attend protest meetings, contribute funds, and campaign among his neighbors in order to awaken the community to go to the polls and "throw the rascals out."

c. Dependence Upon Large Contributors. Parties raise funds chiefly from well-to-do persons and organizations. Such contributors may want favors in return: appointments to office or passage of special legislation. By various laws, the federal government regulates contributions to reduce the political influence of large contributors. To this end, the comprehensive 1974 Federal Campaign Reform Act provides for extensive federal funding of Presidential elections but leaves the funding of Congressional races entirely to private contributors. (Check the Index for "Campaign finances.")

d. Partisanship. With the party out of power seeking to unseat the party in control of the government, the "outs" often denounce the "ins" unfairly.

They may oppose worthwhile measures, raise irrelevant issues, and seek partisan advantage at the expense of the public welfare.

UNDEMOCRATIC FEATURES IN THE ORIGINAL CONSTITUTION

Many of the Founding Fathers feared what they called the "excesses" of democracy. Consequently, they included in the original Constitution several provisions limiting the power of the people. (1) The Constitution provides for the election of the President not by the people, but by an electoral college. In many states, the electors were originally chosen by the state legislatures. (2) The original Constitution provided for the election of United States Senators not directly by the people, but by the state legislatures. (3) The original Constitution left to the states the power to determine who shall vote. It contained no provision outlawing property and religious qualifications for voting and no provision granting voting rights to women.

Furthermore, the original Constitution accepted and protected the undemocratic institution of slavery. It contained provisions (1) counting five Negroes as three whites for purpose of representation and taxation, (2) forbidding Congress for 20 years to interfere with the importation of slaves, and (3) requiring the return of runaway, or fugitive, slaves.

GROWTH OF DEMOCRACY

Since the beginning of the American republic in 1789, Americans have progressed steadfastly toward a more perfect democracy. They have eliminated many undemocratic features of the original Constitution and have expanded the concept of democracy.

1. Political parties, arising under the "unwritten Constitution," have converted the electoral college into a "rubber stamp" so that in reality the people elect the President.

2. Most states, by the mid-19th century, had abolished religious and property qualifications for officeholding and voting.

3. The states ratified amendments to the Constitution that (a) freed the Negro slaves, made them citizens, and gave them the right to vote, (b) provided for direct election of Senators, (c) gave women the right to vote, and (d) enabled District of Columbia residents to vote for President.

4. Spurred by the Depression of 1929, the American people expanded their ideal of democracy from a chiefly political concept to include also economic aspects. The federal government undertook to maintain the economic well-being of the people by minimum wage and Social Security laws.

5. Especially since World War II, American democracy has moved to end racial discrimination and to achieve equality for the Negro. This "civil rights" movement has scored impressive gains: the Supreme Court decision

to prohibit segregation in public schools; the Twenty-fourth Amendment to void the poll tax in federal elections; and federal laws to assure equal voting rights for blacks and to ban discrimination in places of public accommodation and in the sale or rental of most housing. Civil rights leaders contend that these gains mark only the beginning of a massive effort to secure the "blessings of liberty" for blacks in America.

6. The Voting Rights Act of 1970, in addition to protecting black voters against discrimination, also (a) suspended literacy tests across the nation as a qualification for voting, (b) provided a uniform 30-day residency requirement for voting in Presidential elections, and (c) set the voting age at 18 for all federal, state, and local elections. Citing the great importance of protecting black voting rights, President Nixon signed the bill. The President, however, explained that, although he favored lowering the voting age to 18, he believed that such action required a Constitutional amendment. He therefore requested that the law speedily be judged as to constitutionality.

The Supreme Court (a) unanimously upheld the banning of literacy tests as within Congress' power under the Fifteenth Amendment, (b) by 8 to 1, upheld the uniform 30-day residency requirement as within Congress' power to protect the right of individuals to move freely between the states, and (c) by 5 to 4, upheld the vote for 18-year-olds in federal elections but *not* in state and local elections.

Thereupon, Congress overwhelmingly approved a Constitutional amendment lowering the voting age to 18 years for all elections. Ratified in 1971 by 38 states in three months—the fastest ratification ever—it became the 26th Amendment.

EXPERIMENTS IN POLITICAL DEMOCRACY BY STATES

The federal system of government permits individual states to experiment with new ways of furthering democracy. For example, the states were the first to grant suffrage to women, to limit hours of work, and to provide unemployment insurance—reforms subsequently adopted by the federal government. Today, individual states are testing the following practices:

1. **Direct Primary.** This is a preliminary election in which the voters select the party candidates who will run for various offices in the general election. Direct primaries seek to transfer the nomination of candidates from political leaders at party conventions to the voters.

2. **Initiative.** A small percentage of voters (5 or 10 percent) may sign a petition to initiate, or start, a law. Depending on the state, the proposal is submitted to the state legislature or, at the next election, to the people.

3. **Referendum.** A small percentage of voters (usually 5 or 10 percent) may sign a petition, thereby compelling the legislature to submit to the vot-

ers a law already passed. Also, in some states, the legislature may itself submit a proposed law to the voters for their approval or disapproval.

4. Recall. A substantial percentage of voters (usually 25 percent) may sign a petition to recall an official from public office. The official may then present his case to the voters in the special election held to fill the position.

5. Short Ballot. The long ballot, once typical of state elections, listed so many candidates that most voters were unable to determine their qualifications. The short ballot provides that the voters elect only major state officials. The less important officials are appointed by the Governor. By the short ballot, many states have concentrated responsibility in the Governor and made it easier for voters to scrutinize the candidates for election.

6. Unicameral Legislature. Nebraska alone of the 50 states has a unicameral, or one-house, legislature. It makes for greater speed and efficiency, but has the disadvantage of eliminating important checks in lawmaking.

MULTIPLE-CHOICE QUESTIONS

1. Liberal interpretation of the elastic clause has contributed to the fact that (1) a committee system has developed in Congress (2) the Constitution has met the needs of changing times (3) the principle of checks and balances is generally accepted (4) gerrymandering has become an established practice.

2. In authorizing a space exploration program, Congress used (1) an implied power (2) a police power (3) a concurrent power (4) a reserved power.

3. Elimination of the electoral college system for selecting the President of the United States would require (1) a Constitutional amendment (2) an act of Congress (3) a Presidential proclamation (4) a Supreme Court decision.

4. Why have relatively few amendments been added to the Constitution? (1) Necessary changes have been brought about through a broad interpretation of the Constitution. (2) The sole initiative for the amending process resides in the federal government. (3) The federal government has restricted state activity in the amending process. (4) The need for changes has been met by the states.

5. The Constitution provides that amendments may be proposed by (1) Congress (2) the President (3) the governors of the states (4) state conventions.

6. An amendment to the Constitution needs to be ratified by (1) the President and Congress (2) a majority of the Supreme Court Justices (3) legislatures or conventions in three-fourths of the states (4) a majority of the eligible voters.

7. Which has changed from "unwritten" to written Constitution? (1) provision for a President's Cabinet (2) provision for the committee system in Congress (3) formation of political parties (4) limiting the number of terms for any one President.

8. The reason that an amendment was necessary to levy a federal income tax is that (1) the people opposed federal taxation (2) it was a type of tax that had never been used (3) the states were already using this type of taxation (4) it was a direct tax not apportioned according to population.

9. A 19th-century amendment to the Constitution forbids states to (1) deny equality before the law (2) deny the right of suffrage because of sex (3) require the poll tax as a qualification for voting (4) levy an income tax.

10. Citizens living in the District of Columbia (1) elect voting representatives to Con-

gress (2) do not pay personal income taxes (3) are ineligible for civil service positions (4) vote for Presidential electors.

11. Since the adoption of the Twentieth Amendment, Congress convenes every year on (1) December 10 (2) January 3 (3) January 20 (4) March 4.

12. Which is no longer a provision of the Constitution? (1) Three-Fifths Compromise (2) Connecticut Compromise (3) election of the President by electors (4) prohibition of export taxes.

13. That Presidential electors vote separately for President and Vice President was provided in (1) the original Constitution (2) the Presidential Succession Act of 1947 (3) a Supreme Court decision (4) an amendment to the Constitution.

14. A practice that has become a part of our "unwritten Constitution" is (1) the convention method of nominating Presidential candidates (2) Senate approval of Presidential appointments (3) the order of succession to the Presidency (4) the President's power to negotiate treaties.

15. The President makes use of the "unwritten Constitution" when he (1) vetoes a Congressional bill (2) appoints an ambassador to a foreign country (3) calls a special session of Congress (4) summons his Cabinet.

16. The practice that Presidential electors vote for the candidate nominated by their political party is based upon (1) the Constitution of the United States (2) custom and tradition (3) a law of Congress (4) a decision of the Supreme Court.

17. Members of a political party are given a ballot on which they may choose a candidate from among three members of that party—*A, B,* or *C.* This situation is typical of (1) an uncontested election (2) a machine-controlled district (3) a primary election (4) a gerrymandered district.

18. The initiative provides a method for (1) submitting a law to the voters for approval after it has been passed by the legislature (2) removing inefficient public officials (3) enabling voters to propose legislation (4) requiring the Supreme Court to decide the constitutionality of a law.

19. Which democratic ideal was *last* to be achieved in the United States? (1) separation of church and state (2) universal suffrage (3) representative government (4) freedom of speech and press.

ESSAY QUESTIONS

1. Giving *two* examples, show how *each* of the following has helped the federal government meet the needs of changing times: (*a*) amendments to the federal Constitution, (*b*) use of the doctrine of implied powers.

2. For over 175 years the Constitution of the United States has been able to survive in a rapidly changing civilization. Giving *one* specific example for *each,* show how the original Constitution of the United States has been expanded by the following: (*a*) amendments, (*b*) laws of Congress, (*c*) custom and usage.

3. The United States Constitution is a living document. (*a*) Describe a circumstance that led to the adoption of *one* amendment to the federal Constitution in each of *three* of the following periods: (1) 1789–1815, (2) 1860–1875, (3) 1900–1930, (4) since 1930. (*b*) Give *three* examples of the "unwritten Constitution."

4. "The cure for the ills of democracy is not more democracy but more intelligence." (*a*) Give *one* argument for *or one* argument against this statement. (*b*) Discuss *two* attempts to cure the ills of democracy by more democracy.

5. Each state in the United States is a laboratory in which social, economic, and political experiments are constantly being made. Describe *two* experiments that have been tried by various states and later adopted by the national government.

UNIT III. THE YOUNG NATION TACKLES ITS MANY PROBLEMS

Part 1. The Federalists Guide the New Government

GEORGE WASHINGTON: OUR FIRST PRESIDENT

In our first Presidential election, George Washington received the vote of every elector. On April 30, 1789, he took the oath of office in the nation's temporary capital, New York City.

Washington, a dedicated man with a keen sense of duty, sought no personal power. He commanded the loyalty and service of outstanding patriots. With calm and farsighted judgment that rose above petty detail, Washington concentrated upon the larger view: the need to foster national unity, to assure a smoothly functioning administration, and to develop respect for the new government.

FIRST ACTS OF THE NEW GOVERNMENT

1. Judiciary Act of 1789. Congress passed and Washington signed the Judiciary Act of 1789 establishing District and Circuit Courts and specifying that the Supreme Court shall consist of six judges. Washington appointed John Jay to be the first Chief Justice.

2. Bill of Rights. Congress overwhelmingly approved the Bill of Rights —the first ten amendments to our Constitution—and sent them to the states for ratification.

3. Formation of the First Cabinet. Washington appointed capable men to the major offices in the new government. His closest assistants were Thomas Jefferson (Secretary of State), Alexander Hamilton (Secretary of the Treasury), Henry Knox (Secretary of War), and Edmund Randolph (Attorney General). These four men, occasionally called together by Washington for advice, constituted the first Cabinet. The Cabinet officer who exercised the greatest influence on Washington's administration was Alexander Hamilton.

HAMILTON'S FINANCIAL PROGRAM

The new government faced a most urgent problem: organizing its finances. Hamilton, in his reports on public credit and manufacturing, urged that Congress enact the following program:

1. Payment of Debts. According to the Constitution (Article VI, Section 1), the new government assumed responsibility for all debts contracted by the central government during the Revolutionary War and Confederation periods. Hamilton recommended:

   a. Full payment of the domestic debt—government bonds and certificates held by Americans. Hamilton proposed that this debt be "funded," that is, that all old bonds and certificates be exchanged for bonds issued by the new government.

   b. Full payment of the foreign debt—loans extended by our Revolutionary War allies: France, Spain, and the Netherlands.

   c. Assumption of state debts by the federal government, since these debts were incurred in fighting the Revolutionary War.

Such repayments, Hamilton argued, would firmly establish the credit of the United States at home and abroad.

2. Excise Tax. To raise funds, Hamilton proposed an excise tax on various commodities, notably on distilled liquors.

3. Protective Tariff. Congress had already passed a tariff on imports. Hamilton urged that tariffs on manufactured goods be sharply increased to discourage the importation of such goods and to encourage manufacturing in the United States. Although Congress rejected Hamilton's proposal for a protective tariff, it raised rates slightly for revenue purposes.

4. Money Management. Hamilton urged the chartering of a *National Bank*, or Bank of the United States. This would be a private institution with a capital stock of $10,000,000, of which private investors would own 80 percent and the government 20 percent. The Bank would serve the government as its financial agent, holding government moneys, assisting in tax collections, and selling government bonds. Also, the Bank would issue bank notes, or paper money, but with a sufficient backing of specie (gold and silver) to constitute a stable currency. Finally, the Bank would provide loans for manufacturing and other business ventures and facilitate financial transactions throughout the nation.

5. Overall Objectives. Hamilton's program—to establish the national credit, encourage manufacturing, and provide a sound currency—favored men of wealth and enterprise: creditors, merchants, and manufacturers. By giving these groups an economic stake in the new government, Hamilton believed that he was assuring its success.

ADOPTION OF HAMILTON'S PROGRAM DESPITE BITTER OPPOSITION

1. **Repayment of the Domestic Debt.** Speculators had purchased government bonds from their original owners at prices far below face value. The original owners now protested that repaying the domestic debt in full would enrich the speculators. Hamilton argued that the measure was necessary to establish the nation's credit. Hamilton won, and in 1790 Congress passed the Funding Bill.

2. **Assumption of State Debts.** Hamilton's opponents argued that this proposal was unfair to those states, chiefly in the South, that had paid off their indebtedness themselves. Hamilton won adoption of the proposal by logrolling. In exchange for Southern votes, he promised to support the establishment of the nation's permanent capital in the South—on the banks of the Potomac between Maryland and Virginia.

3. **Excise Taxes.** Congress passed Hamilton's excise taxes. The excise tax on whisky chiefly affected farmers on the western frontier, who were converting much of their bulky, low-priced grain into less bulky and higher-priced liquor for shipment to the East.

Farmers in western Pennsylvania refused to pay the whisky tax. In 1794 a group of these farmers put up armed resistance against federal officials, an incident called the *Whisky Rebellion.* Hamilton prevailed upon Washington to recruit 15,000 troops and to crush the rebels. This action, contrasting with the inaction of the Confederation during Shays' Rebellion, demonstrated the power of the new government.

4. **Bank of the United States.** Opponents of the Bank argued for a strict interpretation of the Constitution. Thomas Jefferson pointed out that Congress was not specifically granted the power to establish a National Bank. Hamilton replied that the Bank was "necessary and proper" for carrying out the delegated power to "coin money" and "regulate the value thereof." Hamilton's loose interpretation was accepted by George Washington, who signed the bill chartering the Bank.

RISE OF POLITICAL PARTIES

The bitter struggle over financial matters resulted in the formation of two political parties:

1. **Federalists.** The Federalists were led by John Adams and Alexander Hamilton. (The Federalists are considered the forebears of the mid-19th-century Whig party and of our present-day Republican party.)

2. **Democratic-Republicans.** The Anti-Federalists were led by James Madison and Thomas Jefferson. The Anti-Federalists were also known as the Democratic-Republicans or Republicans. (From this party descended our present-day Democratic party.)

FEDERALIST PARTY	DEMOCRATIC-REPUBLICAN PARTY
1. Consisted of the wealthier people: merchants, bankers, and large landowners.	1. Consisted of the common people: farmers, small shopkeepers, and city workers.
2. Was strongest in the North, especially in New England.	2. Was strongest in the South and West.
3. Believed in government by and for the "rich, well-born, and able," distrusted the common people, and feared what Federalists termed the "excesses of democracy."	3. Believed in government by capable leaders, emphasized that government should work in the interests of the common people, and strongly advocated democratic principles.
4. Favored a strong central government and consequently urged a loose interpretation of the Constitution.	4. Favored states' rights and consequently urged a strict interpretation of the Constitution.
5. Supported Hamilton's financial program as beneficial to the economic interests of the party's supporters.	5. Opposed Hamilton's financial program as harmful to the economic interests of the party's supporters.
6. In foreign affairs, tended to favor Britain, whose government was dominated by the upper classes.	6. In foreign affairs, tended to favor France, whose people had revolted in 1789 for liberty and equality.

FRENCH REVOLUTION STIRS AMERICA

Washington's inauguration coincided with the beginning of a 25-year period of revolution and warfare in Europe. In 1789 began the French Revolution, which led to the Reign of Terror and to an armed struggle between France and a group of conservative European nations: Austria, Prussia, and Great Britain. In 1799 France fell under the rule of the ambitious Napoleon Bonaparte, and until 1815 Europe experienced almost continuous warfare. The prize was the domination of Europe. The chief contestants were France and Britain.

American public opinion quickly divided in regard to the French Revolution.

1. The **Democratic-Republicans** sympathized with the French Revolution, contending that the French were fighting for democracy, and pointing to similarities between the French and American Revolutions. The French (a) had overthrown the authority of their king, (b) had issued the *Declaration of the Rights of Man,* and (c) had proclaimed their democratic ideals as "liberty, equality, fraternity."

2. The **Federalists** were unsympathetic to the French Revolution, pointing to the Reign of Terror as evidence of the "excesses of democracy." In the wars between England and France, the Federalists generally sympathized with England.

WASHINGTON'S PROCLAMATION OF NEUTRALITY (1793)

President Washington deplored the violent division of American public opinion regarding the European war. He also feared that, in accordance with the 1778 Franco-American treaty of alliance, the French Republic would call for American military assistance, especially the use of American ports to outfit expeditions against British ships and colonies.

President Washington believed that for the young nation to become involved in the European war would be suicidal. His views were supported by Hamilton and Jefferson, both of whom urged neutrality. Hamilton further argued that the treaty of 1778 was no longer valid as we had signed it with the French monarchy, not with the French Republic. Washington did not declare the treaty invalid but instead issued a *Proclamation of Neutrality*. In it he urged Americans to be impartial toward the warring nations.

"CITIZEN" GENÊT AFFAIR (1793)

The French Ambassador to the United States, "Citizen" Edmond Genêt, played upon the pro-French sentiments of many American citizens. Defying Washington's Proclamation of Neutrality, he outfitted privateers (privately owned armed ships) in American harbors and commissioned them to raid British ships and colonies.

Fearing that Genêt would involve the United States in a war against Great Britain, Washington ordered Genêt to halt his activities and finally requested Genêt's recall by the French government. Washington thus halted an attempt to breach our neutrality.

JAY TREATY WITH BRITAIN (1794–1795)

1. **Background.** To keep supplies from France, Britain ordered her powerful navy to seize American merchant ships bound for French ports. Such seizures violated the principle of *freedom of the seas*, the right of a neutral nation to trade with belligerents in goods not intended for war use. The British also impressed American sailors into the British navy. Anti-British sentiment in the United States was further aroused because the British still held posts in the Northwest Territory and because the Americans believed that the British were encouraging the Indians to raid American frontier settlements. Washington sent John Jay to London to settle the outstanding issues.

2. **Provisions.** England, confident that the United States would not go to war, made few concessions. The resulting *Jay Treaty* provided that (a) Great Britain withdraw her troops from the American Northwest, and (b) arbitration commissions settle financial claims of Americans against Britain and of the British against the United States.

3. American Reaction to the Treaty. The terms of the treaty further aroused American resentment. The treaty (*a*) did not provide for freedom of the seas, and (*b*) contained no pledge that England would halt the seizure of American ships or the impressment of American sailors. The treaty secured minimal Senate ratification only through the full influence of Hamilton and Washington. In spite of its failings, the Jay Treaty meant peace with Britain.

PINCKNEY TREATY WITH SPAIN (1795)

Spain was alarmed by the Jay Treaty because she feared a secret Anglo-American alliance to seize Spanish territories in North America, especially Florida and the Louisiana Territory. Spain therefore agreed to negotiate outstanding problems with the United States.

The resulting *Pinckney Treaty* (1) established the Mississippi as the western boundary and the 31st parallel as the southern boundary of the United States (see map, page 40), and (2) guaranteed Americans free navigation of the entire Mississippi and the *right of deposit* at New Orleans—the right to transfer goods from riverboats to oceangoing ships without payment of a Spanish tariff. Because the Mississippi River and the port of New Orleans were economically vital to our Western farmers, the Pinckney Treaty was an American triumph.

WASHINGTON'S FAREWELL ADDRESS (1796)

Prior to his retirement as President, George Washington issued his *Farewell Address*. He advised the new nation regarding its future course. In foreign affairs, Washington urged developing commercial relations with all nations but avoiding political entanglements. He stated, "It is our true policy to steer clear of permanent alliances with any portion of the foreign world." He added, however, that the United States could "safely trust to temporary alliances for extraordinary emergencies."

The Farewell Address greatly influenced the United States toward remaining politically aloof from the rest of the world by following a foreign policy of *isolation*. In the early days of the republic, isolation was defended on the grounds that the United States (1) to a large extent was not concerned with Europe's quarrels, (2) was separated from Europe by 3000 miles of Atlantic Ocean, a trip of several weeks, (3) lacked military and naval power, (4) might lose its independence if defeated in a war, (5) was internally divided on foreign policy so that any alliance would endanger national unity, and (6) should devote its energies to developing its lands and other natural resources.

ELECTION OF 1796

1. **Washington Retires.** In 1796 George Washington announced his retirement. Washington was tired of the cares of public office and of the bitter criticisms hurled at him by the Democratic-Republicans. In his Farewell Address, Washington warned that excessive political partisanship endangered the well-being of the nation.

Washington's refusal to run for a third term established the two-term precedent and the principle that no one man is indispensable to the republic. He returned to his home at Mount Vernon, Virginia, where he died a few years afterwards.

2. **Adams Wins the Election.** John Adams, Federalist candidate for the Presidency, defeated Thomas Jefferson, the Democratic-Republican candidate, by the close electoral vote of 71 to 68. However, the Federalist electors split their second-place votes, and Jefferson, with the second largest number of votes in the electoral college, became Vice President. This election marked the only time that candidates of opposing political parties were elected President and Vice President. (A repetition was made unlikely by the Twelfth Amendment, requiring separate ballots for President and Vice President.)

ADAMS FACES DIFFICULTIES WITH FRANCE (1797–1801)

1. **French Hostility.** French resentment at American foreign policy created serious problems for President Adams. The French government had been enraged by (a) Washington's Proclamation of Neutrality and (b) Senate ratification of the Jay Treaty. French warships and privateers attacked and seized American merchant ships. Anti-French sentiment developed in the United States, and many Federalists demanded war.

2. **XYZ Affair (1797).** Seeking peace, President Adams sent a special negotiating mission to Paris. The delegation was insulted by French agents who demanded that, before talks begin, the Americans pay a large bribe. Adams, enraged, reported the episode to Congress, identifying the French agents only as X, Y, and Z. Hence the incident became known as the *XYZ Affair*. American public opinion reacted with the slogan, "Millions for defense, but not one cent for tribute."

3. **Undeclared Naval Warfare (1798–1800).** Congress voted large military funds, especially to build up the navy, and in 1798 established a Cabinet-level Navy Department. American warships and privateers engaged in an undeclared war with France, capturing about 100 French vessels.

Although Hamilton wanted to expand the war, Adams steadfastly desired peace. In 1800 he sent a second mission to France, which was now controlled by Napoleon Bonaparte. Both countries agreed to end the naval conflict and to cancel the 1778 treaty of alliance. Adams lost popularity with pro-war Federalists at home, but he restored the peace.

ALIEN AND SEDITION ACTS (1798)

While the crisis with France was at its height, Federalist partisans in Congress secured the passage of four laws, known as the *Alien and Sedition Acts.* Some Federalists claimed that the laws were meant to protect the United States from alien agitators. However, the chief purpose of the laws was to weaken the Democratic-Republican party.

1. The **Naturalization Act** increased from 5 to 14 years the time required for immigrants to become American citizens. The Federalists wanted to lengthen the naturalization process since most immigrants, upon becoming citizens, voted for Democratic-Republican candidates.

2. The **Alien Act** empowered the President to deport any alien whom he considered dangerous to the United States. The **Alien Enemies Act** authorized detention of enemy aliens in time of war. Although not used by Adams, these two laws caused some aliens to leave the country and frightened others to refrain from speaking out against the Federalists.

3. The **Sedition Act** provided fines and imprisonment for any person who uttered or wrote "false, scandalous, and malicious" statements against Congress or the President. Even Hamilton disapproved this law, and many people considered it a violation of the First Amendment. Nevertheless, the Sedition Act remained in effect and was used to bring to trial and convict ten Democratic-Republican printers and editors.

VIRGINIA AND KENTUCKY RESOLUTIONS (1798-1799)

Instead of weakening the Democratic-Republican party, the Alien and Sedition Acts actually strengthened it. Many people felt that the Federalist party threatened their civil liberties. Democratic-Republican leaders took advantage of the situation to gain votes for their party.

At the urging of Madison and Jefferson, the state legislatures of Virginia and Kentucky passed resolutions condemning these acts as unconstitutional. The Virginia and Kentucky Resolutions presented the states' rights doctrine, claiming that (1) the federal government was created by the states to serve as their agent, and (2) state legislatures could declare laws of Congress unconstitutional and therefore null and void.

Madison and Jefferson intended these resolutions primarily as campaign documents for the 1800 Presidential election. Nevertheless, the idea of *nullification* was to plague the United States until the supremacy of the federal government was conclusively established by the Civil War.

SUMMARY OF THE FEDERALIST ERA (1789–1801)

In the election of 1800, the Federalists lost control of the executive and legislative branches of the government. (However, Federalist judges, appointed for life, remained in office and for many years dominated the Supreme Court. The most important of these was Chief Justice John Marshall.) Never again to win a national election, the Federalist party—but not its ideas—slowly disappeared from American life.

1. Federalist Achievements. During their 12 years in power, the Federalists had (a) used the Constitution to develop a workable system of government, (b) established the nation's credit and fostered economic prosperity, (c) created a court system, (d) demonstrated the ability of the government to enforce laws, (e) admitted three states to the Union, and (f) kept the nation from war and instituted a foreign policy of isolation.

2. Reasons for the Federalist Downfall. The major causes for the defeat of the Federalists were the following: (a) the spread of democratic ideals throughout the nation, especially in the West, (b) the growing realization that the Federalist party distrusted the common people, (c) widespread opposition to Federalist economic measures, (d) opposition to the Federalists' pro-English foreign policy, (e) bitter intraparty rivalry between Adams and Hamilton, and (f) opposition to the Alien and Sedition Acts.

MULTIPLE-CHOICE QUESTIONS

1. President George Washington established a Cabinet in order to (1) help execute the laws of Congress (2) imitate the British Cabinet system (3) carry out a provision of the Bill of Rights (4) obtain the advice of a group of persons in whom he had confidence.

2. Alexander Hamilton based much of his financial program on his belief that (1) the success of the new government required the support of the propertied classes (2) the states should be discouraged from depending on the federal government (3) speculation in government securities had to be prevented (4) land was the most important source of wealth.

3. The *least* controversial of Hamilton's financial proposals was that the national government (1) assume the states' debts (2) pay its debt to foreign investors (3) levy the whisky tax (4) establish a National Bank.

4. Which powers did Congress use to charter the Bank of the United States in 1791? (1) concurrent powers (2) unlimited powers (3) implied powers (4) reserved powers.

5. On which issue were Alexander Hamilton and Thomas Jefferson in closest agreement? (1) establishing a National Bank (2) locating the national capital in the South (3) supporting Britain in her war with France (4) favoring manufacturing over farming interests.

6. Which was a result of Alexander Hamilton's financial policies? (1) issuing of cheap currency (2) extension of participation in government to the people (3) strengthening the credit of the national government (4) default on the nation's foreign debts.

7. The suppression of the Whisky Rebellion (1) constituted the first conflict between the North and the South (2) limited the power of the states to nullify federal laws (3) violated the principle of "no taxation without representation" (4) illustrated the power of the federal government.

8. Political parties appeared in the United States shortly after the adoption of the Constitution because (1) Washington disliked Jefferson (2) the Constitution provides for the two-party system (3) Great Britain had a two-party system (4) differences arose over political and economic issues.

9. Which revolution in Europe was influenced most directly by our American Revolution? (1) Industrial Revolution (2) French Revolution (3) Glorious Revolution (4) Puritan Revolution.

10. President Washington's reason for issuing the Proclamation of Neutrality was his desire to (1) fulfill our obligations to France (2) protect our interests in the Caribbean area (3) safeguard our newly won independence (4) unify the country on foreign policy.

11. In his Farewell Address, Washington warned the United States against (1) expansion westward beyond the Mississippi (2) the imperialistic ideas of Napoleon (3) permanent alliances with foreign nations (4) quarrels with England over commerce.

12. A person who favored George Washington's ideas on foreign policy would be most likely to object to United States (1) recognition of the Soviet Union (2) trade with Common Market nations (3) membership in the North Atlantic Treaty Organization (4) participation in international scientific conferences.

13. Which was a provision of the treaty ending the American Revolution that was *not* carried out by Great Britain until after the Jay Treaty? (1) evacuation of British troops from United States soil (2) determination of the western boundary of the United States (3) freedom of the seas for American merchant ships (4) sharing of the Newfoundland fisheries with the United States.

14. The Pinckney Treaty directly benefited (1) New England merchants (2) farmers in the Ohio Valley (3) Southern plantation owners (4) shipping interests on the Atlantic coast.

15. The XYZ Affair showed that (1) Americans would not tolerate French seizure of Louisiana (2) Americans were developing a sense of national pride (3) our government was pursuing a policy of aggression (4) our government was still bound to its alliance with France.

16. Which represents an effort by the Federalist party to suppress criticism by the Democratic-Republicans? (1) passage of the Alien and Sedition Acts (2) the XYZ Affair (3) the Citizen Genêt episode (4) the Hamilton-Burr duel.

17. Which statement about the Virginia and Kentucky Resolutions is true? (1) They supported the Alien and Sedition Acts. (2) They aimed to prevent sectionalism. (3) They reflected the views of most Federalists. (4) They contributed to the defeat of the Federalists in 1800.

18. Which was a major contribution by the Federalist party to the United States? (1) strengthening of the central government (2) aid to France (3) the states' rights theory (4) a decentralized banking system.

ESSAY QUESTIONS

1. President Hoover said, "The true eulogy of Washington is this mighty nation." (*a*) Describe *two* services of George Washington to the government of the United States. (*b*) State *one* outstanding trait that fitted him to be a leader of democracy.

2. "As Hamilton's measures were debated in Congress, the country gradually divided into two parties, each with its own program." (a) Mention the *two* parties referred to in the quotation and give the names of *two* prominent leaders of each party. (b) State *three* essential differences in the principles advocated by these two parties.
3. It has been said that the principles of Hamilton and Jefferson are still very much alive. (a) Discuss briefly a difference of opinion between Hamilton and Jefferson concerning *two* of the following issues of their day: federal taxation, protective tariff, national control of banking, national debt. (b) Select *two* issues listed in part (a) and show why *each* has been an important problem in the United States during the 20th century.
4. Although the Federalist party compiled a record of considerable achievement while in power, it lost the election of 1800 and thereafter disappeared as a political party. (a) Discuss *three* achievements of the Federalist party. (b) Discuss *two* factors that led to the downfall of the Federalist party.

Part 2. The Democratic-Republicans Take Control and Concentrate on Foreign Problems

ELECTION OF 1800

The Republican candidates, Thomas Jefferson for President and Aaron Burr for Vice President, won the hard-fought election of 1800. However, victory in the election did not assure Jefferson the Presidency. According to the original Constitution, each elector was to cast two ballots. The candidate with the largest number of votes became President; the candidate with the next largest number of votes became Vice President. As each Democratic-Republican elector gave one vote to each of his party's candidates, Jefferson and Burr were tied for the Presidency, and the election was thrown into the House of Representatives. This was not the House elected in 1800 but the Federalist "lame duck" House chosen in 1798. Disliking Jefferson, many Federalists decided to back Burr, and the vote in the House was deadlocked for 35 ballots. On the 36th ballot, a number of Federalists abstained from voting and ensured Jefferson's election. These Federalists were influenced by Hamilton, who considered Burr a scoundrel. Although Hamilton disagreed with Jefferson on political issues, Hamilton believed Jefferson to be an honorable man. One result of this election was the enactment of the Twelfth Amendment, requiring separate ballots for President and Vice President.

JEFFERSON THE MAN

Thomas Jefferson, third President of the United States, was a man of deep and abiding faith in the common people. Considering democracy the ideal form of government, he held that democracy could function best in an agricultural society of small, independent farmers. Jefferson disliked pomp and ceremony in government, preferring simplicity. He believed in strictly limiting the role of government. He favored popular education and careful protection of civil liberties. Although he had urged a strict interpretation of the Constitution in opposing the National Bank, Jefferson was not doctrinaire and supported a loose interpretation when he believed that the national welfare required the purchase of Louisiana. Of his many achievements, Jefferson wished future generations of Americans to remember him for these three: (1) the Declaration of Independence, (2) the Virginia Statute of Religious Freedom, and (3) the founding of the University of Virginia.

Jefferson proclaimed his election as the *Revolution of 1800*. He viewed it as the triumph of the common citizen over the propertied and aristocratic classes.

JEFFERSON AS PRESIDENT (1801-1809)

1. **Reverses Some Federalist Policies.** Jefferson (*a*) secured Congressional repeal of the excise tax on whisky, (*b*) curtailed army and navy expenditures and, with the able assistance of Secretary of the Treasury Albert Gallatin, reduced the national debt, (*c*) secured repeal of the Naturalization Act, thereby restoring the previous five-year waiting period for citizenship; permitted the Alien Act and the Sedition Act to expire; and pardoned persons still imprisoned under the Sedition Act, (*d*) replaced some Federalist officeholders with Democratic-Republicans, and (*e*) secured repeal of the Judiciary Act of 1801, which had created new Circuit Courts. Thus the Democratic-Republicans removed those Federalist judges whom Adams had appointed near the end of his term, supposedly up to midnight of his last day in office—the so-called "midnight judges."

2. **Continues Other Federalist Policies.** (*a*) Except for repealing the whisky tax, Jefferson continued Hamilton's financial program. He continued the full repayment of the domestic debt, including the assumed debt of the states, and he permitted the National Bank to operate undisturbed. (*b*) In his Inaugural Address, Thomas Jefferson reaffirmed Washington's foreign policy of isolation. Jefferson urged the United States to seek "peace, commerce, and honest friendship with all nations, entangling alliances with none." (*c*) When the needs of Western settlers led him to purchase Louisiana, Jefferson moved toward the Federalist view of loose construction of the Constitution.

PURCHASE OF LOUISIANA (1803)

1. **Importance of the Mississippi River and New Orleans.** At the beginning of the 19th century, the settlers west of the Appalachians found it difficult to send their bulky agricultural produce overland to Eastern markets

and seaports. Instead, they depended for transportation upon the Mississippi River and the port of New Orleans. By the Pinckney Treaty with Spain (1795), the Americans had received the right of deposit at New Orleans (see page 113).

2. Napoleon and the Louisiana Territory. In 1800 Napoleon Bonaparte of France secretly secured the vast Louisiana Territory from Spain. In 1802 the right of deposit was suspended. This action, threatening the prosperity of the West, enraged the Western settlers. President Jefferson quickly instructed Robert Livingston and James Monroe to negotiate with France for the purchase of New Orleans. Meanwhile, Napoleon decided to sell the entire territory. His reasons were that he (*a*) needed money to carry on his war against Britain, (*b*) could not defend the territory while the British navy controlled the seas, and (*c*) had abandoned plans for an American empire. Monroe and Livingston readily agreed to a purchase price of $15 million.

3. Constitutional Problem. Jefferson was disturbed by the agreement, for the Constitution did not specifically give the federal government the power to purchase territory. A "strict" interpreter of the Constitution, Jefferson suggested a Constitutional amendment to provide the necessary power. However, he was warned that delay might lead Napoleon to withdraw his

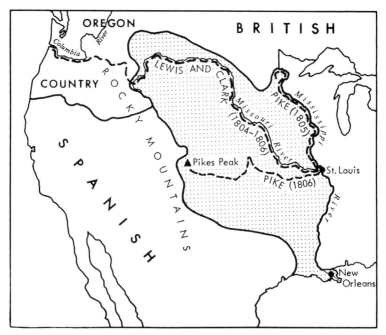

Louisiana Territory and Explorations

offer. Consequently, Jefferson agreed to purchase Louisiana under the Presidential power to make treaties, thus adopting a loose interpretation of the Constitution.

4. Exploration of the Territory. The entire nation was eager to learn of the resources and possibilities of the new territory. Jefferson arranged several journeys of exploration. In 1804 *Meriwether Lewis* and *William Clark* started out from St. Louis, went up the Missouri River and across the Rocky Mountains, and reached the Columbia River and the Pacific Ocean. In 1805 *Zebulon Pike* led an expedition up the Mississippi to look for its source. In 1806 Pike led another expedition to the Rockies in what is today Colorado. Lewis and Clark, as well as Pike, issued optimistic reports and thereby encouraged settlers.

5. Significance. The purchase of Louisiana (*a*) almost doubled the area of the United States, (*b*) was a source of tremendous wealth to the nation, (*c*) gave the United States control of the Mississippi, (*d*) removed French influence in North America, (*e*) established a precedent for future purchases of territory, and (*f*) moved the Democratic-Republicans toward a loose interpretation of the Constitution.

NAPOLEONIC WARS: FRANCE AGAINST GREAT BRITAIN

In 1803 France and Britain renewed their conflict, and for the next 12 years they fought a life-and-death struggle for control of Europe. While, at first, France held supremacy on land, England dominated the seas. Their struggle is often referred to as the battle of "the tiger against the shark."

1. Economic Warfare. While military action was temporarily stalemated, the two countries endeavored to strike at each other economically. Napoleon issued the *Berlin* and *Milan Decrees* (1806–1807) restricting neutral trade with England. The British government issued *Orders in Council* (1806–1807) restricting neutral trade with the French-held Continent. Since Britain had a much stronger navy than France, her blockade of the European Continent was far more successful than France's blockade of the British Isles.

2. Effect Upon the United States. The neutral United States was adversely affected by these blockades. The American merchant marine had grown greatly, and American shippers carried on a prosperous but risky trade with wartime Europe. Profits of ships that got through the blockades more than made up for losses of ships caught. The greater damage to American commerce was inflicted by the British, who, in addition to seizing many American ships, impressed some American sailors into British service, claiming that they were deserters.

3. *Chesapeake-Leopard* **Affair** (1807). Off the Virginia coast the captain of the *Leopard*, a British warship, demanded to search the American navy vessel *Chesapeake*. When the captain of the *Chesapeake* refused, the British fired on the *Chesapeake*, boarded her, and took off four seamen as deserters. Three were American citizens. This indignity inflamed the American public to demand that Jefferson take retaliatory action.

EMBARGO ACT (1807–1809)

To avoid war, Jefferson requested Congress to pass the Embargo Act (1807), which forbade American ships to sail to foreign ports and prohibited American exports to all foreign countries. Jefferson believed that, by depriving England and France of our cotton and foodstuffs, the United States could compel these nations to change their policies toward American shipping. However, the "peaceable coercion" of the Embargo did not sufficiently affect the warring nations.

Meanwhile, the Embargo caused considerable economic damage in the maritime New England states by almost completely destroying their commerce and bringing about widespread unemployment. Jefferson and the Embargo were roundly condemned by New England Federalists. The agricultural sections—South and West—were also somewhat distressed as they lost foreign markets for their farm produce. In 1809, near the end of his second term, Jefferson signed the *Non-Intercourse Act*, repealing the Embargo Act but continuing the prohibition on trade with England and France.

MADISON AND THE DRIFT TO WAR (1809–1812)

1. Efforts for Peace. James Madison, who succeeded Jefferson as President, tried for a while to use diplomatic negotiations to protect American shipping, but he was unsuccessful. Meanwhile, the war spirit in America continued to grow.

2. "War Hawks." In 1810 Southern and Western voters elected to Congress a group of Democratic-Republicans called the "War Hawks." Led by John C. Calhoun of South Carolina and Henry Clay of Kentucky, they demanded war against Britain to acquire Canada and against Britain's ally, Spain, to acquire Florida.

In 1812 Madison surrendered to the war spirit and asked Congress for a declaration of war against Britain.

CAUSES OF THE WAR OF 1812

1. Britain's seizure of American ships and impressment of American sailors. (Madison's war message emphasized these actions as violations of our "freedom of the seas.")

2. American resentment of Britain, dating back to Revolutionary days.

3. The Americans' belief that the British in Canada were arming the Indians and inciting them to raid American settlements.

4. American ambitions to annex Canada and Florida.

Historians have long debated the primary cause of the war: maritime rights or territorial ambitions? The Congressional vote favoring war—by little more than a majority—showed that the Northeast, which was most directly concerned with maritime rights, was mainly opposed to the war. The South and West, which were most strongly for territorial expansion, were wholeheartedly in favor of the war.

MILITARY EVENTS OF THE WAR (1812–1815)

1. The Americans attempted several times to invade and conquer Canada. These attempts all proved unsuccessful.

2. British counterplans to invade the United States from Canada were thwarted when British naval squadrons were defeated by Captain Oliver Perry on Lake Erie and by Captain Thomas Macdonough on Lake Champlain. Perry reported his victory with the message, "We have met the enemy and they are ours."

3. On the high seas American naval vessels and privateers at first won great victories. The achievements of American warships—most notably the *Constitution* (nicknamed "Old Ironsides") and the *United States*—were hailed throughout the country. In time, however, the British navy asserted its superiority and drove the Americans from the seas.

4. The British invaded the Chesapeake Bay area, captured Washington, D.C., burned many government buildings, and then advanced on Fort McHenry at Baltimore. Fort McHenry withstood the British bombardment, inspiring Francis Scott Key to write *The Star-Spangled Banner*.

5. The British attempted an invasion of the American Southwest but were decisively defeated at New Orleans. *Andrew Jackson*, the American commander, overnight became a national hero. (With modern methods of communication, this battle would not have been fought, since a peace treaty had already been signed in Europe.)

TREATY OF GHENT (1814)

At Ghent, Belgium, negotiators arranged a treaty of peace that reestablished the prewar boundaries of the United States. The treaty did not mention the seizure of American ships and the impressment of American sailors. However, since the European war was over, these issues were no longer crucial.

RESULTS OF THE WAR OF 1812

1. **Growth of American Nationalism.** Americans rejoiced in their naval victories on the lakes and on the high seas, and in the triumph at New Orleans. They acclaimed the defense of Fort McHenry and the patriotic words of *The Star-Spangled Banner*. Americans felt greater pride in their country, and, because of this growing spirit of nationalism, the War of 1812 is often called the "Second War for American Independence."

2. **Strengthening of Isolation.** Americans had been directed toward isolation by the foreign policies of both Washington and Jefferson. After the War of 1812, Americans turned still more sharply away from Europe's affairs. They concentrated upon domestic problems, especially the settlement of the West.

3. **Increase in Westward Migration.** Many New Englanders went west, having lost their jobs as the shipping industry declined. Furthermore, several battles in the West destroyed hostile Indian forces, thus making the area safe for settlement.

4. **Encouragement of American Industry.** With the war cutting off imports from England, Americans met the need for goods by greatly increasing domestic manufactures. Also, since the war made shipbuilding and foreign commerce unprofitable, businessmen invested their capital in industrial establishments, chiefly New England textile mills.

5. **Disappearance of the Federalist Party.** The Federalists, who retained political power in the New England states, disapproved the war. They bitterly called it "Mr. Madison's War." The New England states refused to help finance the war and refused to honor the requests of the federal government for troops.

In 1814 the leading Federalists held the *Hartford Convention*. They advocated the doctrines of states' rights and nullification, demanded that the Constitution be changed to require a two-thirds vote of Congress to admit new states or declare war, and hinted at secession. (The Federalist arguments were similar to the Democratic-Republican statements in the Virginia and Kentucky Resolutions. See page 115.)

Almost immediately after the Hartford Convention, the nation learned of Jackson's triumph at New Orleans and of the signing of the Treaty of Ghent. The Federalists were accused of treason for having opposed the war, and soon afterwards the Federalist party went out of existence.

MULTIPLE-CHOICE QUESTIONS

1. A direct result of the election of 1800 was the (1) settlement of differences with France and Britain (2) chartering of the first Bank of the United States (3) provision for separate ballots in the electoral college for President and Vice President (4) split in the Democratic-Republican party.

2. The election of 1800 has sometimes been referred to as a revolution because (1) the Western farmers were in armed rebellion (2) Aaron Burr was tried for treason (3) the Twelfth Amendment was added to the Constitution (4) the incoming administration was more sympathetic to agricultural than to commercial interests.

3. Which characteristic of our country today may be considered a fulfillment of one of Jefferson's principles? (1) an industrialized society (2) popular elections (3) a large public debt (4) a strong central government.

4. On which issue did Thomas Jefferson reverse his opinion of strict construction of the Constitution? (1) the Bank of the United States (2) the purchase of the Louisiana Territory (3) the moving of the capital to Washington, D.C. (4) the appointment of the "midnight judges."

5. The primary reason for our purchase of the Louisiana Territory was to provide (1) people on the frontier with unrestricted use of the Mississippi River (2) Napoleon with money in return for French assistance during the American Revolution (3) New England manufacturers with a source of cheap raw materials (4) land for Indian reservations.

6. Which was a direct result of the purchase of the Louisiana Territory? (1) an amendment to the Constitution permitting the federal government to purchase land (2) the opening of a vast region for fur trading and land development (3) the loss of Canada by France (4) the elimination of Spain from the North American continent.

7. Which economic group most strongly protested the Embargo Act of 1807? (1) New England shippers (2) Southern cotton growers (3) frontier farmers (4) Northern factory workers.

8. The Embargo and Non-Intercourse Acts illustrate the (1) unsuccessful attempt of the United States to isolate itself from a European conflict (2) success of the United States in obtaining recognition of its neutral rights (3) confiscation of British investments in America (4) overwhelming support given by Congress to President Jefferson's policy.

9. Why did the United States declare war on Great Britain rather than on France in 1812? (1) France had aided the United States during the American Revolution. (2) France's democratic revolutionary principles were similar to those of the United States. (3) New England merchants wanted revenge for shipping losses. (4) The "War Hawks" favored the conquest of Canada.

10. The United States government had difficulty financing the War of 1812 because (1) Western farmers refused to pay excise taxes (2) the revenue tariff had been repealed (3) New Englanders were reluctant to lend money to the federal government (4) the internal improvements program had drained the federal treasury.

11. The defense of Baltimore (1814) inspired Francis Scott Key to write (1) *America the Beautiful* (2) *The Star-Spangled Banner* (3) *The Battle Hymn of the Republic* (4) *America*.

12. The Treaty of Ghent failed to prevent the Battle of New Orleans because (1) the United States was determined to destroy the British navy (2) the "War Hawks" continued to be important (3) Madison was eager to win a military reputation (4) communication at that time was slow.

13. One reason why the United States was able to maintain its independence in *both* the Revolutionary War and the War of 1812 was that (1) American troops were better trained than British troops (2) American troops had the support of Indians in the Northwest Territory (3) Great Britain was fighting other enemies (4) the British navy avoided battles with American ships.

14. An important result of the War of 1812 was that it (1) strengthened the Federalist party (2) introduced ironclad naval vessels (3) marked the end of the American policy of isolation (4) encouraged manufacturing in the United States.

15. Two Americans, known as "War Hawks," who were eager for war in 1812 were (1) Jackson and Madison (2) Webster and Clinton (3) Calhoun and Clay (4) Burr and John Quincy Adams.

16. Which of the following events occurred last? (1) adoption of the federal Bill of Rights (2) Hartford Convention (3) election of James Madison as President (4) Whisky Rebellion.

ESSAY QUESTIONS

1. (a) State *two* fundamental principles of the Democratic-Republican party under the leadership of Thomas Jefferson. (b) Show by using a specific illustration how Jefferson modified *one* fundamental principle of his party. (c) Describe *two* ways in which Jefferson's interests went far beyond political affairs.

2. (a) Explain what is meant by our policy of isolation. (b) Explain *two* reasons why the United States adopted this policy in its early history (1789–1830). (c) Give *one* argument for *or one* argument against the maintenance of a policy of isolation at the present time.

3. Some historians claim that the War of 1812 was "rash and unnecessary" for the United States. (a) Evaluate *two* causes of the war to show whether or not each supports the claim of "rash and unnecessary." (b) Discuss *two* results of the war to show whether or not each benefited the United States.

4. During the early history of our national government, its authority was frequently challenged. (a) Show how the authority of the national government was challenged by organized opposition within the United States on *two* occasions between 1790 and 1815. (b) Give a result of each controversy.

UNIT IV. THE NATION IS TORN BETWEEN NATIONALISM AND SECTIONALISM

Part 1. The War of 1812 Is Followed by a Temporary Upsurge of Nationalism

NATIONALISM IN AMERICA

Although some nationalistic and patriotic feeling was evident early in our history, this feeling gained strong momentum in the years following the War of 1812. As nationalism briefly became dominant over sectionalism, most Americans (1) were proud to be known as Americans, rather than as residents of a state or section, (2) gave primary loyalty to the nation, rather than to a state or section, (3) favored extending the powers of the central government, and (4) considered problems from a national, rather than from a sectional, point of view.

ECONOMIC LEGISLATION AND NATIONALISM

By 1815 the Democratic-Republicans in control of the government were considering problems not as representatives of the agricultural South and West, but from the viewpoint of national interest. Discarding their previous positions, the Democratic-Republicans adopted Federalist ideas in enacting the following legislation:

1. Second National Bank. Following 1811, when the charter of the first National Bank expired, the United States experienced financial disorder. State banks, having grown in number, often lacked adequate specie reserves for their paper money and therefore failed to provide a sound currency. Furthermore, the federal government had no safe depository for its funds.

In 1816 Congress passed and Madison signed a law chartering the second Bank of the United States. Although Democratic-Republicans previously had opposed such a bank as unconstitutional, they now supported it in the national interest.

2. Protective Tariff of 1816. Previously, the United States had maintained a revenue tariff, that is, a tariff designed chiefly to provide government income, rather than to protect American industries from competition by low-priced foreign imports. In spite of the lack of protection, American "infant industries," such as New England textile mills and Pennsylvania iron smelters, had prospered before and during the War of 1812, when competition from abroad declined sharply. After the War of 1812, American manufacturers faced renewed competition, as the English planned the deliberate "dumping" of low-priced goods to stifle the new industries. To counter this threat, Congress passed the Tariff of 1816 with its protective rates. It was supported by Congressmen of all sections. Although consumers would have to pay more for American-made goods, the Democratic-Republicans agreed, as Jefferson now stated, that manufactures "are necessary to our independence."

3. Internal Improvements at Federal Expense. In 1806 Congress had approved the construction of the *National* or *Cumberland Road*, running from Cumberland, Maryland, westward across the Appalachian Mountains to Wheeling on the Ohio River. Congress, however, appropriated limited funds, and construction lagged. By 1815 only 20 miles had been completed.

The war years demonstrated that our internal transportation system was inadequate for national needs. In 1816 Congress voted substantial new funds, and, within two years, the Cumberland Road was extended an additional 110 miles to reach Wheeling. Supporters of the Cumberland Road argued that, since the road would help bind the nation together, its cost should be borne by the federal government.

POLITICAL AFFAIRS AND NATIONALISM: THE ERA OF GOOD FEELING

The years 1817–1823, marked by an absence of open political strife, are called the *Era of Good Feeling*. The Federalists disappeared as a national political party following their overwhelming defeat in the election of 1816. James Monroe, the victorious Democratic-Republican candidate, was hailed throughout the country, even in New England. In 1820 Monroe was re-elected, receiving all the electoral votes but one. Having adopted many Federalist ideas, the Democratic-Republicans, the only major political party, reflected national unity. Below the surface, however, bitter sectional strife was brewing, and, following the Presidential election of 1824, the Democratic-Republican party split apart.

FOREIGN AFFAIRS AND NATIONALISM

With the American people strongly nationalistic and enthusiastically supporting the government, the nation's leaders were able to conduct a vigorous foreign policy. In turn, their capable handling of foreign affairs furthered American nationalism.

1. Rush-Bagot Agreement (1817). In this treaty the United States and Great Britain agreed to naval disarmament on the Great Lakes. Later, this agreement was extended to provide for disarmament along the land border between the United States and Canada. Today, the entire 3000-mile United States-Canadian border remains unfortified. A significance of the Rush-

Bagot Agreement was Britain's treatment of the United States as an equal. It was also significant as a sign of mutual trust and understanding, and as an early example of disarmament.

2. Convention of 1818. This treaty fixed the boundary line between the United States and Canada at the 49th parallel of latitude from Lake of the Woods (in northern Minnesota) to the Rocky Mountains. This line became known as the *Treaty Line of 1818.* The treaty also provided that the United States and Britain jointly occupy the Oregon Country.

3. Purchase of Florida (1819)

a. Spanish-Owned Florida: A Trouble Spot. In the hands of Spain, Florida housed pirates, smugglers, runaway slaves, and hostile Seminole Indians. With the Spanish authorities too weak to restrain them, the Indians raided American settlements in the South and then retreated to safety across the Florida border.

In 1818 Andrew Jackson led an American military force into Florida, crushed the Seminole Indians, and captured two Spanish forts. Spain had already lost West Florida to the United States, and she now realized that unless she sold the rest of Florida she might lose it by force.

b. Adams-Onis Treaty. Secretary of State John Quincy Adams and Spanish minister Luis de Onis agreed that Spain sell Florida to the United States for $5 million. Also called the *Transcontinental Treaty,* the Adams-Onis agreement provided that the United States give up claims to Texas and that Spain accept the 42nd parallel as the boundary between Mexico and the Oregon Country.

Although the South would gain the most, the purchase of Florida was supported by the entire country.

4. Monroe Doctrine (1823)

a. Latin American Independence. While Spain was entangled in the Napoleonic Wars, the Spanish colonists in Latin America revolted and began a series of wars for independence. (Brazil, meanwhile, threw off the rule of Portugal.) Spanish attempts to retain control were defeated by the colonists under the leadership of *José de San Martin, Bernardo O'Higgins,* and the "George Washington of South America," *Simon Bolivar.*

The United States hailed Latin American independence because (1) the American Revolution against England had helped inspire the Latin American colonists, (2) the United States preferred having weak independent republics to the south instead of the more powerful monarchical Spain, and (3) American merchants and shippers were building up a profitable trade with the independent Latin American countries. Such trade had previously been barred by Spain, whose mercantilist regulations prohibited her colonies from trading with any country but the mother country.

b. Immediate Causes for Issuing the Doctrine. In 1823 President Monroe was faced with two threats of foreign intervention in the Western Hemisphere. (1) A reactionary European alliance of Austria, Prussia, France, and Russia—all opposed to revolution anywhere—was rumored planning to reconquer Latin America for Spain. (2) Russian expansion southward from Alaska into Oregon and California constituted a threat to ultimate American expansion to the Pacific.

c. Rejection of the British Proposal for a Joint Declaration. Britain too opposed the restoration of Spanish control in Latin America, since British merchants had also built up a profitable trade with the new nations. *George Canning,* the British foreign minister, proposed that Britain and the United States issue a joint declaration warning Europe against any attempt to deny independence to Latin America.

John Quincy Adams, the American Secretary of State, vigorously opposed a joint declaration. He insisted that we act alone, as befits a proud, independent, nationalistic people. Adams did not want the United States to appear as a tiny boat coming "in the wake of the British man-of-war." Adams' point of view and much of his phrasing were accepted by Monroe who, in his annual message to Congress, announced the Monroe Doctrine.

d. Basic Ideas of the Doctrine. (1) The Western Hemisphere was closed to further European colonization. (2) The United States would not interfere with the existing colonies of any European power. (3) The United States would not interfere in the internal affairs of any European power. (4) Any attempt by European powers to intervene in the Western Hemisphere would be regarded as "dangerous to our peace and safety." (This final statement did not commit the United States to a definite course of action in case of European intervention. Instead, it left the American· response up to the discretion of the President.)

e. Significance. The American people approved the Monroe Doctrine for (1) expressing the prevailing spirit of American nationalism, (2) evidencing America's importance in world affairs, and (3) attempting to isolate the entire Western Hemisphere from European affairs. Latin Americans welcomed the Monroe Doctrine as a friendly offer of assistance.

The Russians in 1824 agreed to halt their expansion by accepting the 54° 40′ parallel as the southern boundary of Alaska. The European alliance did not pursue its rumored plans for reconquest of Latin America. Its primary consideration was probably the power of Britain and the British navy. At that time, the United States hardly had the power to enforce the Monroe Doctrine. By 1865, however, when the Doctrine was challenged for the first time, the United States had grown powerful enough to uphold it (see the Maximilian Affair, page 172). To this very day the Monroe Doctrine survives as a cornerstone of American foreign policy.

SUPREME COURT AND NATIONALISM

1. Role of John Marshall. Appointed by President John Adams in 1801, John Marshall, a leading Federalist, served for 34 years (1801–1835) as Chief Justice of the Supreme Court. Marshall dominated the Court, converting to his views many Justices appointed by Democratic-Republican Presidents. Possessing a logical mind and great legal ability, Marshall transformed his nationalistic ideas into court decisions. He (a) elevated the prestige of the Supreme Court, strengthening its powers at the expense of other federal branches, and (b) handed down decisions expanding federal powers at the expense of the states.

Marshall was berated by Jefferson for making the Constitution " a mere thing of wax in the hands of the judiciary." Marshall's decisions, however, have shaped our Constitutional thinking to this very day.

2. Major Cases

a. Marbury vs. Madison (1803)

(1) *Issue.* William Marbury, a Federalist, was appointed as judge by outgoing President Adams in 1801, but was denied his official papers, or commission, by James Madison, the incoming Democratic-Republican Secretary of State. In accordance with the Judiciary Act of 1789, Marbury went directly to the Supreme Court for an order, called a *writ of mandamus*, to compel Madison to deliver the commission.

(2) *Decision.* Speaking for a unanimous Court, Marshall declared that, although Madison was wrong in withholding the commission, the Court could not grant Marbury the requested writ. Marshall explained that the section of the Judiciary Act expanding the Supreme Court's original jurisdiction to include the issuing of writs of mandamus violated the Constitution. Marshall declared that (a) the Constitution is the supreme law of the land, (b) the Supreme Court is the final interpreter of the Constitution, and therefore (c) the Supreme Court may declare unconstitutional and inoperative any law contrary to the Constitution. Marshall thus established the precedent of *judicial review*.

During Marshall's years, the Supreme Court did not invalidate another federal law but did declare several state laws unconstitutional. From Marshall's years to today, the Supreme Court has held some 75 federal laws unconstitutional.

b. Dartmouth College vs. Woodward (1819)

(1) *Issue.* Without the consent of the trustees of Dartmouth College, a New Hampshire law revised the college's original charter of incorporation and placed the college under state control. The trustees objected.

(2) *Decision.* Marshall held: (a) Dartmouth's charter was a contract protected by the Constitutional provision that states may not pass any "law impairing the obligation of contracts." This part of the decision assured not only colleges, but also business interests, that charters, once granted, were fixed and not changeable according to the fancy of state legislatures. (b) The state law revising the Dartmouth charter was therefore unconstitutional. Marshall thus employed the Supreme Court's power of judicial review against a state law.

√c. McCulloch vs. Maryland (1819)

(1) *Issue.* Maryland's legislators, hostile toward the second Bank of the United States, placed a heavy tax upon the Bank's Baltimore branch. McCulloch, a Bank official, refused to pay the tax.

(2) *Decision.* Marshall (a) denied the power of a state to tax a federal agency, declaring that "the power to tax involves the power to destroy," and (b) upheld the constitutionality of the United States Bank, thus supporting the doctrine of loose interpretation and implied powers.

√d. Gibbons vs. Ogden (1824)

(1) *Issue.* Ogden, operating under a New York State monopoly grant, ran a ferry on the Hudson River between New York and New Jersey. Gibbons ran a competing line under a federal license. Ogden sued to halt Gibbons.

(2) *Decision.* The Supreme Court declared invalid New York's grant of a Hudson River monopoly to Ogden. Marshall held that this grant violated the Constitution's delegation of interstate commerce to federal control. Further, he defined commerce in the broadest possible terms. Marshall thus prepared the way for federal regulation of transportation, communication, business organizations, and labor unions—when engaged in interstate commerce.

THE WEST AND NATIONALISM

1. Routes to the West

a. Early Turnpikes and Public Roads. (1) By 1794 settlers were taking the *Lancaster Turnpike,* a toll road from Philadelphia to Lancaster, and then the *Pennsylvania State Road* across the Appalachian Mountains. At Pittsburgh they transferred their goods to a flatboat and floated down the Ohio River. (2) Settlers also crossed the Appalachians by following the *National* or *Cumberland Road.* In 1818 this road, which started at Cumberland, Maryland, reached Wheeling on the Ohio River. By 1852 the road was extended to Vandalia in Illinois. (3) Farther to the south, settlers traversed Appalachian Mountain passes by following state roads such as the *Wilder-*

ness Road. This road went through the *Cumberland Gap,* an often-traveled mountain pass running from North Carolina into Tennessee and Kentucky.

b. Steamboats. In 1807 Robert Fulton built the first successful steamboat, thereby making river transportation quicker and cheaper. By the 1820's steamboats, carrying settlers and cargoes, were plying the Mississippi and Ohio Rivers.

c. Canals. The Erie Canal, completed in 1825 by New York State under Governor De Witt Clinton, was an immediate success. Settlers going west from New York City could travel up the Hudson River to Albany, and then westward on the Erie Canal to Buffalo on Lake Erie. With this all-water route between the Great Lakes and the Atlantic Ocean, Western farmers could ship their produce eastward at greatly reduced cost. New York City, at the mouth of the Hudson, became the leading commercial center on the Atlantic coast.

The success of the Erie Canal spurred an era of canal building, most notably by (1) Philadelphia, which wanted to partake of the Western trade, and

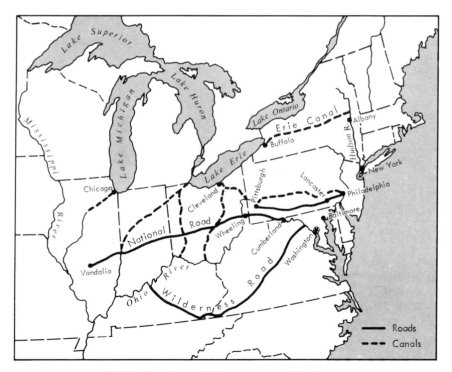

Major Roads and Waterways to the West

(2) Ohio and Indiana, which built canals to connect Lake Erie with the Ohio River and its tributaries.

2. The Growing Frontier Population Is Nationalist. Many people—from the Eastern seaboard and from Europe—migrated to the Western frontier after the War of 1812. Between 1810 and 1820 the number of settlers west of the Appalachian Mountains more than doubled. Between 1816 and 1821 five Western territories achieved sufficient population to be admitted to the Union as states.

The Western settlers, being migrants, possessed little attachment to a state or section but were strongly nationalist. Loyal to the nation, they looked to the federal government for (a) cheap land, (b) internal improvements, especially roads and canals, and (c) protection against the Indians. (For a further discussion of the frontier, see pages 191–198.)

3. Clay's American System. Henry Clay, Congressman from the then Western state of Kentucky, urged making the nation economically self-sufficient by a plan that he called the *American System*. Clay proposed that (a) the West and South support a protective tariff and a national bank to aid industry in the North, and (b) the North support a federal program of roads and canals to unite the country. Clay argued that all sections would benefit as the West and South would exchange their agricultural produce for the manufactured goods of the North. Clay's American System never came into being, since by the middle 1820's the country's nationalist outlook was retreating before the rise of sectional loyalties.

MULTIPLE-CHOICE QUESTIONS

1. The War of 1812 resulted in the (1) growth of American nationalism (2) postponement of the Industrial Revolution in the United States (3) increase in the prestige of the Federalist party (4) decline of British naval power.
2. The nationalism of the Era of Good Feeling is most clearly evident in the (1) widespread support for the Tariff of 1816 (2) appointment of John Marshall to the Supreme Court (3) widespread support for the Hartford Convention (4) refusal of President Monroe to purchase Florida.
3. Spain sold Florida to the United States because Spain was (1) so ordered by Napoleon (2) in great need of funds (3) unable to control the Seminole Indians (4) afraid of losing the territory by force.
4. Which man was *not* a revolutionary leader of the Spanish colonies in Latin America? (1) Luis de Onis (2) Simon Bolivar (3) Bernardo O'Higgins (4) José de San Martin.
5. The main reason for the announcement of the Monroe Doctrine in 1823 was (1) the fear that European countries would try to restore the former Spanish colonies to Spain (2) the desire to annex Texas (3) hostility to Britain (4) the belief that Washington's policy of not interfering in European affairs was no longer sound.
6. The original Monroe Doctrine was part of (1) an act of Congress (2) a treaty with England (3) a message to Congress (4) an agreement with Latin America.

7. One purpose of the Monroe Doctrine in 1823 was to curb (1) Asian expansion in South America (2) Russian expansion in North America (3) British control over Canada (4) the ambitions of Napoleon in Latin America.

8. The Monroe Doctrine declared that (1) the Western Hemisphere was no longer open to further European colonization (2) no European country could own territory in Latin America (3) there could be no trade agreements between Latin America and England (4) Spain should give up her possessions in the Western Hemisphere.

9. The reactionary alliance of European nations did not seriously threaten the Monroe Doctrine because (1) the United States was a great world power (2) Spain was willing to give up her colonies (3) Great Britain supported independence for Latin America (4) Russia had no interest in American affairs.

10. The Monroe Doctrine was (1) a continuation of Washington's foreign policy (2) a reversal of Washington's policy (3) a concession to the Federalists (4) an attempt to open new territory to slavery.

11. The right of judicial review of acts of Congress was first established in the case of (1) *Marbury vs. Madison* (2) *Gibbons vs. Ogden* (3) *Dartmouth College vs. Woodward* (4) *McCulloch vs. Maryland.*

12. In *Gibbons vs. Ogden,* the Supreme Court expanded the meaning of (1) civil rights (2) eminent domain (3) corporate monopoly (4) interstate commerce.

13. In *Dartmouth College vs. Woodward,* the Supreme Court (1) approved loans for educational purposes by the second National Bank (2) limited the taxing power of the states (3) assured corporations that their state charters could not be changed arbitrarily (4) awarded Dartmouth College a federal land grant.

14. The decisions of Chief Justice John Marshall (1) increased the power of the federal government (2) established a strict interpretation of the Constitution (3) strengthened the President's power at the expense of Congress (4) decreased the importance of the Supreme Court.

15. Clay's "American System" was a plan to (1) develop national self-sufficiency through tariff laws and internal improvements (2) drive subversives from the government (3) free the remaining North American colonies held by European powers (4) develop a loyalty program in public schools.

16. One reason why Great Britain supported the Monroe Doctrine in 1823 was that she (1) had declared war on Spain (2) wished to support the reactionary European alliance (3) had a profitable trade with the Latin American countries (4) followed a policy of supporting democratic revolutions.

ESSAY QUESTIONS

1. (a) Discuss *two* reasons why nationalism developed in the United States after the War of 1812. (b) Describe *two* developments during this period that illustrate the growth of nationalism.

2. (a) Name *three* leaders during the Era of Good Feeling (1817–1823). (b) Describe *one* important event in the career of *each* leader that illustrates nationalism.

3. (a) Discuss *two* reasons why the United States in the 1820's opposed the restoration of Spanish control in Latin America. (b) Why did John Quincy Adams advise against a joint declaration with England? (c) State *two* provisions of the Monroe Doctrine.

4. As Chief Justice, John Marshall molded the Supreme Court so that it has played a major role in shaping American institutions. For each of *three* cases decided while Marshall was Chief Justice, (a) state *one* principle that the Supreme Court established, and (b) show why this principle is important in the United States today.

Part 2. The Jacksonian Era Furthers Democratic Reforms

POLITICAL DISPUTES, 1824–1828

By 1824 the Era of Good Feeling was over, and sectional disputes brought the nation upon a lengthy *Era of Hard Feeling*.

1. **Presidential Election of 1824.** The four Presidential candidates, each a sectional favorite, were John Quincy Adams of the North, William H. Crawford of the South, and Henry Clay and Andrew Jackson both of the West. All four candidates were Democratic-Republicans. The people generally voted along sectional lines, and no candidate received a majority in the electoral college. Therefore, the House of Representatives acted to select a President from the top three candidates in electoral votes: Jackson, Adams, and Crawford.

Since Adams advocated strong nationalist policies similar to Clay's American System, Clay, who had run fourth in the electoral college, threw his support to Adams, who had run second. Although Jackson had been the front-runner, the House chose Adams as President. When Adams appointed Clay as Secretary of State, Jackson's supporters bitterly denounced the two men for a "corrupt bargain."

2. **Revival of the Two-Party System.** Embittered by the sectional and personal animosities of the 1824 election, the Democratic-Republicans split into two opposing parties:

a. National Republicans, Later Called Whigs. This party was led by Clay, Adams, and later by Daniel Webster. Although the National Republicans sought mass support, they derived their strength chiefly from the well-established propertied classes: bankers, merchants, manufacturers, and large landowners. Since the National Republicans stood for a strong federal government, a national bank, and a protective tariff, and since they favored the interests of business, they resembled Hamilton's Federalist party.

b. Democrats. Led by Jackson and Martin Van Buren, the Democrats consisted of small farmers, newly emerging businessmen, and city workers. Since the Democrats generally opposed an all-powerful federal government, urged greater democracy, and claimed to represent the common man, they conformed to major Jeffersonian ideals.

3. **Presidential Election of 1828.** In a campaign devoid of a serious discussion of issues but marked by personal abuse and mudslinging, Jackson defeated Adams. Jackson's election has been called a sectional victory, for he lost New England but overwhelmingly carried the South and West. Jackson, who came from Tennessee, was the first President from a state west of the Appalachians.

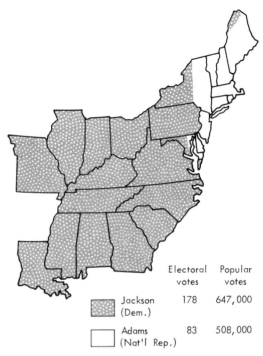

	Electoral votes	Popular votes
Jackson (Dem.)	178	647,000
Adams (Nat'l Rep.)	83	508,000

Election of 1828

REVOLUTION OF 1828

Jackson's election was a victory of the common man—the small farmer and city worker—over the aristocracy of money, factory, and land. The common people viewed Jackson as one of their own. He was the first President to come from a poor family and to have received little formal education. Jackson had risen in the world through his own efforts. "Old Hickory," Jackson's nickname, aroused visions of a tough military hero and a rough frontiersman. Since Jackson opposed special privilege and campaigned as the champion of the people, his election is often referred to as the *Revolution of 1828.*

JACKSON: A COMPLEX MAN

The common man's view of Jackson was in some ways far too simple. Although Jackson was born in poverty, he amassed considerable wealth, owned a large Tennessee plantation with many slaves, and raced fine horses. Although he had little formal education, Jackson learned to read and write at an early age, became a lawyer and judge, and enjoyed an extensive personal library. Although he grew up on the Western frontier, by the time of his election Jackson possessed the manners, dignity, and bearing of a cultured gentleman.

JACKSONIAN DEMOCRACY

The growing democratic ideas and practices that accompanied Andrew Jackson's leadership in American life are together called *Jacksonian democracy*. Jackson himself brought about certain democratic advances. Other advances were encouraged by the democratic atmosphere of the times.

JACKSONIAN DEMOCRACY COMPARED WITH JEFFERSONIAN DEMOCRACY

JEFFERSON	JACKSON
1. Believed that capable, well-educated leaders should govern in the people's interests.	1. Believed that the people themselves should manage governmental affairs.
2. Reflected chiefly an agricultural society.	2. Reflected an agricultural as well as a rising industrial society.
3. Limited democracy chiefly to its political aspects.	3. Expanded democracy from its political aspects to include social and economic aspects.

POLITICAL ASPECTS OF THE JACKSONIAN ERA

1. Democracy in the States. By 1828 most states had (*a*) removed property and religious qualifications for officeholding and voting, (*b*) increased the number of elected rather than appointed state and local officials, and (*c*) given the people a greater check upon elected officials by shortening their terms of office.

2. Democracy in Presidential Elections. (*a*) Beginning with the election of 1832, instead of being named by a *caucus* of a few party leaders, the Presidential candidate of each party was named by a larger number of active party members at a *nominating convention*. (*b*) By 1832 the Presidential electors of all but one of the states were chosen directly by the voters, instead of by state legislatures.

3. Democratic View of the Presidency. Jackson held that the President, the only nationally chosen official, was the servant of the people, elected to further their interests and protect their rights. To achieve these purposes, Jackson used his powers vigorously. (*a*) He employed the veto more often than all the preceding Presidents together. (b) He prepared to use force when South Carolina challenged the authority of the federal government (see pages 143–144). (c) He refused to enforce John Marshall's Supreme Court decision prohibiting Georgia from seizing Cherokee Indian lands. Jackson argued that the decision was contrary to the people's interests.

Jackson's enemies referred to him as *King Veto* and *King Andrew I*. They called themselves *Whigs* as had the 18th-century opponents of monarchical power in England. To the common man, however, Jackson remained both a valiant hero and a democratic servant.

4. Spoils System. Jackson was the first President to employ the spoils system widely. He filled some 20 percent of federal positions with "deserving" members of his own party, replacing the former officeholders. A Jacksonian supporter coined the phrase, "To the victor belong the spoils."

Rotation in office, Jackson believed, was democratic because (a) it prevented a permanent class of officeholders from becoming an aristocracy, and (b) "the duties of public office are so plain and simple that men of intelligence may readily qualify themselves for their performance." (For criticisms of the spoils system leading to the Pendleton Act in 1883, see page 75.)

ECONOMIC ASPECTS OF THE JACKSONIAN ERA

1. Cheap Land. Throughout the early years of the United States, Westerners demanded cheap land. In 1820 settlers had been permitted to purchase as little as 80 acres at $1.25 per acre. However, many settlers considered even this price too high. Many of them merely occupied public land as *squatters*. The *pre-emption laws*, originating during the Jacksonian Era, gave squatters first right to buy the lands they had occupied and farmed.

2. Growth of Trade Unions. During the Jacksonian Era, the trade union movement spread to several large cities, and a National Trades Union existed for a few years. Subsequently, in 1842, the courts for the first time held trade unions and strikes legal. Workers also engaged in politics to further their economic interests. Nevertheless, the labor movement remained weak until well after the Civil War.

SOCIAL ASPECTS OF THE JACKSONIAN ERA

With the political reforms of the Age of Jackson came a growing spirit of social reform. Motivated by humanitarianism, social reformers felt a deep concern for the welfare of the people and acted to improve conditions. Movements arose to secure (1) women's rights, (2) the abolition of slavery, (3) the prohibition of intoxicating liquors, (4) better care of the insane and other unfortunates, and (5) free public education. (For a detailed discussion of social reform, see pages 367–370.)

Part 3. The Rise of Sectional Interests Suppresses Nationalism and Leads to Disputes

MEANING OF SECTIONALISM

In the 1820's nationalism gave way to a growing spirit of sectionalism. Americans now (1) gave their primary loyalty to their state or section rather than to the entire nation, and (2) considered problems from a sectional rather than a national point of view.

Southerners sought to protect their sectional interests by supporting states' rights and opposing federal power. Northerners and Westerners argued that what was good for their section was good for the nation and sought to use federal power to further their interests. The struggle between sectionalism and nationalism eventually resulted in the Civil War and, ultimately, in the triumph of nationalism.

ECONOMIC BASIS OF SECTIONALISM

1. **Industrial Northeast.** Consisting of New England and the Middle Atlantic states, the Northeast pursued shipping, fishing, lumbering, and farming—and industrialized significantly. Industrialization in the North began in 1790 in Rhode Island when *Samuel Slater*, an immigrant from England, constructed the country's first cotton-spinning mill. *Eli Whitney*, in 1798, began to mass-produce guns in Connecticut by assembling them out of interchangeable parts. In Massachusetts, in 1813, *Francis Cabot Lowell* built the nation's first textile factory to combine the steps of processing raw cotton, spinning thread, and weaving cloth.

The leading industrial products of the Northeast were textiles, iron implements, utensils, and machinery.

Industrialization in the Northeast was aided by the following factors: (*a*) Shipbuilding and foreign commerce had declined as a result of the Embargo Act and the War of 1812, and workers and capital were available for the new industries. (*b*) Waterpower was readily available from swift-flowing streams, and steampower from Appalachian coal. (*c*) Factory hands could easily be recruited from farm families discouraged by New England's rocky soil, as well as from among immigrants. (*d*) As the nation's banking center, the Northeast possessed investment capital. (*e*) The South and the West represented a growing market for the Northeast's manufactured goods.

2. **Plantation South.** Consisting of the South Atlantic and Southwestern states, the South contained many small subsistence farmers but was dominated by a small number of wealthy and influential plantation owners. They raised cash crops for the market: tobacco, rice, sugar, and, most impor-

tant, cotton. From 1790 to 1826 cotton production increased from 2 million to 330 million pounds annually.

The rise of *King Cotton* was aided by the following factors: (*a*) Cheap, fertile land was plentiful. As the soil became exhausted by the continuous cultivation of a single crop, planters gradually moved from the South Atlantic states into the fertile lands of the Southwest. (*b*) The cotton gin, invented by Eli Whitney in 1793, provided a simple and inexpensive method of separating the cotton fiber from the seed. It replaced the costly and time-consuming practice of doing the job by hand. (*c*) Cotton-growing was a simple and year-round activity. Negro slaves could therefore be trained easily and kept occupied continuously. (*d*) Northern and English factories provided a growing market for the South's raw cotton.

3. Small-Farm West. Consisting of the Central and Northwestern states, the West emphasized agriculture on the small, family-size farm. Western settlers raised great amounts of wheat, rye, corn, and meat. In producing abundant harvests, Westerners were aided by the following factors: (*a*) Fertile lands were plentiful. (*b*) The federal government sold the Western lands at very liberal prices—first at $2.00 per acre and after 1820 at $1.25 per acre. (*c*) Free men worked hard on their own farms, seeking larger crops so as to better their economic status. (*d*) Northern and English cities represented an ever-growing demand for foodstuffs.

SECTIONAL ISSUES

1. Protective Tariff. The *Northeast* strongly favored a protective tariff in order to protect factory owners and workers against foreign competition. The *South* opposed a protective tariff in order to buy manufactured goods at lower prices. Also, the planters feared that England might retaliate by curtailing purchases of Southern cotton. The *West* generally supported the North on this issue. Although Western farmers disliked the higher prices on manufactures, they wanted a prosperous Northeastern market for their foodstuffs.

2. Second Bank of the United States. The *Northeast* strongly supported the Bank, since manufacturers and bankers benefited from available investment capital and stable currency. The *South* and the *West* both opposed the Bank. Planters, farmers, and debtors generally preferred state banks, since these would bring easy credit, cheap money, and high prices for agricultural products.

3. Internal Improvements at Federal Expense. The *West* favored such projects; farmers needed roads and canals to send their agricultural products to Northeastern markets and seaports. The *South* opposed these federal expenses; planters had satisfactory water routes to Northeastern and English markets and had little need of routes to the West. The *Northeast* generally supported the West on this issue; manufacturers desired improved routes to Western markets. However, many Northeasterners preferred internal improvements through private enterprise or at the expense of the states.

4. Liberal Land Policy. The *West* strongly favored cheap land. Farmers wanted to acquire more land. Also, they wanted to attract new settlers, form new states, and increase the influence of the West in the federal government. The *Northeast* opposed a liberal land policy. Manufacturers feared the loss of factory workers to the West. Northeasterners also feared losing influence in the federal government to the West. The *South* was divided on this issue. Planters wanted cheap lands in the Southwest and yet feared that Western growth would reduce Southern influence in the federal government.

5. Territorial Expansion to the Southwest. The *South* favored annexing Texas and acquiring land from Mexico. Southern planters wanted to secure more slave states and to replace lands exhausted by continuous cotton cultivation. The *Northeast* opposed territorial expansion to the southwest since Northeasterners feared that this would mean new slave states, thereby reducing Northern influence in the federal government. The *West* generally supported the South on this issue. Although Westerners opposed the extension of slavery, they wanted additional sources of cheap fertile land.

6. Expansion of Slavery. The *South* favored the expansion of slavery into new territories. The Southern economy was tied to slavery, and Southerners were anxious to increase the number of slave states. The *Northeast* and most of the *West* utilized free labor. They considered slavery morally wrong and therefore opposed its expansion.

TARIFF ISSUE

THE SOUTH AND THE TARIFF

In 1816, when the first protective tariff was passed, it had the support of all sections including the South, which had visions of becoming industrialized. In 1824, however, the South vigorously but unsuccessfully opposed an increase in tariff rates. Southern Congressmen, realizing that the South was to remain agricultural, argued that the tariff raised the price of manufactured goods and caused foreign countries to curtail their purchases of Southern cotton.

TARIFF OF ABOMINATIONS (1828)

In 1828 Western and Northern Congressmen secured passage of a tariff that provided extremely high rates on imports of raw materials and manufactured goods. Southerners called it a hateful law, a *Tariff of Abominations*.

SOUTH CAROLINA EXPOSITION AND PROTEST (1828)

South Carolina planters, adversely affected by the depletion of their land and by the increased competition from rich cotton land in the Southwest, blamed the decline in their prosperity on the tariff. John C. Calhoun of South Carolina, the leading spokesman of the South, protested the tariff of 1828 and secretly wrote the *South Carolina Exposition and Protest*. This document, patterned after the Virginia and Kentucky Resolutions, presented the following constitutional argument: (1) The federal government was created by a compact among the states to serve as their agent. (2) State conventions have the power to declare laws of Congress, such as a tariff law, unconstitutional. (3) Laws so declared unconstitutional are null and void. Calhoun also believed that, as a last resort, a state could terminate its compact with the other states and secede from the Union.

WEBSTER-HAYNE DEBATE (1830)

The controversy over the nature of the federal Union came to a head in the Senate. Senator Robert Y. Hayne of South Carolina presented the states' rights argument, closely paralleling the *Exposition and Protest*. Daniel Webster of Massachusetts, the leading Northern spokesman, answered Hayne in a speech often considered the greatest ever delivered in the Senate. Webster presented the nationalist point of view: (1) The Constitution and the federal government were created by the people, not by the states. (2) The proper agency for determining the constitutionality of laws is the Supreme Court, not the individual states. (3) No state has the right to nullify a federal law or secede from the Union; otherwise the Union would be an absurdity, a "rope of sand." Webster concluded dramatically with the words, "Liberty and Union, now and forever, one and inseparable."

ATTITUDE OF THE WEST

At the 1830 Jefferson Day dinner, attended by the leaders of the Democratic party, Andrew Jackson aligned the West with the Northeast against the South on the issue of nullification. Looking directly at Calhoun, Jackson proposed a toast, "Our Federal Union: it must be preserved." For the South, Calhoun proposed a counter-toast, "The Union, next to our liberty, most dear."

NULLIFICATION BY SOUTH CAROLINA (1832)

The South was disappointed in the new tariff law, passed in 1832, that provided only modest relief from the Tariff of Abominations. South Carolina thereupon passed an *Ordinance of Nullification*, voiding the new tariff and threatening secession if the federal government attempted to collect tariff duties within South Carolina.

Jackson accepted the challenge. He warned that nullification is "incompatible with the existence of the Union" and asked Congress to pass a *Force Bill*, empowering him to enforce the nation's tariff law in South Carolina by utilizing the army and navy if necessary.

COMPROMISE TARIFF OF 1833

South Carolina did not receive support from the other Southern states, and all sections seemed eager to avoid an armed clash. Henry Clay introduced a Compromise Tariff, which provided for a gradual reduction of rates over a ten-year period to the level of the Tariff of 1816. Congress passed the Compromise Tariff and on the same day passed Jackson's Force Bill. South Carolina withdrew its Ordinance of Nullification, thus making it unnecessary for Jackson to employ armed might. However, to reassert its right to nullify federal laws, South Carolina nullified the Force Bill.

The compromise settled the tariff issue, but Congress did nothing to resolve the more basic issue of states' rights and nullification.

BANK ISSUE

SECOND BANK OF THE UNITED STATES

1. Organization. Chartered in 1816 by a nationalist-minded Congress, the second Bank of the United States was a private, profit-making corporation. Four-fifths of its stock was held by private investors, and one-fifth by the federal government, which also appointed 5 of the Bank's 25 directors. Under *Nicholas Biddle*, its best known president, the Bank prospered and, by 1830, maintained some 29 branches throughout the country.

2. Services. The Bank (a) served as the official depository for government funds and sold government bonds, (b) held private deposits of money and provided loans for business purposes, (c) restrained state banks from overissuing bank notes in relation to their specie (metal) reserves, and (d) issued its own bank notes, which constituted a sound nationwide currency.

THE NORTHEAST FAVORS THE BANK

Northeastern manufacturers and financial interests generally approved the Bank because it (1) paid dividends on the Bank stock they owned, (2) provided business loans, (3) held deposits of their surplus funds, and (4) maintained a sound currency.

THE WEST AND SOUTH OPPOSE THE BANK

State banks, small businessmen, and Western and Southern farmers, planters, and debtors generally opposed the Bank. (1) It prevented state banks from issuing large quantities of bank notes, which would cheapen the value of money, inflate prices of farm crops, and facilitate the payment of debts. (2) Still other Americans opposed all bank notes and expected that the destruction of the Bank would lead to the exclusive use of "hard money"—gold and silver. (3) The Bank refused many loans to small businessmen and farmers who could not provide adequate collateral guaranteeing repayment. (4) By paying dividends, it enriched a few hundred wealthy Northeastern and foreign stockholders. (5) Its opponents claimed that the Bank was illegal, since the Constitution did not specifically authorize such a bank. (6) The Bank engaged in politics by supporting candidates for office, making loans to Congressmen, and retaining Senator Daniel Webster of Massachusetts as its attorney. (7) Opponents of the Bank argued that it enabled a few private individuals, the Bank's officers and directors, to exercise a monopoly over the nation's credit and currency. Referring to its vast economic power, the Bank's enemies called it the "Octopus" and the "Monster."

THE BANK AND THE ELECTION OF 1832

Jackson's enemies, aware of his hostility to the Bank, acted to make the Bank the leading issue of the 1832 election. Nicholas Biddle, president of the Bank, following the advice of Clay and Webster, requested a new charter of Congress although there were four more years left in the term of the old charter. When Congress passed the recharter bill, Jackson met the challenge by vetoing the bill and denouncing the aristocracy of money. Jackson rallied the common people to his support. He won an overwhelming victory in the election, receiving 219 electoral votes to 49 for the National Republican candidate, Henry Clay.

WILDCAT BANKS

Jackson interpreted his reelection as a mandate from the people to destroy the Bank. He ordered government funds withdrawn and placed in state banks, which Jackson's enemies named *pet banks*. The withdrawal of government funds crippled the second Bank of the United States.

With the second National Bank enfeebled, state banks, especially in the West, engaged in an orgy of imprudent banking practices. Nicknamed *wildcat banks*, they (1) made unwise loans, many of which were not secured by adequate collateral and were used for speculation in land, and (2) printed far more paper money than was justified by their reserves of specie. Alarmed by these practices, Jackson in 1836 issued his *Specie Circular.* He instructed federal land agents to accept payment for public lands only in gold or silver.

PANIC OF 1837 AND ITS EFFECTS

Soon after Jackson ended his second term, the nation experienced a financial crisis known as the *Panic of 1837.*

1. Causes. Jackson's Specie Circular was the immediate cause of the panic. State banks, unable to meet the demand for specie, closed their doors, thus bringing on the panic. Other basic causes of the panic were as follows: (*a*) Wildcat banks had made loans to land speculators, who hoped to sell the land at a higher price. However, the speculators found no purchasers and were unable to repay their loans. The banks were left with large uncollectable debts. (*b*) Western states, in particular, had recklessly floated bond issues to finance construction of turnpikes and canals that proved to be unnecessary and unprofitable. Many investors in such projects lost all that they had invested.

2. Independent Treasury System. Martin Van Buren, Jackson's friend and successor as President, did little to ease the panic and the ensuing depression. However, to safeguard government funds, he did influence Congress to pass the *Independent Treasury Act.* By this law, the government established subtreasuries in various cities and kept its funds in its own safety vaults.

3. Election of 1840. Blamed for the panic and depression, Van Buren was swept from office in the election of 1840. The Whigs won easily following a campaign marked by ballyhoo and slogans such as "Van, Van is a used-up man," and "Tippecanoe and Tyler too." General William Henry Harrison, victor over the Indians at the Battle of Tippecanoe, became President, and John Tyler became Vice President.

SIGNIFICANCE OF THE WAR AGAINST THE BANK

The destruction of the second Bank of the United States was a sectional victory for the West and South over the Northeast. To Jackson's supporters, it was also a victory of democracy—of the common people over a powerful economic monopoly. Jackson's war against the Bank left the American people with a heritage of distrust for any central bank.

For over three-quarters of a century, the United States had no centralized banking system. When in 1913 Congress established the *Federal Reserve System,* every effort was made to gain the advantages of sound banking practices without the disadvantages of concentrating banking power in the hands of a few private individuals.

IDENTIFICATION QUESTIONS: WHO AM I?

John Quincy Adams	William Henry Harrison	John Tyler
Nicholas Biddle	Robert Hayne	Martin Van Buren
John C. Calhoun	Francis Cabot Lowell	Daniel Webster
Henry Clay	Samuel Slater	Eli Whitney

1. In a Senate debate, I presented the nationalist viewpoint on the Constitution and called for "Liberty and Union."
2. I benefited from economic discontent to win the 1840 Presidential election.
3. A leading spokesman for the planter aristocracy, I wrote the *South Carolina Exposition and Protest*.
4. An immigrant from England, I built the first cotton-spinning mill in the United States.
5. After serving as Secretary of State under James Monroe, I won the Presidency in the bitterly contested election of 1824.
6. A Connecticut Yankee, I invented the cotton gin and later pioneered the mass production of guns.
7. A Westerner and Whig leader, I proposed the Compromise Tariff of 1833.
8. As president of the second National Bank, I bitterly opposed Andrew Jackson.
9. After succeeding my friend Andrew Jackson as President in 1837, I proposed the Independent Treasury System.

MULTIPLE-CHOICE QUESTIONS

1. Which contributed to the election of Andrew Jackson in 1828? (1) Voters were tired of the Federalist party. (2) Voters wanted to register a protest against John Marshall's decisions. (3) The importance of the West in national elections had increased. (4) Andrew Jackson advocated the spoils system.
2. During the first half of the 19th century, the right to vote was most generally extended by (1) lowering the voting age (2) removing property qualifications (3) outlawing poll taxes (4) amending the federal Constitution.
3. Which two groups most strongly supported Jacksonian democracy? (1) creditors and urban workers (2) supporters of the Bank of the United States and Western farmers (3) New England shipbuilders and Southern plantation owners (4) small farmers and proprietors of small businesses.
4. Andrew Jackson believed that the President should (1) carry out his duties within the strict limits of the Constitution (2) follow the lead of Congress in all matters (3) carry out policies advocated by his party's leaders (4) act as the spokesman of the people.
5. Two achievements of the Jacksonian Era were (1) rotation in public office and further widening of the suffrage (2) promotion of central banking and expansion of states' rights (3) encouragement of states' rights and active involvement in foreign affairs (4) the limitation of Presidential powers and the growth of nationalism.
6. During the period 1830–1860, which is the best example of a minority that exercised great political power within a section? (1) planter class in the South (2) unionized workers in Northern cities (3) farmers in the Northeast (4) shipbuilders in New England.

7. Which of the following would probably have received support from both a New England factory owner and a Western farmer? (1) a liberal land policy (2) a national banking system (3) restrictions on immigration (4) a national program of building roads and canals.

8. Before the Civil War, the South objected to high tariffs because they (1) kept the price of cotton low (2) increased the cost of slaves (3) increased the prices of manufactured goods (4) helped Western farmers at the planters' expense.

9. The history of the tariff between 1800 and 1860 shows that (1) President Jackson supported the South in its stand on the tariff (2) the South consistently opposed a protective tariff (3) the tariff issue contributed to the conflict between North and South over states' rights (4) the tariff restored American industry destroyed during the War of 1812.

10. According to the *South Carolina Exposition and Protest,* a federal law could be nullified by a state because the federal government was (1) dependent on the states for taxes (2) created by the states (3) composed of men elected or appointed from the states (4) limited in its use of power by the Bill of Rights.

11. According to the doctrine of nullification, the right to determine the constitutionality of an act of Congress resides in (1) Congress itself (2) the states (3) the United States Supreme Court only (4) the executive branch of the federal government.

12. President Jackson's action in the nullification controversy (1) antagonized the North (2) brought on the Panic of 1837 (3) won him the support of Calhoun (4) strengthened the power of the national government.

13. President Jackson claimed that the Bank of the United States (1) was supported by the plantation aristocracy (2) was responsible for the Panic of 1837 (3) discriminated against the farmer and the small businessman (4) had become unprofitable.

14. Which action by President Jackson led to the Specie Circular? (1) accepting the Compromise Tariff of 1833 (2) vetoing the recharter bill for the second Bank of the United States (3) advocating the spoils system (4) supporting the seizure of Cherokee lands by Georgia.

15. An important cause of the Panic of 1837 was the (1) end of the frontier (2) shortage of paper money (3) building of the Union Pacific Railroad (4) speculation in Western lands.

16. Westerners opposed the Bank of the United States because they (1) feared inflation (2) believed that the Bank favored the debtor class (3) were forbidden to borrow money from it (4) believed that Easterners received most of the benefits.

17. One immediate effect of President Jackson's Specie Circular was to increase the (1) sale of public land (2) demand for hard money (3) value of paper currency (4) general prosperity of the country.

ESSAY QUESTIONS

1. Both the election of Thomas Jefferson in 1800 and the election of Andrew Jackson in 1828 have been called revolutions. (*a*) Give *two* specific facts to show the extent to which the election of 1800 might be called a revolution. (*b*) Give *two* specific facts to show the extent to which the election of 1828 might be called a revolution. (*c*) Give *one* specific fact to show the difference between these revolutions.

2. The period in American history between the War of 1812 and the Civil War saw first nationalism and then sectionalism. For this period, discuss *one* factor that contributed to the development of nationalism, and *two* factors that contributed to the development of sectionalism.

3. During the Jacksonian Era there were conflicting currents of nationalism and sectionalism, as well as a trend toward democracy. (*a*) Including specific illustrations, explain *two* controversies created by the conflict between nationalism and sectionalism during the Jacksonian Period. (*b*) Show *two* different ways in which democracy was extended during the Jacksonian Era.

4. Some historians have described the administration of Andrew Jackson as "the Reign of King Andrew" and others as "the Era of Jacksonian Democracy." For *each* expression, discuss *two* examples to justify its use as a description of the era in which Jackson was President.

5. The doctrine of states' rights was not limited to any one section of the country. Prove this statement by describing *one* instance of the formal assertion of states' rights in each of *two* different sections before 1860.

Part 4. The Young Nation Expands Across the Continent

MANIFEST DESTINY

Americans, a restless, migratory people seeking new lands, were satisfied temporarily by the relatively easy acquisitions of the Louisiana Purchase and Florida (see pages 119–121 and 129). By the 1840's, Americans had again become expansion-minded. They believed that their country was destined to spread to the Pacific coast, or perhaps over the entire North American continent, a belief known as *manifest destiny*.

Manifest destiny was promoted by (1) land-hungry Americans who eyed tracts of rich but sparsely settled lands, (2) patriots who feared British designs upon such lands, (3) Eastern merchants whose ships trading with Asia needed ports on the Pacific coast, (4) democratic-minded people who believed that American territorial growth meant the speading of freedom, and (5) nationalists who sought American greatness.

EVENTS IN TEXAS

1. Americans in Texas. Americans were invited by newly independent Mexico in 1821 to settle in her northern province of Texas. *Stephen Austin* led the first group of land-hungry Americans. Others soon followed. By 1830 some 20,000 whites with 1000 Negro slaves had come to Texas from the United States. In the 1830's friction developed between the Mexican government and the American settlers, as Mexico attempted to (*a*) halt further American immigration into Texas, (*b*) free the Negro slaves, and (*c*) deprive Texas of local self-government.

2. Texas Revolution (1836). Claiming a parallel with the American Revolution against Britain, the Texans rebelled for independence. At the Alamo, a fortified church mission at San Antonio, a Texan force was besieged and overwhelmed by a Mexican army under General Santa Anna. The bloody massacre of the Alamo defenders further inflamed the Texans, whose battle cry became, "Remember the Alamo!" Led by *Sam Houston*, the Texans won a great victory at the Battle of San Jacinto, capturing Santa Anna and driving his troops out of Texas. The settlers proclaimed the Republic of Texas (the Lone Star Republic), elected Sam Houston as President, and requested annexation by the United States.

ANNEXATION OF TEXAS

1. Delayed by Sectional Rivalry. While Southerners favored the annexation of Texas, Northeasterners opposed it. Northeasterners feared (*a*) the extension of slave territory, (*b*) increased Southern membership in the House of Representatives, and (*c*) the possible division of Texas into several states, which would greatly increase Southern membership in the Senate. In

Annexation of Texas (1845)

1844 Northern opposition and fear of a war with Mexico led the Senate to defeat an annexation treaty.

2. Achieved by Joint Resolution (1845). The annexation of Texas thereupon became an issue in the Presidential election of 1844. Henry Clay, the Whig candidate, straddled the issue. *James K. Polk* of Tennessee, the Democratic candidate, demanded the "reannexation of Texas," arguing that Texas had been part of the original Louisiana Purchase. Polk narrowly won the election.

In 1845, just before Polk took office, President Tyler suggested that Congress admit Texas to the Union by means of a joint resolution. Whereas a treaty requires a two-thirds vote in the Senate, a joint resolution requires only a majority vote, but in each house. The resolution was approved, and Texas joined the Union.

WAR WITH MEXICO (1846–1848)

1. Causes. Mexican patriots resented (*a*) the American annexation of Texas, (*b*) our claim that the southern boundary of Texas was the Rio Grande, rather than the Nueces River, and (*c*) the ambition of American expansionists to acquire additional Mexican territory. In addition, the Mexican government owed money to a number of American citizens. The unstable Mexican government, in response to public opinion, refused to receive the American negotiator John Slidell. The Mexicans refused to listen to Slidell's proposals that the United States purchase their New Mexico and California territories for as much as $30 million and assume Mexico's debts to Americans in exchange for the Rio Grande boundary. Instead Mexican and United States troops entered the disputed area between the Rio Grande and the Nueces River, and in 1846 a minor clash took place.

President Polk, infuriated, informed Congress that "Mexico has invaded our territory and shed American blood upon American soil." Polk requested and secured a declaration of war. Although most Northeastern Congressmen voted for the declaration, many Northeasterners condemned the war as an imperialist plot against a weak neighbor to seize land and extend slavery. Most Southerners and Westerners enthusiastically welcomed the war.

2. Military Events. American volunteer armies soon demonstrated their military superiority. General Zachary Taylor ("Old Rough and Ready") won victory after victory in northern Mexico. General Winfield Scott captured Vera Cruz and Mexico City, the capital. Colonel Stephen Kearny occupied New Mexico and advanced on California. In California, Captain John C. Frémont led American settlers to drive out the Mexican authorities and establish the temporary California (Bear Flag) Republic. Mexico's defeat was complete.

3. Treaty of Guadalupe Hidalgo (1848). Mexico (a) accepted the Rio Grande as the southern boundary of Texas, and (b) gave up California and the province of New Mexico, together called the *Mexican Cession*. (This area was eventually carved up into five states and parts of two others.) The United States agreed to pay Mexico $15 million and to assume the claims of American citizens against the Mexican government. (The terms of the treaty closely paralleled the American proposals that Mexico had refused to hear before the war.)

Territorial Growth of the United States (1783–1853)

GADSDEN PURCHASE (1853)

Five years after purchasing the Mexican Cession for $15 million, the United States paid Mexico $10 million for a small strip of land in southern Arizona and New Mexico. This land, called the *Gadsden Purchase*, provided a favorable railroad route into California. Many Americans felt, however, that the large sum paid for this territory was "conscience money."

MAINE BOUNDARY DISPUTE

Both the United States and Great Britain claimed a territory of 12,000 square miles lying between Maine in the United States and New Brunswick in Canada. By the *Webster-Ashburton Treaty* of 1842, the two nations accepted a compromise boundary. The United States gained 7000 square miles, including the fertile Aroostook Valley.

●OREGON DISPUTE

1. **Conflicting Claims.** Both the United States and Britain claimed the Oregon Country, a huge area extending from the Rockies westward to the Pacific and from the latitude of 42° northward to 54° 40′. British claims were based upon (a) the 16th-century voyage of Sir Francis Drake, (b) the 18th-century explorations of Cook and Vancouver, and (c) the subsequent fur-trading activities of the Hudson's Bay Company. American claims rested upon (a) the discovery of the Columbia River by Captain Robert Gray in 1792, (b) the explorations of Lewis and Clark, (c) the subsequent fur-trading activities of the American Fur Company, owned by John Jacob Astor, and (d) the 5000 Americans who had settled in the territory by 1845, many inspired to migrate there by the reports of the missionary *Marcus Whitman.* For many years the United States and Britain jointly occupied the territory.

2. **Peaceful Settlement of the Dispute.** In the Presidential campaign of 1844, James K. Polk demanded the "reoccupation of Oregon." His support-

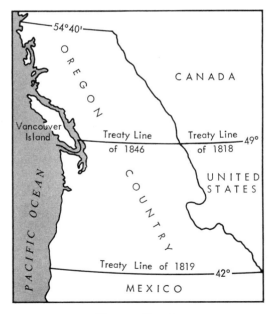

Oregon Country

ers chanted the slogan, "Fifty-four forty or fight." However, when he achieved the Presidency, Polk decided to compromise on the Oregon issue. In 1846 the United States and Britain agreed to divide the Oregon Country at the 49th parallel. This agreement extended the existing boundary between the western United States and Canada westward in a straight line to the Pacific.

MODIFIED TRUE-FALSE QUESTIONS

1. The belief of most Americans in the first half of the 19th century that the United States would expand to the Pacific coast was known as *imperialism*.

2. Americans migrated to Mexico's northern province of Texas in order to get *cheap land*.

3. The battle at the Alamo resulted in a military victory for the *Texans*.

4. *John C. Frémont* was elected President of the Lone Star Republic.

5. The section of the United States most opposed to the annexation of Texas was the *West*.

6. Texas was admitted to the Union by means of *a treaty*.

7. The Americans claimed that the southern boundary of Texas was the *Rio Grande*.

8. The American President who asked for a declaration of war against Mexico was *Andrew Jackson*.

9. An important result of the Mexican War was the annexation of *California*.

10. The *Gadsden Purchase* provided a railroad route into California.

11. An American missionary who helped settle the Oregon Country was *Marcus Whitman*.

12. The Webster-Ashburton Treaty settled our dispute with Great Britain over the *Newfoundland fisheries*.

13. American claims to the Oregon Country were based partly on the explorations of *Lewis and Clark*.

14. English claims to the Oregon Country were based partly on the fur-trading activities of the *American Fur Company*.

15. The Oregon boundary dispute was settled by dividing the land at the *54° 40′ parallel*.

ESSAY QUESTIONS

1. (*a*) What were the boundaries of the United States in 1789? (*b*) Mention *three* additions of territory to the United States between 1789 and 1860. (*c*) Show how *each* of these territories was acquired.

2. (*a*) Discuss *two* reasons why New England opposed the annexation of Texas. (*b*) Discuss *one* reason why James K. Polk felt justified in demanding the annexation.

3. (*a*) Explain *two* arguments used by Americans who opposed the Mexican War. (*b*) Explain *two* arguments of Americans who favored the Mexican War. (*c*) State *two* provisions of the treaty of peace ending the Mexican War.

4. (*a*) Name *four* foreign nations that once owned part of the present territory of the continental United States. (*b*) Show how each of *two* of these nations lost its territory.

Part 5. Slavery and Sectional Crisis Lead to Civil War

SLAVERY IN COLONIAL TIMES

Slavery was practiced in all thirteen colonies but took strongest hold in the South. Tobacco and rice planters needed large numbers of cheap, easily trained workers, and the Southern climate permitted utilizing slaves the year round. By 1763 the English colonies contained 400,000 slaves, three-fourths in the South.

EARLIEST STEPS AGAINST SLAVERY

Many leading Southerners disapproved of the South's dependence upon slavery. Washington and Jefferson, both Southern planters, left wills freeing their slaves. They considered slavery immoral and a danger to the South's ultimate welfare.

In the Northern states slavery was economically unprofitable. Northern farmers owned small, family-operated farms where little work could be done during the severe winter months. Factory owners considered slave labor less efficient than wage labor.

In 1787 Congress prohibited slavery in the Northwest Territory. By 1804 all Northern states had provided for the gradual abolition of slavery. In 1808 Congress halted the importing of slaves into the United States. In the 1820's the *American Colonization Society*, founded by both Northerners and Southerners, sought to transport freed Negroes to *Liberia* on the west coast of Africa. Few Negroes, however, were willing to return to their ancestral continent.

COTTON GIN AND SLAVERY

Meanwhile, in 1793, Eli Whitney, an enterprising Connecticut Yankee, invented the cotton gin. By easily separating the cotton fiber from the seed, this machine made the production of short-staple cotton extremely profitable. The South's economy became tied to cotton. Southern cotton plantations grew rapidly in size and number, and Southern planters became dependent upon slaves for labor. Thus, while slavery declined elsewhere, it fastened its hold upon the economy of the South. Also, as cotton planters acquired landholdings in the Southwest, they spread the institution of slavery.

MISSOURI COMPROMISE (1820)

1. **Issues.** The Missouri Territory, part of the Louisiana Purchase, applied for admission into the Union as a slave state. Missouri's admission would

have upset the balance of 11 free and 11 slave states and would have given the South control of the Senate. The North, by reason of its larger population, already controlled the House of Representatives. Representative James Tallmadge of New York proposed that Congress abolish slavery in Missouri. He thereby set off a bitter sectional debate as to whether Congress had the right to prohibit slavery in a territory or in a state. Both North and South argued vehemently, and Thomas Jefferson wrote that the slavery issue filled him with terror, "like a firebell in the night."

2. Compromise. Henry Clay finally worked out the *Missouri Compromise:* (a) Maine was separated from Massachusetts and entered the Union as a free state, (b) Missouri entered as a slave state, and (c) all other territory in the Louisiana Purchase north of the 36° 30′ parallel was closed to slavery. The Compromise thus left far less territory open to slavery than it closed to slavery.

Missouri Compromise (1820)

ABOLITIONIST MOVEMENT

1. Antislavery Arguments. Abolitionist societies, arising in the 1830's during the era of Jacksonian democracy, were concerned with ending Negro slavery. Most abolitionists demanded the immediate freeing of the slaves without compensation to their masters. The abolitionists argued that slavery (*a*) is morally wrong—that no man has the right to hold a fellow man in bondage, (*b*) transgresses religious teachings and violates the ethics of the Bible, (*c*) results in cruel and inhuman treatment of slaves and their families, (*d*) degrades slaveowners, and (*e*) violates democracy—the equality and the unalienable rights of all men as stated in the Declaration of Independence.

2. Abolitionist Activities. To sway public opinion, the abolitionists conducted meetings and published newspapers. Theodore Parker, a Boston preacher, lectured and wrote against slavery, as did the orator Wendell Phillips, and the authors James Russell Lowell, John Greenleaf Whittier, and Ralph Waldo Emerson. A former slave, *Frederick Douglass*, edited an abolitionist newspaper in Rochester, New York. In Boston, *William Lloyd Garrison*, militant, uncompromising, and the best-known abolitionist, published the leading antislavery newspaper, *The Liberator*.

The abolitionists also organized the *underground railroad*, a network of secret stations by which runaway slaves were smuggled out of the South to freedom in the North and Canada. A leading worker on this "freedom road" was the former slave *Harriet Tubman*.

The abolitionist movement, however, lacked realistic plans for ending slavery and for improving the life of Negroes once they were free.

3. Limited Following Even in the North. In the 1830's the abolitionists in the North were treated roughly. Their meetings were heckled, their newspapers seized, and their leaders attacked.

Most Northerners (*a*) considered the abolitionists as irresponsible fanatics, (*b*) believed that the South should solve the problem of slavery in its own way, (*c*) were anxious not to disturb their profitable business relations with the South, and (*d*) feared tnat freed Negroes would come North and compete for jobs.

As time went on, however, many Northerners accepted the argument that, since slavery is morally wrong, it had to be abolished. They hoped that the United States would follow the British example. In 1833 Great Britain had freed the slaves throughout her Empire peacefully and with compensation to the slaveowners.

THE SOUTH AND SLAVERY

1. **Extent of Slavery.** Of the white families in the South, (a) 80 percent (poor whites, small farmers, and many city dwellers) owned no slaves, (b) 19 percent (mostly small farmers) owned a few slaves, usually five or less, and (c) 1 per cent (large planters) owned 50 or more. These large planters possessed great estates, lived in splendid mansions, and dominated the South socially, economically, and politically.

Psychologically, the non-slaveowning lower classes may have had an interest in maintaining slavery because they (a) could look down upon the slaves as inferior beings, and (b) could hope to rise in status by acquiring slaves.

2. **Treatment of Slaves.** The South's treatment of Negroes varied from urban to rural areas, from small farms to large plantations, and according to the character of the white master. Although cruel treatment existed, especially in the breaking up of Negro families, physical brutality was not the rule. Most slaves received adequate food, clothing, and shelter. Since a male field hand was worth between $1000 and $1800, Negro slaves represented valuable property to be conserved and utilized, not wantonly harmed.

3. **Negro Resistance.** Considerable discontent existed among the slaves. Some ran away, some engaged in deliberate slowdowns or sabotage at work, and some undertook revolts. The fear of slave uprisings haunted Southern whites. In 1822 *Denmark Vesey*, a free Negro, organized an unsuccessful slave conspiracy in South Carolina. In 1831 *Nat Turner*, a slave, led a bloody but unsuccessful insurrection in Virginia.

4. **Proslavery Arguments.** Southern whites defended slavery, not as a necessary evil, but as a positive good. They argued that slavery (a) had existed through the ages and had provided the economic basis of the great civilizations of ancient Greece and Rome, (b) was sanctioned by the Bible, (c) assured continued cotton production and Southern prosperity, (d) meant a better life for the Negroes in the South than in Africa, and (e) provided the Negroes with better treatment and more security than the North granted its factory workers. Furthermore, Southern whites insisted that Negroes were mentally inferior and, if freed, would endanger the lives of Southern whites and would be incapable of caring for themselves.

SLAVERY AND THE MEXICAN CESSION

At the start of the Mexican War in 1846, Representative David Wilmot of Pennsylvania introduced a resolution to prohibit slavery in any territory that might be acquired from Mexico. The *Wilmot Proviso* passed in the House, but met defeat in the Senate. In 1848 the United States acquired the

Mexican Cession, and the North and South resumed the struggle over the status of slavery in federal territory.

In 1848 settlers discovered gold in California, part of the Mexican Cession. The "Forty-Niners," as the incoming fortune hunters were called, soon increased the territory's population to 100,000. Californians drew up a constitution prohibiting slavery and applied for admission to the Union.

COMPROMISE OF 1850

1. **The Issue.** Congress now faced the problem of the status of slavery in California and in the rest of the newly acquired territory. In Congress and throughout the country, Northerners and Southerners debated bitterly regarding the extension of slavery. Finally, Henry Clay, the "Great Compromiser," proposed an acceptable and inclusive plan. In his efforts for compromise, Clay was assisted by Senator Stephen A. Douglas of Illinois and was supported by Senator Daniel Webster of Massachusetts. In defending the Compromise of 1850, Webster declared that he spoke "not as a Northern man, but as an American."

2. **Provisions of the Compromise.** (*a*) California was admitted as a free state. (*b*) The rest of the Mexican Cession was divided into the territories of

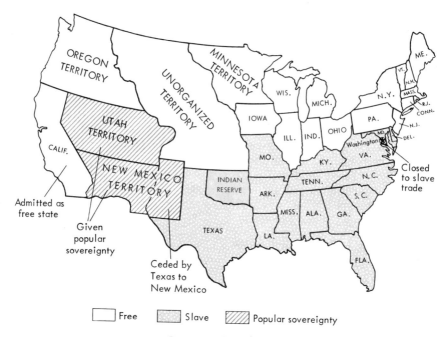

Compromise of 1850

New Mexico and Utah and was to follow the principle of *popular,* or *squatter, sovereignty.* This principle permitted the territorial inhabitants themselves to decide whether or not they wanted slavery. (c) Texas was given $10 million in exchange for a strip of land, most of which was assigned to New Mexico. (d) Slave trade, but not slavery, was prohibited in the District of Columbia. (e) A strict fugitive slave law was adopted to make it easier for Southerners to recover runaway slaves found in the North.

FURTHER GROWTH OF ANTISLAVERY FEELING IN THE NORTH

1. **The Fugitive Slave Law** (1850), with its harsh treatment of suspected runaway slaves, aroused Northern resentment. The law authorized federal commissioners to try Negro suspects without allowing them to testify and without a jury. The commissioner received a double fee if he ruled the suspect a runaway slave rather than a free Negro. To prevent the enforcement of the Fugitive Slave Law, many Northern legislatures passed "personal liberty laws." These laws prohibited state officials from cooperating in the capture of runaway slaves.

2. **Harriet Beecher Stowe,** an abolitionist and worker on the underground railroad, in 1852 wrote *Uncle Tom's Cabin.* This book, with its dramatic picture of Negro suffering in the South, swayed Northern sympathies. Abraham Lincoln supposedly called Mrs. Stowe the "little woman who made the big war."

3. **Horace Greeley,** founder of the New York *Tribune,* aroused Northern opinion by his vigorous antislavery editorials.

KANSAS-NEBRASKA ACT (1854)

1. **Provisions.** Stephen A. Douglas, Senator from Illinois, secured passage of a bill that repealed the Missouri Compromise and, in its place, (a) divided the remaining land of the Louisiana Purchase into the territories of Kansas and Nebraska, and (b) authorized the people in these territories to determine the status of slavery according to the principle of popular sovereignty.

2. **"Bleeding Kansas."** Slaveowners (especially from Missouri) and abolitionists (chiefly from New England) hurried to Kansas, each group seeking to gain control of the territory. These proslavery and antislavery men, resorting to armed violence, began a small-scale civil war. Missouri "border ruffians" attacked free-soil settlements. Abolitionist bands, notably one led by *John Brown,* raided proslavery centers. Reports from "Bleeding Kansas" kept sectional passions inflamed throughout the country.

Status of Slavery in the West After the Kansas-Nebraska Act (1854)

FORMATION OF THE REPUBLICAN PARTY (1854)

Northern antislavery men were shocked by the passage of the Kansas-Nebraska Act. Displeased by the wavering stand on slavery of both the Whig and Democratic parties, antislavery political leaders, meeting in Wisconsin and Michigan, created the present-day Republican party. They pledged to (1) oppose the extension of slavery into new territory, and (2) repeal the Kansas-Nebraska Act.

PRESIDENTIAL ELECTION OF 1856

As their first Presidential candidate, the Republicans in 1856 nominated the famed Western explorer and opponent of slavery, *John C. Frémont.* The

Democrats, again seeking to evade the slavery issue, nominated a Pennsylvanian with Southern sympathies, *James Buchanan.* (A short-lived third party, the American or Know-Nothing party, also ran a candidate.) The Whig party had disintegrated.

Frémont carried 11 Northern states, but Buchanan triumphed in 5 other Northern states as well as in the South and won the election.

DRED SCOTT CASE

1. **Issue.** *Dred Scott,* a Negro slave, had been taken by his master into the Minnesota region, which according to the Missouri Compromise was free territory. He was then brought back to Missouri, a slave state. To create a test case, the abolitionists had Dred Scott sue for his freedom on the grounds that his residence in free territory had made him a free man.

2. **Supreme Court Decision (1857).** The Supreme Court ruled against Scott. Chief Justice *Roger B. Taney* began the majority opinion by stating that a Negro could not be a citizen and that Scott could therefore not bring suit in a federal court. Taney then went beyond this point and ruled on the entire issue of slavery in federal territories. His further conclusions were labeled by antislavery men as an *obiter dictum* (Latin for "something said in passing") and therefore not legally binding. Taney stated that (*a*) slaves are property, (*b*) Congress may not deprive any person of the right to take property into federal territories, and (*c*) the Missouri Compromise, which prohibited slavery in part of the Louisiana Territory, was unconstitutional.

The dissenting opinions in the Dred Scott case pointed out that free Negroes had been considered as citizens in some states and that the Constitution granted Congress the power to make "all needful rules and regulations" for federal territories.

The Dred Scott decision was applauded by the South, denounced by the North.

LINCOLN-DOUGLAS DEBATES (1858)

In 1858 *Abraham Lincoln,* a Republican relatively unknown nationally, contested for the Senate seat from Illinois with the Democratic incumbent, the "Little Giant," Stephen A. Douglas. They engaged in a series of seven remarkable debates. In Freeport, Lincoln forced Douglas to state his view on slavery in the territories. Douglas said that the Dred Scott decision made slavery legal in the territories in theory, but the people of a territory could keep slaves out in practice. Douglas was narrowly reelected Senator, but his *Freeport Doctrine* cost him Southern support for the Presidency in 1860. Abraham Lincoln meanwhile became known throughout the North.

JOHN BROWN'S RAID (1859)

John Brown, a fanatical abolitionist, led a band of some twenty men in a raid against the federal arsenal at *Harper's Ferry* in Virginia. Brown hoped to secure guns, arm the nearby Negroes, and lead a slave rebellion. He was caught, tried for treason, found guilty, and hanged. In the North, Brown was honored for having sacrificed his life for human liberty. In the South, Brown was despised as a dangerous criminal.

PRESIDENTIAL ELECTION OF 1860

1. Issues and Candidates

a. The Democratic party, unable to agree on a platform or a candidate, split into two parts. The Northern Democrats stood for popular sovereignty and nominated Stephen A. Douglas. The Southern Democrats demanded enforcement of the Dred Scott decision and chose John C. Breckinridge.

b. The Republican party opposed the extension of slavery to the territories but promised not to interfere with slavery in the states. The Republicans also appealed to Northern businessmen and Western settlers by pledging a protective tariff, federal aid for internal improvements, a transcontinental railroad, and free homestead farms. In selecting a candidate, the Republicans passed over the outspoken William H. Seward, who saw the struggle over slavery as an "irrepressible conflict." They nominated, instead, the more moderate Abraham Lincoln.

c. The Constitutional Union party, a third party, affirmed its support of the Union and nominated John Bell.

2. Results.
Lincoln polled only 40 percent of the total popular vote but carried the North and West solidly (see map, page 164). He won the election with a decisive majority in the electoral college.

THE SOUTH SECEDES

1. Southern Reaction to the Election.
Southern leaders were outraged by the election of Lincoln, whom they called a "black Republican." Many Southerners ignored the facts that (*a*) the Republicans controlled neither the Senate nor the House of Representatives, and (*b*) pro-Southern judges dominated the Supreme Court.

2. Confederate States of America.
In December, 1860, South Carolina seceded from the Union. She was soon followed by six other Southern states. In February, 1861, the secessionist leaders met at Montgomery, Alabama, and established the *Confederate States of America* with *Jefferson Davis* as President. The Confederacy hastened military preparations in case it would have to use force to defend its independence.

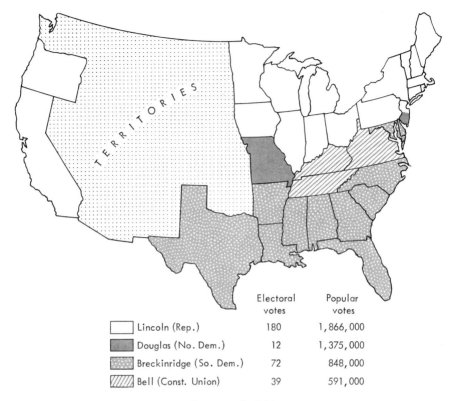

	Electoral votes	Popular votes
Lincoln (Rep.)	180	1,866,000
Douglas (No. Dem.)	12	1,375,000
Breckinridge (So. Dem.)	72	848,000
Bell (Const. Union)	39	591,000

Election of 1860

FEDERAL GOVERNMENT AND THE CHALLENGE OF SECESSION

1. Buchanan's Inaction. Still in office until March 4, 1861, President Buchanan behaved cautiously and ineffectively. He said that states had no right to secede, but he added that the federal government had no right to use force against secession. Buchanan urged compromise but took no decisive action to preserve the Union.

2. Lincoln Takes Office. In his Inaugural Address, Lincoln was both conciliatory and firm. He pledged not to interfere with slavery in the states where it existed, and he promised to enforce federal regulations, including the Fugitive Slave Law. However, he labeled secession as illegal and emphasized his solemn oath to "preserve, protect, and defend" the Constitution. He warned, "In your hands, my dissatisfied countrymen, and not in mine, is the momentous issue of civil war."

In April, 1861, Lincoln notified Southern authorities that unarmed ships would carry food to the federal troops at Fort Sumter in the harbor of Charleston, South Carolina. Nevertheless, Southern guns bombarded the fort and compelled its surrender. The Civil War had begun.

WAS SLAVERY THE MOST IMPORTANT CAUSE OF THE CIVIL WAR?

Slavery (1) presented a dramatic moral issue, since it dealt with human beings and involved individual freedom and democratic ideals, (2) distinguished the South from the North most clearly, and (3) was at the heart of most major issues dividing the two sections.

Nevertheless, we must remember that (1) the overwhelming majority of Southerners did not own slaves, (2) most Northerners were not abolitionists, (3) Lincoln and the Republicans did not threaten slavery where it already existed, and (4) four slave states remained loyal to the Union.

OTHER CAUSES OF THE CIVIL WAR

1. **Economic Differences.** Because of geographical conditions, the South had become agricultural and the North industrial. These economic differences led to bitter sectional rivalry on such issues as slavery and the protective tariff. The aristocratic Southern planters were determined to resist domination by the Northern industrialists and to advance the interests of the South's agrarian economy.

2. **Nature of the Federal Union.** The South insisted that the federal Union was created by the states and that any state had the right to secede. The North insisted that the Union was created by the people and was indivisible, and that no state had the right to secede. Lincoln proclaimed that the primary object of the war was not to abolish slavery, but to preserve the Union.

3. **Control of the Central Government.** To secure control of the central government, both the North and the South had sought the support of new territories. Consequently, the South favored and the North opposed the extension of slavery into the Western territories. In time, most of the West became tied economically to the North by a network of railroads and a mutually profitable exchange of foodstuffs for manufactured goods. Southerners increasingly realized that (a) most Western lands were not suitable for cotton culture, (b) the South was losing the battle for Western support, and (c) the South would remain a minority section in the Union.

4. **Differences in Civilization.** The South had developed a static civilization, dominated by a small aristocracy of influential planter families. Northern civilization was more democratic and dynamic. The clash of civilizations made understanding of each other's point of view difficult.

5. **Fanaticism.** Extremists on both sides sought to exaggerate differences. Northern abolitionists projected unfair stereotypes of Southern slaveowners.

Southern secessionists did likewise with respect to Northern free-soilers and Republicans. In the crucial decade of the 1850's, the nation lacked leaders able to move the sections toward compromise and peaceful solutions. Instead, hysteria and emotion mounted, and the "blundering generation" went to war.

CONCLUSION

No single cause brought about the Civil War. Rather, it resulted from the interrelationship of many complex factors. The causes of the Civil War remain a subject of intense historical research, revision, and debate.

MATCHING QUESTIONS

Column A	Column B
1. Editor of *The Liberator*	a. John Brown
2. Senate advocate of Kansas-Nebraska Act	b. James Buchanan
3. President of the Confederacy	c. Jefferson Davis
4. Editor of New York *Tribune*	d. Stephen A. Douglas
5. President of the United States when seven Southern states seceded	e. Frederick Douglass
6. Leader of raid at Harper's Ferry	f. William Lloyd Garrison
7. Author of *Uncle Tom's Cabin*	g. Horace Greeley
8. Negro abolitionist editor	h. Abraham Lincoln
9. Negro leader of insurrection	i. Harriet Beecher Stowe
10. Chief Justice of Supreme Court in Dred Scott case	j. Roger B. Taney
	k. Harriet Tubman
	l. Nat Turner
	m. David Wilmot

MULTIPLE-CHOICE QUESTIONS

1. Which was a result of the other three? (1) strong Southern support of slavery (2) invention of the cotton gin (3) Industrial Revolution in England (4) abundant supply of good land in this country.
2. The territorial expansion of the United States before the Civil War became a matter for furious political debate because (1) the South would send no troops to acquire free territory (2) Northerners were opposed to any expansion (3) additional states would tend to upset the sectional balance in the Senate (4) no new territory could be admitted until the Texas controversy was settled.
3. In 1860, 19 million bushels of corn went east over the railroads while 4.8 million bushels went south over the Mississippi-Ohio River system. This statement helps to explain the (1) victory of canals over railroads (2) sympathy of the West for the South in the secession movement (3) dislike of Southern cotton farmers for the West (4) support given the North by the West in the Civil War.
4. The Missouri Compromise established the 36° 30' parallel as the boundary between free and slave territories in (1) the Louisiana Purchase only (2) the Northwest Territory only (3) all land west of the Mississippi (4) the entire United States.

5. Many Northerners took serious issue with the abolitionists for (1) attacking slavery as a moral issue (2) writing books about slavery that were sometimes inaccurate (3) demanding the immediate freeing of all slaves (4) advocating that factory owners employ fugitive slaves.

6. Henry Clay is classified as both (1) a Whig leader and a victorious general (2) a "War Hawk" and a "Great Compromiser" (3) a member of the Virginia dynasty and a Presidential nominee (4) an ambassador to France and a Secretary of State.

7. In the Compromise of 1850, the South regarded as its main concession to the North the provision concerning (1) fugitive slaves (2) the admission of California (3) slavery in New Mexico (4) the state of Texas.

8. Which is an expression of states' rights by the Northern states? (1) personal liberty laws (2) the Kansas-Nebraska Act (3) the Fugitive Slave Law (4) the Compromise of 1850.

9. One direct result of the passage of the Kansas-Nebraska Act was the (1) beginning of the abolitionist movement (2) migration of settlers out of the Kansas and Nebraska Territories (3) formation of the Republican party (4) organization of the first underground railroad.

10. In 1857 which act of Congress was declared unconstitutional by the United States Supreme Court in the Dred Scott decision? (1) the Fugitive Slave Law (2) the admission of California (3) the Missouri Compromise (4) the Kansas-Nebraska Act.

11. The significance of the Dred Scott decision was that (1) Congress could not prohibit slavery in the territories (2) only Congress could prohibit slavery in any part of the United States (3) the people of a territory, by popular sovereignty, could outlaw slavery (4) the Fugitive Slave Law was severely weakened.

12. A significant result of the Lincoln-Douglas debates was that (1) Douglas failed to be reelected Senator (2) the Missouri Compromise was repealed (3) Lincoln supported the doctrine of popular sovereignty (4) Douglas lost the support of the South for the Presidency.

13. The chief reason for the opposition of the South to the election of Abraham Lincoln in 1860 was his (1) resistance to secession (2) demand for the immediate abolition of slavery (3) hostility to the extension of slavery (4) insistence on equal education for Negroes and whites.

ESSAY QUESTIONS

1. (a) Describe two economic differences and one difference in political views between the North and the South before 1860. (b) Discuss two factors that have helped to break down sectional differences within the United States since then.

2. Democracy is a series of compromises. (a) Mention three important compromises in our history. (b) For each of two of these compromises, state the main issue and give the major provisions.

3. Show how the North and the South, from 1820 to 1860, differed bitterly in regard to each of the following: (a) tariffs, (b) westward expansion, (c) states' rights theory of government, (d) Uncle Tom's Cabin, (e) Dred Scott decision.

4. Students of American history continue to argue about the fundamental causes of the Civil War. (a) State briefly three fundamental causes for the Civil War that have been advanced by historians. (b) For each cause stated, discuss one argument for agreeing and one argument for disagreeing with the conclusion that this factor brought on the war.

Part 6. The Civil War Marks the Triumph of Nationalism

COMPARISON OF THE NORTH AND THE SOUTH

ADVANTAGES OF THE NORTH

1. The North retained control of more than two-thirds of the states. These included 19 free states and 4 slaveholding border states: Delaware, Maryland, Kentucky, and Missouri. The North also retained the northwestern part of Virginia, whose pro-Union inhabitants in 1863 formed the state of West Virginia. However, strong pro-Southern sentiment existed in the four border states and in the southern parts of Ohio, Indiana, and Illinois.

2. The Northern population totaled 22 million, as compared with the South's 9 million, of whom 3½ million were slaves.

3. Northern manufacturing represented over 90 percent of the country's industry. The North had abundant textile factories, iron and steel mills, and armament plants. The South had few factories and had to depend largely upon imports for manufactured goods.

4. The North contained over 20,000 miles of railroad, more than double the Southern railroad facilities.

5. The North possessed more than three-fourths of the nation's financial resources. Being short of capital, the South had great difficulty in financing the war.

6. The North maintained control of the navy and merchant marine.

ADVANTAGES OF THE SOUTH

1. The South consisted of a geographically compact group of 11 states. The seven states that had seceded following Lincoln's election were joined by four border states: Arkansas, Tennessee, North Carolina, and Virginia. However, the South contained some areas of pro-Union sentiment.

2. Southerners were fighting essentially a defensive war, held the interior, or shorter, lines of communication, and knew their own terrain.

3. The South retained the loyalty of some outstanding military leaders, notably *Thomas J. ("Stonewall") Jackson* and *Robert E. Lee.*

4. Southerners were accustomed to an outdoor life of riding and hunting. They were therefore better prepared than Northern factory workers and shopkeepers for hardships as soldiers.

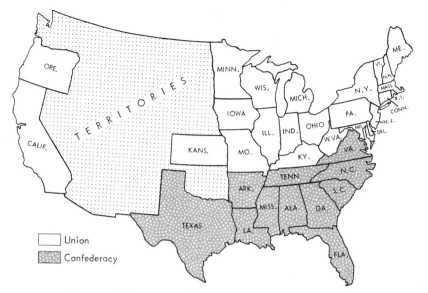

The Divided Nation: The Union and the Confederacy

5. The South had many friends in Britain and France who favored the Southern aristocracy. These nations also depended on imports of Southern cotton. Southern statesmen therefore expected Britain and France to rally to their support.

MILITARY ASPECTS OF THE WAR

WAR ON LAND

1. Stalemate in the East (1861–1863). Northerners expected their troops quickly to capture the Confederate capital of *Richmond*, Virginia, and sweep through the South. These hopes were shattered when a Union army met defeat in the first major engagement of the war, in 1861 in Virginia at *Bull Run.* For the next three years in the East, the Union's *Army of the Potomac* confronted the Confederacy's *Army of Northern Virginia.* Military action took place mainly on Southern soil as Confederate forces repeatedly repulsed Union offensives into the South. The North was twice invaded by Confederate armies under General Robert E. Lee. Union forces repulsed these invasions in bloody battles—in 1862 in Maryland at *Antietam* and in 1863 in Pennsylvania at *Gettysburg.* The Union victory at Gettysburg was the turning point of the war.

2. Northern Victories in the West (1862–1863). General *Ulysses S. Grant* led Union forces to victories on the western front. In 1862 he captured *Fort*

Donelson in western Tennessee, gaining his nickname of "Unconditional Surrender," and repulsed Confederate troops at *Shiloh.* Moving southward into Mississippi in 1863, Grant established Union control of the lower Mississippi River by capturing the Confederate fortress at *Vicksburg.*

3. Final Phase (**1864–1865**). In 1864 Grant received command of all Union forces, while General *William T. Sherman* was placed in charge of the Union army in the West. Sherman captured *Atlanta,* in western Georgia, and started on a 300-mile march through Georgia to the coastal city of *Savannah,* devastating the Confederate countryside. Grant meanwhile led the Union forces in Virginia and launched a relentless attack against Lee's army. In April, 1865, after 11 months of fighting, Grant captured Richmond. Lee realized that the war was lost and in the following week surrendered to Grant at the small Virginia town of *Appomattox Court House.* Grant generously permitted the Confederate soldiers to keep their horses "for the spring plowing" and announced, "The rebels are our countrymen again."

NAVAL WAR

1. Blockade of Southern Ports. Northern strategy called for a coastal blockade of the South to prevent the export of cotton and the import of goods essential to the Southern war effort. Within two years the blockade succeeded in reducing Southern cotton exports from $200 million to $4 million.

2. *Monitor* vs. *Merrimac*: First Ironclad Ships. To break the blockade, the South put iron plates on a wooden frigate, the *Merrimac,* and sent it against the Union fleet. The *Merrimac* easily destroyed two wooden vessels before encountering the ironclad *Monitor.* Designed by John Ericsson, the *Monitor* was described as a cheese box on a raft. The *Monitor* battled the *Merrimac* for hours, until the *Merrimac* withdrew, thus enabling the North to maintain the blockade. These first ironclad ships revealed such superiority in battle that they forecast the doom of wooden fleets.

3. Control of the Mississippi River. In 1862 Admiral *David G. Farragut* led a Union naval force into the mouth of the Mississippi and captured New Orleans. Farragut's victory, together with Grant's success at Vicksburg in 1863, gave the North complete control of the Mississippi, thereby splitting the Confederacy.

4. Confederate Attacks on Northern Merchant Ships. The Confederacy was able to harass Northern commerce on the seas chiefly because of English aid. In violation of her neutrality, England built several cruisers for the South, the most famous being the *Florida* and the *Alabama.* Southern sea raiders sank many Northern merchant ships and brought about a decline of the American merchant marine. Though costly, these Southern raids little affected the outcome of the war.

FOREIGN AFFAIRS DURING THE WAR

RELATIONS WITH GREAT BRITAIN

The North and the South both realized that England's industrial and naval power could tip the scales in the American Civil War. The North sought to keep Britain neutral, while the South worked for active British intervention.

SHARPLY DIVIDED SYMPATHIES IN BRITAIN

The English middle and working classes favored the North, which was the more democratic, and opposed the South, which supported slavery. Sympathy for the Union increased sharply in England after Lincoln issued the Emancipation Proclamation, freeing the slaves in the territories still held by the Confederacy.

The English upper classes favored the South because it (1) was dominated by the aristocracy, (2) maintained class distinctions, and (3) supported free trade with Britain. For these reasons, many leaders of the British government personally favored the South. Furthermore, they saw an advantage for Britain if the United States split into two contending nations in place of one united country.

REASONS FOR BRITAIN'S NEUTRALITY

In spite of the sympathy of British leaders for the South, Britain remained neutral. (1) The London government feared intensifying the sharp divisions within British public opinion. (2) In the early years of the war, English textile manufacturers had no need to import cotton since they held large cotton surpluses. (3) The English populace depended upon the North for imports of wheat. (These considerations of imports are often called "the battle of cotton versus wheat.") (4) In 1863 British military experts predicted that the South would lose the war.

WARTIME CONTROVERSIES BETWEEN THE UNITED STATES AND GREAT BRITAIN

1. *Trent* **Affair** (1861). A United States naval vessel stopped the British steamship *Trent* and took off two Confederate agents, *James Mason* and *John Slidell.* The British government demanded the immediate release of the two men, claimed that the North had violated Britain's rights as a neutral, and threatened war. President Lincoln and Secretary of State William Seward both realized that Great Britain had to be prevented from intervening in the war. The Union government released Mason and Slidell.

2. British-Built Warships for the Confederacy. British shipyards built several cruisers for the Confederacy. Most notable were the *Florida* and the *Alabama*, which were used to prey upon Northern merchant ships. By turning these cruisers over to the Confederacy, Britain violated her obligations as a neutral. Charles Francis Adams, the American minister to Great Britain, repeatedly protested until the British finally halted any further building of ships for the Southern navy.

After the war the United States demanded reparations from Britain for the damage caused by the *Alabama* and other British-built cruisers. In 1871 the two nations agreed to a peaceful settlement of the "*Alabama* claims." In 1872 the United States was awarded $15½ million by an international court of arbitration.

RELATIONS WITH FRANCE

PRO-SOUTHERN POLICIES

The French upper classes and government favored the South. A French banking firm raised several million dollars for the South by selling Confederate bonds in Europe. Napoleon III, the French Emperor, believed that a Southern victory would weaken the Monroe Doctrine and permit him to extend French influence into Mexico.

MAXIMILIAN AFFAIR

In 1862 Napoleon sent an army into Mexico and established a French protectorate under the puppet Emperor *Maximilian*. Secretary of State Seward protested immediately, but the United States could take no action until the end of the Civil War. Thereafter, the United States stationed a large force at the Mexican border and again demanded that Napoleon withdraw his troops. Napoleon did so in 1867, but Maximilian chose to remain. He was soon captured and executed by Mexican troops under the command of their President, *Benito Juarez*.

The *Maximilian Affair* demonstrated the ability and determination of the United States to enforce the Monroe Doctrine.

RELATIONS WITH RUSSIA

PRO-NORTHERN POLICIES

Russia favored the Northern cause, desiring a strong United States as a balance against British power. Czar Alexander II, furthermore, applauded the North's antislavery sentiment, since in 1861 he had emancipated the Russian serfs. In 1863 Russian fleets visited New York City and San Francisco—visits interpreted as friendly gestures to the North and as stern warnings to Britain and France to refrain from assisting the South.

PURCHASE OF ALASKA (1867)

For several years Russia had proposed to sell Alaska to the United States. In 1867, in part out of gratitude for Russia's friendship during the Civil War, Secretary of State Seward agreed to the purchase.

THE HOME FRONT

RECRUITING MEN FOR MILITARY SERVICE

1. In the South. At first, Confederate armies consisted of volunteers. After the initial enthusiasm had worn off, the South in 1862 instituted a conscription, or draft. It provided many occupational exemptions, such as for slave overseers, and permitted conscripts to escape service by hiring substitutes. The draft law aroused considerable defiance and opposition. The lower classes protested a "rich man's war and a poor man's fight." In total, the Confederacy placed under arms approximately 1 million men.

2. In the North. Originally, Union army ranks were also filled by volunteers. When enlistments fell off, the Northern governments—federal, state, and local—encouraged volunteers by offering cash bounties. The bounty system spurred enlistments but also led to *bounty-jumping:* dishonest men would enlist, receive their bounties, desert, and reenlist elsewhere to secure additional bounties.

In 1863 the North, too, passed a draft law, which allowed drafted men to avoid service by hiring substitutes or by paying $300 to the government. Many poor people resented the draft, and riots broke out, most notably in New York City. In total, the Union recruited approximately 2 million men, twice the number of Southern soldiers.

FINANCING THE WAR

1. In the South. Since its wealth consisted chiefly of slaves and land, the South had great difficulty in raising money. The Confederate government (*a*) levied excise taxes, (*b*) sold bonds to its people, and (*c*) issued tremendous quantities of paper money without specie backing. As Southern military prospects declined, the value of its paper money fell. The South sought loans in Europe, but had little success. European bankers doubted the South's ability to repay loans, since the Northern blockade prevented the export of Southern cotton and tobacco.

2. In the North. The prosperous North raised money by the following measures: (*a*) Imposed high excise taxes. (*b*) Passed the *Morrill Tariff Act* (1861), which raised import duties and yielded considerable revenue while giving Northern manufacturers protection against foreign competition. (*c*) Issued $450 million in paper money called *greenbacks.* (Since they were backed by the people's confidence in the government rather than by specie, the greenbacks fluctuated in purchasing power with the North's changing military prospects.) (*d*) Sold government bonds to banks and individuals. (Two bond issues were promoted by the Philadelphia banker *Jay Cooke.*) (*e*) In 1863 passed the *National Banking Act.* This law permitted banks to secure national charters, required nationally chartered banks to purchase government bonds, and authorized them to use the bonds as backing for bank notes. Thus this law provided a sound national currency and also helped the sale of bonds to finance the war.

POLITICAL BATTLES

1. In the South. *Jefferson Davis,* Confederate President, appointed an undistinguished Cabinet and himself lacked qualities of leadership. He proved inflexible, intolerant of criticism, and unable to arouse public enthusiasm. Davis faced attack by personal enemies and political opponents—the more so as the Confederacy moved closer to defeat.

2. In the North

a. Expansion of Presidential Powers. Lincoln used his Presidential powers extensively, especially those powers inherent in his position as commander in chief. He was often accused of acting dictatorially, as he stretched his authority, sometimes beyond constitutional limits. In the first months of the war, before Congress convened, Lincoln proceeded without Congressional sanction to call for army volunteers and spend federal funds that had not yet been appropriated. At the same time, to retain Northern control of Maryland, Lincoln suspended the writ of habeas corpus there.

In coping with the *Peace Democrats,* or *Copperheads,* who urged that the South be allowed to secede, Lincoln exiled their leader, Ohio Congressman Clement L. Vallandigham, to the Confederacy. Also, in regions inhabited by Confederate sympathizers, Lincoln ordered that certain cases be tried by military courts. (In 1866, in the case *ex parte Milligan,* the Supreme Court ruled Lincoln's action unconstitutional. It held that martial law could not be imposed on civilians where civil courts were still operating.)

In 1863 Lincoln declared the slaves under Confederate control free, as he issued the *Emancipation Proclamation.* This unprecedented declaration was designed to inspire the Northern populace, weaken the Southern war effort, and win support abroad.

b. Election of 1864. The Republicans renominated Lincoln and, to broaden their support, chose as their Vice Presidential candidate a pro-Union Democrat, *Andrew Johnson* of Tennessee. The Republicans, who for this election adopted the name of Union party, urged the North to continue the struggle to victory. The Democrats adopted a platform urging an armistice and calling the war a failure. However, General *George B. McClellan,* the Democratic candidate, repudiated this platform.

Lincoln at first feared he would lose the election, but a series of Northern victories in 1864 gained him decisive public support. Lincoln received 55 percent of the popular vote and an overwhelming majority in the electoral college.

LINCOLN'S PLACE IN HISTORY

LINCOLN THE MAN

In March, 1861, when Lincoln was inaugurated, he was little known to his fellow Americans. Today, he ranks as one of the greatest Americans of all time. His claim to greatness rests on his leadership during four long, hard years of civil war. With courage, dignity, and humility, he carried the nation's many burdens. Without hate, he kept steadfastly to his primary purpose—the preservation of the Union. Despite his exercise of almost dictatorial wartime powers, he maintained an unwavering faith in the superiority of the democratic way of life. At all times, he remained close to the people.

LINCOLN'S PHILOSOPHY

1. **Democracy.** In a letter, Lincoln gave a simple yet eloquent definition of democracy: "As I would not be a slave, so I would not be a master. This expresses my idea of democracy." In his debates with Douglas, although disclaiming any intention of introducing social equality between the races, Lincoln insisted that the Negro is the equal of any person as regards "life, liberty, and the pursuit of happiness," and as regards "the right to eat the bread which his own hand earns."

In the *Gettysburg Address* (1863) Lincoln declared that the United States had been "conceived in liberty and dedicated to the proposition that all men are created equal," and he urged Americans to "highly resolve" that "government of the people, by the people, for the people, shall not perish from the earth."

2. **The Union.** Accepting the Republican nomination for the Senate in 1858, Lincoln warned, "A house divided against itself cannot stand. I believe that this government cannot endure permanently half slave and half free."

In his *First Inaugural Address* (1861) Lincoln appealed to the South to remember the "mystic chords" that had held the Union together and to refrain from secession.

3. Second Inaugural Address. When Lincoln began his second term, the war was nearing its conclusion. Looking ahead, Lincoln said, "With malice toward none; with charity for all; with firmness in the right, as God gives us to see the right, let us strive on to finish the work we are in; to bind up the nation's wounds."

LINCOLN'S ASSASSINATION (APRIL, 1865)

Lincoln did not live to carry into effect his humane plans for binding up the nation's wounds and achieving a lasting peace. Shortly after the war's end, he was assassinated by a fanatical Confederate sympathizer, John Wilkes Booth. The death of Abraham Lincoln removed the one man who might have reunited the nation without further bitterness.

MAP QUESTIONS

For each state described on the following page, write *both* its name and the *letter* indicating its location on the map.

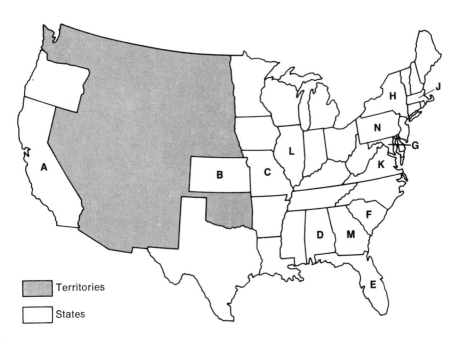

Territories

States

1. As a result of the Compromise of 1820, this state was admitted to the Union as a slave state.
2. This state was the first to secede from the Union.
3. At Appomattox Court House, in this state, General Lee surrendered to General Grant, thereby ending the Civil War.
4. According to the Compromise of 1850, this state entered the Union as a free state.
5. The bloody and decisive Battle of Gettysburg was fought in this state.
6. During the Civil War, keeping this border state in the Union was necessary to prevent the isolation of Washington, D.C., from the Northern states.
7. General William Sherman's march to the sea devastated this state.
8. Formerly part of a territory granted popular sovereignty by a law sponsored by Stephen A. Douglas, this state was admitted to the Union in 1861.
9. In 1858 Lincoln and Douglas engaged in a series of debates while seeking the Senate seat from this state.
10. In this state was located the first Confederate capital.

MULTIPLE-CHOICE QUESTIONS

1. A primary source for the study of the Civil War is (1) an American history textbook (2) *The Dictionary of American History* (3) *Abraham Lincoln: The War Years,* by Carl Sandburg (4) *The Blue and the Gray, The Story of the Civil War As Told by Participants,* edited by H. S. Commager.
2. The chief purpose of the Northern blockade during the Civil War was to prevent (1) English volunteers from reaching the South (2) Confederate officials from escaping to Europe (3) the South from exporting cotton (4) the French navy from aiding the South.
3. The Emancipation Proclamation was (1) a law passed by Congress (2) an amendment to the federal Constitution (3) a Presidential order (4) a joint resolution of Congress.
4. During the Civil War, which action posed the greatest threat to civil liberties? (1) seizure of Mason and Slidell from the *Trent* (2) suspension of the writ of habeas corpus by President Lincoln (3) use of conscription to secure men for the armed forces (4) nomination of General McClellan for the Presidency.
5. Which group in England showed the most sympathy for the Union during the Civil War? (1) large landowners (2) governing classes (3) factory workers (4) merchants.
6. The chief reason why the English commercial class supported the Confederacy instead of the North in the Civil War was that the South (1) was fighting for the preservation of its social structure (2) was more likely to win the war (3) was more likely to repay debts to British citizens (4) was more likely to provide favorable tariff conditions for British goods.
7. England did not recognize the Confederacy during the Civil War because (1) England needed Northern wheat (2) England never had much trade with the South (3) England needed Northern manufactures (4) Russia favored the South.
8. Which dispute involved the United States and France? (1) Florida boundary dispute (2) *Alabama* claims (3) *Trent* Affair (4) Maximilian Affair.
9. Our demand that French forces be removed from Mexico after the Civil War is an example of our enforcement of (1) the federal Constitution (2) the Monroe Doctrine (3) Washington's Proclamation of Neutrality (4) Clay's American System.

10. Which advantage did the North *lack* in fighting the Civil War? (1) large population (2) more industry (3) greater financial resources (4) interior lines of communications in a defensive war.

11. In financing the Civil War, which method did the North *not* employ? (1) higher excise taxes (2) increased price of Western lands (3) issuance of greenbacks (4) selling bonds to national banks.

12. Lincoln's Secretary of State, later responsible for the purchase of Alaska, was (1) John Q. Adams (2) William H. Seward (3) William T. Sherman (4) John W. Booth.

13. The designer of the Union's ironclad ship, the *Monitor*, was (1) John Ericsson (2) David G. Farragut (3) James Mason (4) Clement Vallandigham.

ESSAY QUESTIONS

1. Discuss *two* reasons to support *each* of the following statements: (*a*) The campaign to win the Senate seat from Illinois made Abraham Lincoln a national figure. (*b*) Abraham Lincoln made bold use of his Presidential powers. (*c*) Lincoln's public addresses deserve the praise they have received. (*d*) Abraham Lincoln's views on slavery were moderate in comparison with the views of other leaders of the period.

2. Giving *two* reasons, discuss which item in each of the following pairs did more to win the Civil War for the North: (*a*) the McCormick reaper or the skill of the Union generals, (*b*) the blockade of Southern ports or the attitude of foreign powers, (*c*) the statesmanship of President Lincoln or the superior resources of the North.

3. In regard to the Civil War, discuss (*a*) *two* ways in which writers helped bring about the Civil War, (*b*) *two* reasons why the South seceded from the Union, (*c*) *two* problems faced by the Union in conducting the Civil War, (*d*) *two* problems faced by the Confederacy in conducting the Civil War.

Part 7. An Embittered South Is Brought Back Into the Union

RECONSTRUCTION: MEANING AND PROBLEMS

The term *reconstruction* refers to the years from 1865 to 1877 when the American people reestablished the Southern states as an integral part of the Union. In so doing, Americans had to answer the following questions:

1. What conditions should be placed upon the Southern states before permitting them to return to the Union and to assume their former rights?

2. Which branch of the federal government—executive or legislative— should determine the conditions for the return of the Southern states?

3. What political, economic, and social rights should be granted to the Negroes, and how should these rights be enforced?

LINCOLN'S PLAN OF RECONSTRUCTION

Abraham Lincoln believed that (1) the Southern states had never seceded, since no state could legally leave the Union, (2) the rebellion against the federal government was the work of individual Southerners, (3) reconstruction was a task for the President because of his constitutional power to pardon acts against the government, and (4) reconstruction should be lenient, seeking primarily to regain the South's loyalty to the Union.

In 1863 Lincoln proposed that (1) all Southerners (except high military and government leaders) be pardoned upon taking an oath of allegiance to the Union, and (2) when 10 percent of the voters in a state took this oath of allegiance, they be permitted to form a legal state government. These generous provisions for political reconstruction became known as Lincoln's *10 percent plan.*

JOHNSON RETAINS LINCOLN'S VIEWS ON RECONSTRUCTION

Andrew Johnson, thrust into the Presidency in 1865 by Lincoln's assassination, was a pro-Union Tennessee Democrat. He had been placed on the 1864 ticket with Lincoln in order to attract votes and emphasize national unity. Johnson lacked Lincoln's prestige with the people and Lincoln's influence with the Republican party. Although courageous, Johnson was also stubborn and tactless.

As President, Johnson essentially continued Lincoln's conciliatory reconstruction plan. He offered pardons to most Southerners who pledged allegiance to the Union and who agreed to the abolition of slavery. He accepted the government of every Southern state that disowned its act of secession, that repudiated the Confederate debt, and that ratified the Thirteenth Amendment prohibiting slavery. By late 1865 white Southerners had reestablished all but one of their state governments and had elected Senators and Representatives, including some prominent ex-Confederates, to the federal Congress.

CONGRESS, UNDER RADICAL REPUBLICAN LEADERSHIP, OPPOSES JOHNSON

The Congress that met in December, 1865, soon came under the domination of the *Radical Republicans,* led by Senator *Charles Sumner* and Representative *Thaddeus Stevens.* At the urging of the Radical Republicans, Congress refused to recognize the leniently reconstructed Southern governments and to seat their delegations. The Radical Republicans condemned the entire Lincoln-Johnson reconstruction program for:

1. **Infringing Upon the Powers of Congress.** The Radical Republicans claimed that the Southern states had in fact seceded. Since only Congress

had the power to admit a state into the Union, the Radical Republicans insisted that Congress had the sole power to determine the conditions for Southern readmission.

2. Being Too Lenient. The Radical Republicans argued that the South had to be treated harshly and be severely punished as a conquered province, so as to deter any future challenge to federal authority.

3. Endangering Republican Influence. In the leniently reconstructed Southern states, the Democrats, including former Confederate leaders, regained control. They prevented Negroes from voting, thereby depriving Republicans of their largest potential block of Southern votes. The Radical Republicans feared that Southern and Northern Democrats together would win control of Congress.

4. Abandoning the Negroes. In the leniently reconstructed Southern states, the Negroes were regulated by state laws called *Black Codes.* Most codes, although they listed certain Negro privileges, denied Negroes the right to bear arms, serve on juries, and hold public office. Furthermore, unemployed Negroes might be sentenced to work as "apprentices" to white masters—remindful of pre-Civil War days. The Negroes, the Radical Republicans insisted, needed protection.

CONGRESSIONAL RECONSTRUCTION

1. The **Civil Rights Act of 1866,** passed over Johnson's veto, sought to weaken the Black Codes. The law gave Negroes equal rights with whites and authorized the use of federal troops for its enforcement.

2. The **Freedmen's Bureau Act of 1866,** also passed over Johnson's veto, extended the life of this federal agency. Staffed chiefly by Radical Republican supporters, the Freedmen's Bureau provided the newly freed Negroes with food, clothing, and schooling; found work for them; and protected their civil rights. The new law permitted the Bureau to use military force when necessary.

3. The **Fourteenth Amendment,** proposed in 1866, (a) made the Negroes citizens, by declaring that all persons born or naturalized in the United States are citizens both of the United States and of the state in which they reside, (b) provided that no state may "deprive any person of life, liberty, or property without due process of law," or "deny to any person . . . equal protection of the laws," (c) called for a reduction in the Congressional representation of a state that deprived any of its male citizens of the right to vote, (d) declared the Confederate debt void, and (e) disqualified most former Confederate leaders from holding office unless pardoned by Congress.

As every Southern state except Tennessee refused to ratify the Fourteenth

Amendment, the Radical Republicans became further enraged and pressed on with more stringent reconstruction measures.

4. The **First Reconstruction Act,** passed in 1867 over Johnson's veto, as well as later supplementary measures, rejected as illegal all the reconstructed Southern governments except Tennessee. The legislation divided the South into five military districts, each under a military governor commanding federal troops. To remove military rule and be readmitted into the Union, the states had to meet certain conditions: (*a*) Each state had to conduct an election, open to Negro and white voters, for delegates to a constitutional convention. (*b*) Each new state constitution had to guarantee Negro suffrage and receive the approval of the voters, as well as of Congress. (*c*) The state legislature elected under the new constitution had to ratify the Fourteenth Amendment. An additional requirement, placed upon the four Southern states that had not met these demands by 1869, was ratification of the Fifteenth Amendment prohibiting any state from denying Negro suffrage.

In 1870 the last of the Southern states was readmitted by Congress into the Union. Nevertheless, federal troops, operating under the *Force Acts* (1870 and 1871), remained in the South to protect the rights of Negroes and to support the state governments formed under Congressional reconstruction.

IMPEACHMENT OF JOHNSON

1. **Tenure of Office Act (1867).** Infuriated by Johnson's vetoes and by his public statements denouncing Congressional reconstruction, the Radical Republicans determined to find cause for removing him from office. Again over Johnson's veto, Congress passed the *Tenure of Office Act.* It forbade the President from discharging important government officials without the consent of the Senate. To test the constitutionality of this law, Johnson removed from office his Secretary of War, Edwin M. Stanton, a Radical Republican.

2. **Failure of the Impeachment.** Led by Thaddeus Stevens, the House of Representatives quickly impeached Johnson on grounds of "high crimes and misdemeanors." The House bill of particulars, however, was repetitious, vague, and muddled. The Senate sat as the jury and heard the evidence. As seven Republican Senators voted with the Democrats, the Radical Republicans failed by one vote to secure the two-thirds majority necessary for conviction.

Johnson's acquittal upheld the American principle of Presidential independence of Congress. Johnson's conviction might have started a precedent that the President is responsible to Congress. This would be akin to the British system, in which a Prime Minister may be forced to resign by Parliament.

Johnson remained as President until March, 1869, the end of his term. He was succeeded by General Ulysses S. Grant, who had barely won the election of 1868 as the candidate of the Radical Republicans.

RECONSTRUCTION GOVERNMENTS OF THE SOUTHERN STATES

1. Controlling Political Groups. With the former Confederate leaders barred from office, the Southern state governments during Congressional reconstruction fell into the hands of:

a. Carpetbaggers. Northerners who went South after the Civil War had mixed motives. Some were eager to help the Negroes adjust to freedom. Others sought to further their own fortunes through business and politics. Since many of these newcomers carried their belongings in a traveling bag of carpeting material, Southern whites contemptuously named them *carpetbaggers.* During the Reconstruction Era, carpetbaggers dominated the governments of the Southern states.

b. Scalawags. Some Southern whites, many pro-Union during the Civil War, cooperated with the carpetbaggers. They were labeled by the other Southerners as rascals, or *scalawags.*

c. Negroes. Southern Negroes, who had been enfranchised by the Fifteenth Amendment, were mostly illiterate and inexperienced. Together with some whites, the Negroes provided the votes to elect "carpetbag governments." Negroes, some educated and capable, held a number of public offices, but they never controlled any Southern state government.

2. Criticism of the Reconstruction Governments. The "carpetbag governments" were marked by graft and corruption, wild spending, heavy taxation, and tremendous increases in the public debt. These governments nevertheless remained in power, protected by federal troops. Southern whites referred to Congressional reconstruction as a "tragic era" and a "crime."

3. Defense of the Reconstruction Governments. Supporters of Congressional reconstruction have pointed out that the "carpetbag governments" (*a*) framed liberal constitutions that guaranteed civil liberties, provided universal male suffrage, reapportioned legislative districts fairly according to population, and abolished imprisonment for debt, (*b*) began to rebuild the South by constructing public buildings and roads, and by extending grants to railroads, (*c*) introduced free, compulsory public education, and (*d*) were no more guilty of graft and corruption than governments elsewhere in the nation. (In New York City the *Tweed Ring* defrauded taxpayers of millions of dollars. In Washington the Grant administration, 1869–1877, was honeycombed with dishonesty.)

FACTORS ENABLING SOUTHERN WHITES TO REGAIN CONTROL OF THEIR STATE GOVERNMENTS

1. **Ku Klux Klan.** Southern whites organized secret societies, most notably the *Knights of the White Camelia* and the *Ku Klux Klan*. These organizations operated to drive out the carpetbaggers, to frighten the scalawags, and to intimidate the Negroes so as to keep them from voting. Klansmen, wearing weird, white-hooded robes, threatened Negroes, burned their homes, flogged them, and sometimes lynched them. Increasingly terrorized, Negroes refrained from exercising their political rights. Klan activities were subdued but never completely suppressed by federal forces acting under the Force Acts.

2. **Increased Number of Southern White Voters.** Each year new white voters came of age. Furthermore, in 1872, 160,000 former Confederates regained their political rights as Congress passed the *Amnesty Act*.

3. **Waning Northern Interest in Negro Problems.** Disappointed with the carpetbag governments, Northerners grew weary of reconstruction. Industrialists seeking business in the South wanted an end to social and political turmoil. Reformers turned from the crusade for Negro equality to other issues: curtailing the abuses of big business, securing civil service reform, and aiding the farmer.

Also, Northerners came to believe that the South could not be coerced into changing its traditional attitude toward Negroes and that Southerners themselves should work out the problems of race relations. In both North and South, leaders sought genuine reconciliation, even at the expense of Negro rights.

4. **Presidential Election of 1876.** The Democrats nominated Governor *Samuel J. Tilden* of New York for President against the Republican nominee, Governor *Rutherford B. Hayes* of Ohio. After a bitter contest, Tilden received 184 electoral votes, Hayes received 165, and both candidates claimed the remaining 20 votes: 1 from Oregon and 19 from Louisiana, Florida, and South Carolina. These were the last three Southern states still under carpetbag rule. Congress established an electoral commission of eight Republicans and seven Democrats to assign the disputed votes. The commission, by an 8-to-7 decision, gave all 20 votes to Hayes. Despite Tilden's popular majority of 200,000, Hayes became President by an electoral vote of 185 to 184.

Hayes and his supporters calmed the Democratic opposition by offering to (a) provide federal funds for internal improvements in the South, (b) appoint a Southerner to a Cabinet post, and (c) remove all federal troops from the South. In 1877, soon after taking office, Hayes withdrew the troops, whereupon the remaining carpetbag governments collapsed. Reconstruction was over.

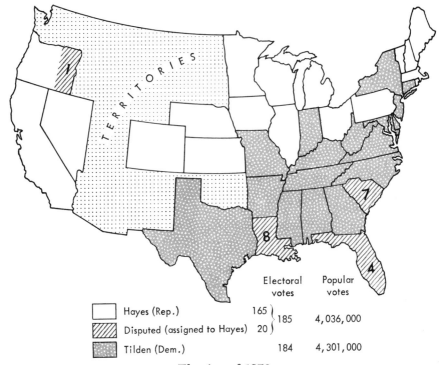

	Electoral votes	Popular votes
Hayes (Rep.)	165 ⎫ 185	4,036,000
Disputed (assigned to Hayes)	20 ⎭	
Tilden (Dem.)	184	4,301,000

Election of 1876

DIFFERING OPINIONS REGARDING RECONSTRUCTION

1. Harsh Aspects. Southern whites suffered the evils of carpetbag government and military occupation. They resented the use of Negroes in the occupation troops. Southern states were compelled to ratify the Fourteenth Amendment and give the illiterate, newly freed Negroes equal political and civil rights while experienced white leaders were barred from office. Some historians believe that Southerners resented the Era of Reconstruction even more than they did the Civil War. Southerners retained a legacy of bitterness toward the North and toward the Negro.

2. Lenient Aspects. Most Southern whites regained their political rights immediately by merely taking an oath of loyalty. Most Confederate leaders were pardoned within seven years, a short period. No Confederate leader was tried or executed for treason. Except for the loss of slaves, Southern whites were not subjected to economic penalties. They were not forced to pay reparations for war damages or to give up plantation lands for distribution to poor whites and landless Negroes. Southern whites experienced military rule and carpetbag government for a short time—depending on the state, from 2 to 10 years. Thereafter, they circumvented the Fourteenth and Fifteenth Amendments and placed Negroes in a subordinate status. Some historians maintain that vanquished rebels have rarely been treated so mildly.

LASTING RESULTS OF THE CIVIL WAR AND RECONSTRUCTION

ABOLITION OF SLAVERY AND CONSTITUTIONAL GUARANTEE OF NEGRO RIGHTS

During the Civil War the slaves constituted a valuable Southern military asset. They worked the farms and plantations, and performed many noncombat army tasks, thus releasing the whites for battle duty. To hinder the Southern war effort, Lincoln in 1863 issued the *Emancipation Proclamation*. It freed the slaves in the states in rebellion, but not in the border states loyal to the Union. In 1865 the Thirteenth Amendment completely abolished slavery. In 1868 the Fourteenth Amendment guaranteed the former slaves the status of citizens and equal protection of the laws. In 1870 the Fifteenth Amendment assured them the right to vote.

DISCRIMINATION AGAINST THE NEGRO IN THE SOUTH

By 1900 Southern whites had found the following ways to evade the Fourteenth and Fifteenth Amendments: (1) Southern states required a poll tax, which discouraged Negroes, most of them being poor, from voting. (2) Southern states established difficult and unfair literacy requirements, which barred Negroes, most of them being poorly educated, from voting. (3) Some states enacted a *grandfather clause*, exempting from literacy requirements persons whose grandfathers had been eligible to vote before the Civil War. Since the Negroes had then been slaves and ineligible to vote, this exemption benefited only the whites. (4) The Democratic party denied membership to Negroes and thus kept them from voting in party primaries. This had the effect of disenfranchising Negroes, since, in the South, the Democratic nomination was equivalent to election. (5) Southern states enacted *Jim Crow*, or segregation, laws. These laws kept Negroes separated from whites in such places as railroads, hotels, restaurants, beaches, and schools. Facilities provided for the Negroes were usually inferior. (For subsequent efforts to gain for the Negro his full rights as an American citizen, see pages 317–332.)

BEGINNINGS OF NEGRO EDUCATION IN THE SOUTH

Formal schooling for Negroes in the South started with the Freedmen's Bureau. This federal agency had spent over $5 million by 1870 to teach

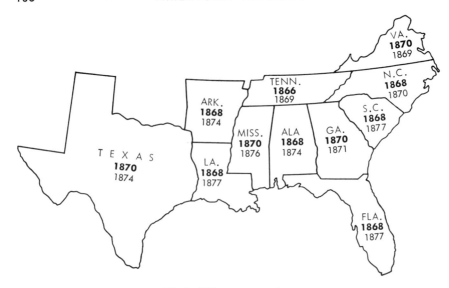

End of Reconstruction

(Dates in boldface indicate readmission to the Union.
Dates in lightface indicate end of carpetbag governments.)

Negroes to read and write. Furthermore, it cooperated with Northern philanthropists in establishing Negro schools of higher learning: *Howard University, Hampton Institute,* and *Fisk University.* In 1881 the *Tuskegee Institute* for vocational training for Negroes began instruction under the leadership of the Negro educator *Booker T. Washington.*

Negroes as well as whites were guaranteed free compulsory public education by the reconstruction constitutions of Southern states. However, after the Southern whites regained control, Negroes received schooling that was segregated and inferior. (For Supreme Court decisions regarding segregation in public schools, see page 319.)

SUPREMACY OF THE FEDERAL GOVERNMENT

The Civil War and the Reconstruction Era marked the triumph of nationalism over sectionalism. Never again has a state threatened to secede. The United States emerged as one nation, indivisible and indissoluble. Further, by the Fourteenth and Fifteenth Amendments, Congress and the Supreme Court gained the power to challenge state activities denying "due process" and "equal protection of the laws."

EXPANSION OF PRESIDENTIAL POWERS IN WARTIME

By suspending habeas corpus and freeing slaves through an executive order, Lincoln exercised powers never before used by an American President. Such expansion of Presidential powers was inevitable because a modern war demands vigorous leadership, and this can come only from the nation's chief executive, the President.

THE "SOLID SOUTH"

Southern whites resented the Republican party because Republicans had controlled the federal government during the Civil War and the Reconstruction Era. Therefore, the South developed a tradition of voting almost solidly Democratic in local, state, and national elections.

The first crack in the "Solid South" appeared in the Presidential election of 1928. Four Southern states voted for the Republican candidate, Herbert Hoover. They rejected Alfred E. Smith, the Democratic nominee, because he opposed prohibition and was a Roman Catholic. Since 1948 various Southern states have denied support to Democratic Presidential candidates, in part because each strongly supported civil rights for Negroes. In the 1960's Southern voters began electing a noticeable number of Republicans to Congress and to state offices. In 1972, the eleven states of the Old Confederacy all went to Richard Nixon, the Republican Presidential candidate. Seemingly, the South has abandoned its 100-year-old legacy of voting solidly Democratic.

DEVELOPMENTS IN THE SOUTHERN ECONOMY

1. **Physical and Economic Devastation.** The South was physically ruined by the war. Its lands were devastated, its railroads demolished, and its cities ravaged by the military campaigns waged on its soil. The Southern economy was destroyed as the war (a) kept Southern cotton from Northern and European markets, (b) exhausted Southern wealth for war needs, and (c) resulted in freeing the slaves without payment to the former owners.

2. **Revival of Southern Agriculture**

   a. Sharecropping. At the close of the Civil War, Southern plantation owners had land but no labor, and the newly freed slaves had no land but needed work. This situation led to the rise of *sharecropping.* The plantation owner (often a merchant who had bought the plantation from the prewar owner) provided the sharecropper—Negro or poor white—with a few acres of land and perhaps a cabin, a mule, and tools. In exchange, the plantation owner received a 50-percent or larger share of the crop. Often the sharecropper also pledged a share of his crop to the local merchant to secure credit to buy foodstuffs, seeds, and tools.

The standard of living and the productivity of the sharecropper were extremely low. He had a meager knowledge of farming techniques, worked with crude equipment, employed little or no fertilizer, and depleted the soil of its minerals by continuous planting of a single cash crop, such as tobacco or cotton. Owing the plantation owner and merchant a large portion of his crop, the sharecropper found himself entrapped in mounting debt and practically bound to his farm.

b. Diversified Agriculture. To end dependence upon a single crop and to halt soil depletion, Southern farmers near the end of the century turned to diversified agriculture. Today, the South raises varied crops, including fruits, vegetables, soybeans, and peanuts.

3. Development of Industry: The "New South." Learning from their experience in the Civil War, Southerners realized the importance of establishing industries. The South had cheap labor, a plentiful water supply, valuable minerals, and agricultural products. Iron and coal gave rise to steel mills; tobacco to cigarette factories; cotton to textile mills; timber to paper mills and furniture plants; oil to refineries and chemical works. Despite low wages and poor working conditions, Southerners left the countryside and flocked to the new factory towns. Birmingham, Alabama, developed into a steel center and became known as the *Pittsburgh of the South.*

Although the industrial growth of the South lagged behind that of the rest of the nation, in 1900 Southern manufacturing output was four times the pre-Civil War level. To describe the industrialization of the South, historians use the term the *New South.*

EFFECTS OF THE WAR ON THE NORTH

1. Economic Prosperity. During the Civil War, Northern industrialists operated their factories at full capacity and even built new factories to meet the unprecedented demand. They overcame labor shortages by rapidly introducing new machinery. Given impetus by the war years, captains of industry soon created tremendous empires in meat-packing, flour-milling, oil-refining, and steel production. The United States entered an age of enterprise (see pages 231–239).

2. Republican Control. The Republican party, largely favorable to Northern business interests, dominated the federal government. Republican legislators furthered business interests by such measures as the *Morrill Tariff Act* (1861), which sharply raised import duties; the *National Banking Act* (1863), which set up a system of banks chartered by the national government; and various laws providing land grants to railroads. For many years after the Civil War, the Republicans retained control of the government.

EFFECTS OF THE WAR ON THE WEST

Western farmers prospered as the war increased the demand for foodstuffs. To overcome labor shortages, farmers purchased improved farm machinery, especially more efficient plows and reapers. Western agriculture was furthered by Congressional acts such as the *Homestead Act* (1862), which gave 160 acres free to any head of a family who cultivated the land for five years; the *Morrill Act* (1862), which encouraged agricultural education by providing for the establishment of land-grant colleges; and land grants for transcontinental railroads. Free homesteads and improved transportation, in addition to the natural resources of the West, attracted many Easterners and immigrants after the Civil War, and the population of the West increased rapidly.

MULTIPLE-CHOICE QUESTIONS

1. President Lincoln's plan for reconstruction was based on the theory that the Confederate States (1) were to be treated as territories (2) could be readmitted to the Union by Congress only (3) had never actually left the Union (4) were to be occupied by Union forces for a period of 20 years.

2. The Radical Republicans in Congress after the Civil War (1) favored Lincoln's ideas on Southern reconstruction (2) passed the Black Codes (3) regarded the Southern states as conquered territories (4) voted against the Tenure of Office Act.

3. The purpose of the Black Codes was to (1) aid the carpetbaggers (2) grant suffrage to Negroes (3) prevent exploitation of freedmen (4) restrict the civil rights of Negroes.

4. An important objective of Congressional reconstruction was to (1) destroy the economy of the South (2) maintain Republican domination of the national government (3) restore pre-Civil War conditions in the South (4) pardon Southern leaders for Civil War activities.

5. Which development was the result of the other three? (1) activities of the carpetbaggers and scalawags (2) formation of the "Solid South" (3) passage of the Reconstruction Acts (4) ratification of the Fourteenth Amendment.

6. During Reconstruction, which branch of the national government attempted to achieve supremacy over another? (1) judicial over legislative (2) executive over judicial (3) legislative over executive (4) legislative over judicial.

7. The impeachment case against President Andrew Johnson was tried in the (1) House of Representatives (2) Court of Appeals for the District of Columbia (3) United States Supreme Court (4) United States Senate.

8. Thaddeus Stevens was the (1) Radical Republican leader in the House of Representatives (2) Radical Republican leader in the Senate (3) Chief Justice of the Supreme Court (4) Secretary of War under President Andrew Johnson.

9. In the Presidential election of 1876, (1) three Southern states each submitted two sets of electoral votes (2) a third party was influential in the outcome (3) the Republican party returned to power for the first time since 1860 (4) the stationing of federal troops in the South had no political effect.

10. An important result of the Civil War was that it (1) discouraged banks from securing national charters (2) strengthened our ties with Great Britain (3) helped make industry rather than agriculture the basis of our economy (4) established equality for the Negro in the South.

11. Sharecropping in the post-Civil War South meant that (1) Southern planters exchanged crops for Northern manufactured goods (2) more than one crop shared the land on a plantation (3) former slaves formed cooperatives to share the costs of buying farms (4) impoverished planters and former slaves supplied each other's need for land and labor.

12. In the South, near the end of the 19th century, (1) cotton growing was abandoned (2) sharecropping disappeared (3) the size of the plantations was increased (4) agriculture became diversified.

13. Which was *not* a method used to keep Negroes from voting? (1) Fifteenth Amendment (2) poll tax (3) literacy test (4) activities of the Ku Klux Klan.

14. The term "New South" refers to all of the following *except* (1) tobacco-processing plants (2) furniture factories (3) textile mills (4) cotton plantations.

15. Which section of the United States was most directly affected by the Homestead Act? (1) South (2) New England (3) West (4) Central Atlantic states.

16. Booker T. Washington was (1) a Negro educator who urged vocational training (2) a former Confederate leader elected Governor of Alabama (3) a Northern capitalist who built the Southern steel industry (4) a carpetbagger active in Louisiana reconstruction politics.

17. Which was *not* a result of the Civil War? (1) abolition of slavery (2) end of Jim Crow laws (3) supremacy of the federal government (4) prosperity in the industrial North.

ESSAY QUESTIONS

1. (*a*) Discuss briefly *two* reasons why Congress rejected President Lincoln's plan for readmission of the Southern states. (*b*) Describe *one* social result and *one* political result that the Reconstruction Period brought about in the South. (*c*) Discuss briefly *two* important economic changes in the South since the Civil War.

2. The extension of democracy, the unification of the nation, and disputes between the President and Congress over the use of power have often been important national issues. For the period of the Civil War and Reconstruction, give specific evidence to show that *each* of these three issues was present.

3. War inevitably has far-reaching effects upon a nation. Show how the Civil War and Reconstruction affected *each* of the following: (*a*) the powers of the states, (*b*) American industry, (*c*) the Negro, (*d*) the powers of the President.

4. Southern whites as well as Negroes have condemned Congressional reconstruction, but for vastly different reasons. (*a*) Explain *two* reasons why Southern whites have condemned Congressional reconstruction. (*b*) Explain *two* reasons why Negro leaders have condemned Congressional reconstruction. (*c*) Briefly evaluate Congressional reconstruction and give *two* reasons to support your evaluation.

UNIT V. THE UNITED STATES CHANGES FROM AN AGRICULTURAL TO AN INDUSTRIAL SOCIETY

Part 1. The Frontier Influences American Development

THE FRONTIER: DEFINITION

The *frontier* in American history refers to the furthermost region of settlement—an imaginary line dividing civilization from wilderness. The United States Census Bureau defined the frontier as that area having less than six but more than two persons per square mile.

For almost 300 years, from colonial times to the end of the 19th century, the frontier was part of the American environment. In 1650 the frontier ran along the Atlantic Coast. By 1750 it spread to the foothills of the Appalachian Mountains. By 1840 it reached the Mississippi River. By 1890 the West was sufficiently populated for the Census Bureau to consider the frontier as closed.

REASONS FOR WESTWARD MIGRATION

1. Adventure. The West, with its Indians, wild animals, rugged country, and unexplored regions, attracted men who sought the thrill of adventure and discovery.

2. Improvement of Economic Conditions. Eastern farmers and city workers considered the West as the land of opportunity. They went west looking for fertile land, fur-bearing animals, timber, and precious minerals—gold, silver, copper, and iron. Southern planters, having exhausted the soil by the continuous growing of cotton, looked to the Southwest for new fertile land. Most Americans agreed with Horace Greeley when he advised, "Go west, young man, and grow up with the country."

3. Greater Social and Political Democracy. In the more settled Eastern states, the lower classes became sharply divided from the wealthier classes and found it difficult to improve their social status. They also resented the slow pace at which state governments extended democratic rights. Many poorer Americans therefore migrated to the West, where they would encounter neither rigid class distinctions nor opposition by the upper classes to the extension of democracy.

PEAK PERIODS OF WESTWARD MIGRATION

1. After the American Revolution. Farmers and workers along the Atlantic seaboard suffered postwar economic distress. Now that the British prohibition of westward migration had been ended, settlers moved west. The population influx enabled three new states to enter the Union—Kentucky, Tennessee, and Ohio.

2. After the War of 1812. Many New Englanders lost their jobs as the shipping industry declined. Meanwhile, Europeans were fleeing the poverty and autocracy of the Post-Napoleonic Era. With the Indian menace lessened by federal troops, settlers went southwest to Mississippi and Alabama, and northwest to Indiana and Illinois.

3. During the Era of Manifest Destiny

a. Mormons in Utah. The *Mormons*, or *Latter-Day Saints*, were a religious sect founded in 1830 in upstate New York by the prophet *Joseph Smith*. The Mormons differed from other Christian sects in that they believed in the *Book of Mormon*, a collection of religious revelation and prophecy. Subjected to persecution in the East, the Mormons continually fled, migrating westward. In 1844 Joseph Smith was murdered in Illinois by an anti-Mormon mob.

Brigham Young, a strong-willed man, assumed leadership. Determined to save the Mormons from further persecution, Young in 1847 led his people far into the unpopulated West to the Great Salt Lake Valley in Utah. (This territory was part of the Mexican Cession soon to be acquired by the United States.)

Despite Utah's inhospitable mountains and deserts, the Mormon settlers survived and prospered. They built irrigation systems, transformed desert land into good farmland, founded Salt Lake City, and sold supplies to migrants traveling the northern route to California.

b. Fortune Hunters. The discovery of gold in California in 1848 brought a gold rush, as the *Forty-Niners* went west to seek their fortunes. Ten years later, discoveries of gold at *Pikes Peak* in Colorado and of gold and silver in the *Comstock Lode* in Nevada set off new stampedes of fortune seekers.

4. After the Civil War

a. Farmers. War veterans were restless for new homes. Farmers desired more fertile lands. Europeans responded to the advertising campaigns of steamship companies seeking passengers. Europeans as well as Easterners answered advertisements by transcontinental railroads seeking to sell lands granted them by the federal and state governments. Migration was further encouraged by the Homestead Act (1862), which granted free federal land to settlers. The federal government also helped the westward movement by sending troops to subdue the Plains Indians.

b. Miners. There was another gold rush in 1875, when gold was discovered in the Black Hills of South Dakota. However, mining in the West was changing, and the individual prospector soon disappeared. By the 1880's big business companies had taken over, buying up claims, systematizing exploration, and introducing the latest mining processes and machinery. These corporations ended the romantic era of the mining frontier.

LAST FRONTIER: THE GREAT PLAINS

LOCATION AND CHARACTERISTICS

The term "Great Plains" refers to a region over 500 miles wide, extending from the first tier of states west of the Mississippi to the foothills of the Rocky Mountains. The soil is fertile and suitable for grazing animals and growing wheat. The Great Plains are generally level and treeless, and receive little rainfall.

RAILROADS CROSS THE GREAT PLAINS

In 1869 the *Union Pacific* and *Central Pacific Railroads* came together at Promontory Point, Utah, to complete the first transcontinental railroad. By the 1890's American railroad men had completed four more transcontinental railroads. The railroads were the fastest and most convenient means of reaching the Great Plains and the Far West.

INDIAN PROBLEM

1. Indian Hostility to Whites. The Plains Indians—such as the Comanches, Cheyennes, and Sioux—were nomadic, horse-riding peoples. From the buffalo, which roamed the Plains in huge herds, the Indians secured food, clothing, and shelter.

The Plains Indians resented (a) white settlers for taking their lands, (b) white hunters for wantonly slaying buffalo for pelts and for sport, (c) white communities for upsetting the traditional migratory paths of buffalo herds, and (d) white traders and government officials for cheating and robbing them, and breaking promises.

2. Indian Wars (To About 1890). For over 25 years the Plains Indians battled wagon trains, settlers, and federal troops in savage guerrilla warfare. In 1876, after white men had invaded an area in South Dakota assigned to the Indians, the Sioux, led by *Sitting Bull*, overwhelmed General *George A. Custer* in his "last stand" at the Battle of Little Big Horn. Despite this and lesser victories, the Indian cause was doomed. The Indians lacked manpower, organization, equipment, and—with the extermination of the buffalo herds— food. By the 1880's most Indians were confined to specific, usually undesirable lands, called *reservations*. They received food, clothing, and shelter from the federal government but were treated as inferiors, or wards.

3. Improved Treatment of the Indians. (*a*) In 1881 *Helen Hunt Jackson* helped awaken Americans to their shameful treatment of the Indians by her book *A Century of Dishonor*. (*b*) In 1887 the *Dawes Act* divided reservation land into 160-acre farms. The Indians who received these farms were required to give up tribal practices and were promised American citizenship. Since the Indians were unfamiliar with farming and were assigned poor lands, they were often unable to secure a living, and many became paupers. Also, most Indians sought to retain their tribal cultures. (*c*) In time, Congress realized that the tribe was basic to the Indian culture and heritage. Therefore, Congress in 1924 granted citizenship to all Indians born in the United States and in 1934 passed the *Wheeler-Howard Act*. This law restored the tribe as the center of Indian life by encouraging tribes to govern themselves and to preserve their culture.

Slowly, the Indians have recovered. The Indian population, estimated at fewer than 300,000 in 1890, exceeds 800,000 today. Since the 1960's, the federal government has acted to revitalize its Bureau of Indian Affairs, to improve Indian school and health facilities, and to increase the authority of Indian tribal councils.

Calling these steps inadequate, Indian "militants" have conducted mass demonstrations and sit-ins to focus public attention on the Indians' plight: inadequate education, poverty and high unemployment, and considerable infant mortality and below-average life expectancy.

CATTLE KINGDOM (TO THE LATE 1880's)

1. Long Drive. In the late 1860's Texas ranchers became aware that their cattle, worth $4 a head in Texas, were worth $40 a head in Chicago. Cowboys began the *long drive* northward—more than a thousand miles—to deliver the cattle to the nearest railroad towns, located mostly in Kansas. They fed the moving herds on the *open range*, which was being rapidly depleted of its native buffalo herds. They fought stampedes, Indians, rustlers, and farmers. Ranchers who completed successful drives made great profits.

2. Collapse (By the Late 1880's). Greedily, cattlemen sent so many herds northward that they overgrazed the open range and oversupplied the market, driving beef prices sharply downward. In addition, farmers, arriving in increasing numbers, fenced in parts of the open range and thus reduced the grazing lands. Cattlemen fought bitter *range wars* with the farmers but to no avail. Before cattlemen could cope with the problem of limited grazing lands, disaster struck. From 1885 to 1887 severe winters and a dry summer destroyed entire herds. The cattle kingdom—romanticized in song and story —came to an end.

Big businessmen took over the cattle industry. They raised herds on fenced-in ranches, improved quality by better breeding, and moved the cattle to market on railroad lines that had been extended southward.

THE FARMER ON THE GREAT PLAINS (TO ABOUT 1900)

1. Factors Encouraging Settlement. (*a*) *Fertile Soil.* Farmers came to realize that the Great Plains, long considered the "Great American Desert," were fertile and were capable of producing abundant harvests. (*b*) *Good Transportation.* The transcontinental railroads provided easy and relatively inexpensive access to the region. (*c*) *Homestead Act (1862).* This act offered a free 160-acre farm to any settler who would cultivate it for five years. However, less than one out of every five settlers secured free homesteads, and these homesteads were usually the less desirable lands. Most settlers were compelled to buy the more desirable lands that were granted to railroads or to the states, or that were acquired, often fraudulently, by land speculators.

2. Science and Invention Aid Settlement. (*a*) Since the Great Plains were treeless, farmers lacked lumber with which to build fences. They therefore welcomed the introduction of barbed wire. (*b*) Since the Great Plains lacked sufficient rainfall, farmers pumped up water from far below the surface by employing windmills. Also, they devised dry farming techniques: plowing deep for subsurface moisture and pulverizing the soil to retard evaporation. (*c*) Since the winters on the Great Plains were severe, farmers planted new, hardier strains of winter wheat. (*d*) Since the Great Plains soil was tough, farmers utilized James Oliver's inexpensive and efficient invention, the chilled-iron plow. Increasingly, Great Plains farmers used machines—grain drills for seeding, as well as harvesters and threshers. Improved farm machinery paved the way for large-scale farming.

3. Effects of Settlement. European immigrants—Swedes, Norwegians, Danes, Germans, and Irishmen—together with Americans from the East and the Midwest, occupied the Great Plains. In three decades (1870–1900) they almost tripled the number of American farms. By 1890 they had brought to an end an environmental factor that for almost 300 years had influenced American life: the frontier.

THE FRONTIER IN AMERICAN HISTORY

INFLUENCE OF THE FRONTIER

Frederick Jackson Turner, a famous American historian, himself born on the agricultural frontier of Wisconsin, wrote the perceptive essay *The Significance of the Frontier in American History.* Turner stated: "The true point of view in the history of this nation is not the Atlantic coast, it is the Great West." He argued that the frontier was the chief influence in shaping a distinctive American way of life.

1. Social Equality. The frontiersman's survival and progress depended on his ability to hunt, fight, and farm. The frontier offered opportunity and free or cheap land to all, so that no man had to work for another. Conditions in the West prevented the rise of class distinctions and promoted the ideal of equality. The West judged a man not by his ancestors, race, religion, or national origin, but by his deeds.

2. Growth of Political Democracy. Frontiersmen believed in political equality, hated special privilege, considered the government as their servant, and insisted that it carry out the wishes of the people. The West originated such democratic reforms as universal manhood suffrage, woman suffrage, direct election of Senators, initiative, referendum, and recall. Turner claimed that democracy in the United States resulted from frontier conditions.

3. Nationalism. The frontiersmen were nationalistic because they depended on the federal government for cheap land, acquisition of new territories, and protection against the Indians.

4. Faith in the Future. Inspired by the resources of the West, the frontiersman looked to the future optimistically. His confidence became typical of most Americans.

5. Economic Independence. The frontier reduced America's economic dependence upon Europe by (a) providing raw materials and foodstuffs for the industrial cities, (b) providing a market for goods manufactured in the East, and (c) serving as a place for investment of surplus capital. Such economic independence enabled 19th-century America to follow a policy of isolation.

6. Safety Valve for Factory Workers. Knowing that workers could leave their jobs and migrate westward, employers in the East offered good wages and working conditions. Labor in the 19th century seldom sought the protection of unions. Workers had a simpler solution to their problems: going to the frontier—the "safety valve."

7. Invention. The frontier encouraged the invention of new machinery. Westward migration threatened to drain the labor market in the East. So factory owners turned to new labor-saving machines. Labor was also scarce in the West. Farmers eagerly turned to new farm machinery to increase their productivity.

8. Wasteful Agriculture. Since land was so easily available, frontiersmen were not mindful of the need for conservation of soil and forests. They cut down trees senselessly and cultivated the land unwisely, destroying its fertility.

EFFECTS OF THE CLOSE OF THE FRONTIER

Turner stated that the close of the frontier, ending the era of cheap or free land, caused many of the problems that face us today.

1. Labor. Discontented factory workers no longer had the "safety valve" of easily available land in the West. These workers therefore remained in the industrial East and turned to labor unions to improve their conditions. The struggle between capital and labor now intensified.

2. Immigration. Immigrants could no longer easily acquire farms. More of them now crowded into the cities and competed for jobs in the factories. Americans began to demand restrictions upon immigration.

3. Conservation. With the close of the frontier, the American people awakened to the need for conservation. Farmers realized that they had to take better care of their land. Timber and mining companies came to the same realization about their resources. Federal and state agencies started projects to conserve the nation's soil, water, timber, and other natural resources.

4. Imperialism. American capitalists, who had looked to the frontier for raw materials, markets, and investment opportunities, now began to look elsewhere. As a result, the United States embarked on a program of economic and political imperialism in the Caribbean, Central and South America, and the Far East.

CRITICISM OF TURNER'S FRONTIER THEORY

Many historians believe that Turner exaggerated the importance of the frontier. They claim that Turner ignored the following facts: (1) American democracy was fostered by our democratic heritage from England and by the demands of workers in the industrial East for a voice in government. (2) England developed a democratic form of government without the existence of a frontier. (3) The Southwestern frontier, settled by cotton planters, developed neither democracy nor nationalism. (4) The frontier did not serve as a "safety valve" for many Eastern factory workers, since they lacked knowledge of farming and the funds necessary to uproot and transport their families, and could not easily secure and equip farms in the West. (5) The frontier itself was the result of industrial expansion in Europe and in the northeastern part of the United States. The demand from industrial areas for raw materials and agricultural produce encouraged Western settlement. (6) Despite the frontier, 19th-century America was never economically independent. It always depended on Europe for markets for its agricultural produce and for capital with which to build up American industry.

Most historians agree that many factors, including industrialism and the factory system as well as agriculture and the frontier, have helped shape modern America.

MULTIPLE-CHOICE QUESTIONS

1. What is the best definition for the term "American frontier"? (1) a fixed boundary line (2) the Atlantic or Pacific coast line (3) a shifting area where pioneer settlement ended (4) the dividing line between French and English settlements.

2. Which one of the following characterizes *all* movements to the frontier? (1) search for religious freedom (2) greed (3) escape from political persecution (4) hardship.

3. The migration of the Mormons to Utah was (1) led by Brigham Young (2) led by Joseph Smith (3) authorized by the Mexican government (4) spurred by the discovery of gold in Utah.

4. Which state lies in the part of the United States that was settled and developed last? (1) Kentucky (2) Ohio (3) Oregon (4) South Dakota.

5. "Long drive" and "range wars" are terms most closely associated with the (1) Indian Wars (2) Forty-Niners (3) cattle kingdom (4) building of the Union Pacific Railroad.

6. The major purpose of the Homestead Act of 1862 was to (1) create future slave states (2) raise revenue for the federal government (3) encourage settlement of public lands for farming (4) provide railroad companies with new land to sell.

7. The policy of the federal government toward the Indians in the period immediately following the Civil War was to (1) move them to reservations (2) drive them from the country (3) require Indian children to attend public school (4) grant Indians full citizenship.

8. What is the generally accepted date for the disappearance of the frontier in American history? (1) 1860 (2) 1890 (3) 1910 (4) 1940.

9. Which historian would be most likely to agree that "the frontier is the most American thing in all America"? (1) James Ford Rhodes (2) George Bancroft (3) Frederick Jackson Turner (4) Arthur Schlesinger, Jr.

10. The government's land policy in the West before 1890 did *not* (1) promote wise use of the land (2) lead to the development of transportation facilities (3) permit most settlers to own their own farms (4) encourage settlers to develop a spirit of independence.

11. The Western frontier contributed to American democracy by (1) establishing the first public elementary schools (2) serving as a symbol of economic opportunity and political equality (3) supporting the establishment of Indian reservations (4) opposing government involvement in internal improvements.

12. Which one of the following was first adopted in the United States on the Western frontier? (1) elementary education (2) the town meeting (3) the granting of suffrage to women (4) separation of church and state.

13. An important influence of the expanding frontier on American life was that it *decreased* (1) our dependence on Europe (2) the growth of nationalism (3) our concern over the slavery controversy (4) our interest in manufacturing.

14. The disappearance of the frontier (1) brought new social and economic problems to the United States (2) decreased American investments abroad (3) discouraged American workers from joining unions (4) made conservation unnecessary.

ESSAY QUESTIONS

1. "Go west, young man" has been important advice for the American people. (*a*) Show *two* different ways in which the westward movement affected life in the Eastern seaboard states. (*b*) Describe *three* effects of the closing of the frontier upon American life. (*c*) What is meant by the statement that there are still frontiers in American life?

2. Giving *one* specific fact, show how each of the following was *either* a cause *or* a result of the westward movement in the 19th century: (*a*) the growth of democracy, (*b*) internal improvements, (*c*) immigration from Europe, (*d*) nationalism, (*e*) the growth of labor unions, (*f*) the development of industry, (*g*) the conservation movement.

3. The expanding frontier has influenced our nation in several ways. Give *two* facts to prove that *each* of the following statements applies to the history of our nation: (*a*) The expanding frontier has helped the growth of democracy. (*b*) The expanding frontier has led to conflicts. (*c*) The expanding frontier has helped the nation to achieve greater economic self-sufficiency.

4. (*a*) Give the provisions of the Homestead Act (1862). (*b*) Describe an effect of the Homestead Act on each of the following: (1) agriculture in the East, (2) immigration, (3) the Indian, (4) the cattle industry.

Part 2. The Farmer Struggles to Increase His Share of the National Income

INTRODUCTION: THE AGRICULTURAL REVOLUTION

BEFORE THE AGRICULTURAL REVOLUTION: COLONIAL FARMERS

The colonial farmers employed primitive implements and methods. They had only a few simple, crudely constructed tools: the rake, hoe, scythe, and wooden plow. They cultivated their farms inefficiently because they (1) had little knowledge of proper soil care, and (2) could secure additional fertile land at low cost. Although they worked long hours, usually at exhausting manual tasks, their harvests remained relatively small; productivity, or output per man, was low. Agricultural methods changed little from father to son.

AGRICULTURAL REVOLUTION: BRIEF DESCRIPTION

1. Meaning. The term *Agricultural Revolution* refers to the change from primitive to modern farming methods: the use of farm machinery and scientific agriculture. In the United States, the Agricultural Revolution began early in the 19th century and continues, at an accelerated pace, to this very day.

2. Farm Machinery. The farmer's most important piece of equipment, the plow, had been made mostly of wood until 1797, when *Charles Newbold* invented a cast-iron plow. In 1814 *Jethro Wood* designed a cast-iron plow that turned soil more easily and more deeply than any plow used before. Still more advanced plows were designed by *John Deere*, who in 1837 invented the self-cleaning steel plow, and *James Oliver*, who in 1877 perfected a plow made from chilled iron.

A pioneer in the invention of other types of farm machinery was *Cyrus McCormick*, who in 1831 invented a reaper. It cut grain many times faster than a scythe. Other agricultural inventions included the thresher to separate grain from the stalk; the harvester to cut and bind the grain; the combine to cut, thresh, and sack the grain; the tractor to pull equipment through the field; the corn planter; the potato digger; the electric milker; and the cotton picker.

3. Scientific Agriculture. Research into agricultural problems led to (*a*) the rotation of crops and the use of artificial fertilizer to renew soil fertility, (*b*) contour plowing to prevent soil erosion, (*c*) the drainage of swamps and the irrigation of dry land to change useless land to land suitable for crops, (*d*) insecticides and germicides to combat insect pests and plant diseases, (*e*) breeding of plants and animals to produce better offspring, (*f*) new uses for agricultural products, and (*g*) processing of canned, frozen, and powdered foods.

SPREAD OF AGRICULTURAL KNOWLEDGE

1. Private Efforts. Agricultural societies, fairs, and journals served to pass new agricultural knowledge on to the American farmer. In 1860 over 900 agricultural societies existed in the United States.

2. Governmental Efforts

a. The *Morrill Act* (1862) offered federal land grants to states for the endowment of colleges whose main object was to be the teaching of "agriculture and the mechanic arts." Eventually, the states received some 12 million acres of land and used the income from selling or renting the land to develop some of our leading institutions of higher learning.

b. Subsequent federal laws provided funds for (1) agricultural experiment stations affiliated with the land-grant colleges (*Hatch Act,* 1887), (2) county agents to bring agricultural information directly to the farmer (*Smith-Lever Act,* 1914), and (3) high school courses in agriculture (*Smith-Hughes Act,* 1917).

c. In 1862 Congress created the *Department of Agriculture.* In 1889 the Department was elevated to Cabinet status. The Department conducted research projects; provided marketing services; and published periodicals, pamphlets, and bulletins.

EFFECTS OF THE AGRICULTURAL REVOLUTION

1. Proportional Decrease in Farm Population. In proportion to the entire nation, our farm population decreased from 80 percent in 1860 to 40 percent in 1900. Nevertheless, farmers produced enough to feed our growing population and, in addition, provided surpluses for export.

2. Increased Production. Farmers increased their output tremendously, in terms of both output per man and total output. From 1860 to 1900, total cotton production rose almost threefold and total wheat production fourfold.

3. Increased Mechanization. As machines took over the heavy, backbreaking tasks, the farmer's work became less wearisome, but he had to learn the mechanical skills of operating and maintaining his machines.

4. End of Farm Isolation. With the invention of the telephone and the automobile, farmers came into closer contact with the world around them. They no longer lived in isolation.

5. Shift From Self-Sufficient to Commercial Farming. Until the middle of the 19th century, most farmers were self-sufficient, or subsistence, farmers. Using family labor, they raised the food for their own tables, and produced their own clothes, furniture, and implements. Many farmers also raised crops for sale. Increasingly after the Civil War, farmers became less self-sufficient and more commercial. They raised large quantities of a few staple crops— such as corn, cotton, or wheat. They sold these crops to industrial regions and depended on these regions for needed manufactured goods.

6. Problems Facing Commercial Farmers as Businessmen. (*a*) *Credit.* Farmers often needed long-term loans to purchase land, livestock, and machinery, and short-term loans to sustain them until harvest-time. (*b*) *Labor.* Farmers employed full-time hired hands and, at peak seasons, migratory labor. (*c*) *Production.* Farmers sought maximum harvests at minimum cost. Since they hired workers and used expensive machinery, farmers achieved greater efficiency by operating large farms. The number of small farms, consequently, steadily decreased. (*d*) **Prices.** Farmers experienced good or bad times depending upon the price their products commanded in the marketplace. (*e*) **Supplies.** Farmers relied upon industry for manufactured goods and upon other farmers for foodstuffs.

AMERICAN AGRICULTURE FROM THE CIVIL WAR TO WORLD WAR I

AGRICULTURAL PROSPERITY DURING THE CIVIL WAR

Northern and Western farmers experienced heavy demand for foodstuffs for the Union armed forces and for the thriving industrial cities. Farmers brought increased acreage under cultivation, employed more machines, and enjoyed relatively high agricultural prices.

COMPLAINTS OF FARMERS FOLLOWING THE CIVIL WAR

1. Low Agricultural Prices. After the Civil War the demand for agricultural produce declined and prices fell. Also, American farmers faced increased competition in world markets from newly plowed lands in Argentina, Australia, and Canada. Nevertheless, American farmers continued to expand their output.

Wheat farmers, who in 1866 received more than $1.50 per bushel, in 1894 received less than $.70. Corn and cotton farmers suffered similar sharp declines in prices. With such low prices, farmers had great difficulty earning a living.

2. Insufficient and Expensive Credit. Since farmers were considered poor credit risks, banks were reluctant to grant them loans. Despite state laws prohibiting usury, farmers often had to pay excessive interest rates, as high as 25 percent per year. Farmers unable to meet their mortgage payments lost their homes and farms.

3. High Rates Charged by Middlemen. Farmers complained that they received only about half the price that city consumers paid for agricultural produce. Farmers blamed this situation on the high rates charged by middlemen: grain storage elevators, packinghouses, insurance companies, wholesale distributors, and especially the railroads. Since each railroad had a virtual monopoly over the transportation of crops from the small farm towns along its tracks, farmers endured poor service and exorbitant rates. The rule that guided railroads in determining their rates was "what the traffic will bear."

4. High Industrial Prices. While farmers received low agricultural prices, they paid dearly for manufactured goods. The farmers blamed high industrial prices upon (a) high tariff rates, which kept out many foreign goods and thus protected American manufacturers from foreign competition, and (b) the growth of business monopoly, which curtailed domestic competition.

AGRARIAN CRUSADE (1865–1900)

To improve their economic conditions, farmers undertook an *Agrarian Crusade*. They joined in organizations—the Grange, the Greenback-Labor party, and the Populist party—to demand help from the states and from the federal government. These movements signaled the beginning of a significant change in American economic thinking: (1) away from the doctrine of *laissez-faire* (that the government should not interfere in economic matters), and (2) toward the doctrine of government responsibility for the economic well-being of the people.

GRANGER MOVEMENT

1. Granger Laws. The Patrons of Husbandry, or *National Grange*, founded by *Oliver H. Kelley* in 1867, was an organization of local farmers' clubs. As farmers became discontented with their economic conditions, they joined their local Granges, and these became active in state politics. Farmers elected Granger spokesmen to state legislatures, and several Midwestern states passed *Granger laws* regulating the rates and practices of grain elevators and railroads. However, in 1886, in the case of *Wabash vs. Illinois*, the Supreme Court ruled that, since railroads were engaged in interstate commerce, they were not subject to regulation by the states.

2. Granger Cooperatives. To eliminate the profits of middlemen, the Grangers established *cooperatives*, or *"co-ops."* Owned and operated by the farmers, these organizations were to do the middleman's work: grading, packing, selling, and shipping crops, and buying farm equipment and other goods at wholesale prices. The profits that the cooperatives earned were to be distributed to their farmer owners. These early "co-ops" failed, in part because of insufficient capital and inexperienced management.

3. Lasting Contributions. The Grange (a) taught farmers to work together to solve their common problems, (b) hastened federal railroad regulation, which started in 1887 with the Interstate Commerce Act (see page 241), (c) stimulated the development of mail-order houses, such as Montgomery Ward and Sears Roebuck, to compete with local middlemen, (d) paved the way for the successful present-day farm cooperatives (see pages 208-209), and (e) still serves rural communities today by providing social activities—meetings, lectures, picnics—and by lobbying in behalf of farmers.

FARMERS DEMAND INFLATION

To arrest the downward trend in agricultural prices after the Civil War, farmers demanded cheap money, or *inflation*. Cheapening the value of money would increase prices and ease the repayment of debts. For example, if wheat sold at $1 per bushel, a farmer would need 5000 bushels to pay off a $5000 mortgage. However, at an inflated price of $2 per bushel, he would need only 2500 bushels—half the amount—to pay off the same debt. True, the farmer would have to pay more for his manufactured goods, but he would benefit in the end. For, while he received higher prices for his agricultural produce, his debts would remain fixed.

Since cheap money could best be attained by having the government increase the amount of currency in circulation, the farmers supported movements for the printing of greenbacks and the coinage of silver.

GREENBACK MOVEMENT

1. Greenbacks and Inflation. During the Civil War the federal government placed into circulation more than $400 million in *greenbacks*. This was paper money supported by confidence in the government but without metallic, or specie, backing. Following the war the government started to recall the greenbacks, and money became scarcer. Farmers protested that the government was hastening the decline of agricultural prices.

2. Specie Resumption Act (1875). In spite of the farmers' protests, in 1875 Congress passed the Specie Resumption Act. It (*a*) fixed the amount of greenbacks in circulation at $346 million, and (*b*) made greenbacks redeemable in gold. This latter provision, raising greenbacks to the value of gold-backed money, continued the trend toward deflation and lower prices.

3. Greenback-Labor Party. In their fight for cheap money, farmers joined the *Greenback-Labor party*. They demanded repeal of the Specie Resumption Act and urged the issuance of more greenbacks. Although the party attracted over a million votes in the Congressional elections of 1878, it declined soon afterwards. Farmers next concentrated on the silver movement.

SILVER MOVEMENT

1. Crime of '73. For years the federal government used two metals, silver and gold, for coinage—a monetary practice called *bimetallism*. The government set the ratio between silver and gold at 16 to 1; that is, the government considered 16 ounces of silver to be worth 1 ounce of gold. Since private silversmiths needed silver commercially and offered a slightly higher price, the government received very little silver for coinage. So Congress passed the *Coinage Act* in 1873, ending the coinage of silver money, that is, *demonetiz-*

ing silver. Shortly afterwards, when miners discovered rich deposits of silver in Nevada and Colorado, the market price of silver fell sharply. Silver interests, which now wanted to sell their silver to the government, vigorously denounced the demonetization of silver as the *Crime of '73*.

2. Silver Purchase Acts (1878, 1890). Silver interests demanded that the government resume the coinage of silver at the ratio of 16 to 1, and their demand received the support of the nation's farmers. The farmers reasoned that the coinage of silver would increase the amount of money in circulation and thus cheapen the value of money. The political alliance of farmers and silver interests mustered sufficient strength in Congress to pass the *Bland-Allison Act* (1878). This law required the government to purchase and coin silver in limited quantities. The law did little to relieve the money shortage, and farmers and silver interests agitated for a further expansion of silver coinage. Congress responded in 1890 by passing the *Sherman Silver Purchase Act,* which increased the amount of silver that the government was required to buy. Like the Bland-Allison Act, it did not halt the decline of agricultural prices.

3. Effects of Silver Purchases on Currency. So much silver was now being mined that its value rapidly declined. It was now advantageous to redeem silver coin and paper money for gold. By 1893 these redemptions reduced the government's gold reserves to a bare minimum. Many people believed that the Treasury would soon be unable to redeem silver currency for gold and that the country would have to go off the gold standard.

CLEVELAND PROTECTS THE GOLD STANDARD

In 1893 the United States suffered a severe depression. President Grover Cleveland, a conservative Eastern Democrat, blamed the depression as well as gold reserve losses upon a single cause: the government's purchase of silver. He claimed that, by paying out gold for silver, the nation had drained its gold reserve and that this had caused the depression. Cleveland (1) secured Congressional repeal of the Sherman Silver Purchase Act, and (2) authorized the Treasury to obtain gold by selling bonds. He permitted the largest sale of bonds to be handled directly through the Wall Street banking house of J. Pierpont Morgan.

Cleveland's actions preserved the gold standard but did little to improve economic conditions. Cleveland was hailed by banking and business interests, which opposed inflation and favored sound money. He was condemned as a "tool of Wall Street" by the silver interests and farmers.

POPULIST PARTY

1. Origin. Farmers came to believe that Eastern industrialists and bankers controlled both the Democratic and Republican parties. Exhorted by agrarian spokesmen to "raise less corn and more hell," farmers in the 1880's established *Farmers' Alliances.* These politically minded organizations evolved into the *People's* or *Populist party.*

2. Program. Meeting in convention at Omaha, Nebraska, in 1892, the Populists adopted the following program: (*a*) Free and unlimited coinage of silver at the ratio of 16 to 1. Populists expected this proposal to increase the amount of money in circulation, then about $20 per person, to at least $50 per person. (*b*) A graduated income tax. Such a tax would bear more heavily on wealthy persons than on farmers and workers, and would provide the federal government with a source of revenue to replace the tariff. (*c*) Government ownership of telephone, telegraph, and railroad systems. Farmers looked to government ownership as a remedy for the abuses of private enterprise in the communication and transportation industries. (*d*) The secret ballot and direct election of Senators. These proposals would provide greater democracy.

To achieve a farmer-labor alliance, the Populists also endorsed pro-labor planks: shorter working hours and restrictions on immigration.

3. Early Vote-Getting Successes. In the 1892 Presidential election, the Populist candidate, General James B. Weaver, received more than one million popular votes and 22 electoral votes, all from Western states. In the 1894 Congressional elections, the Populists increased their voting strength. Elated, they looked forward confidently to the 1896 Presidential election.

ELECTION OF 1896

1. Candidates

a. William Jennings Bryan. Farmers and silver interests gained control of the Democratic nominating convention. They cheered William Jennings Bryan, the "silver-tongued orator" from Nebraska who delivered an emotional attack upon the gold standard in his famous "Cross of Gold" speech, concluding: "You shall not crucify mankind upon a cross of gold." Bryan became the Democratic candidate for President. He also won the Populist nomination.

b. William McKinley. Conservative Eastern business and banking interests controlled the Republican convention. They nominated the skillful Ohio politician William McKinley, who opposed free silver, supported the gold standard, and advocated high protective tariffs.

2. Campaign. Traveling extensively and speaking frequently, Bryan demanded reforms to help the farmer. In a larger sense, however, Bryan crusaded for social and economic justice. McKinley stayed at home, content to issue carefully prepared campaign statements. His campaign was managed by the astute *Marcus A. Hanna*. This wealthy Ohio businessman alerted his friends to warn their workers and mortgagors that they would lose their jobs and farms if Bryan were elected. Hanna received contributions of many millions of dollars for the campaign, at least ten times the amount that Bryan received. McKinley also benefited from the almost unanimous support of the press, which ridiculed Bryan as a radical, irresponsible "boy orator."

The election offered clear-cut issues: McKinley stood for the gold standard, high tariffs, and noninterference by the government with business. Bryan stood for free coinage of silver, lower tariffs, and government responsibility for the economic well-being of the people. McKinley drew his greatest support from bankers and industrialists; Bryan, from silver miners and farmers. McKinley's strength lay in the North and the East; Bryan's, in the South and the West.

3. Results. McKinley carried all industrial states and even won the older agrarian states. With **271** electoral votes to Bryan's **176**, McKinley won the election.

Shortly afterwards, the Populist party disappeared. Some Populist goals were to emerge later in the progressive movement (see pages **391–402**).

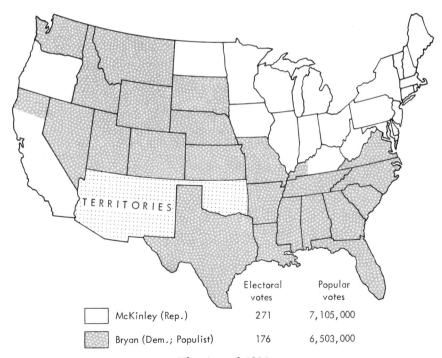

	Electoral votes	Popular votes
McKinley (Rep.)	271	7,105,000
Bryan (Dem.; Populist)	176	6,503,000

Election of 1896

TEMPORARY AGRICULTURAL PROSPERITY

Unexpectedly, after 1896, American farmers entered upon better times. (1) New goldfields were discovered in South Africa, Australia, and Alaska, and methods of gold mining were improved. The considerable increase in the supply of gold permitted an increase in the amount of money in circulation. (2) Crop failures in Europe and India led to increased foreign demand for American agricultural products. (3) Heavy immigration to the United States caused the domestic market to consume more agricultural products.

Farmers, cheered by rising agricultural prices, abandoned their interest in free silver. They offered little opposition when Congress in 1900 passed the *Gold Standard Act*. This act declared that the United States was on the gold standard and made all paper money redeemable in gold.

Farmers considered the pre-World War I years from 1900 to 1914 as the *golden age of American agriculture*.

AGRICULTURE FROM WORLD WAR I TO THE PRESENT

WORLD WAR I AND AGRICULTURE

1. Immediate Effect: Favorable. During World War I, farmers experienced a tremendous demand for agricultural produce for domestic, military, and export use. They enjoyed high prices; for example, wheat, which had sold for less than $.70 per bushel in 1894, now sold at over $2.

2. Long-Range Effect: Unfavorable. To meet the increased demand, farmers sought to increase output by purchasing more land and more farm machinery, paying inflated wartime prices. Since most farmers lacked funds, they borrowed money, often at high interest rates. After the war, demand returned to prewar levels, and prices fell. Desperate, farmers could not afford to allow their land and machines to lie idle, so they continued to produce huge surpluses, which had the effect of driving farm prices still farther downward. Many farmers, unable to meet payments on their mortgages, lost their farms through foreclosure. Having no other home or occupation, they frequently remained on the land as tenants of the new owners, usually banks and life insurance companies.

DEVELOPMENTS AFTER WORLD WAR I

1. Cooperative Movement. Farmers again turned to cooperatives. *Marketing co-ops* graded, stored, packed, sold, and shipped the produce of their members. *Purchasing co-ops* bought supplies for resale to members. Co-ops performed the functions of middlemen and distributed their profits to their members. They benefited from federal and state laws offering them loans and allowing them special tax exemptions. Today, with a membership of several million, co-ops are an essential aspect of American agriculture.

2. Farm Bloc. Congressmen from farm states, Democrats as well as Republicans, joined together as the *farm bloc* to help the farmers. During the 1920's the farm bloc secured laws providing low-interest farm loans and exempting cooperatives from prosecution as monopolies.

3. Agricultural Marketing Act (1929). To tackle the problem of surpluses, President *Herbert Hoover* requested Congress to pass the Agricultural Marketing Act. It created a *Federal Farm Board* with $500 million to lend to farm organizations. They would purchase and store surplus agricultural products until the surpluses could be resold in time of scarcity. The act failed because it made no attempt to limit production, and the Federal Farm Board soon exhausted its funds.

4. Farmers and the Great Depression (Starting in 1929). With the onset of the Depression of 1929, farmers were especially hard hit. From 1929 to 1932 wheat fell from $1.00 to $.38 a bushel; cotton fell from $.16 to $.06 a pound; average farm prices fell more than 50 percent; average cash income per farmer fell about 70 percent. Farmers could not keep up their mortgage payments or buy the necessities of life. Nebraska farmers burned their low-priced corn as fuel. Iowa and Minnesota farmers forcibly prevented mortgage foreclosures. Angry and desperate, the farm belt demanded federal action.

NEW DEAL AND AGRICULTURE

In the Presidential election of 1932, *Franklin D. Roosevelt*, the Democratic candidate, overwhelmingly defeated the incumbent, Herbert Hoover. Roosevelt received widespread support from farmers and laborers as he promised the common man a *New Deal*. Whereas Hoover had employed federal power cautiously and reluctantly, Roosevelt was prepared to experiment boldly with new ideas to solve the nation's economic ills. Roosevelt proposed to involve the government actively in assisting the farmer.

NEW DEAL AND THE PROBLEM OF FARM SURPLUSES

1. Agricultural Adjustment Act (1933). The objective of the AAA of 1933 was to raise agricultural prices in relation to industrial prices so that the farmer would regain the purchasing power he had enjoyed in the prosperous years of 1909–1914. This level of farm prices was called *parity*. If, for example, the price of wheat and the price level of industrial goods were both four times their 1909–1914 average, then wheat was said to be selling at *100* *percent of parity.* However, if the price of wheat had only tripled while the price level of industrial goods had quadrupled, then wheat was said to be selling at *75 percent of parity.*

The law tried to raise farm prices by reducing acreage under cultivation and thereby preventing the production of surpluses. It provided for (*a*) *voluntary curtailment* of production of basic commodities, such as tobacco, corn, cotton, and wheat; (*b*) *cash bounties,* or *bonus payments,* to those farmers who left a percentage of their land idle; and (*c*) *processing taxes*—to be levied on wheat millers, cotton spinners, and meat packers—to raise funds for bonus payments. In 1936 the Supreme Court declared the AAA unconstitutional on the ground that agriculture was an intrastate activity and not subject to federal regulation.

2. Soil Conservation and Domestic Allotment Act (1936). The SCDAA, quickly passed by Congress, replaced the defunct AAA. The SCDAA provided that farmers be paid a bounty for planting a percentage of their land with soil-conserving crops such as clover and alfalfa. Indirectly, this law worked to curtail production of basic agricultural crops. The Supreme Court held that conservation was a legitimate federal power and declared the SCDAA constitutional.

3. Agricultural Adjustment Act (1938). Drawing upon its experience with the two previous laws, the New Deal enacted the extensive AAA of 1938 to control farm surpluses and raise farm prices.

a. The government established *acreage quotas* for basic commodities, and paid the farmers bounties for planting soil-conserving crops on acreage withheld from production.

b. If, despite acreage quotas, farmers raised surplus crops, the government could establish *marketing quotas* with the consent of two-thirds of the farmers producing the commodity. These quotas limited the amount that the farmers could sell.

c. Farmers stored surplus crops under government seal. With the crops in storage as security, the government granted farmers *commodity loans.* The government set the loan value for each commodity at slightly below parity. In good harvest years, to prevent falling prices, farmers placed surplus crops in storage and accepted commodity loans. In bad harvest years, they could take advantage of rising prices by taking surpluses out of storage, selling the commodities, and paying off the loans. This idea, advocated by Secretary of Agriculture *Henry A. Wallace,* was called the *ever-normal granary plan.*

d. Also to bring prices up to the **1909-1914** levels, the government gave the farmers direct subsidies, called *parity payments.*

4. Evaluation of New Deal Farm Surplus Laws

a. In Favor. (1) The New Deal farm laws helped farmers secure higher prices. Between 1932 and 1940 farm income rose from less than $5 billion to over $9 billion. (2) Farmers enjoyed a fairer share of the national income. From 1932 to 1936 the parity ratio of agricultural to industrial prices rose from 55 to 90. (3) The entire nation's economy was lifted, as farmers now had the money to purchase more manufactured goods. (4) Soil conservation was widely practiced. (5) Farmers learned to follow the example of industry and adjust production to demand. (6) The farmer's confidence in the federal government was restored.

b. Against. (1) The New Deal farm laws forced domestic consumers to pay higher prices. (2) Agricultural prices above world levels caused American farmers to lose foreign markets. (3) Taxpayers were burdened with the cost of financing government spending for agriculture. (4) Complex government regulation reduced the farmer's individual initiative. (5) The farm laws proved unable to decrease output sufficiently. Even though he cultivated less land, the farmer was able to increase his total output by sharply raising his productivity per acre. The farmer retired his least fertile lands from cultivation, practiced intensive farming, and expanded the use of fertilizer. From 1930 to 1940 wheat productivity rose from 11 to 15 bushels per acre. (6) The laws brought little benefit to the tenant farmer, the sharecropper, and the migratory worker. In some cases, tenant farmers and sharecroppers were driven off their farms by the landowners, who wanted to withdraw land from production and thus qualify for bounties. (7) The laws tried to curtail agricultural production at a time when many people throughout the world were hungry.

OTHER NEW DEAL FARM MEASURES

1. Credit. The *Farm Credit Administration*, established in 1933, furnished long-term, low-interest loans to farmers to refinance existing mortgages and prevent foreclosures.

2. Electrification. The *Rural Electrification Administration (REA)*, established in 1935, provided low-interest loans to cooperatives for generators and power lines to supply electricity to rural areas not served by private utilities. The REA enabled many farmers and their families to enjoy the convenience of modern electrical appliances.

3. Aid to Tenants and Other Poor Farmers

a. Disadvantages of Tenancy. Of our farm population in the early 1930's, sharecroppers and tenant farmers comprised over 40 percent. This high percentage disturbed New Dealers, who blamed tenancy and sharecropping for much rural poverty. Tenants and sharecroppers (1) received the poorest lands to farm, (2) took poor care of the property since it was not theirs, (3) earned extremely low incomes, often less than $250 in cash per year, and (4) worked their children on the farms instead of sending them to school.

b. Federal Programs. (1) The *Resettlement Administration*, established in 1935, assisted needy farm families in moving from worn-out to more fertile lands. (2) The *Bankhead-Jones Farm Tenant Act* (1937) established the *Farm Security Administration (FSA)*, which took over the functions of the Resettlement Administration. The FSA provided loans to sharecroppers, tenant farmers, and farm laborers for the purchase of land, equipment, and supplies. Loans were made for as long as 40 years and at the low interest rate of 3 percent. (In 1946 the FSA was replaced by a new agency, the *Farmers Home Administration*.)

c. Results. Tenancy and sharecropping were reduced by (*a*) these government efforts, (*b*) the flight of poorer farmers to the city, and (*c*) farm prosperity during World War II. Of our farm population in 1969, sharecroppers and tenant farmers comprised only 13 percent, a substantial decrease from 40 percent in the 1930's.

WORLD WAR II AND AGRICULTURE

With World War II, American farmers again enjoyed a period of prosperity generated by war. The demand for farm produce increased, and prices rose to new highs. To stimulate production, the government (1) removed all restrictions on output, (2) gave special draft deferments to farmers and farm laborers, and (3) guaranteed the farmers 90 percent of parity for two years following the war. Many farmers used their increased earnings to reduce debts, replace equipment, and acquire acreage.

For several years following the war, foodstuffs from the United States were used to help feed the war-torn countries of the world, and demand for American farm goods remained high. In 1949, however, as relief needs overseas tapered off, agricultural prices turned downward. Alarmed, farmers again demanded federal action.

PERIOD OF INEFFECTIVE FARM LAWS (1949–1960)

1. Agricultural Act of 1949. This law (*a*) reaffirmed the provisions of the AAA of 1938 (see page 210) concerning acreage quotas, marketing quotas, and government commodity loans, and (*b*) guaranteed the farmers price supports at 90 percent of parity for the six basic crops: wheat, corn, cotton, rice, peanuts, and tobacco. These price supports were *rigid;* that is, the exact parity ratio was fixed by law.

Congressmen from industrial states severely criticized this law for (a) imposing higher prices for foodstuffs on city consumers, and (b) spending tax moneys to withdraw surplus farm commodities from the market.

2. Agricultural Act of 1954. This law provided for *flexible* price supports. It allowed the Secretary of Agriculture to change the price supports for most basic commodities within a range of 75 to 90 percent of parity. (In 1958 flexible price supports were extended downward to 65 percent of parity for three basic crops.) This approach, adopted over the opposition of the farm bloc, reflected the thinking of President Eisenhower and Secretary of Agriculture *Ezra Taft Benson.* They held that flexible price supports would lower crop prices, thereby (a) discouraging farmers from producing surpluses, but also (b) enabling farmers to sell more produce in the United States and to compete in foreign markets, thus increasing farm income. Secretary Benson saw the solution to the farm problem in the restoration of agriculture to a free-market economy governed by the laws of supply and demand.

3. Soil Bank Act of 1956. This law provided for payments to farmers for transferring substantial acreage—over 10 percent of the 350 million cultivated acres in the United States—from commercial production to conservation uses, such as the planting of alfalfa, clover, soil-binding grasses, and trees. By 1958 farmers had placed 28 million acres in the soil bank, but these were the least fertile lands. Also, the costs of the soil bank were high. For these reasons, Congress halted a major portion of the program.

4. Ineffectiveness of These Laws. From 1947 to 1960 the total income of farmers in the United States declined from $17 billion to $11 billion, a decrease of 35 percent. While the farmer fell behind economically, the rest of the nation advanced. From 1952 to 1960 agricultural prices fell some 25 percent while industrial prices rose 10 percent. The government meanwhile continued its effort to sustain agricultural prices by storing surplus crops. By 1960 the value of the crops stored by the *Commodity Credit Corporation* had reached $9 billion. Despite government efforts, the farmers still produced surpluses, as they offset decreased acreage by increased productivity per acre.

TECHNOLOGICAL SPEEDUP AND AGRICULTURE TODAY

For more than 100 years the Agricultural Revolution has been changing American farming, but since World War II at a quicker pace than ever before. Farmers have utilized the latest technological advances: complex machines, improved fertilizers, pesticides, weedkillers, and better seed varieties. The record since 1940 has been startling:

TRENDS IN AGRICULTURE

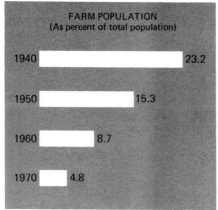

FARM POPULATION
(As percent of total population)

1940   23.2
1950   15.3
1960   8.7
1970   4.8

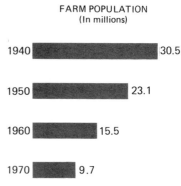

FARM POPULATION
(In millions)

1940   30.5
1950   23.1
1960   15.5
1970   9.7

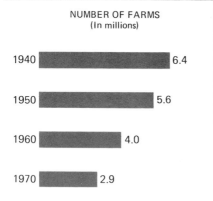

NUMBER OF FARMS
(In millions)

1940   6.4
1950   5.6
1960   4.0
1970   2.9

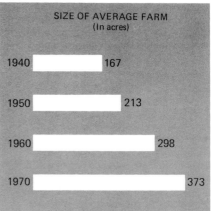

SIZE OF AVERAGE FARM
(In acres)

1940   167
1950   213
1960   298
1970   373

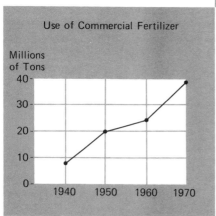

Use of Commercial Fertilizer

Millions
of Tons
40 -
30 -
20 -
10 -
0 -
   1940   1950   1960   1970

NUMBER OF PERSONS
SUPPLIED BY ONE FARMER
(Each figure represents four consumers)

1940

 12

1970

47

1. Increase in Productivity per Acre. The per acre output of wheat increased from 15 to 37 bushels, of cotton from 262 to 630 pounds. Overall crop output more than tripled.

2. Increase in Output per Worker. The number of worker hours needed to produce one bale of cotton fell from 200 to 5. Dramatic drops also were registered for other crops.

3. Rise of the "Superfarm." By the mid-1980's, almost one third of all farm production took place on 27,800 "superfarms"—that is, farms with gross sales of $500,000 or more per year. Only 1.2 percent of farms qualified as "superfarms." The average farm had a gross income of less than $75,000.

4. Problems of Poverty and Hired Workers

a. Impoverished Farmers. Some 2.2 million farms were operating in 1985, down 700,000 in a decade. More than half of these farms had sales totaling under $20,000. While a small percentage of farmers earned high incomes from agriculture, hundreds of thousands of others earned more from off-farm jobs than they did from farming. Many farmers had incomes below the poverty line.

The government has assisted struggling farmers by (1) providing loans for them to expand their landholdings, (2) spurring rural communities to undertake job-creating projects such as constructing water systems, (3) encouraging new industries to locate in rural areas, and (4) granting funds for occupational retraining.

b. Hired Farm Workers. The number of hired farm workers declined from 2.6 million in 1975 to about 1.2 million in 1986. Approximately 200,000 of those were migratory workers who travel from region to region and find employment chiefly on large commercial farms at peak periods such as harvesttime. Working only a few months a year and earning less than $5 an hour, they live in extreme poverty. Many migratory workers come from Mexico and Haiti or are *Chicanos* (Americans of Mexican descent).

Beginning in 1951, Congress permitted Mexican farm workers called *braceros* (laborers) to come to the United States on a temporary basis. Growers supported the *bracero* program because it increased the supply of people willing to work for low wages. Labor unions criticized the program because it increased the difficulty of organizing farm workers into unions. After 1962, temporary foreign farm workers became subject to United States minimum-wage laws, and in 1965 Congress ended the *bracero* program. However, growers continued to hire foreign workers. Under the Immigration Reform and Control Act of 1986, up to 350,000 foreign farm workers per year may enter the United States.

The first union to meet success in organizing farm workers was the *United Farm Workers* (UFW), an AFL-CIO affiliate led by *Cesar Chavez.* In 1965 the UFW called thousands of California farm workers, mainly *Chicanos,* out on strike. Rallying support from segments of the public, the UFW won contracts for improved wages and working conditions from major grape and lettuce growers. The UFW and other unions have had little success in organizing farm workers outside of California. In the mid-1980's, the UFW represented slightly less than 10 percent of California's 200,000 farm workers. Nationwide, less than 1 percent of farm workers belonged to a labor union.

5. The Problem of Food Surpluses. Agriculture in the United States has been too successful for its own good. Each year farmers produce far more food than Americans consume. Since the 1930's, United States farm policy has had two chief aims: (*a*) finding an outlet for food surpluses, and (*b*) finding an acceptable means of bringing farm production down so that the supply of food is in line with the demand for food.

6. The 1970's: Farm Prosperity—For a Time. In the 1970's, a sharp rise in world demand for food opened up new markets for farm products and brought prosperity to many American farmers. The increased demand resulted from (*a*) crop failures in the Soviet Union in 1972 and in other parts of the world in 1974, (*b*) the 1971 devaluation of the dollar that made our products cheaper abroad, (*c*) sharply rising populations in many developing countries, and (*d*) growing prosperity in traditional food-importing countries such as Japan. Exports of United States farm products shot up from $7.3 billion in 1970 to a peak of $43.3 billion in 1981. In the mid-1970's, the prices that farmers received for their crops were quite high in relation to farmers' costs. Flush with prosperity, many farmers expanded their operations by borrowing money and buying new land. As a result, the cost of farmland rose sharply.

a. The Farm Act of 1973. The 1973 farm law started from the assumption that the problem of food surpluses had been solved. It sought to "unleash" farmers so that they could produce more food to meet the rising world demand. The act (1) reduced or eliminated many forms of price supports and other programs designed to hold down production, (2) did away with the New Deal approaches of parity price and complex farm regulations, and (3) protected farmers by assuring them a "floor" under their income based on "target prices" for staple crops such as wheat, corn, and cotton. If market prices should fall below the target prices, the government would make up the difference by crop loans or cash subsidies, limited to a maximum payment per farmer of $20,000. Critics warned that (1) if market prices fell sharply below target prices, the government would have to make large subsidy payments, and (2) farmers would lobby for ever higher target prices. The 1973 act unleashed farmers so successfully that production once again outstripped demand. By 1977 the country again had large crop surpluses.

b. The Farm Act of 1977. This act (1) raised target prices and provided that they be geared to production costs, (2) authorized special subsidies to farmers who agreed to take a percentage of their land out of production, and (3) established a grain-reserve system to store surplus crops on farms. Many farmers thought that the 1977 law did not go far enough. During the winter of 1977–1978, activist farmers drove parades of tractors through farm-belt cities and Washington, D.C., to demand higher benefits.

7. **The 1980's: Crisis on the Farm.** Hard times began to affect some farmers in the late 1970's and spread across the country in the 1980's. Farm exports declined sharply, to about $29 billion in 1985. The reasons for falling revenue included (a) a United States embargo on food exports to the Soviet Union after Soviet troops invaded Afghanistan in 1979, (b) a "green revolution" that enabled developing countries such as India and Thailand to step up food production dramatically, (c) growing competition from other food-exporting areas, especially Europe, Canada, Australia, and Argentina, and (d) an unfavorable exchange rate for the dollar that made our products more expensive in many countries. President Reagan ended the embargo on sales to the Soviet Union in 1981, but Soviet purchases remained low. The Reagan administration also pressured European nations to cut farm subsidies that kept food prices low and reduced opportunities for the sale of American goods in Europe.

With falling demand, the prices received by United States farmers dropped. Farmers who had borrowed heavily in the prosperous 1970's often found themselves unable to keep up payments to banks and other lenders. Many farmers went bankrupt, losing their land and even their homes. The crisis touched many parts of the nation's economy: manufacturers and dealers of farm equipment, grain traders, bankers, and rural merchants.

a. The Farm Act of 1981. While the Reagan administration championed free enterprise, it continued farm subsidies. The Farm Act of 1981 was essentially a renewal of the 1977 act.

b. The Food Security Act of 1985. The 1985 act set the nation's farm policy on a sharply different course. Abandoning the traditional goal of keeping crop prices high, the act sought to lower prices in order to make United States farm exports more competitive. The 1985 act called for (1) sharp cuts in loan rates for major crops and (2) a guarantee of minimum payments (up to $50,000) to help farmers hurt by falling prices. Since market prices are closely affected by interest rates for farm loans, the cuts in rates helped to lower the cost of food. Farmers were eligible to receive "deficiency payments" to make up the difference between market prices and target prices. In return, they had to accept restraints on the amount of land they kept in production.

So many farmers signed up for help under the 1985 law that government outlays for farm price supports reached a record $22.4 billion in 1987.

8. **The Farm Act of 1990.** Partly in response to massive budget deficits, Congress cut subsidies and made other major changes in farm policy. The 1990 act (a) cut back federal farm spending by 25 percent, (b) reduced by 15 percent the amount of land on which farmers could grow subsidized crops, (c) set a limit of $100,000 on subsidy payments to any farmer, (d) cut back loans to debt-burdened farmers, (e) placed a tax on the marketing of milk, sugar, tobacco, peanuts, honey, and wool, and (f) set rules aimed at protecting the environment (for example, by requiring farmers to keep records on pesticide use).

MULTIPLE-CHOICE QUESTIONS

1. Following the Civil War, what effect did the decline of prices have upon the Western farmers? (1) It helped them by lowering the prices of manufactured goods. (2) It helped them by creating a greater demand for their crops. (3) It hurt them by forcing them to pay back a more valuable dollar than they had borrowed. (4) It had no important effect upon them.

2. The denunciation by farmers of what they called the "Crime of '73" reflected their demand for (1) increased regulation of railroads (2) an increase in aid to land-grant colleges (3) federal regulation of wheat markets (4) higher prices through currency expansion.

3. In 1886 a Granger law was declared unconstitutional by the United States Supreme Court. This decision led to the (1) establishment of farm cooperatives (2) acceptance of acreage controls by the farmers (3) ratification of the Sixteenth Amendment (4) passage of the Interstate Commerce Act.

4. In an outline, one of these is a main topic and three are subtopics. Which is the main topic? (1) In 1890 Congress passed the Sherman Silver Purchase Act. (2) Many farmers joined the Greenback and Populist parties. (3) The Grangers secured laws to check the power of the railroads. (4) Agrarian discontent has led to political action in our country.

5. During World War I, farmers helped create some of their later problems by (1) limiting production to raise prices (2) forming cooperatives to market their products (3) borrowing to expand production (4) urging the defeat of the Agricultural Marketing Act.

6. A major *difference* between farmers and industrial producers is the (1) existence of overhead costs for the industrialist (2) need for credit by the farmer (3) need for skilled labor in the factory (4) farmer's difficulty in adjusting production to meet market demand.

7. The 1920's saw the formation of the farm bloc, an organization of (1) Congressmen from the agricultural states (2) agricultural states in the Midwest (3) farmers wanting to start cooperatives (4) banks that held farm mortgages.

8. From 1920 to 1933 the condition of agriculture in the United States was generally characterized by (1) increased tenancy and the production of surplus crops (2) increased land ownership and an increase in farm population (3) much greater increases in farm prices than in farm labor costs (4) a vast expansion of foreign markets for farm products.

9. The New Deal administration attempted to solve the farm problem primarily by (1) purchasing one-half of all farm products (2) sponsoring the cooperative movement (3) increasing the tariff on farm products (4) inducing farmers to curtail production.

10. In applying the principle of parity to farm prices, the government tries to (1) fix prices on farm products (2) provide farmers a purchasing power equivalent to their spending power in a base period (3) establish price levels agreed upon at commodity exchanges (4) reduce imports from low-wage-paying nations.

11. In which area was the New Deal farm program *least* successful? (1) encouraging soil conservation (2) preventing farm surpluses (3) keeping farm surpluses from the market (4) giving stability to farm prices.

12. Which was an important characteristic of the farm policy of President Eisenhower's administration? (1) It rejected the concept of parity payments. (2) It encouraged farmers to produce as much as they could. (3) It provided for flexible price supports for major farm products. (4) It consistently opposed the soil bank program.

13. Which is *not* an economic trend in American agriculture today? (1) large farms (2) large investments in machinery (3) increased productivity per acre (4) increased percentage of farm workers in total population.

14. In the United States, agriculture has posed a persistent problem since the end of the Civil War chiefly because (1) consumers have been buying fewer farm products (2) the federal government has done little to aid the farmer (3) there has been a technological revolution in farming (4) there generally has been insufficient money in circulation.

TIME-LINE QUESTIONS

On the time line the letters *A–F* represent time intervals as indicated. For *each* event listed below, select the *letter* that indicates the time interval within which the event occurred.

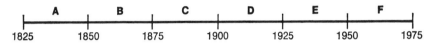

1. Migratory grape pickers in California gained recognition of their union.
2. Oliver H. Kelley founded the National Grange.
3. An Agricultural Adjustment Act introduced a system of parity payments to farmers.
4. Cyrus McCormick patented the mechanical reaper, which helped to revolutionize agriculture.
5. The Rural Electrification Administration was established to bring electricity to neglected farm areas.
6. Cleveland purchased gold bullion and preserved the gold standard.
7. The government offered aid to low-income farmers through rural repair projects and vocational training.
8. Farmers enjoyed prosperous years that later were used as the base period for determining parity prices.
9. The Bankhead-Jones Act was passed to assist tenant farmers.
10. The Morrill Act set up provisions for land-grant college.

DISCUSSION ANALYSIS QUESTIONS

Speakers *A, B, C,* and *D* are discussing the role of a political party in the Presidential election of 1896. Base your answers to the following questions on their statements and on your knowledge of American history.

Speaker A: The members of that political party are radical! Why, they would do away with capitalism!

Speaker B: No. They merely want more direct participation by the people in their government. Perhaps they are far ahead of their times!

Speaker C: Their candidate is a clever politician. A Democrat, he steals their thunder. Then they give him coalition support!

Speaker D: There are factors other than candidates that determine elections.

1. To which political party are the speakers referring? (1) Whig (2) Populist (3) Republican (4) Socialist.

2. The concern of Speaker *A* about capitalism is based on the fact that this party advocated (1) the initiative and referendum (2) bimetallism (3) a substantial increase in the tariff (4) government ownership and operation of public utilities.

3. To which candidate does Speaker *C* refer as a "clever politician"? (1) William Jennings Bryan (2) Franklin D. Roosevelt (3) William McKinley (4) Marcus A. Hanna.

4. The reference by Speaker *B* to this party's being far ahead of its times is supported by (1) its victory in a Presidential election many years later (2) its victory in the following Congressional election (3) its prediction that the United States would adopt a policy of imperialism (4) the subsequent adoption of many of the reforms that it advocated.

5. When Speaker *D* mentions "factors . . . that determine elections," he is referring to the (1) advocacy of the forceful overthrow of government (2) assumption of political power by military leaders (3) control of the Supreme Court by extremists (4) power of pressure groups and vested interests.

ESSAY QUESTIONS

1. Citing *three* specific examples, explain the meaning of this statement: "The Agricultural Revolution had a decided effect on the economic self-sufficiency of the American farmer."

2. (*a*) Discuss briefly *two* major problems that the farmer faces because of the nature of his business. (*b*) Describe *two* attempts that were made by the farmers before 1900 to solve their problems.

3. "When the farmer prospers, the nation prospers." (*a*) Explain the economic truth of the above statement. (*b*) Discuss briefly *two* reasons why the farmer did *not* prosper during the 1920's. (*c*) Describe *two* methods used by the federal government between 1930 and 1940 to help farmers.

4. Use historical evidence to support *or* to refute *each* of the following statements: (*a*) The third-party movement in the West and South in the late 19th century took the form of agrarian revolt. (*b*) The conversion of American agriculture to a commercial basis has made the farmer a specialist. (*c*) Unlike the manufacturer, the farmer has no control over his market or prices. (*d*) Instead of benefiting from the technological revolution in agriculture since World War II, the farmer has been its victim.

5. Discuss *each* of the following statements, giving *two* specific facts to support *or two* specific facts to refute each statement: (*a*) The Industrial Revolution has greatly influenced the life of the farmer. (*b*) Wars have had important effects on the farmer. (*c*) The farmer has always been a "rugged individualist" in that he has made few demands for assistance from the government. (*d*) The farm problem is an important political issue today. (*e*) The surplus of American farm products has been a factor in our foreign relations since World War II.

6. National prosperity is dependent upon the prosperity of all economic groups. Explain and illustrate how a specific law passed by Congress in the interest of American farmers has (*a*) directly benefited farmers, (*b*) indirectly benefited American industrial workers, and (*c*) indirectly benefited American businessmen.

Part 3. Conservation Protects the Nation's Resources

WASTE: AN AMERICAN TRADITION

Americans were blessed with abundant natural resources but used them wastefully. Their squandering habits were encouraged by federal policies of low-cost and free land. (1) Farmers and planters exhausted the soil's fertility. (2) Farmers cleared their lands by chopping down or burning trees wantonly. (3) Lumber companies leveled vast forests without sparing unripe trees and without reforesting. (4) By destroying trees whose roots had served to bind the soil, farmers and lumbermen invited floods and soil erosion. (5) Hunters depleted wildlife, almost completely destroying the vast herds of buffalo. (6) Drillers who struck successful wells burned the escaping natural gas and made little attempt to cap gushers to stop the initial flow of oil. (7) Coal mining companies dug shafts to reach the richest seams and neglected the rest. (8) Cities and factories dumped sewage and wastes into nearby streams and lakes, thereby polluting the waters and killing the fish.

BEGINNINGS OF THE CONSERVATION MOVEMENT

In the late 19th century, as the frontier was drawing to a close, the American people became aware that the nation's resources, although great, were not limitless. Agricultural scientists, forestry experts, nature lovers, and other public-spirited citizens awakened interest in *conservation*—the proper care and wise use of our natural resources.

The government thereupon undertook the following steps toward conservation: (1) In 1872 Congress designated the *Yellowstone* region, lying mostly in Wyoming, as our first national park. From this beginning evolved today's extensive system of national monuments, historical sites, and parks, all administered by the *National Park Service*. (2) In 1891 Congress passed the *Forest Reserve Act*, which permitted successive Presidents to set aside lands as *national forest reserves*.

THEODORE ROOSEVELT AND CONSERVATION

More than any other man, Theodore Roosevelt awakened the American people to the need for conservation. An outdoorsman and a nature lover, Roosevelt had lived in the West and had personally seen the waste and destruction of our natural resources. During his Presidency (1901–1909), Roosevelt promoted the following conservation measures:

1. **Land Reserves.** Roosevelt withdrew from sale about 150 million acres of forest land, 80 million acres of coal land, and 1½ million acres of potential waterpower sites. Under government control, these lands were to be kept from reckless exploitation and used wisely for the national welfare.

2. Newlands Reclamation Act. In 1902 Congress passed the *Newlands Act*, which provided that the federal government use the proceeds from the sale of lands in 16 Western states to finance irrigation projects. This act began a program of government construction of huge dams, the earliest ones being the *Shoshone Dam* in Wyoming and the *Roosevelt Dam* in Arizona.

3. Forest Service. Congress strengthened the *Forest Service*, headed by Roosevelt's friend *Gifford Pinchot*. An ardent conservationist, Pinchot built the Forest Service into a major force for conservation. Forest Service rangers patrol the national forests, fight fires, and replant cutover areas.

4. Governors' Conference. In 1908 Roosevelt invited the governors of all the states and other interested persons to confer with him regarding possible federal, state, corporate, and individual efforts to further conservation. The conference led to the establishment of (a) 41 state conservation commissions, and (b) a *National Conservation Commission* to make an inventory of the nation's resources and to suggest plans for their wise utilization.

OPPOSITION TO CONSERVATION

Theodore Roosevelt's conservation efforts aroused considerable opposition. Coal and lumber companies wanted to take over the government's land reserves. Private utility companies were hostile to the government's dam-building program because they feared competition from government hydroelectric power. Anti-conservationists hoped that, after Roosevelt retired, the public would again become apathetic about conservation.

NEW DEAL AND CONSERVATION

1. Background. In 1933 *Franklin D. Roosevelt* became President and faced (a) the Great Depression, with 13 million persons unemployed, and (b) a series of natural disasters: droughts, dust storms, and floods. A strong supporter of conservation, Roosevelt sponsored a dual-purpose program to provide work for the unemployed and to protect our natural resources.

2. Major Undertakings

a. Civilian Conservation Corps. The CCC, from 1933 to 1942, provided employment for 2 million young men in conservation work. They constructed reservoirs, planted trees, cut forest trails, dug drainage ditches, fought plant diseases, and established forest-fire control systems.

b. Public Works Administration. The PWA, from 1933 to 1939, spent several billion dollars, a considerable portion going for conservation programs. The PWA provided work directly for half a million unemployed on projects for hydroelectric power, sewage treatment, and flood control.

c. Soil Conservation. The New Deal farm laws (Soil Conservation and Domestic Allotment Act of 1936 and Agricultural Adjustment Act of 1938) granted bounties to farmers for planting soil-conserving crops. Also, to encourage efficient use of the soil, the Resettlement Administration moved farmers from unfit lands to more fertile lands. The Soil Conservation Service educated farmers in methods of preventing and halting soil erosion.

d. Multipurpose Dam Projects. The New Deal completed construction, begun during the Hoover administration, of the *Hoover (Boulder) Dam* on the Colorado River. This huge dam provides electric power, irrigation, and flood control. To utilize other Far Western waterpower sites, the New Deal completed such projects as the *Fort Peck Dam* on the Missouri River and the *Bonneville Dam* and *Grand Coulee Dam* on the Columbia River.

e. Tennessee Valley Authority (TVA). Because of its great importance, the TVA is discussed at length below.

TVA: CASE STUDY OF AN ALL-INCLUSIVE REGIONAL APPROACH

1. Background. The Tennessee River Valley, encompassing parts of seven states, was a region of impoverished farmers, eroded soil, cutover forests, and floods. Its rural areas had almost no electricity. But the region had the potential waterpower site at *Muscle Shoals.*

During World War I the federal government began construction at Muscle Shoals of a project for producing nitrates and electricity. Completed in the 1920's, the project caused considerable dispute between public power and private power interests. Senator *George Norris* three times secured Congressional passage of bills providing for federal ownership and operation. The first bill was vetoed by President Coolidge; the second bill, by President Hoover. The third bill, passed in 1933, met with the hearty approval of President Roosevelt, who signed it into law.

2. Organization and Services. The TVA is a government corporation empowered to plan for the "economic and social well-being of the people" in the Tennessee Valley. It represents a *regional approach* to economic development. The TVA consists of a series of dams, reservoirs, nitrate factories, power plants, and electric transmission lines.

A *multipurpose* project, the TVA serves the people by (a) controlling the Tennessee River to prevent floods and permit navigation, (b) encouraging reforestation and soil conservation, (c) producing nitrates for cheap fertilizer, (d) maintaining agricultural experiment stations, and (e) generating electricity, originally by waterpower and later also by the use of coal and nuclear power. The TVA sells its electricity primarily to municipal and cooperative utility companies that resell the electricity to the public, generally at rates below those of private utilities. Many persons view TVA rates as a *yardstick* to measure the fairness of private utility rates.

3. Achievements. The TVA greatly improved the standard of living of the Tennessee Valley people. Farmers diversified their crops, used more fertilizer for higher crop yields, and enjoyed rising incomes. Their homes were brightened by low-cost electricity. Foresters replanted cutover areas. Aluminum and chemical companies, attracted by plentiful low-cost electric power, established plants in the valley and created new jobs. During World War II the TVA produced nitrates for explosives and furnished electric power for the atomic bomb project at Oak Ridge, Tennessee.

4. Opposition. Fearing the competition of the TVA, private utility companies tried to overturn the TVA by legal action. They failed, as the Supreme Court, in a series of cases, upheld the constitutionality of the TVA and its right to sell electricity. Spokesmen fearful of "big government" have also attacked the TVA. President Eisenhower called the TVA an example of "creeping socialism."

The TVA has weathered all opposition, but its enemies have proved sufficiently strong to prevent establishment of other all-inclusive regional projects on the Columbia, Missouri, and St. Lawrence rivers.

DISPUTE OVER PUBLIC DEVELOPMENT OF HYDROELECTRIC POWER

1. Arguments For. (*a*) Being able to borrow large sums of money at low interest rates, the government can undertake projects too expensive for private enterprise. (*b*) The government does not seek to make a profit and therefore can charge lower rates. (*c*) Government-owned utility companies provide a yardstick for measuring the fairness of private utility rates. (*d*) Multipurpose dams not only provide electric power but also further irrigation, navigation, and flood control. (*e*) Federal projects, such as Hoover Dam, Grand Coulee Dam, and the TVA, have proved successful in practice.

2. Arguments Against. (*a*) By competing with private industry, the government is violating our tradition of free enterprise. (*b*) The "big government" resulting from the army of federal officeholders, or *bureaucracy,* threatens our freedom. (*c*) Taxpayers throughout the nation should not have to pay to benefit inhabitants of specific regions.

Also, private utility companies claim that government power projects provide an unfair yardstick of rates because the projects pay no federal income taxes and can produce hydroelectric power more cheaply than private utilities can produce steam-generated power.

ST. LAWRENCE RIVER PROJECT

1. Background. Proposed early in the 20th century, this project called for the construction of (*a*) hydroelectric power dams on the St. Lawrence River, and (*b*) a seaway that would enable oceangoing vessels to sail from the Atlantic Ocean up the St. Lawrence and into the Great Lakes. The project met opposition. (*a*) Railroads feared the loss of freight business. (*b*) Private utilities feared competition from public power. (*c*) Atlantic ports, from Maryland to Maine, feared loss of trade to Canadian and American ports on the Great Lakes. The project was urged repeatedly by Canada but turned down repeatedly by our Congress.

2. Construction of the Project (1954–1959). President Eisenhower recognized the importance of the St. Lawrence project for national defense and economic well-being, but he rejected an all-inclusive regional approach. He authorized New York State to proceed, with the Province of Ontario, in building dams for hydroelectric power. He secured Congressional approval for cooperation between the United States and Canada in dredging the river, and in building canals for the seaway. By 1959 construction was completed on both the seaway and the power projects.

The seaway charges tolls to ships using its facilities. It has substantially increased the amount of cargo carried on the St. Lawrence River and the Great Lakes, made possible low transport rates, and facilitated the economic growth of the Great Lakes area. The New York State Power Authority sells its St. Lawrence power to municipal and cooperative electric systems as well as to private manufacturing and utility companies.

RECENT FACTORS SPURRING PUBLIC INTEREST IN CONSERVATION

1. Postwar Prosperity. Following World War II, affluent Americans had more time and money for recreational purposes. However, the number of campers overwhelmed the limited facilities of national and state parks.

2. Growing Population. From 1940 to 1968 the American population multiplied from 132 million to over 200 million, an increase of over 50 percent. More people meant greater demands upon our shrinking natural resources.

3. Floods. Dwellers along the Mississippi and Missouri Rivers in the 1950's suffered severe floods, with much property damage and loss of life.

4. Water Pollution and Water Shortages. As cities and factories continued to dump sewage and industrial wastes into nearby waters, many people suffered. Magnificent rivers (such as the Hudson and the Potomac) and beautiful lakes (such as Lake Erie and Lake Michigan) became polluted, disease-ridden, and ugly. People found beaches closed and fish dying out.

In the cities of the Northeast, a drought in the 1960's caused water shortages. The people were subjected to restrictions in the use of water for washing cars, sprinkling lawns, and air-conditioning places of business.

5. Air Pollution. Exhaust fumes from automobiles and the smoking chimneys of factories, apartment houses, and private homes have polluted the urban air. Urban dwellers breathe this polluted air, which is often called *smog*. As a result, they suffer eye and nose irritations, and an increased incidence of respiratory ailments and heart trouble.

6. Education. Since World War II, conservationists have redoubled their educational efforts. They have encouraged schools to teach students about conservation, usually as part of biology, geography, or history. They have produced specialized films and published popular articles and books. Fairfield Osborn wrote the book *Our Plundered Planet*, warning that man can survive only if he ends his waste of the earth's resources. Rachel Carson wrote the book *Silent Spring*, warning that the irresponsible use of pesticides harms birds and other wildlife and contaminates our food supply.

Recently, conservation, emphasizing the relationship of people to their surroundings, became known as *environmental protection*.

RECENT PRIVATE EFFORTS IN ENVIRONMENTAL PROTECTION

(1) Large-scale commercial farmers have employed the latest scientific methods of soil conservation. (2) Timber companies have undertaken extensive reforestation programs. They have managed their land as *tree farms*, with annual harvests and with replantings to assure future harvests. (3) Iron and steel companies, after almost exhausting our deposits of high-grade iron ore, have devised techniques for mining and utilizing low-grade *taconite* ore. (4) Oil companies have improved refining techniques to extract more usable products from crude petroleum.

NUCLEAR POWER ISSUE

During the 1970's, electric utility companies turned increasingly to atomic energy. They were influenced by the rising costs of conventional fuels such as coal, oil, and gas, and by technological advances that lowered the costs of nuclear power. By 1978 some 70 nuclear power plants were providing the nation with 13 percent of its electricity. More plants were under construction.

Since then, nuclear power has suffered some major setbacks. Serious accidents took place in 1979 at the Three Mile Island power plant in Pennsylvania, and in 1986 at Chernobyl in the Soviet Union. Opponents charged that nuclear power plants were unsafe, endangered the environment, and produced waste materials for which there were no safe means of disposal. Nuclear advocates denied those charges, insisting that nuclear power posed less danger to people and the environment than coal or electric power, and that scientists had solved the problem of nuclear waste disposal.

In recent years the federal government has set stricter safety standards that sharply increased the cost of nuclear power. Opponents of nuclear power have filed numerous court suits challenging nuclear plants on safety and other grounds. Meanwhile, lower prices for conventional fuels have caused electric utility companies to reconsider the trend to nuclear power.

In the mid-1980's, the United States possessed 102 of the world's 374 operating nuclear power plants. Nuclear power provided about 16 percent of the nation's electricity. However, no new orders for nuclear plants had been placed since 1978.

STATE AND CITY EFFORTS IN ENVIRONMENTAL PROTECTION

Many states and cities undertook conservation activities. They expanded parks, playgrounds, and wildlife preserves; built improved sewage treatment plants; and combatted air pollution. For example: (1) California required that all new cars sold in the state contain exhaust control devices. (2) New York City adopted stringent controls to reduce air pollution, requiring refuse compactors, not incinerators, in new buildings. (3) Pennsylvania, Illinois, Florida, and California all provided stiff fines for polluters. (4) Oregon, New York, and several other states required a deposit on all beverage bottles and cans so as to spur return of the empties and reduce litter.

FEDERAL EFFORTS IN ENVIRONMENTAL PROTECTION

1. **Environmental Protection Laws.** *(a)* The *Wilderness Act* (1964) established a National Wilderness Preservation System of 9 million acres of national forest lands to preserve "an enduring resource of wilderness" as recreational sites for public enjoyment. *(b)* The *Highway Beautification Act* (1965) assigned federal funds for the removal of billboards and junkyards from alongside interstate and primary highways. *(c)* The *Water Quality Act* (1965) and the *Clean Rivers Restoration Act* (1966) empowered the government to set standards of water quality and provided funds to construct sewage treatment plants and to combat water pollution. *(d)* The *Resource Recovery Act* (1970) provided funds for states and cities to build solid-waste disposal systems and to recycle salvageable materials such as aluminum cans. *(e)* The *Clean Air Act* (1970) required the automobile industry to develop an engine that would eliminate 90 percent of noxious auto fumes. *(f)* The *Clean Water Act* (1972) began a program of federal aid for waste-treatment plants, made it illegal to discharge pollutants into United States waters without a permit, and allowed citizens to sue polluters or the federal government. *(g)* A *Clean Air Act* (1990) tightened controls on fumes coming from smokestacks, filling stations, business operations, and motor vehicles.

2. **Agencies.** Two agencies were created: *(a)* the *Council on Environmental Quality,* within the Executive Office (1969), to advise the President and *(b)* the *Environmental Protection Agency (EPA)* in 1970 to enforce laws regarding conservation, environment, antipollution, and *ecology*—the relationship between people and other living things and their surroundings.

ENERGY NEEDS VS. ENVIRONMENTAL PROTECTION

With the 1973 Arab oil embargo against the United States, the American people became aware of their energy crisis. They began to reconsider the matter of environmental protection, suddenly realizing that it brought benefits but also involved costs. They asked questions: (1) Which goal should the nation seek first—energy self-sufficiency or environmental protection? (2) Which standards should environmental protection seek—"absolute" or "reasonable"? These problems are illustrated as follows:

1. **Alaska Pipeline.** With the 1968 discovery of oil in the Prudhoe Bay area of Alaska's North Slope, oil companies planned to construct an 800-mile pipeline to bring the oil southward to Alaska's ice-free port at Valdez. (From there tankers could carry the oil to West Coast refineries.) The pipeline was delayed for several years by conservation groups, which claimed that the pipeline would damage the Alaskan environment. In 1973 Congress passed legislation authorizing construction of the pipeline by private enterprise. It was completed in 1977. Environmentalists' fears were confirmed in March 1989 when an oil tanker sailing out of Valdez ran aground. It spilled 11 million gallons of oil into Prince William Sound, causing untold damage to wildlife and fishing areas.

2. **Strip-Mining of Coal.** Private utility companies have looked to our Western lands—both government reserves and private holdings—for clean, low-sulfur coal that can be dug out by surface, or strip, mining. Conservation groups claimed that strip-mining will scar the land permanently unless costly standards are imposed for restoring the mined land to good condition.

In 1977 the *Surface Mining Control and Reclamation Act* became law. It (a) required coal companies to restore strip-mined land to its original shape, to replant grass and trees, and to prevent the pollution of nearby waters, and (b) placed a tonnage fee on both strip-mined and underground coal to provide funds for restoring land left damaged by previous strip-mining.

Many coal companies argued that the law was an unconstitutional infringement of their property rights. Their criticism lessened in the 1980's when the Reagan administration softened its enforcement of strip-mining rules as a part of a trend to deregulation. Environmentalists urged stricter enforcement of the law and accused strip miners of avoiding regulations.

THE COMPREHENSIVE NATIONAL ENERGY ACT OF 1978

In 1977 President Carter asked Congress for a comprehensive energy bill as necessary for the nation's well-being and as the "moral equivalent of war."

After 18 months of deliberation, Congress enacted a bill whose major provisions were to: (1) permit the price of newly discovered natural gas to rise gradually until controls were removed in 1985, (2) require new electric utility plants to install boilers using coal—not oil or gas, (3) require existing electric utility plants using oil or gas to switch to coal by 1990, (4) provide tax benefits to business firms and homeowners who save energy by use of insulation and solar energy equipment, (5) require manufacturers of household appliances to meet fuel efficiency standards, (6) tax gas-guzzling cars beginning with the 1980 models.

FURTHER CARTER ENERGY PROPOSALS (1979–1980)

By 1979 the United States depended upon foreign imports for 50 percent of its oil needs. The United States consequently was severely affected when revolution in Iran sharply curtailed that country's oil exports and when the OPEC cartel (check the Index) raised oil prices further by about 60 percent.

President Carter proposed the following legislation: (1) Establish a federal agency to develop a synthetic fuels, or *synfuels,* industry. (2) Encourage the use of solar power. (3) Enact a "windfall-profits tax"—an additional levy on the extra profits that oil companies were expected to make as the government in 1981 removed controls on domestic oil.

President Carter's proposals were subjected to considerable criticism: (1) The synfuels program would be in the hands of a government bureaucracy rather than under private initiative. The synthetic fuels so produced would be costly. (2) The windfall-profits tax would deprive oil companies of funds that could be used to uncover new energy supplies.

In 1980 Congress enacted the following laws: (1) Establishing a Synthetic Fuels Corporation to provide subsidies and loan guarantees to private industry to spur construction of plants for converting coal, oil shale, and tar sands into synfuels. (2) Creating a Solar Bank to provide subsidies and loan guarantees for renewable energy projects. (3) Placing a windfall-profits tax on the domestic oil companies.

PRESIDENT REAGAN'S ENERGY POLICIES (SINCE 1981)

President Reagan favored greater reliance on free-market forces and less on government efforts to meet the nation's energy needs. He slashed federal funds for synfuel and solar-energy projects. He also removed obstacles to the development of energy resources on federal offshore and onshore lands. The Reagan administration continued efforts to reduce the nation's dependence on imported oil, mainly by encouraging the growth of domestic production.

Congress passed legislation setting national energy-conservation standards for large appliances such as water heaters and refrigerators. President Reagan vetoed one version of the bill but signed a second version in 1987.

PROPER DISPOSAL OF TOXIC CHEMICAL WASTES

By 1980 the American people were alerted to another public health and environmental problem—the inappropriate disposal of hazardous wastes. This problem received widespread publicity with reports of the health problems of persons living on or near an abandoned chemical dump site—the Love Canal area near Niagara Falls, New York. Further studies indicated that there were, throughout the nation, thousands of abandoned and improperly maintained hazardous-waste dumps spewing poison into the land, air, and water.

In 1980 Congress passed the *Waste Cleanup Act* (1) providing a five-year, $1.6 billion "superfund" to be raised mainly by excise taxes on chemicals, (2) authorizing federal agencies to contract for the removal and containment of chemical wastes, to protect water against contamination, and to relocate people from dangerous sites, and (3) instructing the government to sue companies responsible for the hazardous dumps.

When it became apparent that the problem of toxic wastes was even greater than had been thought, Congress in 1986 expanded the "superfund" to $9 billion. By the early 1990's, the Environmental Protection Agency had cleaned up only a handful of the 1245 "worst" sites. Environmentalists argued that the EPA was moving too slowly. Industry leaders complained that cleanup rules were too strict and that costs were thus unreasonably high.

ANOTHER ENVIRONMENTAL CONCERN: ACID RAIN

When fossil fuels are burned by utilities, factories, homes, and autos, gases containing sulphur dioxide and nitrogen oxide are emitted. These gases combine with moisture in the air to form sulphuric and nitric acids, which fall to the earth with droplets of rain. The acid rain harms all forms of life. It is most serious in the northeastern states and Canada.

The *Clean Air Act of 1990* attacked acid rain by (1) requiring coal-burning power plants to sharply reduce emissions of sulphur dioxide and nitrogen oxide and (2) ordering automakers to greatly improve emissions controls.

MULTIPLE-CHOICE QUESTIONS

1. Which of the following was most important in making Americans aware of the need to conserve their natural resources? (1) the destruction caused by the Civil War (2) the closing of the frontier (3) the work of the Civilian Conservation Corps (4) the demands of the Mexican War upon our natural resources.

2. Who was the first President to draw popular attention to the need for conservation? (1) Theodore Roosevelt (2) William Howard Taft (3) Herbert Hoover (4) Franklin D. Roosevelt.

3. Who is generally recognized as a pioneer of forest conservation in the United States? (1) Rachel Carson (2) Gerald Ford (3) Gifford Pinchot (4) Jimmy Carter.

4. A major stimulus for President Franklin D. Roosevelt's interest in conservation was his desire to (1) set aside more land as an oil reserve for the navy (2) find work for millions of unemployed young men (3) follow the tradition established by Theodore Roosevelt (4) reward the Western states for their support in the election of 1932.

5. The federal government's concern for conservation is best illustrated by the (1) Homestead Act (2) Alaska pipeline (3) Three Mile Island accident (4) Tennessee Valley Authority.

6. The Tennessee Valley Authority has (1) tended to raise the standard of living in the region that it serves (2) established widespread irrigation projects (3) been declared unconstitutional (4) been ineffective in controlling floods.

7. The economic concept of the yardstick is most frequently associated with (1) minimum wages (2) income taxes (3) public utility rates (4) Social Security payments.

8. The St. Lawrence Seaway was built primarily to (1) increase trade between the United States and Canada (2) strengthen the defenses of the United States and Canada (3) increase the prestige of New York State (4) bring more world trade to the Great Lakes.

9. Which was *not* a factor in encouraging conservation after World War II? (1) rapid growth of the American population (2) need for fertile soil to increase cotton crop yields (3) pollution of rivers and lakes (4) increased number of automobiles.

10. By using atomic power, electric utilities further conservation because nuclear reactors (1) contain reusable lead shields (2) use nuclear fuels instead of coal and oil (3) make large dams unnecessary (4) release radiation that kills harmful insects.

11. Recent federal environmental protection laws have been *least* concerned with (1) providing recreational sites (2) protecting the beauty of interstate highways (3) protecting the quality of our water and air (4) establishing regional planning authorities similar to the TVA.

ESSAY QUESTIONS

1. (*a*) Discuss *two* reasons why the conservation of natural resources is more important today than it was 100 years ago. (*b*) discuss briefly *two* ways in which the federal government *or* state governments have promoted conservation. (*c*) Explain *two* ways in which corporations and individuals can promote conservation.

2. (*a*) Show *one* way in which the industrial development of the United States and *one* way in which the westward movement of the American people have affected our natural resources. (*b*) Show *one* relationship between our natural resources and our leadership in world affairs.

3. Show the relation of *each* of the following to the conservation of natural resources: (*a*) Reclamation Act of 1902 (Newlands Act), (*b*) Governors' Conference of 1908, (*c*) Teapot Dome Scandal, (*d*) Tennessee Valley Authority, (*e*) Civilian Conservation Corps, (*f*) any one recent federal environmental protection law.

4. The future development of the natural resources of the United States will come not so much from discovery, as from advances in science and from skill in the utilization of our resources. (*a*) Why can we no longer depend upon discovery as a means of substantially increasing our supply of natural resources? (*b*) Indicate how each of *three* natural resources has been needlessly wasted. (*c*) Show how *each* method—advances in science, skill in utilization—has been used to expand or conserve our supply of raw materials.

Part 4. Big Business Becomes the Dominant Influence in Our Economy

INDUSTRY IN COLONIAL DAYS

LIMITED EXTENT

Over 90 percent of the American colonists pursued agriculture and earned a living directly from the soil. Some few colonists operated small essential enterprises: iron forges, gristmills, sawmills, and tanneries. Usually, the owner and his apprentices, if any, worked side by side, produced goods almost entirely by hand, and sold their products in the local market.

REASONS FOR LIMITED DEVELOPMENT

(1) The colonists lacked capital to build factories and purchase machines. (2) Workers were scarce, for most men preferred to secure their own land and become independent farmers. (3) Markets were limited because the colonies lacked adequate roads for inland transportation. (4) The demand for

factory products was insignificant, since the farmers and their families usually made their own clothing, furniture, and other necessities. (5) The English Parliament passed laws to curtail the growth of colonial industry. In accordance with the principles of mercantilism, England directed the colonists to produce raw materials for, and to purchase manufactured goods from, England. (With victory in the War for Independence, the American people became free of British restrictions upon their economy.)

GROWTH OF AMERICAN INDUSTRY

FACTORS ENCOURAGING INDUSTRIAL GROWTH (TO 1900)

1. Natural Resources. Alexander Hamilton, in his *Report on Manufactures* (1791), argued that our wealth of natural resources made industrial development inevitable. Indeed, nature had endowed the United States with (a) an abundance of raw materials: coal, iron, and lumber, (b) fertile soil for raising foodstuffs, cotton, and tobacco, and (c) swift-running streams for waterpower.

2. Constitution and Government Policies. The original Constitution gave the federal government various powers for assisting the growth of industry. (a) Coining of money made possible a stable currency for business transactions. (b) Regulating interstate commerce made possible nationwide laws to regulate industry and transportation. (c) Levying a tariff on imports made possible protection against foreign competition. (d) Establishing a system of patents encouraged inventors. The original Constitution furthermore forbade the states to tax either imports or exports, thus assuring a nationwide "common market" without man-made barriers to the movement of goods.

The Fifth and Fourteenth Amendments to the Constitution provided that no person could be deprived of property without "due process of law." Thus protected against the arbitrary seizure of private property, American and foreign investors provided capital for American industry.

The government spurred the growth of business by (a) granting land and cash subsidies to railroad builders, (b) levying high tariffs to protect manufacturers, and (c) in most other matters, maintaining a policy of *laissez-faire* almost to the end of the 19th century. Laissez-faire is the government policy of leaving business alone and letting the economy regulate itself.

3. Growing Population. Because of a high birth rate and considerable immigration, the American population in the 19th century almost doubled every 25 years—from 5 million in 1800 to 76 million in 1900. This steady increase meant sufficient workers for industry and expanding markets for goods.

4. New Sources of Power

a. Electricity. Man first learned to use this source of power in the 19th century, when scientists developed the dynamo for converting mechanical energy into electric energy. At first, electricity was used mainly for communication, in the telegraph and the telephone. Later, it was used for lighting and for driving motors.

b. Petroleum. In 1859, in Pennsylvania, *Edwin Drake* drilled the first successful oil well. At first, oil was used for lubrication and lighting. Late in the 19th century, two petroleum products—gasoline and diesel oil—were first used in internal combustion engines, the basis of modern transportation.

5. Introduction of Machinery. The American people eagerly embraced the Industrial Revolution. *Samuel Slater*, an immigrant from England, built America's first cotton-spinning mill. Since textile workers were forbidden to emigrate from England, Slater left England in disguise and built his machines in America from memory. Slater became known as the "father of the American factory system."

6. American Inventors and Inventions. The American people displayed a genius for invention, as follows: (*a*) *Charles Goodyear*—the process of *vulcanizing*, or hardening, rubber, (*b*) *Elias Howe*—the sewing machine, (*c*) *Elisha Otis*—the safety elevator, (*d*) *Gordon McKay*—a machine for sewing shoes, (*e*) *Christopher Sholes* (with Carlos Glidden and Samuel Soulé)—the modern typewriter, (*f*) *Ottmar Mergenthaler*—a typesetting machine, (*g*) *William Burroughs*—a key-operated calculating machine, and (*h*) *Thomas A. Edison*—the phonograph, the electric light bulb, and a motion picture machine.

7. Improved Means of Transportation and Communication

a. Transportation. Invention of the steam locomotive in England inspired railroad building in America. *Peter Cooper* built the *Tom Thumb*, a locomotive that in 1830 traversed the 14 miles of track of America's first railroad, the *Baltimore and Ohio*. Track mileage steadily increased to 30,000 by 1860, almost all of it east of the Mississippi.

Following the Civil War, America stepped up its railroad building. In 1900 the country had five transcontinental railroads and nearly 200,000 miles of track—more than the total trackage in all of Europe. Safety and comfort were increased by using iron and then steel in place of wood for rails and bridges, and by making heavier roadbeds. *George Pullman* invented the sleeping car, and *George Westinghouse* the air brake.

Railroads helped the growth of industry by bringing foodstuffs to city markets, raw materials to factories, and manufactures to consumers throughout the land.

b. Communication. (1) In 1844 *Samuel F. B. Morse* proved the practicability of the telegraph. Later, to provide telegraph service nationally, several telegraph companies merged to form *Western Union*. (2) In 1876 *Alexander Graham Bell* exhibited a successful telephone. His work led to the formation of what is today the world's largest communications company, *American Telephone and Telegraph*.

Rapid communications enabled businessmen to direct their salesmen, contact customers, and take orders quickly and efficiently.

8. Effect of Wars. Industrialization in America was encouraged by wars. (*a*) Because the government needed war materials, industry prospered. (*b*) Because farmers and city workers had more money to spend, consumer goods were in greater demand. (*c*) Because there were not enough workers for America's expanding industries, employers turned to laborsaving machines.

In particular, the growth of industry was promoted by the War of 1812 and the Civil War.

a. The War of 1812 made shipbuilding and shipping unprofitable and cut off imports of English manufactures. New Englanders began to invest in manufacturing, especially textiles. The War of 1812 has been called the "war for economic independence."

b. The Civil War spurred industrial growth, both in the North and the South. Furthermore, the secession of the South left the federal government in the hands of the Republican party, which favored business interests. Congress provided land and loans for transcontinental railroads, established a national banking system, and enacted high protective tariffs.

RESULTS OF INDUSTRIAL GROWTH

1. New Industrial Products and Services. Manufacturers displaced hand- and home-made products with machine- and factory-made products. Investors financed new industries to satisfy the demand for new services and goods: railroad transportation, telegraph and telephone communication, steel, and oil.

2. Higher Standard of Living. Our industrial economy produced a greater volume and variety of goods at lower cost than ever before. The average American enjoyed an ever-increasing array of material comforts.

3. Great Fortunes. Business leaders accumulated great wealth, exercised tremendous economic power, and exerted considerable influence upon the government. Some industrialists returned part of their fortunes to society by financing various philanthropies (see pages 369–370). In noteworthy instances, members of wealthy families devoted their lives to public service.

4. Growth of Cities. Many people flocked to the cities, some to find jobs, others to be near to urban society and culture. Cities faced many problems: clearing slums, constructing housing, preventing fire and crime, providing education, expanding mass transportation, and assuring efficient local government.

5. Increased World Trade and Imperialism. Manufacturers looked abroad for markets and raw materials. American trade with the rest of the world increased. Toward the end of the 19th century, the United States moved away from its policy of isolation and embarked on a policy of imperialism.

6. Serious Economic Problems. The growth of industry gave rise to major domestic problems: preventing monopoly, protecting consumers and small businessmen, improving the living standards of workers, maintaining an effective banking system, levying fair taxes, and leveling out the business cycle.

CORPORATIONS AND BUSINESS CONSOLIDATION

INADEQUACIES OF THE OLD FORMS OF BUSINESS ORGANIZATION

Single proprietorships and *partnerships* proved inadequate to meet the needs of large-scale business. Weaknesses were the (1) inability to raise large sums of money, (2) unlimited financial responsibility of the owners, extending even to their personal assets, for claims against the business, and (3) disruption of the business upon death of the owner or partner. To overcome these weaknesses, businessmen adopted another form of business organization, the *corporation*.

CORPORATION: MEANING

A corporation is a form of business organization created by the grant of a state *charter*. The corporation enables a group of individuals to operate as a single "artificial legal person." The corporation can sue and be sued, hire and fire, buy and sell, manufacture and trade.

ADVANTAGES OF INCORPORATION

1. Securing of Capital. By selling stocks and bonds to the public, the corporation can raise large sums of money. Stockholders are part owners of the corporation and share in the profits, which are paid to them as dividends. Bondholders are creditors who lend money to the corporation and receive interest.

2. Limited Liability. The personal assets of the part owners, or stockholders, cannot be seized in order to satisfy claims against the corporation. Even if the corporation goes bankrupt, the most that the part owner can lose is the money he has paid for the stock.

3. Transferability of Shares. An investor may withdraw from the corporation simply by selling his shares of stock.

4. Perpetual Life. The life of the corporation is not affected by the death of any one of the part owners. The shares of the deceased person are transferable to his heirs, who thus become part owners themselves.

DISADVANTAGES OF INCORPORATION

1. As a state-created entity, the corporation must make public its business and financial records by filing periodic reports.

2. As an "artificial legal person," the corporation is subject to taxes on its profits in addition to taxes paid by its individual part owners on their dividends. This is called "double taxation."

3. Most of our nation's corporations are small, but the corporate form has made possible the growth of business giants. There is no personal contact between the large corporation and its workers and customers.

TURN TO MONOPOLY

Following the Civil War, business leaders increasingly moved to combine competing corporations in order to control prices, production, and sales territory. Such control would give them a *monopoly,* the elimination of competition. A company could then set high prices and thus increase profits at the expense of the consumer. In practice, corporations almost never achieved perfect monopoly.

MONOPOLISTIC PRACTICES IN THE 19TH CENTURY: ILLEGAL TODAY

1. The **pool** was an agreement, usually secret, among competing companies to fix prices and output, or to divide sales territory. In the 1870's and 1880's competing railroad lines often formed pools. By the Interstate Commerce Act (1887), railroad pools were declared illegal.

2. The **trust** was a more permanent consolidation than the pool. Stockholders of competing companies turned their stock over to a board of trustees and in exchange received trust certificates. In this way, the board of trustees gained full control and managed the member companies in such a way as to eliminate competition. The Standard Oil Company (the forebear

of several of today's leading oil companies) originated the trust arrangement with success, and so it was imitated by other giant companies. After the passage of the Sherman Antitrust Act (1890), businessmen abandoned the trust and turned to other forms of consolidation.

The word "trust," however, remained part of our vocabulary, referring to any large and powerful business combination or corporation.

FORMS OF BUSINESS CONSOLIDATION IN THE 20TH CENTURY: LEGAL WITHIN LIMITS

1. The **holding company** buys sufficient voting stock in different companies, called *subsidiaries,* to be able to control them. Some complex forms of the holding company have been declared illegal, but many holding companies legally exist today.

2. The **interlocking directorate** is an arrangement in which one or more men serve on the boards of directors of several companies. Interlocking directorates are legal unless they tend to lessen competition.

3. The **merger** is the consolidation of two companies into a single corporation. The merger is legal unless it causes an unreasonable restraint of trade. It is the most common form of business consolidation today, as corporations try to achieve economy and diversify their interests. In particular, giant corporations have used the merger to branch out into diverse fields. Such corporations are called *conglomerates.*

EXAMPLES OF BUSINESS CONSOLIDATION

1. Railroads

a. Cornelius Vanderbilt acquired the nickname "Commodore" and a fortune in steamboating, and then turned to railroads. He built the *New York Central* and by 1869 had combined a group of small lines into one railroad system running from New York City to Chicago. Vanderbilt improved the safety, comfort, and service of his railroad. However, he was disdainful of the public interest and of government regulations, once proclaiming, "What do I care for law? Hain't I got the power?"

b. James J. Hill built the *Great Northern Railway* westward from Minnesota. In 1893, after a series of mergers, his railroad reached the Pacific coast. Hill did not receive any federal land grand or cash subsidies. To attract settlers to Great Northern territory, Hill farsightedly provided free transportation from the East, easy credit, and expert agricultural advice.

Later, Hill battled another railroad magnate, *Edward H. Harriman,* for control of a competing road, the *Northern Pacific.* After a costly fight, the contestants agreed to compromise. They formed the Northern Securities Company, a holding company, to control the *Great Northern*, the *Northern Pacific*, and the *Chicago, Burlington and Quincy*, a road that provided an entrance from the West into Chicago. In 1904 the Supreme Court ordered the Northern Securities Company dissolved as a violation of the Sherman Antitrust Act.

2. Oil. *John D. Rockefeller*, a food merchant, entered the oil refining business and in 1870 formed the *Standard Oil Company of Ohio*. Rockefeller accumulated strong cash reserves, fought successful price wars, received secret railroad rebates on oil shipments, and, aided by the Depression of 1873, ruthlessly drove out or bought out many competitors. By 1879 the Standard Oil Company controlled over 90 percent of the country's oil refineries. Rockefeller improved his product and distributed it efficiently.

In 1882 Rockefeller combined his various holdings into the *Standard Oil Trust*, but it was ordered dissolved by the Ohio Supreme Court. Reorganized as a holding company, it was ordered dissolved by the United States Supreme Court, which ruled that the 34 member companies had to function as separate units.

3. Steel. *Andrew Carnegie*, a railroad executive and an outstanding salesman, entered the steel business. He built a single company that owned iron ore deposits in the Mesabi Range near Lake Superior, steamships on the Great Lakes, and steel mills in Pittsburgh. He pioneered the use of the Bessemer process for making steel and improved the quality of steel. He undersold competitors and drove them out of business. By 1900 the *Carnegie Steel Company* was producing one-fourth of the country's steel.

To reduce competition, other steel companies planned to form a huge monopoly. *J. P. Morgan*, the investment banker, handled the project. He bought out Carnegie's interests for $500 million and in 1901 combined the various steel companies under a single holding company, the *United States Steel Corporation*. This first billion-dollar corporation in the United States controlled 60 percent of the nation's steel production.

4. Other Industries. Business leaders who formed consolidations in other industries were: *Gustavus Swift* and *Philip D. Armour*—meat-packing; *Charles A. Pillsbury*—flour-milling; *James B. Duke*—cigarette-manufacturing; and *Andrew W. Mellon*—aluminum.

The business leaders of the Post-Civil War Era have been both praised and condemned. For destroying small companies, charging high prices, exploiting workers, manipulating stock, and corrupting government officials, they have been called "robber barons." For organizing new industries, providing better services, improving the quality of their products, supporting philanthropies, and hastening industrialization, they have been called "captains of industry."

ADVANTAGES OF BIG BUSINESS

1. Mass Production. Giant corporations reduced their fixed, or overhead, cost per unit by producing goods in large quantities and applying mass production methods such as the assembly line, division of labor, and standardization of parts. They introduced the most modern machinery, purchased raw materials in large quantities at low prices, and utilized by-products. They could therefore offer the public new, improved, and less expensive products.

2. Wide Distribution. Large corporations increased their profits by using large-scale advertising and by selling their products throughout the entire nation.

3. Efficient Management. Large corporations could afford to hire the most capable executives, maintain costly research laboratories, and raise capital for expansion.

ABUSES BY BIG BUSINESS

1. Elimination of Competition. Large corporations could afford local price wars and use other methods of "cutthroat competition" to drive out small businesses. The mere fact that large corporations can sell at a lower price and even offer a superior product has had the effect of destroying the small businessman.

2. Power Over the Consumer. Once a large company achieved a degree of monopoly, it could force the consumer to pay high prices and accept inferior quality.

3. Exploitation of Workers. By achieving control of the labor market in some communities, large companies were in a position to pay low wages and keep workers from forming unions.

4. Influence Over the Government. Some unscrupulous businessmen have degraded the government by bribing politicians and buying the votes of legislators. By their great concentration of wealth, large corporations have exercised great influence over government policy.

GOVERNMENT AND BIG BUSINESS

GOVERNMENT POLICIES TOWARD BUSINESS

1. Freedom From Government Regulation (Until the End of the 19th Century). *Adam Smith,* a British economist, in 1776 systematically expounded the principles of capitalism in his book *The Wealth of Nations.* He argued that the government should follow a policy of *laissez-faire,* that is, leave business alone. Smith maintained that free competition would lower prices, increase the variety and improve the quality of goods, provide opportunities for new companies, and, in general, further the best interests of society. Smith argued that the government should neither help nor hinder business.

Industrial interests in the United States ignored Smith's arguments against protective tariffs and government subsidies, and asked only that the government not hinder business. To the end of the 19th century, the government therefore followed a policy of fostering industry but not regulating it.

2. Regulation in the Interests of Society (Since the End of the 19th Century). In the post-Civil War period, giant corporations arose and restrained the free competition that was supposed to regulate the economy automatically and thereby benefit society. Big business gained dominance over the economy and committed abuses threatening the public health and welfare, and harming the interests of farmers, laborers, and small businessmen. An aroused people demanded government regulation of industry, a policy that was adopted and that persists to this day.

RAILROADS: THE FIRST REGULATED INDUSTRY

1. Railroad Abuses

a. High Rates. (1) Each railroad, having a virtual monopoly over transportation in its territory, charged "what the traffic will bear." (2) Many railroads issued *watered stock* (stock in excess of the actual worth of the company) and charged high rates in order to pay dividends on their watered stock. (3) Railroads frequently entered into *pooling agreements* to divide business and raise rates. Since no other means of transportation could compete with railroads, shippers had to pay what the railroads charged.

b. Discrimination Regarding Rates. Railroads granted large shippers *rebates*, whereas small shippers—farmers and small businessmen—paid the full rate.

Railroads charged lower rates for freight hauled between big cities, where they faced competing lines, than for freight hauled to or from rural areas, where they faced no competition. As a result, a long haul often cost less than a short haul.

c. Political Corruption. Railroads unduly influenced state and federal politics by the bribery of legislators, campaign contributions to political parties, and free railroad passes to influential people.

Farmers, small merchants, small businessmen, and the general public protested these abuses. The Grange secured several state regulatory laws, but in 1886 the Supreme Court in the case of *Wabash vs. Illinois* declared state regulation of interstate railroads unconstitutional.

2. Beginning of Federal Regulation: Interstate Commerce Act (1887)

a. Provisions. This act (1) forbade discrimination between persons in the form of special rates or rebates, (2) prohibited railroads from charging more for a short haul than for a long haul, (3) prohibited pooling, (4) ordered a ten-day notice and public posting of new railroad rates, (5) declared that railroad rates should be "reasonable and just," and (6) established an enforcement agency, the *Interstate Commerce Commission (ICC)*.

b. Weaknesses. The ICC originally was handicapped by (1) the vague language of the law, (2) the complexity of the railroad business, (3) the shortage of qualified staff, and (4) its inability to enforce its decisions without appealing to the courts, which tended to favor the railroads.

c. Significance. Nevertheless, the Interstate Commerce Act established the precedent of government regulation of private interstate business and paved the way for subsequent and stronger legislation.

3. Subsequent Regulation. The ICC was strengthened by (a) the *Elkins Act* (1903), enabling the ICC to punish shippers as well as railroads engaged in rebating, (b) the *Hepburn Act* (1906), empowering it to set maximum railroad rates, and (c) the *Physical Valuation Act* (1913), empowering it to determine the value of railroad property as a basis for setting fair rates.

To meet the emergency of World War I, the government operated the railroads, coordinating service and eliminating duplication.

The *Transportation Act (Esch-Cummins Act)* of 1920 returned the railroads to private operation. It also empowered the ICC to (a) fix minimum as well as maximum rates, and (b) approve railroad pools and consolidations. Since many railroads were in financial trouble, the ICC was now concerned with the welfare not only of the shippers but also of the railroads.

4. Railroads Today. Railroads no longer have a virtual monopoly, but face fierce competition from bus lines, trucking companies, and airlines. To compete, railroads have introduced new services such as "piggybacking" truck trailers on flatcars. Some large railroads have bought out smaller ones, as railroads seek the economies of larger-scale operations. Meanwhile, railroads have sought greater flexibility in setting their own rates. Under the *Rail Deregulation Act* (1980), Congress gave railroads increased authority to raise freight rates and abandon unprofitable routes. The ICC's regulatory role was thus greatly reduced.

To assure service between heavily populated cities, mainly in the Northeast, Congress in the 1970's created and partly financed two new lines. One was a passenger line, called *Amtrak* (the National Railroad Passenger Corporation). The other was a freight line, called *Conrail* (the Consolidated Rail Corporation). The new railroads took over track of existing private lines. Amtrak operated at a loss and required government subsidies. However, Conrail became profitable and in 1987 the government sold its stock to private investors.

REGULATION OF BIG BUSINESS

1. Sherman Antitrust Act (1890)

a. Provisions. To break up existing monopolies and compel competition, this law (1) declared illegal "every contract, combination in the form of trust or otherwise, or conspiracy, in restraint of trade," and (2) provided penalties for corporations and individuals that violated the act.

b. Weaknesses. In enforcing the law, the Department of Justice was handicapped by (1) the vague language of the law, (2) the ability of business leaders to use forms of combination other than the trust, (3) the lack of sufficient funds, personnel, and executive determination for enforcement, and (4) interpretations by the Supreme Court favoring big business. The Supreme Court held illegal only "unreasonable" restraint of trade, thereby establishing a loophole, called the *rule of reason.*

2. Theodore Roosevelt: "Trust Buster" (1901–1909).
Theodore Roosevelt, who pledged a *Square Deal* for all the people, was the first President who vigorously enforced the Sherman Act. Roosevelt believed that the growth of big business was inevitable. He approved "good" trusts, but he sought to destroy "bad" trusts. Roosevelt instituted over 40 antitrust cases. He won his most famous victory, by a 5-to-4 Supreme Court decision, against the *Northern Securities Company,* a newly formed railroad holding company that threatened to monopolize railroad service in the Northwest.

Roosevelt's successor, William Howard Taft, stepped up the government's trust busting by instituting some 90 antitrust suits.

3. Publicity: Muckrakers.
The trust-busting campaigns of Roosevelt and Taft were aided by a group of writers called *muckrakers.* To arouse the American people to demand reforms, they exposed the evils of big business.

Author	Major Work	Theme
Ida M. Tarbell	*History of the Standard Oil Company*	Ruthless practices of a gigantic monopoly.
Frank Norris	*The Octopus*	Struggle of wheat farmers against the railroad.
Gustavus Myers	*History of the Great American Fortunes*	Corruption and exploitation as practiced by leaders of big business.
Ray Stannard Baker	*Railroads on Trial*	Railroad evils and abuses.
Upton Sinclair	*The Jungle*	Revolting practices of the meat-packing industry.

The Jungle in particular aroused public opinion. In 1906 Congress inaugurated government protection of the consumer by passing two laws. The *Meat Inspection Act* set up sanitary regulations for meat packers and provided for federal inspection of meat-packing plants. The *Pure Food and Drug Act* forbade the manufacture, transportation, and sale of adulterated and poisonous foods and drugs.

4. Woodrow Wilson and Business Regulation. Woodrow Wilson, who pledged the American people a *New Freedom*, secured Congressional enactment of the following business reform laws:

a. Clayton Antitrust Act (1914). This law attempted to strengthen the Sherman Antitrust Act by listing specific illegal practices and combinations: (1) price discrimination toward purchasers, (2) "tie-in" contracts by which a merchant could buy goods from a company only on condition that he would not handle the products of that company's competitors, and (3) certain types of holding companies and interlocking directorates. The law declared these practices and combinations unlawful if they tended "to lessen competition or create a monopoly." This proviso limited the effectiveness of the Clayton Act. As with the Sherman Act, the Supreme Court held illegal only restraint of trade considered "unreasonable." (The Clayton Act prohibited the use of antitrust laws against farm cooperatives and labor unions.)

b. Federal Trade Commission Act (1914). This act established the Federal Trade Commission (FTC) to receive reports from and make investigations of business firms. Its main purpose was to enforce the Clayton Act prohibitions of certain business practices and to prevent other unfair methods of competition.

The FTC has ruled the following practices as unfair: (1) misbranding and adulteration of goods, (2) false and misleading advertising, (3) spying and bribery to secure trade secrets, and (4) closely imitating a competitor's product. To halt such practices, the FTC issues *cease and desist* orders. FTC orders may be challenged by the firm involved and are subject to court review.

INDUSTRIAL GROWTH AND PROBLEMS SINCE WORLD WAR I

BUSINESS FOLLOWING WORLD WAR I: FROM "BOOM TO BUST"

1. Boom Conditions (To 1929)

a. Continued Growth of Big Business. During the war and in the prosperous postwar years, business leaders modernized their plants and promoted consolidations. Modern techniques of production provided an additional stimulus for consolidation, and the concentration of industrial wealth by mergers and the formation of holding companies took place at a rapid pace. The government encouraged consolidation by initiating no new anti-trust suits.

b. Scientific Management. Inspired by the work of the industrial engineer *Frederick W. Taylor,* corporate executives applied the ideas of scientific management: efficient plant organization and time-motion studies. Factories achieved lower production costs per unit and greater productivity per worker.

c. Age of the Automobile. Just prior to World War I, Henry Ford revolutionized the automobile industry by mass-production methods, especially the *assembly line.* Ford workers stood alongside a conveyor, which moved at a steady pace and carried a succession of units for assembly. Each worker, in turn, performed his small task; and, at the end of the assembly line, the completed cars were driven away. Ford's production methods permitted him to reduce the price of his cars so that millions of Americans could afford to buy them. After the war, the American people found that a car was a necessity, and auto production mounted rapidly.

The growth of the automobile industry had widespread effects. Automobile factories required raw materials: rubber, steel, aluminum, and plastics. New enterprises appeared: gasoline and repair stations, garages and parking lots. The popularity of the automobile led to the construction of a vast system of new and improved highways.

d. New Industries. When chemicals from Germany were cut off during World War I, American industrialists expanded the domestic chemical industry. After the war, the government assigned confiscated German patents to American chemical companies and set high tariffs against chemical imports, both measures aiding the growth of the American chemical industry.

Entertainment-seeking Americans delighted in the growth of movies (first "silents" and then "talkies") and radio. The latter invention was made possible by the work of the Italian *Guglielmo Marconi* with wireless telegraphy and of the American *Lee De Forest* with the vacuum tube.

Travelers took to a new and faster means of transportation, the airplane. Invented by *Wilbur* and *Orville Wright* in 1903, the airplane was still in the early stages of commercial development.

Homeowners stepped up their use of electricity in such devices as the refrigerator, radio, phonograph, vacuum cleaner, and toaster.

2. Bust: The Great Depression. In 1929 the American economy entered its most severe depression. By 1933 American business had reached its lowest ebb. Business bankruptcies, bank failures, mass unemployment, and even panic swept the country. This depression sapped the belief in a self-regulating economic system and strengthened the trend toward government regulation. (For causes and other details of this depression, see pages 252–254.)

NEW DEAL AND BUSINESS

To aid the recovery of business, President Franklin D. Roosevelt secured Congressional passage of the *National Industrial Recovery Act (NIRA)*. It (1) established the *National Recovery Administration (NRA)*, (2) empowered the NRA to supervise industry in drawing up "codes of fair competition" providing for minimum wages, maximum hours, price-fixing, production controls, and fair methods of competition, and (3) exempted agreements made under the NIRA from the Sherman and Clayton Antitrust Acts. Thus the NIRA allowed monopolistic practices but kept them subject to government control.

The NIRA was at first welcomed enthusiastically, but it soon drew much criticism. While small businessmen complained that the codes favored the large corporations, large businessmen complained about government "regimentation." (The NIRA also encouraged unionization. See page 277.)

In 1935 the NIRA was declared unconstitutional by the Supreme Court in the *Schechter case*. The Court said that (1) the codes were illegal since they were laws not enacted by Congress, and (2) the federal government had no right to regulate intrastate commerce. Subsequently, the Antitrust Division of the Department of Justice vigorously renewed enforcement of the Sherman and Clayton Acts.

BIG BUSINESS AND WORLD WAR II (1939–1945)

1. **"Miracle of Production."** With the onset of World War II in 1939 and the fall of France to the Germans in 1940, many Americans realized our shocking military unpreparedness. Congress authorized tremendous expenditures for the production of military equipment. When the Japanese attacked Pearl Harbor in 1941, America was drawn actively into the war. American industrialists, displaying great managerial ability and drawing upon the pool of unemployed skilled workers, fulfilled the nation's war needs. From 1940 to 1945 industry almost doubled the production of manufactured goods, thereby supplying our military forces and providing huge quantities of equipment for our allies. American industry significantly helped win the war.

2. **Increased Government Control.** To mobilize and coordinate American industry, the government established the following agencies: (*a*) The **War Production Board** (**WPB**) directed the conversion of industry to wartime production, granted essential industries priorities on raw materials, and brought about the construction of new factories. These new plants increased the production of aluminum, steel, airplanes, and ships, and initiated the production of synthetic rubber and of materials for atomic research. (*b*) The **Office of Price Administration** (**OPA**) combatted price rises and inflation by setting price ceilings and by rationing scarce goods. (*c*) The **War Manpower**

Commission (WMC) directed labor to essential war industries. (*d*) the *War Labor Board (WLB)* settled labor-management disputes.

3. **Evaluation.** Credit for America's "miracle of production" in World War II has been given to the managerial ability of private industry as well as to the centralized planning and controls exercised by government agencies. The American people regained their faith, severely shaken by the Depression of 1929, in American industrial leadership.

BUSINESS SINCE WORLD WAR II: RECENT TRENDS

1. **Protecting the Public.** Since the New Deal, numerous laws and executive actions have sought to protect consumers, workers, and the general public. In 1938 Congress passed the *Food, Drug, and Cosmetic Act* empowering the government to (*a*) prevent adulteration, misbranding, and false advertising, (*b*) require manufacturers to list the ingredients of their products, (*c*) regulate cosmetics as well as food and drugs, and (*d*) require adequate testing of new drugs.

Congress has enacted many other public protection laws: (*a*) The *Truth in Packaging Act* (1966) outlawed deceptive containers, required simpler labels, and set standards for such terms as "family size." (*b*) The *Traffic Safety Act* (1966) empowered the government to enforce minimum safety standards in the design and equipment of new automobiles. (*c*) The *Truth in Lending Act* (1968) required lenders to inform consumers of the full cost of credit in dollars and in annual interest rates. (*d*) The *Consumer Products Safety Act* (1972) created a commission to oversee the safety of household items such as tools and toys. (*e*) The *Nutrition and Labeling Act* (1990) instructed the FDA to set standards for food labeling, especially those that make claims about health and nutrition. (*f*) The *Consumer Products Safety Act* (1990) gave regulators new powers to demand reports from manufacturers about product defects.

2. **Continued Economic Concentration.** Corporations improved their competitive position and diversified their activities by pursuing mergers. While permitting many mergers, the federal government watched for violations of antitrust laws. American companies that acquired or established subsidiaries in other countries became known as *multinational corporations*.

3. **Continued Technological Progress.** Businesses developed many new products, based on innovations in biochemistry, plastics, electronics, and computers. Manufacturing firms employed automatic devices to operate machines, a process called *automation*. By the 1980's this process had extended to the use of computer-run robots to perform many steps in manufacturing.

4. **GNP, GDP, and the Economy.** The *gross national product* (GNP) and the *gross domestic product* (GDP) measure the dollar value of the output of goods and services produced and sold each year. Both are statistical tools used to analyze the health of the economy. The GNP reports all production by U.S. residents, while the GDP reports only production within the U.S. borders. In 1992 the government began using GDP as the basic measure of output.

From 1950 to 1994, the GDP increased twenty-twofold, to more than $6.5 trillion. As measured in terms of the dollar's real purchasing power (to offset price increases caused by inflation), GDP multiplied by three and a half. The growth of GDP was not constant, however. *Recessions* (periods of declining output) occurred eight times during these years.

5. The Reagan Administration and Business

a. Managing the Economy. The Reagan administration persuaded Congress to cut taxes in 1981. The goal was to leave consumers and businesses with more money to invest, thus encouraging economic growth. Meanwhile, Congress approved the Reagan administration's proposals for sharply increasing defense spending while cutting back a variety of social programs.

Federal budget deficits grew dramatically, partly due to increased spending on defense and huge interest payments on the national debt. (Between 1981 and 1989, the national debt jumped from $1 trillion to just under $3 trillion.)

b. Reducing Government Regulation. President Reagan claimed that the "mass of regulations" imposed on businesses add "one hundred billion dollars to the price of things we buy." As part of a program to get the government "off our backs," the Reagan administration greatly reduced regulations.

c. Dealing With Business Mergers and Buyouts. The Reagan administration was more lenient toward business mergers than previous administrations had been, often advising companies on how to fashion mergers to meet its antitrust standards. The 1980's saw a wave of mergers and buyouts.

The Justice Department pursued the effort to break up the monopoly of the huge American Telephone and Telegraph Company (AT&T). In an antitrust case begun under President Ford, a federal judge in 1982 ordered AT&T to splinter into several smaller firms. The breakup led to vigorous competition and caused long-distance rates to fall. However, local rates and service charges rose.

6. The Bush Administration and Business

a. Managing the Economy. Federal budget deficits soared to new heights in the early 1990's, despite deficit reduction efforts.

b. Savings and Loan Bailout. Banking practices came under close scrutiny after the fast and loose practices of the 1980's led to a wave of failures by savings and loan companies. Because savings and loan deposits (as well as other banking deposits) are federally insured, the federal government ended up footing much of the bill. In 1990 Congress created the *Resolution Trust Corporation* to coordinate the multi-billion-dollar savings and loan bailout.

7. The Clinton Administration and Business

a. Managing the Economy. President Clinton struggled to get the economy moving again and bring federal budget deficits down. He tried a mixture of spending increases, spending cuts, and new taxes.

Soon after taking office Clinton proposed a $19.5 billion "economic stimulus" bill, but the Republicans quickly shot it down. The bill would have provided funds for urban development, summer-jobs programs, and extended unemployment benefits. Republicans argued that the bill was too expensive and would increase the deficit. After a brief filibuster by Senate Republicans, Clinton gave up on the bill.

Eventually, Clinton and the Democrats managed to push through Congress in 1993 a five-year economic plan that they claimed would cut $496 billion from the deficit through spending cuts and tax increases. Mainly because of lower interest rates, the deficit declined in 1993 after peaking at a record $290 billion in 1992.

b. Reform of Banking. (1) The Clinton administration proposed to combine four agencies that regulate banks, creating a single regulatory agency. (2) The administration supported legislation in Congress that would allow nationwide banks. Under existing law, banks that want to operate in more than one state must set up a separate subsidiary for each state. That can be expensive.

MULTIPLE-CHOICE QUESTIONS

1. Which factor had *least* to do with the industrialization of the United States in the 19th century? (1) inventions (2) foreign demand for American manufactures (3) abundant natural resources (4) Constitutional protection of private property.

2. The beginning of the "Age of Big Business" in the United States is associated with (1) the War of 1812 (2) the Civil War (3) World War I (4) World War II.

3. Because of the continuing Industrial Revolution, the industrialized nations of the world have been able to (1) raise their standards of living despite increases in population (2) eliminate periods of recession and depression (3) eradicate poverty and hunger among their peoples (4) resist demands to lower trade barriers.

4. Which statement concerning corporations is true? (1) They did not exist before the Civil War. (2) Small businesses seldom incorporate. (3) Businesses incorporate to secure discounts on large purchases. (4) Today, the corporation is the dominant form of business organization in manufacturing.

5. In industries with heavy overhead costs, manufacturers often seek to (1) decrease production so as to use less raw material (2) secure additional money by issuing bonds (3) charge excessive prices (4) increase production to capacity.

6. Company *Q* owns controlling shares of stock in companies *A*, *B*, *C*, and *D*. This is an example of a (1) pool (2) partnership (3) holding company (4) merger.

7. An important reason for the formation of trusts in the latter part of the 19th century was a desire to (1) escape federal regulation (2) eliminate competition (3) reduce prices (4) eliminate the use of rebates.

8. By which technique have most American business consolidations come about in recent years? (1) pooling agreement (2) merger (3) trust (4) trade association.

9. John D. Rockefeller's most significant contribution to business enterprise in the United States was his (1) elimination of wasteful competitive practices (2) introduction of assembly-line techniques (3) ethical approach to business (4) promotion of peaceful settlement of labor disputes.

10. Which pairs an industrial leader with his industry? (1) Vanderbilt—railroads (2) Carnegie—meat-packing (3) Mellon—automobiles (4) Armour—steel.

11. Which policy toward business was generally followed by the federal government before 1880? (1) strict regulation (2) government ownership (3) laissez-faire (4) heavy taxation.

12. Which was the first industry to be regulated by the United States government? (1) railroads (2) hydroelectric power (3) telegraph communication (4) meat-packing.

13. The primary purpose of the Interstate Commerce Act was to (1) grant land to the railroads (2) regulate railroad rates (3) establish government ownership of railroads (4) supervise interstate truck and bus lines.

14. Before 1900 the Interstate Commerce Commission was handicapped by (1) the adoption of the Sherman Antitrust Act (2) the rise of the Populist party (3) court decisions (4) the establishment of the Federal Trade Commission.

15. The most important purpose of the Sherman Antitrust Act (1890) was to (1) encourage competition in business (2) improve relations between big business and the government (3) improve working conditions in factories (4) prevent business from becoming more powerful than labor.

16. An important effect of the Sherman Antitrust Act was that it (1) restored active competition (2) led to the passage of the National Banking Act (3) corrected the weaknesses of the Clayton Antitrust Act (4) caused a change in the forms and techniques of business consolidation.

17. The attitude of Theodore Roosevelt toward business was that the federal government should (1) own public utilities (2) follow a policy of laissez-faire (3) eliminate bad business practices (4) leave the regulation of railroads to the states.

18. In applying the "rule of reason," the Supreme Court ruled that the most important consideration in antitrust cases was the (1) size of the business organization (2) number of stockholders (3) effect on competition (4) type of article manufactured.

19. A literary work associated with the muckrakers is (1) *The Liberator,* by William Lloyd Garrison (2) *Inside U.S.A.,* by John Gunther (3) *The Empire of Business,* by Andrew Carnegie (4) *History of the Standard Oil Company,* by Ida M. Tarbell.

20. Which action was hastened largely because public opinion was aroused by a contemporary novel? (1) ratification of the Sixteenth Amendment (2) establishment of the Interstate Commerce Commission (3) passage of the Sherman Antitrust Act (4) enactment of the Meat Inspection Act of 1906.

21. According to the Federal Trade Commission, which is an example of an unfair business practice? (1) creating a subsidiary corporation (2) lowering prices to meet competition (3) incorporating in one state and doing business in another (4) closely imitating goods sold by a competitor.

22. The National Industrial Recovery Act was declared unconstitutional because (1) Congress has no right to regulate intrastate commerce (2) Congress has no right to regulate interstate commerce (3) no emergency existed (4) the act did not restore prosperity.

23. Since World War II, the railroads have asked the federal government for permission to (1) organize holding companies (2) engage in pooling (3) merge competing systems (4) combine with airlines.

24. "There are acres and acres of machines, and here and there you will find a worker standing at a master switchboard watching lights and dials that tell him what is happening in each machine." This statement best describes (1) consolidation (2) monopoly (3) mass production (4) automation.

25. In the United States, which field of employment has been *least* influenced by automation? (1) domestic services (2) banking (3) baking industry (4) automobile industry.

26. The gross national product (GNP) of the United States is a measure of the (1) total annual production of our mines and factories (2) increase in the number of people living in cities (3) extent to which natural resources have been used up (4) total money value of all the goods and services produced in a year.

27. The gross national product is a (1) means of estimating next year's national debt (2) barometer of the nation's economic growth (3) method of calculating the profits of large corporations (4) method for verifying the Consumer Price Index.

28. The increasing complexity of modern economic life in the United States has tended to (1) cause more government regulation (2) permit corporations to defy the government (3) have little effect upon government regulation (4) strengthen the philosophy of laissez-faire.

29. During the period 1887–1914, the federal government followed the policy that competition among railroads (1) should be maintained (2) was undesirable (3) could not be controlled (4) was of no concern to the federal government.

30. The trend most characteristic of American business since 1900 has been the (1) increase in the size of many business organizations (2) disappearance of small business (3) decrease in government ownership of business (4) decrease in government regulation.

ESSAY QUESTIONS

1. The United States now has the highest standard of living ever attained by man. Giving *two* specific examples, explain how *each* of the following has helped to bring about this high standard of living: (*a*) labor supply, (*b*) inventiveness and ingenuity, (*c*) government policies, (*d*) natural resources.

2. The corporation has made possible the mass production that is characteristic of American industry. (*a*) Explain *two* ways in which the corporation has promoted mass production. (*b*) Discuss briefly *two* reasons why small-scale production continues to exist. (*c*) Explain *two* ways in which mass production has affected the consumer.

3. The so-called "captains of industry" played a major role in the economic development of the United States after the Civil War. (*a*) Show how *each* of the following factors contributed to the success of these industrial leaders: (1) use of natural resources, (2) forms of business organization, (3) the personal characteristics of these leaders. (*b*) Explain *two* effects of the activities of these men on the lives of the American people.

4. In 1887 the federal government began its efforts to regulate big business by the passage of the Interstate Commerce Act. (*a*) Discuss briefly *two* reasons why the federal government generally did not regulate business before then. (*b*) Show *two* ways in which the Interstate Commerce Commission has attempted to regulate big business. (*c*) Show *two* ways in which the increase in government control of business has directly affected the government itself.

5. Big business has occupied a significant place in the affairs of the United States for the past 100 years. (*a*) Discuss *two* reasons why the period after the Civil War was marked by great industrial expansion. (*b*) Discuss *two* specific problems created by

the rise of big business. (c) Show how federal legislation has attempted to solve *each* of the problems given in answer to (b).

6. The policy of the federal government toward business has varied from one period in American history to another. (a) Describe *two* ways in which the federal government aided the growth of business during the period 1865–1890. (b) Explain how *one* federal law passed during the 20th century attempted to regulate business. (c) Discuss *two* basic reasons for the change by the federal government from a policy of aiding the growth of business to a policy of regulating business. (d) Show *two* ways in which business has helped the United States assume a position of leadership in world affairs.

7. Give *one* reason to explain why you agree *or one* reason to explain why you disagree with *each* of the following statements relating to the United States economy: (a) The small businessman must inevitably disappear. (b) The Sherman and Clayton Antitrust laws have proved effective. (c) Since the consumer benefits from competition between corporations, he does not need the protection of the government. (d) Corporation executives today are showing concern for the overall welfare of American society.

Part 5. The Government Concerns Itself With the Business Cycle and Public Finance

BUSINESS CYCLE

PHASES OF THE BUSINESS CYCLE

1. Prosperity: a great output of goods, extensive factory expansion, high prices and profits, easy bank credit, full employment, good wages, and a general feeling of optimism.

2. Recession: a falling off of demand for goods, decreased production, falling prices and profits, the calling in of bank loans, decreasing employment, falling wages, and a general feeling of caution and worry.

3. Depression: low production, low prices, little or no profits, widespread business failures, few bank loans, heavy unemployment, low wages, and a general feeling of pessimism.

4. Recovery: increasing production, rising prices and profits, extension of bank loans, increasing employment, rising wages, and a general feeling of hopefulness.

CAUSES OF BUSINESS CONTRACTION

1. Overproduction. Factory owners and merchants overestimate demand and build up excessive inventories of goods. Eventually, retailers curtail orders, and factory owners reduce production, thereby causing a downturn in business.

2. Underconsumption. Workers and farmers find their incomes insufficient to purchase industry's output of goods. Eventually, this disproportion of industrial supply to consumer demand becomes too great, and the economy slows down.

3. Imbalance Between Savings and Investment. People who save money instead of spending it decrease the demand for consumer goods. These savings, however, are invested in securities or deposited in banks. A sizable proportion of the bank deposits is invested in mortgage loans for the construction of homes and buildings, and in business loans for the purchase of materials and machinery. However, not all savings are invested, since banks may desire to increase their cash reserves or may lack sufficient demand for loans. When a large proportion of savings is not invested, the total demand for goods falls off, and the economy turns downward.

4. Psychological Causes. When pessimism sets in, consumers refrain from buying, businessmen limit expansion, and bankers restrict loans. All these responses cause the economy to worsen and pessimism to deepen.

Economists believe that recessions are not caused by any one factor but by the interaction of several factors. Many economists are convinced, furthermore, that the business cycle is man-made and can be controlled by intelligent human effort.

MAJOR DEPRESSIONS SINCE THE CIVIL WAR

1. The Depression of 1873 was caused by the overexpansion of railroads and industry; the granting of unsound bank loans; insufficient farm purchasing power because of low agricultural prices; and economic distress in Europe. The immediate cause was the failure of Jay Cooke and Company, a leading banking house.

2. The Depression of 1893 was caused by the overexpansion of railroads and industry; continued low agricultural prices; and fear among businessmen for the stability of our currency, due to the shrinking of the gold reserve and the battle for free silver.

3. The Depression of 1929

a. Causes. (1) American industry overexpanded its production facilities. (2) Consumers lacked sufficient income to purchase the total output of industry. Farmers in particular had low incomes following World War I because of the agricultural depression. Workers' wages failed to keep pace with increased productivity. Furthermore, many workers lost jobs because of the introduction of new machinery. (3) Bankers made unsound loans, and these ultimately resulted in bank failures that wiped out the savings of many depositors. (4) "Get-rich-quick" speculators bid up the price of real estate and stocks to unrealistic levels. (5) International trade declined because World War I had hurt Europe's economy and had lessened Europe's ability to purchase goods. Also, high protective tariffs interfered with the flow of goods between countries. (6) The immediate cause was the severe stock market crash starting in October, 1929.

b. Differences From Earlier Depressions. The 1929 depression was the most severe in American history because (1) the United States no longer had the frontier with its economic opportunities, (2) the economy had become primarily industrial, and more Americans were affected by business variations, and (3) the depression was not limited to the United States but was worldwide.

c. Depth of the Depression. By 1932, production, prices, and profits were substantially down, business bankruptcies were numerous, 5000 banks had failed, wages had been slashed, and over 12 million workers, or 25 percent of the labor force, were unemployed.

d. New Deal. In 1933 Franklin D. Roosevelt took office as President and began a concerted attack against the depression. His New Deal included the following approaches (see also pages 413–418):

(1) *Deficit Budgeting and Public Works.* Roosevelt incurred deficit budgets by heavy government borrowing. He used government funds to provide direct relief for the unemployed and, more important, to stimulate business and create jobs. The *Public Works Administration* let out contracts to construction companies for massive programs of public works, which in turn stimulated businesses throughout the economy. The *Works Progress Administration* spent government funds on such programs as statistical surveys, art and theater projects, and some construction work. By thus pumping funds into the economy, the New Deal attempted to invigorate business.

(2) *Banking Reforms.* The New Deal restored public confidence in the banks by insuring depositors' money in case of bank failure and by strengthening the powers of the Federal Reserve Board (see pages 255–257). The Federal Reserve followed an easy-money policy so as to encourage loans for business purposes.

(3) *Production Controls.* To avoid overproduction, New Deal laws encouraged farmers to reduce their output and temporarily suspended the antitrust laws so that businessmen could establish industrywide production controls.

(4) *Encouragement of Consumption.* To promote mass purchasing power, the New Deal legislated minimum wage standards, encouraged the states to establish unemployment insurance systems, and fostered labor unions by guaranteeing collective bargaining. To preserve the future purchasing power of older citizens, the New Deal began Social Security.

(5) *Optimism.* Roosevelt instilled confidence into the people by asserting that the nation was basically sound. His optimism proved contagious.

By 1939 people had regained confidence in our economy, and business had achieved a partial recovery. Unemployment, however, although it had decreased, was still a substantial **17** percent of the labor force, over **8** million persons being out of work. The depression was not fully wiped out until the economy was spurred by national defense and World War II needs.

BUSINESS CYCLE SINCE WORLD WAR II

1. Variations. The economy experienced several postwar recessions. *(a)* The first ones were of short duration and comparatively mild. As measured by GNP, business activity recorded a pause or slight downturn. Unemployment rose, but not above 7 percent. *(b)* The recession of 1973–1975 was more severe, with unemployment above 9 percent and a strong inflation caused in part by the quadrupling of oil prices by the Organization of Petroleum Exporting Countries (OPEC). *(c)* Two back-to-back recessions—in 1980 and in 1981–1982—were most severe, with a sluggish GNP, depressed housing and auto industries, unemployment at 11 percent, severe inflation, and high interest rates.

2. Measures to Level Out Extremes of the Business Cycle

a. Nongovernmental Efforts. (1) Strong labor unions kept wage levels steady even during periods of recession. They divided the available work to keep workers from being laid off, and kept down unemployment due to the introduction of new machines. Unions also sought to assure their members 52 paychecks a year by securing the guaranteed annual wage. (2) Responsible business leaders geared their corporate policies to maintain steady employment and capital investment even during recessions.

During prosperity both unions and management have been urged by the government to exercise restraint regarding wage and price increases.

b. Employment Act of 1946. This law affirmed the "policy and responsibility of the federal government to promote maximum employment, production, and purchasing power." It authorized the President to furnish Congress with economic reports covering current economic conditions and foreseeable future trends, and including, if necessary, recommendations for federal action to halt any extreme swings in the business cycle. To assist the President, the law established a three-person *Council of Economic Advisers.*

c. Government Tax Policies. In 1968 Congress moved to curb serious inflation by extending excise taxes on new automobile purchases and telephone service, and by approving a 10 percent surcharge on individual and corporate income taxes. In 1971, to spur the economy, Congress slightly reduced income taxes of individuals by increasing their personal exemptions, granted business people a tax credit for buying new equipment, and ended the excise tax on new automobile purchases. (For the 1981 tax cut, see pages 259–260.)

d. Built-in or Automatic Stabilizers. Since 1933 the government has enacted significant laws that serve to stabilize the economy once it turns downward. To keep the purchasing power of the consumer strong, these laws provide: unemployment insurance for laid-off workers, Social Security payments to retired workers, price supports for farmers, and minimum wages. Another type of built-in stabilizer is the Federal Deposit Insurance Corporation. The FDIC now guarantees every depositor up to $100,000 per account in case of bank failure. FDIC protection helped restore confidence in our banking system and drastically reduced the number of bank failures.

e. Public Works Programs. During recession periods, the federal government and the states increased the funds spent for public works. Such increased spending pumped more money into the economy and helped reverse the cyclical downtrend. For example, in 1971 President Nixon approved the *Emergency Employment Act,* which provided federal funds for states and localities to create over 150,000 public works jobs.

f. Use of Federal Reserve Powers. The Federal Reserve Board used its bank and credit powers to prevent extremes in the business cycle. A discussion of the Federal Reserve System follows.

FEDERAL RESERVE SYSTEM

Established by Congress in 1913 and strengthened during the 1930's, the *Federal Reserve System* serves as our centralized banking system.

1. Purposes. The Federal Reserve (*a*) supervises banks and helps them serve the general public and the business community, (*b*) serves as the fiscal and banking agent of the federal government by holding government funds, selling government securities, and issuing currency (Federal Reserve Notes), and (*c*) encourages the healthy growth of the national economy by acting to prevent business extremes: runaway prosperity and inflation, as well as serious recession and deflation.

2. Twelve Federal Reserve Banks. The United States is divided into 12 Federal Reserve Districts, each served by its own Federal Reserve Bank. Since the Federal Reserve Banks do business not with individuals or corporations, but only with member banks, they are called "bankers' banks."

3. **Member Banks.** Banks chartered by the federal government must join the Federal Reserve System. Banks chartered by a state may do so if they wish. Today, approximately 5000 federally chartered and 2000 state-chartered banks, doing over 80 percent of the nation's commercial banking, are Federal Reserve members. They provide the capital for the 12 Federal Reserve Banks. All Federal Reserve members must (and other banks may) join the *Federal Deposit Insurance Corporation.*

4. **Board of Governors.** The Federal Reserve System is controlled by its Board of Governors. The Board consists of a chairman and six other members, each appointed for a 14-year term by the President with the consent of the Senate. The Board of Governors, however, is independent of the President and the Senate. It exercises its own best judgment regarding the use of its powers over credit and banking.

FEDERAL RESERVE POWERS

1. **Setting the Reserve Ratio.** Each business day, a bank pays out and receives money. Because on some days it must pay out more money than it receives, it must keep a reserve. The Federal Reserve Board of Governors determines the size of this reserve by setting the *reserve ratio* (the proportion of reserves to deposits).

By raising the reserve ratio, the Federal Reserve Board forces its member banks to increase their reserves. They can therefore lend less money. This causes a decline in business expansion and consumer demand. Conversely, the Board can encourage business expansion by lowering the reserve ratio and thus permitting member banks to lend more money.

2. **Setting the Discount Rate.** If a member bank wants more money, it can borrow from a Federal Reserve Bank. The interest rate charged by the Federal Reserve is called the *discount rate* (or *rediscount rate*). When the Federal Reserve Board raises the discount rate, the member banks in turn raise their interest rate to their customers, and business expansion is slowed down. The Federal Reserve Board can achieve the opposite effect by lowering its discount rate.

3. **Engaging in Open-Market Operations.** The Federal Reserve Banks buy and sell government securities by dealing with individuals and corporations in the open market. When they sell government securities, the Federal Reserve Banks receive payment in checks drawn on the member banks. By cashing these checks, the Federal Reserve Banks decrease the cash reserves of their member banks and thereby reduce the ability of the member banks to make loans. Conversely, by buying government securities, the Federal Reserve Banks increase the cash reserves of their member banks, thus pumping money into the economy.

4. Setting the Margin Requirement. When an investor buys stocks on *margin*, he pays for the securities in part with his own cash and borrows the remainder from his broker. The Federal Reserve Board fixes the margin requirement at a percentage of the dollar amount of the purchase. When the economy is depressed, the Federal Reserve Board reduces the margin requirement in order to encourage investment. When the economy is expanding too rapidly, the Board increases the margin requirement in order to discourage overspeculation.

5. Regulating Installment Buying. In emergency situations, such as World War II and the Korean War, the Federal Reserve Board received temporary powers to regulate installment buying. By requiring a large down payment and giving the buyer little time to complete his payments, the Federal Reserve Board discouraged installment buying and slowed down inflation.

PUBLIC FINANCE

GOVERNMENT EXPENDITURES

1. Local governments spend money to provide schools, libraries, hospitals, public welfare for the unfortunate, police and fire protection, courts of justice, sanitation, local roads and streets, and parks.

2. State governments spend vast sums to provide state police, courts, highways, hospitals, and parks. States also provide *grants-in-aid*, or *state aid*, to local governments for public welfare and education.

3. The federal government spends heavily for national defense, including the armed forces, military equipment, and weapons development. Another sizeable amount is interest paid on the huge national debt. The federal government provides funds for foreign aid, space exploration, and interstate highways; benefit programs for farmers, workers, retirees, and sick persons; and grants-in-aid to states and localities for education, conservation, housing, and antipoverty programs. Those federal payments made on behalf of individuals who are entitled to them under various social welfare programs (such as Medicare and food stamps) are known as *entitlements*.

REASONS FOR THE TREND TOWARD INCREASING GOVERNMENT EXPENDITURES

1. Increasing Population. As the population of the United States has increased, federal, state, and local governments have had to provide services for many more people. As the percentage of the population over 65 and under 21 has increased, governments at all levels have had to increase their spending for aid to the aged and for education.

2. Government Responsibility for Social Welfare. The 1929 Depression led the various governments to accept greater responsibility for the people's welfare. On the federal level, Franklin Roosevelt's New Deal, Harry Truman's Fair Deal, and Lyndon Johnson's Great Society all spurred social welfare programs. Once enacted, these programs grew rapidly in cost. President Reagan in 1981 pledged a "safety net" for the "truly needy" but otherwise acted to lessen the cost of social welfare programs.

3. Cold War. Following World War II the United States became the leader of the free nations in their efforts to contain aggressive Communism. The federal government sharply increased its expenditures for national defense, foreign aid, and localized conflicts, as in Korea and Vietnam.

4. Improvements in Technology. For national defense, the federal government has promoted the development of weapons. The federal government has also assumed the major role in space exploration. Federal agencies have regulated new technological products such as the airplane, television, and nuclear power plants. All levels of government have spent vast sums to provide roads and highways for the growing number of motor vehicles.

GOVERNMENT REVENUES

1. Theories of Taxation. (a) *Ability to Pay.* According to this theory the government should tax individuals according to their income. The person with the greater income has the greater ability to pay and should bear a greater part of the tax burden. This theory underlies the income tax. (b) *Benefit.* According to this theory the government should tax the people according to benefits, or gains, they receive. This theory underlies the gasoline tax in those states in which the funds received from the tax are used for roadbuilding.

2. Tax Rates as Percentages of Income. (a) *Progressive.* The federal income tax is an example of a progressive, or graduated, tax. A person earning a greater income pays taxes at a higher percentage. For example, in recent years families with moderate incomes have paid federal income taxes at a rate of 15 percent. Those with higher incomes have paid 15 percent on part of their income, but up to 39.6 percent on income above a certain level. (b) *Proportional.* An example of a proportional tax would be an income tax that taxed everyone at the same rate. (c) *Regressive.* A regressive tax requires people earning small incomes to pay a higher percentage of their income for the tax than do people with large incomes. An example is a cigarette tax. The laborer who smokes a pack a day pays as much tax as a millionaire who also smokes a pack a day. The tax hits the laborer much harder than the millionaire. By applying this reasoning, economists consider the general sales tax to be a regressive tax.

3. Major Sources of Revenue

a. Local Sources. Local governments generally secure their largest revenue from the property tax, chiefly on real estate. They may also derive income from the sales tax, minor business taxes, transit fares, water service fees, traffic fines, and special assessments. In addition, they receive considerable sums in state and federal aid. In 1966 New York City imposed an income tax on residents and on commuters working in the city.

b. State Sources. State governments secure their largest revenues from two sources: the income tax and commodity taxes. The latter include general sales taxes and taxes on specific items such as gasoline, alcohol, and cigarettes. States also receive revenue from licenses, minor business taxes, and the inheritance, or estate, tax. In addition, they receive grants of federal aid.

c. Federal Sources. The federal government secures most of its revenue from the individual income tax, the corporate income tax, and the Social Security, or payroll, tax. The federal government also levies excise taxes on gasoline, alcohol, tobacco, telephone service, and new car purchases; tariffs on imports; and an inheritance, or estate, tax.

"Taxes," according to Supreme Court Justice Oliver Wendell Holmes, "are what we pay for civilized society."

4. Government Use of Taxation for Social and Regulatory Purposes. The power of taxation may be used to bring about social and economic goals:

a. To further housing construction and attract new industries, local governments sometimes offer limited exemptions from the property tax.

b. To encourage philanthropy, the federal government and the states permit charitable contributions, within limits, to be deducted from taxable income.

c. To aid the elderly, the federal government and states permit persons over 65 to take a double personal exemption from their income taxes.

d. In part to discourage the consumption of liquor and tobacco, both of which may be harmful to the individual, the federal government and most states levy heavy excise taxes on these products.

e. To battle recession and spur economic growth, Congress in several years—1964, 1971, 1975, 1981, and 1986—lowered federal taxes. Laws reducing individual income taxes make it possible for individuals to buy more goods and services, and also provide more funds for investment. Laws reducing corporate income taxes make it possible for corporations to increase dividends to stockholders and to expand their capital investment programs.

f. Congress may also raise taxes to reduce consumer and corporate spending and thus help check rising inflation. Moderate tax increases passed Con-

Berryman in The Washington Star

"Now you must do your duty. . . spend it!"

At what phase of the business cycle might Uncle Sam lower taxes? Would he then want the public to spend or to save its additional income? Explain.

gress in 1982 and 1984. Because higher taxes are unpopular, however, political leaders try to avoid tax increases whenever possible. Congressional leaders and the President depicted the Tax Reform Act of 1986 as "revenue neutral"—neither raising nor lowering taxes.

FEDERAL BUDGET AND THE NATIONAL DEBT

1. Federal Budget. The President, assisted by the *Office of Management and Budget* (formerly the Bureau of the Budget), draws up the annual federal budget and submits it to Congress for approval. The budget is an estimate of income, expenditures, and the allocation of funds among the various government departments and agencies for the following fiscal year. The fiscal year begins on October 1 and ends on the following September 30.

When income exceeds expenditures, the government operates at a surplus and may use the surplus funds for debt reduction. The government is then said to have a *surplus budget.* When income equals expenditures, the government is said to have a *balanced budget.* When expenditures exceed income, the government operates at a deficit and must borrow funds, thereby increasing its debt. The government is then said to have a *deficit budget.*

2. The Federal Budget From 1931 to the Present. Since 1931 the government of the United States has had only seven surplus budgets. The major factors producing deficits since 1931 have been the Great Depression and subsequent recessions, World War II, the Cold War, the Korean War, the space race, the Vietnam conflict, increased spending for human needs, and increased spending on the military. Since 1931 the national debt has risen from $17 billion to over $4 trillion (four thousand billion dollars).

President Reagan, who took office in 1981, had made campaign pledges to increase spending for national defense while balancing the budget through cuts in spending for social services. The Reagan administration carried out the largest peacetime military buildup in United States history. The defense budget rose from $170.7 billion in 1981 to $303 billion in 1989. Meanwhile, the government made sharp cuts in social programs such as welfare, Medicaid, food stamps, student loans, and rental assistance. Nonetheless, domestic spending continued to grow. As a result, rather than cutting deficits, President Reagan presided over the biggest budget deficits in the nation's history—reaching $220.7 billion in 1986 and tripling the national debt in eight years.

3. Efforts to Reduce Federal Budget Deficits. In the 1980's, as the federal debt soared, Americans became concerned that continued federal budget deficits indicated serious problems. Economists warned that federal deficits contributed to inflation and high interest rates—both undermining economic prosperity. Many Americans concluded that federal spending—especially for welfare programs and defense—had ballooned out of control. Demands arose for re-evaluation of government programs, tighter eligibility requirements for welfare, elimination of waste and fraud in defense contracts, and possible transfer of some domestic programs to state and local control. Also voices were raised urging support for a Constitutional amendment to require the federal government to achieve a balanced budget each year.

One approach to reducing deficits was to set a timetable for step-by-step reductions in the annual deficit, reaching zero after a period of years. That was the idea behind the *Gramm-Rudman-Hollings Acts* of 1985 and 1987. They provided for elimination of the deficit by 1991 (later 1993). But that approach didn't work. The deficit soared to new highs, reaching $290 billion in 1992.

Coming to office in 1993, President Bill Clinton called for a combination of spending cuts and tax increases. His efforts were aided by the nation's recovery from recession. More business activity meant more income from taxpayers and thus more revenue for the government. The annual deficit began to drop, although it remained high by pre-1980 standards.

4. Dispute Over Deficit Spending and the Mounting National Debt

a. Arguments Against. (1) By borrowing, the present generation is shifting the burden of payment onto future generations. (2) As the national debt has mounted tremendously, it requires heavy interest payments—about $210 billion annually, or about 14 percent of our current budget expenditures. (3) The government is setting American people a poor example by living beyond its means and constantly borrowing. (4) By its deficit financing, the government pumps additional money into the economy and furthers inflation. If inflation is to be kept under control, the government must move toward a bal-

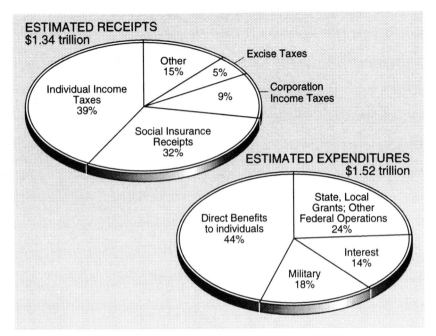

ESTIMATED RECEIPTS
$1.34 trillion

Other
15%

Excise Taxes
5%

Individual Income
Taxes
39%

Corporation
Income Taxes
9%

Social Insurance
Receipts
32%

ESTIMATED EXPENDITURES
$1.52 trillion

State, Local
Grants; Other
Federal Operations
24%

Direct Benefits
to individuals
44%

Interest
14%

Military
18%

The Federal Budget Dollar for 1995

anced budget. (5) By showing neither the ability nor the desire to restrain the rising national debt, the government is risking the loss of confidence in its financial stability.

b. Arguments For. (1) Future generations will benefit from past expenditures—to win World War II, contain aggressive communism, establish national parks, combat pollution, and construct public roads and buildings. Therefore, future Americans should bear part of the cost. (2) Individuals are accustomed to borrowing money or paying on time for a car, or a house, or appliances. They do not feel it is financially unhealthy to be in debt. (3) The American people have rejected the alternatives to deficit spending: raising taxes or cutting back government services. (4) By selling small-denomination savings bonds to average citizens, the government encourages thrift and gives people a personal interest in public finance. (5) By borrowing and incurring budget deficits during business slumps, the government puts funds into the economy. Government spending stimulates production and creates jobs, thereby helping to improve economic conditions. (6) Although by the mid-1990's the national debt has increased to nearly $5 trillion, the debt as a percent of our gross domestic product (GDP) has decreased from 90 percent in 1950 to about 70 percent.

MULTIPLE-CHOICE QUESTIONS

1. Which is *not* typical of depressions? (1) decline in employment (2) increase in government spending for relief (3) increase in bank loans (4) decline in imports.

2. One major cause of the Depression of 1929 was the (1) decrease in the amount of gold bullion in the Treasury (2) contraction of consumer credit by the government (3) decline in consumer purchasing power (4) decline in industrial production.

3. Which was a significant result of the Depression of 1929? (1) elimination of the business cycle (2) establishment by the federal government of certain safeguards against depression (3) failure of the Republican party to win the Presidency since then (4) sharp increase in the proportion of Americans engaged in agriculture.

4. Responsibility for maintaining a healthy economic system in the United States is (1) centralized under the Director of the Budget (2) left to private industry (3) accepted as a function of the federal government (4) delegated entirely to the Federal Reserve System.

5. The President's Council of Economic Advisers is responsible for (1) preparing the budget (2) analyzing business trends (3) reviewing the work of the independent agencies (4) improving the efficiency of government operations.

6. Which procedure would most likely be used to curb inflation? (1) a decrease in personal and corporate income taxes (2) a decrease in margin requirements (3) an increase in the discount rate (4) an increase in spending for public works projects.

7. If the federal government wished to stimulate spending by consumers, the best program to follow would be to reduce (1) corporate taxes (2) inheritance taxes (3) income taxes on upper incomes (4) income taxes on lower incomes.

8. The term "built-in stabilizer" refers to government action designed to (1) reduce the possibility of an economic crisis (2) increase government control over banks (3) maintain a balanced budget (4) equalize the tax burden.

9. Which would be the most valid argument for reducing federal income tax rates despite a deficit budget? (1) Purchasing power will be increased, the economy will be stimulated, and income tax receipts will rise. (2) Those Congressmen supporting the tax cut will benefit politically. (3) Businessmen will invest less, and overproduction will be reduced. (4) Deficit financing will lower the price level and therefore increase consumption.

10. The Federal Reserve System helps to stabilize the economy of the United States by (1) preparing the federal budget (2) insuring deposits in savings banks (3) chartering new banks (4) controlling the credit activities of member banks.

11. If the Federal Reserve System wished to cut down on the loans made by member banks, it could (1) lower the margin requirement (2) lower the rediscount rate (3) raise the reserve ratio (4) order all loans stopped.

12. The term "open-market operations" refers to (1) speculation in stocks and bonds by stock exchange members (2) purchase and sale of government securities by the Federal Reserve Banks (3) making of loans by the Federal Reserve to its member banks (4) regulation of the margin requirement by the Federal Reserve.

13. When the Federal Reserve raises the margin requirement, it is attempting to (1) decrease the reserves of member banks (2) promote consumer spending (3) discourage excessive speculation in securities (4) stimulate a sluggish stock market.

14. Which theory of taxation is the basis for requiring individuals to pay higher taxes on higher incomes? (1) stake in society (2) benefits received (3) ability to pay (4) automatic stabilization.

15. A bridge toll is based upon the taxation principle of (1) ability to pay (2) benefits received (3) controlling consumption (4) regulating business.

16. Which is considered a good example of a progressive tax? (1) a sales tax (2) an excise tax (3) a real estate tax (4) an income tax.

17. Which pairs the major sources of revenue of the federal and local governments in the United States? (1) excise taxes—sales taxes (2) tariffs—inheritance taxes (3) employment taxes—corporation taxes (4) income taxes—property taxes.

18. The federal government obtains the greatest percentage of its revenue from (1) personal income taxes (2) corporate income taxes (3) import taxes (4) excise taxes.

19. The chief argument against the general sales tax is that it (1) does not yield sufficient revenue (2) burdens the poor proportionately more than the rich (3) is too expensive to collect (4) unfairly burdens the rich (who buy more goods).

20. A federal budget represents a (1) legal limit on spending for the fiscal year (2) program to pay back the national debt (3) plan for spending accompanied by an indication of sources of income to meet these expenditures (4) request by Congress for funds from the Treasury Department.

21. Which item in the federal budget costs the American taxpayer the most money? (1) interest payments (2) national defense (3) direct benefit payments to individuals (4) salaries of civil service employees.

ESSAY QUESTIONS

1. The fluctuations of the American economy have been a matter of increasing concern. Show how *each* of the following can help maintain the nation's economic health when depression threatens: (*a*) unemployment insurance, (*b*) the federal tax policy, (*c*) the open-market operations of the Federal Reserve.

2. The following have been used by our federal government to help prevent or control depression: (*a*) public works projects, (*b*) minimum wage laws, (*c*) parity payments to farmers, (*d*) the Federal Reserve Board's control over the volume of money and credit, (*e*) unemployment insurance, (*f*) taxes. For *each* item, (1) state which cause of depression it is designed to prevent or control, and (2) explain how it is expected to work.

3. The business cycle has been a characteristic of economic life in the United States. (*a*) Name *one* phase of the business cycle and describe the characteristic features of that phase. (*b*) Explain *two* controls by which the Federal Reserve Board attempts to stabilize the economy. (*c*) Describe *two* measures passed by Congress in the 1930's to meet the problems of the business cycle.

4. (*a*) Give *one* reason for the increase in expenditures by local governments *and* give *one different* reason for the increase in expenditures by the federal government. (*b*) Give *one* argument for *and one* argument against a reduction of the corporate income tax at the present time. (*c*) Give *one* argument for *and one* argument against the statement that the size of our present national debt is a danger to our economy.

5. Give *one* reason to explain why you would agree *or one* reason to explain why you would disagree with *each* of the following statements: (*a*) The budget of a local government generally reflects the economic and social goals of the community. (*b*) Cuts in personal income taxes will increase the gross national product. (*c*) The growth of the national debt has been a stimulus to the economy. (*d*) All state banks should be compelled to join the Federal Reserve System. (*e*) The automatic stabilizers built into our economic system since 1933 will prevent any severe depression.

Part 6. The Worker Struggles to Increase His Share of the National Income

THE INDUSTRIAL REVOLUTION CREATES LABOR PROBLEMS

With the development of the factory system, workers could no longer labor in their own homes or in small shops. They therefore became dependent upon factory owners for their livelihood. In the early years of the Industrial Revolution, employers took advantage of their dominant position and (1) paid workers low wages for long hours, (2) employed women and children, (3) introduced machines that permitted employers to hire unskilled workers and that made the work monotonous, (4) compelled workers to conform to the speed of the machines, and (5) maintained unsafe, unsanitary, and badly lighted factories.

WORKERS TURN TO UNIONS

Poor conditions aroused widespread dissatisfaction among workers. The worker soon found that by *individual bargaining,* that is, by appealing singly to the employer for better wages and better working conditions, the worker could not very well improve his lot. Under individual bargaining, he did not have the means to compel the employer to meet his demands, and the employer could discharge him without seriously affecting production.

Workers came to realize that they would be in a stronger position by *collective bargaining,* that is, by uniting as a group to make demands upon the employer. Under collective bargaining, workers could threaten to strike, thereby halting production and hurting the employer. In order to bargain collectively with the employer, workers formed labor unions.

LABOR UNIONS BEFORE THE CIVIL WAR

From the 1790's onward, many skilled workers, such as carpenters and printers, organized into craft unions within a city or locality. Following the War of 1812, as industry thrived, some unskilled factory workers organized. These early unions expanded during the era of Jacksonian democracy. However, many unions disappeared as a result of the prolonged depression following the Panic of 1837.

The pre-Civil War labor unions were mostly ineffective because they (1) were small, local, and inexperienced, (2) lacked financial resources, (3) faced great difficulties in attempting to organize women and children, (4) could not deal effectively with the incoming immigrants seeking work at any wage, (5) lost supporters when discontented workers migrated to the frontier, (6) received hostile treatment from the courts, which held them to be "unlawful conspiracies," and (7) found public opinion in the predominantly agricultural society unsympathetic to the worker.

LABOR UNIONS AFTER THE CIVIL WAR

Starting about 1865, labor unions entered a period of growth in membership and power. They were aided by the following factors: (1) The emergence of large corporations destroyed personal contact between the employer and his employees, and made workers realize the necessity of organizing to deal with their employer. (2) The establishment of huge mills and factories drew the workers together and enabled them to discuss their common problems. (3) The courts developed a more favorable attitude toward unions. In the case of *Commonwealth vs. Hunt* (1842), the Supreme Court of Massachusetts ruled that unions were not unlawful conspiracies. After a long struggle, this precedent was finally accepted by the courts of most states. (4) Labor leaders had gained experience. (5) Beginning near the end of the 19th century, no frontier existed to provide workers with a "safety valve."

Post-Civil War workers faced powerful corporations controlling millions of dollars of assets, thousands of workers, and factories throughout the nation. To win concessions from these powerful employers, workers turned to strikes and at times to violence.

RAILROAD STRIKE OF 1877

To protest wage cuts and the blacklisting of union members, railroad employees, beginning with workers on the Baltimore and Ohio, went on strike. The strike led to riots, bloodshed, and destruction of railroad property in several Eastern cities. The strike collapsed after President Hayes called out the federal troops in their first use in a labor-management dispute.

Having found that violence hurt their cause, workers became increasingly concerned with strengthening their economic power by forming strong unions. More and more workers now banded together into nationwide labor organizations.

KNIGHTS OF LABOR

1. **Structure and Early Successes.** Organized by *Uriah S. Stephens* in 1869, the Knights of Labor admitted all workers, both skilled and unskilled, and regardless of race or national origin. Despite differences in occupation and craft, all workers in an area became members of the same local chapter.

Under *Terence V. Powderly* as "Grand Master Workman," the Knights in the 1880's urged an eight-hour day, the abolition of child labor, various political reforms, and the establishment of cooperatives. Although Powderly personally frowned upon strikes, members of the Knights of Labor won several important industrial battles. By 1886 the Knights reached their peak membership of over 700,000. Thereafter, the Knights declined in power and disappeared by 1895.

2. Reasons for Decline

a. Unsuccessful Strikes. Beginning in 1886 the Knights lost several strikes. These had been called without sufficient preparation and without sufficient financial resources.

b. Admission of Unskilled Workers. Unskilled members of the Knights of Labor who went on strike could be replaced easily. Also, workers in local chapters lacked common economic interests, and skilled members were unwilling to strike in support of the unskilled.

c. Failure of Cooperatives. The consumer and producer cooperatives run by the Knights lost money.

d. Haymarket Affair (1886). When Chicago strikers, demonstrating for an 8-hour day, were brutally treated by the police, the workers organized a protest meeting in Haymarket Square. Someone, unidentified to this day, threw a bomb at the police, killing seven people and wounding more than sixty. In an emotionally charged atmosphere, eight radicals were arrested, tried, and found guilty of murder. The Haymarket Affair helped arouse public opinion against organized labor. Although the Knights of Labor condemned the Haymarket Square bombing, public opinion wrongly identified the Knights with violence.

(In 1893 *John P. Altgeld,* newly elected Governor of Illinois, reviewed the case. He pardoned the three convicted men still alive, believing that their trial had been unfair and that the evidence pointed to their innocence.)

AMERICAN FEDERATION OF LABOR

1. Aims and Structure. Organized by *Samuel Gompers* in 1881, the American Federation of Labor shunned political crusades and cooperatives. It emphasized "bread and butter" unionism: the furthering of the economic well-being of its members by means of strong unions.

Gompers' organizational policies made the A.F. of L. more successful than the Knights of Labor. (*a*) The A.F. of L. admitted mostly skilled workers. They could strike with greater hope of success than could the unskilled members of the Knights of Labor. (*b*) The A.F. of L. organized workers into separate *craft unions*. A craft, or trade, union is limited to workers of a particular skill; for example, a carpenter and a plumber would belong to different unions even though they both worked for the same construction company. By combining workers with the same economic interests, A.F. of L. craft unions could serve their members more effectively than the Knights' local chapters.

2. Significant Early Strikes

a. Homestead Steel Strike (1892). Workers at the plant of the Carnegie Steel Company in Homestead, Pennsylvania, were members of an A.F. of L. union. They went out on strike to protest a reduction in wages. The workers fought a bloody battle and drove off 300 Pinkerton detectives hired by the company to guard the plant and help break the strike. To prevent further violence, the Governor of Pennsylvania sent in the state militia. Eventually, the union's resources were exhausted, and the strike collapsed.

b. Anthracite Coal Strike (1902). The United Mine Workers, an A.F. of L. union, went on strike for union recognition, shorter hours, and higher wages. As winter approached, President Theodore Roosevelt summoned both sides to the White House, but the mine owners stubbornly rejected the union's offer to have the dispute arbitrated. The President then threatened to seize the mines, whereupon the owners agreed to accept a Presidential arbitration commission. The commission awarded the workers a wage increase and a 9-hour day, but denied them union recognition.

By thus using Presidential powers to settle a labor-management dispute, Theodore Roosevelt established a precedent and became known as a friend of labor.

3. Growth. Despite occasional setbacks the A.F. of L. prospered. Its membership increased from 100,000 in 1890 to 4 million in 1920 and almost 11 million in 1955. The A.F. of L. faced difficult times during the prosperous 1920's and the early years of the 1929 depression. It experienced great growth during Wilson's administration, the New Deal Era, and World War II. In the 1950's the A.F. of L. consisted of over 100 member unions. Almost all of these were craft unions such as the International Association of Machinists, the United Brotherhood of Carpenters and Joiners, and the American Federation of Musicians.

4. Leaders. Samuel Gompers, an immigrant from England and a member of the Cigar Makers' Union, organized the A.F. of L. and served as its president for some 40 years. A practical man who rejected radicalism, Gompers urged labor to benefit from a capitalist economy by forming strong unions and gaining high wages. His successor, *William Green,* who served from 1924 to 1952, continued Gompers' emphasis on craft unionism but gradually permitted unions to become more active in politics. Green was succeeded by *George Meany,* who later merged the A.F. of L. with the Congress of Industrial Organizations.

CONGRESS OF INDUSTRIAL ORGANIZATIONS

1. Industrial Unionism. An *industrial* union consists of all workers—skilled, semiskilled, and unskilled—in a given industry. In 1935 a small group of A.F. of L. leaders, who headed not craft but industrial unions, urged the expansion of industrial unionism. Notable among these leaders were *John L. Lewis* of the United Mine Workers, *David Dubinsky* of the International Ladies Garment Workers, and *Sidney Hillman* of the Amalgamated Clothing Workers. These leaders condemned the A.F. of L. for its emphasis on craft unions and its consequent neglect of the many semiskilled and unskilled workers in the expanding mass-production industries such as automobiles, steel, rubber, and electrical appliances.

2. Development of a New Nationwide Organization. Supporters of industrial unionism formed the *Committee for Industrial Organization* and unionized the workers at leading mass-production companies such as General Motors, Chrysler, and United States Steel. To organize the workers, the C.I.O. utilized a new weapon, the sit-down strike. The employees not only refused to work, but in addition refused to leave the factories, thereby preventing the companies from operating with strikebreakers. By 1939, when the Supreme Court declared the sit-down strike illegal, C.I.O. unions had won recognition in the automobile, steel, rubber, oil-refining, textile, and shipbuilding industries.

The C.I.O., with its large voting power, represented a threat to the craft unions' control of the A.F. of L. Consequently, the A.F. of L. suspended the industrial unions and ordered the dissolution of their committee. Instead, in 1938 the industrial unions established their own nationwide organization, the *Congress of Industrial Organizations*.

3. Growth. The C.I.O. grew in membership from 3.6 million in 1940 to almost 5 million in 1955. In the 1950's the C.I.O. consisted of over 40 member unions, mostly industrial unions, such as the Textile Workers Union of America, the United Steel Workers, and the United Automobile Workers.

4. Leaders. The first president of the C.I.O. was *John L. Lewis*. An energetic and determined leader, Lewis spurred organizational drives and fought to keep the C.I.O. free of Communist influence. Lewis stepped down in 1940, but his policies were continued by both subsequent heads of the C.I.O.: *Philip Murray* (1940–1952) and *Walter Reuther* (1952–1955).

AMERICAN FEDERATION OF LABOR AND CONGRESS OF INDUSTRIAL ORGANIZATIONS

1. Reasons for Unity. In 1955 the A.F. of L. and the C.I.O. merged to form a single organization, thereby ending the 20-year split in the labor movement. This merger was the work chiefly of a new generation of labor leaders, especially George Meany, President of the A.F. of L., and Walter Reuther, President of the C.I.O. These labor leaders expected that a unified labor movement would (*a*) strengthen labor's influence in political, economic, and social matters and *(b)* bring about harmony among unions by preventing membership raids and jurisdictional strikes (see page 281).

2. Structure. *(a)* The AFL-CIO consists of some 100 affiliated unions with a total membership of about 13.3 million workers. *(b)* It is governed by an executive council composed of the AFL-CIO president, a secretary-treasurer, and 33 vice presidents. *(c)* It finances its activities by taxing each affiliated union a small monthly amount per member. *(d)* Its headquarters are in an impressive marble building located in Washington, D.C.

3. Leaders. George Meany was unanimously elected as the first president of the AFL–CIO. After serving for 24 years, he was succeeded by *Lane Kirkland*. In 1995, *John J. Sweeney* became the union's third president. He promised to greatly increase union organizing, especially among underrepresented groups such as women and minority workers.

INDEPENDENT UNIONS NOT AFFILIATED WITH THE AFL-CIO

(1) The *National Education Association,* representing some 2 million teachers and other educators, is a major independent union. Other teachers belong to an AFL-CIO affiliate, the 750,000-member American Federation of Teachers. (2) The *United Mine Workers* has 186,000 members. (3) The 100,000-member *United Transportation Union,* the largest union of railroad employees, withdrew from the AFL-CIO in 1986. However, many other railroad employees belong to such AFL-CIO affiliates as the Transport Workers Union and the Brotherhood of Railway and Airline Clerks.

Independent unions have a current membership of about 3 million.

UNORGANIZED WORKERS: THE GREAT MAJORITY

1. Extent. The American civilian labor force numbered some 105 million employed wage and salary workers in 1993, 15.8 percent of whom were union members. This represented a decrease from the 20.1 percent who were labor union members in 1983.

2. Reasons

a. Occupational Factors. Self-employed people, such as small storekeepers and repair persons, are both workers and owners. Government employees enjoy civil service status, which provides job security, regular pay increases, sick leave, and retirement benefits. Agricultural laborers and household domestics are often transient workers who go from one employer to the next. Professionals, such as doctors, lawyers, accountants, and engineers, are highly trained, well-paid workers who generally consider unions unbecoming to professional dignity. Many professional groups have societies capable of serving functions similar to those of unions. Workers in the rapidly growing service and technical fields, who utilize high-technology computer and telecommunications equipment, are relatively well-paid.

b. Satisfactory Conditions. Workers feel no need of unions when they have high wages and good working conditions. Often, they owe such good conditions to general economic prosperity, to the spread of union-won benefits to non-union workers, and to the deliberate policy followed by certain employers to keep workers from joining unions. An employer may try to discourage unionization by granting his workers benefits such as profit-sharing plans, medical and hospital care, pensions, and recreational facilities. This policy is called *welfare capitalism.*

c. Anti-Union Sentiment. Some employers are strongly opposed to unions and vigorously combat union organizational drives. This attitude prevails among large commercial farmers in the West and among industrialists in the Deep South.

d. Restrictive Union Practices. To assure employment and decent wages to their present members, some unions severely restrict the admittance of new members. Typical are the "father-and-son" unions, especially in the building and printing trades, which limit new admissions to close relatives of present members.

GOALS OF MANAGEMENT AND LABOR

1. Common Goals. To make possible higher dividends for stockholders and higher wages for workers, management and labor both favor (*a*) a prosperous company with increasing productivity, (*b*) an expanding economy with rising living standards, and (*c*) our system of free enterprise under government regulation. Unlike European labor unions, which have frequently supported Socialist and Communist policies, organized American labor has remained true to Gompers' teachings that labor should benefit from capitalism. Most American workers have rejected anti-capitalist organizations, notably the Industrial Workers of the World (IWW) in the early 1900's and, more recently, the Communist party in America.

2. Goals of Management. Industrialists have consistently aimed at (*a*) managing their companies with as little interference from unions as possible, (*b*) increasing productivity by instituting more efficient methods and utilizing laborsaving machinery, (*c*) requiring unions and workers to live up to the terms of their labor contract, (*d*) hiring, promoting, and firing workers as required by company needs, and (*e*) maintaining an *open shop.* In theory, an open shop permits an employer to hire both union and non-union workers; in practice, most open-shop companies hire non-union workers only.

3. Goals of Labor Unions

a. Traditional Goals. Throughout their history, unions have worked to secure (1) recognition of the union as the sole bargaining agent of the workers, (2) higher wages and shorter hours, (3) good working conditions, including safety devices on machinery and well-lighted, well-ventilated, sanitary factories, (4) job security, including seniority to enable older workers to gain promotions and avoid layoffs, and also including a union voice regarding the introduction of laborsaving machinery, (5) a *union label* to identify union-made products, thus enabling consumers to support unions by buying only goods with this label, (6) the *checkoff* system, which requires an employer to deduct union dues from the workers' pay and forward the lump sum to the union, and (7) union security, through either the *union shop* or the *closed shop.* In a union shop the employer may hire union or non-union workers, but all workers must join the union within a specified time or lose their jobs. In a closed shop the employer may hire only workers who are already union members. (The closed shop was outlawed by the Taft-Hartley Act.)

b. More Recent Goals. In recent years unions have also sought to secure (1) the *guaranteed annual wage* (*GAW*), assuring each worker 52 weekly paychecks a year regardless of whether the employer can provide a full year's work, and (2) *fringe benefits,* including paid vacations and holidays, pay for sick leave, hospital and medical care, group life insurance, and pensions.

PEACEFUL METHODS OF SETTLING LABOR-MANAGEMENT DISPUTES

The overwhelming number of labor-management disputes are settled peacefully, and with little publicity, by the following methods:

1. Collective Bargaining. Employer and union representatives meet, negotiate directly, settle the issues, and complete a labor contract. Sometimes the major employers in a given industry, such as steel, rubber, or clothing, negotiate as a group with the union for contract terms covering the entire industry. Such negotiations are called *industrywide bargaining.*

2. Mediation. A disinterested third party, who has the confidence of both the employer and the union, brings about an acceptable agreement by inducing each side to make concessions. A staff of trained mediators is available through the *Federal Mediation and Conciliation Service.*

3. **Arbitration.** The employer and the union together agree on a neutral third party to hear the dispute and hand down a decision, or *award*. The parties agree in advance to accept the arbitrator's award.

4. **Fact-Finding Board.** In strikes affecting the welfare of the nation, the President may appoint a fact-finding board to hear the dispute and hand down a recommendation. Although the board's recommendation is not binding, the disputing parties usually accept it for fear of adverse public opinion. (The fact-finding method is sometimes used by governors and mayors to settle local labor disputes.)

COSTS OF INDUSTRIAL WARFARE

A small minority of labor-management disputes erupt into industrial battles, frequently accompanied by much publicity. Industrial warfare causes hardship. (1) Employers suffer halted production, decreased profits, and unfavorable publicity. (2) Workers suffer unemployment and loss of income. (3) Consumers endure a shortage of products or a loss of services. (4) The government experiences loss of tax revenues and sometimes a scarcity of goods or services essential to the national welfare.

WEAPONS OF UNIONS

1. **Strike.** Employees refuse to work until the employer yields to union demands.

2. **Strike Fund.** This fund serves to sustain union members and pay for union activities during a strike.

3. **Picketing.** Workers parade outside the strikebound premises. They seek to enlist public support and to deter strikebreakers from taking their jobs.

4. **Boycott.** Workers request consumers not to patronize the strikebound company.

5. **Publicity.** Unions appeal for public support through mass demonstrations, newspapers, radio, and television.

WEAPONS OF EMPLOYERS

1. **Strikebreakers.** To fill the jobs of strikers, the employer hires other workers, called strikebreakers or *scabs*.

2. **Financial Resources.** When a strike halts production and curtails business income, most corporations have sufficient financial reserves to meet their overhead costs and to continue paying dividends to stockholders.

Nonprofit enterprise.

How are strikes costly to the worker, the employer, the public, and the government? What are the other methods of settling labor-management disputes?

3. Lockout. The employer keeps the workers from their jobs until the union accepts his terms.

4. Injunction. Upon the request of either a company or the federal government, a court may issue an order, called an injunction, forbidding the union to strike, picket, or boycott, on the ground that such union action may damage the employer unfairly or harm the national welfare. Violators of the injunction are liable to fine or imprisonment, or both, for *contempt of court.*

Whereas the use of the injunction by the employer was severely limited in 1932 by the Norris-La Guardia Act (see page 277), the use of the injunction by the federal government was expanded in 1947 by the Taft-Hartley Act (see pages 281–282).

5. Publicity. The employer presents his case to the public though mass communications media.

LABOR AND POLITICAL ACTION

1. Early Efforts

a. Unsuccessful Attempts to Build a Labor Party. In the 1830's and again in the 1870's, unions, small and newly organized, undertook to form their own political party or to join in a political party with farmers. Their efforts met with failure.

b. Gompers' Advice. In the 1880's Samuel Gompers urged members of the A.F. of L. to work within the two major parties by punishing enemies and rewarding friends. A.F. of L. leaders and organizations followed Gompers' advice by endorsing pro-labor candidates regardless of party label. However, once elected, these candidates did little to help unions. They owed their nomination and election chiefly to political leaders and therefore felt little obligation to organized labor.

2. Labor Disputes Spur Political Activity

a. Pullman Strike (1894). Workers at the Pullman car plant near Chicago went on strike to protest a wage cut of as much as 40 percent, unaccompanied by any rent reduction in the company-owned town. These workers belonged to the American Railway Union, an industrywide union led by Eugene V. Debs. To support the strikers, railroad employees refused to handle any trains that included Pullman cars. Most railroad transportation out of Chicago halted.

Attorney General Richard Olney, formerly a railroad lawyer, acted to break the strike. Using the Sherman Antitrust Act, he secured an injunction against the union as a "conspiracy in restraint of trade." When Debs violated the injunction by continuing the strike, he was arrested and jailed for contempt of court. President Cleveland meanwhile sent federal troops to Chicago, ostensibly to assure delivery of the United States mail. Cleveland's action was protested as unnecessary by Illinois Governor Altgeld. The arrival of federal troops led to protests by mobs and to violence. With troops on the scene and Debs in jail, the Pullman strike collapsed. It marked the first effective use of the injunction against a labor union.

b. Danbury Hatters Strike (1902). Striking workers of the Loewe Hat Company in Danbury, Connecticut, organized a successful boycott of the company's products. The union and its members were sued by the company, which claimed that the boycott was a "conspiracy in restraint of trade" and therefore a violation of the Sherman Antitrust Act. In a Supreme Court decision in 1908, the union and its members were found guilty and ordered to pay burdensome cash damages.

c. Results. The Pullman and the Danbury Hatters strikes convinced labor leaders that they had to secure legislation to keep the injunction and the antitrust law from being used against labor unions. Labor became increasingly active in political campaigns and in 1912 helped elect Woodrow Wilson as President. Wilson, in turn, brought about the passage of the Clayton Act (see below).

3. More Recently: Considerable Political Activity. Following the formation of the C.I.O., labor took a more active part in politics. In 1943 the C.I.O. empowered Sidney Hillman to organize the *Political Action Committee (P.A.C.)*. The P.A.C. not only endorsed candidates but fought to secure nominations for friends of labor and contributed funds to campaigns. The P.A.C. also engaged in the hard work of politics: ringing doorbells, printing literature, holding rallies, providing speakers, and getting out the pro-labor vote. The success of the P.A.C. encouraged the A.F. of L. to become more active in politics. Following the merger of the A.F. of L. and the C.I.O. in 1955, the AFL-CIO assigned its political efforts to its *Committee on Political Education (COPE)*.

FEDERAL LEGISLATION AIDS LABOR: EARLY 20TH CENTURY

1. Department of Labor (1913). In 1913 Congress created a separate Department of Labor to "foster, promote, and develop the welfare of the wage earners of the United States; to improve their working conditions; and to advance their opportunities for profitable employment." The Department gathers statistics and undertakes special studies on labor problems, publishes labor periodicals and pamphlets, and enforces most federal labor laws.

2. Clayton Antitrust Act (1914). In addition to strengthening the power of the government in fighting monopolistic business practices (see page 243), this act stated that labor is not a commodity and, therefore, legitimate union activities are not subject to antitrust laws. Thus it sought to outlaw suits against unions as combinations or conspiracies in restraint of trade, as in the Danbury Hatters case.

This act also prohibited the use of federal injunctions in labor disputes "unless necessary to prevent irreparable injury." Thus it sought to prevent federal courts from issuing injunctions indiscriminately. Furthermore, the act guaranteed a trial by jury to persons accused of contempt of court for violating an injunction.

Samuel Gompers hailed the Clayton Act as the workingman's "Magna Carta," for the act was intended to aid labor. In practice, the law helped unions very little. The courts applied the "irreparable injury" clause to grant injunctions halting many strikes and boycotts.

3. Adamson Act (1916). To head off a threatened railroad strike, this act legislated an 8-hour day for railroad employees.

4. Norris-La Guardia Act (1932). (*a*) This act prohibited federal courts from granting injunctions against workers who engaged in strikes, boycotts, or peaceful picketing. (*b*) It made *yellow-dog contracts* unenforceable. Under such a contract, a worker seeking employment had been required to state that he was not a member of a union and would not join a union during the term of his employment.

FEDERAL LEGISLATION AIDS LABOR: THE NEW DEAL

Labor began an era of great gains under the New Deal. Having overwhelmingly supported Franklin D. Roosevelt for President, unions now enjoyed his support and encouragement. Furthermore, as a result of the depression, public opinion was becoming increasingly sympathetic to the workingman. Labor and political leaders sensed that the time was ripe for favorable labor legislation.

1. National Industrial Recovery Act (1933). This act called for National Recovery Administration (NRA) codes (see page 245), which prohibited child labor and set maximum hours and minimum wages. Section 7a of the NIRA guaranteed workers the right to "organize and bargain collectively through representatives of their own choosing." To evade Section 7a, however, many employers established *company unions*. These were unions sponsored and dominated by employers. The employer coerced his workers into joining the company union and thus deterred them from joining a union of their own choice.

Because it proclaimed new rights for American labor, the NIRA was a significant measure for social reform. However, in 1935 the Supreme Court declared the NIRA unconstitutional.

2. Wagner (National Labor Relations) Act (1935). This act replaced the defunct Section 7a of the NIRA. The Wagner Act prohibited employers in interstate commerce from committing unfair labor practices relating to collective bargaining. It forbade employers to (*a*) interfere with labor's right to organize, (*b*) interfere in the operation of unions, (*c*) use *blacklists*, which contained the names of active union members to be denied jobs as "troublemakers," (*d*) hire *labor spies* to infiltrate unions and secure confidential information about their membership and plans, (*e*) organize company unions, (*f*) discriminate against union members, and (*g*) refuse to bargain collectively with employees. It created a *National Labor Relations Board (NLRB)* to enforce these prohibitions and to hold elections among the workers to determine their choice of a union, if any, to represent them. (Similar "little Wagner Acts" were passed by most industrial states to regulate labor relations in intrastate commerce.)

By guaranteeing collective bargaining, the Wagner Act was largely responsible for the subsequent growth in legitimate union membership. Over the next six years, more than 300 company unions were dissolved, and the number of workers in genuine unions grew from less than 4 million to over 10 million. Employer groups, led by the National Association of Manufacturers, condemned the Wagner Act for giving too much power to labor. (Its provisions were modified in 1947 by the Taft-Hartley Act. See pages 281–282.)

3. Social Security Act (1935). This act began a modest insurance program to combat economic insecurity due to unemployment and old age. Proponents of Social Security argued that it was self-financing and humanitarian, and that it protected the individuals against hazards over which they had little control. Opponents argued that it was "socialistic," that it substituted government financial assistance for private initiative, and that it weakened the individual's will to work and progress.

With time, as Social Security became accepted overwhelmingly, the original law was amended many times to extend coverage, increase benefits, and expand into the area of medical care for the aged.

a. Old-Age and Survivors Insurance (OASI). See pages 341–342.

b. Unemployment Insurance. The Social Security Act of 1935 encouraged the states to establish their own unemployment insurance systems. The act authorized the federal government to levy a payroll tax on employers and to grant each state 90 percent of the money collected within its borders, on the condition that the state establish a satisfactory unemployment insurance system. Within two years every state had done so.

Systems of unemployment insurance vary from state to state. They cover few workers in agriculture but most workers in industry. (The federal payroll tax does not apply to employers with fewer than four workers.) In general, the state systems grant an unemployed worker a weekly benefit, calculated according to his previous earnings and limited to a certain number of weeks. The worker must report regularly to a State Employment Office, which lists job openings and helps the unemployed find suitable work.

During recent recessions, Congress provided the states with additional funds to extend the unemployment benefits period for jobless workers who had exhausted their regular benefits.

c. Medicare for the Aged. See pages 342–344.

4. Fair Labor Standards (Wages and Hours) Act (1938). This act replaced the defunct NRA codes in regard to fair labor standards. For most workers in interstate commerce, it *(a)* set a minimum wage of 40 cents per hour and a standard workweek of 40 hours, *(b)* required payment for overtime at time and a half, and *(c)* prohibited most child labor.

This act has been revised many times to keep up with the rising cost of living. In 1981 the minimum wage reached $3.35. It became $4.25 in 1991. What effect may these wages have on the hiring of unskilled workers? of youthful workers?

STATE LEGISLATION AIDS LABOR

Most industrial states improved the conditions of labor by laws that provided (1) *workers' compensation,* requiring the employer to take out insurance covering workers in case of occupational disease or job accident, (2) *factory inspection,* requiring the employer to maintain proper sanitation, sufficient lighting, and safety devices on dangerous machinery, (3) *protection of women and children,* limiting their hours of work and prohibiting their employment in hazardous occupations, and (4) *compulsory education,* keeping children in school and out of the labor market.

LABOR AND WORLD WAR II

1. Gains During the War. Labor realized that the war would be fought not only abroad on battlefields but also at home in mines and factories. Victory depended upon an ever-increasing supply of the implements of war: ships, tanks, guns, planes, ammunition. To maintain maximum production, both the A.F. of L. and the C.I.O. pledged a policy of no strikes. To settle labor disputes peacefully, the government established the *War Labor Board (WLB).* In 1942 the WLB permitted workers wage increases totaling no more than 15 percent above prewar levels. This, together with considerable overtime pay, enabled workers, despite rising prices, to improve their living standards. During the war the time lost due to walkouts, mostly not authorized by union leaders, was less than one percent.

The demands of the armed forces for personnel and of industry for workers resulted in labor shortages. The government established the *War Manpower Commission (WMC)* to shift workers from nonessential to essential industries, to "freeze" workers in their jobs in essential industries, and to train new workers, especially women, for jobs in defense industries. Between 1941 and 1945 labor unions increased their membership from 10 million to 14 million.

2. Strikes in the Immediate Postwar Era. Now free of their no-strike pledge, labor unions began walkouts for higher wages. Workers justified their demands because (*a*) take-home pay was sharply reduced by the loss of overtime pay, (*b*) the purchasing power of the dollar was cut by the soaring cost of living, and (*c*) business profits were at an all-time high.

Long and bitter strikes took place in the automobile, steel, coal, and electrical equipment industries. By these strikes, labor unions aroused public resentment. Unions were blamed for delaying the production of long-awaited consumer goods, feeding the forces of inflation, and accepting the leadership of "power-hungry labor bosses."

CRITICISMS OF LABOR UNIONS IN THE POSTWAR ERA

1. Limits Upon Union Membership. Some unions sharply restricted the number of new members, often admitting only relatives of present members, and charged high initiation fees. Also, some unions deliberately excluded Negroes and other minority groups. These practices kept out new workers and prevented them from competing with union members for jobs in closed-shop industries.

2. Opposition to Laborsaving Machinery. Many unions fought the introduction of laborsaving machinery. Although these technological advances reduced the employer's expenses and permitted the consumer more and cheaper goods, unions opposed such machines because they would decrease the number of jobs.

3. Featherbedding. To prevent technological unemployment, some unions forced employers to retain unneeded help. For example, the railroad brotherhoods compelled the keeping of coal-stoking firemen even though no coal was used in the newer oil-burning diesel locomotives.

4. Lack of Union Responsibility. Some unions failed to keep their members from violating the union's contract with the employer. One such contract violation was the *wildcat strike*—a spontaneous walkout by workers without the formal approval of their union.

5. Lack of Financial Statements. A number of unions did not publish financial statements. Their members and the general public had no knowledge of the unions' income and expenditures.

6. Lack of Union Democracy. Some unions were controlled by small groups of insiders. Rank-and-file members, sometimes through indifference and sometimes through fear, had little say in union affairs. Their union resembled a dictatorship rather than a democracy.

7. Racketeer Influence. Racketeers gained control of some few unions and used them for corrupt purposes. They treated union funds as their own and paid themselves excessive salaries. They employed strong-arm methods to suppress critics within the union and to force the union upon employers. In return for monetary "gifts" and other personal favors, they granted employers lenient terms in "sweetheart" labor contracts. (For a further discussion, see Landrum-Griffin Act, pages **282–284**.)

8. Communist Influence. During the depression years of the 1930's, Communists worked hard to gain control of the American labor movement as a means of overthrowing our capitalist economy and democratic government. However, only a few unions fell under Communist leadership.

9. Jurisdictional Strikes. Such a strike came about when two unions competed for control of the same workers. For example, the carpenters' union and the stagehands' union each claimed jurisdiction over workers building movie sets. In the ensuing strike the employer was caught in the middle and suffered from the interruption of production.

TAFT-HARTLEY (LABOR-MANAGEMENT RELATIONS) ACT (1947)

Partly because of the criticisms leveled at labor unions, the Republican-controlled Congress in 1947 passed the *Taft-Hartley Act*. President Truman vetoed the bill, but a combination of Republicans and Southern Democrats overrode the veto. The Taft-Hartley Act provided as follows:

1. Reaffirmed Collective Bargaining. The law reaffirmed the right of workers to organize and bargain collectively.

2. Outlawed the Closed Shop. The law prohibited the closed shop but permitted the union shop, unless it was contrary to state regulations. Section 14b of the Taft-Hartley Act authorized states to bar even the union shop by passing "right-to-work" laws (see page 285).

3. Prohibited Unfair Union Practices. The law prohibited unions from (a) refusing to bargain collectively with employers, (b) engaging in a jurisdictional strike, (c) engaging in a *secondary boycott*, an action against a businessman dealing with a firm involved in a labor dispute (as, for example, when a union requests the public not to buy from a retail establishment that sells goods of a manufacturer whose workers are on strike), (d) protecting jobs by certain forms of featherbedding, (e) charging new members excessive initiation fees, (f) contributing funds to candidates for federal office, and (g) denying responsibility for contract violations by their members, especially wildcat strikes.

4. Established Requirements for Unions. The law required each union to file with the government (a) annual financial reports and details about the operation of the union, and (b) affidavits that union officials were not members of the Communist party.

5. Established New Regulations for Strikes. (a) *Sixty-Day "Cooling-Off" Period.* The law required unions to notify employers of intent to strike and then to wait 60 days. (b) *Eighty-Day Temporary Injunction.* In strikes affecting the national welfare, the federal government was empowered to secure a temporary injunction restraining the union from striking for an additional 80 days. During both the 60-day and 80-day periods, labor and management could seek peaceful settlement of their dispute.

CONTROVERSY REGARDING THE TAFT-HARTLEY ACT

1. **Opposition by Unions.** Most union leaders condemned the Taft-Hartley Act as a "slave-labor" law. They insisted that this law could be used to harass, weaken, and finally destroy the American labor movement. In particular, they opposed (a) the abolition of the closed shop, since, under the union shop, the union had no power over hiring, (b) the right granted to the states to bar even the union shop, (c) the use of a temporary injunction, which revived fears of "government by injunction," and (d) the anti-Communist oath, which union leaders considered an insult, since it was not required of any other segment of American society.

2. **Approval by Major Corporations.** Most corporate leaders hailed the Taft-Hartley Act for (a) prohibiting unfair practices by unions, just as the Wagner Act had prohibited unfair practices by employers, (b) outlawing the closed shop and thus giving employers the right to hire anyone they wanted, (c) providing a cooling-off period to encourage peaceful collective bargaining, and (d) insisting that unions force their members to honor their labor contracts.

3. **Observations.** (a) In spite of the pessimistic predictions of labor leaders, unions made further gains, growing in membership from 14 million in 1947 to 17 million in 1957 and winning higher wages and many fringe benefits. (b) Some 20 states, most of them in the South, have "right-to-work" laws, outlawing the union shop. These laws, union leaders claimed, hampered unions in organizing workers. (c) In many industries, unions unofficially retained the closed shop, as employers voluntarily requested the union to supply additional workers. (d) With the passage of the Taft-Hartley Act, organized labor stepped up its efforts to rid itself of Communist influence. For instance, in 1949 the C.I.O. expelled the United Electrical Workers (UEW) as Communist-led. Also, the C.I.O organized a new non-Communist electrical union. Today, in organized labor, Communist influence is at an all-time low. (e) Employers gained some relief from unfair labor practices.
In general, the Taft-Hartley Act brought little change into the power relationship between unions and employers.

LANDRUM-GRIFFIN (LABOR-MANAGEMENT REPORTING AND DISCLOSURE) ACT (1959)

1. **Background: McClellan Senate Investigating Committee.** Investigating corruption in labor unions, the McClellan Committee concentrated upon the

huge and powerful truckers' union, the *International Brotherhood of Teamsters*. The investigators found Teamster officials to be reluctant witnesses. Nevertheless, the hearings disclosed a shocking picture of racketeering, misuse of union funds, and abuse of union power for personal advantage.

2. AFL-CIO and the Teamsters Union. Following disclosures before the McClellan Committee in 1957, the AFL-CIO acted to enforce its *Ethical Practices Code*. Its executive council (*a*) charged that *James Hoffa* and other Teamster officials associated with gangsters and used the union for personal profit, and (*b*) ordered the Teamsters to get rid of their corrupt leaders. The Teamsters defied the AFL-CIO by overwhelmingly electing Hoffa as president. Thereupon the AFL-CIO expelled the Teamsters. For 10 years Hoffa retained control. (In 1967 he was imprisoned for jury tampering and mail fraud.) By 1987, the Teamsters, with 1.8 million workers, had improved their image and were readmitted to the AFL-CIO.

3. Landrum-Griffin Act. To combat the corrupt union practices uncovered by the McClellan Committee and to assure democracy in union affairs, Congress passed the Landrum-Griffin Act, providing as follows:

a. Union Elections. Union officials must be elected by secret ballot. Elections must be held at least every three years for local offices and every five years for national offices. To insure an honest vote, each candidate must be permitted to inspect the membership lists and have observers at the polls. Criminals convicted of serious offenses may not serve as union officials until five years after being released from prison. Communist party members may not serve as union officials until five years after leaving the party.

b. Bill of Rights. To protect rank-and-file members against coercion by union officials, this "bill of rights" guarantees union members freedom of speech and assembly, and the right to participate in union matters. No union member may be subject to disciplinary action by union leaders without a written statement of charges, time to prepare a defense, and a fair hearing. If these rights are violated, a union member may seek a federal court injunction against the officials of his union.

c. Financial Reports. Unions must file with the Secretary of Labor detailed reports disclosing the handling of union funds, including salaries of union officials, loans to union officials, and loans to business concerns. Union officials must report any monetary benefits received from an employer. Employers must report any loan or payment made to a union or to union officials. Persons filing reports must keep their records for five years.

d. Picketing and Secondary Boycotts. The law (1) prohibited picketing by one union for recognition if an employer has already recognized another union, and (2) strengthened prohibitions against secondary boycotts.

Supporters hailed this law as an effort to curb racketeering and safeguard the rights of union members. Many labor leaders, however, condemned this law, arguing that (a) its "bill of rights" would enable disgruntled members to obstruct legitimate union activities, (b) its prohibition of picketing for recognition would prevent honest unions from ousting racketeer-controlled unions, and (c) it would have no effect on Hoffa's Teamsters Union.

4. The United Mine Workers Elections (1969, 1972). Insurgent rank-and-file miners, whose leader Joseph Yablonski had been murdered, challenged the 1969 reelection of W. A. (Tony) Boyle as president of the United Mine Workers. They charged fraud and other election irregularities in violation of the Landrum-Griffin Act. Their charges were upheld by a federal court which ordered a new union election. Held in 1972 under strict Labor Department supervision, the election enabled the insurgents to oust Boyle and elect their reform candidate. (In 1974 Boyle was found guilty of instigating the murder of Yablonski. In 1977 Boyle won a new trial on the ground that the 1974 court had not heard vital defense testimony. In 1978 he was again found guilty.)

RECENT LABOR TRENDS AND PROBLEMS

1. Weaknesses of the AFL-CIO

a. Internal Dissension. Despite the merger of the A.F. of L. and the C.I.O. in 1955, labor has not achieved internal harmony. The leaders of the AFL-CIO remain divided into two camps, as personality clashes have heightened policy differences. The former A.F. of L. leaders are generally conservative and favor craft unionism. The former C.I.O. leaders are generally more progressive and favor industrial unionism.

In 1967 Walter Reuther, president of the United Automobile Workers, dramatized his dissatisfaction with the AFL-CIO by resigning from its Executive Council. Reuther angrily condemned the AFL-CIO for failing to extend "equal rights and equal opportunities to every American" and for failing to organize the many industrial, farm, and white-collar workers. In 1968 he led the UAW out of the AFL-CIO. (In 1981 the UAW, then under new leadership, reaffiliated.)

b. Failure to Expand Membership. Labor unions represent a declining share of American workers. Unions' share of the nation's labor force reached its highest point, 35.5 percent, in 1945. By 1979, only 24.1 percent of American workers belonged to unions, and the proportion declined further to 15.8 percent in 1993.

AFL-CIO membership, at a peak of 16 million in 1955, was under 14 million in the mid-1990's. Despite the expectations raised by its creation, the AFL-CIO has proved unable to organize the vast majority of workers.

2. **Right-to-Work Laws.** Section 14b of the Taft-Hartley Act permitted states to pass laws to prohibit the union shop. Some 20 states, mostly Southern, have "right-to-work" laws against the union shop. "Right-to-work" measures prohibit compulsory union membership by stating that no worker can be compelled to join a union in order to hold a job.

Supporters of "right-to-work" measures argue that such laws *(a)* protect the democratic right of each worker to join or not to join a union, and *(b)* encourage honest unionism, since workers may resign from corrupt unions without losing their jobs.

Opponents of "right-to-work" measures argue that such laws *(a)* weaken unionism by limiting a union's control over its members, *(b)* deny the democratic principle of majority rule, since a minority of workers may remain outside a union approved by a majority, and *(c)* enable nonunion workers to benefit from the union's efforts without paying a fair share of union costs.

Labor's efforts to secure repeal of Section 14b have so far failed.

3. **Problems of Wages**

a. Money Wages vs. Real Wages. Unions realize that an increase in *money wages,* that is, wages measured in dollars, is often offset by rising prices, which reduce *real wages,* that is, wages measured in purchasing power. For example, if over a three-year period a worker has received a wage increase of 5 percent and if the cost of living has risen 10 percent, the worker is worse off than before. Since World War II, the cost of living has been steadily rising. Some unions consequently secured an *escalator clause* in their labor contracts. This clause provides for an adjustment in wages, according to changes in the cost of living as compiled by the Bureau of Labor Statistics of the Department of Labor in its *Consumer Price Index.* The clause is known by the acronym COLA— *cost-of-living adjustment.*

b. Consumer Price Index (CPI). The CPI measures the change in prices of goods and services as compared to prices in the base year. The CPI currently measures the prices paid by urban consumers for 400 commonly purchased goods and services—*the market basket.* The CPI is not foolproof: (1) a higher price may reflect an improved quality of goods, and (2) the typical market basket may neglect changes in the consumer's purchasing habits. The CPI, nevertheless, remains a highly regarded measure of the "cost of living."

The current CPI uses 1982–1984 as the base period, with an index of 100. Since that base period, the CPI has recorded an almost continuous process of inflation. At the end of 1994, the CPI stood at 147. This meant that the amount of goods bought for $1.00 in 1982–1984 cost $1.47 in 1994, indicating that the dollar's purchasing power had fallen considerably.

4. **Automation.** Following World War II, labor became greatly concerned over automation—the use of automatic devices, chiefly electronic, to control the operation of machines. Unions knew that automation increased productiv-

ity, provided better products at lower cost, and created new, more skilled jobs in the manufacturing, servicing, and using of automatic equipment. But unions feared that automation would displace large numbers of workers. For example, in New York City alone, automatic elevators in skyscrapers replaced some 40,000 elevator operators.

Unions have responded to automation by seeking a voice with management regarding the introduction of automated equipment and also by seeking to provide job security for their current members.

5. **Problem of Strikes Affecting the Public Welfare.** Following World War II the government and public opinion became increasingly concerned over labor-management disputes affecting national security and the public welfare. These included strikes by steelworkers, longshoremen, airline mechanics and ground service crews, and railroad employees. The government employed the 80-day Taft-Hartley injunction, but its use was of questionable effectiveness.

Eric in The Atlanta Journal

"Come any further and I'll strike!"

How can automation help the worker? hurt the worker? What two meanings are contained in the word "strike"?

Some members of Congress proposed legislation to *(a)* outlaw industry-wide strikes and compel unions to deal with only one employer at a time, or *(b)* require labor and management to accept compulsory arbitration, or *(c)* permit the government to seize and operate an essential industry involved in a strike, pending a labor contract.

Unions opposed all these proposals as restrictions on their economic power. Management feared compulsory arbitration as an opening wedge for government price-fixing and suspected that the government would favor unions with their large blocs of votes. Management furthermore considered government seizure of plants as a threat to private ownership. The basic problem remains: How should a democratic society provide for the settlement of labor disputes affecting the national welfare?

6. Givebacks. In the early 1980's, unions were under pressures for concessions from previously won wages and fringe benefits—concessions generally known as *givebacks*. These pressures, which caused a considerable loss of jobs for union members, included: *(a)* An ailing economy. With two recessions coming back-to-back, unemployment among American workers stood at 11 percent, about 12 million persons. *(b)* Foreign competition from low-wage countries such as Brazil in South America, and the Philippines, South Korea, Japan, Taiwan, and Hong Kong in Asia. American auto industry officials claimed that their Japanese competitors—who sell millions of cars in America—pay lower wages of about $8 per hour per worker. This results in a labor-cost advantage per car of $1000 to $1500. American clothing workers' union leaders estimate that more than half of all women's and children's apparel sold in America is not produced by American workers but imported from low-wage countries. *(c)* Failing American companies. A number of companies, unable to compete and operate profitably, have gone out of business—idling their facilities and ending the jobs of thousands of workers. In addition to these pressures upon unions to protect jobs, a number of companies demanded givebacks under threats to move and build new plants in southern and western low-wage areas of the United States, and to farm out work to low-wage countries and purchase supplies from them.

In numerous cases, unions agreed to cut back wages, forgo cost-of-living increases, and reduce paid vacations and pension benefits—sometimes even to make no-strike pledges. In return, unions received company assurances to maintain existing production facilities, to provide a profit-sharing plan for workers, and to offer the union a voice in setting company policy. Do these developments indicate that unions and management are moving from an adversary relationship to one of cooperation?

MULTIPLE-CHOICE QUESTIONS

1. Which statement best describes labor unions in the United States prior to the Civil War? (1) Most labor unions were only local. (2) No unions existed. (3) The courts were hostile to all labor unions and forced them to disband. (4) Most unskilled laborers were organized.

2. An important reason for the decline of the Knights of Labor was the (1) organization of the Socialist party (2) high cost of membership (3) conflict between skilled and unskilled workers (4) passage of antilabor laws by the federal government.

3. During the period 1865–1900, labor-management disputes were often marked by (1) a willingness by both sides to have the disputes arbitrated (2) violence on both sides (3) federal support of the strikers (4) government mediation.

4. At its beginning, the A. F. of L. aimed to (1) unite skilled and unskilled workers into one union (2) establish industrial unions (3) form craft unions of skilled workers (4) campaign actively for the election of its members to public office.

5. Which generalization concerning labor unions in the United States during the period 1890–1910 is true? (1) Newspapers were sympathetic toward them. (2) Court decisions were usually in their favor. (3) They were prosecuted under the antitrust laws. (4) Members were guaranteed the right to vote by secret ballot in union elections.

6. In 1900 among which of the following groups were labor unions the strongest? (1) printers (2) farm workers (3) office workers (4) automobile workers.

7. In the 1930's which issue caused a split within the A. F. of L. and led to the formation of an independent C.I.O.? (1) the sit-down strike (2) the reelection of Franklin D. Roosevelt (3) industrial unionism (4) the National Labor Relations Act.

8. The organizational principles of the Congress of Industrial Organizations reflected the (1) increased need for skilled workers (2) rise of mass-production industries (3) opposition by many labor leaders to the political involvement of the A. F. of L. (4) decline in union membership during the New Deal.

9. Which statement about organized labor is true? (1) All large unions are affiliated with the AFL-CIO. (2) The 1950's saw the most rapid membership increase in labor's history. (3) Less than one-third of the labor force belongs to unions. (4) Craft-industrial union rivalry ceased to be a problem with the merger of the AFL-CIO.

10. Today, which group is most completely unionized? (1) automobile workers (2) office workers (3) teachers (4) farm employees.

11. The procedure by which representatives of employees deal directly with representatives of employers to determine working conditions is known as (1) arbitration (2) collective bargaining (3) injunction (4) mediation.

12. When labor and management agree in advance to settle a dispute by accepting the decision of a third party, they are relying upon (1) arbitration (2) conciliation (3) the checkoff system (4) a secondary boycott.

13. Which two practices are now forbidden? (1) lockouts and injunctions (2) yellow-dog contracts and secondary boycotts (3) secondary boycotts and strikes (4) blacklists and injunctions.

14. A system under which an employer, by agreement with the union, deducts union dues from the wages of his employees and turns them over to the union is known as (1) checkoff (2) collective bargaining (3) processing tax (4) transfer payment.

15. "Fringe benefits" include (1) pensions and paid vacations (2) a worker's right to refuse to join a union (3) labor practices limiting the amount of work that a union member may do (4) a guaranteed annual wage.

16. One provision of the Clayton Act concerning labor resulted from the (1) opposition of the A. F. of L. to the Taft-Hartley Act (2) failure of the Landrum-Griffin Act to end union racketeering (3) Supreme Court decision declaring the National Industrial Recovery Act unconstitutional (4) injunctions issued against labor under the Sherman Antitrust Act.

17. During the 20th century, federal legislation in the area of labor-management relations has most frequently been based on the Constitutional power of Congress to (1) enforce the Fourteenth Amendment (2) levy and collect taxes (3) establish lower courts (4) regulate interstate commerce.

18. The Wagner National Labor Relations Act (1) led to a rapid increase in labor union membership (2) led to a marked decline in the use of the closed shop (3) encouraged the use of injunctions by employers (4) made legal the use of strikes and picketing.

19. One purpose of the Social Security Act of 1935 was to (1) protect workers against accidents on the job (2) provide national health insurance (3) encourage states to set up unemployment insurance programs (4) establish a minimum wage for industries engaged in interstate commerce.

20. In most states, funds for unemployment insurance come from (1) appropriations by Congress (2) appropriations by the state legislature (3) contributions by the employees (4) payments by the employers.

21. The author of the quotation, "Confronted with a contracting number of unionized jobs in an expanding labor force, unions have fought one another for control of work opportunities," is probably trying to prove that (1) unemployment has decreased union strength (2) the A. F. of L. and C.I.O. should again split (3) jurisdictional strife is a major labor problem (4) unions are fighting for an expanded labor force.

22. A work stoppage called without official union approval is known as a (1) lockout (2) wildcat strike (3) sit-down strike (4) closed shop.

23. When a strike threatens the national health and safety, the Taft-Hartley Act empowers the President of the United States to (1) forbid the calling of the strike (2) request an injunction to halt the strike temporarily (3) provide for government operation of the plants threatened by the strike (4) provide for compulsory arbitration.

24. An action against an employer who uses or sells products from an establishment where the workers are on strike is called a (1) lockout (2) general strike (3) jurisdictional strike (4) secondary boycott.

25. The author of the statement, "Railroads would have fewer financial difficulties if unions would permit them to eliminate unnecessary jobs," believes that (1) unions are blocking automation (2) the closed shop is a valuable protection for labor (3) many railroads are owned by labor unions (4) featherbedding is expensive.

26. The Senate committee investigating labor racketeering acted within the Constitution by seeking to (1) destroy the principle of collective bargaining (2) provide evidence for criminal action against labor racketeers (3) provide Congress with information on which to base corrective legislation (4) force the AFL-CIO to expel the Teamsters.

27. A major purpose of the Landrum-Griffin Act was to (1) reestablish the closed shop (2) replace the injunction provisions of the Taft-Hartley Act (3) strengthen the position of the AFL-CIO (4) promote democratic operation within labor unions.

28. A union leader who speaks against "the hourly wage system from which so much of the worker's insecurity stems" most probably supports (1) a piecework wage system (2) a higher federal minimum wage (3) a guaranteed annual wage (4) longer paid vacations.

29. Organized labor opposes "right-to-work" laws because these laws (1) are contrary to the Taft-Hartley Act (2) prohibit the union shop (3) limit unemployment insurance benefits (4) restrict the right to strike.

30. The most reliable basis for measuring changes in the cost of living is the (1) Consumer Price Index of the Bureau of Labor Statistics (2) summary of replies to a public-opinion poll (3) list of quotations on the stock market (4) rediscount rate established by the Federal Reserve Board.

31. An escalator clause in a labor-management contract is usually designed to (1) protect the seniority rights of workers in the event of unemployment (2) provide for a periodic increase in pension benefits (3) keep real wages reasonably stable (4) protect collective bargaining rights not guaranteed by state or federal laws.

32. A generally accepted long-range effect of automation on the labor force is that there will be (1) a decrease in its total size (2) a decrease in the percentage of skilled workers (3) an increase in the percentage of unskilled workers (4) an increase in the percentage of professional and technical workers.

33. "Labor unionism in the United States came into its own in this period. It was also a lean time." This statement best applies to the period (1) 1865–1900 (2) 1901–1920 (3) 1933–1940 (4) 1953–1965.

34. Which of the following demands of labor is of most recent origin? (1) higher wages (2) improved working conditions (3) increased pension benefits (4) shorter working hours.

35. Labor union membership in the United States (1) has increased steadily since the 1930's (2) includes over half of the labor force (3) has sharply increased since the AFL-CIO merger (4) has remained about the same since the AFL-CIO merger.

MATCHING QUESTIONS

Column A

1. First head of merged AFL-CIO
2. Political leader who helped settle coal strike of 1902
3. Head of United Mine Workers and first president of C.I.O.
4. Founder of A. F. of L.
5. First political leader to use federal troops in labor-management dispute
6. Founder of Knights of Labor
7. Labor leader arrested during Pullman strike
8. Senator who sponsored New Deal law guaranteeing collective bargaining
9. **President of United Automobile Workers who led his union out of the AFL-CIO**
10. **Senator who sponsored a law to curtail abuses by labor unions**

Column B

a. Rutherford B. Hayes
b. Walter P. Reuther
c. George Meany
d. John P. Altgeld
e. Robert A. Taft
f. Theodore Roosevelt
g. Franklin D. Roosevelt
h. Robert F. Wagner, Sr.
i. Samuel Gompers
j. Uriah S. Stephens
k. Eugene V. Debs
l. Terence V. Powderly
m. John L. Lewis

ESSAY QUESTIONS

1. (a) Giving *two* specific facts, explain why there was opposition to organized labor before 1900. (b) Show specifically how each of *two* different laws has benefited labor since 1930. (c) Discuss briefly *two* criticisms that have been directed at organized labor since 1950.

2. (a) Discuss *two* causes of the Industrial Revolution in the United States during the 19th century. (b) Discuss *two* facts showing how the steady march of the Industrial Revolution led to the rise of national labor organizations. (c) Explain *two* reasons why the federal government found it necessary to regulate organized labor.

3. Both the Knights of Labor and the Congress of Industrial Organizations (C.I.O.) were industrial unions. (a) Discuss *two* factors that led to the decline of the Knights of Labor. (b) Discuss *three* factors that led to the growth of the Congress of Industrial Organizations.

4. In 1955 the American Federation of Labor and the Congress of Industrial Organizations merged. (a) Describe *two* circumstances that led to the formation of the A. F. of L. (b) Discuss briefly *two* reasons for the merging of the A. F. of L. and the C.I.O. (c) Has the merger of the A. F. of L. and the C.I.O. strengthened the labor movement? Defend your answer by presenting *two* arguments.

5. Show how *each* of the following has been a problem for organized labor: (a) automation, (b) jurisdictional disputes, (c) racketeering, (d) "right-to-work" laws, (e) the civil rights movement, (f) inflation.

6. The federal government has, through legislation, court decisions, and intervention by the executive department, frequently exerted a strong influence on the relations between labor and management. (a) Discuss *two* actions by the federal government that exerted a strong influence on the relations between labor and management during the period 1865–1930. (b) Discuss *two* actions by the federal government that exerted a strong influence on the relations between labor and management during the period from 1945 to the present.

7. (a) State *one* specific provision of the Taft-Hartley Act of 1947 and *one* specific provision of the Landrum-Griffin Act of 1959. (b) Show why you consider each provision you have chosen to be *either* beneficial *or* harmful to labor union members.

8. Discuss each of the following, giving *two* specific facts to support *or* *two* specific facts to refute each statement: (a) During the 19th century, labor experienced difficulties in organizing. (b) Changed conditions contributed to the rapid rise in union membership after 1933. (c) The Taft-Hartley Act marked a change in the government's policy toward labor organizations. (d) Union organizations engage in a wide variety of activities in addition to working for improved wages and hours. (e) Good labor-management relations are essential to the welfare of the United States.

Part 7. Foreign Trade Furthers the Welfare of the Nation

IMPORTANCE OF FOREIGN TRADE TO THE UNITED STATES

1. Imports. *(a)* American consumers purchase imports of foodstuffs (coffee, sugar, cocoa, fish, meat, and fruits and nuts) and manufactured goods (Japanese automobiles, TV sets, and cameras, English textiles, German chinaware, Canadian farm equipment, Italian typewriters, and Swiss watches). *(b)* American manufacturers utilize imports of metals (copper, aluminum, nickel, tin, and iron ore) and other vital products (crude oil, wood pulp, newsprint, and natural rubber). American manufacturers also import large amounts of machinery, especially electrical and textile equipment. From 1966 to 1993, our annual imports rose from $25.5 billion to $580.5 billion.

2. Exports. *(a)* American farmers export much agricultural produce, such as wheat, corn, soybeans, and tobacco. *(b)* American corporations export large amounts of manufactured goods, such as electrical equipment, metalworking machinery, computers, agricultural implements, chemicals, medicinals, paper, textile products, trucks, and automobiles. From 1966 to 1993, our annual exports rose from $29 billion to $465 billion.

Our principal suppliers, and also our chief customers, are Canada, Japan, Mexico, Germany, and Britain.

3. Foreign Trade as an Industry. International trade requires import and export firms, oceangoing freighters, dock and storage facilities, and banking services. These enterprises provide opportunities for business leaders and employment for workers.

THE TARIFF: MEANING OF TERMS

1. A **tariff** is a tax, or duty, placed on goods imported from foreign countries.

2. A **revenue tariff** seeks to provide income for the government. Therefore, its rates are low so as not to discourage imports.

3. A **protective tariff** seeks to protect domestic manufacturers from foreign competition. Therefore, its rates are high so as to discourage imports.

4. Free trade means the international exchange of goods unhampered by any people-made barriers, such as tariffs.

OTHER BARRIERS TO WORLD TRADE

1. Barriers Deliberately Established. In addition to high protective tariffs, nations may employ (a) *import quotas*, limiting the amount of goods permitted to enter the country, (b) *currency controls*, restricting the amount of foreign money available to domestic importers for the purchase of goods from abroad, (c) *embargoes*, halting trade in part or in full with certain countries, and (d) *direct control*, as in Communist nations, where the government itself owns and controls the means of producing and distributing goods.

In recent years nations have used trade as an economic weapon. The United States in 1960 embargoed trade with Communist Cuba and in 1980–1981 temporarily embargoed grain exports to the Soviet Union to express American opposition to the Soviet invasion of Afghanistan. The Soviet Union often directed foreign trade for political purposes, such as bolstering the faltering economy of Communist Cuba.

2. Barriers Due to Economic Conditions. (a) *Similar Products.* Nations with similar products have no reason to trade with one another. For example, Argentina sells little to the United States because we produce an abundance of meat and wheat, Argentina's chief exports. *(b) Poverty in Underdeveloped Nations.* Many developing nations lack sufficient goods to export and funds to buy essential agricultural, industrial, and petroleum imports.

PROTECTIVE TARIFF: EVALUATION

1. Arguments For. (a) By protecting domestic manufacturers from foreign competition, especially from goods produced abroad by cheap labor, the tariff helps business prosper, provides jobs for workers, keeps wages high, and raises the nation's standard of living. (b) It helps "infant industries" to survive the difficult starting years. (c) It encourages diversified industries. This keeps the national economy from becoming dependent on a limited number of products. It also makes a nation self-sufficient, which may be essential in case of war. (d) The abandonment of tariffs on products of industries that have till now been protected by them would cause great hardships to these industries and their workers. (e) While following a policy of high protective tariffs, the United States has become the leading industrial power in the world.

The policy of creating heavy barriers to foreign trade in order to encourage domestic industry is called *economic nationalism.*

2. Arguments Against. (a) By reducing international trade, the tariff discourages *specialization.* By specializing, nations concentrate on those goods that they can produce most efficiently. For example, because of its climate and soil, Brazil grows coffee; because of its mineral deposits, Chile mines copper; because of its technical know-how, the United States produces automobiles. (b) Tariffs prevent healthy competition from abroad. Competition compels manufacturers to modernize their production methods and improve the quality of their products. (c) The tariff enables domestic manufacturers to monopolize the home market and raise prices. (d) Tariffs hurt American exports because foreign nations reciprocate by raising their tariffs on American goods, and because foreign merchants, unable to sell their goods to the United States, lack the dollars with which to buy our goods. A decrease in exports means smaller profits for American corporations and fewer jobs for American workers. (e) By preventing the free flow of goods, the tariff creates ill will among nations.

TARIFF HISTORY OF THE UNITED STATES

1. **Until the End of the War of 1812** (1789–1815). Seeking income, the new government levied only revenue tariffs.

2. **To the Civil War** (1816–1860). To protect the industries that arose with the War of 1812, the government levied high protective tariffs: the Tariff of 1816, the Tariff of Abominations of 1828, and the Tariff of 1832. These tariffs aroused bitter sectional conflict between the industrial North and the agricultural South. With the Compromise Tariff of 1833, the government reduced tariffs but continued its policy of providing some protection.

3. **To the Beginning of the New Deal** (1861–1933). During the Civil War, the Republican party gained control of the government and passed the Morrill Tariff Act (1861), inaugurating an era of very high protective tariffs. For almost 75 years, with two exceptions during Democratic administrations, the general trend of American tariffs was upward. Grover Cleveland urged Congress to lower tariffs, but the resulting Wilson-Gorman Tariff Act of 1894 lowered rates so little that Cleveland let it become law without his signature. In 1913 President Wilson pushed through Congress the much lower Underwood Tariff. Since imports into the United States were sharply reduced by the outbreak of World War I in 1914, the Underwood Tariff had little effect. Following the war, the Republicans regained control of the government and restored high protective tariffs. President Harding in 1922 approved a large increase in our tariffs by signing the Fordney-McCumber Tariff Act, and in 1930 President Hoover approved our highest tariff ever, the Hawley-Smoot Tariff. Hoover's action came at the beginning of the Great Depression and against the advice of over 1000 American economists.

4. **To the Present** (1934–   )

a. *Reciprocal Tariff Acts.* In 1934 President Roosevelt, a Democrat, secured passage of the first *Reciprocal Trade Agreements Act,* providing for lower rates through reciprocity. This law inaugurated a new American policy by (1) authorizing the President to negotiate agreements with foreign countries and set new tariff rates, and (2) permitting reductions up to 50 percent in existing rates. This transfer of rate-making power from Congress to the President displeased the high-tariff lobbyists, who had been able to influence Congressmen by appeals to protect industry in home districts. The

President, they feared, would consider tariff problems not from a local, but from a national point of view.

Under the 1934 act, the United States negotiated agreements with many countries for the reciprocal lowering of tariff rates on each other's exports. As American exports increased, subsequent Congresses extended the reciprocal tariff program and authorized further rate cuts. By 1962 our average reciprocal tariff rates were some 80 percent below Hawley-Smoot levels.

b. Trade Expansion Act of 1962

(1) *Background.* In 1957 six Western European nations (France, West Germany, Italy, Belgium, the Netherlands, and Luxembourg) joined together to form a free-trade area called the *European Economic Community*, or *Common Market*. They agreed to gradually eliminate internal tariff barriers and to establish a unified tariff system on goods imported from outside their common area. Later, the Common Market added more members and evolved into the European Union. In one sense the Common Market drew upon American experience, since the United States under its Constitution is a "common market."

To Americans, the European Common Market was an opportunity and a threat: a prosperous Western Europe would increase its purchase of American goods; a high-tariff Common Market would exclude American goods. Mainly to strengthen our bargaining position with the Common Market, President Kennedy requested a "new and bold instrument of American trade policy." Congress responded by passing the *Trade Expansion Act* (1962).

(2) *Provisions.* The law authorized the President to (a) reduce tariffs up to 50 percent in reciprocal agreements with other countries, (b) raise tariffs on goods from any country that places unreasonable restrictions on U.S. goods, and (c) help domestic industries and workers injured by increased imports.

c. World Trade Negotiations

(1) *Kennedy Round (1964–1967).* Nearly 50 members of GATT (see page 299) agreed to the largest tariff reduction ever. The cuts, which averaged one-third of the rates then in effect, were phased in over a period of five years.

(2) *Tokyo Round (1973–1979).* An enlarged group of 99 GATT members took part in the next round of trade negotiations. They agreed to (a) reduce tariffs on manufactured goods by one-third over eight years, (b) reduce tariffs on agricultural produce, and (c) reduce or remove various nontariff barriers to trade (such as government export subsidies).

(3) *Uruguay Round (1986–1993).* Their numbers swelled by the addition of Communist and formerly-Communist nations, 117 GATT members took part in talks that began in Uruguay and ended in Switzerland. They agreed to (a) cut tariff levels on manufactured goods by about half—from an average of 7 percent to 4 percent, (b) reduce agricultural tariffs, (c) cut farm subsidies, (d) eliminate most textile tariffs in industrial nations over ten years, (e) for the first time put

international restrictions on trade in services, (*f*) protect *intellectual property* such as patents and copyrights, and (*g*) create a new *World Trade Organization* (WTO) to administer trade regulations. The rules are somewhat more lenient for developing nations than for industrial nations.

d. Regional Trade Agreements. The United States has entered into regional trade agreements as follows:

(1) *U.S.-Canada Free Trade Agreement (1988)*. The United States and Canada agreed to eliminate almost all duties and tariffs in three steps over 20 years.

(2) *North American Free Trade Agreement*, or *NAFTA (1993)*. Under a treaty approved by Congress after long debate, the United States and Canada added Mexico to their free-trade area. Tariff reductions began in 1994, with most tariffs on goods and services to end by 2008. In response to criticisms of early drafts, the agreement included side deals to protect consumers and the environment. Critics said NAFTA will siphon off U.S. jobs to low-wage industries in Mexico. Supporters said NAFTA will add more new jobs.

AMERICA'S POSITION IN WORLD TRADE (TO THE 1930's)

1. Definition of Terms

*a. **Balance of trade*** refers to the international flow of goods. If exports exceed imports, a nation is said to have a *favorable* balance of trade; if imports exceed exports, a nation is said to have an *unfavorable* balance of trade.

*b. **Balance of payments*** refers to the international flow of funds. If funds earned abroad exceed funds spent abroad, a nation is said to have a *favorable*, or *surplus*, balance of payments; such a nation is called a *creditor nation*. If funds spent abroad exceed funds earned abroad, a nation is said to have an *unfavorable*, or *deficit*, balance of payments; such a nation is called a *debtor nation*.

2. To World War I: Debtor Nation. In the 19th century the United States was a debtor nation. This was true even though, from the 1870's on, we had a favorable balance of trade, as our exports exceeded our imports. However, our net earnings from trade were insufficient to offset the heavy outflow of funds resulting from foreign investments here. British and other Western European investors had helped finance our economic growth by purchasing government bonds, corporate securities, and real estate. Their earnings on these investments resulted in a continuous outflow of funds from the United States. We remained a debtor nation until World War I.

3. Changes During World War I. Led by Britain and France, the Allies placed large orders for American foodstuffs, war implements, and other manufactures. Impeded by the war, however, European exports to us fell off considerably. The European nations paid for American goods by (a) selling their holdings of American real estate, stocks, and bonds, (b) shipping gold to the United States, and (c) borrowing large sums from American bankers and investors.

4. Following World War I: Creditor Nation. The United States became a creditor nation. (a) During the war, foreigners had sold a large part of their investments here; therefore, their earnings from the United States dropped sharply. (b) The Allies began making payments on their war loans, thereby increasing the inflow of funds into the United States. (c) The value of our exports greatly exceeded the value of our imports. (d) Americans used their favorable financial position to invest in foreign business enterprises, such as plantations, mines, oil wells, and factories. By the end of the 1920's, private investors had placed about $14 billion abroad. The earnings from these investments made for a sizable inflow of funds into the United States, thereby enhancing our position as a creditor nation.

5. Decline of Foreign Trade After 1929. In the early 1930's American foreign trade dropped sharply because (a) the Hawley-Smoot Tariff established our highest rates ever and many foreign countries retaliated by raising their tariffs on American goods, (b) the Depression of 1929 caused a worldwide decline in purchasing power, (c) American investors, fearful for the security of their money, refrained from lending money to foreign countries, which therefore lacked funds to buy American goods, and (d) many foreign countries defaulted on their existing debts to the United States.

FOREIGN TRADE IN THE 1930's: MEANS OF PAYING INTERNATIONAL DEBTS

1. Goods, or Visible Items. International debts can be paid back in goods, called *visible exports* or *visible items*. This is the major method of repaying international debts. In the early 1930's, the debtor nations were unable to sell many goods to the United States because of the depression, which sharply decreased American demand, and because of the exceedingly high rates of the Hawley-Smoot Tariff Act.

2. Services and Other Invisible Items. International debts can also be paid back in *invisible exports*, or *invisible items*. These include services such as insurance protection, shipping facilities, and tourist accommodations. In the early 1930's, because of the depression, debtor nations faced decreased American demand for such services. Other invisible items in international exchange include foreign investments and earnings on such investments. In the early 1930's Americans sent little capital abroad for investments, and Europeans earned little on their limited investments in the United States.

3. Gold. International debts can be paid in gold. In the early 1930's the debtor nations were unable to pay the United States in gold, since the United States already owned most of the world's gold supply. What little gold the debtor nations did possess, they needed as backing for their currencies.

ATTEMPTS TO REVIVE WORLD TRADE

Since 1933 most free nations have accepted, to some extent, the following ideas: (1) International trade is a two-way transaction, meaning that a nation exporting goods must be willing to accept imports in payment. (2) Creditor nations must assist debtor nations by granting them loans. (3) Prosperous and advanced nations must assist poor and developing nations by loans and technical assistance.

These ideas regarding the revival of world trade led to new American policies and new international agencies.

1. United States Reciprocity Agreements. Starting in 1934 the United States took the lead in reviving world trade by negotiating agreements for the reciprocal lowering of tariff rates.

2. United States Export-Import Bank. In 1934 the United States established the *Export-Import Bank,* a government agency to provide low-cost loans to (*a*) foreign governments and companies for purchases of goods from the United States, and (*b*) American businessmen engaging in international trade. The Export-Import Bank has concentrated its loans most heavily in Latin America.

3. Specialized Agencies of the United Nations

a. The *International Bank for Reconstruction and Development,* established in 1945 and more commonly called the *World Bank,* provides loans, especially to underdeveloped nations, for economic development. These include many projects to facilitate the production of goods for export. By 1965 the World Bank had made over 400 loans, totaling almost $9 billion, to about 75 countries and territories.

b. The *International Monetary Fund,* established in 1945, encourages nations to maintain stable currencies in a fixed ratio to each other. To assist a nation that has an excessively unfavorable balance of trade and that has lost much of its gold reserve, the Fund draws upon its own reserves and lends that nation the needed foreign currency. The Fund expects repayment of the loan within five years.

4. United Nations Economic and Social Council. This major U.N. organ, established in 1945, devotes much of its work to international economic matters, including world trade. The Council maintains regional economic commissions to study problems and make recommendations. It also supervises loans and technical assistance through the *U.N. Development Program.*

5. United States Foreign Aid Program. Since 1945 the United States has expended over $220 billion in military and economic aid to about 140 pro-Western and neutral nations. This program stimulated world trade because (*a*) the receiving nations used the major part of these funds to buy goods from abroad, especially from the United States, (*b*) through the *Marshall Plan,* the United States helped revive the post-World War II economies of the nations of Western Europe and thus helped restore them to their place in world trade, and (*c*) through the *Point Four* program, the United States helped raise production and purchasing power in the underdeveloped countries. (For more details on foreign aid, check the Index.)

6. General Agreement on Tariffs and Trade (GATT). In 1947 GATT, originally proposed by the United States, was established by most non-Communist nations. Together, these nations accounted for over 80 percent of the world's trade. GATT represents a multilateral (many nations) approach to the problem of reducing trade barriers. It has three main features: (*a*) a list of existing tariff reductions, (*b*) a code to govern exports and imports, and, most important, (*c*) meetings to further international trade. GATT members have held numerous bargaining sessions at Geneva, Switzerland.

AMERICA'S POSITION IN WORLD TRADE (SINCE 1945)

1. Following World War II: Creditor Nation. After World War II, the United States remained a creditor nation, as it had been after World War I. The United States was an economic powerhouse: In 1950, it produced a whopping 40 percent of the world's goods and services. As war-torn nations recovered, they became good customers for American products. Year after year, United States exports soared, bringing in more money than Americans spent on imports. The United States used its dominant economic position to help build up the economies of the non-Communist nations of Europe and Asia. Its trade surpluses provided funds that the federal government could use in its foreign-aid programs and that businesses could use for investments abroad.

Over the years, however, United States dominance eroded.

2. Our Deficit Balance of Payments. From 1950 through 1967 the United States incurred over $37 billion in balance of payments deficits—the result of the following:

a. Deficit-Producing Factors (1950–1967). (1) *Military Spending.* The United States expended funds to maintain American forces abroad on bases and in battle. (2) *Foreign Economic Aid.* About 25 percent of our foreign aid was not spent in the United States and represented a drain on American funds. (3) *Tourism.* Many Americans went abroad and spent far more money overseas than did foreigners visiting the United States. (4) *Private Loans and Investment.* American creditors placed short-term funds in foreign banks, where they could earn higher interest rates than in the United States. Lured by profitable business opportunities, American corporations invested large sums abroad, building factories and buying foreign companies.

b. Surplus-Producing Factors (1950–1967). (1) *Favorable Balance of Trade.* The United States exported considerably more goods than it imported. (2) *Investment Income.* We received more income on foreign investments than foreigners received on their investments in the United States.

The deficit-producing factors, however, outweighed the surplus-producing factors, and the United States therefore experienced a continual unfavorable balance of payments.

c. Reasons for Concern. From 1958 to 1966 the United States lost $8 billion of gold reserve, bringing its holdings to $13 billion. Even this gold reserve was in jeopardy because foreign governments and individuals held a considerable amount of paper dollars. They could have presented these dollars to the United States at any time and demanded gold in return.

In 1967 our unfavorable balance of payments rose substantially to about $3.5 billion. Thereupon, many foreigners became doubtful about the stability of the American dollar and rushed to exchange their dollars for gold.

d. Steps to Protect the Gold Reserve and Dollar Stability (1968– 1969). The United States acted to protect its gold reserve and assure the stability of the American dollar. *(a)* The United States and six Western European nations (not including France) agreed to a *two-price system* for gold. These nations would use their gold reserves only for intergovernmental transactions at the fixed price of $35 per ounce. They would no longer supply gold to private individuals, who therefore would have to secure gold on the open market at a fluctuating price determined by supply and demand. This agreement meant that private individuals could no longer drain gold away from the United States government. *(b)* The United States, Canada, Japan, and six Western European nations also agreed to establish a means of exchange called Special Drawing Rights, or SDR's. This "paper gold" was to be used, in place of gold, to finance world trade and pay debts among nations.

3. Worsening Trade Balance. Economists use two principal ways of measuring the balance of trade: *(a)* trade in merchandise alone, and *(b)* trade in goods and services. The United States merchandise trade balance had shown a surplus for 75 years. Then in 1971 it slipped into the red. Each year since 1976, the United States has had a substantial deficit in its merchandise trade balance. This is a serious situation. Our favorable merchandise trade balance had formerly enabled the United States to offset, in part or in whole, the deficit-producing factors affecting our balance of payments.

The balance of trade in goods and services was slower to show a deficit. That is because the United States continued to export more services (banking, insurance, shipping, and so on) than it imported. Since 1982, however, the balance in goods and services too has been in deficit.

4. The United States as a Debtor Nation. For the first time since 1914, the United States became a debtor nation in 1985. This resulted from a sharp rise in the flow of foreign funds into the United States. Foreign investors were buying many of the bonds that the federal government sold to finance our huge national debt. Foreign investors were also buying stock in United States businesses. At the end of 1985, foreign investments in this country totaled $1,059 billion while United States investments in other countries totaled $952.4 billion. The deficit of $107.4 billion moved the United States past Brazil and Mexico into the position of the world's leading debtor nation. By 1988 the deficit had surged past $500 billion.

5. Steps to Remedy Imbalances

a. Reduce Foreign Aid. The government cut our foreign aid program, thereby reducing the flow of American dollars out of the country.

b. Devalue the American Dollar. In 1971 the leading non-Communist industrial nations reached agreement for the United States to revalue the American dollar downward, and for Japan and Germany to revalue their currencies upward. By this agreement, the overall devaluation of the American dollar was 12 percent. In 1973 the American dollar was devalued an additional 10 percent. Further devaluations against the Japanese and German currencies became necessary in the mid-1980's.

The devaluation of the American dollar in relation to foreign currencies was intended to have the following effects: (1) Increased exports of American goods. Foreigners would find American goods less costly and therefore would buy more of our products. (2) Decreased imports of foreign goods. Americans would find foreign products more expensive and therefore would buy fewer imported goods. (3) Fewer Americans traveling abroad. Since American dollars would buy less of foreign currencies, American tourists would curtail trips abroad because of the increased expense. (Conversely, European tourists would find trips to the United States less expensive.)

c. Limit Specific Imports. From the late 1970's onward, the government helped bring about limits, or quotas, on imports of shoes from Taiwan and South Korea and on imports of color television sets and automobiles from Japan. The government also acted to stem imports of steel, mainly from the Common Market nations. In addition to reducing imports of such products, these actions were designed to aid domestic manufacturers and workers.

d. Spur Energy Measures to Decrease Oil Imports. Congress enacted various energy laws designed to decrease American consumption of oil and encourage greater use of domestic coal resources. The laws did not accomplish their goal, however. By 1990 Americans imported half of the oil they used.

e. Curtail Inflation. Successive Presidents have taken various steps to reduce inflation. In that way, they have sought to reduce the prices of American exports, making them more attractive to foreign buyers.

f. Expand Markets for United States Exports. The government has negotiated a lowering of tariffs and other people-made barriers to our exports. It has also sought to persuade exporters such as the European Community and Japan, which compete with the United States for customers abroad, to end subsidies to their own farmers and manufacturers. Such subsidies are unfair, United States officials argue, since they make those nations' exports cheaper and thus more attractive to buyers. At the same time, other countries have accused the United States of unfairly subsidizing its own exports through such measures as farm subsidies and export credits.

In passing the Omnibus Trade and Competitiveness Act of 1988, Congress gave the President new powers to impose trade penalties against nations accused of unfairly closing their markets to American goods and companies.

g. Help Solve Developing Nations' Debt Problems. During the 1960's and early 1970's, in their efforts to build up local industries and improve living standards, the developing nations incurred huge international debts. These nations borrowed heavily from private banks in the United States and other industrial countries and from such international agencies as the World Bank and the International Monetary Fund (IMF).

But high oil prices in the late 1970's and a sharp downturn in demand for Third World goods in the early 1980's made it impossible for many developing nations to meet their debt payments. Among the nations with the highest debts were Mexico, Brazil, and Nigeria.

The debt crisis alarmed both bankers (who wanted their money back) and world lenders (who feared the political impact of a widespread economic collapse). The United States and other nations sought ways to resolve the debt crisis and restore growth to the world economy. Only when such growth was restored, said American leaders, would the market for our exports again expand.

As a first step, leaders rescheduled many of the developing nations' debt payments (that is, they stretched out the payments over a longer period). The United States tried to persuade debtor countries to adopt free-market policies and reduce government subsidies for food and services, in exchange for new loans. But many debtor countries resisted such measures, saying they would cause unacceptable increases in hunger and poverty.

RECENT DEVELOPMENTS

1. **The Oil Cartel and International Trade.** Founded in 1960, the Arab-dominated *Organization of Petroleum Exporting Countries (OPEC)* consists of a small number of oil-rich nations in Asia, Africa, and Latin America. OPEC's purpose is to boost oil prices and thus increase its members' revenues.

During the 1973 Arab-Israeli war, Arab members of OPEC cut off shipments to the United States and the price of oil quadrupled. A new surge in OPEC prices occurred in 1979. During the mid-1980's, however, oil prices fell sharply. Reasons included *(a)* a slowdown in the world economy, *(b)* a war between Iran and Iraq (both OPEC members), with both nations stepping up oil production to get desperately needed cash, and *(c)* a price war between OPEC nations and oil-producing nations that did not belong to OPEC.

By the early 1990's OPEC was able to push the price of oil higher once again. Reasons included *(a)* declining oil production in the United States and the Soviet Union, *(b)* a rising demand for oil from industrializing nations of Southeast Asia, and *(c)* the aftermath of war in the Persian Gulf.

2. Free Trade Agreement With Canada (1988). The United States and Canada signed an agreement in 1988 to eliminate almost all duties and tariffs in three steps over a 20-year period. Canada and the United States have long been each other's chief trading partners.

The Bush administration hoped to create a free trade zone in North America to include Canada, Mexico, and the United States. Supporters said it would create jobs for U.S. and Mexican workers. Critics said it would shift jobs away from the United States and relax environmental rules.

MULTIPLE-CHOICE QUESTIONS

1. "At one time the United States normally exported more than it imported, but got such vital materials as tin and uranium from abroad." From this quotation it is correct to conclude that the United States (1) was dependent on other nations (2) had high tariffs (3) was able to "go it alone" (4) was a debtor nation.

2. After 1865, industrialists argued for a high protective tariff because it would (1) increase competition (2) reduce income taxes (3) help the United States gain friends among British manufacturers (4) help the United States become self-sufficient.

3. During the period 1865–1890, the general policy of Congress regarding the tariff was to (1) lower rates (2) raise rates (3) give the President more responsibility for adjusting rates (4) encourage reciprocal trade agreements.

4. One effect of high protective tariffs in the United States was (1) fewer industries (2) lower prices paid by consumers for foreign goods (3) higher prices paid by consumers for domestic goods (4) lower prices paid by consumers for domestic goods.

5. The first tariff act with a considerable reduction in rates after the Civil War was enacted during the administration of (1) Woodrow Wilson (2) Warren G. Harding (3) Herbert Hoover (4) William McKinley.

6. The statement that the United States became a creditor nation after World War I means that (1) our national debt was decreasing (2) the debt of foreign governments to the United States was greater than the debt of the United States to foreign governments (3) our budget was balanced (4) Americans earned more money in foreign countries than foreigners earned in the United States.

7. If the United States lowers tariffs on imports from Britain and if Britain does the same for imports from the United States, such an agreement illustrates (1) cooperative marketing (2) tariff reciprocity (3) the protective tariff (4) free trade.

8. One reason why Congress passed reciprocal tariff legislation in the 1930's was to (1) establish free trade (2) increase our foreign markets (3) help make the United States self-sufficient (4) keep out goods produced by cheap foreign labor.

9. Who was empowered to revise tariff rates under the Reciprocal Trade Agreements Act? (1) the President (2) the Secretary of Commerce (3) the Federal Trade Commission (4) the Interstate Commerce Commission.

10. Brazil exports coffee to the United States, and we export cars to Brazil. Each country concentrates on those goods that it can produce best, thereby illustrating the principle of (1) free trade (2) specialization (3) protectionism (4) mercantilism.

11. The Trade Expansion Act (1962) indicated (1) an increase in protectionist sentiment (2) our willingness to make further trade concessions (3) the growing opposition to foreign aid (4) our unwillingness to continue reciprocal agreements.

12. Under 1962 tariff legislation, the President was granted increased powers chiefly to meet the competition of the (1) Latin American nations (2) European Common Market (3) Sino-Soviet bloc (4) newly independent nations of Asia and Africa.

13. Which has an immediate effect on the balance of payments of the United States different from the effect of the other three? (1) the export of merchandise from the United States (2) Americans traveling abroad (3) grants under our foreign aid program (4) the purchase of foreign securities by Americans.

14. The flow of gold out of this country from 1957 to 1967 indicated that (1) our foreign expenditures were greater than our foreign income (2) the nations of the world were returning to the gold standard (3) European nations were refusing to buy American products (4) our government was removing idle gold from Fort Knox.

15. To reduce the outflow of gold from the United States, Congress in the 1960's (1) took the United States off the gold standard (2) raised tariffs (3) reduced the amount of duty-free goods that American travelers could bring into this country (4) prohibited imports of farm products from nations in the Common Market.

ESSAY QUESTIONS

1. (a) Discuss *two* reasons why some people believe that high tariffs promote prosperity. (b) Giving *two* specific facts, explain why international trade is necessary to maintain a high level of prosperity in the United States today.

2. Discuss the relationship of the tariff issue to each of the following controversies: (a) North against South—from 1824 to the Civil War, (b) industry against agriculture—from the Civil War to 1913.

3. In 1962 President Kennedy secured from Congress a new trade program to meet "new challenges and opportunities." (a) In *two* ways, explain what was "new" about the "challenges and opportunities" confronting the United States in international trade following World War II. (b) Show how *two* provisions of the trade program that was secured by President Kennedy met these "challenges and opportunities." (c) Discuss what is meant by the statement that tariff policy demands a balancing of special interests against the national interest.

4. (a) Explain the difference between an unfavorable balance of trade and an unfavorable balance of payments. (b) Discuss *three* reasons why the United States since the 1950's has had an unfavorable balance of payments. (c) Explain any *two* steps that might help remedy our unfavorable balance of payments.

UNIT VI. THE AMERICAN PEOPLE DEVELOP A DISTINCTIVE WAY OF LIFE

Part 1. The American People Come From Many Lands

UNITED STATES, A NATION OF IMMIGRANTS

Except for the Indians, all Americans are immigrants or the descendants of immigrants. During the colonial period, settlers came by the thousands. From the end of the American Revolution to today, some 45 million people have migrated to our shores.

REASONS FOR IMMIGRATION

1. Economic. European farmers were discouraged as they tried to reap an adequate crop from small and worn-out lands. Farmers were driven from the soil as the Agricultural Revolution brought about a change from subsistence to large-scale commercial farming. European city workers were disheartened by low wages, and many workers faced unemployment as the Industrial Revolution hastened the use of machines. Immigrants looked to America as a land of opportunity, where fertile lands could be acquired at little or no cost and where the expanding economy provided steady employment at decent wages.

2. Political. Most European governments were controlled by the upper classes, and the common people had little or no say in political matters. Immigrants looked to democratic America, where the ordinary citizen had a strong voice in the government.

3. Social. European society was characterized by rigid class distinctions, few educational opportunities for the lower classes, and discrimination against religious minorities. As World War I approached, most governments required young men to serve terms of compulsory military service. Immigrants looked to America as a land of equality, where they could rise in social status, provide an education for their children, practice their religion without fear, and be free of compulsory military service.

HARDSHIPS OF IMMIGRATION

Immigrants were the *uprooted*, having left their friends, relatives, and native lands. Being poor, most immigrants came in the most undesirable sections of ships, where conditions were often crowded and unsanitary. In the

United States, they faced the hardships of having to adjust to a new language and culture. Nevertheless, they were eager to seek their new homeland.

IMMIGRATION FROM THE END OF THE REVOLUTIONARY WAR TO THE CLOSE OF THE FRONTIER (1783–1890)

1. Major Periods of Immigration

a. To the Age of Jackson (1783–1830). At first, immigrants came in a slow but steady stream. Immigration increased as travel became easier with the close of the Napoleonic Wars in 1815. During the years 1821–1830, 143,000 immigrants came to the United States.

b. To the Beginning of the Civil War (1831–1860). In the next three decades, immigrants came in rapidly rising numbers: 1831–1840: 600,000; 1841–1850: 1,700,000; 1851–1860: 2,600,000. Most of these immigrants came from Ireland and Germany. The Irish, long denied self-government by England, received their main stimulus to migrate in the 1840's, when they were afflicted by a potato famine. Germans who had migrated for economic reasons were joined, after the failure of the Revolution of 1848, by German liberals and intellectuals, who came to escape political persecution.

c. To the Close of the Frontier (1861–1890). After being temporarily slowed by the Civil War, immigration again began rising, from 2,800,000 in the years 1871–1880 to 5,200,000 in the years 1881–1890. Immigrants after the Civil War were attracted by the claims of agents and by advertisements of steamship companies and land-grant railroads, and by "America letters" of praise sent by earlier immigrants.

Immigrants continued coming from England, Ireland, and Germany. Farmers came from the Scandinavian countries of Sweden, Norway, and Denmark to look for abundant and fertile soil.

2. Americans Welcomed Immigration. Most Americans considered immigrants an asset to our growing nation. Immigrants represented (*a*) workers for factories, mines, and railroads, (*b*) farmers for Western lands, (*c*) consumers for the products of agriculture and industry, (*d*) men of special abilities, talents, and skills, and (*e*) military strength for the nation.

Americans took pride in their country's tradition as a haven for the oppressed. *Emma Lazarus* expressed the feelings of most Americans in her poem "The New Colossus," which is inscribed on the base of the Statue of Liberty in New York Harbor: "Give me your tired, your poor, your huddled masses yearning to breathe free."

3. Early Opposition to Immigration: The "Know-Nothings." Some Americans disapproved of the Irish and German immigrants for taking jobs away from native Americans, for failing to assimilate into American society, and mostly just for being Catholic. By the 1850's nativist (anti-foreign) and anti-Catholic groups had formed a number of societies, the most influential being the *Know-Nothings.* This society was so called because its members, pledged to secrecy, answered "I know nothing" when asked about the society. The Know-Nothings purported to defend Protestantism against Catholicism and sought to restrict immigration. To further their goals, they ran candidates for political office. Despite initial political gains, the society soon died out, as Americans rejected religious intolerance and concentrated upon the problems of slavery and sectionalism.

4. "Old Immigrants": Characteristics. Historians have traditionally referred to the Europeans coming before 1890 as the "old immigrants." They originated chiefly from northern and western Europe: Great Britain, Ireland, Germany, Holland, France, and the Scandinavian countries of Denmark, Norway, and Sweden. They arrived while the frontier was still open, and many settled on farms in the West. It has been claimed that, since these "old immigrants" possessed customs and traditions similar to those of Americans, they adjusted easily to American ways of life.

IMMIGRATION FROM THE CLOSE OF THE FRONTIER TO THE BEGINNING OF WORLD WAR I (1890–1914)

1. "New Immigrants": Characteristics. Historians have traditionally referred to the Europeans coming after 1890 as the "new immigrants." They came in greater numbers than immigrants had ever come before. From 1901 to 1910 some 8,800,000 persons entered the United States. Unlike the "old immigrants," the "new immigrants" originated chiefly in southern and eastern Europe: Italy, Greece, Austria-Hungary, Serbia, Rumania, Russian Poland, and Russia. They arrived when the frontier was closed and therefore settled chiefly in the cities as factory workers. It has been claimed that, since the "new immigrants" possessed customs and traditions different from those of Americans, they experienced difficulty in adjusting to American ways of life.

2. Typical Migratory Groups. Italians, Serbs, and Greeks fled poverty. Peoples in the despotic Austro-Hungarian and Russian Empires fled heavy taxes and, as World War I approached, compulsory military service. Jews in Russia and in Russian-controlled Poland had long been forced to live in special districts, called the *Pale of Settlement,* and had been subjected to educational restrictions and to legal and economic discrimination. They now fled Czarist-inspired outbreaks of anti-Semitic violence, called *pogroms.*

3. Opposition to Immigration. Many Americans disapproved of the "new immigrants," arguing as follows: (*a*) With the frontier closed, there was no more free or cheap land for immigrants. (*b*) American industry had sufficient workers, and "new immigrants" competed with and took jobs away from native Americans. This argument was emphasized by labor unions. (c) The "new immigrants" were difficult to Americanize. They had little education. They settled in large cities, creating their own ghettos, and felt no need to learn American ways. Their ghettos were becoming breeding places of disease and crime. (d) Some people argued that the "new immigrants" were physically and mentally inferior to the "old immigrants." This was known as the "theory of Nordic supremacy."

4. In Defense of the "New Immigrants." (a) The "new immigrants" assimilated as well as had the Irish and German "old immigrants." Critics of the "new immigrants" forgot that the Germans, too, had clung to their native tongue and that the Irish had been impoverished and uneducated. The Irish and the Germans had also been accused of being clannish and of not assimilating quickly into the American Protestant society. (b) The "new immigrants" who flocked to the cities were joined by native Americans who moved in from the farms. Both groups contributed to the urban problems of slums, disease, and crime. Again, critics of the "new immigrants" forgot that the Irish, too, had settled in the cities. (c) The "new immigrants" provided the additional workers needed by our growing industry. Furthermore, they stimulated industrial growth by enlarging the domestic market for goods. (d) Reputable scientists rejected the theory of Nordic supremacy as false. (e) The "new immigrants" contributed greatly to American life.

EARLY STEPS RESTRICTING IMMIGRATION

1. The Chinese Exclusion Act (1882) began the prohibition of the immigration of Chinese. The law was passed following agitation and riots on the West Coast against cheap "coolie" labor. The prohibition lasted until World War II.

2. The Gentlemen's Agreement (1907) contained a promise by the Japanese government to deny passports to Japanese laborers seeking to migrate to the United States. Negotiated by President Theodore Roosevelt, it followed anti-Japanese race riots in California, and local and state laws discriminating against Japanese immigrants. In 1924 Congress unilaterally ended the Gentlemen's Agreement by prohibiting all Japanese immigration to the United States.

3. The Literacy Test Act (1917) required immigrants to be able to read English or their own language before entering the United States. This act was passed over a veto by President Wilson, who insisted that literacy indicated not mental ability, but merely that an immigrant had received the opportunity to go to school.

RESTRICTIVE IMMIGRATION LAWS FOLLOWING WORLD WAR I

As World War I ended, Americans withdrew emotionally from world affairs, and their isolationist sentiments reinforced their opposition to immigration. Americans experienced a "Red scare," occasioned by the 1917 Communist seizure of Russia, and feared that foreign radicals would infiltrate the United States. The Ku Klux Klan added its voice to demand protection of "white Protestant America." Congress passed the following:

1. **Two Emergency Immigration Acts,** in 1921 and in 1924, began the sharp curtailment of immigration from outside the Western Hemisphere. The 1924 act also contained regulations constituting the 1929 National Origins Plan.

2. **National Origins Plan of 1929**

a. Provisions. This plan (1) permitted no more than 150,000 immigrants from outside the Western Hemisphere to enter the United States per year, (2) allotted each country a quota in proportion to the number of persons in the United States having that national origin according to the census of 1920, (3) granted each eligible nation at least 100 immigrants per year, (4) placed no restrictions on immigration from the Western Hemisphere, and (5) prohibited all immigration from Asian countries. (After World War II, most Asian countries received a quota of 100 immigrants per year.)

b. Effects. The National Origins Plan, coupled with the Depression of 1929, sharply curtailed immigration. From 1931 to 1940, a total of only 530,000 immigrants arrived at our shores. Most quotas remained unfilled.

DISPLACED PERSONS PROBLEM

After World War II, Europe contained many millions of *refugees*, or *displaced persons*, including (1) survivors of the German concentration camps, especially Jews, anti-Nazi Germans, and anti-Nazis of nations overrun by Germany who wanted to start life anew, far from Europe, (2) slave laborers, chiefly eastern Europeans, who had been forced to work in Germany during the war and who refused to return home to Communist rule, and (3) escapees from Communist rule in eastern Europe. The plight of the refugees touched American sympathies. Congress passed several Displaced Persons Acts which by 1956 allowed into the United States some 600,000 refugees above the yearly immigration quotas.

McCARRAN-WALTER IMMIGRATION AND NATIONALITY ACT OF 1952

1. **Provisions.** The new law (a) restated the National Origins Plan by setting a limit of 154,000 immigrants per year and by granting each country a quota based on the 1920 census, (b) allowed each Asian country a quota, usually 100 immigrants per year, (c) required the careful screening of im-

migrants to keep out security risks, and (d) eased the procedures for revoking the citizenship of recently naturalized citizens who joined Communist or Communist-front organizations and for deporting undesirable aliens.

President Truman vetoed the McCarran-Walter Bill as "repressive and inhumane," but Congress overrode the veto. Later, Presidents Eisenhower, Kennedy, and Johnson all requested a revision of our immigration laws.

IMMIGRATION ACT OF 1965 (WITH 1976 REVISIONS)

1. Provisions. For countries outside the Western Hemisphere, the law (a) abolished the National Origins Plan, (b) established a quota of 170,000 immigrants per year, (c) set a limit of 20,000 immigrants per year from any one nation, and (d) provided standards for admitting immigrants according to the following preferences: (1) close relatives of United States residents, (2) scientists, artists, professional people, and skilled and unskilled workers needed to fill labor shortages, and (3) refugees from Communist rule and from natural calamity.

For countries in the Western Hemisphere, the law introduced for the first time a quota of 120,000 immigrants per year and, by the 1976 revisions, subjected them to the same provisions as for other immigrants—a limit of 20,000 per year from any one nation and the same standards of admission.

2. Significant Changes. (a) This law replaced the National Origins Plan, stressing race and nationality, by a preference system emphasizing family relationship, value to the United States, and motive for migrating. (b) It ended the favored position of north and west European nations, and placed them on an equal footing with other countries. Fewer immigrants have come from Great Britain, Ireland, and Germany. (c) It permitted an increase in the number of immigrants from Asia, Africa, and southern and eastern Europe. More immigrants have come from Taiwan, the Philippines, Italy, Greece, and Portugal. (d) The law reduced the number of Western Hemisphere immigrants, which had been about 150,000 in 1965.

THE REFUGEE ACT OF 1980

As countless refugees fled from their native countries—such as Cuba, Haiti, Ethiopia, Somalia, Uganda, Afghanistan, and Vietnam—Congress enacted the 1980 Refugee Act. It (1) defined refugees as people outside their native countries who are unwilling to return because of fear of persecution (this definition did not limit refugees to Communist-ruled nations only); (2) increased the number of refugees to be admitted annually to 50,000—in addition to the existing special programs for Indochinese and Cuban refugees; (3) empowered the President to admit additional refugees in emergency situations; (4) to administer the law, established the position of *United States Coordinator of Refugee Affairs.*

IMMIGRATION REFORM AND CONTROL ACT OF 1986

1. Provisions. (*a*) The law barred employers from hiring illegal immigrants, established civil penalties for each illegal immigrant hired, provided for criminal penalties for employers who showed a "pattern or practice" of hiring illegal immigrants. (*b*) The law made it illegal for an employer to discriminate against legal immigrants. (*c*) The law offered legal status, or amnesty, to immigrants who could prove that they had entered the United States illegally before January 1, 1982, and had resided here continuously since that time. (*d*) The law offered amnesty to illegal immigrants who had worked in the United States for at least 90 days between May 1985 and May 1986. (*e*) The law opened the way for people who benefited from the amnesties to become United States citizens. (*f*) The law provided for the admission of up to 350,000 immigrants for seasonal farm work in fiscal years 1990 to 1993. (*g*) The law set aside funds to help state governments provide assistance to people who benefited from the amnesties.

2. Significance. The 1986 act grew out of a concern that illegal immigration had grown to unacceptable levels. Estimates of the number of illegal immigrants in the country in 1986 ranged between 3 and 5 million. By granting amnesty to many of the illegal immigrants already here and tightening controls against further illegal immigration, officials hoped, in the words of President Reagan, to "regain control of our borders."

IMMIGRATION ACT OF 1990

The most comprehensive revision of laws governing legal immigration since 1924 was passed in 1990. The act increased the maximum number of legal immigrants to 700,000 a year. (In 1995 the number will drop to 675,000.) The act favored the admission of family members (465,000) and individuals with professions and special skills (130,000). It reduced the number of visas allotted to low-skilled workers (from 18,000 to 10,000). Special consideration is given to individuals with large sums of money to invest in new businesses that will provide jobs for ten or more Americans (10,000). Some 40,000 "diversity" visas are set aside for people from 35 countries (mainly in Europe) seen as adversely affected by the 1965 law. Of these visas, 40 percent are specifically for Irish immigrants. The act also eased restrictions on people previously barred because of political beliefs or sexual preference or serious diseases.

RECENT TRENDS IN IMMIGRATION

1. Refugees From All Over.

(a) Europe. (1) During the cold war, thousands fled from Communist rule. Many came from Hungary, where Soviet forces crushed a 1956 revolt, and Czechoslovakia, where Soviet forces intervened in 1968. (2) During the 1970's and 1980's, large numbers of Soviet Jews chose the United States over Israel as a new homeland. (3) After the end of the cold war, large numbers of refugees fled war and economic hardship in places like Bosnia, Croatia, and Armenia.

b. Asia. (1) The Vietnam War and its aftermath sent a wave of Indo-Chinese refugees to the United States. Some 500,000 Vietnamese and tens of thousands of Cambodians and Laotians settled in the United States. (2) Other Asians and Pacific islanders came from places like China, Taiwan, the Philippines, India, Korea, and Samoa. The 1990 census found 2.9 percent of the population to be of Asian background, up from 1.5 percent in 1980.

c. Western Hemisphere. (1) An estimated 1 million Cubans arrived in the three decades that followed Fidel Castro's creation of a Cuban Communist regime in the 1960's. (2) Wars and civil unrest caused tens or hundreds of thousands of people to leave such nations as Nicaragua, El Salvador, Guatemala, and Haiti. Other immigrants seeking economic opportunity left Mexico, the Dominican Republic, and other parts of the hemisphere seeking new homes in the United States.

2. Rising Concerns About Immigration. From 1981 to 1990, 7,300,000 legal immigrants arrived, second only to the record rate of 8,800,000 set between 1901 and 1910. Roughly half of those immigrants settled in California. As more and more Americans lost jobs in the recession of 1990–1991 and after, hostility toward immigrants began to increase. California took steps to limit immigration, and Congress began to consider further restrictive legislation.

IMMIGRANTS AND DISCRIMINATION

Each group of immigrants faced discrimination at the hands of native Americans—themselves descendants of earlier immigrants. Those immigrants who settled in cities and sought factory work were particularly affected. (1) *Economically.* They were the last to be hired, kept at the poorest jobs, and the first to be fired. (2) *Socially.* They were confined to ghettos and slums; excluded from the better hotels, restaurants, and clubs; and often refused admission to institutions of higher learning. Nevertheless, by displaying ability and determination, these immigrants achieved success and entered the mainstream of American life.

CONTRIBUTIONS OF IMMIGRANT GROUPS TO AMERICA

1. Cultural. Immigrants to America brought their different cultural heritages. With time, certain features of those heritages died out while other features became part of American life. In foods, we eat hamburgers and frankfurters named after German cities, English muffins, Irish stew, Hungarian goulash, Chinese wonton soup, Japanese sushi, Jewish delicatessen, Mexican tacos, and Syrian felafel. In music, we listen to Italian operas, Afro-American spirituals, Argentine tangos, Dominican salsa, and Caribbean reggae. In literature, we read the plays of Norway's Ibsen and the novels of Colombia's García Márquez. Perhaps our most important inheritance, an outgrowth of our population diversity, is the American spirit of toleration and fair play.

Because the United States tended to blend different peoples and cultures into a new American nationality and culture, our society has been called a *melting pot*. At the same time, the persistence of cultural influences from other nations has contributed to a sense of *cultural pluralism*. Lately, the term *multiculturalism* has come into use, with much the same meaning as cultural pluralism. Efforts have been made to assure that each of the many strands that go together to create the American heritage receives acknowledgment and fair treatment in textbooks, television programs, and public life.

2. Economic. The immigrants were eager for honest, useful work. Immigrants from each nation found employment in many industries. Nevertheless, many groups have become identified with specific industries. Scandinavians farmed the land. Irishmen and Italians built canals, railroads, and bridges. Jews worked in the garment industry. Poles and other Slavs, as well as Hungarians, mined coal and iron ore, and labored in the steel mills. Mexicans harvested crops. Cubans made cigars.

The immigrants increased the demand for the products of agriculture and industry, thereby further encouraging American economic growth. Also, by coming to the United States in especially great numbers during times of business expansion, immigrants served to prevent any shortage of labor.

MULTIPLE-CHOICE QUESTIONS

1. Which was an important cause of immigration to the United States in the 1840's? (1) the Napoleonic Wars (2) changes in our immigration policy (3) revolutions in Europe (4) completion of the first transcontinental railroad.

2. Which event had the most immediate effect upon immigration to the United States? (1) the defeat of France by Prussia in 1870–1871 (2) the potato famine in Ireland (3) the Crimean War (4) the gaining of independence by Belgium.

3. In which period did the largest number of immigrants enter the United States? (1) 1841–1850 (2) 1881–1890 (3) 1901–1910 (4) 1981–1990.

4. The United States had a liberal immigration policy during most of the 19th century because (1) many Congressmen were foreign-born (2) the population of the United States remained constant (3) there was a shortage of labor in the United States (4) prosperous times in Europe discouraged immigration to the United States.

5. In the latter part of the 19th century, a liberal immigration policy was generally opposed by (1) Eastern manufacturers (2) land speculators (3) labor unions (4) railroad companies.

6. Where can an expression of the philosophy of the United States concerning immigration be found? (1) in Washington's Farewell Address (2) on the base of the Statue of Liberty (3) in the Clayton Act (4) in the Gettysburg Address.

7. Which statement is true of the immigration policy of the United States in the late 19th century? (1) Restrictions were placed on Mexican agricultural workers. (2) Quotas were assigned to European countries. (3) Chinese immigration was prohibited. (4) Japanese immigration was limited.

8. In the early 20th century, immigrants from southern Europe settled chiefly (1) in the cities of the Far West (2) in the cities along the East Coast (3) on the farmlands in the Midwest (4) on the farmlands of the Far West.

9. Which of the following differed in purpose from the other three? (1) Gentlemen's Agreement (2) National Origins Plan (3) Displaced Persons Acts (4) Chinese Exclusion Act.

10. One of the items below is a main topic in an outline, and three are subtopics. Which is the main topic? (1) negotiation of the Gentlemen's Agreement (2) establishment of the quota system (3) passage of the McCarran-Walter Act (4) influence of nativism on American immigration policy.

11. United States immigration legislation from 1920 to 1965 was criticized chiefly on the grounds that (1) there were no quotas for Asians (2) nationality was the major consideration in admitting immigrants (3) annual admissions were reduced to approximately 1,000,000 (4) the proportion of foreign-born in the population of the United States was increasing.

12. Which was true of the McCarran-Walter Act? (1) The quota for Asians was lowered. (2) All literate persons could enter the country and become citizens. (3) Aliens could be deported if they were found to have Communist affiliations. (4) The quota system for Latin America was revised.

13. The Immigration Act of 1965 provided that the United States (1) retain the national origins system (2) prohibit immigrants from the Western Hemisphere (3) admit more German immigrants (4) give high priority to needed professional people.

MATCHING QUESTIONS

Column A—Immigrants
1. Knute Rockne
2. Irving Berlin
3. Lin Yutang
4. William Mayo
5. Igor Sikorsky
6. Albert Einstein
7. John Roebling
8. Pierre L'Enfant
9. Thomas Hunter
10. Arturo Toscanini

Column B—Achievements
a. Physician and surgeon
b. Opera composer
c. Educator
d. Motion picture producer
e. Symphony orchestra conductor
f. Football coach
g. Architect of Washington, D.C.
h. Writer
i. Inventor of helicopter
j. Musical comedy composer
k. Governor of Illinois
l. Theoretical physicist
m. Designer of Brooklyn Bridge

ESSAY QUESTIONS

1. Describe *one* economic, *one* political, and *one* social condition in Europe that led to immigration to the United States. Illustrate *each* case by specific reference to any European country.

2. Explain *one* reason for the attitude of *each* of the following groups toward immigration: (*a*) Know-Nothings, (*b*) railroad builders in the 1860's, (*c*) labor unions of the 1880's, (*d*) the Ku Klux Klan of the 1920's.

3. The immigration policy of the United States has reflected trends in both the development and the problems of our country. (*a*) State our policy in relation to immigration during each of the following periods: (1) 1789–1870, (2) 1880–1910, (3) 1920–1960, (4) since 1965. (*b*) Explain *one* factor that influenced our policy in *each* case.

4. The McCarran-Walter Act, our basic immigration law from 1952 to 1965, was the subject of much dispute. (*a*) Explain *two* arguments in support of this law. (*b*) Explain *two* arguments in opposition to this law.

5. In regard to the Immigration Act of 1965, (*a*) state *three* of its major provisions, and (*b*) for *each* provision stated, explain fully why you approve or disapprove of it.

6. America owes its greatness, in part, to its liberal immigration policy of the 19th and early 20th centuries. (*a*) Discuss *three* ways in which immigrants contributed to America's greatness. (*b*) Explain *two* problems that the liberal immigration policy posed for the United States.

Part 2. Blacks Strive to Attain Their Civil Rights

BLACKS IN AMERICA: FROM COLONIAL TIMES TO WORLD WAR II

1. Importation of Blacks. Like other peoples constituting the American nation, the blacks were not natives of the New World. They were brought from Africa, starting in 1619, when a shipment of blacks arrived at Jamestown in the colony of Virginia. In 1808 Congress outlawed the importation of slaves, but they were smuggled into the United States until 1860. Usually, the slaves were captives taken by other African tribes or were prisoners kidnapped by Arab raiding expeditions. Their captors moved them to the west coast of Africa and sold them to European and American slave traders for transportation to the New World. Crowded into shipholds and treated brutally, only the strongest survived the voyage.

2. Blacks Under Slavery. Sold as slaves, blacks labored chiefly on Southern plantations and received the bare necessities of life. They were considered by their white masters as property and as constituting an "inferior race." Blacks organized several futile insurrections, and occasionally slaves ran away. Sometimes they deliberately slowed down at work. Usually, they just performed their tasks without hope or enthusiasm. (Not all blacks in the United States were slaves. Of the four million blacks living in the United States in 1860, over 10 percent were freemen, half residing in the South, the other half in the North.)

3. Civil Rights: The Reconstruction Amendments. Blacks gained freedom first under the Emancipation Proclamation and then under the Thirteenth Amendment, which prohibited slavery in the entire United States.

Blacks also gained Constitutional guarantees against actions by states infringing upon their civil and political rights. The Fourteenth Amendment granted citizenship to blacks and provided that no state may curtail their privileges, deprive them of "life, liberty, or property, without due process of law," or deny them "equal protection of the laws." The Fifteenth Amendment provided that no state may deny the vote to any citizen because of "race, color, or previous condition of servitude." These amendments, part of the reconstruction program of the Radical Republicans, sought to assure blacks an equal place in American life.

4. Blacks From Reconstruction to World War I: Targets of Southern Discrimination. As reconstruction ran its course, Northerners lost interest in black problems, and Southern whites regained control of their state governments. The Southerners did not attempt to restore slavery, but they proceeded to "put the Negro in his place" as subordinate and inferior. (*a*) *Politically.* Blacks were kept from voting by various devices, such as poll taxes and literacy tests. By 1900 most Southern blacks did not vote. (*b*) *Economically.* Most black farmers were sharecroppers. Practically bound to the soil by heavy debts, they lived in extreme poverty. Black city workers were barred from many labor unions and relegated to the lowest paid occupations, or so-called "Negro jobs." (*c*) *Socially.* By "Jim Crow" segregation laws, blacks were kept separated from whites in railroads, restaurants, and schools. By 1900 "Jim Crow" ruled the South.

5. Blacks During and After World War I: Migration to Northern Cities; Northern Discrimination. During World War I a third of a million blacks moved to Northern cities, lured by jobs in war industries. After the war they continued to come northward, as expanding industries hired black workers. (The white labor supply was now curtailed by restrictive immigration laws.) From 1910 to 1930 the black population in the North more than doubled.

Northern blacks freely exercised their right to vote, but they encountered other forms of discrimination. (*a*) *Socially.* Blacks were crowded into slum areas, or *ghettos,* where they inhabited dilapidated, disease-breeding houses and paid high rents. Their children attended neighborhood schools that were segregated not by law, but in fact (or *de facto*), because of residential patterns. The segregated black schools were often inferior to the white schools. (*b*) *Economically.* Blacks got the lowest paid jobs, had little opportunity to advance, and were still barred from many labor unions.

Since they were generally unskilled and poorly paid, blacks were particularly hard hit by the Depression of 1929. In 1932 they overwhelmingly voted for Franklin D. Roosevelt and his promise of a New Deal. Under Roosevelt, the status of blacks improved, as New Dealers fought the depression and provided jobs and housing for blacks as well as for whites.

MOVEMENT FOR BLACK RIGHTS: STARTING WITH WORLD WAR II

1. **Gains During World War II.** As the United States fought to destroy racist Nazism in Europe, many Americans realized that (a) racial discrimination at home is morally unjust, and (b) black soldiers serving their country in battle deserved equality for themselves and their families. President Roosevelt established a temporary *Fair Employment Practices Committee (FEPC)* to prevent discrimination by defense industries against workers because of "race, creed, color, or national origin." From 1941 to 1945 the number of black workers in war plants quadrupled, and many blacks advanced to more skilled and better paying jobs.

2. **Following World War II: State Anti-Discrimination Laws.** In 1945 New York State passed the first law against discrimination in employment, the *Ives-Quinn Act.* Subsequently, New York State prohibited discrimination in housing and places of public accommodation, and in admission to educational institutions. The *New York State Commission for Human Rights* investigates complaints of discriminatory practices and tries to end discrimination by persuasion, conciliation, mediation, and, if necessary, by orders enforceable in state courts.

Today, about 30 states in the North and West have fair employment practices laws. About 10 states have laws requiring fair practices in the rental and sale of housing units. Also, a number of cities have local anti-discrimination ordinances.

3. **Private Efforts Against Discrimination.** Since World War II, corporations have sought qualified blacks for skilled factory, clerical, and managerial positions. They have also offered on-the-job training to many blacks. Industrial unions have extended membership to blacks. Major league baseball dropped its unwritten color bar in 1947, when *Jackie Robinson* became the first black to play in the major leagues. Movie producers have stopped portraying blacks as happy-go-lucky stereotypes and have started presenting them as human beings. Advertising agencies have begun including blacks in their magazine and television displays. Insurance companies have pledged to invest funds to stimulate building projects and new businesses in ghetto areas.

4. **Federal Efforts on Civil Rights.** President Truman prohibited discrimination in the hiring and promoting of federal employees and began the integration of servicemen in the armed forces. Truman also appointed a *Committee on Civil Rights*, which submitted the historic report "To Se-

cure These Rights." The committee asserted that racial and religious discrimination prevents achievement of the American ideal of democracy. It proposed federal laws to (a) prohibit the poll tax and (b) bar discrimination in voting and employment.

President Truman repeatedly requested such legislation, but could not prevail over Southern Senators armed with the filibuster. Nevertheless, President Truman had elevated civil rights into a major national issue.

Thereafter all three branches of the federal government became increasingly involved in civil rights matters—as discussed in the following pages.

PROBLEM OF SEGREGATION IN EDUCATION

1. **Background.** Because the Fourteenth Amendment guarantees all citizens "equal protection of the laws," the constitutionality of state and local segregation laws has often been challenged before the Supreme Court. In 1896, in *Plessy vs. Ferguson,* which involved a Louisiana law segregating railroad passengers, the Supreme Court held constitutional state laws giving blacks *separate but equal* facilities. Thus fortified, the South pressed forward its program of segregation. However, facilities for blacks were almost always inferior to those for whites. In education, black schools were poorly constructed and equipped, black teachers poorly paid.

2. **The Supreme Court Establishes a New Doctrine That "Separate Educational Facilities Are Inherently Unequal" (1954)**

a. Supreme Court Decision. In 1954, in *Brown vs. Board of Education of Topeka* (Kansas), the Supreme Court unanimously decided that segregation of black children in public schools violates the Fourteenth Amendment. Chief Justice *Earl Warren* pointed out that (1) education plays a vital role in training children for citizenship, employment, and use of leisure, (2) separating black children from others solely on the basis of race "generates a feeling of inferiority" that may affect them "in a way unlikely ever to be undone," and (3) therefore, "separate educational facilities are inherently unequal."

In 1955 the Supreme Court empowered federal District Courts to supervise plans of state and local authorities for achieving school desegregation with "all deliberate speed."

b. Support for the Decision. In the North the Supreme Court decision was praised for upholding American democratic beliefs in human dignity and equality of opportunity. In the South it was (1) accepted by a minority of whites, who urged obedience to the law, (2) praised by many religious leaders, who condemned segregation as morally wrong, and (3) hailed by blacks, who felt that segregation meant second-class citizenship.

c. Opposition to the Decision. (1) *Southern White Groups.* The White Citizens Councils and the Ku Klux Klan defended segregation as part of the Southern way of life. These groups used publicity, economic pressure, threats, and sometimes violence against advocates of integration. (2) *Southern State Legislatures.* Several legislatures approved *interposition resolutions,* defying the desegregation decision on the ground that the federal government has no constitutional power over education. Interposition was based on the pre-Civil War doctrine of nullification (see pages 115 and 143). Some Southern legislatures also appropriated funds for private school systems, thus permitting localities to shut down public schools. Such techniques for evading the Supreme Court decision were held unconstitutional.

d. *Crisis in Little Rock.* In 1957 Governor Orval Faubus used the Arkansas National Guard to prevent nine black children from entering an all-white school in Little Rock. After a meeting with President Eisenhower, Faubus obeyed a court order to withdraw the National Guard. When a mob kept the black children from the school, Eisenhower ordered United States army units to Little Rock to restore order. Under federal protection the nine blacks attended the previously all-white high school.

3. Developments on the Educational Front: In the South

a. *Substantial Acceptance.* Six states with small black populations— Delaware, Kentucky, Maryland, Missouri, Oklahoma, and West Virginia— faced little public opposition to desegregation. The District of Columbia, with its black majority, also achieved desegregation.

b. *Token Acceptance.* The 11 states of the former Confederacy resisted the Supreme Court decision. In 1963–1964 only 2 percent of their black students attended desegregated schools. In the *Deep South* states, where the black population is largest, white opposition to integration was strongest.

c. *Federal Pressure for Integration.* The 1964 *Civil Rights Act* allowed the federal government to deny financial aid to state programs practicing discrimination. The 1965 *Elementary and Secondary Education Act* authorized federal funds for distribution to local school districts. Thereupon, the United States *Office of Education,* in the Department of Health, Education, and Welfare, required Southern school districts desiring federal aid to satisfy certain "guidelines." They were required to submit and begin implementing plans for the desegregation of school faculties and pupils. In 1969 the Supreme Court, now under Chief Justice *Warren Burger,* refused a delay asked for by certain Mississippi school districts and unanimously held that all districts must "terminate dual school systems at once."

d. *Further Integration in the South.* For the 1970–1971 school year, enrollment of blacks in integrated schools in the 11 states of the old Confederacy had risen from 2 percent (1963-1964) to 39 percent. For the 1971–1972 school year, the federal government claimed that over 90 percent of Southern black children were attending desegregated schools. Critics claimed that this figure reflected only the end of dual school systems,

Engelhardt in The St. Louis Post-Dispatch

"This place isn't big enough for both of us, mac."

whereas many black children were still segregated within unitary school systems and only 38 percent were actually integrated. Meanwhile over 400,000, or almost 7 percent, of Southern white students left the public schools for makeshift, underfinanced, understaffed, but all-white private schools.

4. Developments on the Educational Front: In the North

a. Toward School Integration. Most Northern cities contain black residential ghettos, and these cause school segregation not by law—de jure—but in fact—de facto. Public schools in black areas have tended to be more crowded and to have poorer facilities than schools in white areas. Since 1963 several Northern communities have experienced mass demonstrations, picket lines, and boycotts by black groups protesting de facto school segregation. Many school boards thereupon took steps to integrate "fringe area" schools and to permit open enrollment by blacks in underpopulated white schools.

These steps failed to satisfy some civil rights groups. They demanded that all schools achieve racial balance, by mass busing of both black and white pupils if necessary. As some black groups insisted upon total integration, some white parents formed groups to defend the *neighborhood school policy.*

b. Toward "Quality Education." Many school boards made efforts to improve facilities in ghetto schools and provide "quality education." They assigned additional teachers, reduced class sizes, scheduled special classes, and made available more textbooks and other instructional materials. Also, they used funds available under the federal antipoverty program to inaugurate *Head Start* and *Upward Bound* programs (see the Index).

c. Toward School Decentralization. Some civil rights groups, realizing that substantial integration of school systems in large cities would take many years, have demanded school decentralization. These groups seek to control the de facto segregated schools of the ghettos. They wish to replace the centralized school administration, which they claim is bureaucratic and dominated by whites, with local school boards, each controlling its own neighborhood schools. They argue that black community school boards could best provide for the education of black children.

Opponents of decentralization fear that local control would result in a lowering of educational standards. Furthermore, they argue, it might enable extremist groups to dominate ghetto schools, to harass the teaching staff, and to introduce questionable courses of study.

5. The Busing Issue:

a. For Busing. In 1971, in *Swann vs. Board of Education of Charlotte-Mecklenburg* (North Carolina), the Supreme Court unanimously upheld the busing of children as a proper means of overcoming deliberate Southern state-imposed school segregation. Thereafter lower federal courts ordered extensive busing to overcome "de jure" school racial imbalance in the South and also "de facto" imbalance in the Midwest (Indianapolis and Detroit) and in the Far West (Denver and San Francisco). These latter busing orders aroused much public resentment.

b. Limits on Busing.

(1) In 1974 Congress approved a provision that limited busing. Except where necessary to protect the constitutional rights of minority-group chil-

Editorial cartoon by Pat Oliphant. Copyright,
The Washington Star. Reprinted with permission

"Into the bus, off the bus, into the bus,
off the bus—man, what an education!"

dren, the law barred federal courts from ordering busing beyond the school closest or next closest to the child's home.

(2) In 1974 the Supreme Court, in *Milliken vs. Bradley*, decided by 5 to 4 that children should not be bused across school district lines. The decision prohibited the cross-busing of black children in the urban Detroit school district with the white children in the suburban Detroit school districts. The Court majority held that, unless the districts involved had deliberately practiced discrimination, the Constitution did not require interdistrict busing.

(3) In 1982 the Supreme Court upheld a voter-approved amendment to the California constitution that prohibited state courts, in the absence of any violation of civil rights, from ordering compulsory busing.

6. Affirmative Action in Education: The Bakke Case—1978. The 1964 Civil Rights Act prohibited discrimination based on race by any educational institution receiving federal funds. Citing this provision, the Office of Education urged college and university admissions offices to redress past discrimination by programs to benefit minority groups—programs known as *affirmative action*. At the Davis Medical School of the University of California, the admissions office set aside 16 out of 100 positions in the freshman class for members of minority groups—blacks, Chicanos, and Asians.

Allan Bakke, a white engineer who had served with the Marines in Vietnam, determined to become a doctor. He twice applied to the Davis Medical School and was twice rejected—although his medical aptitude test scores were higher than some minority group applicants who gained acceptance. Bakke felt that he was a victim of the Davis admissions program of *minority quotas*, or *reverse discrimination*. He took legal action claiming that he was being denied his constitutional rights under the "equal protection" clause of the Fourteenth Amendment and was being subjected to racial discrimination for being white, in violation of the 1964 Civil Rights Act.

In 1978, the Supreme Court, by a 5-to-4 vote, handed down a complex decision of two major parts: (*a*) Bakke must be admitted to the Davis Medical School, and the Davis affirmative action program with its set quota for minority students is invalid because it is biased against nonminority applicants. (This part of the decision appealed to persons opposed to quotas and in favor of merit selection of applicants.) (*b*) Race and ethnic origins may be considered as one of many factors in establishing programs of college admissions. (This part of the decision appealed to persons who supported affirmative action to assist the victims of past discrimination.)

Many observers held that the Supreme Court decision was ambiguous and confusing, that most affirmative action programs (in education and employment) would continue as is or as revised, and that further lawsuits would be brought to challenge affirmative action programs. (For affirmative action in employment, check the Index for the Weber Case.)

PROBLEMS OF CIVIL RIGHTS IN VOTING, EMPLOYMENT, AND PLACES OF PUBLIC ACCOMMODATION

Encouraged by the Supreme Court decision against school segregation, civil rights groups battled other discriminatory practices.

1. Civil Rights Act of 1957

a. Provisions. (1) A federal *Commission on Civil Rights* was created to investigate the denial of voting rights and violations of "equal protection of the laws." (2) The Attorney General was empowered to secure court orders against persons interfering with the right of any American citizen to vote— such as the refusal by election officials to register qualified black voters.

b. Findings of the Civil Rights Commission. The Commission held hearings and in 1959 reported that (1) many black American citizens did not vote because of threats of violence, economic pressure, and deliberate discrimination in state procedures, and (2) the 1957 Civil Rights Act was inadequate to guarantee voting rights. Congress responded with a new act.

2. Civil Rights Act of 1960

a. Provisions. (1) In cases of obvious voting discrimination, federal courts were empowered to appoint referees who could grant would-be voters certificates entitling them to vote. (2) Persons threatening to use force against blacks trying to register or vote were made subject to federal criminal penalties. (3) It became a federal crime to cross a state line to flee prosecution for a "hate bombing" of a school, church, or other building.

b. Developments. The number of black voters increased, though slowly. Civil rights leaders demanded further laws against discrimination.

3. Continuing Struggle for Civil Rights

a. Nonviolent Protests by Blacks. In 1955–1956, in Montgomery, Alabama, blacks boycotted the city's bus system and won desegregation for city riders. From 1960 to 1963 Southern black "sit-ins" at "for whites only" lunch counters and "ride-ins" on segregated buses furthered desegregation.

b. March on Washington. In 1963 some 200,000 blacks and whites participated in an orderly and peaceful "March on Washington" to demand new civil rights legislation. They heard the Reverend Martin Luther King, head of the Southern Christian Leadership Conference, cry out eloquently, "I have a dream" of equality, of brotherhood, and of freedom and justice.

c. Violence Against Blacks and Civil Rights Workers. Although black leaders stressed nonviolence, the surge of demonstrations aroused violence by white segregationists. Black demonstrators in the South were subjected to strong-arm police tactics: clubbings, fire hoses, and mass arrests. Blacks also experienced threats and violence from private individuals. The houses and churches of blacks were damaged by "hate bombings." Black and white civil rights workers were assaulted, and several were shot and murdered. In the North, blacks faced heckling, fistfights, and counterdemonstrations. "The fury of bigots and bullies," President Johnson said, "served to strengthen the will of the American people that justice be done." In 1964 he secured passage of a comprehensive civil rights measure.

4. Civil Rights Act of 1964

a. Provisions. (1) *Voting.* The law prohibited election officials from applying different standards to black and white voting applicants and declared a sixth-grade education as evidence of literacy. (2) *Public Accommodations.* The law forbade discrimination in most places of public accommodation: hotels, motels, restaurants, lunch counters, retail stores, gas stations, theaters, and sports arenas. (3) *Public Facilities.* The law prohibited discrimination in government-owned or -operated facilities such as parks, swimming pools, and libraries. (4) *Federally Assisted Programs.* The law authorized the federal government to withhold financial aid from state and local programs involving discrimination. (5) *Employment.* The law prohibited discriminatory practices by most employers, employment agencies, and labor unions. To promote voluntary compliance, the law created an *Equal Employment Opportunity Commission.* (6) *Conciliation.* To help communities solve racial problems, the law created a *Community Relations Service.*

b. Developments. Title II of the act, dealing with public accommodations, was immediately challenged by a Southern motel owner. He claimed that he was being subjected illegally to federal regulation, since his business was not sufficiently connected with interstate commerce. The Supreme Court unanimously held Title II constitutional. Referring to John Marshall's reasoning in the 1824 case of *Gibbons vs. Ogden*, Justice Tom Clark asserted that Congress has power over all aspects of interstate commerce.

5. The Twenty-fourth Amendment (1964) prohibited the use of a poll tax as a requirement for voting in a federal election. It affected the five Southern states that still had poll taxes.

6. Voting Rights Act of 1965

a. Background. Amidst much publicity, Southern officials thwarted a black voter registration drive at Selma, Alabama. There, out of 15,000 eligible blacks, the number registered was only 335. Blacks thereupon marched through Alabama from Selma to Montgomery to focus the nation's attention upon Southern racial barriers to voting. The violence with which black and white civil rights workers were treated shocked the nation. Identifying the Ku Klux Klan as a source of the violence, President Johnson denounced its members as a "hooded band of bigots" and insisted that "every American citizen must have an equal right to vote." Congress quickly enacted the *Voting Rights Act of 1965.*

b. Provisions. (1) In any state or county where less than half of the voting-age population was registered or had voted in 1964, all literacy and other qualification tests were suspended. This provision applied immediately to five Southern states and parts of two others. (2) The Attorney General was empowered to send federal examiners to any county practicing voting discrimination. These registrars were authorized to register all would-be voters who met the state's age and residency requirements. This provision replaced the time-consuming court processes required by previous laws. (3) The Attorney General was empowered to file suits challenging the constitutionality of state poll taxes. This provision affected four Southern states.

c. Developments. The Supreme Court almost unanimously held Constitutional the key provisions of the 1965 Voting Rights Act. This law, Chief Justice Warren wrote, was an appropriate means for enforcing the Fifteenth Amendment and wiping out racial discrimination in voting. The Supreme Court also struck down Virginia's state poll tax as a burden irrelevant to voting qualifications and in violation of the Fourteenth Amendment.

7. Overview: Increase of Southern Black Voters. In 1957 the proportion of eligible Southern blacks registered to vote was 25 percent. Thereafter, additional black voters enrolled. They were aided by federal voting laws, federal court decisions, drives by civil rights organizations, cooperation of some Southern registrars, and the efforts of federal examiners who set up registration offices in counties practicing discrimination. By 1970 the proportion of eligible Southern blacks registered had risen to 65 percent.

Since the late 1960's, blacks have been elected to public offices even in the Deep South, and white candidates have appealed for black votes.

RECENT DEVELOPMENTS IN THE BLACK CIVIL RIGHTS MOVEMENT

1. Reasons for Continued Black Discontent. Despite their betterment, blacks remained discontented. They complained that communities were making slow progress in integrating schools and in giving blacks the vote. They also complained that in every phase of life blacks were in an inferior position to whites. (*a*) *Education.* Proportionately fewer black than white students gain a high school and college education. (*b*) **Jobs and Wages.** Blacks are concentrated in low-wage occupations. A disproportionately large number of blacks work as unskilled workers and service workers. (*c*) **Unemployment.** Blacks suffer twice the unemployment rate of white workers. (*d*) **Housing.** Many blacks are confined to slum areas and have no access to decent housing in better neighborhoods. (*e*) **Health.** Blacks have an average life expectancy of 70 years as compared to 74½ years for whites.

STATUS OF BLACKS AS COMPARED WITH WHITES, 1950-1970

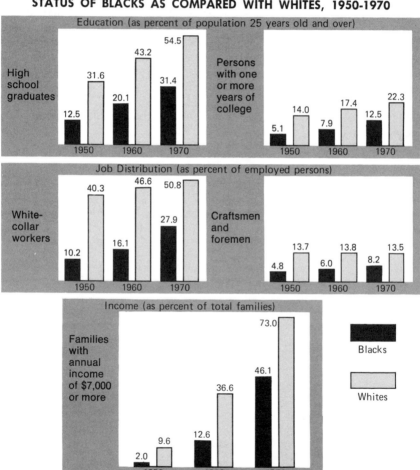

To what extent did blacks improve their status between 1950 and 1970? Did blacks improve their position in relation to whites?

2. Debate Over Black Responsibility. Assistant Secretary of Labor Daniel Moynihan prepared a report on "The Negro Family," contending that the troubles of American blacks stemmed, in part, from unstable families. Moynihan pointed out that because of desertion and divorce, nearly 2 million out of 5 million black families were fatherless and that the children in these families grew up without strong parental guidance. Moynihan urged steps to strengthen black family life, especially providing jobs to enable black men to support their families.

Condemning the Moynihan Report, black civil rights leaders retorted that responsibility for the plight of blacks rested more upon society than upon individual blacks.

3. Organizations to Improve the Black Condition

    a. Civil Rights Organizations: Lawful Efforts to Achieve Black Integration into American Life

    (1) The *National Association for the Advancement of Colored People* (*NAACP*), a biracial group founded in 1909, is the largest and best known of the civil rights organizations. It has worked to stop lynchings, to end school segregation, and to secure laws for fair practices in employment and housing. The NAACP has employed publicity, lobbying, and legal action, which achieved its greatest triumph in the 1954 Supreme Court decision against public school segregation. *Roy Wilkins*, as Executive Secretary, presented the NAACP viewpoint: that blacks want to live as free and equal Americans. (In 1977 Wilkins retired and was succeeded by *Benjamin L. Hooks*.)

    (2) The *National Urban League*, a biracial group founded in 1910, has helped blacks to adjust to city life as they came in from the rural South. It has worked to better conditions for blacks in health, housing, employment, and recreation. In charge of the League's work is its executive director, a position occupied since 1981 by *John E. Jacob*.

    (3) The *Southern Christian Leadership Conference* (*SCLC*), founded in 1957 by a group of Southern black leaders, has opposed discrimination in the use of public facilities, in employment, and in voting. The leading spirit and first president of the SCLC was the Reverend *Martin Luther King*. Inspired by Thoreau's essay "On Civil Disobedience" and by Gandhi's use of passive resistance against British rule in India, King urged blacks to struggle against injustice by nonviolent resistance. King effectively used nonviolent methods many times, starting in 1955–1956 with an economic boycott that compelled Montgomery, Alabama, to desegregate the city buses. In 1964 King was awarded the Nobel Peace Prize, which he accepted as honoring all people of good will who support nonviolent resistance to injustice. In 1968, when King went to lead a protest march for striking sanitation men, mainly black, in Memphis, Tennessee, he was murdered by a white

man. Despite this tragic death, the SCLC reaffirmed its belief in King's philosophy of nonviolence. (The current SCLC head is the Reverend *Joseph E. Lowery*.)

(In 1983 Congress passed and President Reagan signed a bill making King's birthday—to be observed on the third Monday in January—a national holiday. King and George Washington are the only Americans to be so honored.)

In summary, these three groups have stood for operating within the law, employing nonviolence, and seeking black equality and integration into American society. They have supported a policy of "gradualism" in contrast with other groups discussed below that demand "instant" and complete changes and that are considered "militants."

b. The Black Muslims: A Black Nationalist Group to Achieve Black Separation. The Black Muslims are both a religious sect and a nationalist group. Their Muslim religion teaches them to observe clean living and hard work, and to refrain from alcohol, tobacco, and drugs. They have rejected Christianity as the "white man's religion." They hold that white people are evil and therefore seek complete separation from the white world. In some American cities, the Black Muslims maintain their own schools, stores, temples (mosques), and other community facilities. Although the Black Muslims claimed to oppose violence, they were uncompromisingly militant and maintained a trained army-like corps, the Fruit of Islam. In the mid-1970's the Black Muslims eased their antiwhite stand and turned away from militancy.

Elijah Muhammad, the Black Muslim founder, claimed to have met "Allah on earth" in 1929 and thereafter called himself "Allah's messenger." *Malcolm X*, who became a Black Muslim while serving a jail sentence for burglary, was for many years Muhammad's top aide. His *Autobiography of Malcolm X* provides a fascinating view of his life and ideas. In 1963 Malcolm X and Elijah Muhammad had a falling-out, and in 1965 Malcolm X was assassinated by three Black Muslim gunmen. (In 1975 *Wallace Muhammad* succeeded his deceased father as Black Muslim head.)

c. The Black Panthers: A Revolutionary Organization to Overthrow the Existing System and Achieve Black Liberation. Organized in 1966 in Oakland, California, the Black Panther party said that its purpose was to protect ghetto blacks against "police harassment." Claiming to be against violence but for "self-defense," the Black Panthers affected a military stance and prominently displayed guns. They called for a revolutionary struggle of all oppressed peoples, black and white, to overthrow the existing American system, which they labeled as racist, fascist, and imperialist. By conducting antidrug clinics and children's breakfast programs, the Black Panthers spread their influence among ghetto inhabitants.

Many times the Black Panthers came into conflict with the law. This statement applied both to ordinary members and party leaders, especially Minister of Information *Eldridge Cleaver*. While in prison for assault with intent to murder, Cleaver wrote a series of personal and political articles published as *Soul on Ice*. Released on parole, Cleaver later was ordered rejailed as a parole violator, but he fled the United States to find refuge in leftist nations. (In 1975, having abandoned his radical views, Cleaver voluntarily returned to face charges in the United States.)

In the 1970's the Black Panthers moderated their radicalism and placed greater emphasis upon community programs and political action.

4. Destructive Protests in Black Ghettos. In the "long hot summers" of 1964–1967, blacks in Northern and Western cities expressed their discontent by conducting bloody and destructive riots. The most violent riots came in the Harlem section of New York, in the Watts section of Los Angeles, in Newark, and in Detroit. Mobs wantonly destroyed property—belonging to blacks as well as to whites—and maintained a reign of terror leading to many injuries and deaths. The riots perturbed many Americans who supported the civil rights movement but who expected blacks to behave responsibly. President Johnson, while cautioning blacks against violence, appointed an Advisory Commission on Civil Disorders.

5. Report of the Kerner Commission (1968). Governor *Otto Kerner* of Illinois was chairman of the *Advisory Commission on Civil Disorders*. Its eleven members came from major groups in American life: Democrats and Republicans, labor and industry, North and South, white and black. Its black members were Roy Wilkins, head of the NAACP, and Edward Brooke, Senator from Massachusetts. In 1968 the Commission issued a unanimous report.

a. General Conclusions. "Our nation is moving toward two societies, one black, one white—separate and unequal." This trend threatens our "basic democratic values."

b. Riot Findings. The Commission found that the riots were not the result of an organized conspiracy, although it acknowledged that calls for violence by militant black leaders contributed to a climate conducive to rioting. The Commission placed the chief blame for the urban riots on conditions resulting from "white racism." This racism, the Commission wrote, leads to discrimination in employment, education, and housing, and it implants in many blacks a sense of degradation, misery, and hopelessness.

c. Goals. The Commission opposed racial separatism as leading to a permanently inferior status for blacks and a permanently divided country. It favored immediate enrichment of ghetto life and long-range integration of blacks into society outside the ghetto.

d. Recommendations. (1) Creation of additional jobs by governments and private industry. (2) On-the-job training, partly subsidized by the government, for the "hard-core" unemployed. (3) Increased efforts to eliminate de facto school segregation and to improve schools serving disadvantaged children. (4) Public welfare improvements such as federally financed higher payments to the needy and measures to keep black families together. (5) Six million units of decent housing for low- and moderate-income families.

Civil rights leaders approved the report and hailed its conclusion that the riots ought to be blamed on "white racism." Critics generally did not reject the entire report but condemned it for (a) not sufficiently pointing out black progress since World War II, (b) excusing black participants of any blame for the riots, and (c) raising black expectations by recommendations that cannot be implemented because funds are not now available.

6. Civil Rights Act of 1968

a. Background. Despite President Johnson's urging, Congress failed to pass a bill outlawing discrimination in the rental and sale of housing. Southern Congressmen opposed to civil rights legislation received support from some Northern Congressmen, whose constituents feared that the influx of blacks into a white neighborhood would lower property values and destroy the character of the community.

In 1968, faced with a Southern filibuster, the Senate narrowly voted cloture and then easily approved an "open housing" bill. In the House, opponents of the Senate bill were able to delay its consideration.

b. Passage of the Civil Rights Bill. While the bill was stalled, Martin Luther King, in Memphis, Tennessee, was assassinated by a white man. His death, mourned by both whites and blacks, created an emotional atmosphere that spurred quick House approval of the open housing bill. President Johnson hailed the bill as evidence that "America does move forward."

c. Provisions. (1) The law barred discrimination in the rental and sale of 80 percent of the nation's housing. (2) The law provided stiff penalties for persons guilty of intimidating or injuring civil rights workers. (3) It provided penalties for persons who travel from one state to another to incite a riot and for persons who provide firearms for use in a riot.

7. Voting Rights Acts of 1970, 1975, and 1982.

These laws together extended to the year 2007 the provisions of the 1965 act protecting black and other minority voters. The 1970 law also (a) suspended all literacy tests as a voting qualification and (b) set a 30-day residency requirement for voting in Presidential elections. The 1975 law also required—in voting districts where less than half of the voting-age population had registered or voted in 1972 and where more than 5 percent belong to a single-language minority—that election materials be printed, in addition to English, in the minority language.

The 1982 law also required 9 states and parts of 13 others, with a history of voting discrimination, to "preclear" for approval of the Justice Department any changes in their election laws. The affected regions could escape this "preclearance" requirement if, for 10 years, they were free of election discrimination.

8. Affirmative Action in Employment. When it comes to employment, the Supreme Court has tended to place affirmative action plans into two categories—plans that deal with hiring and promotion, and plans that deal with layoffs and firing. The Court has shown a tendency to accept carefully drawn hiring and promotion plans. However, it has tended to reject plans that call for whites and men to be laid off before more recently hired minorities and women.

a. The Weber Case—1979. The Kaiser Corporation and the United Steel Workers Union agreed to establish a voluntary affirmative action plan. This voluntary plan called for special programs to train workers for skilled craft jobs, available to blacks and whites on a 50-50 basis. Brian Weber, a white, worked at the Kaiser Plant in Louisiana where the training program had 13 openings. Weber lacked sufficient seniority to secure one of the six places reserved for whites, but he had more seniority than two of the blacks accepted for the program. Weber brought suit charging "reverse discrimination" in violation of the 1964 Civil Rights Act, which prohibits racial discrimination by employers and unions.

The Supreme Court, by a 5-to-2 vote, decided against Weber and held that the Kaiser plan—with its numerical quota giving special preference to black workers—was legal. The Court majority claimed that the Kaiser plan was within the spirit of the 1964 Civil Rights Act—"to improve the lot of those who had been excluded from the American dream for so long." The Court minority deplored the decision as misreading the 1964 Civil Rights Act.

b. The Memphis Firefighters Case—1984. In *Firefighters Local Union vs. Stotts,* the Supreme Court held, 6 to 3, that the city of Memphis, Tennessee, could not lay off white firefighters with seniority in order to preserve the jobs of black firefighters hired later under affirmative action.

c. The Santa Clara County Case—1987. In *Johnson vs. Transportation Agency,* the Court held, 6 to 3, that an employer could use racial and sexual preferences in hiring and promotion even though there was no proof of past discrimination by that employer. The Santa Clara County, California, Transportation Agency had used an affirmative action plan to try to bring its work force into line with the racial and sexual makeup of the local population. For promotion to the job of dispatching road crews, the agency chose a woman over a man with a slightly higher interview score. The man sued. In rejecting the man's suit, the Court upheld for the first time an affirmative action plan that favored women over men. Justice William J. Brennan, Jr., for the majority, said the Court would judge sex-bias and race-bias cases by a single standard. Justice Antonin Scalia, in dissent, accused the majority of converting the job-discrimination provisions of the 1964 Civil Rights Act into an "engine of discrimination" against men and whites.

9. Other Supreme Court Decisions. (*a*) In *Fullilove vs. Klutznick* (1980), the Supreme Court upheld a Congress-mandated affirmative action program. The Court approved a public works provision that set aside 10 percent of the allotted funds for minority contractors (defined as blacks, Hispanics, Orientals, Indians, and Eskimos)—so as to redress racial discrimination. (b) In *City of Mobile (Alabama) vs. Bolden* (1980), the Supreme Court upheld an at-large or citywide system for electing city commissioners—although this system diluted the voting strength of the city's minority black population. The Court declared that, in the absence of proof of intent to discriminate, citywide (instead of district) voting is constitutional.

"BLACK" OR "AFRO-AMERICAN" REVOLUTION

1. **Meaning.** The above terms encompass the entire post-World War II civil rights movement and the changes in the status of blacks.

2. **Achievements.** Black problems were brought to the attention of the public and became a national issue. Southern blacks made considerable progress in exercising their right to vote. From 1957 to 1971 the proportion of eligible Southern blacks that was registered to vote increased from 25 to 65 percent. Also, progress was made in desegregating public schools and places of public accommodation and in gaining blacks labor-union membership and better employment opportunities. Many blacks entered the middle class and a few the upper class. Significantly, the civil rights movement convinced most Americans that discrimination is morally wrong.

3. **Criticisms and Responses.** Some whites have opposed, in part or in whole, the black civil rights movement. In the South, many whites feel that black aspirations threaten the traditional Southern way of life. In the North, some whites in cities and suburbs feel that black aspirations threaten their jobs and neighborhoods. This hostile reaction among whites, evidenced by demonstrations against civil rights activities and by votes against candidates favoring civil rights, has been called the "white backlash."

a. Criticism. Blacks are demanding too much too soon. They have made considerable gains since World War II. Now, instead of making additional demands, they should learn to use their gains, extend them to all blacks, and give white communities time to adjust to new conditions.

a. Response. Blacks were guaranteed their freedom and their political and civil rights by the Reconstruction Amendments. They have waited over 100 years for these guarantees to be honored. Blacks demand no more than equality with whites and will accept no less.

b. Criticism. Blacks are not making sufficient efforts to lift themselves out of poverty and ghetto life. They demand that the government do for them what they should be doing for themselves. After all, white immigrants faced similar handicaps. But white immigrants worked hard and escaped from the ghetto by their own efforts.

b. Response. Blacks are seeking to improve themselves, but they are deliberately kept down by discrimination, especially in employment and housing. Therefore, they need government help to outlaw discrimination. Also, when the white immigrants arrived, industry needed their unskilled labor; but when blacks came to the cities, industry had become more mechanized and had few jobs for unskilled workers.

c. Criticism. Blacks have rioted in our cities, looted and destroyed property, battled the police, caused injuries and deaths, and fomented disrespect for authority. They must not be permitted to destroy "law and order."

c. Response. Blacks have rioted out of a sense of misery and frustration. They had appealed peacefully to the "white power structure" for help in overcoming their problems—but to little avail. "Law and order" should mean not repression but equality and opportunity.

BLACK CONTRIBUTIONS TO AMERICAN LIFE

know any 3

1. In Military Struggles. Blacks played a role in America's fight for independence and in her subsequent wars. In 1770 *Crispus Attucks* was one of five men killed when British soldiers fired upon a hostile crowd in the Boston Massacre. During the American Revolution, 500 blacks—some freedmen and some slaves—served with the colonial forces.

During the Civil War black freedmen as well as runaway slaves served in the Union forces. At first, blacks were not accepted as fighting men but were assigned essential noncombat duties. With the issuance of the Emancipation Proclamation, blacks were permitted to enlist and were organized into black combat regiments. Over 180,000 blacks saw military service.

Some 1.4 million blacks served in the armed forces in the two world wars, and hundreds of thousands more served in Vietnam. During World War II, *Benjamin O. Davis* became the first black promoted to brigadier general in the United States Army. In 1989 General *Colin L. Powell* became the first black to hold the nation's highest military post: chairman of the Joint Chiefs of Staff.

2. In Government Service. During the Reconstruction Era, blacks were active in Southern politics. They served in all the Southern state legislatures, and one, *P. B. S. Pinchback*, served briefly as acting governor of Louisiana. Fourteen blacks were elected to the United States House of Representatives and two blacks, both from Mississippi, served in the United States Senate.

With the end of Reconstruction, blacks were driven from Southern political life. Only since the 1960's have blacks regained a voice. By 1992, 7,500 African Americans held elective office nationwide—two thirds of them in the South.

As the racial composition of big cities has changed, many have elected black mayors. Blacks have served in increasing numbers in state legislatures, and in 1990 *L. Douglas Wilder* of Virginia became the first elected black governor.

Black politicians have played a growing role on the national stage as well. In 1966 Massachusetts voters elected *Edward Brooke* to be United States Senator, the first black Senator since Reconstruction days. In 1968 *Shirley Chisolm* of Brooklyn became the first black woman elected to the House of Representatives. A black clergyman, *Jesse Jackson*, made a strong showing in campaigning for the Democratic nomination for President in 1984 and 1988. In recent years, African Americans in Congress have included Representatives *Kweisi Mfume* of Maryland, *Ron Dellums* of California, and *Cynthia McKinney* of Georgia and Senator *Carol Mosely-Braun* of Illinois.

Since *Robert Weaver* became the first black Cabinet member in 1966, it has become common for Presidents to select blacks as members of their Cabinet. Blacks also serve in many other appointed federal positions. *Thurgood Marshall*, the NAACP lawyer who won the Supreme Court decision on school desegregation in 1954, became the first black Supreme Court Justice in 1967. *Clarence Thomas* was the second, joining the Court in 1991.

At the United Nations, *Ralph Bunche* won the Nobel Peace Prize for 1950 for his work as mediator of the Arab-Israeli dispute.

3. In the Academic World. In the Post-Reconstruction Era, *Booker T. Washington* headed Tuskegee Institute. He advocated vocational training to enable blacks to improve their economic status. *W. E. B. Du Bois*, a founder of the NAACP, was a pioneer in historical research on American blacks. More recent black scholars have included the psychologist *Kenneth Clark*, the psychiatrist *Alvin F. Poussaint*, the historians *John Hope Franklin* and *Lerone Bennet, Jr.*, and humanities professor *Henry Louis Gates, Jr.* The first African American woman astronaut, *Mae C. Jemison*, was also a chemical engineer.

4. In Sports. For years whites excluded blacks from participation in "white" sports, but slowly blacks began to break the color barrier. Helping to refute the Nazis' "master race" doctrines, *Jesse Owens* set new world records in winning three track events at the 1936 Olympic Games in Berlin. In 1938, *Joe Louis* defended his boxing title as world heavyweight champion by knocking out a German challenger in the first round. *Jackie Robinson* became the first American black to play major league baseball in 1947.

Today blacks are starring players, as well as coaches and managers, in all major sports. Some of the outstanding black athletes of recent decades include:

Baseball—*Willie Mays, Leroy (Satchel) Paige, Henry Aaron, Frank Robinson, Dwight Gooden, Dave Winfield, Eddie Murray.*

Football—*Jim Brown, Herschel Walker, Doug Williams.*

Tennis—*Althea Gibson, Arthur Ashe.*

Basketball—*Wilt Chamberlain, Kareem Abdul-Jabbar, Michael Jordan.*

Track—*Wilma Rudolph, Jackie Joyner-Kersee, Carl Lewis.*

Boxing—*Jack Johnson, Floyd Patterson, Sugar Ray Robinson, Muhammad Ali.*

5. In the Performing Arts. Blacks have enriched American music. *W. C. Handy*, a composer, won acclaim for his "St. Louis Blues." *Marian Anderson*, a singer of spirituals and operatic arias, was world-famed for the beauty of her voice. Other noted black musicians have included *Louis Armstrong, Duke Ellington,* and *John Coltrane*—jazz musicians; *Josephine Baker,* star of Parisian music halls; *Ella Fitzgerald, Lena Horne, Nat King Cole, Jimi Hendrix, Tina Turner,* and *Michael Jackson*—singers of popular music; *Leontyne Price* and *Simon Estes*— opera stars.

In the field of dance, *Katherine Dunham* and *Alvin Ailey* became outstanding. In the theater, actor and singer *Paul Robeson* rose to fame in the 1920's, to be followed later by stars like *James Earl Jones* and *Diahann Carroll.* In the movies, actors *Ethel Waters* and *Sidney Poitier* paved the way for later stars like *Eddie Murphy* and *Whoopi Goldberg,* while *Gordon Parks* and *Spike Lee* became noted directors. In the 1980's, *Bill Cosby, Oprah Winfrey* and *Bryant Gumbel* joined television's superstars.

6. In Literature. Blacks have contributed to American literature from colonial times onward. *Phillis Wheatley,* a slave who was later freed, lived in colonial Boston and wrote lyric poetry. After Reconstruction, *Paul Laurence Dunbar,* the son of former slaves, wrote dialect poems describing black life.

In recent times, black writers have gained a large following. Poets *Langston Hughes* and *Countee Cullen* and folklorist and writer *Zora Neale Hurston* were part of a 1920's flowering of black culture known as the *Harlem Renaissance.* *Richard Wright* wrote *Native Son,* a novel portraying black urban life, and *Black Boy,* an autobiographical work about his Southern childhood. Poet and novelist *Gwendolyn Brooks* was the first black winner of the Pulitzer Prize for poetry, in 1950. *James Baldwin,* essayist, playwright, and novelist, wrote *The Fire Next Time.* More recent black playwrights have included *August Wilson* (who twice won the Pulitzer Prize for drama), *Charles Fuller, Lorraine Hansberry,* and *Imamu Amiri Baraka.* Leading black novelists have included *Ralph Ellison (Invisible Man, Alice Walker (The Color Purple), Ishmael Reed (The Last Days of Louisiana Red),* and *Toni Morrison (Beloved).*

7. In Science. *Benjamin Banneker,* a free black born in colonial Maryland, became an accomplished mathematician and astronomer. He published an almanac that was highly praised by Thomas Jefferson. *George Washington Carver,* who joined the staff of Tuskegee Institute in 1896, was a botanist and chemist. To end the dependence of Southern farmers on the cotton crop, Carver studied the peanut and discovered many commercial uses for it. *Daniel Hale Williams,* a surgeon, did pioneer work in heart operations. *Percy L. Julian,* a chemist and industrialist, did research on hormones and other aspects of organic chemistry. *Charles R. Drew,* a surgeon, devised procedures for the preservation of blood plasma. During World War II, he directed the American Red Cross blood program in New York City.

8. In the Economic World. One fourth of all union members—more than 2 million workers—are blacks, and blacks occupy positions of leadership in the labor movement. *Cleveland Robinson* was president of the Afro-American Labor Council, protecting the interests of black unionists. *A. Philip Randolph* was head of the Brotherhood of Sleeping Car Porters and Vice President of the AFL-CIO. *Mary Hatwood Futrell* was president of the National Education Association, a union for teachers.

For years, black business people specialized in serving the black community. Blacks were teachers, doctors, dentists, lawyers, architects, and bankers. More recently, blacks have moved into important positions in large corporations.

Some, such as publisher *John H. Johnson,* have become wealthy. Johnson's magazines—including *Ebony, Jet,* and *EM*—have a wide readership among blacks. *Earl R. Graves* publishes *Black Enterprise,* a magazine about black business endeavors. In 1987, Wall Street financier *Reginald Lewis* led a group of investors in the $985 million buyout of Beatrice International Foods.

MULTIPLE-CHOICE QUESTIONS

1. The first major surge of black migration to Northern cities took place during the (1) Civil War (2) Reconstruction Era (3) New Deal (4) First World War.

2. In 1954 the Supreme Court handed down a decision involving segregation in the schools. This decision (1) reversed the "separate but equal" doctrine (2) reaffirmed the "separate but equal" doctrine (3) left questions of segregation up to the states (4) gave the federal government control over all private schools.

3. In *Brown vs. Board of Education of Topeka,* the Supreme Court based its decision upon what provision in the Constitution? (1) "privileges and immunities" clause of Article IV (2) "due process" clause of the Fifth Amendment (3) "equal protection" clause of the Fourteenth Amendment (4) elastic clause of Article I.

4. In 1955 the Supreme Court held that integration in the public schools should (1) proceed as rapidly as practicable (2) be left to local school boards to decide (3) be delayed in the Deep South (4) be left to the governors to decide.

5. The Constitutional argument advocated by some sections of the South against federal action for integration in education is based upon (1) delegated powers (2) division of powers (3) the system of checks and balances (4) the elastic clause.

6. Which would segregationist leaders quote today to defend their position? (1) Hamilton's Report on Manufactures (2) the Supreme Court decision in *McCulloch vs. Maryland* (3) Washington's Proclamation of Neutrality (4) the Kentucky and Virginia Resolutions.

7. De facto segregation in Northern schools is brought about primarily by (1) housing patterns (2) legal restrictions (3) voting restrictions (4) transportation facilities.

8. Following 1964, which factor most sped integration in public schools in the Deep South? (1) Southern white opinion shifted in favor of integration. (2) Southern blacks participated in demonstrations. (3) Southern school districts complied with Office of Education "guidelines" in order to qualify for federal funds. (4) Most Southern legislators supported school integration to gain black votes.

9. An objective of the Civil Rights Act of 1957 was to (1) make lynching a federal crime (2) outlaw poll taxes (3) desegregate public transportation (4) protect the voting rights of citizens.

10. Participants in the March on Washington in the summer of 1963 were demonstrating for (1) civil rights (2) government ownership of industry (3) worldwide disarmament (4) federal aid to education.

11. Southern Senators in recent years have tried to block civil rights legislation by the method known as (1) the gag rule (2) lobbying (3) filibustering (4) cloture.

12. Since 1964, a motel owner may legally deny a black's request for a room if (1) there is a local "Jim Crow" ordinance (2) the motel is not directly engaged in interstate commerce (3) the black is not an American citizen (4) there are no vacancies.

13. Which way of protecting black voters was first provided in the Voting Rights Act of 1965? (1) the suspension of literacy tests in certain states (2) court injunctions to prevent unfair voting practices (3) reduction of the number of Representatives of a state that limits black voting (4) use of federal troops on Election Day.

14. Martin Luther King was most closely identified with (1) practicing nonviolent direct action (2) undermining the NAACP (3) investigating the "black power" movement (4) demanding creation of a Civil Rights Commission.

MATCHING QUESTIONS

Column A—Achievements

1. Almanac publisher
2. Baseball star
3. Supreme Court Justice
4. Scientist who discovered many commercial uses for the peanut
5. Vice President of AFL-CIO
6. World heavyweight champion prizefighter
7. Author of *The Fire Next Time*
8. Poet in colonial America
9. United Nations official
10. Singer of classical music

Column B—Blacks

a. George Washington Carver
b. Phillis Wheatley
c. Joe Louis
d. Marian Anderson
e. Booker T. Washington
f. Jackie Robinson
g. Thurgood Marshall
h. Malcolm X
i. A. Philip Randolph
j. James Baldwin
k. Benjamin Banneker
l. Robert Weaver
m. Ralph Bunche

ESSAY QUESTIONS

1. During the past 100 years the issue of civil rights has frequently played a significant role in the United States. Describe *two* ways in which *each* of the following has affected the cause of civil rights: (*a*) Presidents, (*b*) Congress, (*c*) the Supreme Court, (*d*) state legislatures, (*e*) organizations of private citizens.

2. Congress has passed laws—in 1957, 1960, 1964, 1965, and 1970—to assure black voting rights. (*a*) Explain *two* reasons why more than one law was necessary. (*b*) Evaluate *two* provisions of the Voting Rights Act of 1965. (*c*) Discuss *two* effects upon the South attributable, at least in part, to these federal voting laws.

3. Using *two* facts, agree *or* disagree with *each* of the following statements: (*a*) In the United States, blacks were greatly affected by World War II. (*b*) In their efforts to secure equal rights, blacks have had little help from the United States Constitution. (*c*) Blacks in the North face problems different from the problems of blacks in the South. (*d*) Blacks will find their efforts toward improving their conditions hindered by rioting and violence. (*e*) Today, many blacks can improve conditions for themselves and their families through their own efforts. (*f*) Since the end of World War II, blacks in the United States have achieved remarkable gains.

4. For *each* following field, name *one* black and discuss his or her contribution: (*a*) sports, (*b*) literature, (*c*) organized labor, (*d*) government, (*e*) science, (*f*) music.

Part 3. The American People Face Problems Arising From Population Trends

OUR GROWING POPULATION

GROWTH OF THE AMERICAN POPULATION TO 1900

Every ten years the government takes a *census*. A census is the enumeration of all the people. It is taken to comply with the Constitutional requirement for apportioning members of the House of Representatives among the states according to population. At the time of the first census, in 1790, the United States contained almost 4 million people. By 1860 our population had risen to over 31 million, an average increase per decade of almost 35 percent. By 1900 Americans totaled almost 76 million, an average increase of almost 25 percent for each of these four decades.

Our population growth, from 4 million in 1790 to 76 million by 1900, resulted from (1) a comparatively high birth rate, as Americans proved able to feed and clothe large families, (2) some decrease in the death rate, primarily due to medical advances, and (3) a continuous stream of immigrants.

GROWTH OF THE AMERICAN POPULATION IN THE 20TH CENTURY

1. Statistical Data

YEAR	POPULATION IN MILLIONS	INCREASE OVER PRECEDING CENSUS	
		IN MILLIONS	IN PERCENT
1900	76	13	21
1910	92	16	21
1920	106	14	15
1930	123	17	16
1940	132	9	7
1950	151	19	15
1960	179	28	19
1970	203	24	13
1980	227	24	12
1990	250	23	10

Because traditional census-taking procedures undercount certain groups, the Census Bureau takes a postcensus survey to try to catch mistakes. In 1990 the bureau estimated an undercount of 2.1 percent. The undercount was even higher among Hispanics (5.2 percent) and African Americans (4.8 percent). For statistical and political reasons, official figures were *not* changed to correct for the mistakes. If adjusted, the total population would have been 254 million.

2. Analysis

a. From 1910 to 1940 the population increased, but at a declining rate. Fewer immigrants came because of (1) World War I, (2) restrictive immigration laws (1921–1929), and the Depression of the 1930's.

b. From 1940 to the present the population has increased at a higher rate than in the 1930's. During World War II, young people had their lives disrupted, but afterward, finding jobs plentiful, they rushed to marry and raise large families, thereby creating a postwar "baby boom." The high birth rate in America continued to about 1970, then dropped sharply.

3. Aspects of the 1990 Census

a. *Population Shifts.* The region that showed the greatest population growth was the *Sunbelt*—the South and Southwest. The states whose population growth gained them the largest increase in the House of Representatives were California—seven more; Florida—four more; and Texas—three more. The states that lost the most Representatives were New York—three fewer; and Michigan, Illinois, Ohio, and Pennsylvania—each two fewer.

b. Population Density. The average number of persons per square mile is called the *population density.* The greatest population density existed in the small, industrialized North Atlantic states: 995 persons per square mile for New Jersey, 830 for Rhode Island, 728 for Massachusetts, and 657 for Connecticut. The large Rocky Mountain states (whose land is devoted chiefly to mining and grazing) and Alaska (a frontier state) had the lowest population density: about 5 people per square mile for Montana and Wyoming, 11 for Nevada, and less than one person per square mile in Alaska.

For the entire United States, the population density was 69 persons per square mile. This figure was quite high when compared with 6 for Australia and Libya, 7 for Canada, 20 for Saudi Arabia, and 34 for the former Soviet Union. However, the figure for the United States was quite low when compared with 557 for Israel, 564 for Germany, 606 for Britain, 839 for Belgium, and 849 for Japan.

PROBLEMS CREATED BY OUR GROWING POPULATION

As our nation's population continues to grow, we shall need more of everything: (1) more *goods*—food, clothing, homes, and appliances, (2) more *services*—doctors, dentists, teachers, schools, recreational facilities, and transportation, and (3) more *jobs*—to provide employment.

OUR SENIOR POPULATION

INCREASING NUMBER OF PERSONS OVER 65

1. Statistical Data

YEAR	TOTAL POPULATION IN MILLIONS	PERSONS OVER 65	
		IN MILLIONS	IN PERCENT
1850	23	.6	2.6
1900	76	3.1	4.1
1950	151	12.2	8.1
1960	179	16.5	9.2
1970	203	20.0	9.9
1980	227	25.5	11.2
1990	250	31.2	12.0

2. Reasons. The steady increase in the percentage of persons over 65 is due to (a) *improvements in general welfare:* better food, housing, sanitation facilities, working conditions, and recreational opportunities, and (b) *improvements in medical science:* new drugs, advanced surgical techniques, additional medical facilities, and the development of *geriatrics*—a special branch of medicine concerned with older people. As a result, the death rate per 1000 persons fell from 17.2 in 1900 to 8.6 in 1991. Also, the life expectancy of the average American has increased from less than 40 years in 1850 to over 75 years today.

PROBLEMS FACING OUR SENIOR POPULATION

1. Forced Retirement. In the past, many employers required workers to retire at age 65. Other employers gave workers more flexibility in deciding when to retire. In 1978 Congress passed a *retirement age* measure prohibiting forced retirement for most workers in private industry before age 70.

2. Housing. Older people need small, low-cost homes with features to prevent accidents: ramps instead of stairways, handgrips at bathtubs, and nonskid floors. Since the 1950's Congress has passed housing acts with provisions to benefit older persons.

3. Income. Most retired persons face a problem of "making ends meet." Although retired workers have lower living expenses, they no longer receive a wage or salary. They must now depend upon their pensions, savings and investments, and Social Security.

4. Social Security: Old Age and Survivors Insurance

a. Coverage. Social Security, begun in 1935, at first covered only employees working for business concerns. It was gradually extended to include almost all workers. Now self-employed persons (such as farmowners, shopkeepers, lawyers, and doctors), most domestic help, most farm workers, federal civil servants, and all members of the armed forces contribute to Social Security.

b. Benefits. Social Security provides *old-age insurance*. Upon retirement at age 65, insured workers receive monthly payments determined according to earnings, years of work, and number of dependents. Those who retire at age 62 receive lower payments. Social Security also provides *survivors' insurance*. When a worker dies, benefits go to the spouse and children under age 18.

Since 1975, Social Security benefits have gone up automatically each year in step with the Consumer Price Index.

c. Financing the Plan. Social Security and Medicare are financed by a tax on earnings, paid in equal amounts by employee and employer. Unlike the income tax, the earnings tax is regressive. It applies only up to a certain income ($57,600 in 1993), so people whose salaries exceed that amount pay a relatively lower percentage of their total earnings. The tax rate as of 1994 was 7.65 percent each for employer and employed (6.2 percent for Social Security, 1.45 percent for Medicare). Since they had no employer to kick in an equal share, the self-employed paid at almost double that rate.

d. Social Security and the Future. Observers point to the steady aging of the United States population, with relatively fewer working-age people paying into a system that benefits relatively more retired people. Today there are about three workers for every retired person. Some experts predict that by the year 2020 there will be only two workers for every retired person.

5. Political Influence.
The elderly make up one of the most potent voting blocs in the United States. They turn out to vote in far greater proportion than do younger people—and they know how to make their weight felt. If ever members of Congress try to trim Social Security or Medicare benefits, pressure groups like the *American Association of Retired Persons* (AARP) and *Families USA* swing into action.

6. Medical Care

a. Medicare for the Aged Under Social Security.

(1) First proposed in 1945, Medicare was a controversial idea. Liberals and labor unions supported it, while conservatives and doctors' groups like the *American Medical Association* opposed it. Medicare passed Congress in 1965.

(2) *Medicare: Provisions.* Medicare now offers persons over 65 the following: (a) *A basic hospital insurance plan.* The individual must pay the first few hundred dollars of a hospital bill (this is known as a *deductible*). Then Medicare

Ivey in The San Francisco Examiner

Earthbound in the space era.

takes over, covering up to 60 days for each illness. (*b*) *A voluntary medical insurance plan.* The enrollee pays a monthly fee. This plan pays 80 percent of the cost, after a deductible, for services of physicians and surgeons plus certain other medical services. Medicare does *not* generally cover prescription drugs or long-term care in a nursing home.

(3) *Medicare: Costs.* Federal spending for Medicare—hospital and health insurance—shot up from $4.7 billion in 1967 to $178 billion in 1995.

b. Medicaid: Health Insurance for the Needy. For needy persons of all ages not eligible for Medicare, state governments administer programs of health aid called *Medicaid.* Each state sets its own eligibility and benefit standards.

c. Proposals for Universal Health Insurance

(1) *Background.* To help the estimated 34 million Americans who have no health insurance, President Clinton in 1993 submitted a proposal for universal health insurance to Congress, beginning a national debate.

(2) *Competing Plans.* *(a) President Clinton's Plan.* The Clinton plan would have required everyone to get health insurance, with business paying 80 percent of the premiums. Coverage was to be provided by private insurers through regional pools called health alliances. *(b) Single-Payer Plan.* The federal and state governments were to provide health insurance directly to all individuals. The plan was to be financed through taxes. *(c) Voluntary Plan.* Individuals were to be encouraged but not required to pay health insurance through regional purchasing cooperatives. The poor would have received subsidies.

(3) *Debate.* Arguments for universal health insurance include: (1) Medical care is a basic human right; all other advanced industrial democracies have adopted some system of universal health insurance. (2) Too many people are now unable to afford insurance. Arguments against universal health insurance include: (1) If financed by the government, it would add an immense new expense at a time of soaring federal budget deficits. (2) Any universal system would establish a new layer of unwieldy bureaucracy.

(4) *No Resolution.* No plan obtained enough support in Congress to pass, and universal health insurance became another unresolved national issue.

OUR YOUTHFUL POPULATION

AFTER THE "BABY BOOM"

1. Statistical Data

YEAR	TOTAL POPULATION IN MILLIONS	PERSONS UNDER 30	
		IN MILLIONS	PERCENT OF POPULATION
1950	151	74.8	49.7
1970	203	106.9	52.5
1980	227	113.3	50.0
1990	249	112.2	45.1

2. Analysis. From 1950 to 1970, the under-30 population gradually increased to more than half the total population. Because of the post–World War II "baby boom," the 20–29-year age bracket was for a time our fastest-growing group. A new "baby boom" peaked in the early 1990's, with births topping 4 million a year for the first time since the 1960's.

3. Impact of Our Under-30 Population

a. Special Wants. (1) For *consumer goods:* convenience foods, highly styled clothing, flashy cars, rock music, youth-oriented movies, and sports gear; and, upon marriage: homes, home furnishings, appliances, and baby-related items. (2) For *educational facilities:* technical, college, and graduate facilities. From 1965 to 1990, the number of college students more than doubled—from 5.9 million to 13.7 million. (3) For *employment*: additional jobs. Younger people traditionally have a higher unemployment rate than older people.

b. Poverty. People under 18 are the most likely of all Americans to be living in poverty. In the early 1990's, more than 14 million children—one in five—lived in families with incomes below the poverty line. Most were white, although members of minorities like African Americans and Native Americans were more likely than others to be in poverty. The U.S. child poverty rate was double that of other industrial nations.

c. Political Influence. Beginning in the 1960's, the under-30 group—especially college students—showed great interest in political affairs by supporting Presidential candidates and lobbying among members of Congress. In 1971 the Twenty-sixth Amendment assured youths at age 18 of the right to vote in all elections—federal, state, and local.

OUR URBAN POPULATION

URBANIZATION OF THE AMERICAN PEOPLE

1. Statistical Data

YEAR	TOTAL POPULATION IN MILLIONS	DISTRIBUTION BY PERCENT		CITIES OVER 1 MILLION	CITIES OF 100,000 TO 1 MILLION
		URBAN*	RURAL		
1790	4	5.1	94.9	0	0
1850	23	15.3	84.7	0	6
1900	76	39.7	60.3	3	35
1950	151	64.0	36.0	5	101
1960	179	69.9	30.1	5	130
1970	203	73.5	26.5	6	147
1980	227	73.7	26.3	6	163
1990	250	77.5	22.5	8	215

*An urban is area is defined by the Census Bureau as a place with 2500 or more inhabitants.

2. Urbanization: 1990 Census. The 1990 census for the first time showed a majority of Americans living in metropolitan areas of more than one million people. About 27 percent of Americans lived in smaller metropolitan areas. Only 22.5 percent of Americans lived outside metropolitan areas.

Our ten most populous cities were New York, Los Angeles, Chicago, Houston, Philadelphia, San Diego, Detroit, Dallas, Phoenix, and San Antonio. Many cities had large, rapidly growing suburbs (such as Irvine, near Los Angeles) that themselves took on the characteristics of big cities.

REASONS FOR THE GROWTH OF CITIES

1. Industrial Revolution. As industries arose, workers congregated about the factories. These workers added to existing city populations or created new cities. Because urban dwellers needed food, clothing, entertainment, and professional services, still more people came to the cities.

2. Social and Cultural Attractions. Many people were attracted to cities by social and cultural facilities: colleges and universities, theaters and movies, symphonies, libraries, and lecture forums.

3. Improved Transportation and Communication. The railroads, telegraph lines, and telephones that served the cities enabled the city dwellers to (a) obtain foodstuffs and other essentials, (b) distribute the products of city factories throughout the land, and (c) conduct business transactions quickly and efficiently from a central office.

4. Decreasing Farm Population. Farmers and farm laborers were driven from the countryside by the (a) drabness and hardships of farm life, (b) low agricultural prices and difficult times, especially following the Civil War and again following World War I, and (c) increased mechanization and growth of commercial farming.

5. Immigration From Europe. During the 19th century, some "old immigrants" settled in cities. After the close of the frontier in 1890, the "new immigrants" settled chiefly in cities. These urban settlers found jobs in city factories and other businesses. As newcomers unfamiliar with American culture, they preferred to live among fellow immigrants who spoke their native tongue. Ethnic groups congregated in special city sections, thereby forming ghettos.

6. Migration of African Americans and Hispanics

a. Blacks. In the 20th century, blacks left the rural South for urban centers. Some blacks moved to cities in the South, but more moved to cities in the West and North. By 1980, blacks in large numbers inhabited America's most populous cities.

   b. Hispanics. By 1980 Puerto Ricans lived in and about New York City. Mexican-Americans resided mainly in the cities of the Southwest and West. Cubans settled in the Florida cities of Tampa and Miami.

GOVERNMENTAL PROBLEMS OF CITIES

   1. **Corruption and Political Machines.** In the late 19th and early 20th centuries, city "bosses" ruling political machines dominated and victimized a considerable number of cities. They corrupted city governments by selling justice in local courts, giving city franchises and contracts to businessmen in return for presents and favors, and filling city jobs with unqualified political henchmen.

   Most political machines were eventually ousted from power through the combined efforts of reform leaders, crusading newspapers, and an aroused citizenry. In the early 20th century the muckraker *Lincoln Steffens* did much to make the public aware of corruption in city government by his book *The Shame of the Cities.* Today, although occasional cases of corruption among city officials are still disclosed, bossism does not present nearly the problem that it did at the turn of the century.

   2. **City-State Relationship.** City governments are "creatures of the state." They were created by state-granted charters and exercise powers as enumerated in these charters. Some cities complain that the state does not grant them sufficient *home rule.* Cities that do not have home-rule charters must obey state directives on local problems and must secure permission from the state legislature to widen their powers over such matters as transportation and taxation. Many cities, including New York City, also complain that the state treats a city unfairly by collecting more money in state taxes from the city's residents than the state returns to the city in the form of services and state-aid funds.

   3. **Demands for More City Services.** Cities have faced demands from their inhabitants for more and better services. City aid is especially needed in ghettos occupied by disadvantaged blacks and other minorities. As a result, cities have expanded their facilities in recreation, education, housing, transportation, welfare assistance, and public health; and city expenditures have soared.

   4. **Decrease in the City Tax Base.** Especially since the end of World War II, middle-class and upper middle-class families have left the cities for more

spacious homes in the suburbs. They reasoned that they would be escaping the city's crowded living, its social problems, and its taxes, and yet would be living near enough to the city to reach it by auto or commuter train. Businesses, too, fled the major cities, in part to be near the labor supply in suburbs and in part to escape what businessmen called "nuisance" city taxes, such as on commercial rents and gross business receipts.

The outflow of businesses and affluent families decreased the tax base of large cities. This decrease came at a time when the cities' need for revenue was greatest. Cities felt compelled to raise the rates of existing taxes, increase transportation fares, and impose new taxes, such as city income taxes.

PUBLIC HEALTH

Since city dwellers live close together, diseases may spread easily and become epidemics. Consequently, cities maintain health services such as hospitals, clinics, and visiting nurses. In addition, cities ensure a pure water supply and proper sewage disposal, and enforce sanitation laws. Cities also take steps to combat air and water pollution (see page 227).

PREVENTION OF CRIME

The crime rate in cities is high. (1) Cities contain many people and great extremes of wealth and poverty. (2) Runaway children, people with mental problems, and the homeless seek refuge in cities, sometimes turning to crime and vice for income. (3) Social problems such as drug addiction and prostitution greatly burden city social and law enforcement agencies. (4) Violence readily flourishes in the anonymity of city streets.

Cities try to attack the causes of crime by providing aid and counsel to people in need. Many cities have built low-cost housing in an attempt to eradicate slums, but construction has not kept up with population growth.

Every city maintains a police force to uphold law and order, but friction between police and slum residents is often high. Some cities give special training to help police officers become more sensitive to community needs.

MASS TRANSPORTATION

Cities are being "choked to death" by the ever-increasing number of motor vehicles, private and commercial. Streets are too narrow, parking facilities inadequate. Cities have attempted to meet these problems by improving subway and bus services, building expressways around and through the city, and constructing parking areas at the city's outskirts, where commuters can leave their autos and take public transportation.

From The Herblock Gallery (*Simon & Schuster, 1968*)

"Help!"

What problems face our cities? What steps have been taken by the cities to deal with these problems? By the federal government?

The federal government and some states have provided funds to help alleviate city transportation problems. Such funds have been used by urban areas to rebuild and expand subway, bus, and rail lines.

EDUCATION

Cities administer their own educational systems, although these are financed in part by state and federal funds and are subject to state supervision.

Cities have faced demands for (1) *more education:* pre-kindergarten classes, adult education courses, and two- and four-year community colleges, and (2) *better education:* newer buildings, more teachers, and up-to-date teaching materials, such as language laboratories, modern science equipment, and recently published textbooks.

Also, since the 1954 Supreme Court decision in *Brown vs. Board of Education of Topeka,* cities have faced demands that schools be integrated. (For further discussions of education, check the Index.)

HOUSING AND URBAN RENEWAL

1. **Cost of Slums.** Slum areas are typified by *tenement houses*—buildings that are filthy, overcrowded, run-down, poorly ventilated, inadequately heated, and poorly protected against fires. Slum areas usually lack sufficient recreational facilities. Inhabitants generally have few occupational skills and are often unemployed. Compared to the rest of the city, slum dwellers are more susceptible to disease, and more slum youths turn to juvenile gangs and crime. Slum areas therefore require more city services, such as policemen, firemen, and welfare workers.

2. **First Remedial Efforts: Late 19th and Early 20th Centuries.** As cities grew, Americans became increasingly concerned over slums. *Jacob Riis,* a journalist, in 1890 publicized the evils of New York City slums in his book *How the Other Half Lives. Jane Addams* established *Hull House* in Chicago, and *Lillian Wald* established the *Henry Street Settlement* in New York City. These settlement houses, located in slum areas, provided playgrounds, meeting rooms, and libraries, and offered classes at every level from nursery school to adult education.

Cities and states passed *tenement laws,* requiring slum landlords to improve their buildings by providing fire escapes, additional sanitary facilities, and better ventilation, heating, and lighting. However, these laws were not strictly enforced.

While the slums remained, the slum population changed. As the Irish, Polish, Italian, and Jewish immigrants learned American ways and improved their economic status, they gradually moved out of the slums. Their dwellings were taken over by incoming Negroes and Puerto Ricans.

3. **Housing and the New Deal**

a. Purposes. Between 1929 and 1933 housing construction dwindled sharply. During the depression years, President Franklin D. Roosevelt moved to stimulate the building industry so as to (1) provide jobs in construction and in related industries: cement, brick, lumber, and electrical and plumbing supplies, and (2) further social reform. Estimating that one-third of the nation was ill-housed, President Roosevelt wanted to strike at the problem of substandard housing, especially in slums.

b. New Deal Housing Efforts

(1) *Mortgage Insurance.* The *Federal Housing Administration (FHA)*, established in 1934, insured mortgage loans, thus guaranteeing their repayment. This encouraged banks and other credit institutions to lend money for housing construction and home repairs. The FHA set construction standards for builders who desired FHA-guaranteed loans.

(2) *Low-Cost Housing and Slum-Clearance Projects.* The *Public Works Administration (PWA)* provided funds for demolishing slum buildings and constructing housing projects. In 1937 the *United States Housing Authority* took over this work. The USHA could provide up to 90 percent of the cost of approved state and local projects by means of long-term, low-interest loans. The USHA could also make outright grants so as to reduce construction costs and assure low rentals.

c. Significance.
These New Deal housing agencies marked the beginning of federal efforts to solve the housing problem. From 1933 to 1941 they helped bring about a considerable increase in the construction of dwelling units. Construction, however, still remained far below the needs of the people. From 1942 to 1945, as the nation concentrated on winning World War II, housing construction again declined sharply.

4. Housing and Urban Renewal Since World War II

a. Need for Housing.
The American people have needed much additional housing to (1) make up for the limited construction during the years of the depression and World War II, (2) fill the requirements of our growing population, and (3) meet the demands of the rising numbers of urban and suburban dwellers.

b. Private Builders.
The building industry responded by increasing construction to record levels, achieving an average of over 1 million nonfarm dwelling units annually. These businessmen constructed apartment houses for middle- and upper-income families and "mass-produced" one- and two-family houses. They avoided slum clearance and low-income housing, as these projects are financially risky.

c. Federal Efforts.
During Democratic and Republican administrations since 1949, many major laws have been enacted to provide federal programs for housing and urban renewal. These complex laws, involving the expenditure of billions of dollars, were administered until 1965 by various subsidiaries of the *Housing and Home Finance Agency (HHFA)*. In 1965 this agency was replaced by the new Cabinet-level *Department of Housing and Urban Development*, which has charge of the various federal housing programs.

The Department's activities have included the following:

(1) Offering FHA insurance for mortgage loans on house construction.

(2) Assisting local communities to build low-rental public housing by approving projects and granting low-cost loans or outright subsidies to assure low rentals.

(3) Providing loans to colleges and universities for student and faculty housing.

(4) Providing loans and grants to state and local agencies to further housing for the elderly and to spur urban renewal projects.

(5) Enforcing nondiscriminatory practices in the rental and sale of most housing.

d. In Recent Years. During the Reagan administrations of the 1980's, appropriations for federal housing programs were cut by 80 percent. Rising interest rates and inflation pushed up the cost of housing. Home ownership dropped to 64 percent in 1990 from a high of 66 percent in 1980. The early 1990's saw interest rates go down and federal aid to housing remain low.

5. Observations Regarding Housing

a. From 1940 to 1970, according to census reports, America achieved considerable progress in housing. While the population increased 54 percent, from 132 million to 203 million, occupied housing units increased 82 percent, from 35 million to 64 million. Moreover, the number of substandard housing units decreased sharply: from 17 million, or 46 percent of all housing units, to 6 million, or 10 percent. Despite the overall progress, millions of Americans still lacked decent housing.

b. Federal housing programs designed to aid low-income families have proved disappointing. The Housing Act of 1949 set a goal of 810,000 new units of low-rent public housing within six years. Some 18 years later, in 1967, this goal had still not been achieved. Government efforts in eliminating some few slums have been offset by the influx of people crowding into and expanding other slums.

The problem of slum clearance has been complicated by several factors:

(1) Federal spending for slum clearance, currently averaging less than $1 billion a year, has proved inadequate. The cost of wiping out slums has been estimated as high as $100 billion over a 10-year period.

(2) Many people have become indifferent, if not opposed, to low-rent housing projects. Taxpayers resent the seemingly endless demands for government housing funds. Low-income families resent the barracks-like appearance and strict management of housing developments. Social reformers

have found that better housing, by itself, has failed to eradicate juvenile delinquency and crime among project tenants. These objections may help explain why New York State voters several times have defeated measures to extend the state's low-income public housing program.

DEMONSTRATION CITIES ACT

In 1966 Congress approved President Johnson's request for the *Demonstration Cities Act*. It provided funds, to be administered by the Department of Housing and Urban Development, to finance a new approach to the problems of reducing urban slums and helping their inhabitants.

1. Selected "demonstration" cities were to upgrade "run-down" neighborhoods by concerning themselves not only with slum housing but with the slum dweller himself. City planning agencies were to combine programs for new and rehabilitated low-cost housing with social welfare programs. The intent was to change the "total environment" of slum dwellers by improving such facilities and services as libraries, schools, hospitals, recreation centers, and police and fire protection. The planning agencies may draw upon federal funds provided by this act and related federal programs. They may also utilize state and city funds, and may enlist private capital.

2. Cities and their suburbs are encouraged to work together in planning public improvements such as new roads and sewerage systems. Local officials are encouraged to think not in terms of individual communities, but in terms of an entire metropolitan area.

In a 1969 report, a study group appointed by President Nixon endorsed the Model Cities approach for improving urban poverty areas but criticized federal agencies for overregulating and underfinancing the program.

In 1976 the program was phased out.

FAIR REPRESENTATION FOR CITIES: LEGISLATIVE REAPPORTIONMENT

1. **Background: Rural Overrepresentation.** From the late 19th century to the early 1960's, rural voters were overrepresented at the expense of urban voters in the federal House of Representatives and in almost all state legislatures. This disparity arose from the failure of state legislatures to reapportion seats as the population shifted from rural to urban and suburban areas. State legislators failed to reapportion because of inertia, disagreement on new election district boundaries, or deliberate intent to maintain rural control of the state legislature. As a result, in Tennessee, a rural district of 3500 people and an urban district of 78,000 people each elected one legislator.

For many years the Supreme Court held that reapportionment was not a matter to be judged by courts, but rather a political issue to be decided by Congress, state legislatures, and the people.

2. Recent Supreme Court Decisions: More Representation for Urban Areas

a. Baker vs. Carr (1962). The Supreme Court decided that federal courts may consider the constitutionality of state election districts. The Court further held that some districts may be so "arbitrary and capricious" as to violate the Fourteenth Amendment, which requires states to provide "equal protection of the laws."

b. Wesberry vs. Sanders (1964). The Supreme Court, by a 6-to-3 vote, decided that "as nearly as is practicable, one man's vote in a Congressional election is to be worth as much as another's." The majority of the Court held that the Constitution established the principle of equal representation in the House for equal numbers of people.

c. Reynolds vs. Sims (1964). The Supreme Court established the "one man, one vote" rule: that both houses of state legislatures must be apportioned on the basis of population. Chief Justice Earl Warren argued that unequal districts violated the "equal protection" clause of the Fourteenth Amendment.

3. Effects of the Decisions. Most states have acted to reapportion election districts on a more equitable basis. The result has been increased representa-

Flannery in The Baltimore Evening Sun

"It's not going to be easy giving up these seats."

Why were state legislatures for so long under rural domination? What has been the effect of the Supreme Court's "one man, one vote" rule?

tion for cities and suburbs in both houses of state legislatures and in the federal House of Representatives. City officials hope that this change will mean greater attention by legislatures to urban problems.

POVERTY AMONG RURAL AND URBAN PEOPLES

PROBLEMS OF POVERTY

1. Extent of Poverty. In 1960, despite post-World War II affluence, 35 million Americans—20 percent of the total population—lived in poverty. They struggled to secure the necessities of life with family incomes of less than $3,000 a year. In 1995 it took a yearly income of over $15,000 for a family of four to stay above the poverty line. By then, 38 million Americans were poor, but they represented a smaller proportion—14.5 percent—of the population.

2. Causes of Poverty

a. Lack of Training. Millions of Americans have never received vocational or professional training. Filling only low-skill or no-skill jobs, they receive little pay and face frequent unemployment.

b. Worn-Out Farms. Many small farmers, working a few acres of exhausted land, eke out a difficult living. They lack the capital to acquire sizable fertile lands and to buy expensive machines. They live in areas that do not afford adequate health and educational facilities. A number of rural poor have abandoned their farms and moved to the cities, but, lacking education and skills, they remain impoverished.

c. Old Age. With medical science prolonging life, the number of aged has steadily increased. Unable to find work, many old persons find their incomes reduced to the poverty level.

d. Death or Desertion of the Father. Many families are plunged into poverty when the father dies or deserts his family. The mother, lacking job skills and burdened by young children, is unable to support a family by herself.

e. Discrimination. Minority groups, including Puerto Ricans, Mexicans, and blacks, have suffered discrimination in education, housing, and jobs. They suffer poverty both because of discrimination in hiring and because of their lack of skills.

Children of impoverished families are often born into an environment of despair and hopelessness, and do not receive the training necessary to rise out of poverty. From generation to generation, they remain chained to a *cycle of poverty.*

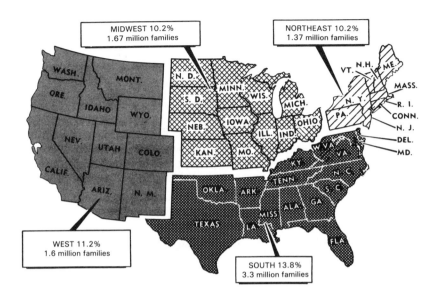

MIDWEST 10.2%
1.67 million families

NORTHEAST 10.2%
1.37 million families

WEST 11.2%
1.6 million families

SOUTH 13.8%
3.3 million families

Poverty in the United States by Region

The U.S. Census Bureau places the poverty level for an urban (nonfarm) family of four at an income of less than $15,000 per year. Boxes show the percentage of population and number of families in each region living below the poverty level.

3. "Pockets of Poverty"

a. Appalachia. In this mountainous area extending from Pennsylvania to Alabama, many coal miners lost their jobs when coal mines were worked out and when the coal industry adopted automatic mining equipment. In addition, many subsistence farmers were fighting a losing battle with the poor soil.

b. New England Textile Towns. Textile workers lost their jobs when many established companies moved to the South, where wages were lower, or to Puerto Rico, where the companies received tax benefits. Other textile mills closed their doors because they were unable to withstand competition from newer domestic and foreign plants.

c. Indian Reservations. American Indians living on government reservations generally have poor land and few vocational skills. In 1966 a Senate committee concluded that "Indians remain at the bottom of the economic ladder" and suffer "chronic poverty."

d. Big-City Slums. Many blacks, Puerto Ricans, Mexican-Americans, and members of other minorities are trapped in slums by poverty and discrimination. Black ghettos include *Harlem* and *Bedford-Stuyvesant* in New York City, *Roxbury* in Boston, and *Watts* in Los Angeles. (For more on slums, see pages 349–352.)

4. Costs of Poverty. *(a)* Poverty-stricken areas have high rates of crime, disease, suicide, and drug addiction. *(b)* Communities must spend heavily on welfare assistance, public health services, and police and fire protection for the poor. Since poor people's earnings are small, they tend to be "taxeaters." *(c)* Poverty-stricken areas do not contribute proportionately to the nation's production of goods and services. *(d)* Impoverished Americans may find little reason to support an "American way of life" that has shut them out.

ANTI-POVERTY MEASURES OF THE KENNEDY ADMINISTRATION (1961–1963)

President Kennedy secured legislation chiefly to train job-seeking youths and retrain jobless workers. (1) The *Area Redevelopment Act* (1961) provided funds to attract industries to depressed areas and retrain chronically unemployed workers in these areas. (2) The *Manpower Development and Training Act* (1962) expanded the retraining program to jobless workers outside of depressed areas. Later amendments offered training to illiterates and school dropouts. (3) The *Vocational Education Act* (1963) provided funds to states and communities to expand vocational education, especially for unemployed and underprivileged youths.

PRESIDENT JOHNSON AND THE "WAR ON POVERTY" (1964–1969)

As part of his *Great Society,* President Johnson moved to arouse the national conscience by declaring "unconditional war on poverty." In response, Congress passed the *Economic Opportunity Act* (1964), authorizing anti-poverty programs and creating the *Office of Economic Opportunity (OEO).*

1. OEO Programs. *(a)* The *Job Corps* enlisted youths who were out of school and unemployed, and gave them remedial education and job training at special camps. *(b)* The *Neighborhood Youth Corps* provided underprivileged youths with summer and part-time community jobs, as in libraries and parks. *(c) VISTA (Volunteers In Service To America),* also known as the *domestic Peace Corps,* supplied volunteers to counsel, train, and, in various

ENGELHARDT
Engelhardt in The St. Louis Post-Dispatch

"A hand is better than a hand-out, right?"

other ways, assist impoverished Americans. (*d*) **Community Action Programs** undertook local projects with federal funds to provide health services, legal services, job training, and work for needy persons. (*e*) **Project Head Start** provided training to help disadvantaged pre-school children so that they could succeed in their schooling. (*f*) **Operation Upward Bound** offered a remedial study program to youths who came from poor families and did not have a good high school record, but who seemed to have the potential for attending college. (*g*) The **College Work Study** program provided part-time jobs to enable needy students to remain in college.

    2. Other Anti-Poverty Laws. The *Appalachian Redevelopment Act* provided funds for aid to Appalachia: road-building, land improvement, and the construction of health centers. The *Regional Development Act* provided funds for similar aid to other depressed areas.

    3. Debate Over the "War on Poverty." Critics condemned the Office of Economic Opportunity for squandering government funds, encouraging boondoggling (valueless work), permitting graft and corruption, providing political patronage, and tolerating administrative mismanagement. Sargent Shriver, first OEO Director, conceded mistakes—the result of starting "too much, too fast, getting too many people excited." Supporters, however, insisted that the "war on poverty" awakened the nation to realize the problem and was directly and indirectly helping millions of impoverished Americans.

RECENT POVERTY DEVELOPMENTS AND DATA

1. President Nixon in 1973 acted to dismantle the Office of Economic Opportunity. Citing the need to improve efficiency and avoid duplication of services, he transferred most OEO activities to other federal agencies. For example, the Job Corps was moved to the Labor Department and Head Start to Health, Education, and Welfare. President Ford in 1975 established the *Community Services Administration (CSA)* to replace the OEO. President Reagan in 1981 abolished the CSA as Congress voted reduced funds for the states to continue various community services.

2. President Nixon secured from Congress the 1973 *Comprehensive Employment and Training Act (CETA)*. It authorized federal grants to local and state agencies to operate their own manpower programs. Under the Reagan administration, CETA's activities were sharply reduced by budget cuts and in 1982 CETA was permitted to expire. It was replaced by the less expensive *Job Training Partnership Act* that called for the annual training of 1 million persons—mainly unskilled youths and unemployed workers—but did not offer any public works employment.

3. Cutbacks in government spending and changes in society during the 1980's widened the gap between rich and poor. Social changes included a rise in the number of single-parent families, an increase in the number of jobs paying minimum wages or below, and the entry of more women into the work force.

The table below divides the American people into five equal groups based on income. Each group represents one-fifth of the population. The table shows the percentage change in income (adjusted to take inflation and family size into account) for each of those groups between 1979 and 1987. Income includes government assistance such as welfare payments, food stamps, and old-age insurance.

Poorest people	−9.8%
Next poorest people	−0.5%
Middle group	+5.2%
Next to wealthiest	+9.3%
Wealthiest	+15.6%

MULTIPLE-CHOICE QUESTIONS

1. At the present time, the population of the United States is (1) stationary (2) declining (3) increasing at a lower rate than in the 19th century (4) increasing at a higher rate than in the 19th century.

2. In 1990 the population of the United States reached about (1) 60,000,000 (2) 75,000,000 (3) 160,000,000 (4) 250,000,000.

3. According to the 1990 census, which area showed the most rapid rate of population growth? (1) Sun Belt (2) Middle West (3) Northeast (4) Middle Atlantic.

4. The most densely populated area in the United States is the (1) South (2) Far West (3) Rocky Mountain region (4) Northeast.

5. Of the following, the *least* densely populated country is (1) Australia (2) England (3) Japan (4) the United States.

6. Which is true of population trends in the United States? (1) The closing of the frontier marked an end of major population shifts. (2) The population of the United States is characterized by immobility. (3) Population shifts have political effects. (4) Economic development has had little effect on population trends.

7. The percentage of people over 65 in the United States has doubled since 1900. This is largely due to (1) an increase in immigration (2) improvements in medical science (3) the adoption of Social Security (4) more homes for the aged.

8. The purpose of Social Security is to (1) provide cheap life insurance (2) curtail employers' profits (3) help relieve workers of the fear of destitution (4) provide more business for the big insurance companies.

9. A group *not* protected by Social Security is (1) workers in interstate industries (2) white-collar workers (3) workers in the building industries (4) federal employees hired before 1984.

10. Over the years, the Social Security tax has (1) gone up (2) gone down (3) been paid entirely by the employer (4) remained fixed at the present level.

11. A period of inflation would probably have the most unfavorable effect on (1) the owner of a small business (2) a person living on a pension (3) an industrial laborer (4) a common stockholder in a corporation.

12. Which of the following statements regarding Medicare is *not* correct? (1) It was first officially proposed by President Truman. (2) It was supported by the American Medical Association. (3) It is financed through Social Security taxes. (4) It provides plans for paying hospital costs as well as doctor bills.

13. At present the majority of the people in the United States live in (1) cities with a population of over 1,000,000 (2) suburbs with a population of over 100,000 (3) communities with a population of 2500 or more (4) rural areas.

14. Jane Addams is well known for (1) writing *The Shame of the Cities* (2) devising the commission type of city government (3) establishing a settlement house in Chicago (4) founding Oberlin College.

15. Jacob Riis was chiefly interested in advancing (1) slum clearance (2) old age insurance (3) urban mass transportation (4) civil rights for minority groups.

16. The term "home rule" deals with the relationship of (1) cities to suburbs (2) cities to state governments (3) cities to the federal government (4) states to the federal government.

17. Which is an important result of the movement of people from the cities to the suburbs? (1) an increase in the proportion of low-income families in the cities (2) a decline in the urban crime rate (3) a decline in urban renewal and planning (4) a decline in the cost of public transportation in the cities.

18. City governments do *not* deal with the problem of (1) tariffs (2) fire protection (3) sanitation (4) education.

19. The agency placed in charge of directing President Johnson's "war on poverty" was (1) the Job Corps (2) Project Head Start (3) the Office of Economic Opportunity (4) Operation Upward Bound.

20. The federal government has sponsored programs of public housing because (1) the Constitution prohibits states from enacting housing laws (2) there is a surplus in the Treasury (3) there is a need to provide adequate housing for low-income groups (4) private builders have urged public housing projects.

21. The Federal Housing Authority has encouraged private investors in housing by guaranteeing (1) profit to the builder (2) a buyer for the property (3) the repayment of mortgage loans (4) rent controls.

22. Which principle was involved in the Supreme Court decision on reapportionment in *Baker vs. Carr?* (1) separation of church and state (2) separation of powers (3) "separate but equal" (4) equal protection of the laws.

23. The Supreme Court decision on reapportionment in *Reynolds vs. Sims* has helped bring about (1) a shift in political power from rural to urban areas (2) an increase in Republican strength in state legislatures (3) better representation of farm interests in state legislatures (4) an increased representation in Congress for states with growing populations.

24. In 1960 what percent of our total population was considered impoverished? (1) 5 percent (2) 10 percent (3) 20 percent (4) 40 percent.

25. Which area probably contains the *smallest* percentage of impoverished families? (1) an Indian reservation in New Mexico (2) a ghetto in Los Angeles (3) a textile town in Massachusetts (4) a suburb of Detroit.

ESSAY QUESTIONS

1. An important population shift in the United States during the 20th century has been from rural to urban or suburban areas. (*a*) Explain briefly *two* reasons for this shift in population. (*b*) Discuss *three* problems facing cities as a result of this shift.

2. (*a*) Show how slums are costly to (1) slum inhabitants, (2) the community, (3) the nation. (*b*) Give *one* argument for *and* one argument against government slum-clearance projects.

3. (*a*) Discuss *two* reasons why the percentage of persons over 65 in our population has more than doubled since 1900. (*b*) State *two* problems that face our senior citizens. (*c*) For *each* problem stated, discuss *one* effort that can be made either by the individual or by the government to provide a solution.

4. (*a*) Explain *one* argument for *and* one argument against Medicare under Social Security. (*b*) Describe *two* kinds of protection received by persons over 65 from Medicare.

5. The housing problem in American cities has two aspects: insufficient housing and inadequate housing. (*a*) Explain *each* of these aspects of the housing problem. (*b*) Show how *each* of the following either helped or hindered the solution of the housing problem: (1) tenement laws, (2) World War II, (3) private builders, (4) Federal Housing Administration (FHA), (5) Negro migration into Northern cities.

6. President Johnson has proclaimed an "unconditional war on poverty." (*a*) Discuss *three* factors that have kept many American families living in poverty. (*b*) Describe *three* programs sponsored by the federal government to break the "cycle of poverty." (*c*) Do you think that poverty can be completely eliminated? Give *two* arguments to defend your answer.

Part 4. The American People Create a Rich and Varied Culture

EDUCATION

DEVELOPMENT OF THE FREE PUBLIC SCHOOL: ELEMENTARY AND SECONDARY EDUCATION

1. In the Young Nation (1789–1829). Most early American leaders, including Washington and Jefferson, believed that the success of the American republic depended upon an educated citizenry. Nevertheless, education was left largely to towns and to religious and other private groups. Children of well-to-do families that could afford to pay the tuition fees went to private schools. Some children of poorer families attended religious schools or, especially in New England, public primary schools maintained by towns. The majority of American children, however, attended no school at all.

2. From the Jacksonian Era to the Civil War (1829–1860). The spirit of Jacksonian democracy brought with it an educational awakening. The average citizen, having received the right to vote, demanded free, tax-supported public schools. City workingmen, in particular, favored this movement, since it would (a) provide free education for their children, and (b) take children out of the labor market. By 1860, despite some opposition, the free public elementary school had become prevalent, especially in the North. Two leaders in this educational awakening were Horace Mann and Henry Barnard.

Horace Mann was selected in 1837 to be the secretary of the newly founded Massachusetts Board of Education. Serving in this office for 11 years, Mann (a) aroused the public to the need for free, tax-supported schools, (b) raised professional standards by establishing the first state-supported teacher-training school, and (c) introduced compulsory attendance, less rigid discipline, and a more varied curriculum. Horace Mann is known as the "father of the American public school."

Henry Barnard greatly improved the public school systems in Connecticut and Rhode Island. In 1867 he was appointed the first United States Commissioner of Education.

3. From the Civil War to the Present. In the last hundred years, educators and political leaders have greatly expanded free public school systems by (a) providing elementary schools throughout the nation, (b) developing public high schools and gradually raising the age for compulsory education to 16, and, in a few states, to 17 or 18 (whereas in 1900 only 11 percent of youths 14 to 17 years old attended high school, today the comparable figure is 93 percent), (c) equipping schools with facilities such as libraries, science laboratories, museums, gymnasiums, vocational shops, and homemaking and business-machine rooms, and (d) enlarging the scope of the high school to include—in addition to the traditional preparation for college—training for citizenship, for the use of leisure time, and for gainful employment.

BRIEF SURVEY OF HIGHER EDUCATION

1. **To the Civil War.** Before 1860 various religious groups founded about 200 colleges. Originally, these schools prepared students for the ministry and taught Latin, Greek, grammar, and philosophy. Later, as they began preparing students for other vocations, they expanded their courses of study. Also, a few states, such as Georgia and Virginia in the South, Vermont in New England, and Michigan in the Midwest, founded state universities, which offered courses in the liberal arts and in various professional subjects.

2. **Developments to the Present.** Since 1860 American colleges and universities have grown in number and broadened their scope. (a) The *Morrill Act* (1862) granted federal lands to states to support colleges teaching agriculture and the mechanical arts. This act helped increase the number of state colleges and universities. Furthermore, it stimulated the movement toward more practical subjects such as agricultural science, veterinary medicine, and engineering. Among the well-known land-grant colleges today are the state universities of Wisconsin, Illinois, Texas, and California. The University of California, which has campuses throughout the state and enrolls over 120,000 full-time students, is one of the largest institutions of higher learning in the world. (b) *Technical schools*, usually privately endowed, were founded and have maintained high standards in training chemists, physicists, architects, and engineers. One example is the Massachusetts Institute of Technology. (c) *Charles Eliot*, President of Harvard, permitted students considerable freedom in selecting their courses of study, thereby originating the *elective system*. (d) *Daniel Gilman*, President of Johns Hopkins University, established a graduate school, where students pursuing advanced studies concentrated on research. At Johns Hopkins, Gilman also helped found the most advanced medical school of his time.

3. **Higher Education Today.** The United States today contains over 2000 colleges and universities. They may be classified as follows: (a) Slightly more than one-third are church-controlled institutions, mostly Protestant and Roman Catholic. (b) Slightly less than one-third are privately controlled. (c) One-third are publicly controlled—by states, cities, or school districts. Among the largest is the State University of New York, consisting of a number of colleges throughout the state with a total enrollment of over 340,000.

American colleges and universities may also be classified according to their programs: (a) Slightly more than two-thirds offer a four-year course, and many of these institutions offer graduate work. (b) Slightly less than one-third are community, or junior, colleges. These schools, which grew rapidly after World War II, offer a two-year course, enabling students to prepare for a technical career or to transfer to a four-year college.

The number of students in today's colleges and universities totals about 11 million. Whereas in 1900 only 4 percent of youths 18 to 21 years old were enrolled in college, today the comparable figure is about 48 percent.

RECENT EDUCATIONAL PROBLEMS

1. **Integration.** See pages 318–323.

2. **Adult Education.** More and more adults have gone to school in recent years. Adults take courses to earn high school diplomas, improve their written and spoken English, learn new vocational skills, and earn college diplomas and advanced degrees. Colleges and universities, in particular, have welcomed "nontraditional students" as a valuable addition to the educational scene.

3. **The Soviet Challenge.** Americans were startled by the Soviet Union's early leadership in the space race when, in 1957, the Soviets launched the world's first artificial satellite, *Sputnik I*. Americans asked: Is something wrong with our educational system? Why aren't we producing more scientists, engineers, and technicians? In response, Congress passed the *National Defense Education Act of 1958*. The act provided (a) grants to states for the purchase of materials to strengthen the teaching of science, mathematics, and foreign languages, (b) grants to states for programs to locate and encourage gifted students, (c) loans and graduate fellowships for college students, especially for those interested in teaching. The act was later expanded to include grants for the purchase of instructional materials for English and history.

4. **The Japanese Challenge.** During the 1970's and 1980's, Americans began to cast worried glances across the Pacific, as Japan's bustling economy became a major competitor on the world stage. Observers cited studies showing that Japanese inventors were pulling ahead of American inventors in such fields as electronics, biotechnology, and automotive design. Noting the rigorous standards and challenging tests that are central to Japanese education, Americans asked: Are our schools too easy? Will Americans lose out to a rising generation of Japanese inventors and managers? Will Japan control the technology of the 21st century? Some wanted to make American schools more like Japanese schools, with (a) longer school weeks, (b) harder tests, and (c) more homework. Others said Japan's system is a product of a society that is very different from our own, and that copying it would be a mistake. Critics argued that Japanese schools suffered from such problems as (a) regimentation, (b) an emphasis on rote memorization, and (c) a squelching of the individual creativity needed to blaze new trails in science, technology, and human relations.

Partly in response to the Japanese challenge, American schools (a) began to experiment with year-round classes, (b) boosted salaries to attract the most talented teachers, and (c) put increased stress on homework and basic subjects such as reading, writing, history, geography, and mathematics.

5. Availability of College Facilities. After 1945, college attendance increased as (a) several G.I. Bills of Rights offered financial assistance for veterans to go to college, (b) more people became aware of how a college degree could boost their future earnings, and (c) a rising birth rate enlarged the college-age population. Colleges expanded rapidly, often with federal help.

By the end of the 1980's, "boom babies" had finished college and enrollments grew more slowly or declined. Colleges also faced decreasing federal aid as the Reagan administration curtailed funds for constructing college facilities and providing loans and grants to students.

6. The Supply of Teachers. From the 1940's to 1970, teachers were in short supply, due to rapidly expanding enrollments, poor working conditions, and low salaries. Then, for a time in the 1970's, the supply of teachers exceeded the demand, although mathematics and science teachers were still in short supply. Experts predicted that more teacher shortages might develop in the 1990's. That might mean more rapid increases in teacher salaries to attract qualified people away from jobs in industry.

7. Finances for Elementary and Secondary Schools

a. State and Local Support. Public education has been financed mainly by state and local taxes. In the mid-1990's, the average annual expenditure for public education was nearly $5,500 per pupil. This average figure, however, had wide variations from state to state. Relatively wealthy states spent considerably more than other states. Alaska, New York, and Connecticut spent more than $8,000 per pupil. The poorer Southern states of Alabama and Mississippi each spent under $4,000, and Utah spent closer to $3,000.

b. Debate Over Federal Aid
(1) *Supporters.* Many educators and political leaders urged that federal funds be used for the overall improvement of public education. They argued that federal funds are necessary to bring education in the poorer states up to the national level.

(2) *Opponents.* Advocates of states' rights feared that federal aid might lead to federal control of education, thereby further reducing the powers of the states. (Roman Catholic leaders opposed any federal program that omitted funds for parochial schools. They rejected the argument that the First Amendment to the Constitution, separating church and state, prohibited government grants to church-controlled schools.)

c. Elementary and Secondary Education Act (1965). By gearing federal education aid to the "war on poverty," President Lyndon Johnson gained quick Congressional passage of this law. It provided (1) a program of grants to the nation's public school districts based on their number of children from impoverished families, (2) a program of grants to states for the purchase of textbooks, library books, and audiovisual aids to be used by public, private and parochial school students, and (3) a program of grants to create public education centers for special instruction on a "shared-time" basis for public, private, and parochial school students.

This act (1) satisfied Roman Catholic leaders by providing instructional materials and educational centers for parochial students, (2) satisfied advocates

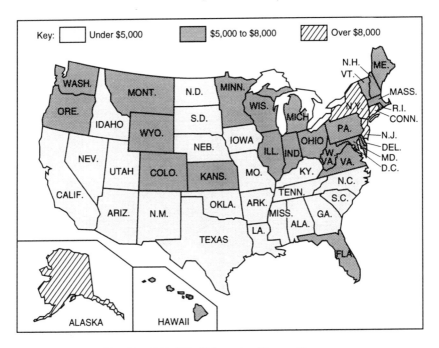

Per Pupil Public Education Expenditure

of separation of church and state by giving public officials control of the shared resources and by granting aid to parochial students rather than to parochial schools, and (3) established a precedent of direct federal aid for overall improvement of the public schools. (This act continues to be funded by renewed federal appropriations.)

8. **Court Decisions Affecting Educational Finances.** (*a*) In *Robinson vs. Dicenso* (1971) the Supreme Court declared unconstitutional the Rhode Island

law that provided state funds to help pay salaries of parochial school teachers of nonreligious subjects. The Court held that such a law violated the First Amendment by requiring the state to keep parochial schools under surveillance, thereby causing "excessive entanglement." (b) In 1971 several lower courts held unconstitutional the reliance upon local property taxes for financing public education. Within a state, poor districts obtained much less money

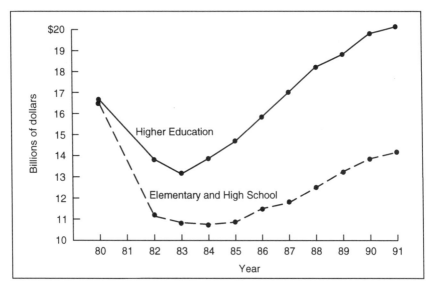

Federal Spending for Education

per child for education than did rich districts. In *Rodriguez vs. San Antonio School District* (1973) the Supreme Court upheld the property tax as a method of financing public school systems. (c) One response to complaints of unequal financing was for states to assume more of the burden. For the first time, states passed local districts as the main source of educational funding in 1979. In the late 1980's and early 1990's, a number of state courts struck down school financing systems on grounds that they violated state constitutions.

9. **Recent Criticisms of American Education.** In 1983 there were a number of reports on American education—all critical. Typical was the report of the bipartisan federal *National Commission on Excellence in Education.* It warned that our nation was threatened by a "rising tide of mediocrity" in education. It proposed the following reforms: (a) Set higher standards in basic subjects—both for high school study and college admission. (b) Require more time in school by extending the school day and school year. (c) Assign "far more homework" to high school students. (d) Increase salaries for teachers. (Other reports urged merit pay increases for superior teachers.) (e) Offer financial

THE AMERICAN PEOPLE

incentives to attract "outstanding students" into teaching. The commission warned that "excellence costs, but in the long run mediocrity costs far more."

10. Other Educational Issues:

(a) Should the Cabinet-level Department of Education be abolished and some of its functions transferred to other federal agencies?

(b) Should federal education funds be given as block grants without federal regulations so as to permit greater educational decision-making by the states and localities?

(c) Should the federal government grant tuition tax credits to parents that they could use to pay for their children's education in either private or public schools?

(d) Does the Supreme Court decision in *Lau vs. Nichols* (1974)—ordering the public schools to take extra steps to educate students who lack an adequate understanding of English—require that these students be given a bilingual education (in their native tongue and English) or an intensive course in English as a second language?

(e) Should prayer be permitted in the public schools? If yes, what steps might overturn the Supreme Court decision in *Engel vs. Vitale* (1962) holding unconstitutional a nondenominational public school prayer?

SOCIAL REFORM

HUMANITARIANISM: MEANING AND AMERICAN ORIGINS

Humanitarians feel deep concern and seek to improve the welfare of the unfortunate. The earliest humanitarian movements in the United States arose amidst the democratic atmosphere and industrial growth of the Jacksonian Era. (1) Since democracy teaches respect for the life of each individual, it encouraged Americans to concern themselves with helping unfortunates. (2) The early Industrial Revolution called attention to unfortunates, as it accentuated certain evils such as slums, poor working conditions, and child labor. (3) By creating wealth, the Industrial Revolution provided humanitarians with money and time to combat social injustices.

MOVEMENTS FOR HUMANITARIANISM AND SOCIAL REFORM

1. **Improved Treatment of the Insane and Criminals.** In the 1840's *Dorothea Dix* worked to secure better treatment of the insane, improve conditions in prisons, and abolish imprisonment for debt. In her day the insane were treated as criminals. Prisons were filthy, and prisoners were often treated cruelly. Today special hospitals treat the insane as mentally sick persons. Prisons provide criminals with training to help prepare them for earning an honest livelihood. Imprisonment for debt has been ended.

In 1971 revolts by inmates in various prisons, notably at *Attica*, New York, indicated that the prisoners were greatly dissatisfied with conditions and far from society's desired goals of their reform and rehabilitation.

2. Care for Sick and Wounded Soldiers. *Clara Barton* aided Civil War soldiers by providing medical and nursing care. In 1881 she organized and for many years headed the *American Red Cross*. Today the American Red Cross serves not only war casualties but also peacetime disaster victims.

3. Care for the Physically Handicapped. Many private charitable organizations collect funds to help the physically handicapped: the ill, the blind, and the crippled. The federal government and the states provide funds for state-administered programs to help these unfortunate persons.

4. Prohibition of Intoxicating Beverages. Beginning in the early 19th century, many Americans urged prohibition of alcohol to protect the home against drunkenness and to prevent workmen from squandering their wages at the corner saloon. In 1851 *Neal Dow* secured prohibition in Maine, and this example was followed by several other states. In 1874 *Frances Willard* helped found the nationwide *Woman's Christian Temperance Union* (*WCTU*). Another prohibition group was the *Anti-Saloon League*.

During World War I, when grain used in making liquor was needed for food, Congress proposed the *Eighteenth Amendment* prohibiting the manufacture and sale of intoxicating beverages. Overwhelmingly adopted, this amendment was hailed in 1928 by Herbert Hoover as a "great social and economic experiment, noble in motive." Nevertheless, it was defied by the public, opened a profitable field for bootleggers and gangsters, and led to general disrespect for the law. In 1933 the Eighteenth Amendment was repealed by the *Twenty-first Amendment*. Today, all states have ended prohibition but exercise supervision over the sale of intoxicating beverages.

5. Women's Rights

a. To the Mid-19th Century: Status Inferior to Men. In the early years of our nation, women were (1) denied the right to vote and otherwise participate in political affairs, (2) hindered in educational pursuits, especially on the higher level, (3) denied equal opportunity in business and the professions, and (4) legally limited in the right to own property.

b. Struggle for Suffrage. (1) *Leading Suffragettes. Susan B. Anthony,* the leader of the movement to give women the vote, wrote, lectured, and organized supporters. She was ably assisted by other feminists, including *Lucy Stone, Lucretia Mott,* and *Elizabeth Cady Stanton.* (Most suffragettes also supported temperance, abolition of slavery, and other social reforms.)

(2) *Major Events.* In 1848 the *Women's Rights Convention*, at Seneca Falls, New York, drafted a declaration stating that "all men and women are cre-

ated equal." In 1869 the Territory of Wyoming granted the vote to women. By 1900 four states permitted women to vote. In 1920, recognizing women's efforts in World War I, the states ratified the *Nineteenth (Susan B. Anthony) Amendment* guaranteeing women suffrage. (3) *Notable Women in Political Life. Frances Perkins*, Secretary of Labor under President Franklin D. Roosevelt, was the first woman Cabinet member. *Eleanor Roosevelt*, wife of Franklin D. Roosevelt, helped promote laws to benefit underprivileged groups. She also served as first chairman of the United Nations Human Rights Commission. *Margaret Chase Smith* of Maine was a respected member of the United States Senate.

   c. Higher Education for Women. In 1821 *Emma Willard* provided higher education for women by opening the Troy Female Seminary. In the 1830's *Oberlin College* in Ohio became the first coeducational college. In 1837 *Mary Lyon* founded a women's college, *Mount Holyoke*, in Massachusetts. Today women may enroll in most colleges and universities.

   d. Other Aspects of the Women's Rights Movement. In most states women have achieved legal gains, especially the right to own property and, in case of divorce, to retain custody of children. Women are gaining acceptance in business and in the professions.

   e. Women's Liberation Movement. In recent years militant feminists have led the struggle for women's rights. *Betty Friedan* founded the *National Organization for Women (NOW)*. *Gloria Steinem* presented the women's viewpoint in a new magazine, *Ms.* "Women's Lib" demanded that women be treated equally with men as to jobs, wages, child care, housework, and higher education.

   f. Changing Laws. Congress passed a number of laws in the 1960's and 1970's expanding women's rights: (1) The Civil Rights Act of 1964 banned job discrimination against women. (2) The Fair Housing Act of 1974 barred sexual discrimination in the sale or rental of housing. (3) The Depository Act of 1974 and the Equal Credit Opportunity Act of 1975 sought to make it easier for women to secure credit. (4) A 1976 law provided for equal opportunity for women in school and college activities such as sports. Court decisions also expanded women's rights.

   In 1972 Congress proposed an Equal Rights Amendment (ERA) stating that "equality of rights under the law" shall not be denied on account of sex. Supporters argued that this amendment would assure women full equality with men. Opponents feared that this amendment would subject women to the draft, deny them preference in child-custody cases, and ban laws prohibiting women from working in hazardous occupations. The ERA died when only 35 of the necessary 38 states had ratified the amendment by a 1982 deadline.

   6. Philanthropy. Philanthropists are persons of great wealth who donate large sums of money to promote the welfare of society. Notable philanthropists include: ***Peter Cooper,*** an inventor and a leader in the iron industry, promoted the arts and encouraged scientific training by founding *Cooper Union,* a school and cultural center in New York City. *Andrew Carnegie,* steel magnate, provided free public libraries and established the *Carnegie Endowment for International Peace.* He also built the *Hague* (Holland) *Peace Palace,* which today houses the International Court of Justice. *John D. Rockefeller,* oil millionaire, endowed the *University of Chicago.* Through the *Rockefeller Foundation,* he provided grants to other colleges and universities and encouraged research programs in the social sciences and humanities. He also founded an institute for medical research, now called *Rockefeller University. Andrew W. Mellon,* banker and aluminum manufacturer, gave funds for establishing the *National Gallery of Art* in Washington, D.C. *Henry Ford,* automobile manufacturer, established the *Ford Foundation.* It grants funds to universities, medical schools, and hospitals and finances studies of such problems as civil liberties and international peace.

7. Other Social Movements. Discussed throughout the book are other humanitarian and social reforms: abolition of slavery, settlement houses in slums, free public schools, low-cost public housing, and Social Security.

SCIENCE

OBSERVATIONS ON SCIENCE IN AMERICA

1. American scientists have emphasized practical rather than pure science. *Pure* or *basic scientists* seek knowledge for its own sake. *Practical* or *applied scientists* are chiefly concerned with inventing new machines and developing new products. Because science and industry are interdependent, many American corporations spend large sums on research laboratories.

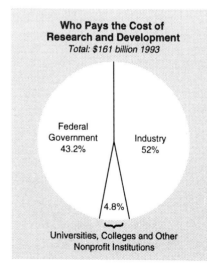

Who Pays the Cost of Research and Development
Total: $161 billion 1993

Federal Government 43.2%

Industry 52%

4.8%

Universities, Colleges and Other Nonprofit Institutions

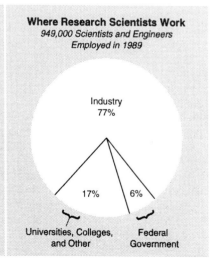

Where Research Scientists Work
949,000 Scientists and Engineers Employed in 1989

Industry 77%

17%   6%

Universities, Colleges, and Other   Federal Government

2. American science knows no boundaries of race, religion, or nationality. For example, to produce an atomic bomb during World War II, the United States mobilized scientists from all over the world: Albert Einstein, a refugee from Nazi Germany; Edward Teller, from pro-Nazi Hungary; Enrico Fermi, from Fascist Italy; and Niels Bohr, from Nazi-occupied Denmark; as well as native-born Americans, such as J. Robert Oppenheimer and Harold C. Urey.

AMERICAN SCIENTISTS

MEDICAL SCIENTISTS	CONTRIBUTIONS
Virginia Apgar	Devised Apgar Test to judge infants' health.
William Morton	Use of ether as an anesthetic during surgery.
Walter Reed	Discovery of mosquito as carrier of yellow fever.
Helen Brooke Taussig	Developed operation to cure "blue-baby" condition.
Selman Waksman	Antibiotic "wonder drug" streptomycin.
Alice Hamilton	Pioneer in industrial toxicology.
Jonas Salk	First polio vaccine, given by injection.
Albert Sabin	Second polio vaccine, taken by mouth.
Rosalyn S. Yalow	Nobel Prize (1977) for hormone research.

ATOMIC SCIENTISTS	CONTRIBUTIONS
Albert Einstein	Theory of relativity, including the formula $E = mc^2$ (tremendous energy from small amount of matter); advised President Roosevelt in 1939 to build atom bomb.
Harold C. Urey	Discovery of "heavy" hydrogen for nuclear research.
Ernest O. Lawrence	Cyclotron, a machine for studying the atom.
Enrico Fermi	First nuclear chain reaction (Chicago, 1942).
Leona M. Libby	Work on Manhattan Project to build first nuclear reactor.
J. Robert Oppenheimer	Head of Los Alamos group of men who built first atom bomb.
Edward Teller	Research leading to hydrogen bomb.
Glenn T. Seaborg	New chemical elements and radioactive isotopes.
Maria Goeppert-Mayer	Nobel Prize (1963) for analyzing the structure of atomic nuclei.

OTHER SCIENTISTS	CONTRIBUTIONS
John J. Audubon	Detailed paintings printed as *The Birds of America*.
Asa Gray	Study of plants in North America.
Louis Agassiz	Study of glaciers, fossils, and fishes.
Maria Mitchell	Discovery of comet (1847), later named for her.
Luther Burbank	New and improved varieties of plants by crossbreeding.
Albert Michelson	Accurate measurement of speed of light.
Robert H. Goddard	First liquid-fuel rocket (1926)—later used for space exploration.
Wallace Carothers	Nylon, developed in DuPont Company laboratories.

LITERATURE AND THE ARTS

OBSERVATIONS ON LITERATURE AND THE ARTS IN AMERICA

1. The history of American culture goes back to colonial times. As many colonists acquired wealth, they became interested in the arts. Theatrical performances and concerts took place in leading cities. A few American painters received recognition in England as well as in America. The leading writers turned out some excellent political and religious writing.

2. The 19th century produced the first significant American fiction and poetry. Writers dealt with our past, current issues, and broad philosophical questions. Painters portrayed famous Americans and scenes of everyday life.

3. In the 20th century, American writers sought to explore human motivation and to understand individuals in their complex societies. Painters experimented with new forms, notably abstract art. Composers produced traditional classical works and tried new forms, such as electronic music. Other composers developed the musical comedy into a major American art form.

4. Since World War II, more and more Americans have gained access to literature and the arts, a development called the *cultural explosion*. Television producers presented fine documentaries, dramas, concerts, and educational programs. Publishers expanded the market for books by producing less expensive paperbacks. Municipal leaders, using public and private funds, helped build new museums and cultural centers. Since 1965 Congress has encouraged culture through the federally funded *National Endowment for the Arts*. The endowment stirred controversy in the late 1980's when some members of Congress complained that it had supported exhibitions of "obscene and indecent art." Some said the government should not subsidize art that the public might find offensive. Others said the government had no right to censor art.

AMERICAN WRITERS: COLONIAL PERIOD

Cotton Mather and Jonathan Edwards, New England clergymen, wrote on religious themes. Benjamin Franklin praised hard work, thrift, and sound judgment in his *Poor Richard's Almanac* and in his *Autobiography*. In political affairs, Thomas Paine urged independence in his pamphlet *Common Sense;* Thomas Jefferson wrote the *Declaration of Independence;* Alexander Hamilton, James Madison, and John Jay defended the federal Constitution in essays published together as *The Federalist*.

AMERICAN WRITERS: 19TH CENTURY

WRITERS	TYPICAL WORKS
Washington Irving	*The Legend of Sleepy Hollow* and *Rip Van Winkle,* stories based on folklore of the Hudson River valley.
James Fenimore Cooper	*The Last of the Mohicans* and *The Deerslayer,* adventure novels of frontiersmen and Indians.
Harriet Beecher Stowe	*Uncle Tom's Cabin,* novel about the plight of slaves.
William H. Prescott	*History of the Conquest of Mexico.*
George Bancroft	*A History of the United States,* extolling democracy.
Ralph Waldo Emerson	*Self-Reliance, Experience,* and *Fate,* essays on the dignity of the individual; *Concord Hymn,* a poem.
Nathaniel Hawthorne	*The Scarlet Letter* and *The House of the Seven Gables,* novels set in New England.
Henry Wadsworth Longfellow	*The Song of Hiawatha* and *The Courtship of Miles Standish,* poems based on American folklore and history.
Edgar Allan Poe	*The Fall of the House of Usher,* short story of horror and mystery; *The Raven* and *Annabel Lee,* poems.
Emily Dickinson	"I'm Nobody, Who Are You?", "Because I Could Not Stop for Death," and other poems about the self and destiny.
Henry David Thoreau	*Walden* and *Civil Disobedience,* autobiographical works urging individual freedom and self-reliance.
James Russell Lowell	*Biglow Papers,* poems against the Mexican War and slavery.
Louisa May Alcott	*Little Women* and *Little Men,* novels about childhood.
Walt Whitman	*Leaves of Grass,* poems on democracy and individualism.
Herman Melville	*Moby Dick,* a novel about whaling.
Samuel L. Clemens (Pen name: Mark Twain)	*The Adventures of Huckleberry Finn,* novel of youthful adventure on the Mississippi.

AMERICAN WRITERS: 20TH CENTURY

NOVELISTS	TYPICAL WORKS
Edith Wharton	*Ethan Frome,* a New England tragedy.
Upton Sinclair	*The Jungle, Oil,* and *Boston,* stories of social protest.
Willa Cather	*O Pioneers!,* about life on the fading frontier.
Sinclair Lewis	*Babbit* and *Main Street,* criticisms of middle-class life.
William Faulkner	*The Sound and the Fury,* about the decay of Southern society.
Ernest Hemingway	*For Whom the Bell Tolls,* against Fascism.
John Steinbeck	*The Grapes of Wrath,* about farm workers of the 1930's.
Mary McCarthy	*The Group,* tracing the experiences of eight women.
James Baldwin	*Go Tell It on the Mountain,* story of a childhood in Harlem.
Alice Walker	*The Color Purple,* story of a black woman's trials.

POETS	TYPICAL WORKS
Robert Frost	*Mending Wall* and *Birches,* about rural New England.
Carl Sandburg	*Chicago Poems* and *The People, Yes,* praising the common man. (also a biography of Abraham Lincoln)
Edna St. Vincent Millay	"The Harp Weaver," about a mother's love for her son.
Stephen Vincent Benét	*John Brown's Body,* about the Civil War.
Gwendolyn Brooks	Poet and novelist of black urban life.

PLAYWRIGHTS	TYPICAL WORKS
Eugene O'Neill	*Ah, Wilderness!,* analysis of human character.
Lillian Hellman	*The Children's Hour,* psychological drama.
Robert Sherwood	*Abe Lincoln in Illinois,* about his early career.
Tennessee Williams	*The Glass Menagerie,* study of human emotions.
Lorraine Hansberry	*A Raisin in the Sun,* first Broadway play by a black author.
Arthur Miller	*Death of a Salesman,* concerned with moral questions.

Historians	Typical Works
Frederick Jackson Turner	*The Frontier in American History.*
Vernon L. Parrington	*Main Currents in American Thought,* weaving together history and literature.
Charles A. Beard	*An Economic Interpretation of the Constitution.*
Margaret Leech	*Reveille in Washington,* on the Civil War; *In the Days of McKinley,* on the late 19th century.
Bruce Catton	*The Centennial History of the Civil War,* a multivolume work, including *Never Call Retreat.*
Barbara W. Tuchman	*The Guns of August,* on the causes of World War I.
John Gunther	*Inside U.S.A.,* journalistic anecdotes.
Arthur M. Schlesinger, Jr.	*The Age of Jackson; The Age of Roosevelt; A Thousand Days,* about the Kennedy Administration.
Frances FitzGerald	*Fire in the Lake,* about Vietnam.

AMERICAN COMPOSERS

Composers	Typical Works
Stephen C. Foster	*My Old Kentucky Home, Oh! Susanna,* and *Old Black Joe,* songs.
John Philip Sousa	*Semper Fidelis* and *Stars and Stripes Forever,* marches.
Amy Marcy Cheney (Mrs. H. H. A. Beach)	*Gaelic Symphony,* first symphonic work by an American woman (1896).
Victor Herbert	*Babes in Toyland* and *Naughty Marietta,* operettas.
Edward MacDowell	*Woodland Sketches* for piano; *Indian Suite* for orchestra.
Irving Berlin	*Annie Get Your Gun,* musical comedy; *White Christmas* and *God Bless America,* songs.
George Gershwin	*Porgy and Bess,* folk opera of Negro life; *An American in Paris* and *Rhapsody in Blue,* symphonic jazz.
Aaron Copland	*Billy the Kid, Rodeo,* and *Appalachian Spring,* ballets.
Ruth Crawford Seeger	*Sacco-Vanzetti* and *Chinaman, Laundryman,* works on political and social themes.
Richard Rogers	*Oklahoma!, South Pacific, The King and I,* and *The Sound of Music,* musical comedies.
Leonard Bernstein	*Wonderful Town* and *West Side Story,* musical plays.

AMERICAN PAINTERS

PAINTERS	TYPICAL WORKS
John Singleton Copley	Portraits of colonial Americans such as Paul Revere.
Gilbert Stuart	Portraits of early Americans such as George Washington.
Mary Cassatt	"The Boating Party" and "In the Park," scenes of leisure.
James McNeill Whistler	*Portrait of My Mother;* also landscapes.
Winslow Homer	*The Herring Net,* seascapes.
Thomas Hart Benton	Historical murals; also scenes of the Midwest.
Grant Wood	Scenes of the Midwest such as *American Gothic.*
John Steuart Curry	Midwest scenes such as *Baptism in Kansas* and *Tornado.*
Georgia O'Keeffe	Stark paintings of objects such as rocks and clouds.
Jackson Pollock	Abstract paintings with new techniques.

AMERICAN SCULPTORS

SCULPTORS	TYPICAL WORKS
Augustus Saint-Gaudens	The standing Lincoln in Lincoln Park, Chicago.
Malvina Hoffman	The 100 life-size bronze statues in "Races of Mankind" exhibit, Field Museum of Natural History, Chicago.
Daniel Chester French	*The Minuteman* at Concord; the seated Lincoln in Washington, D.C.
Louise Nevelson	"Scavenger art" using such materials as wheels and furniture parts.
Alexander Calder	Abstract sculpture; stabiles and mobiles.

AMERICAN ARCHITECTS

ARCHITECTS	TYPICAL WORKS
Henry H. Richardson	New York State Capitol at Albany (Romanesque features).
Louis Sullivan	Early modern skyscrapers.
Cloethiel Woodward Smith	Laclede Town, St. Louis; townhouses in Reston, Virginia.
Frank Lloyd Wright	Johnson Wax Building in Racine, Wisconsin; Guggenheim Museum in New York City.

IDENTIFICATION QUESTIONS: WHO AM I?

Susan B. Anthony	Dorothea Dix	John D. Rockefeller
Henry Barnard	Charles Eliot	Eleanor Roosevelt
Clara Barton	Mary Lyon	Margaret Chase Smith
Andrew Carnegie	Horace Mann	Elizabeth Cady Stanton
Peter Cooper	Frances Perkins	Frances Willard

1. I was a pioneer for free public education. I made the school system of Massachusetts a model for other states.
2. To provide higher education for women, I founded Mount Holyoke.
3. I organized and for many years served as president of the American Red Cross.
4. I was an untiring advocate of giving the vote to women. An amendment to the Constitution has been named for me.
5. I donated money to establish free public libraries.
6. I brought about important reforms in the treatment of insane people and criminals.
7. As president of the Woman's Christian Temperance Union, I fought the evils of intoxicating liquor.
8. I established a New York City school to serve as a civic center and to train students in the arts and sciences.
9. I endowed the University of Chicago and founded an institute for medical research.
10. A prominent public figure of the 1930's, I later headed the U.N. Human Rights Commission.

MULTIPLE-CHOICE QUESTIONS

1. During the period 1825-1860, which was an important factor in the movement for a tax-supported public school system? (1) unpopularity of religious schools (2) heritage of state-supported schools brought from Europe (3) leadership of wealthy groups who believed in equal opportunity for all (4) influence of the wage-earning class in the cities.
2. The Morrill Act of 1862 aided education by giving (1) to each state the right to control its own schools (2) to colleges funds for research (3) to each state public land, the income from which was to be used for agricultural colleges (4) to the federal government a grant of money to set up an office of education.
3. Today, most policy decisions affecting public schools in the United States are made by (1) federal courts (2) Congress (3) local boards of education (4) the Secretary of Health, Education, and Welfare.
4. Which event spurred Congress to pass the National Defense Education Act of 1958? (1) the Soviet launching of Sputnik I (2) China's explosion of her first atomic bomb (3) the seizure of power in Cuba by Fidel Castro (4) French expulsion from Vietnam.
5. Beginning in the 1950's the federal government has aided college education by all of the following *except* (1) loans for construction of college classrooms (2) grants for purchase of equipment (3) special tax exemptions for parents supporting children at college (4) scholarships for needy students.
6. Which statement regarding the Elementary and Secondary Education Act of 1965 is *not* true? (1) It was related to the "war on poverty." (2) It granted money to states for the purchase of instructional materials to be used by parochial school students. (3) It began federal aid to public education. (4) It provided federal aid directly to school districts.

7. Today, public education in the United States is supported by (1) local governments only (2) state governments only (3) the national government only (4) local, state, and national governments.

8. With which one of these 19th-century reform movements were women closely associated? (1) civil service reform (2) conservation of national resources (3) lowering the tariff (4) temperance.

9. Which one of these government positions has been held by a woman? (1) Chief Justice of the United States Supreme Court (2) Cabinet member (3) Vice President of the United States (4) Speaker of the House of Representatives.

10. In its statement that "all men and women are created equal," the Seneca Falls Convention was paraphrasing (1) the Declaration of Independence (2) the Preamble to the Constitution (3) Calhoun's Exposition and Protest (4) Lincoln's Gettysburg Address.

MATCHING QUESTIONS: SCIENCE

Column A—Achievements

1. Used ether as an anesthetic
2. Developed antibiotic streptomycin
3. Propounded theory of relativity
4. Constructed first nuclear reactor
5. Discovered how yellow fever is spread
6. Developed cyclotron
7. Created first polio vaccine
8. Studied nature through glaciers and fossil fishes
9. Developed hydrogen bomb
10. Launched first liquid-fuel rocket

Column B—Scientists

a. Louis Agassiz
b. John J. Audubon
c. Luther Burbank
d. Albert Michelson
e. Albert Einstein
f. Enrico Fermi
g. Robert H. Goddard
h. Ernest O. Lawrence
i. J. Robert Oppenheimer
j. Walter Reed
k. Jonas Salk
l. Edward Teller
m. Selman Waksman
n. William Morton

MATCHING QUESTIONS: LITERATURE

Column A—Themes

1. Pursuit of a white whale
2. Fascism anywhere as a threat to liberty everywhere
3. Praise of hard work and thrift
4. Experiences of frontier settlers and Indians
5. Poems in praise of democracy and individualism
6. Conditions of migratory farm workers
7. Account of a boy's life on the Mississippi

Column B—Literary Works

a. *Poor Richard's Almanac*
b. *The Adventures of Huckleberry Finn*
c. *Moby Dick*
d. *The Federalist*
e. *Go Tell It on the Mountain*
f. *Leaves of Grass*
g. *For Whom the Bell Tolls*
h. *The Grapes of Wrath*
i. *Inside U.S.A.*
j. *The Last of the Mohicans*

MATCHING QUESTIONS: LITERATURE AND THE ARTS

Column A	*Column B*
1. Biography of Lincoln	*a.* Irving Berlin
2. *Porgy and Bess*	*b.* Henry David Thoreau
3. *Main Street*	*c.* Ralph Waldo Emerson
4. *American Gothic*	*d.* Bruce Catton
5. Guggenheim Museum building in New York City	*e.* Carl Sandburg
	f. Daniel Chester French
6. *Walden*	*g.* Eugene O'Neill
7. *God Bless America*	*h.* Sinclair Lewis
8. Statue of the seated Lincoln in Washington, D.C.	*i.* Frank Lloyd Wright
	j. Robert Frost
9. *The Centennial History of the Civil War*	*k.* Winslow Homer
10. *Mending Wall*	*l.* George Gershwin
	m. Grant Wood

ESSAY QUESTIONS

1. Throughout the history of the United States, our practices and policies in the field of education have been influenced by our national ideals and by historical developments. Give *two* specific examples to prove the truth of this statement for *each* of the following periods: (*a*) 1829–1860, (*b*) 1860–1945, (*c*) 1945–present.

2. The United States today faces the problem of equalizing educational opportunities. (*a*) Show in *two* ways how this problem arose out of conditions in American life. (*b*) Describe in *one* way how this problem affects the welfare of the American people as a whole. (*c*) Illustrate *two* ways by which this problem is being tackled by the federal government.

3. Women have come to play an increasingly important role in American life. (*a*) For *three* of the following fields, name an American woman who has gained distinction *and* explain briefly how *each* of these women has been outstanding in her field: (1) education, (2) politics, (3) literature, (4) humanitarian work. (*b*) Discuss *two* reasons why new opportunities have opened to women during the 20th century.

4. "Who reads an American book or goes to an American play or looks at an American picture or statue? What does the world yet owe to American physicians or surgeons? What new substance have their chemists discovered?" This was a criticism by an English writer in 1820.
   For each of *three* of the areas indicated above (such as literature, medicine, science, sculpture, painting), discuss *two* achievements to prove that the United States, by today, has increased or has influenced the world's knowledge.

5. Since 1900, significant changes have occurred in the United States in the areas of (*a*) painting, (*b*) literature, (*c*) architecture, (*d*) music, (*e*) the theater. Select *three* of the areas above, and for each area selected show how *two* specific Americans influenced the area chosen.

6. For *each* of the following fields, mention *one* American who has made an important contribution: (*a*) medicine, (*b*) social welfare, (*c*) education, (*d*) science, (*e*) music, (*f*) literature, (*g*) architecture, (*h*) painting. Show how *three* of these contributions have influenced the life of the American people.

UNIT VII. POLITICAL DEVELOPMENTS MIRROR A CHANGING AND COMPLEX AMERICA

Part 1. The Republicans Dominate the Post-Civil War Period (1869–1885)

BRIEF SURVEY OF NATIONAL DEVELOPMENTS

1. Economic Developments. (*a*) Business leaders transformed America from an agricultural to an industrial nation. In business, they achieved wealth and power; they disdained the men who devoted themselves to politics. (*b*) Settlers occupied the last frontier, the Great Plains. (*c*) Employed by large, impersonal corporations and paid low wages, workers turned to nationwide labor organizations, first the Knights of Labor and then the American Federation of Labor. (*d*) Faced with unfair railroad practices and falling agricultural prices, farmers formed the Granger movement and joined the Greenback-Labor party.

2. Social Developments. (*a*) Workers flocked to the cities for jobs. Increasingly, Americans experienced the problems of urbanization. (*b*) After being slowed down by the Civil War, the flow of immigrants picked up rapidly.

3. Political Developments

a. Major Parties and Their Supporters. The Republicans were the party of Eastern businessmen and bankers, of Western farmers, and of pro-Union patriots. The Democrats found strong support among Southern whites and Northern urban dwellers. In times of economic distress, the Democrats also made inroads among the Western farmers.

b. Issues. Having preserved the Union, the Republicans sought to keep war hatreds alive by "waving the bloody shirt." The Democrats urged the nation to forget the bitterness of the war. In 1877 this issue disappeared. On economic matters, the two parties differed only in that the Republicans favored higher tariffs than did the Democrats. Both parties favored the laissez-faire doctrine that the government should not interfere with business. Neither party came to grips with the newly emerging economic and social issues: abuses by big business and the needs of workers, farmers, and immigrants. In Presidential elections, the parties largely neglected issues and concentrated on personalities and emotions. From 1868 through 1880 the Republicans won each Presidential election, but they failed to maintain control of both houses of Congress for any length of time.

GRANT ADMINISTRATION: 1869–1877 (REPUBLICAN)

MAJOR POLITICAL ASPECTS

1. Election of 1868. General Ulysses S. Grant, who accepted the Radical Republican reconstruction policies, received the Republican nomination. Following a bitter "bloody shirt" campaign, Grant defeated the Democratic candidate, the former Governor of New York, Horatio Seymour.

2. Grant and the Presidency. Inexperienced in politics, inept in choosing assistants, insensitive to public needs, and inclined to defer to Congress, Grant has been judged among the least successful of Presidents. Although personally honest, Grant permitted his administration to be marked by corruption.

3. Election of 1872. The Republicans renominated Grant despite internal party opposition. A Liberal Republican group, seeking honesty in government and a more lenient policy toward the South, chose their own Presidential candidate, *Horace Greeley*, the editor of the New York *Tribune*. The Democrats also nominated Greeley, although he long had been their bitter critic. Grant's wartime record, the "bloody shirt," heavy campaign contributions by businessmen, and Democratic distaste for Greeley, all combined to give Grant an easy reelection.

4. Corruption: A Period of "National Disgrace." (*a*) Grant's private secretary was connected with a scandal in which Treasury officials accepted bribes not to collect taxes from a group of St. Louis distillers, the *Whisky Ring*. (*b*) Grant's Secretary of War took graft from agents he appointed to posts on Indian reservations. (*c*) Grant's Vice President and several Congressmen received bargain-priced stock to prevent investigation of a fraud by a railroad construction company, the *Crédit Mobilier*.

The Grant Era was also marked by corruption on the state level (by Southern carpetbag governments) and on the municipal level (notably by the *Tweed Ring* in New York City).

Grant has not been blamed for causing such corruption. It probably resulted from the lowering of ethical standards during the war and from the postwar emphasis by businessmen upon material gains. However, Grant has been blamed for assisting guilty officials to escape punishment and for failing to fight for honesty in public life.

IMPORTANT DOMESTIC LEGISLATION

LAWS	PURPOSES
Force Acts (1870–1871)	Use federal troops to protect Southern Negroes.
Amnesty Act (1872)	Restore rights of most Confederate leaders.
Coinage Act (1873)	End coinage of silver.
Specie Resumption Act (1875)	Redeem greenbacks in gold.

SIGNIFICANT FOREIGN AFFAIRS: THE *ALABAMA* CLAIMS

Grant's Secretary of State, Hamilton Fish, a capable official, negotiated an agreement with England for an international court of arbitration to settle the *Alabama* claims. The United States received compensation for damages caused by British-built war vessels turned over to the Confederacy.

HAYES ADMINISTRATION: 1877–1881 (REPUBLICAN)

MAJOR POLITICAL ASPECTS

1. Election of 1876

a. Candidates and Issues. The Republicans nominated the honest and conscientious Governor of Ohio, *Rutherford B. Hayes.* The Democrats chose the reform Governor of New York, *Samuel J. Tilden,* who had smashed the corrupt Tweed Ring. Both candidates represented the business community, supported sound money, urged civil service reform, and favored ending Radical reconstruction. In the campaign, the Republicans "waved the bloody shirt," and the Democrats emphasized the corruption of the Grant Era.

b. The Disputed Electoral Vote. Tilden received 184 electoral votes, Hayes received 165, and both candidates claimed the remaining 20 votes: 1 from Oregon and 19 from the three Southern states that still had carpetbag governments. Congress established an electoral commission whose eight Republicans outvoted its seven Democrats and assigned all 20 votes to Hayes. Despite Tilden's 200,000 popular majority, Hayes became President. Hayes was denounced by the Democrats as "His Fraudulency" and "Old Man Eight to Seven."

c. End of Reconstruction. To appease the Democrats, Hayes promised to withdraw federal troops from the South. Once in office, Hayes did so. The remaining carpetbag governments collapsed, and reconstruction was over.

2. **Beginnings of Civil Service Reform.** Hayes antagonized the regular, or "Stalwart," Republicans by trying to curtail political patronage: dismissing unneeded and incompetent employees; forbidding officeholders from being assessed political contributions; and naming as his Secretary of the Interior the Liberal Republican advocate of civil service reform, *Carl Schurz.*

3. **Hayes' Anti-Labor Acts.** (*a*) Hayes employed federal troops in 1877 against the railroad strikers. (*b*) Hayes vetoed a Chinese exclusion bill, claiming that it violated our treaty with China. He was condemned as favoring cheap "coolie" labor.

IMPORTANT DOMESTIC LEGISLATION: SILVER COINAGE

The *Bland-Allison Act* (1878), passed over Hayes' veto, provided that the government purchase and coin a limited quantity of silver.

GARFIELD-ARTHUR ADMINISTRATION: 1881–1885 (REPUBLICAN)

MAJOR POLITICAL ASPECTS

1. **Election of 1880.** The Republican convention, split between rival factions, turned on the 36th ballot to a compromise candidate, Ohio Congressman *James A. Garfield.* The Democrats nominated a former Union general, *Winfield S. Hancock.* The campaign was undistinguished as to issues, but the Republicans were well organized and expended heavy funds. Despite a very slim lead in popular votes, Garfield won easily in the electoral college.

2. **Assassination of Garfield (1881).** In office less than four months, Garfield was fatally shot by a disappointed officeseeker. He was succeeded by his Vice President, *Chester A. Arthur.*

3. **Arthur as President (1881–1885): The Office Makes the Man.** Though he had been a machine politician, Arthur rose to the responsibilities of his office by maintaining an able and honest administration. He began modernization of the American navy by constructing steel warships; fought corruption; and strongly supported civil service reform.

IMPORTANT DOMESTIC LEGISLATION

(1) The *Chinese Exclusion Act* (1882), passed after revision of our treaty obligations with China, suspended the immigration of Chinese laborers. (2) The *Pendleton Act* (1883) set the basis of our present federal civil service system.

Part 2. Seesawing Election Results Reflect a Period of Turmoil (1885–1901)

BRIEF SURVEY OF NATIONAL DEVELOPMENTS

1. **Continuation of Post-Civil War Economic and Social Trends.** (*a*) Business leaders continued to expand their industrial empires. In 1901 steel magnates and bankers formed America's first billion-dollar corporation, the United States Steel Corporation. (*b*) By the turn of the century, settlers completed the closing of the frontier. (*c*) Immigrants entered in increasing numbers. Many were "new immigrants" from southern and eastern Europe. (*d*) Workers, more discontented than ever before, joined unions and engaged in strikes. They lost the Homestead Steel strike (1892) and the Pullman strike (1894). (*e*) Agricultural prices continued to fall, causing farmers to create the Populist party.

2. **Political Developments.** (*a*) *Issues.* In 1884 both parties emphasized personalities and appealed to emotions. In subsequent elections, the parties paid increasing attention to issues, such as the tariff and currency. (*b*) *First Moves Away From Laissez-Faire.* Congress began government regulation of the economy with the Interstate Commerce Act (1887) and the Sherman Antitrust Act (1890). (*c*) *Populist Party.* This third party, which advocated many reforms, had a brief existence. Created in 1891, it disappeared after losing the 1896 Presidential election.

FIRST CLEVELAND ADMINISTRATION: 1885–1889 (DEMOCRATIC)

MAJOR POLITICAL ASPECTS

1. **Election of 1884.** The Republican convention nominated the former Congressman from Maine and Secretary of State, *James G. Blaine.* Republican reformers, dubbed the "Mugwumps," refused to support Blaine, since he had been linked to political dishonesty. The Democrats nominated a reform candidate, *Grover Cleveland.* As Mayor of Buffalo and Governor of New York, Cleveland had won a reputation for integrity.

The campaign highlighted bitter personal attacks. Just before the election, a Blaine supporter in New York labeled the Democrats as the party of "Rum, Romanism, and Rebellion." This prejudiced attack, most historians believe, rallied Roman Catholic voters to Cleveland. He carried New York State by slightly more than 1000 out of 1,125,000 votes and won the election narrowly by 219 electoral votes to 182 for Blaine.

2. **Cleveland and Civil Service Reform.** Cleveland doubled the number of federal positions filled by merit examinations. However, as the first post-

Civil War Democratic President, he also had to satisfy his party's demand for patronage. Cleveland provided jobs for "deserving Democrats," but he insisted that they be honest and capable. Cleveland proclaimed that "public office is a public trust."

3. Restored Prestige of the Presidential Office. Cleveland reasserted executive independence of the legislature. He fought efforts by the Republican-controlled Senate to limit executive appointive powers. He vetoed many special pension bills for Civil War veterans, claiming that the bills were based on dishonest or farfetched claims. Cleveland guarded the public interest by compelling the return of 80 million acres of public land held illegally by lumber and railroad companies.

Cleveland devoted his annual message to Congress in 1887 to demanding lower tariff rates. When the Senate rejected such a measure, Cleveland had a major issue for the 1888 Presidential election.

Cleveland has been criticized for viewing his Presidential role as chiefly negative (the prevention of dishonesty) and, except for the tariff issue, for not providing constructive leadership. Nevertheless, Cleveland is considered outstanding among the 19th-century Presidents following Lincoln.

IMPORTANT DOMESTIC LEGISLATION

(1) The **Hatch Act** (1887) provided for agricultural experiment stations. (2) The **Dawes Act** (1887) offered land and citizenship to Indians. (3) The **Interstate Commerce Act** (1887) began federal regulation of railroads.

HARRISON ADMINISTRATION: 1889–1893 (REPUBLICAN)

MAJOR POLITICAL ASPECTS

1. Election of 1888. The Democrats renominated Grover Cleveland and endorsed tariff reform. Cleveland therefore lost support among protectionist Democrats.

The Republicans nominated Indiana's *Benjamin Harrison.* A grandson of former President William Henry Harrison, he had been a Union general and supported high tariffs. His campaign benefited from lavish funds contributed by industrialists favoring protection. Part of these funds was used for bribes and other dishonorable election tactics. Although Cleveland outdrew Harrison by 100,000 popular votes, Harrison narrowly carried many large states and won the election by an electoral vote of 233 to 168.

2. Harrison and the Presidency. Harrison did not assert Presidential authority but deferred to the wishes of the Republican party leaders. In making appointments to major posts, Harrison carried out his campaign managers' election deals. He allowed party leaders to distribute the many post office jobs to loyal party workers. In legislation, Harrison permitted the Republican Congressmen to set their own goals.

3. First Billion-Dollar Congress (1889–1891). With Republicans controlling both houses, Congress (a) reduced federal revenues by raising tariff rates to a level that decreased imports, and (b) increased federal expenditures by voting "pork barrel" public works and by authorizing veterans' pensions previously vetoed by Cleveland. These measures wiped out the surplus of federal funds. This Congress authorized expenditures of almost $1 billion.

4. Congressional Elections of 1890. The Republicans overwhelmingly lost control of the House of Representatives. Consumers blamed the high Republican tariff for a sharp rise in the cost of living. Farmers blamed the Republicans for failing to raise agricultural prices. Especially in the Midwest, farmers deserted the Republican party to vote for candidates of the Farmers' Alliances, the forerunners of the Populist party.

IMPORTANT DOMESTIC LEGISLATION

(1) The *McKinley Tariff Act* (1890), providing high rates, was passed by logrolling between Eastern protectionist Republicans and Western farm and silver interests. (2) The *Sherman Silver Purchase Act* (1890) increased government purchases and coinage of silver. (3) The *Sherman Antitrust Act* (1890) declared business efforts in "restraint of trade" illegal.

SIGNIFICANT FOREIGN AFFAIRS: THE PAN-AMERICAN CONFERENCE

Secretary of State James G. Blaine organized and in 1889 presided over a Pan-American Conference, held at Washington, D.C.

SECOND CLEVELAND ADMINISTRATION: 1893–1897 (DEMOCRATIC)

MAJOR POLITICAL AND ECONOMIC ASPECTS

1. Election of 1892. The Republicans renominated Harrison, although he lacked public appeal. The Democrats selected Cleveland. Both major party platforms straddled the currency issue. The Populists presented their first Presidential candidate, General *James B. Weaver*. The Populists' *Omaha Platform* demanded unlimited coinage of silver and other reforms.

In polling over 1 million popular votes and 22 electoral votes, the Populists cut considerably into Republican strength in the Midwest. Thus aided,

Cleveland defeated Harrison by an electoral vote of 277 to 145. He became the only President to serve two non-consecutive terms.

2. Cleveland Faces Economic Problems. A conservative, sound-money, business-oriented Easterner, Cleveland had little contact with the discontented groups: Far Western silverites, Midwestern farmers, and urban workers. To deal with complex economic problems, Cleveland possessed only a limited knowledge.

a. Panic of 1893. Cleveland took the oath of office as the nation experienced the *Panic of 1893*, which began a severe depression. Railroads, banks, and industrial enterprises went into bankruptcy. Farmers suffered further declines in agricultural prices. Workers suffered sizable wage cuts, and some 20 percent were unemployed.

b. Cleveland Antagonizes Silverites and Farmers. Cleveland blamed this depression on a single cause: the government's purchase of silver. Therefore, he pressured Congress to repeal the Sherman Silver Purchase Act and authorized the Treasury to obtain gold by selling bonds. Cleveland's actions preserved the gold standard but did not noticeably improve economic conditions.

c. Cleveland Antagonizes Workers. Cleveland ignored the demands of Populist *Jacob Coxey* that the government provide the unemployed with work on a national road-building program. When *Coxey's Army* of 500 demonstrators arrived in Washington, Coxey was arrested for walking on the Capitol grass, and his "army" melted away. Cleveland further antagonized labor by using troops and an injunction in the Pullman strike.

3. Congressional Elections of 1894. The Democrats suffered heavy losses, as the Republicans regained control of the House of Representatives and as the Populists increased their vote substantially.

IMPORTANT DOMESTIC LEGISLATION

(1) The **repeal of the Sherman Silver Purchase Act** (1893) ended the government's buying of silver for coinage. (2) The **Wilson-Gorman Tariff Act** (1894) lowered tariff rates so little that Cleveland, disgusted, permitted it to become a law without his signature. It also provided for a small income tax, which the Supreme Court in 1895 declared unconstitutional.

SIGNIFICANT FOREIGN AFFAIRS

In 1895 Cleveland's new Secretary of State, Richard Olney, intervened in a boundary dispute between British Guiana and Venezuela. The dispute led to an expansion of the Monroe Doctrine by the *Olney Interpretation*.

McKINLEY ADMINISTRATION: 1897–1901 (REPUBLICAN)

MAJOR POLITICAL AND ECONOMIC ASPECTS

1. Election of 1896. Dominated by Marcus A. Hanna, a wealthy business-man turned politician, the Republican convention nominated the ex-Congressman and Governor of Ohio, *William McKinley,* who supported the gold standard and opposed free silver. Meanwhile, silver and farm leaders had wrested control of the Democratic party from Cleveland and the conservative business interests. The Democratic convention chose ex-Congressman *William Jennings Bryan* of Nebraska. The Populists, in a supreme effort to achieve free silver, also nominated Bryan. With huge campaign funds and with Hanna's skillful managing, McKinley won the election by an electoral vote of 271 to 176.

2. Return of Economic Prosperity. (*a*) *Farmers* experienced rising agricultural prices. Foreign markets grew, as crop failures struck Europe. Currency expanded, as the supply of gold increased with new gold discoveries in Alaska, Australia, and South Africa, and with improved gold-mining methods. (*b*) *Businessmen,* having recovered from the depression, increased production and achieved higher profits. (*c*) *Workers* found more jobs and earned higher wages.

3. Disappearance of the Populist Party. Following the 1896 election and the revival of farm prosperity, the Populist party fell apart. Some Populist leaders and policies reappeared later in the progressive movement.

4. Election of 1900. The Republicans renominated William McKinley, claimed credit for economic prosperity, and pledged to maintain the "full dinner pail." The Democrats renominated William Jennings Bryan, who renewed his call for cheap money and condemned as imperialism the territorial acquisitions following the Spanish-American War. By an even greater margin than previously, McKinley defeated Bryan.

IMPORTANT DOMESTIC LEGISLATION

(1) The **Dingley Tariff Act** (1897) raised tariff rates to new highs. (2) The **Gold Standard Act** (1900) made all paper money redeemable in gold.

SIGNIFICANT FOREIGN AFFAIRS

1. Turn to Imperialism. Responding to public pressure over events in Cuba, McKinley led the United States into war with Spain (1898). The Spanish-American War marked the emergence of the United States as a world power with colonial possessions. McKinley also secured a joint resolution in Congress approving the annexation of Hawaii (1898).

2. Concern Over Trade With China. John Hay, Secretary of State, announced the *Open Door Policy* (1900) to assure all nations equal trading rights in China. Shortly afterwards, Hay persuaded the nations that suppressed the Boxer Rebellion in China not to annex Chinese territory.

MULTIPLE-CHOICE QUESTIONS

1. "In an age characterized by few statesmen and by Presidents and lawmakers now half-forgotten, history was made by economic giants." This is a quotation from someone who is probably (1) opposed to the Republican party (2) questioning a democratic form of government (3) supporting socialism (4) attempting to interpret an era.

2. During the period 1865–1900, big business (1) was strictly regulated by federal laws (2) lost many important strikes (3) experienced substantial growth (4) developed friendly relations with labor unions.

3. The industrial growth of the United States between 1865 and 1890 was aided by the (1) government policy of protective tariffs (2) financial policies of the Federal Reserve Banks (3) dominance of the Populist party in national politics (4) passage of laws to restrict immigration from Europe.

4. During the period 1865–1900, the federal government did *not* take any action to (1) curb big business (2) relieve human distress during a depression (3) curb the activities of labor unions (4) regulate railroads.

5. Which was a significant characteristic of politics in the United States during the quarter century following the Civil War? (1) beginning of the abolition of the spoils system (2) greater concern by Presidents for foreign affairs than for domestic affairs (3) disappearance of third-party movements (4) domination of national politics by the Democratic party.

6. The policies of the Republican party in the period following the Civil War were most favorable to the interests of (1) Southern farmers (2) Northern industrialists (3) wage earners (4) debtors.

7. Between the Civil War and the Spanish-American War, the most controversial domestic issue in the United States was (1) internal improvements (2) labor unions (3) cheap money (4) treatment of the Indians.

8. If you had been a member of the Republican party in the 1880's and had advocated reform, you would have been called a (1) Mugwump (2) muckraker (3) carpetbagger (4) scalawag.

9. Which was the major issue in the Presidential campaign of 1896? (1) government ownership of railroads (2) monetary policy (3) imperialism in the Far East (4) removal of troops from the South.

10. "The change came in the nineties, and it was more than mere coincidence that it accompanied the coming of age of our industrial system." This statement refers to the period in which the United States (1) began a policy of westward expansion (2) adopted a policy of isolation (3) became involved in imperialism (4) first enforced the Monroe Doctrine.

11. Which factor best explains the disappearance of the Populist party? (1) adoption of unlimited silver coinage (2) ratification of the income tax amendment (3) return of farm prosperity (4) government ownership of railroads.

12. Which of the following terms has the *least* relationship to Presidential campaigns from 1868 through 1900? (1) "the bloody shirt" (2) "Alabama Claims" (3) "Old Man Eight to Seven" (4) "Rum, Romanism, and Rebellion."

IDENTIFICATION QUESTIONS: WHO AM I?

Chester A. Arthur	James A. Garfield	Rutherford B. Hayes
James G. Blaine	Ulysses S. Grant	William McKinley
William Jennings Bryan	Horace Greeley	Horatio Seymour
Grover Cleveland	Benjamin Harrison	Samuel J. Tilden

1. I was victorious in a disputed election. I alienated many members of my party by withdrawing the last remaining federal troops from the South.

2. During my administration, the United States won a short war and acquired an overseas empire. The slogan "the full dinner pail" was used in one of my campaigns.

3. I was the first Democrat elected to the Presidency after the Civil War. I supported the principle that "public office is a public trust."

4. I was the editor of the New York *Tribune.* I received both the Liberal Republican and Democratic nominations for the Presidency in 1872, but I lost the election to the regular Republican candidate.

5. President for less than four months, I was assassinated by a disappointed officeseeker. My death hastened passage of a civil service reform law.

6. I won an electoral college majority although my opponent received more popular votes than I did. The first Congress of my administration voted expenditures of close to one billion dollars.

7. A Democrat and reform Governor of New York, I lost the disputed Presidential election of 1876.

8. Despite my oratorical abilities and my claims to speak for the masses of farmers and workers, I lost two successive Presidential elections to the same Republican candidate.

ESSAY QUESTIONS

1. Allan Nevins gave his biography of Grover Cleveland the subtitle "A Study in Courage." (a) Discuss *three* of Cleveland's actions as President to prove he was a man of courage. (b) For each of the actions discussed above, give *one* argument supporting *or one* argument opposing Cleveland.

2. In the era from the end of the Civil War to 1901, three major economic developments were (1) the growth of big business, (2) discontent among workers, and (3) discontent among farmers. (a) Describe *one* specific event illustrating *each* development. (b) Show how a federal action or law attempted to deal with a problem created by *each* development.

3. Two issues that faced the United States after the Civil War were civil service reform and the tariff. (a) Compare the attitude of Hayes with the attitude of Arthur toward civil service reform. (b) Compare the attitude of Cleveland with the attitude of McKinley toward the tariff.

4. The following statements all refer to the era from the end of the Civil War to 1901. Agree or disagree with each statement, giving *two* reasons to support your point of view: (a) Presidential elections emphasized personalities rather than issues. (b) President Grant must be blamed for the corruption that marked his administration. (c) The McKinley administration reflected the interests of the business community. (d) The United States had little interest in foreign affairs. (e) The power and prestige of the Presidency were not high.

Part 3. The Progressive Era Marks an Upsurge of Reform (1901–1921)

THE PROGRESSIVE MOVEMENT

PROGRESSIVISM: MEANING AND OBJECTIVES

Permeating the early 20th century, progressivism was a movement to improve American life by expanding democracy and achieving economic and social justice. Progressives were optimistic and forward-looking. They generally did not seek to restore the rural America of the past, but rather they accepted urbanization and industrialization. They hailed the benefits of the machine age but sought to correct its evils.

1. Political Reforms. Shocked by the sorry state of everyday politics, progressives planned (*a*) to wipe out such practices as graft, machine politics, and business domination of government, and (*b*) to set up political procedures to assure the people closer control over the government. The remedy for the evils of democracy, progressives believed, is more democracy.

2. Social and Economic Reforms. Appalled by the poverty afflicting many Americans, progressives planned (*a*) to eliminate practices harming farmers, workers, tenement dwellers, and consumers, and (*b*) to expand government regulation over our economy so as to further the public interest.

SOURCES OF PROGRESSIVE STRENGTH

1. Farmers. Although they had abandoned the Populist party, farmers retained the Populist heritage. They wanted tighter regulation of railroads, lower tariffs, and easier credit.

2. Urban Middle Classes. Many professional people, shopowners, and small businessmen were alarmed by the power of giant trusts and political machines. They favored lower tariffs, more government regulation of industry, and the extension of democracy.

3. Workers. Laborers looked to the government for laws regulating work by women and children, protecting workers from dangerous machinery, and easing the financial hardships caused by industrial accidents.

4. Writers. Men of letters critically analyzed American society and indicated the need for reform. These writers included Frank Norris, Gustavus Myers, Ida Tarbell, Ray Stannard Baker, Upton Sinclair, and Lincoln Steffens; they are generally known as *muckrakers.*

5. Political Leaders. Progressives were found not only in the short-lived Progressive party of 1912, but more significantly in both major parties. Progressive leaders achieved office and furthered reform at all three levels of government.

REFORMER	PARTY	MAJOR OFFICE
Tom Johnson	Democrat	Mayor of Cleveland
Samuel "Golden Rule" Jones	Republican; Independent	Mayor of Toledo
Robert La Follette	Republican	Governor of Wisconsin
Charles Evans Hughes	Republican	Governor of New York
Hiram Johnson	Republican	Governor of California
Theodore Roosevelt	Republican	President of the United States
Woodrow Wilson	Democrat	President of the United States

ACCOMPLISHMENTS OF THE PROGRESSIVE MOVEMENT

1. Political Reform

a. City and State Action. (1) *Direct primaries* enabled voters rather' than party bosses to nominate candidates. (2) *Corrupt practices laws* regulated political contributions and campaign spending. (3) The *Australian ballot* allowed citizens to vote in secrecy. (4) The *initiative* and *referendum* provided voters with a greater voice in making laws. (5) The *recall* enabled voters to oust an unsatisfactory elected public official. (6) The *commission* and *city manager* forms of municipal government reduced the power of political machines. (7) Municipal and state *civil service examinations* reduced the number of positions available to political machines for patronage. (8) *State woman suffrage* extended democracy.

b. Federal Action. (1) *Direct election of Senators* was achieved by the Seventeenth Amendment (1913). (2) *Nationwide woman suffrage* was guaranteed by the Nineteenth Amendment (1920).

2. Social and Economic Reform

a. City and State Action. (1) *State regulation of intrastate railroads and public utilities* improved service and reduced rates. (2) *Consumer protection laws* assured honest weights and unadulterated foods. (3) *Fair tax laws,* by taxing incomes, relieved the burden on owners of real estate. (4) *Child labor laws* set a minimum age for employment and prohibited children from working in dangerous occupations. (5) *Woman labor laws* set minimum wages and maximum hours for women workers. (6) *Welfare benefits* were enacted for dependent children, widows, and the aged. (7) *Factory inspection laws* improved sanitation, lighting, and safety. (8) *Workmen's compensation laws* protected workers and their families in case of on-the-job accidents.

b. Federal Action. (1) Expanded federal *regulation of railroads, industrial combinations, and banks* protected the public interest. (2) *Conservation measures* preserved America's natural resources. (3) *Consumer protection laws* required pure foods and drugs. (4) An *income tax* was authorized by the Sixteenth Amendment (1913). (5) *Legitimate union activities* were exempted from antitrust prosecution, and the use of injunctions in labor disputes was limited. (6) Federal funds were used for long-term, low-interest *loans to help farmers.*

WEAKNESSES OF THE PROGRESSIVE MOVEMENT

1. Uneven Pattern of Reform. In some states, the progressives achieved very little; in other states, with vigorous leaders, the progressives achieved much. The leading progressive states included New York, New Jersey, California, Oregon, Michigan, Ohio, and Wisconsin.

2. Court Roadblocks. The courts at first held illegal considerable progressive legislation affecting economic matters such as minimum wages for women. The states claimed that such laws were a valid exercise of the states' "police powers." The courts, however, frequently ruled that such laws violated the "due process" clause of the Fourteenth Amendment.

3. Survival of Political Machines. The progressives failed to end the power of political machines. Party bosses learned to evade the reform laws. The progressives were unable permanently to overcome public apathy, which continued to be the greatest enemy of successful democratic government.

DISAPPEARANCE OF THE PROGRESSIVE MOVEMENT

By the early 1920's, progressivism had died out because many progressive reforms had become law and the public had lost its enthusiasm for further reforms. Also, the American people had turned their attention from domestic matters to foreign affairs with the coming of World War I. After the war, Americans were tired of public affairs and looked on reform with apathy.

HERITAGE OF THE PROGRESSIVE MOVEMENT

(1) The progressives promoted the belief that government has the responsibility to act for the people's welfare. The Progressive Era marked the transition from laissez-faire to government regulation of the economy. (2) The

progressives demonstrated the ability of our democratic institutions to meet problems arising out of urbanization and industrialization. Further, they showed the need for tackling such problems on the city and state levels as well as on the federal level. (3) The progressives believed that a President should provide strong and effective national leadership. This concept was illustrated, for the first time since the days of Abraham Lincoln, by both progressive Presidents: Theodore Roosevelt and Woodrow Wilson.

THEODORE ROOSEVELT ADMINISTRATION: 1901–1909 (REPUBLICAN)—THE "SQUARE DEAL"

MAJOR POLITICAL AND ECONOMIC ASPECTS

1. Roosevelt Becomes President. President McKinley was assassinated six months after his second inauguration. He was succeeded in office by his Vice President, Theodore Roosevelt.

2. Roosevelt's Background and Personality. A member of an aristocratic family and a graduate of Harvard, Roosevelt early decided upon a career in politics. He acquired considerable experience, serving as a New York State Assemblyman, a federal Civil Service Commissioner, a New York City Police Commissioner, and Assistant Secretary of the Navy. During the Spanish-American War, Roosevelt organized and led a volunteer cavalry regiment, the *Rough Riders*. Elected Governor of New York in 1898, Roosevelt achieved civil service and tax reforms, and demonstrated his independence from state Republican leaders, who became eager to be rid of him. He was "kicked upstairs" in 1900, receiving the nomination for the Vice Presidency, a position without power or influence. With McKinley's assassination, Roosevelt at the age of 42 became our youngest President ever.

Roosevelt was a man of tremendous energy and varied activities: rancher and outdoorsman, historian of the West, and politician. A dramatic and popular figure, Roosevelt was affectionately acclaimed by millions as "Teddy."

3. Roosevelt's Views

a. Strong Leadership. Roosevelt considered himself morally bound as President to further the interests of the people. During his tenure he focused public attention upon national problems and won public support for progressive solutions. Roosevelt effectively utilized the power and prestige inherent in the office of President to provide strong leadership.

b. "Square Deal." Roosevelt believed that the government should (1) assure honesty and fairness in both government and business, and (2) give greater economic opportunity to the individual. He proclaimed that the theme of his administration was to afford all groups—businessmen, laborers, farmers, and consumers—a "square deal."

4. Election of 1904. Roosevelt's Square Deal and his strong leadership evoked great public enthusiasm. In the election of 1904, he overwhelmingly defeated the colorless and little-known Democratic candidate, Judge Alton B. Parker. Now President by election, Roosevelt proceeded even more vigorously, and although Congress was controlled by conservative Republicans, he secured significant progressive legislation.

5. Roosevelt's Relationship to Progressivism. Roosevelt did not create the progressive movement, but he supported many progressive reforms as essential to save our democratic, capitalist system from both the extreme left and the extreme right. He opposed Socialists and other radicals who urged an end of private enterprise. At the same time, Roosevelt condemned those men of wealth who resisted change and who abused their power. He accused them of "arrogant stupidity" and called them "malefactors of great wealth." Roosevelt represented the middle-class progressives, whose method was moderate reform.

6. Roosevelt Provides Vigorous Government

a. Curbing "Bad" Trusts. Roosevelt insisted that big business adjust to the public welfare. Roosevelt approved "good" trusts but condemned "bad" trusts. In 1902 Roosevelt instituted an antitrust suit against a railroad holding company, the *Northern Securities Company.* Roosevelt won dissolution of this monopoly by a 5-to-4 decision of the Supreme Court. Roosevelt hailed the decision as indicating the power of the federal government to regulate business combinations. In all, Roosevelt began over 40 antitrust suits. He thus gained his reputation as a "trust buster."

b. Settling the Anthracite Coal Strike (1902). The United Mine Workers went out on strike in 1902 for union recognition, shorter hours, and higher wages. With coal scarce and winter approaching, Roosevelt summoned mineowners and union leaders to the White House. Union chief John Mitchell offered to submit the issues to arbitration, but the mine owners refused. When Roosevelt threatened to seize the mines, the owners agreed to accept a Presidential arbitration commission. Its decision, reflecting moderate progressivism, awarded the workers a wage increase and shorter hours but denied them union recognition.

In contrast with Cleveland during the Pullman strike, Roosevelt emerged as a friend of labor. Also, by settling the strike, Roosevelt established a precedent for expanded Presidential powers.

c. Conserving Natural Resources. Roosevelt had lived in the West and personally witnessed the depletion of natural resources. As President, Roosevelt (1) increased substantially the national reserves of forests, coal lands, and waterpower sites, (2) secured passage of the *Newlands Act* (1902) to finance irrigation projects, (3) encouraged the conservation efforts of the

Forest Service, directed by the able Gifford Pinchot, and (4) in 1908 summoned a *Governors' Conference* at the White House to spur conservation. By his leadership, Roosevelt propelled conservation into national significance.

d. Protecting the Consumer and the Railroad User. To achieve these ends, Roosevelt urged and secured legislation from Congress.

IMPORTANT DOMESTIC LEGISLATION

LAWS	PURPOSES
Newlands Act (1902)	Finance construction of irrigation dams.
Pure Food and Drug Act (1906)	Protect the consumer.
Meat Inspection Act (1906)	Protect the consumer.
Hepburn Act (1906)	Expand the powers of the Interstate Commerce Commission.

SIGNIFICANT FOREIGN AFFAIRS

Roosevelt envisioned the United States as a major power playing a leading role in an interdependent world. Advocating that the United States "speak softly and carry a big stick," Roosevelt modernized the army, built a strong navy, and pursued an active foreign policy.

1. Revolt in Panama (1903). Roosevelt aided the successful revolt of the province of Panama against Colombia. By a treaty, the United States then gained control over the Panama Canal Zone.

2. Roosevelt Corollary to the Monroe Doctrine (1904). This statement declared the United States the international policeman of the Western Hemisphere. It arose out of the Venezuela debt dispute and the Dominican Republic debt default.

3. Settlement of the Russo-Japanese War (1905). Roosevelt arranged for Russia and Japan to end their war by a peace conference at *Portsmouth,* New Hampshire. For this effort, Roosevelt received the 1906 Nobel Peace Prize.

4. Gentlemen's Agreement (1907). Roosevelt halted immigration from Japan by negotiating the *Gentlemen's Agreement* with that nation.

TAFT ADMINISTRATION: 1909–1913 (REPUBLICAN)

MAJOR POLITICAL ASPECTS

1. Election of 1908. The Republican convention, at the recommendation of Roosevelt, nominated his Secretary of War and good friend, *William*

Howard Taft. Promising to continue Roosevelt's policies and benefiting from Roosevelt's popularity, Taft defeated William Jennings Bryan, whom the Democrats selected as their candidate for the third and last time.

2. Taft: Background and Personality. Taft had served as federal judge, Governor of the Philippines, and Secretary of War—all appointive positions that afforded him little experience in dealing with legislators and voters. A jovial, easygoing man, Taft lacked the personality to dramatize issues, to arouse public support, and to battle with Congress for his program. Furthermore, he held a limited view of the President's role and was unwilling to utilize fully his powers as chief executive. Taft recognized the need for further progressive measures, but he was basically a conservative.

Taft displayed personal integrity and a keen legal mind. Although these qualities later (1921–1930) enabled Taft to serve effectively as Chief Justice of the Supreme Court, they did not suffice to let him master the problems facing him as President.

3. Taft Antagonizes the Progressives

a. Tariff Issue. Taft called Congress into special session to lower tariff rates. However, by fighting only halfheartedly to keep Senate protectionists from enacting high rates, Taft dismayed the progressives. When Taft signed the resulting Payne-Aldrich Tariff and acclaimed it the best ever, he further alienated the progressive Republicans, now known as "insurgents."

b. Conservation Issue. Taft supported his Secretary of the Interior, Richard Ballinger, in a conservation controversy with Roosevelt's friend, Gifford Pinchot, head of the Forest Service. Although Taft favored conservation, his role in this controversy widened the breach between Taft and the progressives, who favored Pinchot.

c. Issue of Reform in the House of Representatives. Taft failed to support the Republican progressives in their effort in 1910 to limit the power of the Speaker of the House of Representatives, the conservative *Joseph G. "Uncle Joe" Cannon.* Nevertheless, when the Republican insurgents joined with the Democrats, they ended Cannon's dictatorial rule. They stripped the Speaker of his power to appoint members of House committees and excluded him from membership on the powerful Rules Committee.

By Taft's handling of these issues, he heightened the division in the Republican party between the "Old Guard" conservatives and the insurgents.

4. Split Between Taft and Roosevelt. While Taft moved closer to the Old Guard, Roosevelt voiced support for the insurgents. Differences in personality accentuated the political issues between the two men, and they became bitter enemies. In 1912 Roosevelt challenged Taft for the Republican Presidential nomination, announcing: "My hat is in the ring."

5. Accomplishments of the Taft Administration. (*a*) Although in office only half as long as "trust buster" Roosevelt, Taft instituted twice as many antitrust suits. (*b*) Taft increased the number of federal employees under civil service. (*c*) Congress proposed the Sixteenth Amendment for a national income tax, and the Seventeenth Amendment for the direct election of Senators. (In 1913 both amendments became part of the Constitution.) (*d*) Congress increased the powers of the Interstate Commerce Commission.

IMPORTANT DOMESTIC LEGISLATION

(1) The *Payne-Aldrich Tariff Act* (1909) maintained high import duties. (2) The *Mann-Elkins Act* (1910) authorized the Interstate Commerce Commission to regulate telephone and telegraph companies. (3) The *Physical Valuation Act* (1913) empowered the Interstate Commerce Commission to determine the value of each railroad's property as a basis for setting fair rates.

SIGNIFICANT FOREIGN AFFAIRS

Taft encouraged Americans to look for investment and trade opportunities in Latin America, especially in Honduras, Haiti, and Nicaragua. In 1911 Taft sent marines to Nicaragua to protect American investments. By giving strong diplomatic and military support to American business interests abroad, the Taft administration became identified with the practice of *dollar diplomacy*.

WILSON ADMINISTRATION: 1913–1921 (DEMOCRATIC)— THE "NEW FREEDOM"

MAJOR POLITICAL ASPECTS

1. Election of 1912. President Taft dominated the Republican convention and won renomination on the first ballot. Roosevelt's supporters claimed fraud, hastily created the new *Progressive party*, and with great fervor nominated Theodore Roosevelt. Because Roosevelt often said that he was as "strong as a Bull Moose," the new party became known as the *Bull Moose party*. After a bitter struggle between conservatives and progressives, the Democratic convention nominated the choice of the progressives, *Woodrow Wilson*.

In many ways, Wilson's and Roosevelt's programs were similar: greater political democracy and more social and economic reforms. Roosevelt and Wilson differed, however, in that Roosevelt supported high tariffs, considered business consolidation inevitable, and urged that giant corporations be per-

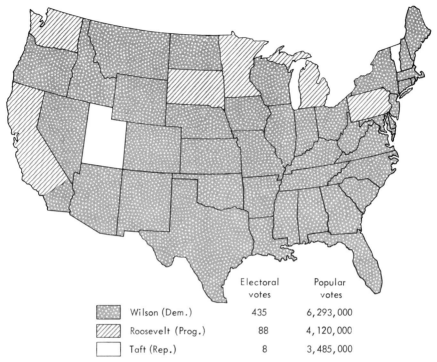

	Electoral votes	Popular votes
Wilson (Dem.)	435	6,293,000
Roosevelt (Prog.)	88	4,120,000
Taft (Rep.)	8	3,485,000

Election of 1912

mitted to exist, but under government regulation; Wilson favored lower tariffs, opposed business consolidation, and urged the government to break up giant corporations.

Wilson won the election (see map above). The combined popular votes for Roosevelt and Taft showed that the Republican split made Wilson's election possible. However, the combined popular votes for Wilson and Roosevelt indicated a victory for progressivism.

2. Wilson: Background and Personality. The son of a Southern minister, Woodrow Wilson received a fine education, excelling in politics and public speaking. When he became a professor of history, he compared the American and British political systems in his famed study *Congressional Government*. In 1902 he was appointed President of Princeton University. By his efforts to improve education and to end snobbish eating clubs at Princeton, Wilson attracted public attention. Elected Governor of New Jersey in 1910, he pushed a progressive program through the legislature.

A "scholar in politics," Wilson personified intellect, reason, and logic. He was a man of high moral principles and an idealist who found it difficult to compromise on basic issues. Although he lacked warmth in his personal relationships, Wilson could sway crowds by his eloquent prose and effective oratory.

3. Wilson's Views

a. Strong Leadership. Believing that the President of the United States should give the country strong leadership, Wilson utilized his Presidential powers to the fullest. In 1913 he called Congress into special session and appeared personally before Congress—a practice unused since Jefferson's day —to request legislation. He employed the power of patronage to swing necessary Senate votes, and he appealed to the people and won public support to influence wavering Congressmen. For his strong leadership in securing legislation, Wilson is rated a highly successful President.

b. "New Freedom": A Progressive Program. Wilson distrusted the extremes of great wealth and radical agitation. His *New Freedom* sought to preserve and strengthen our democratic, capitalistic society by progressive reforms: lower tariffs, an improved banking system, stronger regulation of business, and protection for unions and workers.

4. Election of 1916.

Wilson narrowly defeated the Republican candidate, Charles Evans Hughes. Both candidates represented the progressive viewpoint, but Wilson won reelection with the slogan "He kept us out of the war." Nevertheless, in 1917 the United States entered World War I. As Americans turned their energies from reforms to war, the Progressive Era came to an end.

IMPORTANT DOMESTIC LEGISLATION

Laws	Purposes
Underwood Tariff Act (1913)	Reduce tariff rates; institute an income tax.
Federal Reserve Act (1913)	Create an effective national banking system.
Clayton Act (1914)	Strengthen antitrust regulations; exempt unions from antitrust suits; limit injunctions in labor disputes.
Federal Trade Commission Act (1914)	Prevent unfair business practices.
La Follette Seamen's Act (1915)	Improve working conditions on American merchant vessels.
Adamson Act (1916)	Establish an 8-hour day for railroad workers.
Federal Farm Loan Act (1916)	Provide low-interest loans for farmers.

SIGNIFICANT FOREIGN AFFAIRS

1. **Difficulties With Mexico.** When Wilson took office in 1913, Mexico was seething with revolution. Wilson refused to recognize the military regime of General Huerta and instead adopted a policy of *watchful waiting*. After a dispute with Huerta involving American sailors, Wilson ordered the navy to occupy the port of Vera Cruz. Soon afterwards, the reformer Carranza became President of Mexico.

In 1916 Wilson ordered American troops under General John J. Pershing to cross into Mexico to hunt the bandit Pancho Villa, who had conducted raids into the United States. In 1917 Wilson withdrew our troops from Mexico and recognized the Carranza regime as the *de jure* (rightful) government.

2. **Interest in the Caribbean.** Wilson claimed to oppose "dollar diplomacy," but he continued Taft's policies in Nicaragua and also sent troops to Haiti and the Dominican Republic. In 1917, to protect the Panama Canal, the United States paid Denmark $25 million for the Virgin Islands.

3. **World War I.** In 1914, when World War I began, Wilson urged Americans to remain neutral. He protested violations of our "freedom of the seas" both by British warships and by German submarines. In 1917, as a result of Germany's unrestricted submarine warfare, Wilson asked Congress for a declaration of war. Wilson inspired Americans to a victorious war effort.

In 1918 Wilson proposed his idealistic *Fourteen Points* for a postwar settlement. Wilson helped draw up the *Treaty of Versailles*, the peace treaty with Germany, and incorporated in it his plan for a *League of Nations*. In 1919, to arouse public support for the treaty, Wilson undertook a speaking tour, which ended when he suffered a paralytic stroke. Thereafter, the Senate rejected the treaty.

WILSON ADMINISTRATION AFTER WORLD WAR I (1918–1921)

1. **End of the Progressive Movement.** The progressive spirit disappeared as (*a*) popular attention centered upon the battle over the Treaty of Versailles, and (*b*) Wilson fell seriously ill and could not provide effective leadership, although he remained President till March, 1921. Among the last measures reflecting progressive influence were the Eighteenth Amendment (prohibition) and the Nineteenth Amendment (woman suffrage).

2. **Transition to a Peacetime Economy and Labor Strife.** As the government quickly ended all wartime economic controls, the cost of living rose sharply, and the United States experienced postwar inflation.

Labor unions, seeking to maintain their members' living standards, called a series of strikes. The steelworkers and the Boston police lost their strikes. The coal miners won a partial victory. Equating strikes with radicalism, public opinion turned against labor unions.

3. Public Hysteria: The "Red Scare." Alarmed by the Communist seizure of Russia in 1917, the American people feared "Red" threats within the United States. Attorney General A. Mitchell Palmer conducted raids seeking subversive aliens and Communists. He arrested and held many innocent persons, often in violation of their constitutional rights. By the end of 1920, however, public hysteria subsided.

MULTIPLE-CHOICE QUESTIONS

1. The best description of the progressive movement of the early 20th century is that it was a movement to (1) free the individual from dependence on the government (2) solve the political and social problems created by industrialism (3) preserve an agrarian America (4) provide government ownership of the major industries.

2. A major objective of the progressive movement was to (1) end overseas expansion (2) increase the supply of money (3) assure more democracy in government (4) end government ownership and operation of the post office.

3. The progressive movement urged (1) the use of the initiative and referendum (2) consolidation in industry (3) more financial aid to the railroads (4) close ties between government and business.

4. Which correctly pairs a progressive governor and his state? (1) Charles Evans Hughes—California (2) Robert La Follette—Wisconsin (3) William Jennings Bryan —Nebraska (4) Hiram Johnson—Texas.

5. The progressive movement (1) urged a policy of laissez-faire (2) had the support of a group of influential writers (3) had no success at the city government level (4) eliminated political machines as an influence in American government.

6. Which statement best represents Theodore Roosevelt's attitude toward trusts? (1) "Good" trusts should be allowed to exist but under government supervision. (2) There should be no interference with the organization of trusts. (3) The federal government should encourage the formation of trusts. (4) All trusts should be abolished.

7. Which statement best expresses an opinion of Theodore Roosevelt? (1) Combinations in industry are a result of economic law and must be protected. (2) Latin American nations can conduct their own affairs without interference from the United States. (3) Natural resources must be used for the benefit of all the people. (4) The states and not the federal government must protect public welfare.

8. In which area did Theodore Roosevelt exert *least* influence? (1) conservation (2) tariff reform (3) railroad regulation (4) antitrust actions.

9. In the Spanish-American War, Theodore Roosevelt (1) commanded the American army (2) led a volunteer regiment, the Rough Riders (3) served as Secretary of the Navy (4) negotiated the treaty of peace with Spain.

10. An office *never* held by Theodore Roosevelt was (1) Governor of New York State (2) federal Civil Service Commissioner (3) Vice President of the United States (4) Mayor of New York City.

11. Which term is *not* associated with Theodore Roosevelt? (1) square deal (2) big stick (3) red scare (4) trust buster.

12. In 1908 Taft secured the Republican Presidential nomination (1) with Theodore Roosevelt's aid (2) by battling against Theodore Roosevelt (3) as a dark horse following a convention deadlock (4) as the candidate of the "Old Guard."

13. The Progressives were most antagonized by President Taft when he (1) signed the Payne-Aldrich Tariff Act (2) instituted antitrust suits (3) urged adoption of the Sixteenth Amendment (4) placed additional federal employees under civil service.

14. President Taft's foreign policy was most closely associated with the term (1) watchful waiting (2) strenuous life (3) dollar diplomacy (4) hands off Cuba.

15. Which was a third party that played a prominent part in the election of 1912? (1) Greenback-Labor (2) Populist (3) Democratic (4) Progressive.

16. Woodrow Wilson entered politics following a successful career as (1) historian and educator (2) minister and religious reformer (3) lawyer for large corporations (4) banker engaged in foreign investments.

17. As part of his New Freedom, Wilson advocated (1) repeal of restrictions on immigration (2) broader responsibility of government in social and economic areas (3) passage of anti-discrimination laws (4) open diplomacy instead of secret treaties.

18. President Wilson did *not* request Congress to enact a law to (1) lower tariff rates (2) establish the Federal Reserve System (3) inaugurate Social Security (4) create the Federal Trade Commission.

19. Which Constitutional amendment *least* reflected an objective of the progressive movement? (1) the income tax (2) direct election of Senators (3) two-term limitation upon any one person as President (4) nationwide woman suffrage.

20. Which of the following had most to do with the decline of the progressive movement? (1) Wilson's belief in weak Presidential leadership (2) American participation in World War I (3) disappearance of the Progressive party (4) the Senate's rejection of the Treaty of Versailles.

ESSAY QUESTIONS

1. In the early 20th century the United States experienced an era of reform resulting from the progressive movement. (*a*) Show *one* way in which the progressive movement was similar to *and one* way in which it was different from the earlier Populist movement. (*b*) Describe *two* political and *two* social or economic reforms achieved by the progressive movement. (*c*) Explain *two* weaknesses of the progressive movement. (*d*) Describe *one* way in which the progressive movement has had an influence upon American life today.

2. State whether you agree or disagree with *each* of the following statements and give *two* facts to support your point of view: (*a*) Theodore Roosevelt deserved the title of "trust buster." (*b*) Theodore Roosevelt awakened the United States to the need for conservation. (*c*) Theodore Roosevelt was a pioneer in the efforts of the United States to promote world peace. (*d*) Theodore Roosevelt followed the same philosophy in regard to the power of the President as did James Buchanan.

3. In connection with the life of Woodrow Wilson, discuss *each* of the following: (*a*) *two* outstanding aspects of his career before 1912, (*b*) *one* reason why he was able to secure the Democratic Presidential nomination in 1912, (*c*) *one* reason why he won the election of 1912, (*d*) *two* important domestic reforms achieved during his administration, (*e*) *one* reason why his administration marked the decline of the progressive movement.

4. For *each* of the following comparisons, state which President, you think, handled the matter better and defend your answer: (*a*) Theodore Roosevelt and Cleveland in regard to a labor dispute, (*b*) Taft and Cleveland in regard to the tariff issue, (*c*) Theodore Roosevelt and Taft in regard to enforcing the antitrust law, (*d*) Theodore Roosevelt and Wilson in regard to securing progressive legislation.

Part 4. The Republicans Dominate the Post-World War I Era (1921–1933)

BRIEF SURVEY OF NATIONAL DEVELOPMENTS

ECONOMIC DEVELOPMENTS

1. **"Golden Twenties": Booming Business.** Following a brief depression in 1920–1921, the American people entered upon an era of prosperity. Corporations grew bigger as executives constructed new plants and concluded mergers. Enterprising businessmen ventured into new fields: automobiles, chemicals, radio, and movies. Output and profits increased, as did employment opportunities and wages. The American economy enjoyed widespread public confidence.

2. **Flaws in the Business Boom.** Not sharing in the general prosperity were a number of "sick" industries, such as coal mining and textiles. In addition, agriculture experienced overproduction, and railroads faced competition from newer means of transportation. Furthermore, consumers found their purchasing power not rising sufficiently to absorb the increasing output of goods. Finally, many Americans, seeking to "get rich quick," speculated excessively in real estate and in the stock market.

3. **Great Depression (Beginning in 1929).** In late 1929 the values of stocks fell abruptly. This stock market crash signaled the onset of the Great Depression. Production, prices, and profits declined sharply, as did wages and employment. The mood of most Americans veered swiftly from confidence to despair.

SOCIAL DEVELOPMENTS

1. **New Nativism.** As an outgrowth of the "Red Scare" of 1918–1920, a new nativist, anti-foreign movement arose. The most notorious group, the Ku Klux Klan, which had been revived in 1915, grew in membership and spread bigotry against minority groups: foreigners, Negroes, Catholics, and Jews. However, by the late 1920's, the influence of the Klan declined, as the American people recoiled against the Klan's lawlessness, corruption, and intolerance.

2. **Prohibition Era.** With the ratification of the Eighteenth Amendment in 1919, the United States inaugurated nationwide prohibition. Instead of improving American life, prohibition provided profitable opportunities for criminal syndicates, encouraged bootleggers and speakeasies, fostered alliances between gangsters and corrupt politicians, and bred public disrespect for the law. In 1933 the Twenty-first Amendment repealed prohibition.

3. Loss of Idealism. Americans of the "Golden Twenties" lost the social concern characteristic of the Progressive Era. In foreign affairs, they wished to withdraw into isolation. In domestic affairs, they saw little need for reform.

4. Undercurrent of Protest. Many intellectuals and youths rejected conformity and complacency. *Sinclair Lewis*, typical of the protesting writers, criticized American culture and values. Young people rebelled against uniformity by acclaiming a new musical form, jazz. Many young women, called "flappers," defied social standards by unconventional dress and behavior. These young people, who felt out of place in postwar America, constituted the "lost generation."

POLITICAL DEVELOPMENTS

(1) The **Democratic party** was enfeebled by factional quarrels. Progressives battled conservatives, and Eastern big-city political bosses contended against Southern and Western rural leaders. The Democrats lost three successive Presidential elections: 1920, 1924, and 1928. (2) The **Republican party** was dominated by conservative businessmen (who supplied the campaign funds) and by "Old Guard" professionals (who provided political leadership). The Republicans won the three successive Presidential elections with Warren G. Harding, Calvin Coolidge, and Herbert Hoover.

HARDING ADMINISTRATION: 1921–1923 (REPUBLICAN)

MAJOR POLITICAL ASPECTS

1. Election of 1920. The Democratic convention, after a bitter struggle, gave a 44th-ballot nomination to Governor *James M. Cox* of Ohio. Heeding Wilson's plea that the election be a "great and solemn referendum," Cox campaigned vigorously for the League of Nations.

When the Republican convention failed to select a nominee on the first six ballots, a small group of political bosses met privately in a "smoke-filled room" and threw their support to a "dark horse" candidate, Senator *Warren G. Harding* of Ohio. He was nominated on the 10th ballot. Campaigning from his front porch, Harding dealt with the League issue evasively. He failed also to spell out his domestic policies. He did, however, capture the public mood with his promise of a "return to normalcy." Harding won the election overwhelmingly.

2. Harding and the "Return to Normalcy." An easygoing man, Harding possessed a limited understanding of national problems. He ignored the developments of the Progressive Era and returned to the domestic policies of the Republican party of McKinley's time. He favored (a) less government: reduced federal spending and the restricted use of Presidential powers, (b) pro-business policies: higher tariffs, lower taxes, and inactivity by government regulatory agencies, and (c) a foreign policy tending toward isolation.

3. Scandal at the National Level. Harding was an honest but pliable man who, like Grant, was unable to protect his postwar administration from scandal. (a) *Charles R. Forbes,* head of the Veterans Bureau, pocketed millions through various shady deals. (In 1925 Forbes was sentenced to prison.) (b) *Harry M. Daugherty,* Harding's political patron and Attorney General, was involved, together with others, in substantial kickbacks following the rigged sale of government property. (Eventually, one man committed suicide and another went to jail, but Daugherty was saved twice by a hung jury.) (c) *Albert Fall,* Secretary of the Interior, secretly gave private businessmen liberal leases to government oil reserves at *Elk Hills,* California, and *Teapot Dome,* Wyoming. In return, Fall received considerable "loans" and gifts. (Subsequently, the leases were cancelled, and Fall was sentenced to jail, the first Cabinet officer so dishonored.)

In 1923, soon after the public became aware of this corruption, Harding suffered a severe illness and died. He was succeeded by his Vice President, *Calvin Coolidge.*

IMPORTANT DOMESTIC LEGISLATION

(1) The **Emergency Quota Act** (1921) severely restricted immigration. (2) The **Veterans Bureau Act** (1921) created a single agency to administer veterans' benefits. (3) The **Fordney-McCumber Tariff Act** (1922) provided high tariffs.

SIGNIFICANT FOREIGN AFFAIRS

1. Return to Isolation. Harding interpreted his election to mean rejection of the League of Nations. To replace the Treaty of Versailles, Harding arranged a separate peace treaty with Germany that did not provide for American membership in the League.

2. Washington Conference (1921-1922). Charles Evans Hughes, Secretary of State, summoned and presided over this international conference. It concluded the *Five-Power Agreement,* providing for partial naval disarmament, and the *Nine-Power Agreement,* pledging respect for the territorial integrity and independence of China.

COOLIDGE ADMINISTRATION: 1923–1929 (REPUBLICAN)

MAJOR POLITICAL AND ECONOMIC ASPECTS

1. Calvin Coolidge: Background and Personality. Calvin Coolidge, a descendant of New England colonists, rose slowly in Massachusetts politics and in 1918 became Governor. Coolidge won national attention when he called up the state National Guard to maintain order during a Boston police strike and proclaimed, "There is no right to strike against the public safety." Coolidge received the Republican Vice Presidential nomination in 1920, and, upon Harding's death, he became President. He "cleaned house" by prosecuting the Harding appointees involved in scandals. For many Americans, Coolidge came to represent "normalcy" combined with honesty.

2. Election of 1924. The Republican convention gave a first-ballot nomination to the President and urged the nation to "keep cool with Coolidge." The Democratic convention, deadlocked for more than 100 ballots, finally named a "dark horse" candidate, the conservative corporation lawyer *John W. Davis*. Both the Republican and the Democratic nominees disappointed reform groups, who established a new Progressive party and nominated Senator *Robert La Follette* of Wisconsin.

While Coolidge claimed credit for prosperity and Davis attacked the Harding scandals, La Follette concentrated upon vital issues and proposed reforms: more aid for farmers, further curbs on the use of injunctions in labor disputes, government ownership of railroads and waterpower resources, and higher income taxes. La Follette polled almost 5 million votes, more than polled by any previous third-party candidate; Davis received almost 8½ million; Coolidge, however, won easily with more than 15 million.

3. Business Administration. Insisting that "the business of America is business," Coolidge believed that the government should encourage business but regulate it as little as possible. Coolidge favored reduced government spending and low taxes, and vetoed government aid for farmers and government operation of the power plant at *Muscle Shoals*. He made no effort to restrain stock market speculation. Although the Coolidge years were prosperous, Coolidge's failure to act in economic matters helped bring on the Great Depression.

IMPORTANT DOMESTIC LEGISLATION

(1) The **Immigration Act** (1924) tightened immigration restrictions. (2) The **Soldiers' Bonus Act** (1924), passed over Coolidge's veto, provided World War I veterans with paid-up life insurance policies.

SIGNIFICANT FOREIGN AFFAIRS

Secretary of State Frank B. Kellogg and Foreign Minister Aristide Briand of France arranged for over 60 nations to sign a pact "outlawing" war. The *Kellogg-Briand Pact (Pact of Paris)*, although it lacked any provision for enforcement, was welcomed by Americans.

HOOVER ADMINISTRATION: 1929–1933 (REPUBLICAN)

MAJOR POLITICAL AND ECONOMIC ASPECTS

1. **Election of 1928.** After Coolidge announced "I do not choose to run," the Republican convention gave a first-ballot nomination to his Secretary of Commerce, *Herbert Hoover*. A "dry" (supporter of prohibition) and a successful businessman, Hoover told the American people that they were nearer than ever before to "the final triumph over poverty."

The Democratic convention nominated New York's Governor *Alfred E. Smith*. A grandson of Irish immigrants, Smith had risen from the "sidewalks of New York" to the Governor's Mansion and had provided efficient and humane state government.

As a Presidential candidate, however, Smith labored under several handicaps. As a Roman Catholic—the first nominated by a major party—Smith lost votes because of religious bigotry, especially in Ku Klux Klan strongholds in the South. As a "wet" (anti-prohibitionist), and as a big-city man, Smith was mistrusted by the predominantly "dry" Southern and Midwestern rural voters. Most important, Smith could not overcome the Republicans' claim that they had engendered prosperity. Smith pulled almost double the vote of the 1924 Democratic candidate and carried many large cities. However, Hoover handily won the election and was the first Republican since Reconstruction to carry five states of the "Solid South."

2. **Hoover: Background and Views.** Educated at Stanford University as a mining engineer, Hoover became a successful businessman and a self-made millionaire. During and after World War I, he directed food relief programs for the Belgians and other European peoples, gaining renown as an administrator and humanitarian. His work as Secretary of Commerce (1921–1928) further enhanced his reputation.

Hoover credited America's greatness and prosperity to free enterprise and "rugged individualism." He argued that government interference in business endangered economic progress and personal liberty. The government, he held, should serve business by levying high tariffs and low taxes, practicing economy, and maintaining a balanced budget.

3. **Hoover's Efforts to Combat the Depression.** (*a*) When the Depression of 1929 began, Hoover at first believed that the economy was basically

sound and would recover, as in the past, through the workings of natural economic factors. Nevertheless, to halt the depression, Hoover requested business leaders voluntarily to maintain employment, wage scales, and capital investment. However, faced by falling prices, production, and profits, they were unable to do so. As conditions worsened, the Democrats made substantial gains in the 1930 Congressional elections. (b) Thereafter, Hoover secured increased appropriations for a federal public works program. Although modest, this program was greater than any attempted previously. Also, through the Reconstruction Finance Corporation, Hoover provided federal loans to hard-pressed banks, life insurance companies, railroads, and other businesses. Hoover's efforts proved inadequate to stop the depression, which reached its lowest depth in the years 1932–1933.

4. Hoover's Rejection of Additional Measures to Combat the Depression. (a) Hoover opposed proposals for direct federal relief to the unemployed. (b) Hoover refused to expand the federal public works program. (c) He opposed the request of unemployed veterans for immediate payment of their World War I bonus (not due until 1945).

In these times of despair, surprisingly few Americans turned to violence or to radical political parties. Americans overwhelmingly remained faithful to their traditions and patiently awaited the Presidential election of 1932.

IMPORTANT DOMESTIC LEGISLATION

(1) The *Agricultural Marketing Act* (1929) tried to raise farm prices by establishing a Federal Farm Board with funds to purchase surplus produce. (2) The *Hawley-Smoot Tariff Act* (1930) raised tariffs to the highest levels ever. (3) The *Reconstruction Finance Corporation Act* (1932) established the RFC to make loans primarily to distressed railroads, life insurance companies, and banks.

SIGNIFICANT FOREIGN AFFAIRS

1. Improving Relations With Latin America. Hoover refused to intervene in Latin America to protect American economic interests, thus rejecting dollar diplomacy. In 1933 he withdrew American marines from Nicaragua.

2. Furthering Naval Disarmament. At the *London Naval Conference* (1930), the United States, England, and Japan extended for five years the limits on their navies.

3. Voicing Opposition to Japanese Aggression. When Japan invaded China's northern province of Manchuria in 1931, Secretary of State Henry L. Stimson informed Japan that the United States would not recognize any seizure of territory by force.

MULTIPLE-CHOICE QUESTIONS

1. "The public mood zigzagged from one extreme to the other: first hysteria over radicalism, then complacency over good times, and finally gloom when the depression began." Which period is being described? (1) 1860's (2) 1890's (3) 1920's (4) 1930's.

2. In the "return to normalcy" following World War I, a policy of the government was to (1) keep federal expenditures at a minimum (2) prosecute monopolies (3) encourage the growth of labor unions (4) follow a low-tariff policy.

3. In the 1920's the domestic policies of the federal government were primarily concerned with (1) protecting business interests (2) furthering social reform (3) negotiating reciprocal trade agreements (4) improving the national banking system.

4. During the 1920's Congress and the President approved legislation providing for (1) conservation of natural resources (2) increases in tariff rates (3) regulation of the sale of stocks and bonds (4) guaranteed prices for farm products.

5. A study of the 1920's reveals that (1) the people preferred Presidents who exerted the full power of the office (2) the people favored a continuous buildup of armaments (3) law enforcement was difficult in the face of opposition from a large segment of the population (4) social reform movements tended to increase because of prosperity.

6. In the 1920's which policy was most inconsistent with the fact that we were a creditor nation? (1) our tariff policy (2) our neutrality policy (3) our disarmament policy (4) our policy toward Latin America.

7. In which national election was the "Solid South" first broken? (1) 1920 (2) 1924 (3) 1928 (4) 1932.

8. The Teapot Dome Scandal involved (1) import duties on tea (2) excise taxes on the sale of beverages (3) overcutting in government forest lands (4) liberal leases of government oil reserves.

9. Before becoming President in 1929, Herbert Hoover had been all of the following *except* (1) mining engineer (2) administrator of Belgian food relief (3) Governor of California (4) Secretary of Commerce.

10. The most dramatic event that occurred during Hoover's first year as President was the (1) stock market crash (2) beginning of our Social Security system (3) Japanese invasion of Manchuria (4) repeal of prohibition.

MODIFIED TRUE-FALSE QUESTIONS

1. In 1920 a group of Republican political bosses meeting in a "smoke-filled room" arranged for the Presidential nomination of *James M. Cox.*

2. The Presidential candidate of the Progressive party who in 1924 polled almost 5 million votes was *Theodore Roosevelt.*

3. A position held by both Charles Evans Hughes and Frank B. Kellogg was *Secretary of State.*

4. The author of the statement, "I do not choose to run," issued in 1927, was *Calvin Coolidge.*

5. The first Roman Catholic to be nominated by a major party for the Presidency was *Alfred E. Smith.*

6. In the elections of 1930, the *Progressive* party substantially increased its representation in Congress.

7. In spite of a protesting petition of over 1000 economists, President Hoover signed the *Fordney-McCumber* Tariff Act.

8. To provide loans to distressed railroads, banks, and life insurance companies, President Hoover approved the establishment of the *Federal Trade Commission*.

ESSAY QUESTIONS

1. The years from 1921 to 1929 have been characterized as an era of *political conservatism, economic prosperity,* and *social conformity.* For *each* of the *italicized* terms in the preceding sentence, discuss *one* fact to support *and one* fact to refute the accuracy of the statement.

2. Warren G. Harding has been associated with the term "return to normalcy." (*a*) Discuss *two* reasons why the voters in the election of 1920 welcomed Harding's promise of a "return to normalcy." (*b*) Discuss *one* domestic and *one* foreign policy of the Harding administration, showing how each reflected the search for "normalcy." (*c*) Were the scandals of the Harding administration part of or alien to "normalcy"? Give *one* argument to support your point of view. (*d*) The Coolidge administration has been considered as representing "normalcy" combined with honesty. Agree or disagree with this statement, giving *two* arguments to support your point of view.

3. Agree or disagree with *each* of the following statements, giving *two* reasons to support your point of view: (*a*) In his career until 1928, Herbert Hoover received excellent training for the Presidency. (*b*) Hoover had great difficulty in winning the Presidential election of 1928. (*c*) President Hoover provided effective leadership to combat the Depression of 1929. (*d*) In foreign affairs, the Hoover administration compiled a successful record.

Part 5. The Democrats Introduce the "New Deal" and Then the "Fair Deal" (1933–1953)

BRIEF SURVEY OF NATIONAL DEVELOPMENTS

ECONOMIC DEVELOPMENTS

1. Partial Recovery With the "New Deal." The Democrats under Franklin D. Roosevelt began the *New Deal,* a program of strong government intervention in the economy to combat the depression. By 1939 five million persons previously unemployed were back at work, industrial and farm prices were up significantly, as were workers' wages, and the total national income had almost doubled. The recovery, nevertheless, was only partial, and relief needs remained heavy, since over eight million workers were still unemployed.

2. Full Recovery With World War II. After war started in Europe in 1939, the United States hurried its own military preparedness and offered "all aid short of war" to England. In 1941 the United States was forced into active battle. War needs stimulated industry to produce to capacity and to absorb the remaining unemployed. Wartime prosperity carried over into the postwar years.

SOCIAL DEVELOPMENTS

1. Restoration of Confidence. Abandoning the despair of the depression, the American people reasserted their natural optimism. When faced by Fascist and Communist ideologies, the American people reaffirmed their faith in their own institutions: regulated capitalism and democratic government.

2. Cultural Developments. Through its *Works Progress Administration,* the New Deal provided work for destitute artists, musicians, writers, and actors. Apart from the WPA, novelists and playwrights tackled current problems, thereby heightening social consciousness. Their messages, as well as purely escapist stories, reached wide audiences by means of the newly developed "talking" motion picture. Also, Americans depended increasingly on the radio for entertainment, newscasts, and political addresses. In the years after World War II, the radio was to an extent replaced by television.

3. Post-World War II "Red Scare." With the beginning of the cold war between the United States and Soviet Russia, the American people once more became concerned with the danger of domestic Communists. Their fears were heightened by the disclosure of several spy cases, the most notable involving a former State Department employee, Alger Hiss.

a. Laws Against Subversion. In 1948–1949 the Justice Department successfully prosecuted 11 top Communists for violating the *Smith Act,* which prohibited teaching the violent overthrow of the government. In the *Dennis case,* which arose from this prosecution, the Supreme Court upheld the constitutionality of the Smith Act. The majority opinion held that the Communists constituted a "clear and present danger" of an attempt to overthrow the government by force. For the minority, Justice William O. Douglas said that free speech should not be denied to these "miserable merchants of unwanted ideas." In 1950 Congress passed the *Internal Security (McCarran) Act,* placing further restrictions upon domestic Communists and their organizations. The major provision of the law required Communist and Communist-front organizations to register with the Department of Justice. (The Supreme Court later held that Communists could not be compelled to register because of the Fifth Amendment protection against self-incrimination.)

b. Congressional Investigations. Meanwhile, House and Senate committees conducted hearings to uncover Communist agents in strategic positions. Senator *Joseph McCarthy* of Wisconsin made newspaper headlines by charging that the State Department contained a large number of Communists. McCarthy's charges, investigated by a special Senate committee, were found to be half-truths and untruths. Undaunted, McCarthy continued his attack, accusing Secretary of State George C. Marshall of disloyalty and charging the Democratic administrations with "twenty years of treason." McCarthy's supporters praised his efforts to alert the nation to the danger of Communist subversion. McCarthy's detractors labeled him a demagogue whose wild and reckless charges divided the nation and fanned public hysteria. (Later, McCarthy directed his charges against members of the Republican administration of President Eisenhower. In 1954 McCarthy was officially condemned by the Senate for "unbecoming" conduct, and his influence rapidly declined.)

POLITICAL DEVELOPMENTS

1. Democrats: A Victorious Coalition. Starting in 1932 the Democratic party forged a successful coalition: factory workers, liberal businessmen, ethnic minorities, and intellectuals, mostly in the big cities; traditional Democrats in the South; and small farmers. The Democratic party won five consecutive Presidential elections.

2. Republicans: Defeated and Divided. The Republicans labored under severe handicaps. At first, they were blamed for the so-called "Hoover depression" and were identified with upper-class interests. Later, they were split on New Deal reforms. Many Republicans urged total rejection of the New Deal; others favored retention of certain New Deal measures. Then, as the nation approached World War II, the Republicans were split on foreign policy between Midwestern isolationists and Eastern internationalists. After the war, the Republicans gained strength, but not sufficiently to capture the White House in 1948.

FRANKLIN D. ROOSEVELT ADMINISTRATION: 1933–1945
(DEMOCRATIC)—THE "NEW DEAL"

MAJOR POLITICAL AND ECONOMIC ASPECTS

1. Election of 1932. Although aware that the public blamed President Hoover for the depression, the Republican convention renominated him. The Democratic convention gave a fourth-ballot nomination to Governor *Franklin D. Roosevelt* of New York. The two candidates disagreed basically regarding the economy. Roosevelt insisted that the government should take firm steps to insure the well-being of the people. Hoover argued for the continuation of only limited interference in the economy. Roosevelt won overwhelmingly, and the Democrats also secured substantial majorities in both houses of Congress.

2. Franklin D. Roosevelt: Background and Personality. A member of a wealthy New York landowning family, Franklin D. Roosevelt was educated at Harvard University and Columbia Law School. He served a term in the New York State legislature and in 1912 supported Woodrow Wilson, who appointed him Assistant Secretary of the Navy. Roosevelt demonstrated resourcefulness and also absorbed Wilsonian progressivism and idealism. Nominated for Vice President in 1920, Roosevelt, together with Presidential nominee James M. Cox, battled unsuccessfully for the League of Nations. In 1921 Roosevelt was paralyzed by an attack of polio. He fought back and, although never again able to walk unaided, he recovered sufficiently to resume political activity. In 1928, while Presidential candidate Alfred E. Smith lost the election and failed to carry New York State, Roosevelt narrowly won the New York Governorship. His progressive administration provided care for the aged and aid for the unemployed.

Roosevelt possessed personal warmth, self-confidence, tremendous energy, and a zest for life. A master politician and a skilled orator, Roosevelt commanded widespread public loyalty.

3. Roosevelt Provides Strong Leadership. Like his distant cousin "Teddy" Roosevelt, Franklin Roosevelt used the Presidency as an office of moral and political leadership.

a. Bank Holiday. For a month before his inauguration, Roosevelt had observed that depositors, fearful of bank failures, were making "runs" on their banks to withdraw cash, thereby compelling many banks to shut their doors. Immediately upon taking office, Roosevelt closed all banks by declaring a *bank holiday.* He called Congress into special session and quickly obtained legislation empowering Treasury officials to examine the banks and reopen those that were solvent. Roosevelt's vigorous action restored public confidence not only in the banks but also in the federal government.

b. The "Hundred Days." The banking act was the first of many laws enacted by Congress during the three months of its special session. Roosevelt proposed many new laws and, using his position as party leader and public spokesman, secured passage of every major proposal. This period of the New Deal has become known as the "Hundred Days."

c. Press Conferences. Roosevelt held frequent press conferences and utilized them to present his ideas to the public and to dominate newspaper headlines.

d. "Fireside Chats." Roosevelt used the radio to reach into the American home with his "fireside chats." In an informal manner, he addressed his listeners as "my friends" and gained public support for his programs.

Roosevelt reestablished the Presidency as a position of leadership. In doing so, he stirred vigorous controversy, and no President since Lincoln has evoked so much public love or hate. Most historians agree that Roosevelt ranks among our greatest Presidents.

4. Roosevelt Constructs the New Deal

a. Concern With the "Forgotten Man." Roosevelt pledged himself to "a new deal for the American people." He offered help for the average citizen, the "forgotten man at the bottom of the economic pyramid."

b. Use of the "Brain Trust." Respecting academic scholarship, Roosevelt sought the help of a group of college professors, who were soon dubbed by the newspapers as the "brain trust." From the clash of ideas among these and other advisers, Roosevelt was able to evaluate alternative proposals and to determine the government's course of action.

c. Disregard of Laissez-Faire. To combat the depression, Roosevelt committed the government to an ever-increasing role in the economy. His New Deal completed the transition from laissez-faire to regulated capitalism.

d. Pragmatic, or Practical, Approach. In his 1933 Inaugural Address, Roosevelt said, "This great nation will endure, revive, and prosper. . . . The only thing we have to fear is fear itself. . . . This nation asks for action and action now." Roosevelt favored bold experimentation: "Above all, try something." He adopted the pragmatic approach of trial and error.

e. New Deal Goals: Relief, Recovery, Reform. The New Dealers sought (1) *relief*—to assist distressed persons through direct money payments, jobs, and mortgage loans, (2) *recovery*—to lift the nation out of the depression through aid to farmers, businessmen, and workers, and (3) *reform*—to eliminate abuses in the economy and to prevent future depressions through protection of bank depositors, investors, consumers, the aged, and the unemployed.

f. Growth of Federal Power. The federal government greatly expanded its role in our society. The full extent of federal activity is revealed best by the listing of New Deal laws and agencies (see page 418).

5. Election of 1936. The American people overwhelmingly reelected Roosevelt over the Republican candidate, Governor Alfred M. Landon of Kansas. Roosevelt won all but two states and almost **61** percent of the popular vote.

6. New Deal and the Supreme Court

a. The Supreme Court Temporarily Checks the New Deal. Dominated by a conservative majority, the Supreme Court threw out several early New Deal laws, notably, in 1935, the National Industrial Recovery Act and, in 1936, the Agricultural Adjustment Act. Roosevelt complained that the Supreme Court was living in the "horse and buggy" age, and he feared for the fate of other New Deal laws.

b. Roosevelt's Court Plan Is Rejected by Congress. Encouraged by his overwhelming reelection in 1936, Roosevelt proposed a court reorganization plan that would have permitted him to appoint up to six additional Supreme Court Justices. Roosevelt's enemies labeled his plan "court-packing" and accused the President of trying to upset our traditional separation of powers. The court bill was defeated in Congress, as Republicans and many Democrats voted against it.

c. The Supreme Court Reverses Itself. Meanwhile, the Supreme Court adopted a more liberal position. In 1937, by a vote of 5 to 4, the Court held constitutional two major New Deal laws: the National Labor Relations Act and the Social Security Act. Thereafter, a conservative Justice resigned, enabling Roosevelt to appoint a New Dealer to the Court—the first of several such appointments. Roosevelt later claimed that he had lost the battle but won the war.

7. End of the New Deal (By 1939).

Although Roosevelt remained in office until 1945, by 1939 he had ceased to expand the New Deal. (a) Southern Democrats, mainly conservative, had split from the liberal wing of the party in the 1937 Supreme Court fight. They were further alienated in 1938 by the Wages and Hours Act, which they viewed as a threat to the use of cheap labor by Southern industry. Thereafter, Southern Democrats in Congress joined with Republicans to create a formidable opposition to any further New Deal proposals. (b) Because the economy had achieved some recovery, the public lost its enthusiasm for further reforms. (c) Americans shifted their attention from domestic to foreign affairs, as international crises pointed toward a second World War.

8. Evaluation of the New Deal

a. Arguments For. Supporters praised the New Deal for (1) restoring courage and optimism to the people and improving the economic status of most Americans, (2) providing work relief, which enabled the unemployed to retain their self-respect and which enriched the nation with roads, public buildings, dams, and parks, (3) increasing government spending, thereby offsetting declines in private spending and helping the economy to recover from the depression, (4) reducing unemployment by 5 million and treating the remaining unemployed humanely, (5) successfully regulating capitalism and introducing laws of permanent value, and (6) expanding federal power over our economic system and yet maintaining democratic methods and personal freedoms.

b. Arguments Against. Critics condemned the New Deal for (1) failing to gain the confidence of the business community, (2) wasting money on valueless make-work, or "boondoggling," through its work-relief projects, (3) unbalancing the budget and increasing the national debt through a program of deficit spending, (4) failing to eliminate unemployment, which stood at 8 million in 1939, (5) interfering excessively with free enterprise, engaging in "socialistic" experiments, and passing unconstitutional and highly controversial laws, and (6) increasing the number of federal employees and creating a bureaucracy of agencies with vast powers over the economy.

c. Revolution or Evolution? (1) Critics, pointing to deficit spending and the growth of federal power, especially over the economy, claimed that the New Deal was a revolution—a break with American tradition. (2) Supporters, pointing to our Populist and Progressive heritage, and to the preservation of our capitalist democracy, claimed that the New Deal represented evolution—in harmony with American tradition.

9. Breaking the Two-Term Tradition

a. Election of 1940. The Democratic convention focused its attention upon the world crisis. Nazi German armies had overrun France and were threatening England; and Japan was overrunning China. To retain experienced leadership, the Democrats nominated Roosevelt for an unprecedented third term. Meanwhile, the Republicans nominated *Wendell Willkie*, the president of a large utility company, and a liberal and internationalist. Willkie supported most of Roosevelt's foreign policies and also many New Deal reforms. However, he opposed federal ownership of power plants, as in the TVA, and the breaking of the two-term tradition. Roosevelt won the election by a substantial margin.

Roosevelt's third term was chiefly concerned with foreign affairs and with America's participation in World War II.

b. Election of 1944. The Democrats nominated Roosevelt for a fourth term. The Republicans selected the young and energetic Governor of New York, *Thomas E. Dewey*. Being mildly liberal and internationalist, Dewey raised few issues. He charged the fourth-term candidate with being "tired" and insisted that it was "time for a change." Roosevelt demonstrated his popularity by easily winning the election.

Within three months after his fourth inauguration, President Roosevelt suffered a massive stroke and died. He was succeeded by his Vice President, *Harry S. Truman*.

IMPORTANT NEW DEAL LEGISLATION AND AGENCIES

Laws	Purposes
Federal Emergency Relief Act (1933)	Provide grants to states for relief of destitute persons.
Agricultural Adjustment Act (1933)	Raise farm prices by curtailing production.
National Industrial Recovery Act (1933)	Speed business recovery by codes of fair competition.
Reciprocal Trade Agreements Act (1934)	Increase foreign trade by reciprocal lowering of tariffs.
National Labor Relations Act (1935)	Guarantee workers the right to organize and bargain collectively.
Social Security Act (1935)	Protect workers by insurance for unemployment and old age.
Soil Conservation and Domestic Allotment Act (1936)	Raise farm prices by curtailing production through soil conservation programs.
Agricultural Adjustment Act (1938)	Same as above.
Fair Labor Standards Act (1938)	Establish minimum wages and maximum hours; prohibit most child labor.
Food, Drug, and Cosmetic Act (1938)	Protect consumers by proper labeling and advertising.

Agencies	Purposes
Civilian Conservation Corps (CCC)	Provide work for the unemployed.
Public Works Administration (PWA)	Same as above.
Works Progress Administration (WPA)	Same as above.
Home Owners Loan Corporation (HOLC)	Provide mortgage loans for homeowners facing foreclosure.
Federal Deposit Insurance Corporation (FDIC)	Protect depositors in case of bank failure.
Tennessee Valley Authority (TVA)	Improve economic conditions in the Tennessee Valley through development of hydroelectric power.
Securities and Exchange Commission (SEC)	Protect investors by supervising issuance of securities and regulating stock exchanges.
Rural Electrification Administration (REA)	Bring low-cost electricity to farm families.
United States Housing Authority (USHA)	Lend funds to local governments for slum clearance and low-cost housing.

SIGNIFICANT FOREIGN AFFAIRS

1. **Good Neighbor Policy Toward Latin America.** By pursuing the *Good Neighbor Policy*, Roosevelt (*a*) expanded our Latin American trade so as to combat the depression, and (*b*) won Latin American friendship so as to unite the Western Hemisphere against Fascist aggression.

2. **Recognition of Communist Russia (1933).** Roosevelt recognized the 16-year-old Soviet regime, but our relations with Russia remained unfriendly. The United States and Russia did not increase trade with each other nor, until 1941, did they cooperate against the Axis menace.

3. **From Isolation to Leadership of the Free World.** Roosevelt alerted the American people to the danger of aggression by the Rome-Berlin-Tokyo Axis. After World War II began in Europe (1939), Roosevelt extended all aid short of war to Great Britain and other nations fighting the Axis. Following the Japanese sneak attack upon Pearl Harbor (1941), Roosevelt led the United States to military victory and helped plan the *United Nations.*

TRUMAN ADMINISTRATION: 1945–1953 (DEMOCRATIC)— THE "FAIR DEAL"

MAJOR POLITICAL AND ECONOMIC ASPECTS

1. **Harry S. Truman: Background and Personality.** A Missouri farmboy by birth, Truman held various jobs and, during World War I, served as an army officer. After an unsuccessful haberdashery store venture, Truman turned to politics and was elected county commissioner. He administered county affairs efficiently, and in 1934 was elected to the United States Senate. As chairman of the Senate committee investigating military contracts, Truman saved government funds, sped war production, and gained a national reputation. At the 1944 Democratic convention, Truman defeated *Henry A. Wallace* for the Vice Presidential nomination. (Wallace, a former Secretary of Agriculture and Roosevelt's third-term Vice President, was considered by many Democrats as too liberal.)

Well-read in American history, Truman viewed the Presidency as an office of power and leadership. He acted with authority and demonstrated intelligence, imagination, and courage. Truman was above all a "fighter" and a champion of the average citizen. According to historians, Truman "grew on the job" and fulfilled his responsibilities competently. His record contrasted sharply with those of Grant and Harding, who were also postwar Presidents.

2. **Transition to Peacetime.** (*a*) Bowing to strong public pressure, Truman permitted the hasty demobilization of the armed services. To adjust to civil-

ian life, veterans availed themselves of the *Servicemen's Readjustment Act* (1944), popularly called the *G. I. Bill of Rights*. Under this law, servicemen were entitled to unemployment pay; medical care; loans for buying a home, farm, or business; and payments for continuing their education. (*b*) Heeding the business community, Congress denied Truman's request for continuation of strong price controls. Meanwhile, labor unions won strikes for considerable wage boosts. With prices and wages rapidly rising, the nation experienced serious inflation.

3. Election of 1948. The Republicans, confident of victory, again nominated Governor Thomas E. Dewey of New York. Republican confidence was based upon their success in 1946, when they had gained control of both houses of Congress, upon predictions of public-opinion polls, overwhelming newspaper support, and dissension in the Democratic party.

The Democratic convention nominated President Truman. Thereupon, Southern Democrats, who opposed Truman's strong stand on civil rights, organized the *States' Rights* or *Dixiecrat party* and named Governor *J. Strom Thurmond* of South Carolina for the Presidency. Left-wing Democrats, who opposed Truman's efforts to halt the spread of Russian influence, founded a new *Progressive party* and nominated Henry A. Wallace. His candidacy fell increasingly under Communist domination.

While Dewey waged a colorless campaign to avoid offending voters, Truman fought vigorously. He undertook "whistle-stop" railroad tours, berated the "do-nothing" Republican Congress, and projected an image as an unassuming but concerned human being. Truman won an upset victory, with 24 million popular and 303 electoral votes to Dewey's 22 million popular and 189 electoral votes. (Thurmond and Wallace each polled slightly over 1 million popular votes, and Thurmond also won 39 Southern electoral votes.)

4. "Fair Deal"

a. Relationship to the New Deal. Truman knew that Wilson's New Freedom had ended with World War I. He was determined that Roosevelt's New Deal should survive World War II and continue, improved and expanded, as the *Fair Deal*.

b. Opposition in Congress: The Conservative Coalition. During Truman's two terms in office, the conservative coalition of Republicans and Southern Democrats mustered sufficient votes to defeat Fair Deal proposals for (1) civil rights legislation: an anti-lynching law, an anti-poll-tax law, and a Fair Employment Practices Committee (FEPC), (2) compulsory health insurance, and (3) federal aid to education.

Congress also rebuffed President Truman by overriding his strongly worded vetoes of measures designed to (1) curb labor unions, (2) protect internal security, and (3) continue the national origins system for immigration.

c. Accomplishments

(1) *Improvement of Existing Laws.* Truman secured passage of Fair Deal proposals to expand Social Security coverage and benefits, raise the minimum wage, provide funds for slum clearance and low-income housing projects, and maintain farm price supports.

(2) *New Laws.* Truman secured the passage of laws establishing the Atomic Energy Commission, unifying the armed services, and committing the government to a policy of full employment.

(3) *Civil Rights.* Truman appointed a *Committee on Civil Rights,* which in 1947 issued the historic report "To Secure These Rights." It called the nation's attention to the unfinished business of ending racial and religious discrimination. Truman incorporated the recommendations of the committee into his legislative program. (Through an executive order, he had already begun desegregating the armed services.) Truman's efforts awakened the nation's conscience to the problem of discrimination.

5. Other Developments. *(a)* **Loyalty Program.** Truman established loyalty boards to investigate federal employees and remove disloyal persons and other security risks. Of almost 3 million government employees investigated, some 2000 resigned and 200 were dismissed. *(b)* **Steel Strike of 1952.** After union and management had failed to agree upon a new labor contract, Truman ordered his Secretary of Commerce to seize the steel mills. Before the Supreme Court, (1) the steel companies challenged the seizure as a violation of the Fifth Amendment, which prohibits the federal government from taking private property without "due process of law," and (2) attorneys for the Secretary of Commerce defended the seizure as a war measure necessary to assure steel production for the Korean fighting front. The Supreme Court declared the seizure illegal, thus checking the power of the executive branch. The steel mills were returned to their owners, and the workers went out on strike and after two months secured a new contract.

IMPORTANT DOMESTIC LEGISLATION PASSED WITH TRUMAN'S APPROVAL

(1) The **Employment Act** (1946) affirmed the responsibility of the federal government to "promote maximum employment" and established the *Council of Economic Advisers.* (2) The **Atomic Energy Act** (1946) ordered government control over atomic research and production, and established a civilian *Atomic Energy Commission (AEC).* (3) The **National Security Act** (1947) unified the armed forces—Army, Navy, and Air Force—by creating a single *Department of Defense.*

IMPORTANT DOMESTIC LEGISLATION PASSED OVER TRUMAN'S VETO

1. The *Taft-Hartley (Labor-Management Relations) Act* (1947) placed restrictions upon labor unions. (Congress did not agree with Truman's veto message that the law showed prejudice against unions.)

2. The *McCarran (Internal Security) Act* (1950) called for strict regulation of pro-Communist activities within the United States and created the *Subversive Activities Control Board*. (In his veto message, Truman claimed that this law punished men not for committing crimes, but for holding unpopular opinions.)

3. The *McCarran-Walter (Immigration and Nationality) Act* (1952) restated the national origins quota system. (Truman argued that this law unfairly restricted immigration from much of the world.)

SIGNIFICANT FOREIGN AFFAIRS

1. **Japanese Phase of World War II and the Atomic Bomb.** To speed the end of the war and save countless American battle casualties, Truman authorized the use of the newly developed atomic bomb. Eight days after the bombing of the Japanese city of Hiroshima, Japan surrendered.

2. **United Nations.** Truman signed the U.N. Charter and obtained overwhelming Senate ratification of American membership in the world organization.

3. **Cold War.** As Russia expanded her power in Europe and Asia, Truman countered with the American policy of *containment*. The Truman administration originated the *Truman Doctrine*, the *Marshall Plan*, and the *Point Four Program*. It helped establish the NATO military alliance. In the Far East, Truman began the non-recognition policy toward Communist China and sent American forces to help repel the North Korean Communist invasion of South Korea.

MULTIPLE-CHOICE QUESTIONS

1. The major reason why Franklin D. Roosevelt won the Presidential election of 1932 was (1) his oratorical ability (2) the split in the Republican party (3) the support of his distant cousin, Theodore Roosevelt (4) the fact that the public associated the depression with Hoover.

2. Which statement about Franklin D. Roosevelt before 1932 is *not* true? (1) He was born into a wealthy family. (2) He was the Democratic Vice Presidential candidate in 1920. (3) He supported Theodore Roosevelt in the election of 1912. (4) He served as Governor of New York.

3. Which term is *not* associated with the New Deal? (1) rugged individualism (2) the forgotten man (3) the brain trust (4) fireside chats.

4. The careers of Theodore Roosevelt and Franklin D. Roosevelt were similar in that each man (1) led the cause for peace but involved the United States in a major war (2) led the fight for progressive ideas (3) succeeded to the Presidency upon the death of the previous President (4) successfully mediated a dispute between major world powers.

5. The policies of Theodore Roosevelt and Franklin D. Roosevelt that differed most dealt with the (1) conservation of natural resources (2) protection of the consumer (3) power of the Presidency (4) countries of Latin America.

6. The statement, "Like Franklin D. Roosevelt, this President concerned himself primarily with domestic reform during his first years in office, and with foreign affairs in subsequent years," applies most accurately to (1) Woodrow Wilson (2) Herbert Hoover (3) Harry S. Truman (4) William McKinley.

7. Woodrow Wilson and Franklin D. Roosevelt were alike in that both (1) were Republican (2) favored creating an organization for world peace (3) requested Congress to establish the Tennessee Valley Authority (4) died in office.

8. Why did President Franklin D. Roosevelt ask Congress to increase the number of Supreme Court Justices? (1) The Court had declared several New Deal laws unconstitutional. (2) There was too much work for nine men. (3) More experienced men were needed on the Court. (4) Until 1932 there had usually been more than nine judges on the Supreme Court.

9. An important reason for the opposition to Franklin D. Roosevelt's proposal to "reform" the United States Supreme Court was that this change would have (1) encouraged the appointment of inexperienced justices (2) been contrary to a tradition established by President Washington (3) lengthened the terms of the Justices of the Supreme Court (4) weakened the system of checks and balances.

10. Which group most consistently opposed New Deal legislation? (1) industrialists (2) labor-union members (3) farmers (4) Negroes.

11. New Deal legislation helped protect investors by (1) nationalizing all banks (2) preventing the practice of buying on margin (3) regulating the issuance of securities (4) determining dividend rates.

12. A feature of our economic life during the period 1933–1945 was that (1) the United States shifted from a creditor to a debtor nation (2) there was an increase in our farm population (3) there was a decrease in the output of goods (4) the number of persons at work increased.

13. An important criticism of the New Deal was that it (1) greatly increased the national debt (2) weakened the power of the Chief Executive (3) did not deal with important issues (4) promoted the idea of laissez-faire.

14. Which was an idea of the New Deal? (1) Rights of states have priority over rights of the federal government. (2) Development of electric power should be the concern solely of private enterprise. (3) Supreme Court Justices should be responsible to the President. (4) The federal government has a major responsibility for insuring economic prosperity.

15. A reason for Roosevelt's election to a fourth term in 1944 was the (1) strength of his running mate, Henry A. Wallace (2) support given him by powerful third parties (3) ratification of the Twentieth Amendment (4) reluctance of voters to change leaders in the midst of a great crisis.

16. The administrations of Grant, Harding, and Truman were similar in that all three (1) were Republican (2) were marked by a return to isolationism (3) were followed by the election of a President from a different party (4) faced problems resulting from a recent war.

17. Which is the chief reason why the leaders of the Communist party in the United States were convicted of violating the Smith Act? (1) They had pledged allegiance to a foreign nation. (2) They had given government secrets to Soviet Russia. (3) They had conspired to overthrow the government of the United States by force. (4) They had ridiculed the courts and government of the United States.

18. An aim of the federal internal security program was to (1) remove subversives from government positions (2) provide for workmen's compensation in industry (3) train able-bodied male citizens for military duty (4) restrict the use of wiretapping.

19. In winning the Presidential election of 1948, Truman was most helped by (1) the endorsement of Henry A. Wallace (2) the strong support of Southern Democrats (3) editorial support of most newspapers (4) his own determination to carry his campaign to the voters.

20. Truman's views regarding Presidential powers were most similar to those of (1) Harding (2) Wilson (3) Coolidge (4) McKinley.

21. Which term is *not* associated with the career of Harry S. Truman? (1) whistle-stop campaign (2) policy of containment (3) the hundred days (4) "To Secure These Rights."

22. One Fair Deal proposal *not* passed by Congress during the Truman administration was to (1) provide federal aid for education (2) expand Social Security benefits (3) raise the minimum wage (4) provide federal funds for low-income housing projects.

23. One measure passed by Congress during the Truman administration that became law with the President's signature was the (1) Taft-Hartley Labor-Management Relations Act (2) McCarran Internal Security Act (3) McCarran-Walter Immigration Act (4) Atomic Energy Act.

24. President Truman (1) initiated important foreign policies (2) gave little support to the United Nations (3) requested Senator Joseph McCarthy to investigate federal employees for security risks (4) advocated a return to isolation.

25. Which was an outstanding achievement of the Truman administration? (1) passage of civil rights legislation (2) revision of the Taft-Hartley Act (3) formation of the NATO alliance (4) termination of the Korean War.

ESSAY QUESTIONS

1. Designed to meet the domestic problems of the United States in the 1930's, the New Deal continues to shape our way of life today. (*a*) Explain *two* conditions that helped to produce the Great Depression in the United States. (*b*) Show how *three* New Deal laws passed in the 1930's still affect us today.

2. The administration of Franklin D. Roosevelt was marked by various reform measures. (*a*) Discuss briefly an important law that was passed in relation to *each* of the following: (1) conservation, (2) housing, (3) labor, (4) agriculture. (*b*) In regard to a dispute that arose between the executive department and the United States Supreme Court during this period, describe the main issue and the outcome of the dispute.

3. Agree or disagree with *each* of the following statements, presenting *two* arguments to support your point of view: (*a*) Franklin D. Roosevelt was well-qualified for the Presidency. (*b*) Franklin D. Roosevelt made excessive use of Presidential powers. (*c*) The New Deal had much in common with the progressive movement of the early 20th century. (*d*) The New Deal was more successful in achieving reform than in promoting recovery.

4. (*a*) In connection with the life of Harry S. Truman, discuss *each* of the following: (1) *two* domestic problems that faced him as President and the steps that he took to solve each problem, (2) *one* reason why he won the Presidential election of 1948, (3) *one* reason why he was unable to secure Congressional passage of much Fair Deal legislation, (4) *two* foreign policies initiated during his administration. (*b*) How would you rate Truman in comparison with Warren G. Harding, the President following World War I? Present *two* facts to support your answer.

Part 6. Americans Choose as Leaders Both Republicans and Democrats (1953 to the Present)

BRIEF SURVEY OF NATIONAL DEVELOPMENTS

ECONOMIC AND SOCIAL DEVELOPMENTS

1. Prosperous America. Despite moderate inflation, heavy taxation, and several mild recessions, Americans continued to enjoy unprecedented prosperity. Their affluence was reflected in the growth of suburbs; the rising sales of automobiles, home appliances, and television sets; the expansion of airplane transportation; and the increase in leisure time. Nevertheless, considerable numbers of our people still lived in poverty.

2. Problem of Improving American Life. Critics of our "affluent society" urged Americans to be less concerned with seeking consumer goods and more concerned with improving their communities. This criticism stirred public discussion and eventually led to government action. Cities and states raised their taxes to improve public services. In the 1960's the federal government undertook new programs to fight poverty, expand medical care, combat the pollution of our air and water, and improve education.

3. Emphasis Upon Education. As Americans entered upon the "age of automation," the "atomic age," and the "space age," they became increasingly concerned with education. Parents and citizens viewed education as essential for individual advancement and national survival. In the 1960's local governments increased their educational expenditures, and the federal government greatly expanded its aid to education.

4. Civil Rights Movement. Negroes made progress toward overcoming discrimination, exercising their right to vote, and improving their economic status. These gains resulted from a favorable climate of public opinion, from the work of civil rights organizations, and from the activities of business and labor leaders, various state governments, and the federal government.

POLITICAL DEVELOPMENTS

1. Major Parties and Their Supporters. The Republican and Democratic parties each consisted of diverse groups functioning in a loose coalition. Each party reflected the same wide spectrum of political and economic opinion, although with different emphasis. The Republicans tended to outdraw the Democrats in attracting conservatives, business leaders, and well-to-do farmers. In contrast, the Democrats tended to lead the Republicans in attracting liberals, laborers, and small farmers.

2. Issues. In Presidential elections, each party generally sought to occupy the "middle-of-the-road" positon in order to appeal to the greatest number of voters. Both parties supported American leadership in world affairs. They differed as to degree and method rather than as to goals. The Republicans generally accepted basic New Deal-Fair Deal reforms. Presidential campaigns tended to blur issues and to emphasize each candidate's personality and experience.

In the 1980's President Reagan argued that the federal government had become too large and too involved in our daily lives. He therefore urged that its role in American life be lessened.

EISENHOWER ADMINISTRATION: 1953–1961 (REPUBLICAN)

MAJOR POLITICAL AND ECONOMIC ASPECTS

1. Election of 1952. The Republican convention witnessed a bitter struggle between "Mr. Republican," Senator *Robert A. Taft* of Ohio, and the popular General *Dwight D. Eisenhower.* The Senator was the candidate of the more conservative and isolationist "Old Guard" Republicans; the General was supported by the party's liberal and internationalist wing. The convention gave a first-ballot nomination to Eisenhower and then selected, as his running mate, Senator *Richard M. Nixon* of California. Eisenhower promised to lower taxes and to reduce government regulation of the economy. He criticized the Truman administration for excessive spending, incompetence, petty corruption, and its conduct of the Korean War. Republicans argued that, after 20 years of Democratic control of the Presidency, it was "time for a change."

The Democratic convention, wide open because President Truman refused to run again, nominated Governor *Adlai E. Stevenson* of Illinois. Stevenson pointed to the nation's prosperity, defended the Democratic conduct of foreign affairs, and warned the people that no easy solutions existed for our many complex problems. Eisenhower, who presented a fresh face in politics and a promise of new leadership, especially to bring an end to the Korean War, easily won the election.

2. Election of 1956. Again, Eisenhower and Stevenson contested for the Presidency. This time, Eisenhower campaigned on his record of "peace and prosperity." Stevenson attacked Eisenhower for favoring big business and mishandling· foreign affairs. The Democrats also warned the nation that Eisenhower, having suffered a heart attack in 1955 and undergone an intestinal operation in 1956, could be only a "part-time President." Stevenson, however, was fighting a losing battle. By a somewhat greater margin than in 1952, Eisenhower repeated his election triumph.

3. Observations Upon the Election Results

a. Eisenhower twice carried several states of the traditionally Democratic "Solid South." Many white Southern voters deserted the Democratic party because they opposed its strong civil rights program. Also, they favored Eisenhower's opposition to the further growth of federal power.

b. In 1956 Eisenhower received a heavy Negro vote in Northern cities. Many Negroes supported Eisenhower because they (1) acclaimed the Supreme Court decision against segregation, handed down during his first term in office, and (2) felt that the Democratic party was dominated by Southerners, who opposed civil rights legislation.

c. Eisenhower's impressive victories testified to his popularity among the American people, who affectionately called him "Ike." However, other Republican candidates ran far behind Eisenhower, and the Republicans controlled Congress for only two of Eisenhower's eight years in office.

4. Eisenhower: Background and Personality. "Ike" was brought up in Kansas and held a night job while at high school. He secured an appointment to West Point, graduated in 1915, and subsequently served in varied army positions. During World War II, Eisenhower was advanced by President Roosevelt, over numerous senior officers, to the command of American forces in Europe. Eisenhower led the invasion of North Africa (1942) and the assault across the English Channel into France (1944). After the war Eisenhower served briefly as President of Columbia University and in 1950 was appointed by President Truman to be the first commander of the military forces of NATO.

Eisenhower had a warm personality with the ability to get diverse people to work together. Honest, sincere, and unpretentious, Eisenhower was one of our most popular Presidents.

5. Eisenhower Favors Bounds Upon Presidential Power. Eisenhower disapproved the practice, identified with his predecessors Roosevelt and Truman, of strong Presidential leadership. Eisenhower urged restoration of the traditional separation of powers between the executive and Congress. He proposed legislative programs, but he held that Congressmen should vote according to their own views and remain free from executive pressures. Eisenhower was willing to exercise leadership by "influencing people," but he refrained from "desk-pounding."

6. Eisenhower Advocates "Modern Republicanism." Eisenhower defined "modern Republicanism" as a middle-of-the-road approach which was "conservative when it comes to money and liberal when it comes to human beings." The chief principles of "modern Republicanism" were the following:

a. Accepting Basic New Deal–Fair Deal Reforms. Eisenhower secured measures to expand Social Security benefits and coverage, to raise the minimum wage, to further slum clearance and low-cost public housing, and to extend the reciprocal tariff program.

b. Limiting Federal Power. Eisenhower opposed the expansion of federal activity as leading to "statism" and threatening personal liberties. He favored making the federal government "smaller" by transferring some of its activities to the states and to private enterprise.

(1) *To Expand the Power of States.* Eisenhower approved a law shifting from the federal government to individual states the title to offshore lands. California, Texas, and Louisiana thus received lands rich in oil. He also authorized New York State, instead of the federal government, to cooperate with the Canadian Province of Ontario in building hydroelectric power plants on the St. Lawrence River.

(2) *To Encourage Private Enterprise.* Eisenhower ended the price and wage controls of the Korean War period. He secured flexible instead of rigid price supports for agriculture as a step toward withdrawing all government controls. He condemned the Tennessee Valley Authority as "creeping socialism" and urged that, in the future, waterpower sites be developed by private enterprise. Further, to assure a "smaller" federal government, Eisenhower urged reducing expenditures and balancing the national budget. (Despite rising defense and space needs, Eisenhower was able to balance the budget in three of his eight years as President.)

c. Maintaining American Leadership in World Affairs. See pages 429–430.

7. Other Developments

a. Eisenhower's Illnesses. During his Presidency, Eisenhower suffered three serious illnesses: a heart attack, an intestinal obstruction, and a mild stroke. These illnesses made the public realize that, if the President were disabled, there was no Constitutional way to replace him. (This situation was remedied, in 1967, by the adoption of the Twenty-fifth Amendment.)

b. Civil Rights. The Eisenhower years witnessed considerable activity in civil rights. In 1954 the Supreme Court outlawed segregation in public schools. In 1957 Eisenhower ordered army units to Little Rock, Arkansas, to prevent mob rule and enforce federal court orders for school integration. In 1957 and in 1960, Congress enacted civil rights laws.

c. Space Program. In 1957 Russia seized initial leadership in space by orbiting the world's first man-made satellite, *Sputnik I.* To speed up American efforts in space, Eisenhower secured from Congress (1) increased appropriations for space programs, (2) establishment of the *National Aeronautics and Space Administration (NASA),* and (3) the National Defense Education Act.

IMPORTANT DOMESTIC LEGISLATION

LAWS	PURPOSES
Civil Rights Acts (1957, 1960)	Protect voting rights of all Americans.
National Defense Education Act (1958)	Improve teaching of science, mathematics, and foreign languages.
Landrum-Griffin Labor-Management Act (1958)	Further democracy in labor unions and prevent union corruption.
Acts granting statehood to Alaska and Hawaii (1958, 1959)	Give full rights of citizenship to Alaskans and Hawaiians.

SIGNIFICANT FOREIGN AFFAIRS

1. **Far East.** (*a*) *Korea.* The Eisenhower administration concluded truce talks in 1953 ending the war in Korea and thereafter signed a mutual defense treaty with South Korea. (*b*) *Indo-China.* The United States attended the 1954 Geneva Conference on Indo-China, but we did not sign the final agreements, which partitioned Vietnam. Thereafter, Eisenhower gave aid to the non-Communist regime of South Vietnam, and Secretary of State John Foster Dulles helped create the *Southeast Asia Treaty Organization (SEATO).*

2. Atoms for Peace. Eisenhower's plan for peaceful uses of atomic energy led to the creation of the *International Atomic Energy Agency.*

3. Middle East. (*a*) *Egypt.* Eisenhower opposed the invasion of Egypt by Israel, Britain, and France in 1956. Eisenhower's stand caused a sharp but temporary split with our traditional allies. (*b*) *Eisenhower Doctrine.* In 1957 Eisenhower offered any Middle Eastern nation economic aid, and, if threatened by Communist aggression, military aid. In 1958 Eisenhower sent American troops to help sustain the government of Lebanon.

4. Summit Conferences. Eisenhower met twice with the leaders of Britain, France, and Russia to seek to ease international tensions. The *Geneva Conference* of 1955 radiated cordiality but brought no concrete results. The *Paris Conference* of 1960 collapsed when Soviet Premier Khrushchev made an issue of an unarmed American U-2 spy plane downed over Russia.

5. Cuba. In 1959 Eisenhower recognized the new Cuban regime of Fidel Castro. In January, 1961, after Castro seized American property and harassed American officials, Eisenhower broke off diplomatic relations.

KENNEDY ADMINISTRATION: 1961–1963 (DEMOCRATIC)—
THE "NEW FRONTIER"

MAJOR POLITICAL AND ECONOMIC ASPECTS

1. Election of 1960. The Democratic convention gave a first-ballot nomination to Senator *John F. Kennedy* of Massachusetts. Kennedy had actively sought the nomination and had proved his vote-getting ability by winning seven Presidential primaries. To strengthen the ticket in the South, Kennedy selected Senator *Lyndon B. Johnson* of Texas as his running mate.

The Republican convention gave Vice President *Richard M. Nixon* the Presidential nomination on the first ballot. He had the overwhelming support of party workers and the public endorsement of President Eisenhower. For the Vice Presidential nomination, Nixon decided upon the American Ambassador to the United Nations, *Henry Cabot Lodge.*

The election of 1960 introduced a new campaign technique. Kennedy and Nixon met in a series of four television encounters, popularly called "debates." Both candidates answered questions posed by panels of newsmen, but the candidates did not cross-examine each other directly. The debates were viewed by an audience of over 80 million Americans.

Kennedy charged that, under the Eisenhower administration, the United States had suffered a decline in world power and prestige. Nixon answered that "American prestige is at an all-time high." The candidates also differed regarding ways to spur the nation's economic growth. Kennedy urged increased government action to "get the country moving again." Nixon called for economic growth through private enterprise and individual initiative.

John F. Kennedy won the election: Kennedy—34,227,000 popular votes and 303 electoral votes; Nixon—34,109,000 popular votes and 219 electoral votes. (Senator Harry Byrd of Virginia received 15 electoral votes from unpledged Southern electors.) Despite the narrow popular margin of Kennedy's victory, the Democrats retained substantial control over Congress.

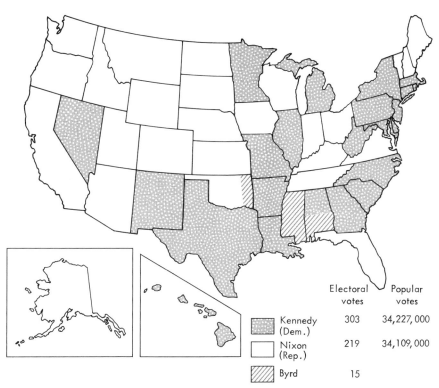

	Electoral votes	Popular votes
Kennedy (Dem.)	303	34,227,000
Nixon (Rep.)	219	34,109,000
Byrd	15	

Election of 1960

2. Observations Upon the Election Results

(a) Kennedy became the first Roman Catholic and, at age 43, the youngest man ever to be elected President. (b) Kennedy's Roman Catholicism played a part in the election, although both candidates deplored religion as a campaign issue. Kennedy's religion probably helped him in the large industrial states, especially in the Northeast, where the Catholic population is large. His religion probably lost him votes in the small rural states, especially in the South and Midwest, where the Catholic population is small and anti-Catholic prejudice strong. (*c*) Kennedy won overwhelming support from minority groups and labor unions. These people believed that Kennedy's election would bring strong civil rights laws and government action to improve economic conditions. (*d*) Like Truman and Stevenson before him, Kennedy failed to hold the "Solid South" intact. The Democratic ticket lost Virginia, Tennessee, and Florida to the Republicans and also lost unpledged electors from Alabama and Mississippi. White Southerners who deserted the Democratic party did so chiefly because of Kennedy's stand on civil rights and his religion.

3. Kennedy: Background and Personality. John F. Kennedy was the great-grandson of an immigrant who had left Ireland during the potato famine of the 1840's. He was the son of Joseph Kennedy, a self-made millionaire who was active in Democratic politics and served under President Franklin Roosevelt as chairman of the Securities and Exchange Commission and as Ambassador to England. The elder Kennedy instilled in his children a strong sense of family loyalty, a competitive spirit, and an interest in public service. Young "Jack" Kennedy majored in political science at Harvard University and graduated with honors. During World War II he served courageously in the navy. Returning to Massachusetts, Kennedy won election in 1946 to the House of Representatives, and in 1952 to the Senate.

Attractive and youthful-looking, Kennedy displayed dignity and self-assurance. Possessing a sense of history, Kennedy had written two books: *Why England Slept,* discussing Britain's appeasement of Nazi Germany, and *Profiles in Courage,* describing valiant deeds of American Senators. Kennedy adhered to the Roosevelt-Truman view that the President should exercise strong leadership.

4. Kennedy's Inaugural Address (1961). Kennedy reaffirmed America's determination to "pay any price, bear any burden, meet any hardship, support any friend, oppose any foe to assure the survival and the success of liberty." Speaking to "those nations who would make themselves our adversary," Kennedy asked "that both sides begin anew the quest for peace." Kennedy concluded with an appeal to his fellow Americans: "Ask not what your country can do for you—ask what you can do for your country."

5. "New Frontier"

a. Meaning. As the frontier of the 19th century had provided Americans with opportunity in the West, so the "new frontier" of the Sixties meant opportunity in the areas of technology, science, and social relations. Kennedy used this term to describe the program of his administration.

b. Accomplishments. Kennedy secured Congressional approval for the modernization of existing programs: expanding Social Security coverage and benefits, raising the minimum wage, furthering slum clearance and public housing, and lowering tariff barriers. Kennedy also won approval for some less controversial new measures: combatting mental retardation, improving medical education, and assisting economically distressed persons.

c. Opposition in Congress. On more controversial measures, Kennedy faced strong opposition from the conservative coalition of Republicans and Southern Democrats. He did not secure legislation for (1) tax reduction, (2) federal aid to elementary and secondary education, (3) medical care for the aged under Social Security, and (4) voting rights and equal treatment for Negroes in places of public accommodation. (During Johnson's administration, Congress enacted all these Kennedy proposals.)

6. Assassination of President Kennedy (November, 1963)

a. Tragic Events. In Dallas, Texas, President Kennedy met death from a sniper's bullet. His suspected assassin, Lee Harvey Oswald, was quickly arrested by the police. Oswald, who had lived in the Soviet Union and who claimed membership in a pro-Castro group, denied the charge. Two days later, as Oswald was being moved to the county jail, he was shot and killed by a Dallas resident who had greatly admired the late President.

b. The New President. Within two hours after the assassination, Vice President Johnson was sworn in as President. Johnson moved quickly to express the nation's grief and to restore public determination to move "toward a new American greatness."

c. Investigating Commission. At President Johnson's request, Chief Justice Earl Warren headed a special commission to investigate the Kennedy assassination. After conducting a 10-month inquiry and evaluating the testimony of over 500 persons, the Warren Commission concluded that Oswald was the assassin and that he had acted alone.

IMPORTANT DOMESTIC LEGISLATION

Laws	Purposes
Area Redevelopment Act (1961)	Help economically depressed areas.
Manpower Development and Training Act (1962)	Retrain destitute farmers and chronically unemployed workers.
Trade Expansion Act (1962)	Permit tariff reductions, enabling the United States to bargain effectively in the "Kennedy Round" of trade negotiations.
Medical Education Act (1963)	Provide student loans; improve teaching facilities in medicine and related fields.
Mental Retardation and Health Centers Act (1963)	Provide funds for research and treatment of mental retardation.

SIGNIFICANT FOREIGN AFFAIRS

1. Peace Corps. President Kennedy created this agency to send skilled and idealistic Americans to assist underdeveloped nations.

2. Cuba. In 1961 Kennedy permitted American-trained Cuban exiles to invade Castro's Cuba at the *Bay of Pigs*. The invaders were crushed. In 1962 Kennedy ordered a naval quarantine of Cuba and secured from Soviet Premier Khrushchev the removal of offensive missiles from Cuba.

3. Alliance for Progress. Kennedy initiated this program of aid and reform to improve the living conditions of the masses of Latin America.

4. Limited Nuclear Test Ban Treaty. In 1963, after many years of negotiations, the United States, Great Britain, and Russia agreed to ban all but underground nuclear tests.

5. Vietnam. Kennedy stepped up military aid to the government of South Vietnam, which was battling Communist guerrillas, the *Vietcong*.

JOHNSON ADMINISTRATION: 1963–1969 (DEMOCRATIC)—
THE "GREAT SOCIETY"

MAJOR POLITICAL AND ECONOMIC ASPECTS

1. Johnson: Background and Personality. The son of a Texas farmer, Lyndon B. Johnson attended Southwest Texas State Teachers College and worked to help pay his way through school. After teaching for a year, Johnson turned to politics. In 1937 Johnson won election to the House of Representatives. Johnson was the first Congressman to enlist in World War II and served with distinction in the navy.

In 1948 Johnson won election to the Senate, and in 1953 he was chosen Senate Democratic Leader. As Senate Majority Leader during the last six years of the Eisenhower administration, Johnson cooperated with the executive branch in furthering legislation. In particular, he helped overcome Southern opposition to the Civil Rights Acts of 1957 and 1960.

In 1960 Johnson made a bid for the Democratic Presidential nomination but lost to John F. Kennedy. Thereafter, Johnson accepted Kennedy's invitation to take second place on the ticket. As Vice President, Johnson assisted Kennedy in major governmental matters.

A determined yet sensitive man, Johnson desired public approval, but not at the price of abandoning his principles. Johnson excelled in working with people of divergent views and achieving satisfactory compromises. He often quoted the Biblical prophet Isaiah, "Come now, and let us reason together."

2. Johnson's Views

a. Strong President. Johnson believed in strong Presidential leadership, having admired Franklin D. Roosevelt as "one of the giants of all times." Johnson welcomed power and used it to further his goals for the public welfare. In dealing with Congress from 1964 to 1966, Johnson, in the words of one historian, "rang up a remarkable record" by a "furious display of coaxing, cajoling, compromising, and plain arm-twisting."

b. Desire for Consensus. A goal of political leadership, Johnson held, is to make the people aware of their "fundamental unity of interest, purpose, and belief." He asked his supporters and his opponents to remember that "there are so many more things in America that unite us than can divide us." Johnson sought broad national agreement, or *consensus*.

3. Election of 1964. The Democrats nominated *Lyndon B. Johnson* for President and Senator *Hubert H. Humphrey* of Minnesota for Vice Presi-

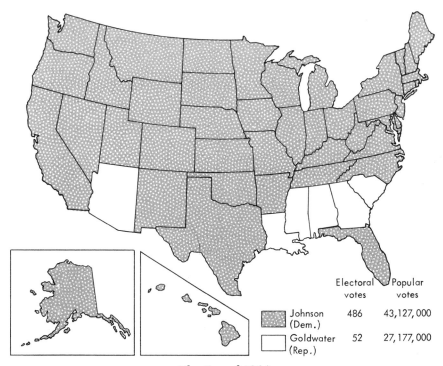

	Electoral votes	Popular votes
Johnson (Dem.)	486	43,127,000
Goldwater (Rep.)	52	27,177,000

Election of 1964

dent. The Republicans nominated Senator *Barry M. Goldwater* of Arizona for President. The Goldwater nomination was a victory for Republican conservatives over the party's previously dominant liberal wing. Goldwater received only lukewarm support, if any, from many liberal Republicans.

Goldwater claimed that he offered voters "a choice not an echo." He urged a tougher foreign policy toward the Communist world. He opposed the growth of federal power as threatening personal freedom and claimed that civil rights matters belonged to the states.

Johnson argued that his foreign policy, being tough but flexible, furthered world peace. He insisted that the expansion of federal power was essential to protect civil rights and to further the nation's liberty and progress.

The American people gave Johnson a landslide victory: Johnson—43 million popular votes, 44 states, and 486 electoral votes; Goldwater—27 million popular votes, 6 states, and 52 electoral votes.

4. Observations Upon the Election Results

(*a*) Johnson's popular vote—43 million, or 61 percent of the total—was greater than that polled by any previous Presidential candidate. (*b*) Johnson swept many other Democrats into House and Senate seats. The Democratic gains in the House were considered sufficient to break the power of the conservative Republican-Southern Democratic coalition. (*c*) Goldwater polled some 7 million votes fewer than Nixon in 1960, indicating that many Republicans had deserted him.

5. "Great Society"

a. Meaning. Johnson asserted that man now possesses the capacity to end war, eradicate poverty and racial injustice, dispel ignorance, share abundance, overcome disease, revitalize cities, and, in general, permit mankind to enjoy a life of freedom and prosperity. To describe the goals of his administration, Johnson employed the term *Great Society*.

b. "Great Society" Congress (1965–1966). Controlled by huge Democratic majorities, the 89th Congress responded favorably to Johnson's requests for far-reaching legislation. According to some historians, this first Great Society Congress could be compared with great productive Congresses of the past: the first New Freedom Congress of the Woodrow Wilson administration and the first New Deal Congress under Franklin D. Roosevelt.

c. Ninetieth Congress (1967–1968). As a result of the Congressional elections of 1966, the Democrats retained control of both houses of Congress but with significantly reduced majorities. The Democratic setback was attributed to a "white backlash" against strong civil rights legislation, protests against inflation, and uneasiness regarding Vietnam.

IMPORTANT DOMESTIC LEGISLATION

Laws	Purposes
Civil Rights Act (1964)	Prohibit discrimination in voting, employment, and places of public accommodation.
Economic Opportunity Act (1964)	Inaugurate programs for the "war on poverty."
Voting Rights Act (1965)	Strengthen previous voting rights laws.
"Medicare" Act (1965)	Provide medical care for the aged under Social Security.
Elementary and Secondary Education Act (1965)	Grant funds directly to public schools; provide instructional materials for public, parochial, and private school students.
Higher Education Act (1965)	Continue grants for college construction and student loans.
Appalachian Development Act (1965)	Aid the distressed Appalachian region.
Immigration Act (1965)	Admit immigrants on the basis of family relationships and national needs.
Clean Rivers Restoration Act (1966)	Provide funds for sewage treatment plants.
Demonstration Cities Act (1966)	Rebuild deteriorated urban areas.
Traffic Safety Act (1966)	Require car manufacturers to meet auto safety standards.
Truth in Packaging Act (1966)	Require accurate labeling of foods, drugs, and cosmetics.
Meat Inspection Act (1967)	Improve inspection of intrastate meat-processing plants.
Civil Rights Act (1968)	Ban racial discrimination in the sale and rental of most housing.
Truth in Lending Act (1968)	Require lenders to state the true cost of consumer credit.
Safe Streets and Crime Control Act (1968) and Gun Control Act (1968)	Grant funds to improve local law enforcement; ban interstate mail-order sales of handguns, shotguns, and rifles; prohibit their sale to minors.
Wholesome Poultry Act (1968)	Improve poultry inspection standards.

SIGNIFICANT FOREIGN AFFAIRS

1. Dominican Republic (1965). Fearing that a Dominican civil war might lead to a Communist take-over, President Johnson intervened with American troops. Although Johnson's action was resented by many Latin Americans, it helped restore peace on the island and enabled the Dominican people to elect a pro-Western regime.

2. Vietnam. Johnson began air strikes against North Vietnam and sharply increased American forces in the South. He also launched "peace offensives" seeking negotiations. These were spurned by Hanoi.

Johnson's Vietnam policies faced criticism at home from "hawks," who demanded stepped-up military effort, and from "doves," who urged a reduction in military activity. Also, the cost of the Vietnam War retarded the programs of Johnson's Great Society. In 1968 Johnson again halted the bombing of North Vietnam, whereupon Hanoi agreed to peace negotiations.

NIXON ADMINISTRATION: 1969–1974 (REPUBLICAN)

MAJOR POLITICAL AND ECONOMIC ASPECTS

1. Election of 1968

a. The Candidates. The Republican convention gave a first-ballot nomination to *Richard M. Nixon*. A middle-of-the-roader, Nixon was acceptable to both liberal and conservative wings of the Republican party. To strengthen the ticket in the South, Nixon selected as his Vice Presidential running mate Governor *Spiro T. Agnew* of Maryland.

The Democratic convention gave a first-ballot nomination to *Hubert H. Humphrey*. When President Johnson had announced that he would not run again, Vice President Humphrey fell heir to the President's political support: labor unions, and city and state party organizations. For the nomination, Humphrey was opposed by Senators Eugene McCarthy of Minnesota and Robert F. Kennedy of New York, both outspoken critics of the Vietnam war, who clashed in five successive primaries. (Humphrey entered the race too late to run in any Presidential primaries.) Kennedy won all but one of these primaries, but, immediately after his victory in California, he was assassinated by an Arab immigrant from Jordan, presumably incensed by Kennedy's pro-Israel statements.

Humphrey's delegates controlled the convention. They nominated Humphrey and his Vice Presidential choice, Senator *Edmund S. Muskie* of Maine.

George C. Wallace, former Governor of Alabama and advocate of segregation and states' rights, ran as a third-party candidate. In most states, his name was listed under the banner of the American Independent party.

b. The Campaign. Nixon blamed the Johnson-Humphrey administration for the Vietnam war, the high crime rate, and the urban riots. He urged the voters to elect "new men" with "new ideas." Humphrey asserted that the voters could "trust" him to lead the nation to peace and prosperity. Wallace urged a return to "law and order" by strengthening the power of the police to deal with crime and with student and Negro riots. Wallace also called for the repeal of federal laws on "open housing" and voting rights, and for the end of federal efforts to desegregate the public schools.

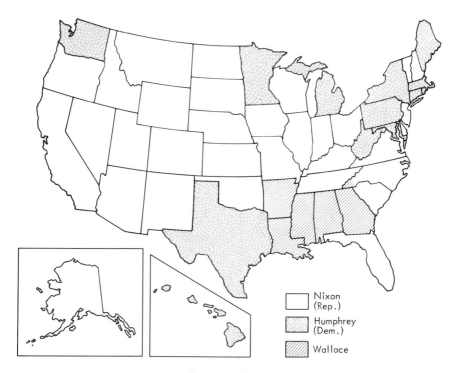

Nixon
(Rep.)

Humphrey
(Dem.)

Wallace

Election of 1968

c. The 1968 Election Results: A Close Victory for Nixon

CANDIDATE	POPULAR VOTE		STATES WON	ELECTORAL VOTE
	IN NUMBER	IN PERCENT		
Nixon	31,770,000	43.4	32	301**
Humphrey	31,271,000	42.7	13*	191
Wallace	9,897,000	13.4	5	46

* Plus the District of Columbia.
** Although Nixon won the popular vote in North Carolina, one elector from that state
voted for Wallace.

2. Observations Upon the 1968 Election Results

(a) Nixon won a close victory. Of 73 million popular votes cast, his
lead over Humphrey was about 500,000. His percentage of the popular vote

(43.4) was the smallest of any successful Presidential candidate since 1912, when Woodrow Wilson was elected, also in a three-way contest. (*b*) Despite Nixon's victory, both branches of Congress remained strongly Democratic. (*c*) In what had traditionally been the Democratic Solid South, Humphrey carried only Texas; Nixon and Wallace each won five states. (*d*) Wallace polled 9.9 million popular votes (13.4 percent of the total), half of them from the South.

3. Election of 1972. The Republican convention renominated Nixon and Agnew, almost unanimously, for a second term.

The Democrats nominated *George McGovern* of South Dakota. McGovern had headed a Democratic reform commission that required convention delegations to give greater representation to women, young people, and ethnic minorities. A challenge to McGovern from the right ended when a would-be assassin shot and paralyzed Alabama Governor George Wallace, thereby ending Wallace's campaign for the Democratic nomination. McGovern selected as his running mate Senator *Thomas Eagleton* of Missouri. After Eagleton revealed that he had been hospitalized for mental depression, McGovern dropped him and selected *Sargent Shriver* as Vice Presidental candidate.

In the campaign, McGovern received only tepid support from many labor leaders and state political bosses. He called for immediate peace in Vietnam, sharp cuts in military funds, and sweeping social reforms. Meanwhile, the Nixon team campaigned on the administration's record: in foreign affairs—withdrawal of half a million soldiers from Vietnam, the journeys to Peking and Moscow, and the SALT pacts limiting missiles; in domestic matters—efforts to stop inflation and opposition to busing pupils to achieve racial integration.

During the campaign, Republican partisans broke into the Democratic Headquarters at the Watergate complex in Washington and were caught trying to "bug" the telephones. Voters paid little attention at the time. However, after the election, the *Watergate Affair* became a major scandal.

Nixon won an overwhelming victory: Nixon—46 million popular votes, 49 states with 521 electoral votes; McGovern—29 million popular votes, 1 state (Massachusetts) and the District of Columbia with 17 votes. Nonetheless, the Democrats kept control of both houses of Congress by substantial margins.

4. Nixon: Background and Views. A native of California, Nixon studied history at Whittier College and compiled an excellent record at Duke University Law School. During World War II he rose to the rank of lieutenant commander in the Navy. Elected to the House of Representatives in 1946, he gained attention as a member of the House Un-American Activities Committee, which investigated Communist influence in the United States. In 1950 he was elected to the Senate. He served as Vice President under Dwight Eisenhower from 1953 to 1961.

As the Republican Presidential nominee in 1960, Nixon lost a close race to Democrat John F. Kennedy. Two years later, Nixon lost a race for Governor of California. Campaigning for Republican Presidental candidate Barry Gold-

IMPORTANT DOMESTIC LEGISLATION

Laws	Purposes
Coal Mine Health and Safety Act (1969)	Reduce coal mine hazards; provide benefits for disabled miners.
Clean Air Act (1970)	Produce a 90-percent pollution-free auto engine.
Organized Crime Control Act (1970)	Increase federal powers over interstate gambling and organized crime; make bombings a federal offense.
Voting Rights Act (1970)	Set voting age at 18 for all elections. (Supreme Court disallowed this provision for state and local elections, making necessary the 26th Amendment.)
National Cancer Act (1971)	Allot funds to expand cancer research.
Social Security Act (1972)	Raise Social Security taxes; increase benefits; provide for future "cost of living" benefits tied to Consumer Price Index.
Product Safety Act (1972)	Create a commission to enforce safety standards for many household items.
Revenue-Sharing Act (1972)	Distribute federal funds to state and local governments for use as they see fit.
Clean Water Act (1972)	Clean up rivers and lakes by providing federal funds to state and local governments mainly for sewage plants.
Agricultural Act (1973)	Provide direct cash subsidies to farmers if "target prices" of basic crops fall below market prices.
Alaska Pipeline Act (1973)	Construct Alaska oil pipeline; bar environmental suits opposing the pipeline.
War-Powers Resolution (1973)	Require the President to secure Congressional approval for any extended combat use of American forces abroad.

water in 1964 and for Congressional candidates in 1966, Nixon built a broad base of support within the Republican party, which served him well in 1968.

MAJOR DOMESTIC EVENTS

1. Supreme Court Appointments. Nixon appointed four Justices to the Supreme Court, all within his first term. As Chief Justice he named Warren Burger. As Associate Justices he named Harry Blackmun, Lewis Powell, and William Rehnquist. In contrast to the previous Warren Court majority, which had been liberal and interpreted the Constitution broadly, the four Nixon appointees were considered conservatives who favored a stricter interpretation of the Constitution and judicial restraint.

2. Revenue-Sharing. Nixon persuaded Congress to put federal aid to the states on a new footing. The *Revenue-Sharing Act* of 1972 gave states and local governments more leeway in using federal money.

3. Energy Problems

a. Background. The American people for years benefited from cheap and plentiful supplies of energy—coal, natural gas, and oil. With 6 percent of the world's population, Americans accounted for 30 percent of all the energy used by the world's people. In the early 1970's, experts warned that the nation was using more energy than it was producing and would soon face an energy crisis.

b. Arab Oil Embargo (1973–1974). Check the Index.

c. American Energy Plans. To deal with the oil shortage caused by the Arab embargo, President Nixon urged people to set their thermostats lower, drive no faster than 50 miles an hour, and form more car pools. For the long run, he proposed (1) building new electric plants to use coal and nuclear fuel; (2) tapping fossil fuel supplies more aggressively (building the Alaska oil pipeline, increasing offshore oil drilling, and strip-mining more coal), and (3) pursuing new energy sources (solar energy, shale-oil deposits, and coal-to-gas conversion).

4. Fight Against Inflation. The oil embargo and other factors caused prices to rise sharply. The Nixon administration battled inflation by such traditional methods as cutting federal spending (to reduce demand) and raising interest rates (to discourage borrowing). It also imposed temporary wage and price controls—with little success. The cost of living rose 42 percent from 1968 to 1974. Inflation remained serious and showed little sign of easing.

5. Reducing Pollution. The *Environmental Protection Agency* was created in 1970 to enforce laws aimed at protecting the environment. Congress passed the *Clean Air Act* of 1970 and the *Clean Water Act* of 1972 to reduce pollution.

6. Resignation of Agnew as Vice President. Vice President Spiro Agnew came under investigation for alleged kickbacks, fraud, and income tax evasion while Baltimore County Executive and Maryland Governor. He resigned as Vice President late in 1973 after pleading "no contest" to a charge of tax evasion. Agnew was sentenced to three years' probation and a fine. He was the first Vice President to resign because of criminal charges.

Acting under the Twenty-fifth Amendment, President Nixon nominated Gerald R. Ford to replace Agnew. Congress approved, and Ford became Vice President.

WATERGATE AND THE NIXON RESIGNATION

1. Background. Overshadowing President Nixon's second term was *Watergate*—a word that carried two meanings. (*a*) In general, Watergate meant a series of political scandals affecting the Nixon administration. The *Committee to Reelect the President* had accepted secret and illegal contributions from corporations and dairy cooperatives that could benefit from administration favors. The committee also had financed "dirty tricks" to discredit Democrats. White House officials had used the Internal Revenue Service to harass administration "enemies." (*b*) Specifically, Watergate meant the June 1972 break-in at Democratic national headquarters at the Watergate complex, and the subsequent efforts to hide involvement of top administration officials by a cover-up. Caught in the break-in, Republican partisans were arrested and put on trial.

2. Highlights. For almost two years Watergate dominated the news and revealed a complicated, often confusing sequence of political intrigue. The highlights were as follows:

a. Investigations. Two newspapers, the *Washington Post* and the *New York Times*—both considered anti-Nixon—pursued investigations of Watergate. The Senate established a bipartisan committee, led by Senator *Sam Ervin* of North Carolina, that held hearings and uncovered evidence damaging to the administration. A *special prosecutor* named by the Attorney General investigated the Watergate affair and brought criminal charges against a number of administration officials, most of whom had already resigned from office.

b. Court Actions. Some of those charged pleaded guilty and offered to provide evidence for the prosecution, hoping to receive lighter sentences. Others received jury trials. Some 30 persons charged with various Watergate offenses—including burglary, obstructing justice, fraud, and lying to a grand jury—were found guilty and given jail sentences.

c. The Tapes. A witness before the Senate investigating committee revealed that President Nixon had ordered the taping of all White House conversations. In response to requests from the committee and the special prosecutor for specific tapes, the President released some tapes and turned over edited transcripts of other tapes. Soon afterward Special Prosecutor *Leon Jaworski* requested further tapes, but President Nixon said no. The President based his refusal on the doctrine of *executive privilege*. Under this doctrine, which is not stated in the Constitution but is implied by the system of separation of powers, Nixon claimed a right to keep Presidential records confidential. Jaworski then took his case to the federal court.

In July 1974 the Supreme Court in an 8-to-0 decision ordered the President to surrender the tapes. Chief Justice Warren Burger stated that the doctrine of executive privilege must yield to the need for evidence in the Watergate trials. Although expressing disappointment, Nixon agreed to obey the decisions.

d. The Impeachment Proceedings. Meanwhile the bipartisan *House Judiciary Committee* had been holding hearings to consider possible impeachment charges against the President. With several Republicans joining the Democrats, the committee approved two Articles of Impeachment. The first dealt with Nixon's role in the Watergate cover-up. The second accused Nixon of abusing Presidential powers for personal purposes. While the committee was acting, Nixon complied with the Supreme Court order by turning over more tapes, one of which revealed that he had halted an FBI investigation of the Watergate break-in immediately after it occurred. Since Nixon had previously denied knowledge of the Watergate cover-up for its first nine months, this revelation undercut the President's credibility and eroded his support in Congress. Republican leaders advised Nixon that impeachment was likely.

e. The Resignation. On August 9, 1974, Richard M. Nixon resigned—the first President in American history to do so. In a televised speech, Nixon said some of his judgments had been wrong, insisted that at all times he had been concerned with the best interests of the nation, and explained that he was resigning because he no longer had a "strong enough political base in Congress." Nixon's successor, Gerald Ford, upon being sworn in as President, called upon the nation to "bind up the internal wounds of Watergate" and asserted that "our long national nightmare is over."

3. Significances

a. Bad Effects. The Watergate affair (1) increased public cynicism toward politicians generally and the political system generally, (2) endangered the ability of the Republican party to function effectively, and (3) was a scandal comparable to Teapot Dome in the Harding administration and the various corruptions that marred the Grant administration.

b. Good Effects. The response to Watergate showed the strength and competence of our democratic institutions: (1) *Freedom of the press worked.* Protected by the First Amendment, newspapers focused attention upon Watergate scandals. (2) *The two-party system worked.* The Democrats in control of Congress functioned effectively and reasonably in opposition to the Republican administration. (3) *Checks and balances worked.* The Congress was able to check the executive by investigating the actions of top administrative officials. The House was able to check the President by starting the impeachment process. The Supreme Court was able to check the President by deciding that the Presidential claim of executive privilege to withhold tapes was in this case not valid. (4) *Government by law worked.* Ours is a government of laws, not of persons. The laws must be enforced, fairly and impartially, regardless of the individuals involved. No one, not even the President, is above the law. The Constitutional procedures inscribed almost 200 years earlier proved resilient. They provided the methods and agencies to investigate the scandals, to punish the wrongdoers, to compel a President to resign, and to effect a smooth transition of executive power to a new President. Upon taking the Presidential oath, Gerald Ford noted the strength of our political democracy, saying, "Our Constitution works. Here the people rule."

c. Further Effects. (1) *The powers of the Presidency were weakened and the powers of Congress were strengthened.* This reversed a 20th-century trend, at least for the time being. Congress reasserted its authority, not only by investigations and impeachment proceedings but also by the following legislative actions: The *Budget Reform Act* gave Congress a larger voice in the budget-making process. The *War-Powers Resolution,* passed over Nixon's veto, required the President to get Congressional approval for any extended combat by American troops abroad. (Check the Index.) (2) *Public esteem for Congress rose.* (3) *Campaign laws were changed.* Almost all states passed campaign reform laws, as did Congress for federal elections. In general, these laws set limits on campaign contributions so as to reduce the influence of wealthy donors on candidates for office.

SIGNIFICANT FOREIGN AFFAIRS

1. Vietnam. President Nixon sought a negotiated peace that would preserve American vital interests. Nixon's national security adviser, *Henry Kissinger,* undertook secret talks with the North Vietnamese. In 1973 a detailed truce agreement was signed and the United States withdrew from Vietnam. Nixon thus brought to an end a long and costly war that had deeply divided the American people. (For details on what followed, check the Index for Vietnam.)

2. Congress and Foreign Affairs. With Nixon under attack because of Watergate, Congress reasserted its authority over foreign affairs. Using its power to withhold funds, it compelled Nixon to stop all bombing in Cambodia in August 1973. In November 1973 it passed the *War-Powers Act* (check the Index).

3. Asian Policy. Announcing the *Nixon Doctrine* at Guam in 1969, the President said the United States would cut back its involvement in Asian affairs. He said we would keep our treaty commitments and provide economic and military help. However, except for a nuclear threat, we would expect Asian nations to provide the military forces for their own defense.

4. Middle East. In the 1973 Arab-Israeli War, President Nixon resupplied the Israelis with essential military equipment. Henry Kissinger (who became Secretary of State in 1973) negotiated troop disengagement agreements for the Israeli-Egyptian and Israeli-Syrian fronts.

5. Detente With the Soviet Union. In 1969 President Nixon declared that Soviet-American relations were ready to move from confrontation to negotiation in a new era of *detente,* or relaxation (check the Index). Nixon visited Moscow in 1972 and U.S.-Soviet relations took a turn for the better.

6. Arms Limitations. The Nixon administration began negotiations with the Soviets in the *Strategic Arms Limitation Talks (SALT).* In 1972 in Moscow, President Nixon signed two SALT I pacts limiting missiles. (Check the Index.)

7. Improved Relations With China. President Nixon ended more than two decades of isolation between the United States and China. In 1972 he visited China, a trip he called a "journey for peace."

FORD ADMINISTRATION: 1974–1977 (REPUBLICAN)

MAJOR POLITICAL AND ECONOMIC ASPECTS

1. Ford Takes Office (August 9, 1974). Immediately upon Nixon's resignation, Vice President Gerald R. Ford was sworn in as President. Ford delivered a brief and simple Inaugural Address. Since he had become Vice President by provisions of the Twenty-fifth Amendment and President by resignation of his predecessor, Ford remarked, "I am acutely aware that you have not elected me as your President by your ballots. So I ask you to confirm me as your President with your prayers."

2. Ford: Background and Views. Ford was a star football player at the University of Michigan. He served 13 terms as a member of the House of Representatives from Michigan. In 1965 his fellow Republican Representatives elected Ford as House minority leader. Ford described his political outlook in these words: "I would say I am a moderate on domestic issues, a conservative in fiscal affairs, and a dyed-in-the-wool internationalist in foreign affairs."

3. Ford's Initial Moves

a. *Rockefeller for Vice President.* With the Vice Presidential office again vacant, Ford acted quickly, under the Twenty-fifth Amendment, to nominate his choice—oil millionaire and former New York Governor Nelson Rockefeller. Congress overwhelmingly approved the nomination.

b. *Unconditional Pardon for Nixon.* Ford granted Richard Nixon an unconditional pardon for all federal offenses that he "committed or may have committed or taken part in" while President.

4. The 1973–1975 "Inflationary Recession." This recession was the longest and most severe since World War II. Recessions usually bring falling prices, but this one brought a business slump with strong inflation.

President Ford, a Republican, held that the best way to improve the economy was to curtail inflation. To this end he sought to limit government services and hold down federal spending. Congress, heavily Democratic, wanted to stimulate the economy and reduce unemployment by increased government spending. In 2½ years in office, Ford used the veto—on economic and other bills—66 times and was overridden 12 times. This sixth postwar recession ended in 1975.

IMPORTANT DOMESTIC LEGISLATION

1. Campaign Reform Act (1974): provide substantial federal funding of Presidential campaigns; establish a Federal Elections Commission; limit contributions by wealthy individuals.

2. "Government in Sunshine" Act (1976): require some 50 government agencies to conduct their activities in full view of the press and public.

3. Other Legislation: (*a*) restrict busing for integration to no farther than the school next closest to the child's home, (*b*) provide federal funds to states and cities for urban mass transit, (*c*) provide federal loans to New York City to help stave off bankruptcy, (*d*) extend American jurisdiction over fishing in waters up to 200 miles offshore.

OTHER DEVELOPMENTS

1. Stalemate Over Energy. President Ford proposed removing all price controls on oil and natural gas to spur the search for new domestic energy resources. Congress favored maintaining price controls to protect consumers.

2. Investigations of Intelligence Agencies. Select committees of the House and Senate held hearings on abuses by the CIA and the FBI. The CIA had kept Americans under surveillance (although this was specifically prohibited by law) and engaged in assassination plots abroad. Both the CIA and the FBI had illegally opened mail, maintained wiretaps, and conducted break-ins.

Both agencies reorganized to eliminate illegal activities. Also, President Ford issued an executive order to limit the agencies' domestic activities and to establish a Civilian Oversight Board to check on the CIA and the FBI.

SIGNIFICANT FOREIGN AFFAIRS

1. Vietnam. In 1975 Hanoi, in violation of the Paris truce agreement, mounted a massive offensive and gained control of South Vietnam. President Ford secured funds from Congress to bring some Vietnamese refugees to the United States.

2. Angola. Learning that the United States was covertly aiding one side in Angola's civil war, Congress passed the *Clark Amendment* to prohibit such aid.

CARTER ADMINISTRATION: 1977–1981 (DEMOCRATIC)

MAJOR POLITICAL AND ECONOMIC ASPECTS

1. Election of 1976. The Democrats nominated James Earl (Jimmy) Carter, a former governor of Georgia. As his running mate, Carter selected *Walter Frederick (Fritz) Mondale*, a liberal Senator from Minnesota.

President Ford won the Republican nomination, narrowly withstanding a challenge by former California Governor *Ronald Reagan*, the idol of Republican conservatives. To restore party harmony, Ford named as his running mate for the Vice Presidency a conservative Kansas Senator, *Robert Dole*.

In the campaign, Ford stressed his Presidential record: restoring confidence in the integrity of government, curtailing inflation, and leading the nation out of a recession. Carter said it was "time for a change" and claimed to represent a "fresh face"—not one of the Washington insiders—who would curtail bureaucracy and improve government operations.

2. Observations on the 1976 Election Results. (*a*) Carter won a narrow victory, carrying the South and most industrial states of the Northeast and Midwest. (*b*) The Democrats retained overwhelming control of both branches of Congress. (*c*) Carter was the first candidate from the Deep South to be elected President since Zachary Taylor in 1848. Observers interpreted Carter's victory to mean that Americans had overcome prejudices arising out of the Civil War and Reconstruction. (*d*) Carter's victory was significantly helped by the Campaign Reform Act of 1974. Relatively unknown nationally and having limited financial support, Carter greatly benefited from federal funds.

ELECTION OF 1976

| CANDIDATE | POPULAR VOTE | | STATES WON | ELECTORAL VOTE |
	IN NUMBER	IN PERCENT		
Carter	40,300,000	51	23*	297
Ford	38,600,000	49	27	241

*Plus the District of Columbia.

3. Carter: Background and Views. A graduate of the United States Naval Academy, Carter served in the Navy's nuclear submarine service. Upon the death of his father in 1953, Carter returned to Georgia to manage the family agribusiness. He won election to the state senate and in 1970 became Governor.

Moved by deep religious convictions (he was a Southern Baptist who considered himself "born again"), Carter saw himself as an activist President. He frequently referred to moral imperatives in his Presidential addresses.

4. Economic Problems. The Carter administration had to confront high unemployment, mounting inflation, high interest rates, an unfavorable balance of trade, and other economic problems. By 1980, the situation had worsened.

5. Tensions Between the Administration and Congress. Carter had difficulty getting his programs through Congress even though he and the majority in Congress were Democrats. Congress was still asserting its own authority against the executive branch—a process that began during the Watergate scandals. Also, Carter was an "outsider" and inexperienced in dealing with Congress.

IMPORTANT DOMESTIC LEGISLATION

1. Strip-Mining of Coal Act (1977): permit most strip-mining of coal, provided the land is restored to good environmental condition.

2. Comprehensive Energy Act (1978): permit the price of newly discovered natural gas to rise gradually until controls are removed in 1985; give tax breaks to homeowners who save energy by insulating their homes; put a special tax on gas-guzzling cars; encourage industry to expand its use of coal.

3. Further Energy Measures (1980): spur production of synthetic fuels; place a "windfall-profits tax" on domestic oil companies.

4. Waste Cleanup Act (1980): provide for cleaning up chemical waste dumps.

5. Other Legislation: (*a*) raise the minimum wage, in four steps, to $3.35 by 1982, (*b*) reform the civil service to ease regulations for discharging incompetent workers, (*c*) broaden the definition of refugees and permit additional refugees to enter the United States, (*d*) prohibit U.S. companies from participating in the Arab trade boycott against Israel, (*e*) raise the mandatory retirement age for most workers in private industry from 65 to 70, (*f*) provide loan guarantees to help the Chrysler Corporation avoid bankruptcy, (*g*) create two new Cabinet-level departments—of Energy and Education, (*h*) partially deregulate the banking, trucking, and railroad industries, and (*i*) strengthen safety standards for nuclear power plants.

SIGNIFICANT FOREIGN AFFAIRS

1. Human Rights. Carter launched a human rights campaign, arguing that since all U.N. members were pledged to respect human rights, their treatment of political prisoners and dissidents was a matter of international concern.

2. Panama Canal Treaties. The President secured Senate ratification, by a narrow margin, of treaties providing for the transfer of ownership and management of the canal to Panama by the year 2000.

3. Camp David Summit Meeting (1978). The President acted as mediator for talks between President Sadat of Egypt and Prime Minister Begin of Israel. He hailed two agreements as a major advance toward peace in the Middle East.

4. Diplomatic Recognition of China. In 1979 Carter gave diplomatic recognition to China while keeping economic ties with Nationalist China on Taiwan.

5. Soviet Invasion of Afghanistan. President Carter condemned the Soviet invasion of Afghanistan in 1979 and imposed various economic and political sanctions. He asked Congress to delay consideration of the SALT II Treaty.

6. Carter Doctrine. Carter warned the Soviet Union in 1980 that any attempt to gain control of the oil-rich Persian Gulf region "will be regarded as an assault on the vital interests of the United States" and "will be repelled by any means necessary, including military force."

7. Iran Hostage Crisis. To gain the release of some 50 American diplomatic personnel held hostage in Iran, Carter applied pressures against Iran. The hostage crisis hurt Carter politically, contributing to his defeat in 1980.

REAGAN ADMINISTRATION: 1981–1989 (REPUBLICAN)

MAJOR POLITICAL AND ECONOMIC ASPECTS

1. Election of 1980. President Carter withstood a belated challenge to his renomination by Massachusetts Senator Edward (Teddy) Kennedy. The President secured an easy first-ballot renomination at the Democratic convention; also renominated was his running mate, Walter Mondale.

Former California Governor Ronald Reagan racked up a series of victories in Republican primaries over rivals who included George Bush, John Anderson, Howard Baker, and Robert Dole. The Republican convention chose Reagan on the first ballot. As his running mate he chose *George Bush*, a former member of Congress, director of the CIA, and ambassador to the U.N.

Anderson, a Republican Congressman from Illinois, ran in the November election as an independent candidate for President.

In the election campaign, Carter emphasized that he had maintained peace, was experienced, and represented the liberal traditions of the Democratic party; also he portrayed Reagan as a "dangerous" leader. Reagan blamed Carter for the nation's economic woes—double-digit inflation, heavy unemployment, high interest rates—and for America's "humiliation" over the hostages held in Iran. Portraying Carter as a "weak" leader, naive about Soviet intentions, Reagan called upon the voters to choose strong, conservative leadership.

ELECTION OF 1980

CANDIDATE	POPULAR VOTE		STATES WON	ELECTORAL VOTE
	IN NUMBER	IN PERCENT		
Reagan	43,900,000	51+	44	489
Carter	35,500,000	41+	6*	49
Anderson	5,700,000	7	0	0

*Plus District of Columbia

2. Observations on the 1980 Election Results. (*a*) Although pollsters had predicated a close election, Reagan won an easy victory. He won the votes of many traditionally Democratic voters—union members, ethnic and religious minorities, Southerners, and urban dwellers. (*b*) The Republicans gained control of the Senate for the first time in 26 years. Although Democrats continued to control the House of Representatives, the Republicans gained 35 seats, enabling them to win votes on certain issues when Republicans and conservative Democrats joined forces.

3. Election of 1984. The Republicans again nominated Reagan and Bush. Senator Gary Hart of Colorado and Jesse Jackson, a black clergyman, made a strong showing in the Democratic primaries, but former Vice President Walter Mondale led the field and won the nomination. As his running mate, Mondale chose Representative *Geraldine Ferraro* of Queens, New York. She was the first woman on the national ticket of a major party.

4. Congressional Election of 1986. Democrats recaptured control of the Senate while retaining a strong majority in the House of Representatives. For the rest of his term, President Reagan had to deal with a Democratic Congress.

5. Reagan: Background and Views. Born into a poor family, Ronald Reagan grew up in Illinois in a small-town environment. He attended Eureka College, where he majored in economics and won letters in three major sports. After graduation in 1932, Reagan worked as a radio sportscaster, then as a Hollywood movie star and television host. He was head of the Screen Actors Guild.

Reagan became a conservative Republican and served as governor of California from 1967 to 1975. Reagan was 69 years old when elected president in 1980—the oldest person ever elected to that office.

Reagan said that the federal government had become too large and too involved in people's lives. He worked to reduce government involvement in social and economic life and to build up the nation's military power.

MAJOR DOMESTIC EVENTS

1. Cuts in Social Spending. President Reagan got Congress to make sharp cuts in social programs such as welfare grants, Medicaid, food stamps, and student loans. Critics said the cuts caused widespread suffering among the poor. Reagan and his supporters said the cuts had removed "fat" from the budget and that a "safety net" remained to protect the poor.

2. Tax Changes. Under President Reagan, income taxes on individuals and businesses were lowered significantly, while payroll taxes were increased. Payroll taxes go for Social Security and Medicare; they hit working-class and middle-class people the hardest. By 1990, nearly three fourths of all Americans were paying more in payroll taxes than in income taxes.

a. Income Tax Cuts. In 1981 President Reagan secured Congressional approval for a cut in income taxes, in line with the theory of *supply-side econom-*

ics. The goal was to make more money available to individuals and businesses, thereby promoting economic growth.

   b. Payroll Tax Rise. To restore the Social Security System to financial health, bipartisan measures cut Social Security benefits and increased the payroll taxes that provide the system's income. By 1990, employees and employers each paid a 7.65 percent tax on the first $51,300 of wages or salary.

   c. Income Tax Reform. Under the bipartisan *Tax Reform Act of 1986*, basic income tax rates were simplified and reduced, and many deductions and tax breaks were eliminated. (See page 258.)

   3. Budget Deficits. Budget deficits soared to new heights during the Reagan years, as receipts lagged behind spending and the government had to borrow billions each year to pay for its programs. President Reagan proposed a Constitutional amendment to require a balanced budget. Instead, Congress approved the *Gramm-Rudman-Hollings Act of 1985*, which called for automatic, across-the-board cuts each year. (See page 261.)

   4. Drugs. President Reagan and Congress stepped up the war on illegal drugs. The *Omnibus Drug Act of 1988* permitted the death penalty for drug-related killings and authorized $2.8 billion for drug education, rehabilitation, and interdiction. The armed forces began apprehending drug smugglers.

   5. Business Deregulation. Reagan continued the process of deregulation begun during the Carter years, extending it to airlines and other industries.

   6. Immigration. The *Immigration Reform and Control Act of 1986* offered amnesty to illegal immigrants who had lived in the United States for more than four years. It barred the hiring of illegal immigrants. (See page 311.)

   7. Farm Subsidies. The Reagan administration tried to trim government farm programs. Nonetheless, government spending on farm programs reached record levels as farmers suffered a prolonged drought crisis. Under the *Food Security Act of 1985*, the government paid higher subsidies to farmers while holding grain prices down in an effort to boost grain exports. (See page 217.)

   8. Supreme Court Appointments. In 1981 President Reagan appointed *Sandra Day O'Connor*, the first woman Justice. In 1986 he appointed *Antonin Scalia*. The President elevated Justice *William H. Rehnquist* to the position of Chief Justice upon the retirement of Warren Burger in 1986.

   9. Welfare Reform. In 1988, the President and Congress worked out a major overhaul of welfare laws. A key goal: to require many welfare recipients to either get a job or take part in job-training programs.

FOREIGN AFFAIRS

   1. Arms Buildup and "Star Wars." At President Reagan's urging, Congress stepped up military spending and expanded the nation's nuclear arsenal.

The President called for a large new space-based defense system—the *Strategic Defense Initiative*, or "Star Wars." (See page 651.)

2. Soviet Union. At first President Reagan took a hard line against the Soviet Union, calling it an "evil empire." However, tensions eased after Mikhail Gorbachev took over as Soviet leader in 1985 and began reforms. In 1987 Reagan and Gorbachev signed the Intermediate Nuclear Forces (INF) Treaty. In 1989, Soviet troops pulled out of Afghanistan.

3. El Salvador and Nicaragua. The Reagan administration took measures to oppose what it called Communist expansionism in Central America. It stepped up aid to the government of El Salvador battling leftist rebels. It organized a force of Nicaraguan guerrillas (the *contras*) to oppose the leftist government of Nicaragua. Congress often disagreed about these policies.

4. Iran-Contra Affair. In an attempt to procure the freedom of American hostages in Lebanon, the Reagan administration secretly sold arms to Iran (a nation that presumably had influence with the hostage takers). Profits from the Iran arms sales were then diverted to Nicaraguan contras, at a time when Congress had cut off military aid to the contras. President Reagan denied knowing of the diversion of funds. National Security Adviser *John Poindexter* and an assistant, *Oliver North*, were later convicted on criminal charges resulting from the Iran-contra events.

5. Reagan Doctrine. The administration announced it would support "freedom fighters" opposing hard-line leftist and Communist regimes. Besides the contras, the United States aided guerrillas in Afghanistan and Angola.

6. Caribbean Aid. Under the *Caribbean Basin Initiative*, friendly nations around the Caribbean received trade privileges and economic aid.

7. Grenada. United States troops led an invasion of the Caribbean island nation of Grenada in 1983, ousting a Marxist government.

8. Middle East.

a. Lebanon. The United States criticized Israel's 1982 invasion of Lebanon, but continued to supply Israel with economic and military aid. President Reagan sent Marines to Lebanon to help deal with the chaotic conditions that followed Israel's 1982 invasion. After a suicide truck-bombing killed 241 Marines in 1983, Reagan withdrew the troops.

b. PLO. In 1988 the United States opened direct talks with the Palestine Liberation Organization (PLO). The talks began after PLO leader Yasir Arafat eased the PLO's traditional position by renouncing terrorism.

c. Libya. Accusing Libya of major responsibility for international terrorism, the United States in 1986 bombed Libyan cities and air bases.

9. Trade Problems. Arguing in favor of free trade, the Reagan administration opposed protectionist measures that some members of Congress proposed for dealing with massive trade deficits. Through talks and various pressures on Japan, the European Community, and others, the administration sought to increase American exports while holding down imports. The *Omnibus Trade and Competitiveness Act of 1988* gave the administration new powers aimed at bolstering its negotiating position. Also, the United States and Canada signed a free-trade treaty in 1988 to eliminate almost all duties and tariffs. (See pages 302–303.)

10. Philippines. The United States disavowed Philippine President *Ferdinand Marcos*, a longtime ally, after he was accused of election fraud in 1986. President Reagan welcomed Marcos's successor, *Corazon Aquino*.

11. South Africa. President Reagan denounced South Africa's *apartheid* system of racial separation under white minority-rule, while cooperating with South Africa in a policy of *constructive engagement*. Over Reagan's veto, Congress applied economic sanctions against South Africa in 1986. The Reagan administration and the Soviet Union helped work out agreements in 1988 for the independence of Namibia (which South Africa had ruled).

12. Panama. The United States applied economic sanctions against Panama, accusing dictator Manuel Noriega of drug smuggling. (See pages 473–474.)

BUSH ADMINISTRATION: 1989–1993 (REPUBLICAN)

MAJOR POLITICAL AND ECONOMIC ASPECTS

1. Election of 1988. Beating back a challenge by Senator Robert Dole of Kansas, Vice President George Bush easily won the Republican nomination. His surprise choice for running mate was Senator *Dan Quayle* of Indiana.

Massachusetts Governor *Michael Dukakis* gained a strong lead in the Democratic primaries, with all of his opponents except civil rights activist Jesse Jackson dropping out before the convention. To balance his own liberal views, Dukakis picked a conservative senator from Texas, *Lloyd Bentsen*, as his running mate.

During the fall campaign, both candidates were criticized for "attack ads" that substituted appeals to raw emotion for reasoned political dialogue.

ELECTION OF 1988

CANDIDATE	POPULAR VOTE		STATES WON	ELECTORAL VOTE
	IN NUMBER	IN PERCENT		
Bush	48,886,097	53	40	426
Dukakis	41,809,074	46	10*	111

*Plus the District of Columbia.

2. Observations on the 1988 Election Results. (*a*) Bush's victory was the fifth Republican win in the last six Presidential elections. (*b*) For the first time since Martin Van Buren in 1836, a serving Vice President had won election as President. (*c*) Democrats won majorities in the Senate and the House.

3. Bush: Background and Views. Bush grew up in a prominent New England family. At 18 he became the Navy's youngest commissioned pilot in World War II, and he won the Distinguished Flying Cross after being shot down by a Japanese gunner. After the war, Bush made a fortune as a Texas oilman.

Bush became active in Republican politics, representing a Texas district for two terms in the House of Representatives. Later he served as ambassador to the U.N., chairman of the Republican National Committee, and head of the CIA.

More pragmatic than the ideological Reagan, Bush was distrusted by many in the conservative wing of the Republican party. However, he shared Reagan's desire to hold down social spending and taxes. One of Bush's most memorable lines in the 1988 campaign was "Read my lips: no new taxes," in response to assertions that the government would need higher taxes to tame its budget deficits.

MAJOR DOMESTIC EVENTS

1. Banks. To rescue the nation's savings and loan banks, which were beset with staggering losses, President Bush and Congress began a plan to shut down and sell off failing S&L's. Congress and the President negotiated over further plans for far-reaching banking reforms (check the Index).

2. Drugs. President Bush called the war on drugs "the toughest domestic challenge we've faced in decades." Congress appropriated even more than Bush asked for the war on drugs.

3. Deficits and Taxes. President Bush and Congress circled warily around each other, hesitating to attack high budget deficits with either massive spending cuts or new taxes. However, two years after pledging no new taxes, the President agreed to a modest increase in the income tax as well as higher taxes on luxury boats, gasoline, cigarettes, beer, wine, and spirits. Despite the new taxes, budget deficits soared higher than ever.

4. Rights of the Disabled. With support from Bush, Congress passed the *Americans with Disabilities Act* of 1990 to fight discrimination against people with disabilities.

5. Civil Rights. The President and Congress agreed on a 1991 bill to expand the rights of workers to sue on claims of job discrimination. (See page 329.) President Bush had vetoed a 1990 version, calling it a "quota bill."

6. Education. Saying he wanted to be known as "the education president," Bush worked with state governors to institute national standards for evaluating students' progress. The President also proposed giving parents more choices about which schools their children attend.

7. Supreme Court Appointments. President Bush appointed *David Souter* in 1990 and *Clarence Thomas* in 1991. Thomas, who succeeded Thurgood Marshall, became the second African American to sit on the Supreme Court.

8. Environment. The *Clean Air Act of 1990* was the most important new antipollution law in many years. (For its provisions, check the Index.) Separately, President Bush asked Congress to convert the Environmental Protection Agency into a new Department of the Environment.

FOREIGN AFFAIRS

1. Collapse of Communism in Eastern Europe. With stunning rapidity, the nations of Eastern Europe began ousting Communist rulers and adopting multiparty political systems late in 1989.

2. German Reunification. East Germany merged with West Germany in 1990, making Germany a united nation for the first time since World War II. The new Germany, with a democratic government, promised to follow a peaceful path.

3. Collapse of the Soviet Union. Soviet President *Mikhail Gorbachev* encouraged the evolution of Eastern Europe. He also began changes in the Soviet Union. But events seemed to spin out of Gorbachev's control after an unsuccessful attempt by hard-liners to oust him in a 1991 coup. The central structure of the Soviet Union then collapsed. In the chaotic months that followed, Russia and the other regions that had made up the Soviet Union struggled to piece together a loose new confederation of republics. They faced the immense task of reviving the country's desperate economy and assuring firm control over its nuclear weapons.

4. End of the Cold War. President Bush and other leaders proclaimed that the cold war was over. After the Soviet Union collapsed, the United States and its allies offered economic aid to Russia and other former Soviet republics to pave the way for the free-market reforms.

5. Nicaragua. President Bush hailed the results of Nicaraguan elections in 1990 that replaced the leftist Sandinistas with an American-backed coalition led by *Violeta Barrios de Chamorro.*

6. Panama. United States troops invaded Panama in December 1989 and ousted the dictator Manuel Noriega. (Check the Index for Panama.)

7. Trade. President Bush opened three-way talks aimed at linking Canada, Mexico, and the United States in a North American trade union. He pressed the European Community to maintain open doors as it advanced to new stages of economic and political unity.

8. Japan. President Bush continued efforts to gain greater access to the Japanese economy for American businesses. Many Americans no longer saw Japan as a longtime cold war ally, but rather as a serious economic rival.

9. South Africa. The Bush administration praised South African President *F. W. de Klerk* for easing *apartheid* and for freeing imprisoned black nationalist leader *Nelson Mandela*.

10. Persian Gulf War. With United Nations backing, the United States led a coalition of nations that attacked Iraq early in 1991, five months after Iraq had invaded and occupied its oil-rich neighbor, Kuwait. The brief *Perisan Gulf War* consisted of protracted air attacks followed by an invasion carried out by allied ground forces. Iraq surrendered six weeks after the first air strikes and 100 hours after the ground operation began. A U.N.-supervised program to destroy all Iraq's weapons of mass destruction then began.

11. Middle East Peace Talks. The United States and the Soviet Union served as co-sponsors of Middle East peace talks that began in 1991. The talks brought together Israelis, Palestinians, and other Arab representatives.

12. Indochina. In 1991 the major powers helped to negotiate a cease-fire after two decades of war in Cambodia. The Cambodian government and rebel factions agreed to U.N.-supervised elections in 1993. Meanwhile, the United States took steps to resume normal relations with Vietnam.

13. Somalia. Shortly before leaving office, President Bush sent U.S. troops to Somalia, a nation in eastern Africa that was torn by civil war. His goal was to protect relief workers supplying food to starving people.

ELECTION OF 1992

| CANDIDATE | POPULAR VOTE | | STATES WON | ELECTORAL VOTE |
	IN NUMBER	IN PERCENT		
Bush	39,104,545	37	18	168
Clinton	44,909,899	43	32*	370
Perot	19,742,267	19	0	0

*Plus the District of Columbia.

CLINTON ADMINISTRATION: 1993–   (DEMOCRATIC)

MAJOR POLITICAL AND ECONOMIC ASPECTS

1. Election of 1992. The voters turned to Democrats *Bill Clinton*, governor of Arkansas, and his running mate *Al Gore, Jr.*, U.S. Senator from Tennessee, to pull the country out of economic stagnation and move it in a new direction. President George Bush had come under attack from conservatives for having reneged on his no-new-taxes pledge, and he and Vice President Dan Quayle finished second in a three-way race. H. Ross Perot, a wealthy Texas businessman, ran as an independent. He stirred great excitement among a segment of the electorate.

2. Observations on the 1992 Election Results. (a) Bush lost despite the fact that many voters had considered him a hero in 1991 for leading the United States to victory in the Persian Gulf War. (b) Political analysts said that a recession in 1990–1991, followed by economic stagnation, was the largest factor in Bush's defeat. Ironically, statistics released after the election showed that the economy had begun to perk up during the summer of 1992—too late to save Bush's candidacy. (c) President Bush became only the third elected incumbent in this century to lose a reelection bid. (The others were Herbert Hoover in 1932 and Jimmy Carter in 1980.) (d) Ross Perot reported spending $60 million of his own money, mainly for television time. He did remarkably well for a candidate with no party behind him. (e) Clinton succeeded in winning back many Democratic conservatives and moderates ("Reagan Democrats") who had supported Republicans in the three previous elections. (f) The campaign generated unusual interest, with 55 percent of the voting-age population casting ballots.

3. Clinton: Background and Views. A native of Hope, Arkansas, William Jefferson Clinton became fascinated with politics after participating in Boys' Nation and shaking President Kennedy's hand on a trip to the nation's capital. After graduating from college, he was a Rhodes scholar at Oxford University in England and received a law degree from Yale.

Clinton entered Arkansas politics as a liberal and won the governorship in 1978, but lost a re-election bid two years later. Shifting his position toward the political center, he made a comeback and served four more terms as governor.

In the Clinton White House, the President's wife, *Hillary Rodham Clinton*, took an unprecedented role in policy formation. She was especially active in the administration's campaign for universal health insurance.

4. Clinton Administration

a. Domestic Affairs

(1) *Deficits and Taxes.* By the narrowest of margins, President Clinton won approval in 1993 for a five-year plan to reduce the deficit by cutting spending and raising taxes. The military took the brunt of the spending cuts. Upper-income taxpayers paid more income tax, while everyone paid higher fuel taxes.

(2) *Universal Health Insurance.* Check the Index.

(3) *Supreme Court Appointment.* Clinton appointed *Ruth Bader Ginsburg* as Associate Justice in 1993. She became the second woman on the Court. In 1994 the President nominated *Stephen G. Breyer* to replace retiring Justice Harry A. Blackmun.

(4) *Whitewater Investigation.* In 1994 Special Prosecutor *Robert B. Fiske* began a formal investigation into Arkansas land dealings by Bill and Hillary Clinton. The Clintons had been partners with another couple in a failed real-estate venture called the Whitewater Development Company.

b. Foreign Affairs

(1) *Bosnia.* As Serbs, Croats, and Muslims engaged in a cruel civil war in Bosnia, President Clinton tried to get European nations to openly provide military aid to Bosnia. In 1995 the United States supported NATO air strikes against Bosnian Serb troops that had repeatedly violated cease-fires in certain Bosnian Muslim safe areas. In November 1995 the United States hosted a peace conference in Dayton, Ohio. The three warring states signed an agreement that divided Bosnia into a Bosnian-Croat federation and a Bosnian-Serb republic, with a central government in Sarajevo. To keep the peace, 60,000 NATO troops (one third of them Americans) were to be stationed in Bosnia.

(2) *Somalia.* U.S. soldiers in Somalia withdrew after 18 Americans died in an October 1993 street battle in the Somali capital, Mogadishu. U.S. and United Nations soldiers had become openly hostile to one side in Somalia's civil war.

(3) *Trade.* Overcoming strong opposition from labor unions, environmentalists, and political independent Ross Perot, the Clinton administration won Congressional approval for the *North American Free Trade Agreement (NAFTA).* NAFTA is a three-way trade pact linking Mexico, Canada, and the United States. (Check the Index.) In other trade-related issues, the administration (*a*) saw to a successful conclusion the Uruguay Round of world trade talks and (*b*) stepped up pressure on Japan to open its markets to U.S. goods.

(4) *Russia.* The Clinton administration continued President Bush's policy of working closely with Russian President Boris Yeltsin. The United States offered economic assistance not only to Russia but also to other former Soviet republics, such as Ukraine and Georgia, seeking to bolster their independence.

(5) *Middle East.* Israeli President Yitzhak Rabin and Palestinian leader Yasir Arafat shook hands at the White House to seal a historic 1993 agreement creating a framework for peace in the Middle East. As a first step, Palestinian self-rule occurred in the city of Jericho and the Gaza Strip. A second step was taken in 1995 when an agreement was reached about the West Bank.

(6) *Vietnam.* President Clinton dropped a ban on U.S. trade with Vietnam that had been in effect since the Vietnam War. He said Vietnam had been cooperating in U.S. attempts to find out what happened to Americans still missing in action. Many U.S. businesses had been eager to invest in Vietnam.

(7) *Haiti.* The Clinton Administration supported exiled President Aristide and opposed the right-wing military officers who had seized power. A trade embargo and threats of U.S. invasion finally convinced the military to step down and allow Aristide to return in 1994.

MULTIPLE-CHOICE QUESTIONS

1. Since 1952 the United States has (1) experienced a severe depression (2) successively elected three Republican candidates to the Presidency (3) placed increased emphasis upon improving education (4) lost interest in European affairs.

2. Which statement regarding the Presidential election of 1952 is *least* valid? (1) Eisenhower enjoyed great popularity. (2) Stevenson defended Truman's record. (3) Settlement of the Korean War was a major issue. (4) The Republican candidates for the Senate and House of Representatives helped assure Eisenhower's victory.

3. Which term is *not* associated with the career of Dwight D. Eisenhower? (1) modern Republicanism (2) Atoms for Peace (3) time for a change (4) a choice not an echo.

4. During the Eisenhower administration, Congress passed laws affecting all of the following *except* (1) civil rights (2) education (3) protection of the consumer (4) admission of new states.

5. Which was a major aim of the Eisenhower administration? (1) balancing the budget (2) compulsory health insurance (3) rigid price supports for farm products (4) raising tariffs.

6. In foreign affairs, the Eisenhower administration (1) ended American aid to South Vietnam (2) sent American troops to Egypt (2) achieved a truce in Korea (4) refused to take part in summit conferences.

7. Which of the following was *not* a factor in the Presidential election of 1960? (1) the religion of the Democratic candidate (2) television "debates" (3) a split in the Republican party (4) Negro demands for additional civil rights legislation.

8. John F. Kennedy was *not* (1) a mining engineer and self-made millionaire (2) author of *Profiles in Courage* (3) in the navy during World War II (4) United States Senator from Massachusetts.

9. Presidents Eisenhower and Kennedy were *least* in agreement regarding (1) raising the minimum wage (2) support for the U.N. (3) lowering tariff barriers (4) the use of Presidential powers.

10. Which foreign policy did President Kennedy inherit from his predecessors and carry to a successful conclusion? (1) establishment of the Peace Corps (2) limited nuclear test ban (3) war in Vietnam (4) reunifying Germany.

11. Which statement regarding Lyndon B. Johnson is *not* true? (1) He was born in Texas. (2) He was educated at the Naval Academy at Annapolis. (3) He greatly admired Franklin D. Roosevelt. (4) He served as Senate Majority Leader.

12. Lyndon B. Johnson and Andrew Johnson, on succession to the Presidency, each faced the problem of (1) limiting the power of the Supreme Court (2) providing foreign aid to Europe (3) insuring civil rights for minority groups (4) appointing a Vice President.

13. President Johnson's desire for a consensus refers to his (1) disregard of public opinion (2) distrust of public opinion polls (3) seeking of strong public support for his policies (4) advocacy of extreme measures to achieve his goals.

14. Which man served as Secretary of State under both President Nixon and President Ford? (1) Arthur Goldberg (2) John Foster Dulles (3) Robert McNamara (4) Henry Kissinger.

15. Which measure, first proposed by President Truman, was achieved during the Johnson administration? (1) St. Lawrence Seaway (2) medical care for the aged under Social Security (3) aid to Appalachia (4) reciprocal tariff program.

CHRONOLOGY QUESTIONS

The following are the names given to five successive Presidential administrations:

(*A*) New Deal of Franklin D. Roosevelt

(*B*) Fair Deal of Harry S. Truman

(*C*) Modern Republicanism of Dwight D. Eisenhower

(*D*) New Frontier of John F. Kennedy

(*E*) Great Society of Lyndon B. Johnson

For each of the following events, select the *letter* of the Presidential administration during which the event took place.

1. Supreme Court decides the case of *Brown vs. Board of Education of Topeka*.
2. President calls for a "war on poverty."
3. Congress passes immigration bill over President's veto.
4. President looks forward to tariff negotiations with the Common Market as he signs the Trade Expansion Act.
5. Federal Deposit Insurance Corporation begins operations to protect savings.
6. President opposes America's traditional allies on their invasion of Egypt.
7. Invasion of Cuba at the Bay of Pigs is crushed.
8. Congress passes immigration bill to end the national origins system.
9. National Aeronautics and Space Administration takes charge of space research.

ESSAY QUESTIONS

1. (*a*) For each of the following fields, describe briefly a problem faced by President Eisenhower: (1) agriculture, (2) segregation, (3) labor-management relations, (4) the cold war. (*b*) Show *one* way in which the Eisenhower administration attempted to deal with each of these problems.

2. The frontier of the 1800's was a vast, unexplored region of adventure and opportunity. The New Frontier of the Kennedy administration referred to another avenue of opportunity, that of technological, social, and scientific development. (*a*) Show *two* ways in which the federal government played an important part in the development of the frontier from 1783 to 1890. (*b*) Show *two* ways in which the Kennedy administration attempted to solve the problems of the New Frontier of the 1960's.

3. Choose *three* of the following aspects of the Great Society program: (*a*) aid to education, (*b*) aid to the creative arts, (*c*) civil rights, (*d*) Social Security, (*e*) urban development, (*f*) anti-poverty projects. For each aspect chosen, explain (1) how it represents a continuation of a policy adopted by a previous administration, and (2) how it marks an advance in the intellectual or economic well-being of the United States.

4. In recent years, attention has been focused on the office of Vice President of the United States. (*a*) State *one* specific duty or power of the Vice President that is provided for by the federal Constitution. (*b*) Explain *two* reasons why the office of Vice President has become more important in recent years. (*c*) Name *two* Presidents of the United States who succeeded to the Presidency following the death of the previous President. For *each* of the Presidents named, give *two* facts to show that he was either successful or unsuccessful in office.

UNIT VIII. AMERICAN FOREIGN POLICY MOVES FROM ISOLATION TO WORLD LEADERSHIP

Part 1. Introduction

MAKING OF FOREIGN POLICY TODAY

1. Preeminent Position of the President. The President determines and carries out American foreign policy. His authority derives from his Constitutional powers to receive ambassadors (and therefore to recognize foreign governments), to command the armed forces, to negotiate treaties, and to appoint officials concerned with foreign affairs.

The President also has extraconstitutional powers: to rally public opinion, to visit foreign countries, and to sign *executive agreements*. (Such agreements, between the President and the head of a foreign nation, do not have the stature of treaties and therefore do not require Senate ratification. An example was the Destroyer-Naval Base Deal in 1940 between the United States and Britain.)

2. The President's Assistants. The President receives information and advice from the President's assistant for national security affairs, the Secretary of State, American ambassadors to foreign countries, and American representatives to international organizations; from the Secretary of Defense and the *Joint Chiefs of Staff* of the armed services; and from the *Central Intelligence Agency (CIA)*, which coordinates American intelligence activities related to national security. The President and his key advisers on foreign policy and national defense together constitute the *National Security Council*. The President, however, makes the final decisions on foreign policy and bears the final responsibility.

3. Role of Congress. The "advice and consent" of the Senate are necessary to approve Presidential appointments, including foreign service personnel, and to ratify treaties. Appointments require a majority vote; treaties, a two-thirds vote. Approval of both houses of Congress is necessary for expenditures in the area of foreign affairs. Both the Senate Foreign Relations Committee and the House International Relations Committee hold hearings, question witnesses, and make recommendations. Congress also has the power to regulate commerce with foreign nations, to voice its opinion upon foreign policy by means of a joint resolution, and to declare war. Finally, Congress may restrict the power of the President as commander of the armed forces by insisting that he comply with the provisions of the War-Powers Resolution (check the Index).

4. Other Influences. The President may be influenced by the policies of his predecessors, the views of our allies, the efforts of the United Nations, the pressures of lobbying groups, and, most important, public opinion. No matter how great his powers, no President has long maintained a foreign policy at sharp variance with public opinion.

REVIEW OF AMERICAN FOREIGN POLICY FROM 1789 TO 1865

√1. **Policy of Isolation.** George Washington, in his *Farewell Address* (1796), urged the young republic to further its foreign trade but avoid permanent alliances with foreign nations. Labeled a policy of isolation and endorsed by subsequent American statesmen, Washington's advice guided American foreign policy for over 100 years. It did not prevent the War of 1812, which involved the United States in the Napoleonic Wars. But, thereafter, it enabled the American people to concentrate upon domestic issues and upon foreign affairs affecting the Western Hemisphere—especially the independence of Latin America and our expansion westward to the Pacific.

2. **Monroe Doctrine.** James Monroe, in his message to Congress in 1823, stated that (*a*) the Western Hemisphere was no longer open to European colonization, (*b*) the United States would not interfere in the internal affairs of European nations, and (*c*) any attempt by a European power to intervene in the Americas would be regarded as "dangerous to our peace and safety."

The American people approved the Monroe Doctrine as a logical extension of our policy of isolation, since it attempted to isolate the entire Western Hemisphere from European affairs. Latin Americans, who had just won their independence, welcomed the Monroe Doctrine as an offer of assistance against would-be European aggressors. The first real application of the Monroe Doctrine was the Maximilian Affair, in which the United States persuaded France to withdraw her troops from Mexico.

†3. **"Manifest Destiny."** Many Americans in the early 19th century believed that the United States had a *manifest destiny* to expand to the Pacific coast. James Polk, in his Presidential campaign in 1844, demanded the "reannexation of Texas" and the "reoccupation of Oregon." Just before Polk took office, Congress approved the annexation of Texas. Thereafter, Polk led the United States in a war against Mexico and secured the Mexican Cession. He compromised with England and agreed to divide the Oregon Country at the 49th parallel. Polk's expansionism enabled the United States to reach the Pacific coast.

Part 2. The United States Undertakes a Policy of Imperialism

REASONS FOR AMERICA'S TURN TO IMPERIALISM any 2

Following the Civil War, and especially in the 1890's, the United States began to extend its control over "backward" or weaker areas in the Caribbean, Central America, South America, and the Pacific. The following were the major reasons:

1. Industrial Revolution. Spurred by Civil War needs, American industry continued to grow tremendously. Industrialists began to look abroad for (a) new sources of raw materials, (b) additional markets for manufactured goods, and (c) places to invest surplus capital.

2. Close of the Frontier. By 1890 the American West was sufficiently populated for the frontier to be considered closed. This development motivated American manufacturers and investors to look beyond our borders for economic opportunities.

3. Example of European Nations. The major as well as many lesser European powers were engaged in imperialist ventures. Britain purchased control of the Suez Canal, established domination over Egypt, and planned a "Cape-to-Cairo" empire in Africa. France annexed Indo-China. Russia secured border territories from China. Belgians took over the Congo. Such developments stimulated American interest in empire-building.

4. American Nationalism. Expansionists in the United States urged that America assume its rightful place as a great power by embarking upon a policy of imperialism. Most influential were the lectures and writings of Captain *Alfred Mahan*. In his book *The Influence of Sea Power Upon History*, Mahan urged the United States to "look outward": to expand foreign markets, construct a powerful navy, and acquire overseas bases. (Mahan had a notable admirer in Theodore Roosevelt.)

FIRST COLONIAL ACQUISITIONS

1. Alaska

a. Purchase From Russia (1867). Russia proposed to sell Alaska to the United States, and Secretary of State William Seward agreed to the purchase. Seward's reasons were (1) gratitude to Russia for her support of the Union during the Civil War, and (2) a desire to reduce foreign possessions in North America. Because many people thought the territory a "barren icebox," Alaska, costing $7.2 million, was called "Seward's Folly."

b. Statehood (1959). Alaska received the status of an *incorporated territory* in 1912 as a step toward statehood. In 1959 Alaska became our 49th state.

Alaska ranks first in area (being more than twice the size of Texas) but last in population (having about 225,000 inhabitants). About one-sixth of the population consists of native Eskimos and Indians.

c. Importance. Alaska is important for (1) its natural resources of timber, fur, fish, coal, oil, and gold, and (2) its location along North Polar air routes to northern Europe or Asia. Also, Alaska lies close to Russian Siberia. Alaska contains air bases at Fairbanks, Anchorage, Nome, and Dutch Harbor, as well as several missile warning systems.

2. Samoan Islands and Midway. The Samoan Islands in the South Pacific served American merchant ships as supply harbors and coaling stations. Starting in 1872 the harbor of Pago Pago came under American control. In 1899 several of the islands were formally annexed by the United States. Also in the 19th century, the United States annexed the Central Pacific island of Midway. Today, American Samoa and Midway are American colonies and provide the United States with naval and air bases.

3. Hawaii

a. Acquisition (1898). Hawaii, a group of islands in the Central Pacific, 2400 miles off the California coast, (1) served American merchant ships as a supply and refueling station, (2) drew American missionaries, who converted the natives to Christianity, and (3) attracted American investors into Hawaiian sugar plantations. Almost all the sugar grown in Hawaii was sold in the United States.

In 1893 revolutionists, consisting mainly of American settlers, overthrew the anti-American native Queen Liliuokalani. The revolutionists established a temporary republic and asked for annexation by the United States. Annexation was delayed by the opposition of President Cleveland, who believed that most native Hawaiians preferred independence. In 1898, however, with McKinley in the White House, the United States annexed Hawaii by a joint resolution of Congress.

b. Statehood (1959). Hawaii, our last incorporated territory, long sought admission to the Union. In 1959, with the approval of Congress and the President, Hawaii became our 50th state.

Today the islanders total 630,000, of whom 32 percent are white, 32 percent Japanese, and the rest Hawaiian, Chinese, or Filipino.

c. Importance. Hawaii is important because it (1) produces sugar and pineapples, (2) attracts many tourists, and (3) contains the major American military installations in the Central Pacific, including the naval base at *Pearl Harbor.*

SPANISH-AMERICAN WAR (1898)

1. Cuban Background of the War

a. Early American Interest. Americans had long been interested in the Spanish colony of Cuba. They recognized Cuba's strategic location, within 90 miles of the Florida coast, and its importance as a key defense base on the Caribbean and the Gulf of Mexico. Americans feared for our security if Cuba passed from Spanish into stronger European hands.

Before the Civil War, Southerners wanted to annex Cuba as another pro-slave state. In 1854 three American diplomats wrote a memorandum known as the *Ostend Manifesto.* It declared that, if the United States could not purchase Cuba, we would be justified in seizing Cuba by force. Although the Ostend Manifesto was repudiated by the United States government, it reflected considerable American sentiment. After the Civil War, American interest in Cuba temporarily subsided.

b. Despotic Spanish Rule. Spain denied the Cubans civil liberties and political rights, levied heavy taxes, restricted foreign trade, and ruthlessly suppressed all rebellions. In 1876, after combatting a lengthy insurrection, Spain promised a number of reforms. Ten years later Spain finally abolished slavery but still denied the Cubans self-government. In 1895, as a depression hit the island, Spain faced another Cuban revolt for independence.

2. Causes of the Spanish-American War

a. Humanitarianism. Americans sympathized with the desire of the Cuban people for independence. Americans were outraged when Spain's General Valeriano Weyler placed Cuban civilians in concentration camps to prevent them from aiding the revolution. Some 200,000 concentration camp inmates died of hunger and disease.

b. Economic Interests. American merchants traded with Cuba to the amount of $100 million per year. American investors had placed $50 million in Cuban sugar and tobacco plantations. Our trade and investments suffered from unsettled conditions. (However, many American investors opposed war with Spain. They feared wartime destruction of their property and laws harmful to their enterprises if Cuba gained independence.)

c. "Yellow" Journalism. The "yellow" press—especially William Randolph Hearst's New York *Journal* and Joseph Pulitzer's New York *World*—sought to increase newspaper circulation by sensational treatment of news from Cuba. Journalists exaggerated stories of Spanish atrocities and falsified news pictures while playing down atrocities by the Cuban revolutionaries. The yellow press also gave sensational treatment to the *De Lome Letter.* Written by the Spanish minister in Washington to a friend in Cuba and stolen from the Havana post office, this private letter belittled President

McKinley as a weak, incompetent politician. By its treatment of such news stories, the yellow press served to enrage the American people against Spain.

d. Sinking of the "Maine." In February, 1898, the American battleship *Maine*, visiting in Havana, Cuba, was blown up with a loss of 260 American lives. The cause of the explosion remains unknown, but the American people placed the blame on Spain. They were goaded to do so by the yellow press and by other groups eager for war: jingoists, who boasted of the nation's strength, and imperialists, who wanted the United States to acquire an overseas empire.

3. Outbreak of the War. President McKinley had sought to avert war and urged Americans to remain calm regarding Cuba. Now, with the sinking of the *Maine*, McKinley demanded that Spain proclaim an armistice, end the concentration camps, and negotiate with the rebels. Although Spain's reply was conciliatory, McKinley finally yielded to American public sentiment for war. At his request, Congress approved the use of American armed forces in Cuba. Congress also recognized the independence of Cuba and, in the *Teller Resolution*, declared that the United States would not annex Cuba but would leave "control of the island to its people."

4. Conduct of the War. With "Remember the *Maine!*" as their battle cry, American forces swept quickly and easily to victory. In the Pacific, a fleet under Commodore *George Dewey* destroyed the Spanish fleet at Manila, the capital of the Philippines, and an American army took possession of the city. In the Caribbean, American naval forces destroyed the Spanish fleet at Santiago, Cuba. Meanwhile, American forces captured this city after a battle famed for the heroic dash up San Juan Hill by Theodore Roosevelt and his Rough Riders.

In this "splendid little war," as the American diplomat John Hay called it, more American soldiers died from tropical diseases than from Spanish guns. (After the war, *Walter Reed*, an army surgeon, studied yellow fever and discovered that the disease is transmitted by a certain kind of mosquito. This discovery led to the wiping out of yellow fever.)

5. Treaty of Paris (1898). Thoroughly beaten, Spain agreed to the following peace terms: (*a*) Cuba was freed of Spanish control, (*b*) Puerto Rico, in the Caribbean, and Guam, in the Pacific, were ceded to the United States, and (*c*) the Philippine Islands, in the Pacific, were sold to the United States for $20 million.

(Later, the United States annexed the unclaimed Wake Island, principally to serve as a station for a cable from San Francisco to Manila.)

6. Significance. The United States emerged from the Spanish-American War as a world power with colonies in the Caribbean and the Pacific. Anti-imperialists were alarmed. In the Presidential election of 1900, Democrat William Jennings Bryan warned that imperialism abroad would lead to despotism at home. Disregarding this warning, the people reelected William McKinley, who represented imperialism but who had campaigned on the issue of the "full dinner pail."

AMERICAN RELATIONS WITH CUBA

1. **Temporary American Occupation.** After the Spanish-American War, the United States temporarily took charge of Cuba, establishing schools, building roads, providing sanitation, and wiping out yellow fever. Americans also assisted the Cubans in drawing up a democratic constitution. In 1902, in keeping with the Teller Resolution, American forces withdrew from the island.

2. **American Protectorate Over Cuba: The Platt Amendment.** Under strong American pressure, the Cubans included in their constitution the *Platt Amendment*. It provided that Cuba would (*a*) not sign any foreign treaty that threatened her independence, (*b*) allow the United States to intervene to preserve Cuban independence and to protect life, liberty, and property, and (*c*) grant the United States naval bases. Under the last provision, Cuba leased to the United States the strategic naval base at *Guantanamo Bay*.

The Cubans lacked political experience; for years their governments alternated between weak, inefficient regimes and tyrannical military dictatorships. The island abounded with corruption, fraud, violence, and revolt.

Using the Platt Amendment, the United States intervened four times to restore order in Cuba and safeguard American lives and investments. Our interventions aroused resentment among Cuban nationalists. In 1933, however, although Cuba was in the midst of another revolt, President Franklin D. Roosevelt did not intervene. Instead, in 1934, as part of his Good Neighbor Policy, he abrogated (abolished) the Platt Amendment. With Cuban consent, the United States retained the naval base at Guantanamo Bay.

3. **Economic Ties.** Although the Platt Amendment was ended, the United States continued to dominate the Cuban economy. Americans had over $1 billion invested in Cuban public utilities, railroads, iron and nickel mines, and sugar and tobacco plantations. The United States provided the chief market for Cuban agricultural and mineral exports, and was the chief source of Cuban imports of manufactured goods. American tourists flocked to Cuban vacation resorts.

The Cuban economy could provide her people with no more than a very low living standard. Few farmers owned their own land, and farm workers received low wages. Because Cuba was largely dependent upon the sugar crop, the entire economy frequently suffered from world competition and low prices.

4. Hostility (Since 1959). In 1959 rebels led by *Fidel Castro* overthrew the dictatorship of Fulgencio Batista and seized power. As Castro aligned himself with the Communist world, relations between Cuba and the United States deteriorated. (For details, check the Index for "Cuba, under Castro.")

PUERTO RICO: AN AMERICAN SHOWCASE

1. Political Evolution: From Colony to Commonwealth

a. Foraker Act (1900). With this law, Congress assigned Puerto Rico the status of an *unincorporated territory*. This meant that Puerto Rico was not destined for statehood. Congress provided that the President of the United States appoint the island's governor and the upper house of the Puerto Rican legislature but that the Puerto Ricans elect the lower house.

b. Jones Act (1917). In this law, Congress granted the Puerto Ricans American citizenship and the right to elect both houses of the Puerto Rican legislature.

c. Elected Governor (1948). In 1947 Congress passed a law to permit the Puerto Ricans to elect their own governor. The following year, the Puerto Ricans chose, as their first elected governor, *Luis Muñoz Marín*. Elected for four consecutive terms until he retired in 1965, Muñoz Marín helped shape modern Puerto Rico. He furthered economic progress and achieved Commonwealth status for the island.

d. Commonwealth Status (Since 1952). Congress empowered the Puerto Ricans to draw up their own constitution. Under Muñoz Marín's leadership, the islanders overwhelmingly chose to become freely associated with the United States as a self-governing *Commonwealth*. (1) Puerto Ricans elect their own legislators and governor, who pass and enforce local laws. (2) Puerto Ricans are American citizens. However, as long as they reside in Puerto Rico, they do not vote in Presidential elections and do not elect Congressmen. They do, however, send a Resident Commissioner to Washington with power to speak, but not to vote, on measures before the House of Representatives. (3) Puerto Ricans are subject to most federal laws. They serve in the American armed forces, and their products enter the mainland free of tariff duties. However, individuals and corporations on the island are exempt from federal income taxes.

e. Political Developments. Until recently, a majority of Puerto Rican voters approved the Commonwealth status; very few desired independence. But a large minority favored statehood, which would mean voting in federal elections—and also paying federal income taxes. In the 1976 elections, the Puerto Ricans narrowly elected as governor *Carlos Romero Barceló*, an advocate of statehood. This surprising result, although probably reflecting economic discontent, spurred interest in statehood.

In 1979 President Carter, citing "humane considerations," freed from American prisons four Puerto Rican independence nationalists—one who in 1950 had attempted to assassinate President Truman and three who in 1954 had sprayed gunfire into the House of Representatives and wounded five Congressmen. Their unconditional release was opposed by Puerto Rico's governor as encouraging terrorism and menacing public safety.

In 1980 Romero Barceló narrowly won reelection, but in 1984 he was defeated by the pro-Commonwealth Popular Democratic party leader, *Hernández Colón*.

2. Economic Developments

a. Problem of Poverty. Despite the fertile soil, a favorable climate, and good crops of sugar and tobacco, the Puerto Ricans subsisted for a long time at minimal living standards. (1) The island lacked sufficient area to support its rapidly growing population in agriculture. In contrast to a population density of 51 inhabitants per square mile for the United States, Puerto Rico has a population density of over 750. (2) Most Puerto Rican land was held by American corporations. Eighty percent of the islanders were landless. (3) The island's economy depended upon sugar. A drop in world sugar prices meant depression.

b. Operation Bootstrap: Efforts to Improve Conditions. In the early 1940's Puerto Rico initiated a program to improve its economy. Since Puerto Rico was trying "to lift itself by its own bootstraps," the project became known as "Operation Bootstrap." (1) *Limits on Landholdings.* Puerto Rico began enforcing a law, passed in 1900, limiting corporate land ownership to 500 acres. The government bought up the excess holdings and distributed the land to agricultural cooperatives and individual farmers. (2) *Tourism.* The Puerto Rican government encouraged the building of hotels and developed the island as a resort area. Beaches, gambling casinos, the *Pablo Casals Music Festival*, and touches of Spanish culture all attracted American vacationers. (3) *Social Welfare Projects.* The Puerto Rican government paved roads, built hydroelectric plants, provided public health facilities, constructed low-income housing projects, and substantially increased educational expenditures. Instruction is in Spanish; the chief second language studied is English. Literacy has risen to about 95 percent of the population. (4) *Industrialization.* "Operation Bootstrap" especially emphasized attracting American capital and industry. The Puerto Rican government offered new factories, easy credit, and vocational training of workers. Most important, corporations in Puerto Rico are exempt from federal income taxes.

Over 1000 new enterprises, manufacturing textiles, electrical equipment, plastics, chemicals, and many other products, were set up on the island and provided many jobs.

  c. *Results.* Today, Puerto Rico's income derived from manufacturing exceeds its income from agriculture. The people's standard of living has risen substantially; it is among the highest in Latin America. On the other hand, the unemployment rate in Puerto Rico is almost 20 percent, and the per capita income of Puerto Ricans remains considerably below that of Americans on the mainland.

  3. **Emigration to the Mainland.** As American citizens, Puerto Ricans may move freely to the mainland. Starting in 1940 they came in large numbers, chiefly to east coast cities, and found jobs in industry during the war and the postwar boom. By 1960 about one million Puerto Ricans resided on the mainland, mostly in New York City. The Puerto Rican migrants faced many problems: a culture different from their own; a language barrier, which complicated the education of their children; a lack of vocational skills, which meant low-paying jobs and considerable unemployment; and discrimination in housing. To ease the adjustment of the migrants, agencies in Puerto Rico and on the mainland developed various information and aid programs.

  Starting in the early 1960's the number of Puerto Ricans returning to the island roughly equaled those coming to the mainland. The returnees were motivated by (*a*) discrimination and unemployment on the mainland, (*b*) improved living standards and job opportunities on the island, and (*c*) a desire to raise their children within the Spanish culture.

PANAMA CANAL

  1. **American Interest.** Americans long desired a canal across the Isthmus of Panama to connect the Atlantic and Pacific Oceans. They pointed out that, by eliminating the long voyage around South America, a canal would shorten the boat trip between our east and west coasts and would lower the cost of transporting goods. The Spanish-American War pointed up the need for a canal (*a*) to provide greater mobility for our naval fleets, (*b*) to protect our new colonial empire, and (*c*) to further commerce with the Far East.

  2. **American Diplomatic Moves**

  a. With Great Britain. In the *Clayton-Bulwer Treaty* (1850) the United States and Great Britain agreed to share control of any canal across Central America. In 1901 Secretary of State John Hay negotiated the *Hay-Pauncefote Treaty*, by which Britain permitted the United States to go ahead without her in building and operating the canal. In return the United States pledged to let ships of all nations use the canal.

b. With the French Canal Company. A private French company, under *Ferdinand de Lesseps*, builder of the Suez Canal, had attempted to construct a canal in Panama but had failed. After the ratification of the Hay-Pauncefote Treaty, the United States agreed to pay $40 million to the French company for its property and its franchise rights.

c. With Colombia. In 1903 Secretary Hay negotiated a treaty with Colombia to pay that nation $10 million and an annual rental of $250,000 for the right to build a canal across her northern province of Panama. The treaty was rejected by the Colombian Senate, which hoped for better terms the following year when the French company's franchise would expire. Rejection of the treaty worried the French canal company, inflamed the people of Panama, and enraged President Theodore Roosevelt.

d. Roosevelt and the Panama Revolution. Roosevelt privately expressed the wish to see Panama independent of Colombia. Shortly afterwards, a revolt broke out. The United States openly aided the revolt by sending naval vessels to prevent Colombian troops from entering Panama. Later, Roosevelt boasted, "I took the Canal Zone." Roosevelt's actions earned us ill will throughout Latin America. (In 1921 the United States attempted to placate Colombia by paying her $25 million.)

e. Treaty With Panama. Hay now negotiated a treaty with the new Republic of Panama, whose minister was the former official of the French canal company, *Philippe Bunau-Varilla*. The Hay–Bunau-Varilla Treaty (1903) provided for (1) American control, "in perpetuity," of the Canal Zone, a strip of land 10 miles wide across the isthmus, (2) American intervention in Panama when necessary to preserve order, and (3) payment to Panama of $10 million and an annual rental of $250,000 for the Canal Zone. (The annual rental was increased several times up to $2.3 million.)

3. Building the Canal

a. George W. Goethals, an army engineer, had charge of building the canal. To solve the problem of the uneven terrain, Goethals built huge locks to raise and lower ships. In 1914 the 50-mile canal was opened to traffic.

b. William C. Gorgas, an army medical officer, wiped out malaria and yellow fever in the Canal Zone. By maintaining proper sanitation, Gorgas enabled the workers to complete the canal.

4. Protecting the Canal. The United States (*a*) fortified the Canal Zone, (*b*) extended our influence over the nations bordering the Caribbean, thus converting the Caribbean into an "American lake" (see pages 474-476), (*c*) maintained American military bases throughout the Caribbean, notably in Puerto Rico and at Guantanamo Bay in Cuba, and (*d*) in 1917 purchased from Denmark an additional Caribbean military base, the *Virgin Islands*.

5. Panamanian Nationalism and the Canal Zone. By the 1960's Panamanians strongly resented American control over the Canal Zone "in perpetuity" as well as the comfortable life of American personnel, in contrast with the poverty of most Panamanians. In 1964 a Canal Zone incident involving the unauthorized flying of the American flag by American high school students sparked a series of anti-American riots. Thereafter the United States and Panama began negotiations to revise the status of the Canal Zone.

6. The 1977 Treaties. After 13 years of intermittent talks spanning four American Presidential administrations, United States and Panama negotiators agreed to replace the 1903 Hay-Bunau-Varilla pact with two new treaties. The *"Transfer of Ownership"* treaty provided that (*a*) the United States transfer ownership and control of the canal to Panama by the year 2000, (*b*) until then the United States operate the canal but assign an increasing role to Panamanians, (*c*) soon after ratification, Panama assume control of most of the Canal Zone—those areas not essential for defense or operation of the canal, and (*d*) Panama receive $50 to $70 million annually out of canal tolls and also extensive American economic aid. The *"Neutrality"* treaty (*a*) guaranteed the neutrality of the canal from the year 2000 onward and (*b*) gave the United States (as later spelled out) the right to intervene militarily to defend the canal's neutrality.

Although some Panamanians feared the provision giving the United States the right to intervene militarily, Panamanian voters approved the treaties.

In the United States, President Carter exerted much political pressure to secure ratification. Ronald Reagan and other conservatives bitterly opposed the treaties, arguing that they amounted to a surrender of American rights. Critics said the canal was vital to American security, which would be endangered by Panamanian control. In 1978, the Senate ratified the two treaties in close votes.

7. Opposing Noriega. In the 1980's, relations between the United States and Panama deteriorated when American leaders fell out with General *Manuel Noriega,* a longtime "asset" of American intelligence services who had become Panama's de facto ruler as head of the army. Americans accused Noriega of (*a*) funneling illegal drugs to the United States and (*b*) using brutal methods to suppress democracy in Panama. To bring down Noriega, President Reagan applied stiff economic pressures beginning in 1988. Although the American sanctions devastated Panama's once-bustling economy, Noriega held on to power.

8. American Invasion (1989). In 1989 Noriega nullified a presidential election that appeared to have been won by opposition leader *Guillermo Endara.* Seven months later, President George Bush sent an invasion force of 14,000 American troops into Panama, where they joined 13,000 troops already based there. The goal of the invasion was to oust Noriega and put Endara in power.

The attack in December 1989 was the largest American military operation since the Vietnam war. Although the invasion drew condemnation from both the Organization of American States and the United Nations General Assembly, it met its goals. Endara became president and promised to restore democracy.

After taking refuge for a time in the Vatican embassy, Noriega was arrested and brought to the United States to be tried on drug-trafficking charges. His lawyers called the invasion illegal, terming it a "war crime" because of a high death toll. The exact figures were disputed, with American officials setting the toll at about 50 Panamanian soldiers, 202 Panamanian civilians, 23 American soldiers, and 3 American civilians. Other estimates ranged from "less than 600" (by President Endara) to several thousand (by Noriega supporters).

Critics claimed the invasion's toll in lives lost and property damaged far outweighed the advantages of arresting Noriega. Supporters of the invasion said it had allowed Panama to return to democratic rule.

EXPANSION OF THE MONROE DOCTRINE IN THE CARIBBEAN

In 1823 the United States issued the Monroe Doctrine to keep European powers from extending their control in the Western Hemisphere. Beginning in 1895, the United States interpreted the Monroe Doctrine so as to justify its own political and economic domination of the Caribbean area.

1. Venezuela Boundary Dispute (1895). Great Britain and Venezuela had long disputed the boundary between Venezuela and British Guiana. The disputed area, where gold was discovered, extended north to the mouth of the Orinoco River. Britain had rejected several proposals for arbitration.

In 1895 *Richard Olney,* Secretary of State under President Cleveland, demanded that England submit to arbitration. Olney (*a*) claimed that British pressure on Venezuela violated the Monroe Doctrine, and (*b*) asserted that the United States may intervene in all Western Hemisphere affairs because "the United States is practically sovereign on this continent"—the *Olney Interpretation* of the Monroe Doctrine. Britain dismissed Olney's arguments, but, after Cleveland indicated that the United States was ready to use force, Britain agreed to arbitration. British Guiana was awarded most of the disputed territory, but Venezuela retained the mouth of the Orinoco River.

The Olney Interpretation greatly perturbed the Latin American nations, who foresaw intervention by the United States in their internal affairs.

2. Venezuela Debt Dispute (1902). Venezuela defaulted on debts owed to citizens of Italy, Great Britain, and Germany. The European powers sent warships to compel repayment of the debt by blockading Venezuelan ports. President Theodore Roosevelt feared that the naval display might lead to permanent occupation of Venezuela, in violation of the Monroe Doctrine. Roosevelt secured arbitration of the dispute and withdrawal of the warships.

3. Dominican Debt Default (1904–1905). The Dominican Republic (sometimes called Santo Domingo) failed to repay loans to European credi-

Caribbean Area

tors. President Roosevelt opposed European intervention as a violation of the Monroe Doctrine, but he authorized intervention by the United States to protect the European creditors. In 1905 the United States took control of Dominican finances and initiated the repayment of Dominican debts.

Roosevelt justified his interference in Dominican affairs by asserting that, in case of "chronic wrongdoing" by any Western Hemisphere nation, the United States would exercise "international police power." This *Roosevelt Corollary* to the Monroe Doctrine was part of Roosevelt's "big stick" policy, a term derived from his expression, "Speak softly and carry a big stick."

The Roosevelt Corollary pleased European and American investors, for it indicated that we would intervene, if necessary, to protect their investments. It enraged Latin Americans by implying that they needed help from the United States to manage their affairs. (In opposition to the Roosevelt Corollary, the Latin American nations denied the right of any country, European or American, to use force to collect foreign debts.)

4. "Dollar Diplomacy." President Taft endorsed the Roosevelt Corollary and expanded our role as "policeman" of the Western Hemisphere. Taft offered American businessmen in the Caribbean the full military and diplomatic support of the government, a policy called *dollar diplomacy.* Taft encouraged American bankers to expand their loans to Honduras, Haiti, and Nicaragua. After disturbances in Nicaragua, Taft in 1912 sent marines to that country to protect American lives and property, and to restore order.

President Wilson continued American intervention in Latin America. In 1915 Wilson sent marines to occupy Haiti, and the United States took control of Haiti's finances. In 1916 he ordered marines to safeguard American interests and restore peace in the Dominican Republic.

American economic interests had by now become firmly entrenched in most Caribbean nations. Wilson's greatest Latin American problem, however, was Mexico.

AMERICAN RELATIONS WITH MEXICO: AN UNEVEN RECORD

1. Relations in the 19th Century. The annexation of Texas by the United States and the Mexican War of 1846–1848 left Mexicans with considerable ill will toward the United States. Mexican sentiments changed when the United States, after the Civil War, invoked the Monroe Doctrine to help overthrow a French protectorate in Mexico under the Emperor Maximilian.

2. American Investments in Mexico. *Porfirio Diaz*, who ruled as dictator from 1884 to 1911, favored the landowning aristocracy and welcomed foreign, especially American, investors. Diaz issued a code granting landowners the right to subsoil minerals. Americans invested over $1 billion in Mexican cattle ranches, railroads, mines, and oil wells.

3. Mexican Revolution of 1911. Many Mexicans were dissatisfied with Diaz. Peons (peasants who worked on large estates) wanted their own land; nationalists resented foreign investors; and supporters of democracy demanded representative government. In 1911 revolutionists ousted Diaz, and Mexico entered upon an era of turmoil. In 1913 an army strongman *Victoriano Huerta* seized control. His dictatorial regime was opposed by reform-minded Mexicans under *Venustiano Carranza*.

4. Wilson's Policies Toward Mexico

a. "Watchful Waiting." Wilson refused to recognize the Huerta regime, claiming that it lacked the consent of the Mexican people. Wilson also resisted demands to send troops into Mexico to protect American lives and property. Instead, he applied various pressures against Huerta: ordering American forces to occupy the Mexican seaport of Vera Cruz so timed as to keep European arms from Huerta and permitting the shipment of American arms to Carranza. Huerta finally fled from Mexico. Wilson's policy toward Mexico under Huerta became known as "watchful waiting."

b. Pursuit of Pancho Villa (1916–1917). After Wilson recognized the Carranza government, a rival Mexican leader, Pancho Villa, led several raids into the United States and murdered a number of Americans. Wilson ordered American forces under General John Pershing into northern Mexico to seize Villa, but he eluded capture.

5. Troubled Relations (Following 1917). The Mexicans resented Wilson's occupation of Vera Cruz and the pursuit of Villa into Mexican territory. They further feared "Yankee imperialism" and American economic power. During World War I Mexico was unfriendly toward the United States.

In turn, many Americans disliked the actions of the Mexican government. American Catholics protested Mexico's seizure of Church lands and the closing of parochial schools. American oil interests objected to Mexico's nationalization in 1938 of all foreign-owned oil properties.

6. The Good Neighbor Policy (Since 1933). President Franklin D. Roosevelt acknowledged Mexico's right to seize the oil properties but demanded fair compensation for the foreign investors. Mexico complied with this request. The friendly conclusion to this dispute improved Mexican-American relations. In World War II, Mexico was a firm ally of the United States.

7. Mexican-American Relations Today

a. Energy Supplies. In the 1970's, Mexico discovered huge new deposits of natural gas and oil. Mexico became the leading supplier of United States oil imports.

b. Economic Troubles. Mexico's economic prosperity, fed by the oil boom, lasted until the early 1980's, when its economy plunged into recession. Declining oil prices in the mid-1980's made the recession worse. Mexico struggled to keep up payments on its massive foreign debt, which in 1986 passed the $100 billion mark. Officials voiced concern that the economic troubles in Mexico would lead to increased illegal immigration into the United States.

c. Illegal Immigrants. In the mid-1980's, United States immigration officials were taking more than one million Mexicans a year into custody at the border with Mexico and deporting them as illegal immigrants. Many other Mexicans crossed the border illegally without being detected. Mexicans made up by far the largest portion of the officially estimated 3 million to 5 million illegal immigrants living in the United States. (Other estimates put the figure much higher.) Illegal immigration had become a major source of friction between the two nations. Many in the United States argued that Mexican "illegals" were taking jobs away from American citizens, depressing wages, and adding to welfare costs. Mexicans, on the other hand, argued that the immigrants benefited the United States economy by taking jobs no one else wanted and provided a "safety valve" for Mexico's political and economic woes. Mexican officials argued that the United States should have negotiated with Mexico on the issue of illegal immigration rather than dealing with it through the Immigration Reform and Control Act of 1986. (See page 311.)

d. Illegal Drug Traffic. United States officials claim that Mexico has become a major source of the illegal drugs entering this country.

e. Assembly Plants in Border Towns. Taking advantage of Mexican wage rates that are much lower than United States rates, many American businesses have set up assembly plants just across the border in northern Mexico.

Part 3. The Good Neighbor Policy Replaces Imperialism in Inter-American Affairs

MOVEMENT FOR PAN-AMERICANISM

1. Aims. *Pan-Americanism* fosters cooperation among the nations of the Western Hemisphere to achieve common goals such as improved trade relations, greater political stability, military defense, and cultural interchange.

2. Beginnings. *Simon Bolivar*, the Latin American liberator, issued the call for the first Pan-American conference. Held in 1826, this first meeting was a failure, and interest in Pan-Americanism declined afterwards.

3. Revival (In the 1880's). *James G. Blaine*, American Secretary of State, revived the idea of inter-American cooperation by calling for another Pan-American conference. Convened in 1889, this meeting of American republics agreed to establish an information center, which later developed into the *Pan-American Union*. This organization was housed in Washington, D.C., in a magnificent building donated by Andrew Carnegie.

4. Limited Accomplishment. Subsequent Pan-American conferences to 1928 achieved little of practical value. The Latin American nations mistrusted the United States. They feared that our support of Pan-Americanism was designed to further American domination of the Western Hemisphere.

REASONS FOR LATIN AMERICAN MISTRUST OF THE UNITED STATES

The following actions by the United States aroused mistrust in Latin America: (1) our annexation of Texas, (2) the Mexican War and our annexation of the Mexican Cession, (3) the Olney Interpretation of the Monroe Doctrine, asserting the right of the United States to intervene in any Western Hemisphere matter, (4) the Spanish-American War and our annexation of Puerto Rico, (5) the Platt Amendment, making Cuba a protectorate of the United States, (6) our role in the revolt of Panama against Colombia, (7) the Roosevelt Corollary to the Monroe Doctrine, asserting that the United States was an international policeman in the Western Hemisphere, and (8) our intervention in the Dominican Republic, Nicaragua, Haiti, and Mexico.

AMERICAN EFFORTS TO DISPEL MISTRUST

Under Herbert Hoover the United States moved to improve Latin American relations. As President-elect, Hoover made a successful goodwill tour of

Latin America. His State Department in 1930 issued the *Clark Memorandum,* disowning the Roosevelt Corollary. Despite several Latin American revolutions and debt defaults, Hoover refused to intervene. In 1933 he withdrew American marines from Nicaragua.

GOOD NEIGHBOR POLICY (STARTING IN 1933): OBJECTIVES

President Franklin D. Roosevelt and his Secretary of State, Cordell Hull, labored to win Latin American goodwill by the "policy of the good neighbor." Their objectives were as follows: (1) *Friendship.* By respecting the rights of others, Americans hoped to overcome the hostility that many Latin Americans felt toward the United States. (2) *Trade.* With the United States in the midst of the Great Depression, Americans hoped to increase trade with Latin America and spur our economic recovery. (3) *Defense.* As the Nazis rose to power in Germany and as war clouds gathered over Europe and Asia, Americans wanted to strengthen hemispheric defenses. They sought to forestall Nazi influence in Latin America and to assure inter-American military cooperation.

GOOD NEIGHBOR POLICY IN PRACTICE

1. Retreat From Imperialism. (*a*) In 1934 American marines were withdrawn from Haiti, and the United States gave up its protectorate over Cuba by abrogating the Platt Amendment. (*b*) In 1936 the United States surrendered its right to intervene in the internal affairs of Panama. (*c*) In 1938 Secretary of State Hull acknowledged Mexico's right to expropriate American oil properties.

2. Pan-Americanization of the Monroe Doctrine. (*a*) At the Montevideo Conference (1933), the American republics declared that "no state has the right to intervene in the internal or external affairs of another." By endorsing this declaration, the United States formally abandoned the Roosevelt Corollary. (*b*) At the Buenos Aires Conference (1936), the American republics pledged to consult together in case of a threat to the peace of the Americas. At the Lima Conference (1938), they further agreed that a threat to the peace of any one of them would be considered a threat to all. Thus the *unilateral* (one-nation) interpretation of the Monroe Doctrine was replaced by a *multilateral* (many-nation) interpretation. The Monroe Doctrine became a Pan-American doctrine to be interpreted and enforced not by the United States alone, but by all 21 American republics.

3. Strengthening Economic Ties. (*a*) In 1934 the United States created the Export-Import Bank. This agency granted low-cost, long-term loans to Latin American nations for building roads and for developing their natural resources. It also provided credit facilities to encourage inter-American trade. (*b*) In 1934 Congress passed the Reciprocal Trade Agreements Act. Hull negotiated trade agreements, providing for the mutual lowering of tariff barriers, with a number of Latin American nations.

4. Strengthening Social and Cultural Ties. The United States and its neighbors to the south used literature, art, music, science, education, radio, the press, movies, and goodwill tours to promote better understanding. In 1941 the United States established the *Office of Inter-American Affairs*, under Nelson Rockefeller, to strengthen hemispheric bonds.

EFFECTIVENESS OF THE GOOD NEIGHBOR POLICY AS DEMONSTRATED DURING WORLD WAR II

With the chief exception of Argentina, the nations of Latin America supported hemispheric solidarity during World War II and cooperated with the United States.

1. Upon the Outbreak of War (1939). At the Panama Conference the American republics declared their neutrality and forbade belligerents from entering a safety zone that ranged from 300 to 1200 miles off the coast of the Americas.

2. Following the Nazi Conquest of Western Europe (1940). When Nazi Germany overran France and Holland, the American republics feared that the Nazis would try to occupy the colonies that these two nations had in the Western Hemisphere. These consisted of (*a*) in South America: Dutch Guiana and French Guiana, and (*b*) in the Caribbean: Aruba and Curaçao, both Dutch; and Guadeloupe and Martinique, both French. At the Havana Conference the American republics agreed that they would jointly take control of these colonies if necessary to prevent seizure by Nazi Germany.

3. Following the Japanese Attack on Pearl Harbor (1941). At the Rio de Janeiro Conference the American republics declared the Axis powers a threat to the liberty and independence of the Americas, and recommended the severing of diplomatic relations.

Thereafter, the nations of Latin America, except for Argentina, gave valuable assistance to the United States. They (*a*) severed diplomatic relations with Italy, Germany, and Japan, and declared war against them, (*b*) arrested Axis agents, seized Axis airplanes and ships, and prohibited Axis propaganda, (*c*) granted the United States military bases, and (*d*) increased the production of strategic raw materials. (In addition, Mexico and Brazil sent troops to the fighting fronts.)

4. With Victory Assured (1945). At the Mexico City Conference, the American republics (*a*) approved proposals to create the United Nations, and (*b*) adopted the *Act of Chapultepec*, pledging joint action in case of aggression against any American nation. The Conference also urged Argentina to cooperate with the other nations of the Western Hemisphere and to declare war against Germany.

(For later Pan-American developments, including the establishment of the Organization of American States, check the Index for "Latin America, and cold war era.")

REASONS FOR ARGENTINE OPPOSITION TO THE UNITED STATES

1. Hemispheric Leadership. Intensely nationalistic, Argentina considered herself the logical leader of the nations of Latin America. Consequently, Argentina resented American leadership in the Pan-American movement.

2. Economic Competition. Both Argentina and the United States exported much wheat and beef, and competed for world markets. Argentina found the chief market for her exports in Europe, particularly England and Germany. In turn, England invested tremendous sums of money in Argentina. Consequently, Argentina was economically more closely tied to Europe than to the United States and looked on the United States as an economic competitor.

3. Nazi Influence. Argentina was the target of German efforts during the Hitler regime to spread Nazi propaganda and implant Nazi influence. This campaign was furthered by the German and Italian immigrants in Argentina, by the economic ties between Germany and Argentina, and by Argentine army men, many of whom had been trained by Germans. During World War II, Argentina served as a center of Axis activity in the Western Hemisphere. Not until 1944, when Germany's defeat appeared inevitable, did Argentina break relations with Germany.

MULTIPLE-CHOICE QUESTIONS

1. Which power of the President is related *least* to his control of foreign policy? (1) commanding the armed forces (2) calling Congress into special session (3) negotiating treaties (4) receiving ambassadors.

2. Because of the treaty-making procedure provided in the Constitution, some Presidents have (1) negotiated executive agreements instead of treaties (2) vetoed proposed Constitutional amendments curbing the treaty power (3) obtained advisory opinions from the Supreme Court before submitting treaties to the Senate (4) referred treaties to the House of Representatives instead of to the Senate.

3. Which is an important check on the President's control of foreign policy? (1) Congress must approve appropriations. (2) The House of Representatives must approve Presidential appointments. (3) The Senate can remove ambassadors. (4) The Central Intelligence Agency must approve the admission of foreign diplomats to the United States.

4. United States foreign policy in the 19th century was influenced most by (1) the Civil War (2) Washington's Farewell Address (3) dollar diplomacy (4) the Gentlemen's Agreement.

5. The United States had few foreign investments before 1890 because (1) Americans did not believe in imperialism (2) Congress had prohibited all loans to foreign countries (3) the development of the West offered a profitable field for the investment of capital (4) foreign countries did not need capital.

6. In the years following 1900, United States foreign policy in the Caribbean was determined largely by (1) the decline of our foreign trade (2) the economic growth of our country (3) the demands of our farmers for markets (4) our desire for cheap manufactured goods from abroad.

7. The earliest colonial acquisition of the United States was (1) Alaska (2) Hawaii (3) Puerto Rico (4) the Virgin Islands.

8. Since World War II, Alaska's strategic importance has increased because of (1) the discovery of new gold mines (2) the large-scale mining of uranium deposits (3) the air routes across the Arctic (4) her achievement of statehood.

9. The admission of Hawaii as our 50th state (1) granted equality with the older states to an area with an Asian majority (2) extended our defenses against Red China to the mid-Pacific (3) eliminated the tariff on Hawaiian sugar (4) permitted unlimited Hawaiian immigration to the mainland.

10. The United States declaration of war on Spain is an example of (1) Presidential leadership in the face of Congressional disapproval (2) army maneuvers making war inevitable (3) the influence of the press on popular opinion (4) the unanimous opinion of businessmen in favor of war.

11. By the treaty ending the Spanish-American War, the United States acquired (1) Hawaii, the Philippines, Guam (2) the Philippines, Guam, Puerto Rico (3) Haiti, the Philippines, Guam (4) Cuba, Puerto Rico, Guam.

12. An important result of the Spanish-American War was that it (1) strengthened American control in the Caribbean (2) increased the rivalry between the United States and Russia (3) forced Spain to recognize the Monroe Doctrine (4) assured the election of Theodore Roosevelt as President in 1900.

13. The Platt Amendment provided that the United States (1) annex Cuba (2) maintain a protectorate over Cuba (3) withdraw American investments from Cuba (4) send an American to serve as President of Cuba.

14. Puerto Rico is represented in the United States House of Representatives by (1) its Governor (2) an elected commission of three (3) a delegate who may speak but not vote (4) one elected Representative.

15. Which term is used to describe Puerto Rico's relationship to the United States today? (1) colony (2) state (3) trust territory (4) Commonwealth.

16. The Hay-Pauncefote Treaty between the United States and Great Britain was concerned with the (1) boundary between Maine and Canada (2) building of a canal across the Isthmus of Panama (3) disposition of the Samoan Islands (4) Bering Sea seal fisheries.

17. A major reason why the United States built the Panama Canal was to (1) improve the defense of the United States (2) increase the prosperity of Central America (3) force the reduction of railroad rates (4) fulfill our treaty obligations with Great Britain.

18. In 1917 the United States purchased the Virgin Islands because the islands (1) were a source of tropical products (2) provided a naval base on the Caribbean Sea (3) were suitable as an air base for trans-Atlantic aviation (4) were occupied by American settlers.

19. Which occurred during the last quarter of the 19th century? (1) Maximilian Affair (2) Venezuela boundary dispute (3) occupation of Vera Cruz (4) opening of the Panama Canal.

20. Which combines a period in United States history with a phase of foreign policy dominant at that time? (1) 1865–1890—active leadership in world affairs (2) 1890–1903—rejection of opportunities for imperialism (3) 1904–1910—active role in Caribbean area (4) 1910–1918—isolation from world struggles.

21. Which idea was a corollary to the original Monroe Doctrine? (1) The Western Hemisphere is closed to further colonization. (2) The United States has the right to intervene in Latin America. (3) The United States will not intervene in the affairs of Europe. (4) The United States will respect European colonies already established in the New World.

22. The United States used the Roosevelt Corollary to justify (1) intervention in Cuba's rebellion against Spain (2) requests to Latin American countries to join in enforcing the Monroe Doctrine (3) reversal of the policy followed in the Maximilian Affair (4) intervention in the financial affairs of certain Caribbean republics.

23. Dollar diplomacy was used by both President Taft and President Wilson to (1) provide aid for developing nations in Asia (2) protect United States investments abroad (3) promote an economic union of European nations (4) encourage adoption of reciprocal tariff agreements.

24. During the late 1920's and early 1930's, United States foreign policy changed most significantly in respect to (1) Canada (2) Great Britain (3) Latin America (4) Germany.

25. As Secretary of State, James G. Blaine is best remembered for his (1) weak foreign policy (2) desire to annex Mexico and Canada (3) frequent clashes with France (4) efforts to establish friendlier relations with Latin America.

26. Pan-Americanism is chiefly a movement to (1) unite the countries of North America under one government (2) strengthen our military bases in Canada (3) bring about cooperation among the republics of the Western Hemisphere (4) protect the Panama Canal.

27. A sharp contrast in our relations with Latin America is evident between (1) dollar diplomacy and our intervention in Nicaragua (2) the Roosevelt Corollary and our intervention in Haiti (3) the Olney Interpretation and the Good Neighbor Policy (4) "watchful waiting" and nonrecognition of the Huerta government.

28. The United States carried out the Good Neighbor Policy by (1) reviving dollar diplomacy (2) intervening in Guatemala (3) negotiating reciprocal trade agreements (4) supporting a revolutionary movement in Argentina.

29. The Good Neighbor Policy was promoted by the (1) Platt Amendment (2) "big stick" policy (3) Roosevelt Corollary (4) multilateral interpretation of the Monroe Doctrine.

30. The United States does not trade extensively with Argentina because Argentina (1) exports goods that we also export (2) does not want more foreign trade (3) has nothing to export (4) is tied to the Russian trade bloc.

31. Which of the following countries gave us the *least* cooperation during World War II? (1) Venezuela (2) Brazil (3) Mexico (4) Argentina.

MODIFIED TRUE-FALSE QUESTIONS

1. The American battle-cry in the Spanish-American War was *"Remember the Alamo!"*

2. The effort by the government of Puerto Rico to improve economic conditions on the island was called *Operation Bootstrap*.

3. The President who first proclaimed the "big stick" policy was *William McKinley*.
4. The President at the time of the Venezuela boundary dispute was *Richard Olney*.
5. In the *Foraker Act,* Congress declared that the United States would not annex Cuba.
6. The army surgeon who discovered that yellow fever is transmitted by a certain kind of mosquito was *Alfred Mahan*.
7. The naval base that Cuba leased to the United States is located at *Santiago*.
8. The army engineer who had charge of building the Panama Canal was *George W. Goethals*.

MAP QUESTIONS

For each area described below, write *both* its name and the letter indicating its location on the map.

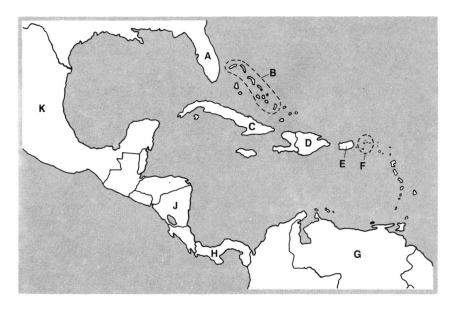

1. Acquired by the United States as a result of the Spanish-American War, this area now has the status of a Commonwealth.
2. This area, a protectorate of the United States from 1901 to 1934, later experienced a revolution led by Fidel Castro.
3. Conditions in this area, once ruled by Maximilian, caused President Woodrow Wilson to adopt a policy of "watchful waiting."
4. This area has been considered as an alternate canal route; it was occupied by United States troops for most of the years from 1912 to 1933.
5. In 1917 the United States strengthened its naval control of the Caribbean region by purchasing this area from Denmark.
6. This area gained its independence with the aid of President Theodore Roosevelt, who was interested in acquiring the right to build a canal.
7. A boundary dispute in this area led to the issuance of the Olney Interpretation.

ESSAY QUESTIONS

1. Discuss the Spanish-American War, including (*a*) *two* reasons for the war, (*b*) *three* provisions of the Treaty of Paris ending the war, (*c*) *two* effects of the war upon American foreign policy.

2. The relations between the United States and Latin America are vital to the future welfare of the Western Hemisphere. (*a*) State specifically *two* policies of the United States toward Latin America as expressed in the Monroe Doctrine of 1823. (*b*) Discuss *two* actions of the United States in the period 1890–1930 that aroused ill feeling in Latin America. (*c*) Describe *two* activities of the United States in the period 1930–1945 that fostered goodwill in Latin America. (*d*) Describe *two* reasons for the shift in our policies toward Latin America during the period 1930–1945.

3. Giving *one* specific reason in each case, explain why *each* of the following either improved or worsened relations between Latin America and the United States: (*a*) Wilson's policy toward Mexico, (*b*) Pan-Americanization of the Monroe Doctrine, (*c*) reciprocal trade agreements, (*d*) Venezuela boundary dispute, (*e*) economic and political conditions in Puerto Rico today, (*f*) plans for a second interoceanic canal.

4. World War II provided a test for the effectiveness of the Pan-American movement. (*a*) What is meant by Pan-Americanism? (*b*) Discuss *two* ways in which Latin America aided the United States during World War II. (*c*) Explain *one* reason why Argentina was unwilling to support a policy of hemispheric solidarity.

Part 4. The United States Pursues National Interests in the Far East

AMERICAN INTERESTS IN THE FAR EAST

1. Economic Interests. In 1783, the year the American Revolution ended, an American sailing ship began the first successful voyage to China. Thereafter, American merchants created a small but thriving trade with the Far East, delivering furs and textiles, and bringing back tea, silk, and spices. Following the Civil War, as the United States became more industrial, American manufacturers and investors looked to the Pacific area for markets, raw materials, and investment opportunities.

2. Religious Interests. American missionaries supplied Western medical and agricultural knowledge to the Asians and sought to convert them to Christianity.

3. Colonial Acquisitions. Between 1867 and 1899 the United States gathered a colonial empire in the Pacific: purchasing Alaska, annexing Hawaii, securing Guam and the Philippines as a result of the Spanish-American War, and acquiring Midway, Wake, and part of the Samoan Islands. In 1914 the United States completed the Panama Canal, which provided a shorter, quicker route between the eastern United States and the Pacific.

4. Defense. American military leaders utilized our possessions in the Pacific to establish army, navy, and air bases.

PHILIPPINES

PEOPLE AND ECONOMY

Located in the western Pacific, 7000 miles from California, the Philippines has a population of over 66 million. As a result of Spanish rule, the Filipinos are principally Roman Catholic. As a result of American rule, the Filipinos have an elementary school system, and most of the population is able to read and write. The Filipinos have a standard of living low compared to Americans, but good compared to most Asians.

The Filipinos are engaged chiefly in agriculture, raising rice, manila hemp, tobacco, coconut oil, and sugar. The islands contain relatively undeveloped mineral deposits of gold, silver, copper, chromium, and iron. Their industrial plants are concerned chiefly with processing agricultural and forest products. The Philippines trades extensively with the United States.

AMERICAN ANNEXATION

1. **Reasons.** As a result of the Spanish-American War, the United States annexed the Philippines for (a) *economic reasons:* trade, raw materials, investments, (b) *military reasons:* a strategic base in the Far East, and (c) *humanitarianism:* a desire to educate and "civilize" the Filipinos.

2. **Filipino Opposition.** Many Filipinos had expected the United States to withdraw after 1898 and grant them independence. *Emilio Aguinaldo* led the embittered islanders in revolt against American rule. After three years of fighting and at great cost, American forces suppressed the Filipino rebels.

AMERICAN ACHIEVEMENT IN THE PHILIPPINES

1. **Economic Development.** American investors furthered the development of Filipino resources and processing industries. American authorities promoted extensive public works and helped peasants purchase small farms.

2. **Conquest of Disease.** American health officials started a number of sanitation programs, wiped out cholera and smallpox, and built hospitals and health centers.

3. **Education.** By establishing a system of free public schools, the United States substantially reduced illiteracy.

4. **Gradual Self-Government.** The United States trained the islanders for self-government. Beginning in 1907 the Filipinos elected the lower house of their legislature. By the *Jones Act of 1916*, they received the right to elect both houses of the legislature and were promised eventual independence from the United States.

STEPS TO PHILIPPINE INDEPENDENCE

1. American Support for Independence: Reasons. Americans came to realize that most Filipinos desired independence. Also, American producers of sugar and edible oil wanted tariff protection against Philippine sugar and coconut oil. American workers on the Pacific coast wanted to halt the influx of Filipino immigrants. American taxpayers wanted to end federal spending in the Philippines. Finally, American military leaders, concerned by the distant location of the islands, wanted to end American responsibility for Philippine defense.

2. Tydings-McDuffie (Philippine Independence) Act—1934. This act offered the Filipinos independence after a transition period. It also empowered the Filipinos to write a constitution and establish a democratic government.

3. Philippines in World War II. In December 1941, immediately after bombing Pearl Harbor, Japan invaded the Philippines and quickly overran the islands. General *Douglas MacArthur,* commander of the American forces in the Far East, fled to Australia but pledged, "I shall return." In 1944 MacArthur, with a powerful military force, returned and liberated the islands.

PHILIPPINES AS AN INDEPENDENT NATION

1. Independence. In 1946, at Manila, the Philippines formally received independence from the United States. It also received extensive postwar economic aid, as well as favorable tariff treatment for its exports.

2. Friendship for the United States. In 1947 the Philippines granted the United States military bases, and in 1951 the two nations signed a treaty of mutual defense. To support the American effort in South Vietnam, the Philippine government sent a token force of troops, chiefly engineers.

3. Presidency of Ferdinand E. Marcos (1965–1986). After being elected president of the Philippines in 1965, Marcos acted as follows:

a. Foreign Policy Shifts. Marcos moved somewhat away from a pro-American and toward an independent foreign policy. In 1979 and 1983, Marcos secured revisions in the agreement regarding American military bases in the Philippines. While allowing the United States "unhampered" military use, the revisions acknowledged Filipino sovereignty over the bases and stepped up United States economic and military assistance to the Philippines.

b. Moves Against Muslim Guerrillas. Marcos tried to crush a guerrilla movement that demanded a separate state for the Philippines' Muslim minority.

c. Communist Insurgency. After the defeat of a Communist insurgency movement called the *Hukbalahap* (or "Huk"), in the 1950's, Philippine Communists reorganized. A group called the New People's Army launched a second rebellion in 1969. By 1986 the movement had an estimated 20,000 guerrillas.

d. Authoritarian Rule. Marcos declared martial law in 1972, ruthlessly suppressing opposition and ruling by authoritarian methods. Although martial law ended in 1981, Marcos held firmly to power. The nation's economy limped from bad to worse. Corruption in high places fed public unrest.

e. Marcos's Fall. The leading opposition figure, *Benigno Aquino,* returned from self-exile in 1983, only to be shot dead as he stepped from an airplane. *Corazon Aquino,* the slain leader's wife, took his place as leader of the opposition. She ran against Marcos in 1986 in a hotly contested election. Although officials said Marcos had won, Aquino's outraged followers thought otherwise. They took to the streets in mass demonstrations. United States leaders, who up to that point had backed Marcos, now joined in accusing him of election fraud. When several high Philippine military leaders switched their support to Aquino, Marcos and his wife Imelda fled to Hawaii. Marcos died in 1989.

4. Presidency of Corazon Aquino (1986–1992). Aquino faced many problems: *(a)* repeated military uprisings, *(b)* Communist and Muslim insurgencies, and *(c)* the Philippines' large foreign debt and shaky economy. In 1987 the legislature approved a new constitution, hoping to stabilize the country's uncertain democracy. With the rejection of the treaty for Subic Bay, the United States decided to close its naval base there. Aquino did not run for reelection.

CHINA

APPEAL TO MODERN IMPERIALISTS (FROM THE MID-19TH CENTURY)

China, a land occupying much of eastern Asia, attracted imperialist nations for several reasons: (1) China's huge population offered a tremendous market for manufactured goods and cheap labor for foreign-owned enterprises. (2) China's untapped mineral resources—coal, iron, and tin—attracted investors. (3) China's tea and silk found ready European markets. (4) China's Manchu government was inefficient and lacked military power.

VICTIM OF MODERN IMPERIALISM

Britain, by the *Opium War* (1839–1842), compelled China to (1) allow imports of opium, a habit-forming narcotic, (2) open additional ports to British trade, (3) cede Hong Kong to Britain, and (4) grant British citizens the privilege of *extraterritoriality.* (This entitled an Englishman accused of a crime in China to be tried in a British court. Extraterritoriality, soon conceded to other foreign nations, offended Chinese justice and pride.) Britain later established a *sphere of influence* over the Yangtze River valley. (A sphere of influence was a region over which an imperialist nation maintained an *economic monopoly:* licensing businesses, controlling tariff rates, and determining railroad and harbor fees.)

Other foreign nations secured trading and extraterritorial rights in China, annexed Chinese territory, and acquired spheres of influence. France gained a sphere of influence in southeastern China, as did Germany in the Shantung Peninsula. Russia annexed territory in northern China and established a sphere of influence over Manchuria. Japan annexed Taiwan (Formosa).

The imperialist nations seemed poised to annex their respective spheres of influence, thereby threatening further to dismember China.

AMERICAN RELATIONS WITH CHINA

The United States had long conducted a small but profitable trade with China. In 1844 *Caleb Cushing* negotiated a treaty with China securing for Americans the trading and extraterritorial privileges extended to other foreigners. However, unlike most other foreign nations in China, the United States annexed no territory and claimed no sphere of influence. American relations with China therefore remained friendly.

OPEN DOOR POLICY (1899)

With the acquisition of the Philippines in 1898, Americans anticipated an increase in our China trade. Such trade was threatened, however, by the existence of spheres of influence and by the prospect of China's dismemberment. *John Hay*, the American Secretary of State, therefore suggested the *Open Door Policy*. It proposed equal trading rights in China for all nations. Later, the Open Door Policy also came to mean the preservation of China's independence and territory.

The "open door" was accepted by the imperialist nations in principle, but not in practice. However, it earned us China's goodwill and, for many years, served as the cornerstone of American policy toward the Far East.

(Some historians have contended that, by committing us to safeguard China's territorial integrity, the Open Door Policy was a long-range American blunder. They argue that America's trade with China was too small to justify our entanglement in Far Eastern affairs. They further point out that, once a single nation became dominant in the Far East, as Japan did, the United States had to face the choice either of abandoning the Open Door Policy or of fighting to uphold it.)

BOXER REBELLION (1900)

The *Boxers*, a Chinese society encouraged by Manchu leaders, staged an uprising to drive out all foreigners and restore China to isolation. They wrecked foreign property and killed foreign citizens, chiefly missionaries, businessmen, and diplomatic officials. The Boxers were suppressed by an international military force comprised of European, Japanese, and American troops.

When the foreign nations demanded damages from China, Secretary of State Hay urged that China pay not by surrendering territory, but by giving a monetary indemnity. The other nations agreed. (When the foreign powers imposed excessive indemnities, the United States returned half of its money to advance education in China and to enable Chinese students to attend American colleges.)

BRIEF SURVEY OF DEVELOPMENTS IN CHINA TO WORLD WAR II

In 1911–1912 the *Kuomintang*, or *Nationalist party,* under *Sun Yat-sen,* overthrew the feeble Manchu Dynasty and proclaimed a republic. Thereafter, the Nationalists struggled to subdue the local warlords. By 1928 General *Chiang Kai-shek* had led the Nationalist armies to victory over the warlords, but he now faced a greater threat, the Chinese Communists. Following a period of civil war, the Nationalists and Communists arranged a temporary truce to meet the challenge of Japanese imperialism. (Check the Index for "Japan, to World War II.")

JAPAN

OPENING OF JAPAN (1853–1854)

By the mid-17th century, feudal Japan had withdrawn into isolation, and for 200 years she remained unaffected by Western civilization.

In 1853–1854 Commodore *Matthew C. Perry,* heading an American naval squadron, convinced Japan to open certain ports to American trade. Soon afterwards, the leading European powers demanded and received similar trade rights. In 1857–1858 *Townsend Harris,* America's first consul to Japan, skillfully negotiated treaties expanding diplomatic and commercial relations between the two countries.

WESTERNIZATION OF JAPAN (STARTING IN 1867)

In 1864 European and American warships bombarded a Japanese seaport in retaliation against antiforeign outbreaks. Impressed by Western military might and fearful of foreign domination, the Japanese rapidly transformed their country from medieval feudalism to modern nationhood. In so doing, they demonstrated a talent for learning from the West and for adapting Western institutions to Japanese needs.

The Japanese (1) established a strong central government with a constitution that concentrated power in the hands of the Emperor and the military leaders, (2) created a powerful army and navy, (3) ended serfdom and enabled many peasants to become landowners, and (4) encouraged a sweeping program of industrialization. Japan soon produced textiles, steel, machinery, and ships, and became a major trading and manufacturing nation.

JAPAN TURNS TO IMPERIALISM

1. Reasons. (*a*) Japanese industrialists needed raw materials—especially cotton, iron ore, and oil—and markets for their manufactured goods. (*b*) Japanese nationalists sought honor for the Emperor and glory for the military forces. They thought that colonies would raise Japan to the rank of a big power. (c) Densely populated and lacking arable land, Japan wanted colonial outlets for her surplus population. (d) Japan's location placed her within easy reach of the underdeveloped nations of eastern Asia, especially China.

2. Sino-Japanese War (1894–1895). In a short war Japan overwhelmed China and acquired Taiwan and a sphere of influence in Korea. (In 1910 Japan annexed Korea.)

3. Russo-Japanese War (1904–1905). Caused by imperialist rivalries over Manchuria and Korea, this war was fought on Chinese territory and in the nearby Pacific waters. Japan, to the world's surprise, defeated Russia.

    a. Treaty of Portsmouth (New Hampshire). President Theodore Roosevelt brought the warring nations together to negotiate the *Treaty of Portsmouth.* Japan gained the southern half of Sakhalin Island, Russia's lease of Port Arthur (in China), and Russia's sphere of influence in southern Manchuria. Roosevelt was pleased that the Treaty of Portsmouth did not violate the Open Door Policy. (For his efforts, Roosevelt received the 1906 Nobel Peace Prize.)

    b. Significance. (1) Japanese militarists were cheered by their victory, the first in modern times of an Asian nation over a European power. They became determined to place eastern Asia under Japanese domination. (Later, they promised to bring a *New Order* to this *Co-Prosperity Sphere.*) (2) Although Japanese officials were satisfied with the treaty, many Japanese resented the lack of any war indemnity and were dissatisfied with their territorial gains. They blamed President Roosevelt and staged anti-American riots. (3) American government officials realized that Japan had become the major power in the Far East. They feared for the safety of the Philippines and the maintenance of the Open Door Policy. To demonstrate American power, President Theodore Roosevelt sent the American navy on an around-the-world tour with a significant stop at Tokyo, where the navy received a friendly welcome. (4) American people became aroused over what was loosely termed the "yellow peril."

JAPAN AND THE UNITED STATES COME INTO CONFLICT

1. Japanese Resentment of American Immigration Policies. Japanese immigrants, residing chiefly in California, were dependable workers who accepted low wages. They were berated by organized labor, denounced by newspapers, and subjected to various forms of discrimination. In 1906 Japanese schoolchildren in San Francisco were segregated by order of the City Board of Education. This act angered Japan, and the Japanese government protested to Washington.

Although President Roosevelt had no legal authority over California officials, he pressured San Francisco into reversing its action. At the same time Roosevelt secured the *Gentlemen's Agreement* (1907), by which Japan pledged to halt the emigration of laborers to the United States.

The San Francisco school dispute, subsequent state laws restricting Japanese landownership, and the Immigration Act of 1924, which ended the Gentlemen's Agreement and excluded all Japanese immigrants, all contributed to bitter feelings. However, they were minor irritations when compared to the basic conflict of interests: support of the Open Door Policy by the United States versus Japan's ambition to dominate China.

2. Japan's Twenty-one Demands Upon China (1915). During World War I, while the Western powers were preoccupied in Europe, Japan tried to turn China into a protectorate by making the *Twenty-one Demands*. Despite American protests, Japan compelled acceptance of most of these demands by weak, defenseless China.

After the war the United States called the *Washington Conference* (1921–1922) to discuss naval and Far Eastern problems. The American Secretary of State, Charles Evans Hughes, presided over the conference and guided its deliberations. Under Western persuasion, Japan joined in the *Nine-Power Treaty*, pledging to respect the principles of the Open Door: (*a*) equal trade rights in China, and (*b*) China's territorial integrity and independence.

3. Japanese Invasion of Manchuria (1931). In violation of the Nine-Power Treaty, Japan invaded the outlying Chinese territory of Manchuria, rich in coal, iron, and fertile soil. The *Lytton Commission*, investigating for the League of Nations, condemned Japan and recommended that she withdraw her troops. Instead, Japan withdrew from the League.

Henry L. Stimson, the United States Secretary of State, informed Japan that America disapproved of the aggression in Manchuria. He declared that the United States would recognize no seizure of territory by force—a declaration that became known as the *Stimson Doctrine*. Neither the League nor the United States took further action.

By 1932 Japan exercised full control over Manchuria, which was now the puppet state of *Manchukuo*. In violation of the Open Door Policy, the Japanese expelled foreign business interests and monopolized the region's economic development. They built railroads, developed hydroelectric power, and created a sizable iron and steel industry, thereby increasing Japan's economic and military power.

4. Japanese Invasion of China (1937). Japan invaded China proper, seeking to control the entire country. Initially, Japanese armies met with success and occupied most of coastal China. By 1939, however, their advance into the interior was slowed, often to a standstill, by Chinese guerrilla resistance. Meanwhile, the United States, in support of China, (a) extended loans for the purchase of war materials, (b) permitted American volunteer pilots to fight for China as the *Flying Tigers,* and (c) in 1940 embargoed the sale to Japan of scrap metal and aviation gasoline. Also, many American importers and consumers boycotted Japanese goods.

5. Japanese Attack on Pearl Harbor (December 7, 1941). Japanese leaders believed that they had to drive out Great Britain and the United States in order to dominate the Far East. In 1937 Japan joined the Axis alliance of Fascist Italy and Nazi Germany. When World War II began in 1939, Japanese leaders believed that their opportunity was at hand. Britain was at war against Germany; the United States was busy supplying military equipment to the Allied nations in Europe. Consequently, on December 7, 1941, Japan staged a surprise attack against the American naval base at Pearl Harbor, Hawaii. Japanese armies invaded British-owned Malaya and the American-owned Philippines. (For Japan's defeat in World War II, check the Index under "Japan, and World War II.")

MULTIPLE-CHOICE QUESTIONS

1. American merchants began trading with the Far East (1) after the Open Door Policy was announced (2) just prior to the Civil War (3) just after the Revolutionary War (4) during the administration of Theodore Roosevelt.

2. The American record in the Philippines includes all of the following *except* (1) training the Filipinos for self-government (2) developing a highly industrialized economy (3) reducing illiteracy (4) improving health conditions.

3. During the 1920's some Americans urged independence for the Philippines because (1) the Filipinos are brown-skinned (2) the Communists were very powerful in the islands (3) Filipino products were entering the United States without payment of any tariff (4) the islands had no need of American military protection.

4. Since independence, the Philippines has followed a foreign policy that (1) favors Communist China (2) opposes entangling alliances (3) supports the United States (4) seeks strict neutrality in the cold war.

5. A sphere of influence, in the history of China, was a region (1) annexed by a foreign power (2) ruled by foreign missionaries (3) nominally Chinese but controlled economically by a foreign power (4) lacking in Chinese courts.

6. The United States decided on its Open Door Policy at a time when China (1) was in danger of being partitioned by foreign nations (2) refused to trade with non-Asian powers (3) was engaged in a civil war between Communists and Nationalists (4) was undergoing rapid industrialization.

7. The Open Door Policy indicated that the United States was primarily interested in (1) acquiring a colonial empire in the Far East (2) protecting United States trade in China (3) applying the Monroe Doctrine to Asia (4) protecting United States bases in the Philippines.

8. The United States won the friendship of China immediately after the Boxer Rebellion by (1) encouraging Japanese expansion into Manchuria (2) returning a portion of the indemnity payments (3) allowing the admission of Chinese immigrants on a quota basis (4) refusing to recognize Chiang Kai-shek.

9. Commodore Perry's visit to Japan was made primarily to (1) open Japanese ports to American merchant ships (2) prevent Japanese domination of China (3) break the British monopoly of Japanese trade (4) settle the controversy over the seal fisheries.

10. An important reason for Japan's emergence as a modern world power was her (1) involvement in World War II (2) reliance on the teachings of Buddha (3) imitation of Western technology and institutions (4) great wealth of oil and iron ore.

11. American policies toward the Far East during the period 1900-1914 (1) aroused Japanese resentment (2) encouraged German ambitions (3) produced a united China (4) weakened British influence.

12. Which event marked the emergence of Japan as a major power? (1) Sino-Japanese War (2) Russo-Japanese War (3) Twenty-one Demands (4) Washington Nine-Power Treaty.

13. The Gentlemen's Agreement between the United States and Japan dealt primarily with the problem of (1) racial discrimination (2) trade (3) immigration (4) naval disarmament.

14. The major cause of tension between the United States and Japan during the 1930's was Japan's (1) violation of the Open Door Policy (2) expulsion of American missionaries from Japan (3) refusal to trade with the United States (4) military pact with Russia.

15. The Stimson Doctrine (1) had little effect on Japanese aggression in the 1930's (2) was issued when Japan annexed Formosa (3) placed an embargo on the sale of scrap metal to Japan (4) opposed efforts by the League of Nations regarding Manchuria.

MATCHING QUESTIONS

Column A	*Column B*
1. Formulated Open Door Policy	*a.* Emilio Aguinaldo
2. Overthrew Manchu regime	*b.* Chiang Kai-shek
3. Was first American consul in Japan	*c.* Caleb Cushing
4. Led Filipino revolt against United States	*d.* Townsend Harris
5. Stated that the United States would recognize no seizure of territory by force	*e.* John Hay
6. Opened Japan to Western trade	*f.* Douglas MacArthur
7. Sponsored bill to offer independence to Philippines	*g.* Ferdinand Marcos
8. Commanded American army forces in the Far East	*h.* Matthew C. Perry
	i. Theodore Roosevelt
9. Led Chinese Nationalists against warlords and then against Communists	*j.* Henry L. Stimson
	k. Sun Yat-sen
10. Received Nobel Peace Prize for efforts in ending Russo-Japanese War	*l.* Millard Tydings

ESSAY QUESTIONS

1. As a result of the Spanish-American War, the United States acquired the Philippines. Discuss (a) *two* reasons why the United States annexed the Philippines, (b) *two* problems that the Philippines posed for the United States after annexation, (c) *two* reasons why the United States later offered the Philippines independence, and (d) *one* way the Philippines was affected by World War II.

2. The United States championed the Open Door Policy with regard to China. (a) Briefly state the terms of the Open Door Policy. (b) Describe *one* circumstance that led to the issuance of the Open Door Policy. (c) Describe *one* incident in which Japan threatened the Open Door Policy during the period 1905–1945, and explain *one* action taken by the United States government to resist this threat.

3. Describe *one* action taken by the United States as a result of *each* of the following developments in the Far East: (a) emigration from the Far East to the United States between 1875 and 1929, (b) Boxer Rebellion, (c) Russo-Japanese War, (d) Twenty-one Demands, (e) Japan's seizure of Manchuria, (f) Japan's invasion of China proper.

Part 5. The United States Becomes Involved in World War I

EUROPE GOES TO WAR (1914)

Divided into two hostile alliances, the major European nations had provoked each other in a series of international crises. They had turned Europe into a "powder keg" ready to explode into war. When in 1914 a Serb (Yugoslav) assassinated the heir to the Austro-Hungarian throne, World War I began. In the initial stage of the war, the conflicting nations were (1) the **Central Powers**—Germany and Austria-Hungary—against (2) the **Allies** —Great Britain, France, Russia, Serbia, and Belgium.

FUNDAMENTAL CAUSES OF WORLD WAR I

1. Nationalism. (a) France was determined to recover from Germany the French-inhabited provinces of Alsace and Lorraine. (b) Subject nationalities sought independence. Yugoslavs, Czechs, and Slovaks sought freedom from Austria-Hungary. Poles, divided among Russia, Austria-Hungary, and Germany, longed to re-create a self-governing Polish state. (c) Intense patriotism assured popular support for warlike measures.

2. Imperialism. (a) France and Germany clashed over Morocco. (b) Russia and Austria-Hungary were rivals in the Balkans. (c) Britain and Germany competed for imperialist control in Africa and the Middle East, and for markets throughout the world.

3. **Militarism.** (*a*) By peacetime conscription, the Continental European nations each sought military superiority. (*b*) Germany had a military tradition and extolled armed might. (*c*) Britain, which relied heavily upon her navy for protection, felt threatened by Germany's huge naval building program.

4. **International Anarchy.** (*a*) No international organization existed with authority to compel nations to obey its decisions. (*b*) The *Hague Court of Arbitration,* a tribunal to settle international disputes, depended on voluntary acceptance of its authority and was ineffective.

OTHER NATIONS ENTER THE WAR

1. The **Central Powers** were joined by Turkey and Bulgaria.

2. The **Allied Powers** were joined by more than 25 nations. Most notable were (*a*) in 1914, Japan, which acted primarily to seize German territories in the Pacific, (*b*) in 1915, Italy, which had refused to honor her alliance with the Central Powers and which was now won over to the Allies by a secret treaty promising her territorial gains, and (*c*) in 1917, the United States.

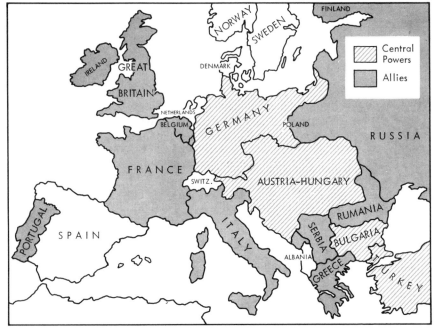

Europe: The Opposing Sides in World War I

AMERICAN ENTRANCE INTO WORLD WAR I: REASONS

When war started in 1914, President Woodrow Wilson urged the American people to be "neutral in fact as well as in name" and issued a *Proclamation of Neutrality.* However, Americans could not help but take sides. Except for some Irish-Americans, traditionally anti-English, and some German-Americans, most people overwhelmingly sympathized with the Allies.

In November, 1916, Wilson narrowly won reelection with the slogan, "He kept us out of war." In April, 1917, only five months later, Wilson asked Congress to declare war on Germany. The main reasons, according to historians, were the following:

1. Unrestricted Submarine Warfare by Germany. To blockade England and to counteract British superiority in surface vessels, the Germans resorted to *unrestricted submarine warfare.* The United States contended that German submarines, or *U-boats,* violated international law by interfering with our *freedom of the seas:* (*a*) the right of American merchant ships to trade with belligerents in goods not intended for war use, and (*b*) the right of American citizens to sail on the merchant ships of belligerents . The American people were outraged as German U-boats violated our neutral rights and took an increasing toll of American lives. Before the United States entered the war, over 200 Americans, most traveling on Allied merchant ships, perished as a result of Germany's submarine warfare.

a. Sinking of the Lusitania (1915). A German U-boat sank the *Lusitania,* an English passenger liner, without first searching for contraband war goods and without providing for the safety of the crew and passengers. More than 1000 persons lost their lives, including over 100 Americans. The United States vigorously protested this "illegal and inhuman act." The Germans replied that the *Lusitania* had carried contraband and that Americans had been warned, by a newspaper advertisement, to stay off the ship.

b. Sussex Pledge (1916). A U-boat torpedoed an unarmed French vessel, the *Sussex,* injuring several American passengers. When President Wilson threatened to sever diplomatic relations, the German government gave the *Sussex Pledge,* not to sink merchant vessels without first attempting to save human lives.

c. Unrestricted Submarine Warfare Again (1917). Believing that they now had enough U-boats to starve Britain, the German leaders took the risk of war with the United States and renewed their unrestricted submarine warfare. U-boats soon sank several unarmed American merchant ships. President Wilson ordered guns placed on our ships and shortly afterwards asked Congress to declare war.

(In spite of our protests, Britain blockaded our trade with the Central Powers, forced American ships into British ports to be searched, and intercepted American mail. However, Americans were less angered by British than by German acts, since British interference with our neutral rights did not endanger American lives.)

2. Allied Propaganda. Americans were receptive to Allied propaganda. (*a*) We felt a kinship for England, based upon a common language and culture. (*b*) Our friendship for France went back to French support of the colonial cause in the American Revolution.

3. Hostility Toward Germany. The American people became increasingly hostile toward Germany because the Germans (*a*) invaded Belgium in violation of a treaty guaranteeing Belgian neutrality, (*b*) waged unrestricted submarine warfare, (*c*) attempted to sabotage American industries, and (*d*) plotted to draw Mexico into war against the United States, as evidenced by the *Zimmermann Note.* (German Foreign Minister Zimmermann in early 1917 sent instructions to the German minister in Mexico. In the event of German-American hostilities, he was to induce Mexico to declare war against the United States. Mexico might then regain Texas, New Mexico, and Arizona. Intercepted by the British, this secret German message inflamed American war sentiment.)

4. American Economic Interests. Because Britain effectively blockaded the Central Powers, Americans sold foodstuffs and manufactured goods almost entirely to the Allies. Our manufacturers, workers, farmers, and exporters all shared in a period of prosperity. When the Allies exhausted their funds, American investors extended them substantial loans. Americans feared that, if Germany won the war, American loans to the Allies might never be repaid.

5. American Idealism. Americans felt that a better world would emerge if the Allied nations triumphed over the autocratic Central Powers. President Wilson called World War I the "war to end all wars" and proclaimed that "the world must be made safe for democracy."

6. American Security. Germany, if victorious, would have replaced democratic England as the dominant European power on the Atlantic. From this location, aggressive, militaristic Germany could have threatened the security of the United States.

AMERICA AT WAR: THE HOME FRONT

1. Increasing Presidential Powers. Wilson provided strong wartime leadership. He received from Congress broad emergency powers to direct the economy and spur the war effort. Wilson commanded an array of government agencies representing a tremendous expansion of federal and executive power.

√2. **Mobilizing the Economy.** The *War Industries Board,* headed by Bernard Baruch, allocated raw materials, eliminated waste, and expanded war production. The *War Labor Board* mediated labor disputes so as to prevent work stoppages. The *Railroad Administration* took control of the railroads, unifying and improving their operations. The *Shipping Board* built a "bridge of ships" to transport men and materials to the European fighting fronts. The *Fuel Administration* stepped up the production of coal, gas, and oil, and combatted wastefulness in their use. The *Food Administration,* headed by Herbert Hoover, increased farm output, encouraged the public to observe "wheatless" and "meatless" days, and popularized the slogan, "Food will win the war."

3. **Influencing Public Opinion.** The *Committee on Public Information* contrasted American idealism with German militarism and aggression. The Committee reached the public through lectures, pamphlets, press releases, and posters. Its efforts heightened support for the war effort but sometimes led superpatriots to excesses such as banning German as a school subject and renaming sauerkraut "liberty cabbage."

4. **Punishing Espionage and Sedition.** (*a*) The **Espionage Act** (1917) provided severe penalties for spying, sabotage, and obstructing the war effort, and banned the mails to anti-war materials. (*b*) *The* **Sedition Act** (1918) punished persons who spoke or wrote against the American form of government or the war effort. These laws, which led to the arrest of some 1500 pacifists and pro-Germans who criticized the war, reflected wartime unwillingness to tolerate dissent.

5. **Financing the War.** The government (*a*) raised income taxes and levied new and heavier excise taxes, securing $11 billion, or one-third of the cost of the war, and (*b*) borrowed from the American people by selling them *Liberty* and *Victory Bonds,* securing $21 billion, or two-thirds of the war's cost. From these funds, the United States lent the Allies $10 billion to purchase war supplies.

6. **Providing Military Manpower.** Congress passed several *Selective Service Acts.* Our armed forces consisted of almost 3 million draftees together with 2 million volunteers. The dispatch of army units to Europe was hastened by desperate Allied appeals for American manpower to turn the tide of battle.

MILITARY ASPECTS OF THE WAR

1. **Worldwide Involvement.** For the first time in history, all major nations throughout the world were involved in the same war. Peoples from all over the world provided combat forces.

2. New Weapons. The following devices were introduced into warfare: dirigibles, submarines, giant artillery guns, tanks, poison gas, and, most significant, the airplane. It was employed at first mainly for observation purposes but later for small-scale bombings and for attacks on ground forces.

3. Naval Warfare. The British navy, aided by the French, maintained control of the Atlantic shipping lanes, combatted the German submarine menace, and effectively blockaded the Central Powers. In 1916 the British navy in the North Sea turned back the major German attempt to break the blockade in the famous *Battle of Jutland*. In 1917 the American navy under Admiral *William S. Sims* bolstered the Allied fleets. Together, they convoyed merchant and troop ships to Europe and substantially decreased losses due to German submarines.

4. Europe: Major Theater of Warfare

a. Eastern Front. Russian forces suffered crushing defeats, inflicted chiefly by German armies. In 1917 Russia experienced two revolutions and came under Communist rule. In early 1918 Russia withdrew from the war by accepting from Germany the harsh *Treaty of Brest-Litovsk*.

b. Southern Front. By 1917 the Central Powers had overrun most of the Balkans but had won no decisive battle in Italy. In 1918 the Allies won back much of the Balkans, and an Italian offensive compelled Austria-Hungary to surrender.

c. Western Front. In 1914 German armies overran Belgium and northern France until halted by desperate French and British resistance at the *Battle of the Marne*. Then the opposing armies dug into the ground for *trench warfare;* the western front became deadlocked. In 1916 the Germans attempted to smash the Allied defenses but were thrown back at *Verdun* and the *Somme*. In 1918 the war-weary Allied forces were reinforced by fresh American troops and unified under the command of the French *Marshal Foch*.

5. American Military Contribution. The *American Expeditionary Force (AEF)*, totaling 2 million men and led by General *John J. Pershing*, turned the tide of battle in France. In 1918 American soldiers helped halt a German offensive at *Château-Thierry* and *Belleau Wood*. Later they led the Allied end-the-war counteroffensive at *St. Mihiel* and in the *Argonne Forest*.

6. German Surrender. By late 1918 the German High Command under Generals *von Hindenburg* and *Ludendorff* realized that the German armies, although still fighting on foreign soil, had lost the war. Germany sued for peace and on November 11, 1918, ended hostilities by accepting an *armistice*.

PRESIDENT WILSON'S FOURTEEN POINTS

In 1918, before the end of the war, President Wilson addressed Congress on American war aims. His program, which evoked enthusiasm among peoples throughout the world, called for a lasting peace based upon *Fourteen Points:* (1) open covenants (treaties) of peace openly arrived at, (2) freedom of the seas, (3) removal of international trade barriers, (4) reduction of armaments, (5) impartial adjustment of colonial claims with due regard for the interests of the native peoples, (6–13) adjustment of European boundaries in accordance with the principle of nationality, that is, the right of any national group to self-determination regarding its own government and the formation of an independent national state, and (14) establishment of a League of Nations.

Allied statesmen approved Wilson's Fourteen Points only with significant reservations. In particular, each statesman upheld his nation's claims to territorial gains specified in secret treaties.

TREATY OF VERSAILLES WITH GERMANY (1919)

1. Different Allied Objectives. The "Big Four," the Allied leaders who dominated the peace conference, each sought different objectives. (*a*) *David Lloyd George,* Prime Minister of Great Britain, sought to expand Britain's colonial empire, preserve her naval and industrial supremacy, and "make Germany pay for the war." (*b*) *Georges Clemenceau,* Premier of France, sought to make France safe against future German invasion and weaken Germany by imposing military limitations, financial payments, and territorial losses. (*c*) *Vittorio Orlando,* Premier of Italy, sought to enlarge Italy's territory in Europe and expand her empire overseas. (*d*) *Woodrow Wilson,* President of the United States, sought to provide a just peace and create a better world by implementing his Fourteen Points.

Out of these different and often conflicting objectives emerged the *Treaty of Versailles,* the result of months of struggle and compromise.

2. Major Treaty Provisions

a. Territorial Changes. Germany surrendered (1) Alsace-Lorraine to France, (2) the Saar Valley to League of Nations authority and Saar coal mines to French control, with the provision that, after 15 years, the Saar inhabitants decide their political future by a plebiscite (in 1934 they voted for union with Germany), (3) minor border regions to Denmark and Belgium, (4) parts of Posen and West Prussia, including a corridor to the Baltic Sea, to the new nation of Poland (this "Polish Corridor" cut off East Prussia from the rest of Germany), (5) Danzig, a Baltic seaport bordering on Poland. This city was placed under League of Nations authority as a "free city" for Polish use.

The Saar and Danzig, predominantly German-inhabited, were transferred for economic considerations. Saar coal mines were to compensate France for property destruction caused by the German invasion. Danzig was to provide Poland with her only seaport. The other territorial changes were in accord with the principle of nationality. The territory granted to Poland, however, contained a considerable German minority.

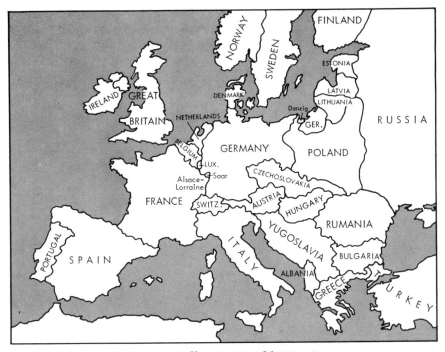

Europe Following World War I

b. Colonial Losses. Germany ceded all her colonies to the Allies, to be held as League of Nations mandates.

c. Disarmament. The German army was limited to 100,000 volunteers. Conscription was forbidden. The Rhineland, in western Germany, was demilitarized. The German navy was reduced to a few small ships. Submarines, military aircraft, and war industries were prohibited. These military restrictions were intended to prevent Germany from again waging war.

d. War Guilt and Reparations. Germany accepted sole responsibility for causing the war and agreed to pay reparations for war damages. (Germany made a few payments until 1931 but afterwards repudiated the remainder of the debt.)

e. League of Nations. The first article of the treaty provided for the establishment of the League of Nations (see pages 507-509).

3. Differing Views of the Treaty

a. Arguments Against: A Harsh Treaty That Planted the Seeds of World War II. The treaty took German-inhabited territory away from Germany, forced Germany to give up all her colonies, and compelled her to accept sole "war guilt." It forced Germany to be unarmed while other nations remained armed, and it wounded German pride. Later, by attacking the treaty, the Nazi party gained the support of the German people, achieved power, and brought on World War II.

b. Arguments For: A Fair Treaty That Was Not Enforced. The treaty transferred German territory chiefly on the basis of nationality, assigned German colonies as League of Nations mandates with the objective of eventual independence, disarmed Germany as a start toward world disarmament, and provided for a League of Nations. The treaty alone cannot be blamed for the German people's later support of Nazism. Furthermore, if the military provisions of the treaty had been enforced, Nazi Germany would not have been able to wage war.

TREATIES WITH THE OTHER DEFEATED NATIONS

The Allies signed separate treaties with each of the other Central Powers. Most significant were the treaties with Austria and Hungary breaking up the Austro-Hungarian Empire. (1) Austria and Hungary became independent national states. (2) Czechoslovakia, a new republic, was created entirely out of Austro-Hungarian territories. (3) Italy, Rumania, Poland, and Yugoslavia secured areas inhabited by their own nationals.

Both Austria and Hungary were required to limit their armies and pay reparations. Also, Austria was forbidden *Anschluss,* or union with Germany.

RESULTS OF WORLD WAR I

1. Social. (*a*) Almost 10 million soldiers were killed and over 20 million wounded. (*b*) Millions of civilians died as a result of the hostilities, famine, and disease. (*c*) The world was left with a legacy of hatred, intolerance, and extreme nationalism.

2. Economic. (*a*) The total cost of the war was over $350 billion. Paying for the war brought heavy taxation and lower living standards to European peoples. (*b*) After the war, international trade suffered because nations raised tariffs and sought economic self-sufficiency. (*c*) In Russia, the Communists seized power and introduced a new economic system. (*d*) The

United States changed from a debtor to a creditor nation. (*e*) Economic dislocations caused by the war helped bring on the Great Depression.

3. Political. (*a*) Three major European dynasties were dethroned: the Hohenzollerns of Germany, the Hapsburgs of Austria-Hungary, and the Romanovs of Russia. (*b*) New nations arose in central Europe. Several contained minority groups (subject nationalities), such as the German-speaking populations of Poland and Czechoslovakia. (*c*) Beset by economic and political discontent, many European nations—notably Russia, Italy, and Germany—turned to dictatorship. (*d*) The League of Nations was established to solve international problems and advance world peace. (*e*) The United States emerged as a leading world power, though reluctant to assume international responsibilities.

MULTIPLE-CHOICE QUESTIONS

1. The division of the major European powers into two rival alliances in the years preceding 1914 resulted in a (1) reduction of world tensions (2) decline of imperialism (3) decrease in military expenditures (4) series of international crises.

2. The suppression of subject nationalities contributed to the outbreak of World War I. This statement can be illustrated by (1) Austro-Hungarian domination of part of present-day Yugoslavia (2) German domination of Danzig (3) French domination of Alsace and Lorraine (4) German and French domination of Morocco.

3. Which was a characteristic of the period 1900–1914? (1) a series of armament races involving European nations (2) a series of Communist revolutions in central Europe (3) an international organization that fostered discussion of common problems (4) the rise of dictatorships in Italy and Germany.

4. President Wilson's policy at the beginning of World War I was to (1) send lend-lease aid to nations attacked by Germany (2) declare war against the Central Powers (3) prohibit trade with warring nations (4) issue a Proclamation of Neutrality.

5. Immediately following the sinking of the *Lusitania,* President Wilson (1) signed a secret treaty to give aid to Britain (2) presented his Fourteen Points as a basis for promoting world peace (3) refused to be stampeded into any hasty act leading to war (4) prohibited Americans from traveling on ships of belligerents.

6. The immediate cause for the entry of the United States into World War I was Germany's (1) attempt to arrange an alliance with Mexico (2) invasion of Belgium (3) resumption of unrestricted submarine warfare (4) campaign of sabotage in the United States.

7. Which is *not* considered a factor that influenced the United States to enter World War I? (1) financial commitments to the Allies (2) desire to gain overseas possessions (3) desire to repay France for her assistance during our Revolutionary War (4) concern over the survival of democracy.

8. The United States raised money to carry on World War I primarily by (1) high protective tariffs (2) the sale of government-owned property (3) loans obtained from the American people (4) loans obtained from the Allied nations.

9. One of the aims of the United States during World War I was (1) the defeat of Japan (2) the collection of indemnities (3) freedom of the seas (4) the division of Germany into two countries.

10. Which would be consistent with one of President Wilson's Fourteen Points? (1) the formation of new independent African states (2) the permanent separation of East Germany and West Germany (3) a secret military alliance between the United States and Japan (4) an increase in the United States tariff rates to keep out German goods.

11. Which principle of Wilson's Fourteen Points was incorporated in the Treaty of Versailles? (1) open diplomacy (2) removal of economic barriers (3) limitation of armaments for all signers of the treaty (4) a League of Nations.

12. An important result of World War I was that in many European nations (1) living standards rose (2) foreign trade increased (3) nationalism became less intense (4) dictators seized control.

13. Another result of World War I was that the United States (1) became a creditor nation and world power (2) abandoned its interests in the Caribbean area (3) initiated a policy of imperialism in the Far East (4) feared Germany's emergence as an Atlantic power.

MODIFIED TRUE-FALSE QUESTIONS

1. The "Lusitania," sunk by a German submarine during World War I, was *an American* ship.

2. In winning the Presidential election of 1916, Woodrow Wilson was aided by the slogan, *"The world must be made safe for democracy."*

3. The Zimmermann Note called for a German offer of American territory to *Japan*.

4. The head of the American Expeditionary Force during World War I was General *John J. Pershing*.

5. In 1918 pacifists in the United States who spoke against American participation in World War I were subject to prosecution under the provisions of the *Sussex Pledge*.

6. Allied territorial claims, often in conflict with the principles of the Fourteen Points, were based upon *secret treaties*.

7. In returning Alsace and Lorraine to France, the Treaty of Versailles was *in accord with* the Fourteen Points.

8. The Treaty of Versailles limited Germany to an army of *one million* men.

ESSAY QUESTIONS

1. (a) Briefly discuss *three* reasons why the United States entered World War I. (b) Evaluate these three reasons, explaining which one you consider most important, which one second in importance, and which one least important.

2. Describe *one* way in which the United States dealt with *each* of the following problems during World War I: (a) expanding industrial and agricultural production, (b) providing men for the armed forces, (c) mobilizing public opinion.

3. (a) List *five* important provisions of the Treaty of Versailles. (b) Discuss *two* reasons why Germany criticized this treaty. (c) Would you agree or disagree with each of the German criticisms? Explain your answer.

4. Describe *two* important results of World War I in *each* of the following areas: (a) social, (b) economic, (c) political.

Part 6. The United States Is Torn Between Isolation and International Cooperation (1919–1939)

OPPOSING VIEWPOINTS ON AMERICAN FOREIGN POLICY

1. Isolation: The Predominant Sentiment

a. Disillusionment With World War I. Many Americans were disappointed with the results of the war. It had proved costly in American lives and money. Instead of making "the world safe for democracy," it had led to major European dictatorships. Instead of being a "war to end all wars," it had apparently planted the seeds for another world conflict.

b. American Tradition of Isolation. Isolationists claimed that, except for World War I, the United States had successfully pursued a policy of isolation since the days of George Washington. Now they demanded a "return to normalcy" by strict adherence to this traditional policy.

c. Peace Through Isolation. Isolationists argued that America could have peace only by shutting herself off from the rest of the world. Let Uncle Sam "stay on his side of the street" while Europe "stews in its own juice."

Isolationist sentiment was powerful during the 1920's as well as during the depression years, when Americans concentrated upon domestic problems. It found expression in books, plays, and newspapers, and it received strong support from a powerful group of Senators.

2. International Cooperation: The Minority View

a. Defense of World War I. Internationalists defended American entrance into World War I by emphasizing Wilsonian idealism and national security. They claimed that, by rejecting world leadership, the United States endangered its own security and lost the opportunity to assure world peace.

b. Failure of Isolation. Opponents of isolation insisted that isolation had not worked in the past, since the United States had been involved in the Napoleonic Wars (by the War of 1812) and World War I. Now that economic factors and scientific progress had made nations more dependent on each other than ever before, internationalists argued, isolation was unrealistic.

c. Peace Through International Cooperation. Internationalists argued that America could have peace only by cooperating with peace-loving nations against aggression. We cannot "stop the world and get off."

Sentiment for cooperation grew in the late 1930's, as Americans observed Fascist militarism and aggression. President Franklin D. Roosevelt, who had served under and admired Wilson, worked cautiously but deliberately to swing public opinion away from isolation. However, not until England stood alone in World War II did international cooperation achieve acceptance by a majority of Americans.

UNITED STATES REFUSAL TO JOIN THE LEAGUE OF NATIONS

1. Brief Survey of the League of Nations

a. Establishment. Woodrow Wilson believed that the single most important step toward world peace was the League of Nations. Wilson succeeded in placing the League Covenant (Charter) into the Treaty of Versailles.

b. Purposes. The aims of the League were (1) to provide a world organization and thus eliminate international anarchy, (2) to prevent war by encouraging disarmament and by settling international disputes peacefully, and (3) to solve economic and social problems through international cooperation.

c. Procedures to Prevent War. To settle disputes peacefully, the League called for (1) arbitration by neutral third parties, or (2) judicial decision by the World Court, or (3) inquiry and recommendation by the League Council. If an aggressor nation refused to submit to peaceful settlement, the League could advise, but could not force, its member nations to employ coercive measures, called *sanctions*. These might be diplomatic, such as withdrawing ambassadors; economic, such as halting trade; and, finally, military. (The League, in its brief existence, never attempted military sanctions.)

2. Senate Defeat of the Treaty of Versailles and the League

a. Republican Opposition. In control of the Senate, the Republicans consisted of (1) a small group of extreme isolationists, notably *William Borah, Hiram Johnson,* and *Robert La Follette,* and (2) a large group of more moderate Senators, most of whom supported the chairman of the Foreign Relations Committee, *Henry Cabot Lodge, Sr.* Bitterly hostile to Wilson, Senator Lodge determined to humiliate the President, to "republicanize" the Treaty of Versailles, and to protect American sovereignty by adding strong *reservations* to the treaty. Lodge held lengthy committee hearings to delay action and win support from the public and the Senate.

b. Arguments Against the League. Lodge and his supporters offered the following arguments: (1) The League might involve the United States in a war, thereby violating the American Constitution, which gives Congress the exclusive power to declare war. (2) The League might interfere in domestic matters, such as tariff and immigration policies. (3) The League would be under the disproportionate influence of Great Britain, since Britain and each of her dominions had its own vote in the League Assembly. (4) League membership would involve us in world problems and thus violate America's traditional policy of isolation.

   c. Wilson's Countermoves. Wilson denounced the Lodge reservations. To arouse the people and to bring pressure on the Senate, Wilson undertook an extensive speaking tour. His efforts ended abruptly when, overworked and exhausted, he suffered a paralytic stroke. From his sickbed, Wilson instructed the Democrats in the Senate to reject the Lodge reservations.

   d. The Senate Votes. The Senate overwhelmingly defeated the Treaty of Versailles with the Lodge reservations and then also rejected the unamended treaty. In a third and final vote, some Democrats disregarded Wilson's instructions and supported the treaty with the Lodge reservations. The amended treaty, however, fell seven votes short of the required two-thirds majority. (Later, the United States negotiated a peace treaty that ended the war with Germany but that did not provide for a League.)

   √*e. Who Defeated the Treaty and the League?* The Treaty of Versailles was defeated by (1) Lodge, by his insistence on reservations, (2) Wilson, by his refusal to compromise, and (3) the American people. At first, most people probably favored League membership, but they did not speak out with sufficient strength. As the League debate raged, Americans became confused, disillusioned, and unwilling to assume the burdens of world leadership.

   3. Election of 1920 and the League. Appealing to the voters again, Wilson requested that the Presidential election of 1920 be a "great and solemn referendum" on the League. James M. Cox, the Democratic candidate, campaigned vigorously for the League. Warren G. Harding, the Republican candidate, urged a "return to normalcy" but took no definite stand on the League.

   The voters were influenced by other factors, all working against the Democrats: falling farm prices; growing unemployment; disillusionment with the war; and the resentment of various national groups who blamed Wilson for treating Germany harshly, denying territory to Italy, and failing to secure independence for Ireland. Harding won an overwhelming triumph. He interpreted the result to mean that the American people opposed League membership.

HISTORY OF THE LEAGUE: A FAILURE

1. Reasons for Failure

   a. Membership. The League did not include all major nations. The United States never joined. Russia entered the League in 1934 but was expelled in 1939. Germany and Japan withdrew in 1933, as did Italy four years later.

b. Voting. League decisions required *unanimous* votes.

c. Powers. The League lacked the power of taxation and the power to draft an army. Although the League could request money, men, and support from its members, each state was free to respond according to its own national interests. The League was an association of independent nations. It was not a world government, but a weak *confederation*.

2. Record of Failure. Although the League settled minor disputes between small nations, it failed in major crises to (*a*) stop the Japanese invasion of Manchuria, (*b*) halt the Italian conquest of Ethiopia, and (*c*) prevent German rearmament in violation of the Treaty of Versailles, and German territorial seizures.

In 1946 the League disbanded and transferred its properties to the new world organization, the United Nations.

LIMITED INTERNATIONAL COOPERATION BY THE UNITED STATES

1. The United States Cooperates With the League. The United States cooperated with the League by (*a*) joining the *International Labor Organization (ILO)*, a League agency to gather labor statistics and improve world labor conditions, (*b*) working with other League agencies to wipe out disease, suppress slavery, and establish standards in communication and transportation, and (*c*) supporting the League during the crisis over Manchuria. (Check the Index for "Stimson Doctrine.")

2. The United States Joins in Naval Disarmament

a. Early Agreements. To reduce the tax burden and to avoid a naval armaments race, which had helped cause World War I, the United States cooperated with other naval powers in seeking a reduction of naval forces.

(1) *Washington Conference (1921–1922).* The United States, Great Britain, Japan, France, and Italy agreed to stop building capital ships (large warships) for 10 years and to maintain capital ships for each nation in a ratio of 5:5:3:1.67:1.67, respectively.

(2) *London Naval Conference (1930).* The United States, Great Britain, and Japan agreed to a ratio of approximately 10:10:7, for five years, for cruisers and destroyers as well as capital ships.

b. Eventual Failure. At the *London Conference* (1935), the United States and England faced a Japanese demand for a 10:10:10 ratio, or *parity*. The democracies refused on the ground that Japan had no need of such naval power unless for aggression. No agreement was reached; soon afterwards Japan started a new naval race.

3. The United States Joins in International Pacts

a. Nine-Power Treaty at the Washington Conference (1921–1922). The United States, Japan, Britain, France, and five smaller nations agreed to support equal trading rights in China and to respect China's independence, thus reaffirming the Open Door Policy.

✓ *b. Kellogg-Briand Pact (1928).* *Frank Kellogg,* American Secretary of State, and *Aristide Briand,* French Foreign Minister, proposed a pact to settle all disputes peacefully and to outlaw war "as an instrument of national policy." Most nations, including Germany, Japan, and Italy, signed this idealistic statement, also called the *Pact of Paris.*

c. Failure of International Pacts. In the 1930's militarist Japan, Fascist Italy, and Nazi Germany all violated the Kellogg-Briand Pact. Japan also violated the Nine-Power Treaty. Without provision for enforcement and without restraining action by the other signatories, these agreements proved worthless.

FURTHER EVIDENCES OF ISOLATION BY THE UNITED STATES

1. Refusal to Join the World Court. The World Court was established by the League to settle disputes between nations according to international law. Despite the requests of four successive Presidents—Harding, Coolidge, Hoover, and Roosevelt—Senate isolationists managed to keep the United States from membership in the World Court. They insisted that the World Court was a "back door" into the League.

2. Immigration Restrictions. Congress passed a series of immigration laws reversing our "open house" policy and drastically limiting admissions. Congress thus expressed American sentiment for fewer world contacts—an aspect of isolationism.

3. High Tariff Policy. Congress restored high import duties and in 1930 passed the highest rates ever. By such protectionism, Congress reflected the isolationist view in economic matters.

4. Insistence Upon Repayment of War Debts. During World War I the European Allies—mainly Britain, France, and Italy—had borrowed $10 billion from the United States. Thereafter, the Allies suggested that the United States cancel the war debts because they (*a*) had spent the money, chiefly for American war materials, to secure victory for the United States as well as for themselves, (*b*) could not repay as long as America's high tariffs made it difficult for them to secure dollars, and (*c*) could not repay unless they received reparations from Germany. (To facilitate the payment of reparations, the *Dawes Plan,* 1924, provided for orderly payment by Germany, and the *Young Plan,* 1929, reduced the debt substantially. Germany made a few payments until 1931, but afterwards repudiated the remainder of the debt.)

The United States refused to cancel the war debts, arguing that the Allies (*a*) had borrowed the money, (*b*) could afford to pay as proved by their spending of large sums for armaments, and (*c*) had no right to relate war debts to reparations.

By 1934, in the midst of the worldwide economic depression, all debtor nations except Finland had defaulted on their war debts. Resentful, Congress passed the *Johnson Debt Default Act,* prohibiting public or private loans to any foreign government that had defaulted on debts to the United States.

5. American Neutrality Acts (1935, 1937). As Germany and Italy became more and more aggressive, Americans sensed that Europe was again headed toward war. Congress passed two *Neutrality Acts* which (*a*) prohibited the sale of war implements to belligerents, (*b*) prohibited loans to belligerents, (*c*) prohibited Americans from sailing on ships of belligerents, and (*d*) restricted the entry of American merchant ships into war zones.

These acts surrendered traditional American claims to freedom of the seas. But Congress hoped that neutrality would prevent the economic and emotional entanglements that, many believed, had involved the United States in World War I.

6. Unfavorable Response to President Roosevelt's "Quarantine" Speech (1937). After Japan's invasion of China proper, President Franklin D. Roosevelt braved isolationist sentiment by delivering his "quarantine" speech. Citing "the present reign of terror and international lawlessness," Roosevelt warned, "let no one imagine that America will escape . . . that this Western Hemisphere will not be attacked." He compared world lawlessness to an "epidemic of physical disease" and proposed that the aggressor nations be subjected to "quarantine." Deliberately vague, Roosevelt wanted to test the readiness of the American people to support efforts against the aggressors.

Public and press reaction to the speech was generally unfavorable. Americans still believed that they could avoid war by retreat into isolation. Extreme isolationists called Roosevelt a "warmonger." Shortly thereafter, the American people became alarmed when Japanese planes over China bombed the American gunboat *Panay,* but Americans were relieved when Japan issued an apology.

Part 7. The Allies Win World War II

AXIS NATIONS

Imperial Japan was controlled by the military, Fascist Italy was led by the dictator *Benito Mussolini,* and Nazi Germany was headed by the dictator *Adolf Hitler.* These nations—Japan, Italy, and Germany—(1) engaged in one act of aggression after another, thereby violating, without any effective opposition, the major international peace agreements: the Treaty of Versailles, the Covenant of the League of Nations, the Nine-Power Treaty, and the Kellogg-Briand Pact, (2) withdrew from membership in the League, and (3) joined together to form a military alliance, the *Rome-Berlin-Tokyo Axis.*

RECORD OF AXIS AGGRESSION
any 2

1. Manchuria. In 1931–1932 Japan invaded and conquered China's northern province of Manchuria. Japan flouted the mild efforts put forth by the League of Nations to halt her aggression. Some historians maintain that, by first revealing the weaknesses of the League, the Manchurian invasion marked the beginning of World War II.

2. Ethiopia. In 1935 Italy invaded the African nation of Ethiopia. The League of Nations branded Italy an aggressor and voted minor economic sanctions but failed to recommend an embargo on Italy's most essential import, oil. Undeterred by such feeble opposition, Mussolini conquered and annexed Ethiopia.

3. German Remilitarization. Nazi Germany violated the Treaty of Versailles in 1935 by reintroducing conscription and in 1936 by remilitarizing the Rhineland. Hitler encountered no serious Allied opposition although Germany's military strength was then still slight.

4. Spain. In 1936 General *Francisco Franco* began a revolt against the legally elected left-of-center government of Spain. While the Loyalists, who supported the elected government, received limited aid from Russia, Franco received extensive support of troops and military equipment from Italy and Germany. After three years of civil war, Franco won complete control and established a military dictatorship friendly to Germany and Italy. The Spanish civil war served Nazi Germany as a testing ground for new weapons and military tactics, such as dive-bombings and tank assaults, later used in World War II.

5. China. In 1937 Japanese forces from Manchuria invaded China proper. The Japanese overran China's coastal areas but failed to penetrate far into the interior. The Chinese continued their resistance, receiving limited aid from Britain and the United States.

6. Austria. In 1938 Hitler invaded and annexed Austria on the ground that all German-speaking people belonged within one German nation. *Anschluss* (union) of Germany and Austria violated the World War I peace treaties. Furthermore, Anschluss was never approved by the Austrian people in an honest plebiscite.

7. Czechoslovakia

a. Hitler Demands the Sudetenland. Later in 1938 Hitler claimed the *Sudetenland*, a region in Czechoslovakia bordering on Germany and inhabited by German-speaking people. Although the Sudeten people had not been oppressed, Nazi propagandists manufactured stories of Czech "atrocities." The Czech government refused to yield. It counted on its alliances with Russia and France, and expected British support. However, Britain and France decided not to risk war but to appease Hitler.

b. Munich Conference. British Prime Minister *Neville Chamberlain* and French Premier *Edouard Daladier*, meeting at Munich with Mussolini and Hitler, agreed to let Hitler annex the Sudetenland. Deserted by her friends, Czechoslovakia yielded. Chamberlain returned to England and proclaimed that he had preserved "peace in our time." Hitler promised that he would demand no more territory.

c. Hitler Seizes the Rest of Czechoslovakia. Six months later, however, Hitler seized the Slavic-inhabited remainder of Czechoslovakia. In England, the Chamberlain government at last realized that Hitler could not be trusted to keep his promises. Britain and France joined in a military alliance and guaranteed protection to Germany's next probable victim, Poland.

8. Albania. In 1939 Mussolini invaded and annexed the Balkan country of Albania, giving Italy control of the Adriatic Sea.

9. Poland

a. Hitler's Demands. In 1939 Hitler demanded the return of Danzig and the Polish Corridor on the ground that they were inhabited by German-speaking people.

b. Russo-German Non-Aggression Pact. Before Poland responded, Nazi Germany and Communist Russia announced a 10-year *Non-Aggression Pact*. The world was surprised because Hitler had always preached hatred of Communism, and Joseph Stalin, the Russian dictator, had always condemned Fascism. (1) The pact enabled Russia to avoid (for the time being) involvement in a major war and, by its secret clauses, gave Stalin a free hand over eastern Poland and the Baltic states of Estonia, Latvia, and Lithuania. (2) The pact protected Germany against a two-front war and promised Hitler foodstuffs and war supplies from Russia.

c. Start of World War II. On September 1, 1939, German troops invaded Poland. Two days later, Britain and France honored their guarantee to Poland and declared war on Germany. World War II had started.

BASIC CAUSES OF WORLD WAR II: AXIS PHILOSOPHY AND AGGRESSION

1. Totalitarianism. The Axis nations (Germany, Italy, and Japan) were totalitarian dictatorships. They scorned the democratic ideals of civil liberties, of the dignity of the individual, and of world peace; and they openly declared their intent to destroy democracy.

2. Militarism. The Axis nations spent vast sums on armaments, devised new weapons and battle techniques, built huge military organizations, and psychologically prepared their peoples for war. They proclaimed war a glorious adventure and death for the Fatherland the highest honor.

3. Nationalism. Japanese Shinto teachings, Italian dreams of a revival of the Roman Empire, and German "master race" doctrines all fostered a narrow and bigoted nationalism. The Axis nations considered themselves superior and destined to rule over "lesser peoples."

4. Imperialism. The Axis powers embarked upon imperialism with the excuse that they lacked land and resources and were *have-not* nations. Japan expanded into Manchuria and China proper to establish a Japanese-dominated "New Order" in Asia. Italy enlarged her African empire and planned to make the Mediterranean an "Italian lake." Germany annexed Austria and Czechoslovakia as first steps toward domination of Europe and eventually, perhaps, of the world.

SUBSIDIARY CAUSES OF WORLD WAR II

1. Failure of Appeasement. Britain and France followed a policy of *appeasement*—that is, making concessions to the dictators in the hope that they would eventually be satisfied and stop their aggression. Anxious for peace, democratic peoples failed to understand that each concession strengthened the aggressors and emboldened them to make further demands. The chief advocate of appeasement was Neville Chamberlain, and the final application of appeasement was the transfer of the Sudetenland to Germany by the Munich Conference.

2. Lack of Collective Security. Peace-loving nations, by coordinating their military strength and acting collectively, might have protected each other from aggression. However, the democratic peoples shrank from any kind of military action. The United States was determined to remain neutral. Britain and France delayed the formation of a firm alliance until 1939.

Communist Russia urged collective security because she feared attack by Nazi Germany. Democratic nations, however, were reluctant to enter into collective security pacts with the Soviet Union because they (*a*) doubted Russia's sincerity, (*b*) feared Communist plans for world revolution, and (*c*) were not eager to protect the Soviet Union. Indeed, some people felt that a Russo-German war would lessen both the Communist and Fascist threats to Western democracy. In 1939, however, Russia saw an opportunity to turn the Nazi war machine against Britain and France. Thereupon, Russia terminated her support of collective security and concluded the Stalin-Hitler Non-Aggression Pact.

3. American Neutrality Legislation. By prohibiting loans and the sale of war implements to all belligerents, the Neutrality Acts actually favored the well-armed aggressor nations over their ill-equipped victims. Furthermore, these laws implied that Americans would not intervene to check Axis aggression in Asia and Europe.

SECOND WORLD WAR (1939–1945)

1. Initial German Successes (1939–1940)

a. Conquest of Poland. German armies, employing massive air bombings and tank assaults, unleashed a "lightning war," or *blitzkrieg.* They speedily rolled across the open plains of Poland and destroyed all resistance. Germany annexed western Poland. (As agreed in the Hitler-Stalin Pact, Russia seized eastern Poland and annexed the Baltic countries. After a four-month war, Russia also secured territory from Finland.)

b. Conquest of Denmark and Norway. Nazi armies next overran neutral Denmark and Norway. Germany thus gained valuable submarine bases on the Atlantic Ocean. In Norway, Nazi armies received assistance from traitors, called *fifth columnists,* led by *Vidkun Quisling.*

c. Conquest of France. Nazi armies invaded northern France in 1940 by going through the plains of neutral Holland and Belgium. By this route, the Germans bypassed the Franco-German border with its mountainous terrain and French defensive fortifications, the *Maginot Line.* Nazi armies easily defeated the Allied defenders. The British miraculously evacuated most of their troops to England. French resistance collapsed, and French forces fled southward. With Mussolini confident that victory was already won, Italy entered the war. As the German forces continued their advance southward, France surrendered.

The Germans established military rule over half of France, including the whole Atlantic and English Channel coasts. For the rest of France, the Germans permitted an antidemocratic government at *Vichy*, headed by Marshal *Henri Pétain*. In England, General *Charles de Gaulle*, determined to liberate France, established the *Free French* movement.

2. Britain Stands Alone (1940–1941)

a. Leadership of Churchill. Winston Churchill, who had repeatedly opposed appeasement of the Nazis, succeeded Chamberlain as Prime Minister. Churchill inspired the English people to courage and determination, as he called upon them to save the world from the "abyss of a new dark age." "I have nothing to offer," he said, "but blood, toil, tears, and sweat."

b. Battle of Britain. Hitler ordered his *Luftwaffe* (air force) to soften England for invasion. For three months England was subjected to devastating air attacks. The *Royal Air Force (RAF)*, however, drove off the Luftwaffe. By maintaining control of the air lanes, the RAF compelled the Nazis to shelve their plans for an invasion of England. Instead, the Nazis turned southward, overrunning the Balkans and placing an army in North Africa to support the Italians.

3. American Preparedness and Aid to the Allies (1939–1941)

a. Neutrality Act of 1939. Soon after World War II started, President Franklin D. Roosevelt requested Congress to pass the Neutrality Act of 1939. This law permitted belligerents to purchase war materials on condition that they paid cash and carried the goods away in their own vessels. *Cash and carry* was designed to give limited assistance to the Atlantic sea powers (France and Britain) and, at the same time, maintain American neutrality.

b. Changes in Public Opinion. President Roosevelt labored to awaken the American people to the threat to their national security. When France fell in 1940, Americans finally realized that England alone stood between them and a hostile Fascist world. For America's self-defense, Congress supported a vast military buildup and aid to Britain by *all measures short of war*.

c. Military Preparedness. Congress authorized a two-ocean navy and a huge air force, and passed the 1940 *Selective Service Act*. It provided for America's first peacetime conscription.

d. Destroyer-Naval Base Deal (1940). President Roosevelt traded 50 "over-age" destroyers to Britain in exchange for military bases on British territory in the Western Hemisphere from Newfoundland to British Guiana. Britain needed the destroyers to combat German submarines; the United States used the bases as defensive outposts. (Fearful of delay in the Senate,

Roosevelt negotiated this exchange by an executive agreement rather than by a treaty, which would have required Senate approval.)

e. Lend-Lease Act (1941). Realizing that Britain's cash was almost exhausted, President Roosevelt requested new legislation to maintain the United States as the "arsenal of democracy." Congress passed the *Lend-Lease Act* authorizing the President to lend or lease goods to any nation whose defense he deemed necessary for the defense of the United States. Immediately, Roosevelt extended substantial aid to Britain; he later gave aid to other Allies, including Russia. (Total lend-lease aid amounted to $50 billion.) Also, Roosevelt ordered that merchant ships carrying lend-lease materials be convoyed by the United States Navy part way across the Atlantic. When convoys were attacked by German submarines, American warships responded with fire, thus beginning a limited naval war.

f. Embargo on Strategic Materials to Japan. As an advocate of the Open Door Policy, the United States opposed Japan's plans for an empire in eastern Asia. In 1940–1941 the United States protested Japanese occupation of French Indo-China. Since protests proved ineffective, President Roosevelt embargoed the sale of aviation gasoline, scrap iron, and other strategic materials to Japan and "froze" Japanese assets in the United States.

4. The Axis Makes Two Mistakes (1941)

a. German Attack Upon Russia (June 22, 1941). Despite the Russo-German Non-Aggression Pact, Hitler ordered a blitzkrieg against Russia to acquire the grain, coal, and iron of the Ukraine and the oil of the Caucasus. Hitler expected a quick victory, but Russia proved to be a formidable foe. The Nazis occupied much territory but were unable to crush the Soviet armies.

b. Japanese Attack Upon the United States (December 7, 1941). Japan staged a sneak attack upon the American naval base at *Pearl Harbor,* Hawaii, forcing the United States actively into the war. Under General *Hideki Tojo,* the Japanese government planned to humble the United States and assure Japanese domination of eastern Asia. Japan's Axis partners, Germany and Italy, immediately declared war on the United States.

Axis strategists hoped that, if they forced the United States into a Pacific war, the United States would be unable to complete her military preparations and would be forced to curtail lend-lease aid to Great Britain and Russia. However, the Axis reckoned without the American people. They closed ranks behind Roosevelt to "win the war and the peace that follows."

5. The United States Organizes for Victory

a. Presidential Leadership. Franklin D. Roosevelt showed confidence and determination in directing the national war effort. As commander in chief he planned the overall war strategy: first beat Hitler, then Japan. He met with top Allied leaders in several wartime conferences. On the home front, Roosevelt established an array of government agencies to direct the economy toward winning the war.

b. Economic Mobilization. (1) The *War Production Board (WPB)* ordered military equipment, shifted peacetime plants to war production, set up priorities for raw materials, and built new plants, most notably to produce aluminum and synthetic rubber. During the war years, total industrial production almost doubled. (2) The *War Labor Board (WLB)* settled labor-management disputes, permitted wage increases to help offset the rising cost of living, and endeavored to prevent strikes. With a few exceptions, unions adhered to their no-strike pledge. (3) The *War Manpower Commission (WMC)* trained workers and channeled them into essential industries, supervised the Selective Service system, and recruited new workers, including several million women. (4) The *Fair Employment Practices Committee (FEPC)* encouraged maximum use of labor by combatting racial and religious discrimination in employment. (5) The *Office of Price Administration (OPA)* combatted inflation by imposing price and rent ceilings and by rationing scarce consumer goods, such as sugar, meat, shoes, and gasoline. From 1939 to 1945 the cost of living rose about 30 percent, far less than during World War I.

c. Civil Liberties. Except for the forced removal of Japanese-Americans from the West Coast to interior relocation centers, civil liberties survived the war strains. Compared to World War I, the nation experienced less war hysteria. The press and the people remained free to criticize the government, and vigorous debate marked the Presidential election of 1944, in which Roosevelt won a fourth term.

d. Wartime Finances. The federal government greatly increased corporate and individual income tax rates and for the first time taxed individuals in the low-income brackets. The number of taxpayers rose from 8 million to almost 55 million. The government introduced a pay-as-you-go system by which employers *withheld* (deducted in advance) the estimated tax from each worker's paycheck. The government also raised and expanded excise taxes.

Of the total war cost of $330 billion, taxes provided one-third. The rest, the government borrowed through the sale of *war bonds*. From 1940 to 1945 the federal debt rose from less than $50 billion to over $250 billion.

e. Military Manpower. With draft boards under the Selective Service system providing most of the recruits, the armed forces enrolled 15 million Americans. At peak strength the army totalled 8½ million men, the navy 3½ million, and the marines half a million. To release men for frontline duty, women's branches—Army Wacs, Navy Waves, and Women Marines—took over necessary noncombat duties.

6. Victory in Europe

a. From North Africa to Italy. In October, 1942, a British army under General *Bernard Montgomery* defeated the Germans and Italians at *El Alamein,* Egypt, and began pursuing them westward. In November, 1942, an Anglo-Canadian-American army under General *Dwight D. Eisenhower* invaded French North Africa and moved eastward. By thus placing the enemy in a vise, the Allies destroyed the Axis African armies. In 1943 the Allies crossed the Mediterranean and invaded Sicily and southern Italy. Mussolini's Fascist government collapsed, and Italy surrendered unconditionally. To resist the Allied advance northward, Germany rushed troops into Italy.

b. Russian Counteroffensive. In early 1943, following a six-month battle, the Russians annihilated a 300,000-man Nazi army deep inside the Soviet Union at *Stalingrad.* Following this great victory Russian armies seized the initiative, materially assisted by huge amounts of American lend-lease, especially motor vehicles and airplanes. The Communists drove the Nazis from Russia and pursued them through Rumania, Bulgaria, Yugoslavia, Hungary, Austria, Czechoslovakia, and Poland. In 1945 the Russians reached eastern Germany and stormed into Berlin.

c. Anglo-American Invasion of France. To prepare the way for invasion, American and British airmen bombed Nazi-held Europe, and underground patriots sabotaged Nazi factories and harassed Nazi forces. On June 6, 1944 (D-Day), American and British forces, led by General Eisenhower, crossed the English Channel and landed in *Normandy* in northern France. This greatest waterborne invasion in history established a major *second front.* The invading forces met a powerful German army, which had been kept from the Russian front in anticipation of the attack. Allied forces pushed back the Nazi army, recaptured Paris, and drove the Germans from France.

d. Surrender of Germany. In 1945 Anglo-American armies crossed the Rhine River in Germany and continued to the Elbe. Here they met the Russians driving in from the east. After Hitler committed suicide, Germany surrendered unconditionally.

7. Victory in the Pacific

a. Initial Japanese Offensive. In 1941–1942 Japanese forces overran the Philippines, the Malay States, the Dutch East Indies, and part of New Guinea. Poised just north of Australia, they were halted by American naval forces in a major battle in the *Coral Sea.* Soon afterwards, American forces won a second major naval victory, in the Central Pacific at *Midway.*

b. Allied Counteroffensive. In August, 1942, General *Douglas MacArthur* started the Allied forces (chiefly American) on an "island-hopping" offensive on the road to Japan. Overcoming fierce resistance, Allied troops seized *Guadalcanal* in the Solomon Islands; the *Gilbert, Marshall,* and *Caroline Islands;* and *Guam.* In 1944, while the American navy was winning a decisive victory at *Leyte Gulf,* American forces returned to the Philippines. In early 1945 they also captured *Iwo Jima* and *Okinawa.* From these island bases, American airmen launched destructive raids upon Japan.

c. Atom Bomb and Surrender of Japan. President Truman approved the use of the atom bomb against Japan, thereby expecting to save countless American (and Japanese) casualties that would result from a seaborne invasion of Japan. In August, 1945, the United States dropped a single atom bomb—the first used in war—on the Japanese city that contained Japanese army headquarters and munitions factories—the city of *Hiroshima.* The bomb killed or injured 130,000 people. Two days later Russia declared war against Japan and invaded Japanese-held Manchuria. The following day the United States dropped a second atom bomb, this time on the industrial and shipbuilding city of *Nagasaki.* Defenseless against atomic bombings and without allies, Japan surrendered.

SIGNIFICANT FACTS DESCRIBING WORLD WAR II

1. Total War. The war was fought not only by armed forces at the battle-front but also by civilians in factories and in the home. Even schoolchildren took part, collecting scrap metal, rubber, and newspapers; helping air-raid wardens; and assisting in war bond drives.

2. Global War. This most extensive war was fought on all major seas and in Africa, Asia, and Europe. It involved almost 60 nations, seven of them on the side of the Axis. To plan global military strategy, top Allied leaders held a series of conferences, such as the ones at Teheran, Yalta, and Potsdam.

3. Scientific Progress. Scientists and engineers devised or adapted for war purposes such inventions as radar, guided missiles, jet-propelled planes, magnetic mines, and atom bombs. World War II witnessed the use of blood plasma, penicillin, and sulfa drugs to save lives.

4. Major Role of the Airplane. Fleets of airplanes attacked troop and naval units, destroyed railroads and industrial centers, and prepared the way for invasion. Control of the air was essential to offensive military action.

RESULTS OF WORLD WAR II

1. Economic. (*a*) The war—the most costly in history—exacted military expenditures of over $1100 billion and caused property damage of over $230 billion. (*b*) European and Asian nations, ravaged by military action, faced difficult problems of economic recovery. (*c*) The Communist economic system spread from Russia to eastern and central Europe, and to several Asian nations.

2. Social. (*a*) The war—the most destructive in history—left over 22 million servicemen and civilians dead, and over 34 million wounded. For the United States alone, the dead and wounded totaled over one million. (*b*) Several million *refugees* and *displaced persons*, uprooted by the war, needed assistance to rebuild their shattered lives.

3. Political. (*a*) Germany, Italy, and Japan met complete military defeat, and their totalitarian systems were overthrown. (*b*) The United States and Russia emerged as the major world powers and soon came into a conflict called the *cold war*. (*c*) Russia acquired an empire of Communist satellite nations. (*d*) The Asian and African colonial peoples became intensely nationalistic and hastened the downfall of Western imperialism. (*e*) Great Britain and France declined as world powers and gradually relinquished major portions of their empires. (*f*) The atomic age brought the problem of achieving international control of atomic energy. (*g*) To preserve peace, the Allies formed a new international organization, the *United Nations*. (*h*) The United States joined the United Nations and otherwise actively assumed the responsibility of world leadership.

MULTIPLE-CHOICE QUESTIONS

1. In the 1920's American public opinion was (1) opposed to all international cooperation (2) predominantly isolationist (3) predominantly internationalist (4) equally divided between isolationism and internationalism.

2. The United States Senate rejected the Treaty of Versailles mainly because the treaty (1) contained the Covenant of the League of Nations (2) made Germany assume sole guilt for the war (3) required Germany to pay reparations (4) provided for the return of Alsace-Lorraine to France.

3. Republican leaders in the Senate opposed the unamended Treaty of Versailles because they (1) wanted Germany to pay reparations to the United States (2) considered the treaty too harsh on Germany (3) feared infringement upon American sovereignty (4) feared a revival of German militarism.

4. In which area was the League of Nations most successful? (1) improvement of health conditions (2) achievement of European disarmament (3) arbitration of the Italian-Ethiopian dispute (4) withdrawal of Japanese forces from Manchuria.

5. In 1934 the United States became a member of the (1) World Court (2) Pan-American Union (3) Munich Conference (4) International Labor Organization.

6. "The high contracting parties . . . condemn recourse to war for the solution of international controversies, and renounce it as an instrument of national policy." This quotation is taken from the (1) Treaty of Versailles (2) Kellogg-Briand Pact (3) Nine-Power Treaty (4) Munich Pact.

7. The Kellogg-Briand Pact failed to accomplish its purpose because it (1) was not signed by Germany (2) was signed by too few nations (3) had no provisions for enforcement (4) was rejected by the League of Nations.

8. European nations claimed that they were unable to pay their war debts because the United States did not (1) join the League of Nations (2) sell them enough goods (3) lower its tariff rates (4) join the World Court.

9. A nation that does not give aid to either side in a controversy is said to be (1) a belligerent (2) a buffer state (3) an aggressor (4) a neutral.

10. One similarity between the Embargo Act of 1807 and the Neutrality Act of 1937 is that both (1) distinguished clearly between aggressor and victim (2) showed United States determination to fight (3) abandoned substantially the principle of freedom of the seas (4) discouraged aggression in Europe.

11. The main purpose of the United States in the Neutrality Acts of 1935 and 1937 was to (1) stay out of war (2) increase foreign trade (3) cooperate more closely with the League of Nations (4) protect the rights of neutrals in wartime.

12. The United States contributed to world peace during the period between World War I and World War II by (1) opposing the League of Nations (2) supporting naval disarmament (3) joining the World Court (4) adopting free trade.

13. *Not* a concern of the Washington Conference of 1921–1922 was (1) the burden of naval armaments (2) the Far Eastern imperialistic ambitions of the great powers (3) Japan's economic penetration into China (4) the payment of war debts due the United States.

14. During the 1930's the leaders of Germany, Italy, and Japan promoted a warlike attitude among their peoples by (1) stressing the huge indemnities required of them by the Treaty of Versailles (2) playing upon nationalist feelings (3) condemning the League of Nations for refusing them membership (4) pointing to their loss of territory as a result of World War I.

15. Germany's rearmament, starting in 1935, was (1) essential to the policy of collective security (2) encouraged by France (3) in violation of the Treaty of Versailles (4) approved by the London Naval Conference.

16. Hitler argued that Germany should annex the Sudetenland to (1) protect the German-speaking population (2) reduce French influence in central Europe (3) gain control of additional munitions factories (4) prevent Communist seizure of the area.

17. During the Spanish Civil War, General Franco received military aid from (1) Germany and Russia (2) Germany and Italy (3) Italy and France (4) the United States and Great Britain.

18. The term "appeasement" is often used to describe the (1) Munich Pact (2) Destroyer-Naval Base Deal (3) Stimson Doctrine (4) Rome-Berlin-Tokyo Axis.

19. An international policy whereby nations agree to take joint measures against an aggressor nation is called (1) unilateral action (2) an offensive alliance (3) benevolent neutrality (4) collective security.

20. The Non-Aggression Pact of 1939, preceding the outbreak of World War II, was between (1) Germany and Poland (2) Germany and the United States (3) Germany and Russia (4) Great Britain and the United States.

21. World War II started in 1939 when Germany invaded (1) England (2) France (3) Poland (4) Russia.

22. During the period 1939–1941, United States foreign policy can best be described as (1) consistently internationalist (2) aimed at avoiding war at all costs (3) moving steadily toward isolation (4) moving from isolation to active aid for the Allies.

23. In 1940 the United States leased naval bases from Great Britain to (1) cancel Great Britain's debts from World War I (2) build adequate defenses in the Western Hemisphere (3) give our investors markets for exports (4) secure sources of uranium.

24. President Roosevelt urged that the United States remain the "arsenal of democracy" when he called for the (1) Neutrality Act of 1939 (2) Selective Service Act of 1940 (3) Destroyer-Naval Base Deal of 1940 (4) Lend-Lease Act of 1941.

25. The Lend-Lease Act of 1941 authorized the President to (1) declare war against Germany (2) trade destroyers for British naval bases in the Western Hemisphere (3) supply equipment to the countries fighting the Axis nations (4) send an expeditionary force to Europe.

26. A widely adopted means of solving the manpower problem in industry during World War II was to (1) use forced labor (2) raise the immigration quotas (3) employ women (4) abolish relief payments.

27. The United States financed World War II by (1) borrowing from Britain (2) confiscating factories engaged in defense production (3) increasing tax rates and selling war bonds (4) increasing tariff rates.

28. During World War II, the United States (1) gave substantial lend-lease aid to Russia (2) requested Russia to send an army to the North African front (3) sent troops to the Russian front (4) granted recognition to the Communist government in Russia.

29. The first city ever atom-bombed was (1) Munich (2) Tokyo (3) Hiroshima (4) Nagasaki.

30. Which two countries were on our side in World War I and were our enemies in World War II? (1) Italy and Japan (2) Germany and Japan (3) Russia and Japan (4) Austria and France.

31. The two nations that emerged as major world powers following World War II were (1) the United States and Great Britain (2) the United States and the Soviet Union (3) the Soviet Union and Germany (4) the Soviet Union and China.

IDENTIFICATION QUESTIONS: WHO AM I?

Neville Chamberlain	Dwight D. Eisenhower	Henri Pétain
Winston Churchill	Warren G. Harding	Franklin D. Roosevelt
James M. Cox	Henry Cabot Lodge, Sr.	Harry S. Truman
Charles de Gaulle	Douglas MacArthur	Woodrow Wilson

1. As chairman of the Senate Foreign Relations Committee, I led the fight for reservations to the Treaty of Versailles.

2. I delivered my "quarantine" speech to alert the American people to the danger of aggression.

3. I became Prime Minister of Britain in 1940. I offered my people "blood, toil, tears, and sweat."

4. As Presidential candidate in 1920, I took no clear-cut stand regarding the League of Nations.

5. As commander of the Anglo-American forces in Europe, I led the invasion of Normandy.

6. After the fall of France in 1940, I fled to England and established the "Free French" movement.

7. As Prime Minister of Britain I made concessions to Hitler at the Munich Conference. I believed that my policy was preserving "peace in our time."

8. I commanded the Allied forces in the Southwest Pacific. In 1944 I kept my pledge to return to the Philippines.

9. To shorten the war and save American lives, I ordered the use of the atom bomb against Japan.

ESSAY QUESTIONS

1. (a) Describe *two* events or circumstances in the period 1919–1920 that kept the United States from membership in the League of Nations. (b) Give *two* arguments for *and two* arguments against the entrance of the United States into the League. (c) Explain *two* reasons why the League was unable to prevent war.

2. (a) Explain *one* reason why the United States adopted the policy of isolation early in its history. (b) Give *two* reasons for the change in sentiment between 1919 and 1941 regarding the policy of isolation. (c) Referring to these years, describe (1) *one* American action illustrating isolation, and (2) *one* American action illustrating international cooperation.

3. In the 1930's some Americans proposed that, in case of a foreign war, the United States maintain neutrality by cutting off all trade relations with the warring powers. (a) Show how this proposal developed out of our experience during the years 1914–1917. (b) State *two* provisions of the Neutrality Acts of 1935 and 1937. (c) Explain *one* reason why such neutrality legislation failed to keep the United States out of World War II.

4. In the period between World War I and World War II, democracies and dictatorships were rivals. (a) Describe *three* instances of aggression by totalitarian states before World War II. (b) Discuss *one* reason why the democracies declared war on Germany when that country attacked Poland. (c) Discuss *two* basic causes of World War II.

5. The United States has played a major role in the worldwide struggle against totalitarianism. (a) Discuss *two* reasons why the American people are opposed to totalitarianism. (b) Describe *three* factors that made it possible for the United States to be the "arsenal of democracy" during World War II.

6. Similar foreign problems arose during the administrations of Woodrow Wilson and Franklin D. Roosevelt. Describe *two* foreign policies of Franklin D. Roosevelt and show how *each* either resembled or contrasted with a foreign policy of Woodrow Wilson.

7. State whether you agree or disagree with *each* of the following statements and give *two* facts to support your point of view: (a) Preparedness for war is the best guarantee of peace. (b) The United States was right in not joining the League of Nations. (c) Appeasement of dictators can preserve the peace. (d) The failure of the League proves that wars cannot be prevented by an international organization. (e) The causes of World War II were very different from those of World War I.

UNIT IX. IN THE COLD WAR ERA AND AFTER: THE UNITED STATES AS A SUPERPOWER

Part 1. The United States Takes an Active Part in the United Nations

HOPES FOR A BETTER WORLD

In 1941 President Roosevelt said the United States looked forward to a world founded upon *Four Freedoms:* (*a*) freedom of speech, (*b*) freedom of religion, (*c*) freedom from want, and (*d*) freedom from fear. To achieve this goal, the Allied powers moved to create the United Nations.

STEPS TOWARD THE UNITED NATIONS

1. Atlantic Charter (1941). Roosevelt and Churchill, meeting on board ship in the Atlantic, issued a statement of principles, the *Atlantic Charter*. Remindful of Wilson's Fourteen Points, this document stated that Britain and the United States (*a*) desired no territorial gain, (*b*) respected the right of all peoples to choose their own form of government, (*c*) hoped that all men would live in freedom from fear and want, (*d*) believed that nations must abandon the use of force, and (*e*) would seek to establish a "system of general security," implying an international organization.

In 1942 the Allied nations met at Washington, pledged support for the Atlantic Charter, and adopted the name *United Nations* (U.N.).

2. Yalta Conference (February, 1945). The Big Three—President Roosevelt, Prime Minister Churchill, and Premier Stalin—decided upon procedures for voting in the U.N. Security Council and called upon the United Nations to send delegates to San Francisco to prepare the final Charter.

3. San Francisco Conference (April–June, 1945). Despite the unexpected death of President Roosevelt just before the conference, delegates representing 50 nations met as planned. They completed the U.N. Charter.

The United States became the first nation to ratify the Charter, as the Senate overwhelmingly approved American membership. Also, the United States provided the U.N. with headquarters, located in New York City.

PURPOSES OF THE UNITED NATIONS

The United Nations has as its goals to (1) maintain international peace and security, (2) by collective action, remove threats to the peace and suppress acts of aggression, (3) develop friendly relations among nations, (4) promote respect for human rights without distinction as to race, sex, language, or religion, and (5) encourage international cooperation in solving economic, social, cultural, and humanitarian problems.

ORGANIZATION OF THE UNITED NATIONS

1. General Assembly: The International Forum

a. Membership and Voting. The General Assembly consists of all U.N. member nations, now totaling about 184, each having one vote. General Assembly decisions on "important questions" require a two-thirds majority.

b. Powers. The General Assembly has the power to (1) discuss international problems fully and freely, (2) make recommendations to member nations, to the Economic and Social Council, to the Trusteeship Council, and to the Security Council, (3) elect members of other U.N. organs, (4) with the prior recommendation of the Security Council, suspend or expel any member nation persistently violating U.N. principles and admit any "peace-loving" nation to membership, (5) approve the U.N. budget and apportion expenses among the member nations, and (6) propose U.N. Charter amendments, which come into effect when ratified by two-thirds of the member nations, including all permanent members of the Security Council.

c. Sessions. The General Assembly meets in *regular* session annually, for about three months. If necessary, however, the Assembly may be summoned into *special* session.

2. Security Council: The Executive Agency

a. Membership. The Security Council consists of fifteen members: (1) Five are *permanent:* the United States, Great Britain, France, Russia, and China. (Until 1971 China's seat was held by the Nationalist regime, which since 1949 controlled only the island of Taiwan. In 1971, as the United States and Red China moved toward a better relationship, the General Assembly voted, with American support, to admit Red China as representative of the Chinese people and, despite American opposition, to expel the Nationalist delegation as representative of Taiwan.) (2) Ten are *nonpermanent,* each elected for a two-year term by the General Assembly. Until a Charter amendment in 1965, the Security Council had included only six nonpermanent members. The increase to ten reflected the large rise in Afro-Asian membership in the U.N. and the demand for Security Council seats according to "equitable geographical distribution."

b. Voting. Decisions by the Security Council on important matters require the affirmative vote of nine members, including the five permanent members. Thus, by a negative vote, any one of the Big Five can defeat a Security Council decision, that is, exercise its *veto power.* Abstention from voting by a permanent member is not considered a veto.

c. Powers. The Security Council bears primary responsibility for maintaining international peace and security. It has the power to (1) investigate disputes that endanger world peace, (2) make recommendations for peaceful settlement, and (3) if necessary, call upon U.N. member nations to take economic or military action against an aggressor nation.

d. Sessions. To be able to deal instantly with any international crisis, the Security Council functions *continuously.*

e. Agencies Directly Under the Security Council. (1) The *Military Staff Committee* was established to advise the Council regarding the use of military force to preserve international peace. (2) The *Disarmament Commission* was set up to prepare plans for the regulation and reduction of conventional and nuclear weapons.

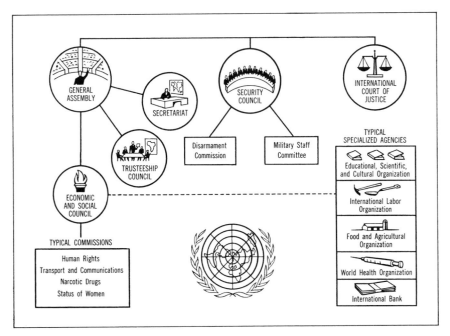

Organization of the United Nations

3. Secretariat: The Civil Service

a. Personnel and Duties. The Secretariat consists of the *Secretary General* and his staff. They are charged with primary loyalty to the United Nations. The Secretary General is appointed (usually for a five-year term) by the General Assembly upon the recommendation of the Security Council. The Secretary General selects and directs his staff, numbering several thousand employees, to perform U.N. clerical and administrative work. In addition, the Secretary General is authorized to (1) bring to the attention of the Security Council any matter threatening world peace, and (2) perform any other task entrusted to him by major U.N. organs, such as the Security Council or the General Assembly. Such tasks have included the undertaking of special diplomatic missions and the directing of U.N. emergency military forces.

b. Persons Serving as Secretary General. *Trygve Lie* of Norway served as first Secretary General. In 1953 he was succeeded by Sweden's *Dag Hammarskjold.* In 1961 Hammarskjold died in an airplane crash while on a U.N. peace mission to the Congo. Hammarskjold's successor was Burma's *U Thant.* From 1972 to 1981 the Secretary General was the Austrian *Kurt Waldheim.* Peruvian diplomat *Javier Pérez de Cuéllar* served from 1982 to 1991. *Boutros Boutros-Ghali* of Egypt started his service in 1992.

4. International Court of Justice: The Court for Nations. The International Court of Justice consists of 15 judges who decide cases by majority vote. The Court has the power to (*a*) settle legal disputes between nations, and (*b*) grant U.N. organs advisory opinions on legal questions. Nations submitting disputes to the Court agree in advance to accept its decisions.

5. Trusteeship Council: For Protection of Colonial Peoples

a. Membership and Voting. The Trusteeship Council consists now of the five permanent Security Council members: Four do not administer any trust territories; the United States administers the sole remaining trust territory—certain Pacific islands. (A trust territory is a colonial area that the U.N. has placed under the administration of a member nation.) This council's decisions require a simple majority.

b. Powers. The Trusteeship Council was established to supervise trusteeships so as to safeguard colonial peoples. It received power to (1) consider reports submitted by the administering nations, (2) examine petitions from the peoples of the trust territories, (3) with consent of the administering nation, send an investigating committee, and (4) report to the General Assembly. As trust territories gained independence, the work of the Trusteeship Council diminished.

6. Economic and Social Council (ECOSOC): For Mankind's Welfare

a. Membership and Voting. The Economic and Social Council consists of 54 members, each elected for a three-year term by the General Assembly. Decisions require a simple majority, each member nation having one vote.

b. Powers. The Economic and Social Council is concerned with improving economic, social, cultural, educational, and health conditions throughout the world. ECOSOC may conduct studies and make recommendations to U.N. member nations and to the General Assembly. Through ECOSOC's efforts, the U.N. hopes to eliminate the underlying causes of war.

c. ECOSOC Commissions and Committees. To further its objectives, ECOSOC organized (1) the *Commission on Human Rights,* which seeks to encourage respect for human rights and fundamental freedoms for all persons, regardless of race, sex, language, or religion, and (2) other commissions and committees concerned with such problems as control of narcotics, prevention of crime, and the status of women. ECOSOC also receives reports from the U.N. Children's Fund (UNICEF), the High Commissioner for Refugees, and the U.N. Development Program, which provides technical assistance to developing nations.

SPECIALIZED AGENCIES

The specialized agencies are independent organizations, some predating the United Nations, that came into existence by intergovernmental agreement. They include most (but not all) nations as members; they secure their funds chiefly by voluntary contributions from member nations; they directly serve only those nations that request assistance; and they coordinate their efforts with the U.N. through the Economic and Social Council.

The United States joined all the specialized agencies, actively participated in their work, and provided them with substantial financial contributions.

1. The **United Nations Educational, Scientific, and Cultural Organization** (**UNESCO**) seeks to promote the worldwide exchange of information on education, science, and culture. UNESCO undertakes projects to raise educational standards and to combat ignorance and prejudice. UNESCO bases its work on the belief stated in its Charter: "Since wars begin in the minds of men, it is in the minds of men that the defenses of peace must be constructed."

2. The **International Labor Organization** (**ILO**) endeavors to improve world labor conditions. ILO defines minimum labor standards and assists countries in formulating labor laws.

3. The **Food and Agriculture Organization (FAO)** attempts to raise world food and nutrition levels. FAO provides information to improve methods of growing and distributing food.

4. The **World Health Organization (WHO)** seeks to improve world health standards. WHO surveys health conditions, combats mass diseases and epidemics, and helps nations improve public health services.

5. The **International Monetary Fund** tries to promote world trade by helping nations to maintain stable currencies.

6. The **International Bank for Reconstruction and Development (World Bank)** encourages world economic progress by providing loans for large-scale projects, such as electric power plants, railroads, and highways.

7. Other specialized agencies include (*a*) the **International Civil Aviation Organization (ICAO)**—to expand and improve civil aviation facilities and to standardize laws regarding use of air lanes, (*b*) the **Universal Postal Union (UPU)**—to provide uniform mail procedures, and (*c*) the **World Meteorological Organization (WMO)**—to coordinate data on weather and develop weather-forecasting services.

MAJOR ACTIONS TAKEN BY THE UNITED NATIONS

U.N. ACTIONS PERTAINING TO SOCIAL AND ECONOMIC MATTERS

1. Children's Fund. In 1946 the General Assembly created the *United Nations International Children's Emergency Fund (UNICEF)*. It provides food, vitamins, and medicines to millions of needy children; and it trains nurses to help mothers in proper child care. UNICEF's activities, now permanent, are financed by voluntary contributions of governments and individuals. (American youngsters raise funds for UNICEF by Halloween "trick or treat" collections and by UNICEF greeting card sales.)

2. Declaration of Human Rights. In 1948 the General Assembly overwhelmingly approved the *Declaration of Human Rights*, drawn up by the Commission on Human Rights of ECOSOC. The Declaration states that all human beings are born free and equal and, without discrimination of any kind, are entitled to (*a*) *civil rights:* life; liberty; freedom of religion, speech, and assembly; and a voice in their government; (*b*) *legal rights:* freedom from arbitrary arrest and the right to a fair trial; (*c*) *economic rights:* employment, participation in labor unions, an adequate living standard, private property, and leisure time; and (*d*) *social rights:* education and a cultural life. Although these ideals will not soon be realized throughout the world, they provide a "standard of achievement for all peoples and all nations."

To put human rights in binding form, the U.N. General Assembly in 1966 unanimously adopted two covenants, or treaties—(1) on civil and political rights, and (2) on economic, social, and cultural rights. These *International Covenants on Human Rights* went into force in 1976. The United States is one of the few industrial nations that has yet to ratify them.

In 1993, the U.N. sponsored a World Conference on Human Rights in Vienna to review progress on human rights over the 25 years since the 1948 Declaration, and to discuss continuing violations of human rights in all parts of the world. Also in 1993, the General Assembly created the new position of U.N. High Commissioner for Human Rights. The High Commissioner's job is to make sure human rights are respected. The first person appointed to the position was *Jose Ayala Lasso* of Ecuador.

3. Genocide Convention. In 1948 the General Assembly adopted the *Genocide Convention*, drawn up by the Commission on Human Rights. This Convention declared illegal the deliberate extermination of any human group (as the Nazis had attempted with the Jews and the gypsies) and provided that violators be tried before an international court. The Convention, ratified by over 60 nations, represents an attempt to rally world opinion in favor of granting all people freedom from fear.

4. Technical Assistance. Since 1949, the United Nations and several specialized agencies have sent thousands of technical experts to assist developing nations in improving social and economic conditions.

5. Law of the Sea Convention. This 1982 convention set national offshore limits—12 miles for national sovereignty, 250 miles for exclusive rights to marine life, 350 miles for exclusive rights to oil and gas resources. In addition, it called for unhampered transit of all ships through international straits. More controversially, the convention declared minerals (such as manganese, nickel, copper, and cobalt) lying on the ocean floor to be the "common heritage of mankind" and established a consortium (joint body) to mine the seabed on behalf of the world's nations.

While more than 150 nations ratified the treaty, the United States, Britain, Germany, and some other industrial nations refused, arguing that the treaty undercut private enterprise and required industrial nations to share their technology. U.S.-led efforts were underway in the 1990's to revise the treaty.

6. Protecting the Environment. In 1992 the U.N. sponsored an *Earth Summit* at Rio de Janeiro, Brazil, to discuss ways of protecting the environment. The summit produced international conventions to protect plant and animal species and curb global warming. Following up, the U.N. General Assembly created the Sustainable Development Commission.

U.N. ACTIONS ON INTERNATIONAL DISPUTES

With the destruction of World War II fresh in mind, people hoped for a better world, to be achieved in part through the United Nations. The U.N. recorded some major achievements.

1. Iran (1946). Security Council discussions spurred the Soviet Union to withdraw its troops that had been stationed in Iran during World War II.

2. Greece (1946–1948). The General Assembly requested the Communist nations to cease aiding guerrilla rebels in northern Greece. After Yugoslavia broke with the Soviet Union and stopped helping the guerrillas, the rebellion collapsed.

3. Palestine (1948–1949). The General Assembly approved the partition of Palestine into an Arab state and a Jewish state. When Israel—the new Jewish state—was attacked by the Arab nations, U.N. mediator *Ralph Bunche* arranged temporary armistices.

4. Indonesia (1947–1949). The Security Council assisted in negotiations that led to Indonesia's independence from the Netherlands.

DISPUTES INVOLVING STRONG SOVIET CONCERNS (1948–1980'S)

1. Korea (1948–1953). In 1948 a U.N. commission to unify Korea by elections was denied admission to Soviet-occupied North Korea. In 1950, when North Korea invaded the South, the Security Council was able to approve a resolution for a U.N. army to help South Korea—only because the Soviet Union was absent from the session. (Check the Index for "Korea, since World War II.")

2. Hungary (1956). The General Assembly approved a resolution that condemned Soviet suppression of a revolt by the Hungarian people.

3. Soviet Intervention in Afghanistan. In 1979–1980, Soviet forces invaded Afghanistan in support of a pro-Soviet government (check the Index for Afghanistan). The Soviets vetoed a U.N. Security Council resolution calling for "the withdrawal of all foreign troops." A similar resolution passed the General Assembly, 104 to 18. Each year thereafter until Soviet troops withdrew in 1989, the assembly passed a similar resolution.

DISPUTES AFFECTING FORMER BRITISH EMPIRE AREAS

1. Kashmir (Since 1948). The U.N. has worked to ease hostilities between India and Pakistan over Kashmir.

2. Cyprus. An island in the eastern Mediterranean that gained independence in 1960, Cyprus contains two antagonistic groups—Greek Cypriotes (80 percent of the population) and Turkish Cypriotes (20 percent). In 1963, tensions between Greek and Turkish Cypriotes erupted into civil war. Greece and Turkey threatened to intervene. A U.N. peace force arrived in 1964 and helped to restore order. In 1974, new fighting broke out when Greek Cypriote forces, hoping to unite Cyprus with Greece, overthrew Cyprus's President (a Greek Cypriote, Archbishop Makarios). Turkish troops invaded Cyprus and gained control of 40 percent of the island; Greek forces did not intervene. In 1983 the

Turkish Cypriotes declared their territory to be an independent republic, although only Turkey recognizes it as such. The U.N. peace force still separates Greek and Turkish sections of the island. (Check the Index.)

3. Zimbabwe (Southern Rhodesia). Britain insisted that the white-minority regime in its African colony of Southern Rhodesia move toward rule by the black majority. Instead, in 1965, Southern Rhodesia declared its independence. At Britain's request, the Security Council voted economic sanctions against the breakaway colony. Harassed by black guerrilla groups and weakened by the sanctions, the white regime agreed in 1979 to free elections in which blacks and whites shared. The elections led to independence under a black prime minister in 1980. The country took the name Zimbabwe.

4. India-Pakistan War and Creation of Bangladesh (1971). India and Pakistan both gained independence in 1947. Pakistan consisted of two regions 1000 miles apart, with India in between. Aside from the Islamic religion, West Pakistanis and East Pakistanis had little in common. The West Pakistanis controlled the government and in 1971 sent the army into East Pakistan to suppress demands there for autonomy. The East Pakistanis declared their region independent as the nation of *Bangladesh*. In support of Bangladesh, India sent its army there and easily defeated the Pakistani forces.

The Soviet Union vetoed three Security Council resolutions for a cease-fire and withdrawal of forces. India ignored a similar General Assembly resolution.

ARAB-ISRAELI DISPUTES

As United Nations membership increased over the years, a sizable bloc of nations lined up against Israel. Those nations included Arab, Muslim, Communist, and Third World countries. The United States often—but not always—used its veto in the Security Council to defend Israeli positions.

1. Israeli-French-British Invasion of Egypt (1956). In 1956 Egypt was invaded (*a*) by Israel, which sought to stop border raids by Arab guerrillas and to end a shipping blockade by Egyptian guns commanding the Gulf of Aqaba, and (*b*) by Britain and France, which hoped to undo Egyptian nationalization of the Suez Canal. The United States and the Soviet Union both opposed the attacks.

The invading nations heeded a General Assembly resolution and pulled back their forces. To maintain peace in the area, the General Assembly created a *United Nations Emergency Force* (U.N.E.F.).

2. Arab-Israeli War of 1967. Israel made major territorial gains in a 1967 war that began with Israeli attacks in response to threatening moves by Syria and Egypt. Both sides eventually accepted Security Council calls for a cease-fire. In a resolution, the General Assembly declared Israel's unification of Jerusalem to be invalid. The Security Council later adopted *Resolution 242* calling for (*a*) withdrawal of Israeli forces from the occupied territories, (*b*) right of every Middle Eastern state to live in peace within secure boundaries and free from acts of force, (*c*) free navigation of international waterways, and (*d*) just settlement of the refugee problem.

3. Arab-Israeli War of 1973

a. The Security Council Cease-Fire. Israel held its own in a war that began when Egypt and Syria attacked on the Jewish religion's holiest day, Yom Kippur. The United States (which backed Israel) and the Soviet Union (which backed the Arabs) jointly secured adoption of a Security Council resolution (*a*) calling for a cease-fire, (*b*) reaffirming Resolution 242 of 1967, and (*c*) urging negotiations for a "just and durable peace." A new *U.N. Emergency Force (U.N.E.F.)* of 7,000 men separated the opposing armies.

b. Subsequent General Assembly Votes:

(1) *On the Palestine Liberation Organization (P.L.O.).* In 1974 the General Assembly invited the P.L.O. to take part in a debate on the "Palestine question." P.L.O. leader *Yasir Arafat* addressed the assembly, wearing a holster on his hip. The General Assembly overwhelmingly approved a resolution declaring the right of the Palestinian people to national independence. Israel condemned the resolution for not affirming the right of Israel to exist. The United States and a few other nations backed Israel's position.

(2) *On Zionism.* The movement for a Jewish homeland in Palestine is known as Zionism. In 1975 the General Assembly approved an Arab-sponsored resolution condemning Zionism as "a form of racism and racial discrimination." In support were 72 nations—mainly Arab, Moslem, or Communist; in opposition were 35 nations—mainly the industrial countries.

The resolution, perhaps the most controversial ever adopted at the U.N., drew a stinging rebuke from the United States. Israel condemned the resolution as reminiscent of Nazi anti-Semitism. And U.N. Secretary General Waldheim deplored the resolution as worsening divisions "at a time when the need for understanding . . . is more than ever necessary."

In 1991, the General Assembly repealed the anti-Zionist resolution.

4. Israel's Invasions of Lebanon. To stop cross-border attacks by Palestinians, Israel twice invaded Lebanon (check the Index).

a. 1978. The U.N. Security Council sent a peacekeeping force, the *U.N. Interim Force in Lebanon (U.N.I.F.I.L.).* The Israelis withdrew from southern Lebanon within a few months, leaving a pro-Israeli Lebanese army in control. U.N.I.F.I.L. troops remained on the scene.

b. 1982. The peacekeeping force could do nothing to block Israeli troops in a 1982 invasion. The Israelis swept north to the capital, Beirut, and forced the bulk of P.L.O. troops to leave Lebanon. Israel did not heed unanimous Security Council resolutions calling for a cease-fire and immediate Israeli withdrawal. The United States later vetoed a Security Council resolution threatening sanctions against Israel. The General Assembly overwhelmingly condemned the Israeli invasion.

5. Israeli Raid on an Iraqi Nuclear Reactor (1981). The Security Council voted to "strongly condemn" the raid and urged Israel to open its nuclear power plants to inspection by the International Atomic Energy Agency.

6. Israeli Annexation of the Golan Heights (1981). Israel formally annexed the Golan Heights, a territory taken from Syria in the 1967 war. In a unanimous vote, the Security Council called the annexation illegal.

7. Palestinian Uprising (1989). In 1989 the United States vetoed a Security Council resolution deploring Israeli repression of the Arab *intifada* in Israeli-occupied territories. The General Assembly later condemned Israel by a vote of 140 to 2 for "violating the human rights of the Palestinian people."

8. Accords for Peace (1993). The General Assembly endorsed agreements on a framework for peace that were signed by Israel with both the Palestine Liberation Organization (P.L.O.) and Jordan in September 1993 (check the Index). For the first time in 20 years, the Assembly refrained from criticizing Israel in a resolution on an overall peace settlement. Israeli's ambassador called the resolution "a turning point in the United Nations history in dealing with the Middle East and Israeli affairs." The resolution requested U.N. members to offer financial aid to help carry out the agreements.

OTHER DISPUTES

1. Eritrea (1952–1993). The United Nations placed Italy's former African colony of Eritrea in a federation with Ethiopia in 1952. After Eritrean guerrillas fought a long and victorious war against Ethiopian control, U.N. observers monitored elections in 1993 that set up an independent Eritrea.

2. The Congo/Zaire (1960–1961). In 1960 Belgium granted independence to the Congo (since renamed Zaire). Unprepared for independence, the African nation erupted into bloody wars, complicated by the cold war rivalries of the major powers. A large U.N. emergency force served in the Congo from 1960 to 1964, helping to fend off bloodshed and violence.

The Soviet Union accused Secretary General Dag Hammarskjold of taking sides in Congolese affairs. It demanded that he be replaced by a *troika*—a three-person board of Western, Soviet, and neutralist representatives, each with a veto. Western nations strongly defended Hammarskjold's impartialty. After Hammarskjold was killed in a plane crash while visiting the Congo, the Soviets dropped their demand for a troika.

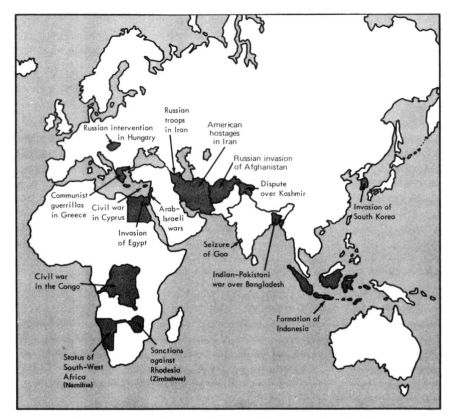

International Disputes Considered at the United Nations

3. Iran (1979). In 1979 militant Iranians seized the American embassy in Teheran and took 50 staff members hostage. The U.N. Security Council and the World Court declared the seizures to be illegal.

4. Falkland Islands (1982). An island group in the South Atlantic, some 300 miles from Argentina, the *Falklands* have been under British rule since the 1800's, and the islanders are chiefly of British descent. Argentina also claims the islands, which it calls the *Malvinas*. In 1982, Argentina's military government seized the islands by force. The Security Council demanded that Argentina withdraw its troops. Although the United States supported Britain, Secretary of State *Alexander Haig* tried to mediate the dispute through shuttle diplomacy. He failed, and Britain sent an armada to recapture the islands. After a war that lasted several weeks, Britain secured the surrender of more than 11,000 Argentine troops and reoccupied the islands.

5. Namibia (South-West Africa). South Africa received a League of Nations mandate in 1920 to rule the former German colony of South-West Africa.

Later South Africa refused to change the mandate into a U.N. trusteeship. In 1966 the General Assembly (*a*) declared South Africa's mandate over South-West Africa ended, (*b*) ordered the territory placed under U.N. control, and (*c*) created a committee to suggest ways for leading South-West Africa to freedom.

Opponents of South African rule organized the South-West Africa People's Organization (SWAPO) and began a war for independence. In 1973 the General Assembly declared SWAPO to be the "authentic representative of the Namibian people." In 1978, the Security Council called for U.N.-supervised elections leading to independence.

In 1988 the United States helped work out a regional settlement calling for South Africa to pull out of Namibia while Cuba withdrew troops backing the government of neighboring Angola. A U.N. observer force oversaw the transition to independence, including elections that SWAPO won with 57 percent of the vote.

6. Cambodia (1978–1994). The General Assembly annually condemned the Vietnamese occupation of Cambodia that lasted from 1978 to 1989. A typical resolution (1988) called for the country's rival factions to unite under the leadership of Prince Norodom Sihanouk, the former monarch. Forces loyal to Sihanouk were among three factions fighting against the pro-Vietnamese Cambodian government in a prolonged civil war.

In 1991 a U.N.-mediated cease-fire went into effect. The agreement provided that the U.N. would (*a*) supervise a partial demobilization of rival groups, (*b*) take charge of five key departments under a coalition government in which rival groups shared power, and (*c*) organize 1993 elections for an assembly to draw up a new Cambodian constitution.

U.N. observers monitored the May 1993 elections. The U.N. role ended when an elected government took over Cambodia in September 1993. (Check the Index.)

7. Iran-Iraq War (1980–1988). In 1987 the Security Council ordered a cease-fire in a war between Iran and Iraq that had begun in 1980. Initially, Iran rejected the proposal on grounds that the resolution did not brand Iraq as an aggressor. Finally, U.N. Secretary General Javier Perez de Cuellar helped to arrange a cease-fire, which went into effect in 1988. A force of several hundred U.N. observers monitored the cease-fire.

8. South Africa. For years the General Assembly criticized the rule over South Africa of a white-minority government committed to *apartheid*, or racial separation. Expressing the view that apartheid was racist and abhorrent to the world community, the General Assembly after 1974 refused to allow South Africa's white-minority government to occupy the nation's seat in the General Assembly. From 1977, the United Nations banned arms sales to South Africa. Individually, many nations imposed limited economic sanctions in 1986.

F. W. de Klerk, who became prime minister of South Africa in 1989, phased out apartheid. He opened negotiations with *Nelson Mandela* and other black leaders, leading to agreement on a transition to majority rule. In 1994 Mandela was elected President in South Africa's first multi-racial election.

9. U.S.-Led Intervention in Grenada. The General Assembly condemned the 1983 invasion of Grenada by a multinational force led by the United States (check the Index). The United States vetoed a Security Council resolution "deeply deploring" the invasion, which overthrew a Marxist government.

10. Central America. The Security Council voted in 1989 to send a small observer force to monitor a plan by Central American nations for cutting off outside aid to rebels fighting against governments in El Salvador and Nicaragua. It was the first U.N. peacekeeping operation for the Western Hemisphere. Later, U.N. observers monitored Nicaragua's 1990 election.

The Security Council sent a peacekeeping force to El Salvador to disarm rebel troops as part of a 1992 settlement that ended 12 years of civil war (check the Index). The troops remained to monitor 1994 elections. In addition, a U.N.-sponsored commission investigated human rights abuses during the war; it recommended far-reaching changes in the country's military and courts.

11. Persian Gulf War (1991). After Iraq's 1990 invasion of Kuwait, the Security Council ordered an embargo on trade with Iraq. At the urging of the United States, the council then authorized the use of military force to expel the Iraqi invaders. (Check the Index for Persian Gulf War.) After Iraq's defeat, the council (a) demanded that Iraq pay reparations for war damages, (b) ordered protection of Iraqi opposition groups such as Kurds and Shiites, and (c) forbade Iraq to possess nuclear, biological, or chemical weapons. Agents for the International Atomic Energy Agency made inspections.

12. Western Sahara (Since 1991). U.N. peacekeepers enforced a cease-fire between Moroccan troops and rebels seeking independence for Western Sahara. The U.N. prepared a referendum aimed at deciding the territory's future.

13. Angola (1991). After the parties in Angola's civil war reached a peace agreement in 1991, a U.N. peacekeeping force helped to oversee elections in September 1992 (check the Index). When new fighting broke out after the elections, U.N. observers worked to arrange a more permanent settlement.

14. Wars in the Former Yugoslavia (Since 1991). Wars broke out in Croatia and Bosnia after the breakup of Yugoslavia in 1991–1992 (check the Index). The United Nations joined the European Community in sending mediators to try to help the warring parties reach a solution. The Security Council (a) imposed trade and other sanctions on what remained of Yugoslavia to force it to stop backing Serbian forces in Croatia and Bosnia, (b) imposed an arms embargo on all of the former Yugoslavia, (c) sent more than 20,000 peacekeeping troops to Bosnia and Croatia (and a much smaller number of troops to Macedonia), and (d) created an international war crimes tribunal to weigh atrocity charges leveled against various parties in the Balkan wars. However, the U.N. was criticized for not doing more to prevent the widespread loss of life.

15. Wars in the Former Soviet Union (After 1991). After the breakup of the Soviet Union in 1991 (check the Index), the Security Council sought to help end wars in Nagorno-Karabakh (Azerbaijan) and Abkhazia (Georgia).

16. Haiti (Since 1991). Military officers ousted Haiti's elected President Jean-Bertrand Aristide in September 1991. In June 1993 the Security Council placed an oil embargo on Haiti and worked to persuade military leaders to agree to Aristide's return.

17. Mozambique (1992). A 7,500-person peacekeeping force was created in 1992 to help monitor a cease-fire between Mozambique's government and rebel forces. Other goals: disarm the two sides and organize elections.

18. Somalia (1992). In 1992 the U.N. sent more than 20,000 troops to Somalia to protect relief operations in a civil war. The Security Council authorized the troops to use all the force necessary to accomplish their mission. Thus, the Somalia operation was an *enforcement action* and not just a peacekeeping mission. It was the first U.N. enforcement action under U.N. command. (Earlier enforcement actions in the Korean and Persian Gulf Wars had been under U.S. command.)

19. Criticism of U.S. Embargo on Cuba (1992). In response to a tightening of a 30-year-old United States embargo on trade with Cuba, the General Assembly in 1992 and 1993 demanded that the embargo be removed.

20. Rwanda (1994). The U.N. in 1993 sent a peacekeeping force to the border between Rwanda and Uganda to monitor the smuggling of weapons to rebels fighting against Rwanda's government. In 1994 the fighting escalated. It was estimated that 400,000 civilians had been killed.

ACTIONS PERTAINING TO TERRORISM

1. Background. Extremist groups have used terrorism—deliberate violence against innocent civilians—to further the extremists' political goals. Terrorist groups have been active in many parts of the world—from Northern Ireland to Spain, from India to the Philippines, from South Africa to Libya, from Canada to Peru. They have included leftists and rightists, opponents and supporters of the United States, people who claim to act from religious conviction and people who claim to have no religious beliefs.

Hostility between Israelis and Arabs gave rise to many incidents of terrorism: the slaying of 11 Israeli athletes at the 1972 Olympic Games in Munich, Germany; the murder of more than 20 schoolchildren at the Israeli town of Ma'alot in 1974; the killing of 30 civilians in a Palestinian raid on the Israeli coast in 1978; the hijacking of the cruise ship *Achille Lauro* and the killing of an American passenger in October 1985; an attack at the Vienna and Rome airports in December 1985 that killed 20 people; the killing of 20 people in a hijacked Pan American jet at Karachi, Pakistan, in September 1986; the killing

UNITED NATIONS PEACEKEEPING FORCES

For years, U.N. forces have been serving around the globe. The 10,000-member peacekeeping forces won the Nobel Peace Prize for 1988.

LOCATION	YEAR(S)	DUTIES
Middle East	1948–present	Patrol borders between Israelis and Arabs.
Kashmir	1949–present	Monitor cease-fire between India and Pakistan.
Egypt	1956–1967	Monitor cease-fire between Egypt and Britain, France, and Israel.
Congo (Zaire)	1960–1964	Prevent civil war; secure withdrawal of Belgian and other foreign troops.
West New Guinea	1962–1963	Monitor peace between Netherlands and Indonesia.
Yemen	1963–1964	Oversee withdrawal of Arab forces in Yemen civil war.
Cyprus	1964–present	Stop fighting between Greek and Turkish Cypriotes; keep buffer zone between sides.
India-Pakistan	1965–1966	Supervise cease-fire along borders.
Sinai peninsula	1973–1979	Monitor cease-fire between Egypt and Israel.
Golan Heights	1974–present	Monitor cease-fire between Syria and Israel.
Southern Lebanon	1978–present	Provide buffer between Israel and Lebanon.
Afghanistan	1988	Monitor Soviet troop pullout.
Persian Gulf	1988–present	Oversee cease-fire between Iraq and Iran.
Namibia	1988–1990	Oversee transition to Namibian independence.
Nicaragua	1989–1990	Check fairness of 1990 Nicaraguan elections.
Central America	1989–1990	Monitor demobilization of contra guerrillas.
Middle East	1991–present	Oversee peace proposals in Persian Gulf region.
Angola	1991–present	To separate rival forces and to monitor elections held in September 1992.
El Salvador	1991–present	To disarm rebels and to monitor the peace process.
Western Sahara	1991–present	To prepare a referendum at which voters could choose between independence and annexation by Morocco.
Former Yugoslavia	1992–present	To provide buffer zones and oversee relief efforts.
Mozambique	1992–1994	To monitor an agreement to end civil war and to prepare free elections.
Somalia	1993–present	To enforce peace between rival factions in a civil war and to guard relief operations.
Rwanda	1993–present	To monitor a cease-fire between government and rebel troops and coordinate relief efforts.

of 22 Jews at a synagogue in Istanbul, Turkey, in September 1986; the fire-bombing of an Israeli bus in 1988 that killed a woman and her three small children; the assassination in New York in 1990 of Rabbi Meir Kahane, a right-wing Israeli legislator; and the massacre by an Israeli settler of more than 30 Arabs in a mosque in Hebron, on the West Bank, in 1994. Israeli commandoes tracked down and killed PLO leaders in Britain, France, Italy, and Lebanon; they once mistakenly gunned down a Moroccan waiter in Norway who had no connection to the PLO. In 1988 Israeli commandoes assassinated Abu Jihad, a high PLO official, at his home in Tunis, Tunisia.

Other incidents of terrorism have included the kidnapping and murder of Italian Premier *Aldo Moro* by leftists in 1978; the assassination of Egyptian President *Anwar Sadat* by Islamic militants in 1981; a bomb blast that killed Lebanese President-elect *Bashir Gemayel* in 1982; the assassination of India's Prime Minister *Indira Gandhi* by Sikh guards in 1984 and of her son, former Prime Minister *Rajiv Gandhi*, by Tamil extremists in 1990; the bombing in a New Zealand harbor in 1985 by French agents of a ship owned by the environmentalist organization Greenpeace, killing one person; a bomb explosion in 1985 that killed 329 people on an Air India plane flying from Canada to India (police suspected Sikh militants); the bombing of Pan Am flight 103 over Lockerbie, Scotland, in December 1988, killing 259 on board and 11 on the ground; the alleged bombing of a Libyan passenger plane on the fourth anniversary of the Lockerbie bombing, killing all 157 people aboard; and the bombing of the World Trade Center in New York in February 1993, killing six people and wounding more than 1,000.

2. Condemnation of All Terrorism. While most governments condemn terrorism, at least in public, some people argue that terrorism is a legitimate weapon of the powerless against the powerful. In 1985 the U.N. General Assembly unanimously voted to condemn all international terrorism as criminal.

3. Sanctions Against Libya. The Security Council applied economic sanctions against Libya in 1993 when that North African nation refused to turn over for trial two suspects in the 1988 Lockerbie bombing.

EVALUATION OF THE UNITED NATIONS

1. Optimistic View: Effectiveness of the U.N.

a. Almost Universal Membership. The U.N. is the world's most representative body of nations. It mirrors the hopes and fears of humanity.

b. Availability of Forum. The U.N. provides a forum where any member nation may present its point of view on world problems. Non-governmental groups also have a chance to be heard.

c. Uniting-for-Peace Resolution (1950). This resolution asserts the right of the General Assembly to deal with a threat to world peace if a veto prevents the Security Council from acting. It states that the General Assembly may be summoned into emergency session and may recommend, by a two-thirds vote, that U.N. members take collective action, including the use of armed force.

   d. Solution of International Problems. Through the U.N., many international problems have been solved or brought closer to a solution. Examples of U.N. achievements include (1) the withdrawal of invading forces from Egypt in 1956, (2) the independence of Zimbabwe and Namibia under freely elected governments, and (3) the Cambodian ceasefire of 1991.

   e. U.N. Military Forces. The U.N. has secured the military cooperation of a number of member nations. Examples include (1) the formation of a U.N. army to repel aggression against Korea in 1950, (2) the creation of U.N. emergency forces for the Middle East, Cyprus, and other trouble spots, and (3) the expulsion of Iraqi invaders from Kuwait by an international coalition in 1991.

   f. Economic and Social Progress. The Economic and Social Council, the specialized agencies, and the technical assistance programs have worked to improve economic and social conditions in underdeveloped countries.

   g. Colonial Independence. Through the Trusteeship Council, the General Assembly, and other organs, the U.N. has helped pave the way for an end to colonial rule.

   h. Prevention of International Anarchy. The U.N. keeps the world from reverting to international anarchy. It enables quarreling nations to speak to one another and gives smaller nations a role in addressing world problems.

   i. Mediation. U.N. leaders sometimes offer their *good offices* (assistance as a mediator) in helping to resolve international disputes. For example, Secretary General Javier Perez de Cuellar helped to win the release of hostages held by Middle Eastern terrorists in the early 1990's.

2. Pessimistic View: Problems Besetting the U.N.

   a. Blocs Within the U.N. Throughout the cold war, the U.N. was divided into three blocs: (1) The *Western bloc* (about 50 nations) included the United States, Western Europe, most of Latin America, Japan, and other nations. (2) The *Communist bloc* (10 to 20 nations) consistently followed Soviet policy. (3) The *nonaligned movement* (eventually numbering more than 100 nations) fiercely opposed colonialism but held diverse views on most other international issues.

   b. Self-Serving Use of U.N. Organs and Specialized Agencies. U.N. members often consider international problems on the basis of individual or bloc interests, rather than on the basis of U.N. principles.

   In the 1970's Communist and Arab nations, with Third World support, "politicized" the work of U.N. specialized agencies. At the ILO, the Communist nations secured condemnation of the military regime in Chile for "denying trade

Bear market.

*Crawford. Reprinted by permission of
Newspaper Enterprise Association*

*"Bear market" denotes values
that are sharply falling.
What is the cartoonist saying
about U.N. prestige? about
what has caused this trend?
What other factors might be
considered? How could the
U.N. reverse this trend?*

union rights." Using a double standard, the ILO did not say a word about the denial of such rights in Communist and many Third World nations. At WHO the Arab nations secured rejection of a report by WHO experts that Israel had improved the health conditions of Arab peoples under Israeli control. At UNESCO the Arab nations secured condemnation of Israel for archaeological excavations in Jerusalem and achieved UNESCO expulsion of Israel. In 1976, by a maneuver, UNESCO readmitted Israel.

Also at UNESCO, Soviet-bloc and Third World nations secured approval for the preparation of a so-called New World Information Order that would empower UNESCO to draw up a code of journalistic ethics, to regulate the flow of world news, and to "license" journalists. The Western world's free news organizations viewed these proposals as attempts to justify government censorship and to restrict Western-type press freedom. In 1981 they vowed to oppose UNESCO's efforts to curtail the "free circulation of news."

In late 1983 the United States gave the one-year required notice of intent to withdraw from UNESCO.

In a 1974 speech, the chief American representative to the United Nations deplored bloc voting and self-serving use of the U.N. by Communist, Arab, and Third World nations. He warned that, by adopting unrealistic, one-sided positions and resolutions, the General Assembly was eroding support for the U.N. in the American Congress and among the American people. He further declared that "when the rule of the majority becomes the tyranny of the majority, the minority will cease to respect or obey it." The American representative urged the General Assembly to fulfill its true function: "to bridge the differences among its member states."

In 1975, at AFL–CIO and business prodding, the United States gave the required two-year notice of intent to withdraw from the ILO. The United States was particularly incensed that the ILO did not apply its labor standards equally to all nations, including Communist and Third World countries, and that the ILO accepted government delegates as worker representatives from countries that had no free labor unions. In 1977 the United States withdrew, thereby ending its ILO financial support (about 25 percent of ILO's budget) and expressing American displeasure with the "politicizing" of the U.N. and the specialized agencies.

(In 1980, as the ILO seemed to be abandoning its "politicizing" activities and returning to its original purpose—improving the condition of workers—the United States rejoined the organization.)

In 1984 the United States withdrew from UNESCO—charging that organization with mismanagement, financial excesses, and "politicizing" of issues.

c. Veto Power. During the cold war, the Soviet Union used the veto more than 100 times and the United States more than 60 times, thereby limiting the effectiveness of the Security Council. Soviet vetoes were more common in the early years of the U.N., when the Western bloc dominated U.N. activities. With the rise of Third World influence, American vetoes became more numerous. Since the end of the cold war, vetoes occur less frequently.

Some examples of Soviet vetoes: (1) More than 40 times in the early years of the U.N., the Soviet Union vetoed membership applications by nations it considered pro-American. (2) On at least two occasions the Soviet Union vetoed a candidate for Secretary General. (3) In 1980 the Soviets vetoed a call for withdrawal of Soviet troops from Afghanistan. (4) In 1983 the Soviets vetoed a resolution condemning their shooting down of a South Korean passenger plane.

Some examples of American vetoes: (1) In 1972 the United States vetoed a resolution condemning Israeli raids on Palestinian guerrillas in Lebanon without mentioning the provocation—the murder of 11 Israeli athletes at the Munich Olympics. (2) In 1974 the United States, with Britain and France, vetoed a plan to expel South Africa from the U.N. (3) In 1983 the United States vetoed a resolution deploring its invasion of Grenada. (4) In 1989 the United States (with Britain and France) vetoed a resolution opposing its invasion of Panama.

d. Defiance of U.N. Resolutions. Many nations have defied U.N. resolutions, claiming that the issue involved was a domestic matter not subject to U.N. authority or insisting that they were protecting their national interests.

e. Lack of Permanent Military Power. The U.N. has never created a permanent military force. It depends upon member nations to honor resolutions requesting armed personnel. Only 16 nations—at that time constituting about one-fourth of the U.N. membership—heeded the call for troops to aid South Korea in 1950.

f. Financial Difficulties. The U.N. secures funds for its regular budget by assessing member nations according to their ability to pay. Separate assessments are made for the U.N.'s peacekeeping costs. The United States is billed the most (about 25 percent of the regular budget and 30 percent of the peacekeeping budget). Member nations also make voluntary contributions for special activities. The U.N. has often run short of money because (1) some nations have not kept up their payments and (2) the U.N. has been expanding its costly peacekeeping operations. In the mid-1990's some 80,000 peacekeepers were on duty in a dozen nations.

Bankruptcy threatened the U.N. in the mid-1980's when the United States withheld more than $500 million. Its reasons: concern about massive United States budget deficits and a desire to have more say in U.N. spending policies. Under the *Kassebaum Amendment* (1986), the United States reduced its contribution from 25 percent to 20 percent. The General Assembly agreed to change budget-making procedures, giving big contributors a veto. Presidents Reagan and Bush then asked Congress to restore the cuts.

Like the United States, the Soviet Union held back funds to underline political objections to various aspects of U.N. spending during the cold war. In 1987 the Soviet Union began paying its arrears of $197 million.

In the mid-1990's the money shortfall totaled about $2 billion, more than half of which was for peacekeeping forces. The U.S. remained the largest debtor nation in the U.N.

Secretary General Boutros-Ghali reduced the U.N. staff and imposed stringent cost-cutting measures on U.N. operations. The United States and other nations have called for further economies.

3. Realistic View. The United Nations is not meant to be a world government; it is a loose confederation whose member states retain their sovereignty. The United Nations is only an instrument available for their use.

MULTIPLE-CHOICE QUESTIONS

1. "They hope to see established a peace . . . which will afford assurance that all the men in all the lands may live out their lives in freedom from fear and want" is quoted from the (1) Atlantic Charter (2) Genocide Convention (3) United Nations Charter (4) UNESCO Charter.

2. The Atlantic Charter was most similar in its provisions to the (1) Platt Amendment (2) Fourteen Points (3) Stimson Doctrine (4) Kellogg-Briand Pact.

3. The conference that completed the United Nations Charter met in (1) New York (2) Yalta (3) San Francisco (4) Moscow.

4. Which U.N. body provides a forum for expression by all U.N. members? (1) Security Council (2) Trusteeship Council (3) General Assembly (4) World Court.

5. The General Assembly meets (1) in continuous session (2) at least once a year (3) only when called by the Secretary General (4) only in time of emergency.

6. Each nation's voting strength in the General Assembly is according to (1) area (2) population (3) military strength (4) the principle of one vote per nation.

7. Which organ of the U.N. was given primary responsibility for investigating situations that threaten world peace? (1) the Economic and Social Council (2) the Secretariat (3) the Security Council (4) the Trusteeship Council.

8. The nonpermanent members of the Security Council are selected by the (1) General Assembly (2) Economic and Social Council (3) five permanent members of the Council (4) Secretary General.

9. The Security Council has the power to (1) veto decisions of the General Assembly (2) cancel treaties made by member nations (3) recommend the use of force to stop aggression (4) elect the Secretary General.

10. The veto power in the U.N. is held by (1) each member of the Security Council (2) each member of the General Assembly (3) only the Soviet Union and the United States (4) the five permanent members of the Security Council.

11. The country that most often blocked action in the U.N. by the use of the veto is (1) France (2) the Soviet Union (3) Great Britain (4) the United States.

12. To fill the office of Secretary General of the U.N., a person must be (1) recommended by the Security Council and appointed by the General Assembly (2) recommended by the General Assembly and appointed by the Security Council (3) nominated by the Soviet Union and the United States, and elected by the Security Council (4) recommended by the Security Council and elected by the International Court.

13. One function of the Economic and Social Council is to (1) settle boundary disputes (2) promote respect for human rights (3) direct the economics of underdeveloped nations (4) regulate the use of atomic energy.

14. The specialized agency that seeks to promote cultural cooperation and understanding among nations is (1) UNICEF (2) Trusteeship Council (3) WHO (4) UNESCO.

15. The United States' explanation for withdrawing from UNESCO in 1984 was that (1) Russia had become a member (2) UNESCO had condemned Chile (3) UNESCO was interfering in U.S. domestic issues (4) UNESCO was "politicizing" issues.

16. "Since wars begin in the minds of men" is a phrase used in the UNESCO Charter to emphasize the need for (1) encouraging regional agreements on trade (2) expanding educational opportunities (3) controlling newspapers that stir up controversies (4) stopping research on atomic weapons.

17. A territory under the protection of the U.N. but administered by a member nation is called a (1) trusteeship (2) protectorate (3) mandate (4) sphere of influence.

18. A leading member of the United Nations that was *never* a member of the League of Nations is (1) Italy (2) Russia (3) France (4) the United States.

19. The United Nations has (1) admitted many new member nations (2) adopted a plan by which nations may withdraw from the U.N. (3) outlawed atomic weapons (4) established a permanent U.N. military force.

20. Which was an achievement of the U.N.? (1) technical aid to underdeveloped regions (2) release of Hungary from the control of the Soviet Union (3) awarding of Kashmir to Pakistan (4) establishment of U.N. control over South-West Africa.

21. The Secretary General who was attacked by the Soviet Union for his conduct of the U.N. Congo operation was (1) Trygve Lie (2) Dag Hammarskjold (3) U Thant (4) Ralph Bunche.

22. Until 1971, the admission of Red China to the United Nations was most vigorously opposed by (1) Egypt (2) Russia (3) India (4) the United States.

23. The Uniting for Peace resolution has tended to transfer power from the (1) Security Council to the General Assembly (2) Security Council to the Secretary General (3) Gen-

eral Assembly to the Security Council (4) General Assembly to the International Court of Justice.

24. In 1950 the Security Council was able to pass a resolution calling upon the North Korean Communists to withdraw from South Korea because (1) Russia approved the resolution (2) Russia was absent from the meeting (3) Russia was prohibited from voting since she was directly concerned with the issue (4) the veto power had not yet gone into effect.

25. The U.N. role in Afghanistan involved (1) organizing an international force to oppose aggressors (2) providing election observers (3) sending a peacekeeping force (4) helping with peace talks.

26. The U.N. finances its regular budget chiefly by (1) charging admission to visitors (2) assessing member nations (3) placing a tax upon citizens of U.N. member nations (4) selling U.N. stamps and souvenirs.

27. A cause of the U.N.'s financial crisis in the 1980's was (1) the cost of military operations (2) extravagant living styles of U.N. delegates (3) a boycott of the U.N. by Third World nations (4) a refusal by the United States and the Soviet Union to pay their full assessments.

28. A major criticism of the voting procedure in the Security Council is that (1) Russia has as much voting power as the United States (2) a veto by any permanent member can prevent or delay action (3) the permanent members have more votes than the nonpermanent members (4) most member nations have no voting power in the Security Council.

29. In getting member states to heed its requests, the United Nations closely resembles (1) the United States under the federal Constitution (2) the United States under the Articles of Confederation (3) England in relation to the first English settlements in the New World (4) a holding company in relation to its subsidiaries.

ESSAY QUESTIONS

1. Giving *one* specific example for *each*, show how the United Nations has sought to achieve the following objectives stated in its Charter: (*a*) "to maintain international peace and security," (*b*) "to promote social progress and better standards of life," (*c*) "to reaffirm faith in fundamental human rights."

2. Using *one* specific fact, show why *each* of the following represents a problem for the United Nations: (*a*) use of the veto, (*b*) withdrawal of Indonesia, (*c*) raising funds to finance U.N. activities, (*d*) defiance of U.N. resolutions.

3. The U.N. represents an effort to solve the problems of international tension in an age of extreme danger. (*a*) Describe *two* ways in which the U.N. represents an improvement over the League of Nations. (*b*) Discuss *two* different ways in which the U.N. attempts to maintain world peace. (*c*) Show how the United States has cooperated with the U.N. in meeting *two* international crises. (*d*) Explain *two* limitations on the ability of the U.N. to meet world problems.

4. (*a*) State *two* functions of *each* of the following specialized agencies associated with the United Nations: (1) WHO, (2) FAO, (3) ILO, (4) UNESCO. (*b*) Discuss *two* weaknesses that hinder the work of the specialized agencies.

5. At a discussion on the United Nations, the following arguments were given:

For the United Nations	*Against the United Nations*
a. The United Nations Charter has avoided the weaknesses of the Covenant of the League of Nations.	a. Since the United States pays about 25 percent of the cost of running the United Nations, our country might just as well "go it alone."

b. The wars in Korea and the Persian Gulf have tested the strength of the United Nations and proved that it can stop aggression.

c. The U.N. serves as a safety valve where nations may talk out problems rather than resort to war.

b. The frequent use of the veto has made the United Nations helpless.

c. By passing partisan and unrealistic resolutions, which nations defy, the General Assembly has destroyed U.N. prestige.

Agree or disagree with any *two* of the arguments above, giving *two* specific facts for each to support your point of view.

Part 2. The United States and the Communist Challenge

AMERICAN LEADERSHIP IN WORLD AFFAIRS

The Japanese attack on Pearl Harbor, involving us in World War II, ended our traditional policy of isolation. The American people finally realized that the United States had become a major world power and could not achieve security by a policy of isolation. American public opinion encouraged the government to pursue a new foreign policy: active American participation and leadership in world affairs.

BIPARTISAN APPROACH

This new foreign policy was *bipartisan*, formulated and supported by both of our major political parties. In spite of occasional disagreements, Republican and Democratic leaders have cooperated to analyze our international problems and to establish a foreign policy best suited to American interests.

RECENT OBJECTIVES OF AMERICAN FOREIGN POLICY

1. Safeguard the national interests of the United States.

2. Avoid the outbreak of another world war.

3. Promote democracy throughout the world.

4. Help other nations improve their social and economic conditions.

5. Protect our friends and allies against Communist expansion.

COLD WAR

1. Origins. The "cold war" originated immediately after World War II as a struggle between the Western nations, led by the United States, and the

Communist nations, led by the Soviet Union. Americans were alarmed by *(a)* the expressed Soviet aim of communizing the world and *(b)* the expansion of Soviet power into Central Europe. The Soviet people were alarmed by *(a)* overwhelming American economic and military might and *(b)* the Marxist assumption that American capitalism had to expand to survive. President Truman began the American policy of keeping the Soviet Union from gaining control of any additional territories—a policy called *containment.*

2. **Weapons.** The cold war was fought by means of *(a) propaganda*—in newspapers, on radio and television, in street demonstrations, and at the U.N.; *(b) diplomatic moves,* including international conferences and military alliances; *(c) scientific competition,* reflected in the development of nuclear weapons and missiles and in the undertaking of space flights; *(d) economic competition,* especially aid to underdeveloped countries; *(e) espionage,* conducted by extensive spy rings, intelligence-gathering ships, and data-gathering space vehicles; and *(f) subversion,* by encouraging dissent and disruption within each other's spheres.

The cold war also was marked by localized military action but not by all-out war. The world lived under an uneasy armed truce—an absence of total war but also an absence of genuine peace.

3. **Today: After the Cold War.** Although the cold war divided the world into an American bloc and a Soviet bloc, that simple division no longer exists. Each bloc experienced strains, and the Soviet bloc disintegrated.

a. Western European nations have become less dependent militarily and economically upon the United States. Over the years, American allies such as France and Britain have occasionally differed with the United States on important issues. Since the late 1980's, fast-paced changes within Eastern Europe have presented new problems and new opportunities to the nations of Western Europe. The United States and its allies began a searching reassessment of their relationship, seeking new ways of pursuing their economic and military partnership.

b. As early as the late 1940's, disunity and discontent troubled the Communist world, as Yugoslavia broke sharply with Stalin and adopted its own milder form of communism. In the 1950's, China challenged Soviet leadership. Then in the 1980's, the Soviet Union eased its hard-line policies, and the Soviet bloc underwent sweeping change. In the 1990's, the entire Soviet bloc crumbled.

TWO SUPERPOWERS: THE SOVIET UNION AND THE UNITED STATES— A COMPARISON (During the Cold War)

1. **Government: Dictatorial vs. Democratic Traditions**

a. Political Parties

(1) *Soviet Union.* Until 1990, the Communist party was the only party permitted to exist; it exercised supreme power dictatorially. After 1990 other parties were legally free to organize and to propose candidates for public office.

(2) *United States.* Many political parties exist, the two major parties being the Democrats and the Republicans. The major and minor parties check upon each other, present candidates and issues to the people, and compete for support. No one party monopolizes the government.

b. Power Over the Country

(1) *Soviet Union.* Traditionally, Communist party leaders debated among themselves and then decided upon a *party line* that determined Soviet policies. The party dominated every aspect of Soviet life. Under the reforms of Soviet President *Mikhail Gorbachev,* party and government functions were held to be separate, although power was still highly centralized.

(2) *United States.* National officials set American policies, but these are subject to public criticism. Public policies are influenced by leaders in such fields as industry, agriculture, labor, race relations, education, and the information media. Because power is diffused, no one group or political party dominates the country.

c. Civil Liberties

(1) *Soviet Union.* The Soviet constitution guaranteed various civil liberties, but the power of the state was unrestrained by any system of checks and balances. As a result, citizens' rights were widely abused.

(2) *United States.* The federal Constitution and state constitutions guarantee the civil liberties of citizens and noncitizens alike. Americans can turn to the courts to protect their rights.

2. Economy: Communist vs. Capitalist

a. Industry

(1) *Soviet Union.* The government owned and operated all industry. The Communists transformed Russia from an agricultural nation into a major industrial nation through a series of *Five-Year Plans.* These emphasized heavy industry and military equipment rather than consumer goods. Having concluded that the traditional Soviet system failed, reformers of the 1990's tried to introduce market mechanisms and rudiments of free enterprise.

(2) *United States.* Private entrepreneurs—individuals and corporations—own and operate most industry. Competition and the *profit motive* provide personal economic incentives. The government acts chiefly to prevent abuses. The United States, the world's leading industrial nation, exceeded the Soviet Union in output of capital goods and consumer products.

b. Labor

(1) *Soviet Union.* Traditionally, the Communist party dominated the unions to which almost all Soviet workers belonged. The unions spurred the workers to greater productivity. However, they had no say in determining wages and no right

to strike. Although the standard of living of Soviet workers was higher than in Czarist times, it remained low by Western standards.

(2) *United States.* One-sixth of American workers belong to unions, which are free of government domination although subject to regulation. Unions bargain collectively with employers regarding wages and working conditions; the right to strike is guaranteed by law. American workers enjoy a considerably higher living standard than Soviet workers did.

c. Agriculture

(1) *Soviet Union.* The Soviet Union employed 23 percent of its labor force in agriculture. Farmers traditionally have worked on vast state-owned farms or in farm communities called *collectives.* Farm families often resented collectivization and concentrated on their own small garden plots, and the Soviet Union had to import grain. Reforms in the 1980's sought to give farm workers more rights and to promote individual initiative and profit-making.

(2) *United States.* The United States employs less than 4 percent of its labor force in agriculture. Farmers own their own land or work on giant commercial farms. American farmers use much machinery and fertilizer, and employ the latest production methods. They receive government aid to maintain soil fertility, achieve fair prices, and secure agricultural knowledge. American farmers produce more than enough for domestic consumption and export large quantities of food to other nations.

3. Culture: Regimentation vs. Freedom

a. Education

(1) *Soviet Union.* The central government controlled education. All children received compulsory schooling for at least eight years. Capable students were encouraged to study further, especially in mathematics and the sciences. The Soviet Union produced more engineers and scientists than did the United States. In the humanities, students were traditionally trained to follow the Communist party line rather than think for themselves.

(2) *United States.* The states and localities control education, although the federal government grants funds to expand school facilities, improve instruction, and aid capable students. Most children receive compulsory education to at least the age of 16. The United States turned out far more college graduates than did the Soviet Union. In the humanities, students are encouraged to pursue independent, nonregimented thinking.

b. Literature and Art

(1) *Soviet Union.* The Soviet government encouraged writers and artists, but traditionally demanded that they propagandize for Communism. Dissident writers long tried to escape conformity by privately circulating their own works in a form called *samizdat* (self-published). Reforms in the 1980's allowed greater freedom for writers and artists to deviate from official positions.

(2) *United States.* The Constitution prohibits the federal government and state governments from interfering with free expression. American writers and artists produce works that represent their own tastes and their own outlook on life. Their works may praise or criticize aspects of American culture and governmental policy.

BRIEF HISTORY OF SOVIET-AMERICAN RELATIONS

1. 1917–1941: Unfriendly. The Communists resented (*a*) American aid to anti-Communist forces following the Russian Revolution, and (*b*) America's refusal until 1933 to recognize the Soviet Union.

The United States resented (*a*) the Soviet withdrawal from World War I, enabling the Germans to concentrate their military forces on the western front, (*b*) Russian efforts to spread unrest and revolution in non-Communist countries by means of an organization called the *Comintern*, and (*c*) Russia's Non-Aggression Pact of 1939 with Nazi Germany—an agreement that encouraged Germany to start World War II.

2. 1941–1945: Cooperative. During World War II, Russia and the United States found themselves fighting against a common enemy, Germany. To create amity with her democratic allies, Russia dissolved the Comintern. To assist Russia, the United States (*a*) provided her with $11 billion of lend-lease equipment, and (*b*) led the Western allies in opening other fronts in Europe by invading southern Italy and northern France. Also, Russia, the United States, and Britain coordinated military strategy and planned postwar arrangements at top-level conferences at *Teheran, Yalta,* and *Potsdam.*

3. Post-1945: The Cold War Era. After World War II, cooperation broke down and the two former allies entered a period of intense hostility. Stalin pursued a hard line toward the West, but his successors urged *peaceful coexistence.* They did not, however, abandon the Soviet goal of communizing the world. American leaders (*a*) held the expansion of Soviet power to be a threat to the rest of the world and (*b*) predicted that peaceful competition would lead to the ultimate triumph of societies committed to democracy and capitalism.

4. 1971–1992: Détente and Great Change. In the early 1970's, Soviet and American leaders began to move from confrontation to negotiation in an era of relaxation, or *détente.* Détente recognized the basic differences between the two superpowers, but it also recognized their mutual interest in improving relations and avoiding a nuclear war. Over a decade of détente, the two nations achieved a certain number of understandings, but they continued cold-war-style confrontations in many parts of the world. (Check the Index for Détente.)

During the 1980's, Soviet leader *Mikhail Gorbachev* began a major liberalization of economic, political, and military policies that spread to Eastern Europe and brought a new warmth to Soviet-American relations. Suddenly, in 1991, the new policies undermined the Communist system and broke up the Soviet Union.

RECORD OF COMMUNIST EXPANSION FROM 1939 TO 1992

OUTRIGHT ANNEXATIONS	LOCAL COMMUNIST PARTIES SEIZE CONTROL
BY THE SOVIET UNION 1. *Countries:* Estonia, Latvia, and Lithuania. 2. *Territories:* from Czechoslovakia, Finland, Germany, Japan, Poland, and Romania. BY CHINA 1. *Country:* Tibet.	1. *In Europe:* Albania, Bulgaria, Czechoslovakia, East Germany, Hungary, Poland, Romania, and Yugoslavia. 2. *In Asia:* Cambodia, China, Laos, Mongolia, North Korea, South Yemen, and Vietnam. 3. *In America:* Cuba 4. *In Africa:* Angola, Ethiopia, and Mozambique.

THE SOVIET UNION AND ITS SATELLITES

1. **Meaning of Satellites.** A *satellite* is a heavenly body that orbits a larger body. People used the word throughout the cold war to describe the Soviet-dominated nations of Eastern and Central Europe: Bulgaria, Czechoslovakia, East Germany, Hungary, Poland, and Romania. Their relationship to the Soviet Union was similar to that of protectorates to a mother country.

The satellite nations (self-proclaimed *people's republics*) had governments that essentially imitated Soviet practices. (*a*) They were dictatorships, each controlled by its own Communist party. (*b*) They nationalized industry, tried to collectivize agriculture, and adopted centrally controlled economies. (*c*) They denied many civil liberties and restricted free cultural expression. (*d*) In Poland and Hungary, both predominantly Roman Catholic, the governments harassed the Catholic Church and at times arrested members of the clergy, most notably Hungary's Cardinal *Mindszenty*.

2. **Establishment of Satellites.** To help local Communist parties take over and maintain control, the Soviet Union (*a*) fostered Communist regimes in Eastern and Central Europe as its armies pursued the retreating Germans in the final phase of World War II, (*b*) trained local Communists in tactics and leadership, (*c*) provided military equipment and advisers for local Communist forces, and (*d*) kept Soviet troops in Eastern and Central Europe.

3. **Methods of Soviet Control.** (*a*) Soviet specialists in political, economic, and military matters "advised" the satellite governments. (*b*) The Soviet Union tied the satellite economies to its own by trade treaties. (*c*) Soviet military forces were stationed in some satellite countries; on occasion they intervened to compel satellite conformity to Soviet policy. (*d*) Soviet generals headed a unified military command of Soviet and satellite forces in the *Warsaw Pact*.

✓ IRON CURTAIN

As part of the cold war, Communist regimes kept their people from free contact with Western ideas. They established restrictions on visitors, newspapers, magazines, books, and movies; they jammed Western radio broadcasts, especially *Radio Free Europe* and *Radio Liberty*. Speaking at a time when this barrier between the Communist nations and the West was first appearing, British leader Winston Churchill called it the "iron curtain."

CHANGES IN THE COMMUNIST WORLD

1. **National Communism in Yugoslavia Since 1945.** *Josip Broz,* known as *Marshal Tito,* Communist ruler of Yugoslavia, defied Stalin and pursued nationalist policies. Tito was able to act independently because Yugoslavia was not occupied by Soviet troops and does not border on the Soviet Union.

Stalin and his allies sought to overthrow Tito by economic pressure, propaganda, and subversion. Those efforts failed. After Stalin's death, the Soviet Union patched up relations with Yugoslavia to a degree. Nonetheless, Yugoslavia remained free of Soviet domination.

To enable Yugoslavia to resist Soviet pressure, Western nations extended aid: loans, food, trade, diplomatic support, and even military equipment.

Yugoslavia used a federal form of government to unite six regions (called republics) with a history of quarreling. Until Tito's death in 1980, differences among the republics were kept in check. Afterward, separatist tendencies appeared. Smaller republics like Slovenia and Croatia resented what they saw as an attempt by Serbia, the largest republic, to become dominant.

2. **Power Struggle Following Stalin's Death in 1953.** The death of Joseph Stalin touched off a bitter struggle for power among the top Soviet communists. *Nikita Khrushchev* became First Secretary of the Communist party, a position that Stalin had used to rise to absolute power. Khrushchev eliminated his chief rivals. One was executed; others were deposed from positions of importance. In 1958 Khrushchev assumed the premiership of the Soviet Union.

The struggle for power after Stalin's death gave the world an unusual glimpse of the conflict that could exist within the Soviet dictatorship—a conflict that was usually kept well hidden below the surface.

3. **Downgrading of Stalin (1956).** Stalin used every means of propaganda to encourage hero-worship of himself as a great teacher, leader, and military genius. In 1956 Khrushchev began an all-out attack to downgrade Stalin in the eyes of the Soviet people. Khrushchev condemned Stalin for *(a)* purges of military and political leaders on false charges, *(b)* blunders in foreign affairs, *(c)* terror against innocent Soviet citizens, and *(d)* personal cowardice during World War II. After Khrushchev's denunciation of Stalin, the Communist party spread the new anti-Stalin line.

In Eastern Europe the anti-Stalin campaign strengthened the Titoist doctrine of national communism and helped set off upheavals, especially in Poland and Hungary.

4. Uprising in Poland (1956). The Polish people engaged in strikes and demonstrations (a) to achieve better living conditions and (b) to end Soviet domination. *Wladyslaw Gomulka,* who had been imprisoned as a Titoist, regained the leadership of the Polish Communist party and announced that Poland would seek its own road to socialism. Khrushchev was alarmed by Poland's trend toward independence, but Gomulka reassured him that Poland would remain Communist and allied with the Soviet Union. Khrushchev thereupon pledged not to interfere in Poland's internal affairs.

By this bloodless revolution Poland achieved (a) a measure of independence in domestic matters, enabling Gomulka to end the forced collectivization of agriculture, and (b) expulsion of Soviet agents from positions of authority over the Polish army, economy, and government.

5. Revolution in Hungary (1956). The Hungarian people revolted for (a) better living conditions, (b) the withdrawal of Soviet troops, and (c) full national independence. *Imre Nagy,* a Titoist, became head of the government, appointed non-Communists to his cabinet, and demanded the immediate withdrawal of Soviet forces. Nagy announced Hungary's neutrality in the cold war and withdrawal from the Warsaw Pact.

Such anti-Soviet moves were more than Khrushchev would permit. Soviet troops seized all of Hungary and suppressed the Hungarian *freedom fighters.* Thousands of Hungarians were killed or deported to Siberia; almost 200,000 fled their native

**Having trouble
keeping them in orbit.**

Ellenwood in the Arizona Daily Star

land. The Soviets smashed the Nagy government, replacing it with a puppet Hungarian regime under *Janos Kadar*.

6. Split Between the Soviet Union and China (By 1963). See pages 598–599.

7. Removal of Khrushchev (1964). In a surprise development, Khrushchev was removed, by collective action of the other top Communists, from his positions as First Secretary of the Communist party and as Premier. In *Pravda*, the Communist party newspaper, Khrushchev was denounced for "harebrained scheming, immature conclusions, and hasty decisions." Khrushchev was succeeded as First Secretary by *Leonid Brezhnev*. Khrushchev's removal, according to Western observers, was caused by his worsening of the dispute with Communist China and his failure to improve the economy.

8. Invasion of Czechoslovakia (1968). *Alexander Dubcek* became head of the Czechoslovak Communist party and began a program of liberalization. Dubcek lifted censorship of press, radio, and television and permitted non-Communists to form political groups. He said that Czechoslovakia would seek trade and loans from the West. To reassure the Soviet Union, Dubcek asserted that Czechoslovakia remained Communist and loyal to the Warsaw Pact.

Soviet leaders, however, feared that the Czechoslovak reforms might spur similar movements in the other satellite nations. Soviet forces, supported by troops of four Warsaw Pact nations—East Germany, Poland, Hungary, and Bulgaria—occupied Czechoslovakia. The Soviets compelled Czechoslovakia to reestablish censorship, ban non-Communist political groups, accept Soviet advisers, consent to the stationing of Soviet troops, and replace Dubcek as head of the Czechoslovak Communist party with the more amenable *Gustav Husak*.

The Soviet invasion of Czechoslovakia, condemned by many Western and neutral nations, was also condemned by three Communist states—Yugoslavia, Romania, and China—and by West European Communist parties. Those Communist groups rejected the Soviets' claim to have saved Czechoslovakia from "counter-revolutionary forces." They also rejected the Soviet assertion that whenever a Communist nation endangered socialism at home or in other Communist countries, the Soviet Union had the duty to intervene with military force—an assertion termed the *Brezhnev Doctrine*.

9. Recurrent Unrest in Poland

a. 1970–1979. Polish workers felt their earnings threatened by a new wage incentive system. When the government upped the prices of food, fuel, and clothing in 1970, workers rioted. Another increase in food prices in 1976 touched off more riots.

Religion also played a role in the Poles' resistance to Communist rule. Karol Cardinal Wojtyla of Poland was elected Pope in 1978 and took the name *John Paul II*. He was the first Polish pontiff in history. In 1979 the Pope visited his heavily Roman Catholic homeland, where he was warmly received by huge crowds. The Pope's visit spurred Polish nationalism, intensified religious fervor, and raised expectations of greater personal freedom.

b. 1980–1984. Aroused by sharp meat price increases, workers walked off their jobs. In Gdansk, a Baltic seaport, shipyard workers selected a strike committee headed by *Lech Walesa*. The workers demanded a free and independent labor union with the right to strike. After two months of turmoil, the Polish regime accepted most of the workers' demands. *Solidarity*—the 10-million-member independent Polish labor union headed by Lech Walesa—developed a measure of power and authority separate from the Communist party.

COLLAPSE OF COMMUNISM IN EASTERN EUROPE (1989–1990)

Responding to economic disasters and public unrest, several nations of Eastern Europe began reforms in the 1980's. As early as 1982, for example, Hungary began taking steps to decentralize its economy and promote private enterprise on a limited scale. Few observers, however, predicted the revolutionary upheaval that broke out in Eastern Europe in 1989 and swept aside Communist rule in almost all the countries of this region in less than six months' time. The Soviet Union did not interfere.

1. Free Elections in Poland. In June 1989, in Poland's first free elections since 1947, Solidarity won many more legislative seats than the Communists. A Solidarity member, *Tadeusz Mazowiecki*, became Premier. In December 1990, voters elected Lech Walesa, the Solidarity leader, to be Poland's President.

2. Pattern of Revolt in Other Countries. Following Poland's example, people in other East European countries demanded immediate change. Typically, Communist power collapsed in three stages. (*a*) Yielding to public pressure, the old-guard leaders stepped down in favor of younger, reform-minded Communists. (*b*) The new leaders agreed to multiparty systems. (*c*) In free elections, non-Communists overwhelmingly defeated Communist candidates.

By the end of 1989, the first two stages of this process were successfully accomplished in Hungary, Bulgaria, East Germany, and Czechoslovakia. The third stage, free elections, came in early 1990. The last of Eastern Europe's Communist governments to fall was that of Albania in 1991.

In only one nation did the popular revolt against communism take a violent turn. In Romania, revolutionaries captured the Communist dictator, *Nikolai Ceausescu*. They hastily executed him and his wife Elena in December 1989.

3. Fall of the Berlin Wall. The most dramatic episode in the collapse of European communism was the pulling down of the wall that had divided the two sections of Berlin since 1961. On November 9, 1989, Berliners gleefully attacked the wall with sledgehammers when East Germany's Communist leaders announced that people could freely cross the borders into West Germany. On December 7, East Germany set free elections for May 1990. In late 1990, East Germany and West Germany were reunified as one Germany.

IMPACT OF CHANGE ON EASTERN EUROPE

While celebrating the end of Communist dictatorships, the countries of Eastern Europe faced severe economic and political challenges as they tried to adjust to the demands of a rapidly changing world.

1. Adjusting to a Free-Market Economy. Having lived for more than 40 years under communism, the new leaders of Eastern Europe considered heavy-handed state control of the economy to be an unworkable system. They were eager to adopt the ways of the free market. But changing from one system to its complete opposite was excruciatingly difficult.

Poland's new government removed subsidies and price controls. Food prices soared. Many workers lost their jobs. Rebelling against the painful changes, Polish voters replaced a reform government in 1993 with one led by the *Democratic Left Alliance (DLA)*, a party dominated by former Communists. The DLA promised to slow down (but not reverse) the pace of reforms.

Poland's problems were not unique. Other countries in the region experienced similar pain.

2. Ethnic Splintering. Another development was the breakup of some countries due to rivalries among their many ethnic groups and nationalities.

a. Civil War in Yugoslavia. Four of Yugoslavia's six republics—Slovenia, Croatia, Bosnia-Herzegovina, and Macedonia—declared independence in 1991 and 1992. Only two republics remained in the Yugoslav federation—Serbia, which had dominated the old union, and Montenegro.

Civil wars broke out as Croatia and Bosnia divided along linguistic and religious lines—Roman Catholic Croats vs. Orthodox Christian Serbs vs. the many Muslims of Bosnia-Herzegovina. Serbs (in Croatia and Bosnia) and Croats (in Bosnia) objected to their minority status within the newly independent republics. Those groups formed armies and fought against the newly independent governments. They demanded more autonomy—(1) separate regional governments having self-rule within the new nations, or (2) independence for their own "mini-states," or (3) reattachment of their regions to a "homeland" (either Serbia or Croatia).

The civil wars have greatly alarmed other nations—after all, the Balkan wars of 1912–1913 are often considered a major cause of World War I. The U.N., the European Union, and NATO all took part in efforts to restore peace.

b. Division of Czechoslovakia. Seventy-four years after Czechoslovakia's birth, which united the Czech and Slovak peoples in a federation, the country divided peacefully on January 1, 1993. Many Slovaks, who had made up one third of the population, resented what they saw as domination by the Czechs. The split was worked out by elected leaders of the Czech Republic and Slovakia, who rejected demands for a referendum. Polls had indicated that a majority of the Czechoslovak people did not favor the breakup.

RESHAPING THE SOVIET UNION

1. **The Old Order Crumbles.** President Gorbachev's program of reforms unleashed a whirlwind of debate and dissent within the Soviet Union. In 1991 Communist hard-liners tried to overthrow Gorbachev. The coup aroused popular indignation and failed within a week. Shortly after, the Communist party lost its grip on power, and the central government collapsed. A new group of self-styled democrats—such as *Boris Yeltsin,* the elected president of the Russian republic—came to the forefront.

2. **The New Order.** Each of the 15 republics of the Soviet Union claimed the right to run its own affairs. In 1992 most decided to become part of a *Commonwealth of Independent States* proposed by Russia, Belarus, and Ukraine. Gorbachev resigned from office, and power in the new Commonwealth shifted to Russian President Yeltsin. (Russia is the largest republic. In the past, the names Russia and the Soviet Union were used interchangeably. Now the name Russia refers only to the republic.)

The republics are going through the difficult and painful process of developing a *market economy* patterned after economic systems in Western industrial nations. Such an economy encourages private enterprise and lets producers and consumers, instead of the central government, determine what should be produced and at what price.

Part 3. The United States Promotes the Economic and Military Strength of the Free World

FOREIGN AID

TRUMAN DOCTRINE

1. **Purpose.** In 1947 Greece, in economic chaos as a result of Axis occupation in World War II, was under attack from Communist guerrilla bands. Turkey was under pressure from Russia for concessions in the Dardanelles, the straits connecting the Black Sea and the Mediterranean. If successful, these Communist efforts would have expanded Russian influence into the eastern Mediterranean. President Truman therefore announced that "it must be the policy of the United States to support free peoples" against direct and indirect Communist aggression. This statement became known as the *Truman Doctrine*. Congress responded by overwhelmingly approving economic and military aid for Greece and Turkey.

2. **Effects.** *(a)* With American economic aid, Greece revived its economy. With American military aid, Greece put down Communist guerrilla attacks. Also, Yugoslavia halted aid to the Greek guerrillas following Tito's split with Russia. *(b)* Bolstered by American economic and military aid, Turkey withstood Russian demands for control of the Dardanelles.

MARSHALL PLAN

1. Reasons for Offer. In 1947 Secretary of State *George C. Marshall* offered American economic aid to all European nations (including Russia and its satellites) to enable them to recover from the destruction of World War II. He said, "Our policy is directed not against any country or doctrine but against hunger, poverty, desperation, and chaos."

The United States wanted to help Europe in order to (a) improve living conditions, (b) end the need for continued American relief funds, (c) revive a mutually profitable trade between the United States and Europe, and (d) lessen the danger of Communism in Western Europe. (Especially in France and Italy, Communist parties had a considerable following.)

2. European Recovery Program (ERP). The Marshall Plan, officially the *European Recovery Program,* aided most non-Communist nations of Europe: Great Britain, France, Austria, Belgium, Denmark, Greece, Iceland, Ireland, Italy, Luxembourg, the Netherlands, Norway, Portugal, Sweden, Switzerland, Turkey, and West Germany. They cooperated with each other and with the United States to achieve "recovery, not relief." The United States provided $12.5 billion, most of which was spent in this country for foodstuffs, raw materials, and machinery.

3. Achievements. During its four years (1948–1951) the Marshall Plan helped strengthen non-Communist Europe. It (a) promoted strong economic recovery, (b) furthered political stability, (c) reduced Communist influence, and (d) encouraged West European economic unity.

4. Russian Opposition. Russia condemned the Marshall Plan as a scheme of American capitalists to gain economic and political control over Europe and announced that it would exert every effort to defeat the Plan. (a) Russia and its European satellite nations refused America's offer of Marshall Plan aid. (b) Russia initiated an economic aid program of its own, the *Council of Mutual Economic Assistance (COMECON).* This program competed with the Marshall Plan by bringing about closer economic relations between Russia and its satellites.

POINT FOUR PROGRAM

In his 1949 Inaugural Address, President Truman reaffirmed America's opposition to Russian expansion. As *Point Four* in America's effort to contain Communism, Truman proposed a "bold new program" to utilize our scientific and industrial knowledge to give technical assistance to underdeveloped nations.

Under the Point Four Program, Congress annually has appropriated considerable sums of money to meet the requests of developing nations in Latin America, the Middle East, Africa, and Asia. The United States has sent technical specialists to help increase agricultural and industrial output, encourage urban development, improve government administration, promote public health, and advance education. The Point Four Program has made gratifying contributions in bettering conditions in underdeveloped lands.

EISENHOWER DOCTRINE

In 1957 President Eisenhower warned that the economic and political instability of the Middle East made it vulnerable to Communist infiltration. Eisenhower offered the Middle East nations (1) a program of economic and military aid, and (2) armed assistance, upon request, to repel open Communist aggression. The *Eisenhower Doctrine* was welcomed by Lebanon and Saudi Arabia but was denounced by Egypt and Syria as an American plot to dominate the Arab world. (Under the Eisenhower Doctrine, the United States in 1958 sent troops into Lebanon to protect that nation's government.)

PEACE CORPS

In 1961 President Kennedy set up a new foreign aid agency, the Peace Corps. It enrolls idealistic volunteers who receive token pay, work in needy countries, and live as do the local people. Peace Corps volunteers range from new college graduates to experienced technicians and business people.

The Peace Corps was conceived as a double-barreled tool: (1) for helping people in need, and (2) for countering Soviet influence in the developing nations. Most projects were in Africa, Asia, and Latin America. After the cold war ended, Russia and other formerly Communist nations invited Peace Corps volunteers to help teach business skills to budding entrepreneurs.

More than 90 countries have welcomed Peace Corps workers.

AMERICAN FOREIGN AID: AN OVERVIEW

The United States continues to spend substantial sums for foreign aid—annually several billion dollars, which amounts to 3 percent or less of our national budget. Currently, American military aid is administered by the Defense Department and economic aid by the State Department's *Agency for International Development (AID)*.

From 1945 to the present, the United States has extended over $220 billion in aid to some 140 countries. Of this total, 34 percent has been for military supplies and services and 66 percent for economic and technical aid. One-third of American aid has been in the form of loans that are repayable; two-thirds has been in the form of grants that are outright gifts.

At first U.S. foreign aid went chiefly to Europe, especially Britain, France, and West Germany. As Europe recovered from World War II, the United States extended economic and technical aid to the developing nations. As a result of Communist aggression in Korea in 1950, military aid went to Asia, especially South Korea, Japan, Taiwan, and South Vietnam. In the 1960's the United States extended aid to most countries of Latin America. During the 1970's and

1980's, aid flowed heavily to the Middle East, especially Israel and Egypt. Since the end of the cold war, Russia and other former Communist nations have joined the list of recipients of U.S. aid.

CRITICISMS OF OUR FOREIGN AID PROGRAM

American leaders argue that foreign aid serves the national interest and helps U.S. farmers and businesses make sales abroad. However, critics claim that foreign aid (1) burdens American taxpayers, (2) diverts funds from projects at home, (3) worsens the U.S. trade deficit, (4) is characterized by inefficient administration, waste, and corruption, and (5) creates competition for American manufactures and farmers.

Once the cold war ended, critics of U.S. foreign aid observed that the containment of communism was no longer a major goal. Congress began to cut back on foreign aid in the 1990's.

FOREIGN AID PROGRAMS OF OTHER NATIONS

Many other industrial nations also have extensive foreign aid programs. In 1989, for the first time, Japan exceeded the United States in the amount of foreign aid dispensed.

At the height of the cold war, Communist leaders boasted that their systems would outstrip capitalism in peaceful competition. Communist nations challenged the industrial democracies by offering economic and military assistance to many developing nations. Soviet and Chinese aid was chiefly in the form of loans, skilled personnel, and military hardware. It went both to Communist-ruled countries like Cuba and North Korea and to non-Communist countries like Argentina, India, Egypt, Indonesia, Iraq, and Syria.

Cuba, in particular, suffered after the collapse of the Soviet Union resulted in a cutoff of aid and a sharp drop in trade. (Check the Index.)

EUROPEAN ECONOMIC UNITY

THE EUROPEAN UNION

1. First Steps. The *Inner Six* West European nations—Belgium, France, Italy, Luxembourg, the Netherlands, and West Germany—having cooperated under the Marshall Plan, moved toward further economic unity. In 1952 the six established an authority to manage their coal and steel resources in the interests of the entire community. In 1957 they formed a European Atomic Energy Commission to spur atomic research and increase the production of electric power.

2. Common Market. In 1957 the Inner Six agreed to join in a tariff union. They set up a *European Economic Community* to (*a*) eliminate internal tariff barriers and (*b*) establish a unified tariff system on imports from outside the tariff union area. European leaders wanted a free-trade area—a *Common Market* without human-made barriers to the movement of goods, capital, and labor. The EEC created a federal structure with a weak parliament (the *European Parliament*) and a weak executive (the *European Commission*). The main decision-making body was a *Council of Ministers* in which each member nation had one vote.

3. Expansion. Over the years the community added new members and took further steps toward unity. Britain, Ireland, and Denmark officially joined the Community in 1973. Three relatively poor nations from southern Europe—Greece, Spain, and Portugal—joined in the 1980's. In 1994 the community assumed a new name, the *European Union*. It admitted Sweden, Finland, and Austria in 1995, raising its membership from 12 to 15. Other nations—Turkey and the former Communist nations in Eastern Europe—also want to join.

4. Lowering Barriers. At the end of 1992, the Community removed most barriers to the movement of people and goods among member nations. Leaders planned further steps, such as creating a central bank and a common currency.

A RIVAL TRADE GROUP: EFTA

In the 1950's, some countries feared that joining the Common Market would force them to give up economic sovereignty. Seven nations, known as the *Outer Seven*, created the *European Free Trade Association (EFTA)* in 1960. The original members were Austria, Denmark, Great Britain, Norway, Portugal, Sweden, and Switzerland.

1. EFTA's Goals. EFTA's goals were limited to (*a*) reducing tariffs and quotas and (*b*) encouraging bilateral agreements to lower barriers to agricultural trade. EFTA did not create uniform external tariffs. It had no parliament and only a small administration.

2. Growth and Change. EFTA later gained new members: Finland, Iceland, and Liechtenstein. But it also lost members to the European Union.

CREATING A EUROPEAN ECONOMIC AREA

The EEC and EFTA agreed in 1991 to join in a new, more extensive common market known as the *European Economic Area*, effective in 1993. EEC and EFTA kept their own identities within the new, 19-nation trading bloc, with the EEC continuing its march toward greater economic and political unity. Some 380 million people lived in the 19 nations. National parliaments had to ratify the treaty before it took effect.

The European Economic Area provided for (1) free movement of goods, services, capital, and people; (2) acceptance by the EFTA nations of EEC rules on such matters as consumer protection, environmental protection, and labor rules,

(3) establishment of a new European court for the settlement of disputes, and (4) creation of a joint *Council of Ministers*.

MILITARY ALLIANCES

NORTH ATLANTIC TREATY ORGANIZATION (NATO)

1. Free World Fears. In 1948 the free world nations were shocked by three Russian-inspired aggressions: (1) a coup d'etat in Czechoslovakia that eliminated democratic leaders and gave the Communists complete control of the country, (2) pressure upon Finland to accept a mutual assistance pact with the Soviet Union that in effect compelled Finland to adhere to Russian foreign policy, and (3) a Russian attempt to drive the Western powers out of Berlin by a surface route blockade. Made fearful by these Russian moves, the free world nations formed the North Atlantic Treaty Organization.

2. Defensive Military Alliance. In 1949 twelve nations—Britain, France, Belgium, the Netherlands, Luxembourg, Denmark, Iceland, Italy, Norway, Portugal, Canada, and the United States—signed the *North Atlantic Pact*. They declared that (*a*) they would consider an attack on any one of them as an attack on all, and (*b*) they would come to the defense of the attacked member nation with armed force if necessary. The American Senate overwhelmingly ratified the pact.

NATO admitted Greece and Turkey in 1952, West Germany in 1955, and Spain in 1982, bringing its membership to 16.

3. NATO Army. In 1950 the member nations authorized a NATO army. Its head, the *Supreme Allied Commander in Europe (SACEUR)*, has always been an American. NATO headquarters, located in Belgium, are known as the *Supreme Headquarters of the Allied Powers in Europe (SHAPE)*.

The United States assigned over 300,000 personnel—army, navy, and air force—to Europe as part of the NATO military establishment and gave much military equipment for NATO use. Other member nations also assigned personnel and equipment to the NATO command. NATO's military strength, however, was far less than that of the Soviet Union and its European satellites.

4. Strains in the NATO Alliance

  a. Nuclear Fears. People in NATO nations worried that, in case of a Soviet-American conflict, Western Europe would suffer nuclear devastation. Some Europeans opposed such NATO policies as (1) *forward defense*, which called for maintaining large armies in Europe to block any Soviet invasion at the East German border, and (2) *flexible response*, under which NATO may use conventional, nuclear, or chemical arms to respond to an attack by conventional forces.

  b. The Suez Crisis of 1956. The United States opposed a British-French attack on Egypt and occupation of the Suez Canal in coordination with an Israeli

Europe: Cold War Alliances

attack on Egypt's Sinai region. Pressure from the United States helped force all three to withdraw. (See pages 532–533.)

    c. French Nationalism and Withdrawal from NATO Command. President Charles de Gaulle of France was a French nationalist who resented American dominance of NATO. In 1966 de Gaulle claimed that NATO was obsolete because (1) the development of missiles with nuclear warheads had made NATO defenses insignificant, and (2) the Soviet Union had adopted a policy of peaceful coexistence. Accordingly, de Gaulle withdrew all French forces from NATO command and demanded the removal of NATO troops, chiefly American and Canadian, from French soil. However, de Gaulle pledged that France would remain a member of the North Atlantic Pact. While other NATO members deplored de Gaulle's moves, they had no choice but to yield to his demands. All NATO troops left France, and SHAPE headquarters moved from near Paris to Belgium. French presidents following de Gaulle have maintained his NATO policies.

    d. The Vietnam War. Many Europeans opposed American policy in Vietnam, and NATO governments were reluctant to offer full support. (Check the Index.)

    e. The 1973 Arab-Israeli War. The major European members of NATO, yielding to Arab oil embargo threats, refused permission to the United States to use facilities on their soil for transporting military equipment to Israel. Their refusal compelled the United States to transport the equipment by a more difficult route.

f. Hostility Between Greece and Turkey over Cyprus. Although Greece and Turkey both belong to NATO, the two countries have traditionally been enemies. In recent years they have clashed over the island of Cyprus in particular. In 1974 Greece's military rulers backed a Cyprus coup that aimed to unite the island with Greece. The coup failed as Turkish armies responded by occupying 40 percent of the island. In Greece, the military government collapsed, and Greece returned to civilian and democratic rule.

During the Cyprus dispute, Greece and Turkey both criticized the United States. Greece blamed the Americans for not preventing the Turkish invasion of Cyprus. Turkey condemned the action of the United States Congress—cutting off military aid to Turkey—and ordered American forces out of posts in Turkey used to monitor Soviet military activities. Congress lifted the embargo on Turkey in 1978, after three years. Greece withdrew its forces from NATO's military wing in 1974 but rejoined in 1980.

In 1983 Turkish Cypriotes declared their portion of Cyprus an independent republic—the *Turkish Republic of Northern Cyprus.* This move was condemned by the Greek Cypriotes, Greece, Britain, and the United States. Turkey immediately recognized the new republic, although the United States warned that the action would cause problems for NATO and weaken relations with the United States.

g. Poland. When Poland's Communist regime instituted martial law in 1980 and later banned the independent Solidarity union, the United States imposed economic sanctions against both Poland and the Soviet Union. France and West Germany, in particular, were concerned over their considerable trade with the Soviet Union and declined to take comparable action.

h. The Medium-Range-Missile Issue. In 1979 the NATO members in Western Europe, considering the almost 400 Soviet SS-20 nuclear missiles already aimed at them, agreed to accept American Pershing 2 missiles. But, in many European countries, public opposition to the decision was strong.

The United States and the Soviet Union began negotiations in 1981 on the reduction or elimination of medium-range missiles like the SS-20 and Pershing 2. These *Intermediate Nuclear Force (INF) Talks* took place in Geneva. When the first Pershing 2 missiles arrived in Europe in 1983, the Soviets broke off the INF talks, but the discussions resumed in 1985. Agreement was finally reached and an *INF Treaty* signed by the superpowers in 1987, calling for a complete ban on medium-range missiles.

i. Efforts to Restrict Technology Exports. In order to restrict the export of high technology to the Communist bloc, the United States and 16 industrial allies (14 Western European countries, Japan, and Australia) founded the *Co-ordinating Committee for Multilateral Export Controls (COCOM),* which must approve any exports of sensitive items. The United States has tended to want a more restrictive policy than European nations and businesses want. In recent years the American monopoly on high technology has declined, and other nations have grown more assertive in pushing for liberalized export policies.

In the early 1980's, the United States opposed Western European participation in construction of a 2,800-mile natural gas pipeline from Siberia across the Soviet Union and Czechoslovakia to Western Europe. Despite American objections, West Germany, France, and Italy signed contracts for the purchase of Siberian gas. West German and French manufacturers agreed to sell the Soviets necessary pipeline equipment, and a group of French banks provided a large loan. The pipeline began delivering gas to Western Europe in 1984.

Since 1985, COCOM has significantly eased controls on exports to China.

j. Role of Communists in NATO Governments. In the 1970's and 1980's, Communist party representatives participated as junior partners in coalition governments in some NATO nations. American leaders tried to discourage such cooperation, with little success. However, Communists later left the governments as a result of political changes within the nations involved.

(1) *Portugal.* In 1974 an army coup ended right-wing dictatorial rule but plunged Portugal into political chaos. For a time the Portuguese Communist party seemed likely to gain control, but an attempted leftist coup was suppressed in 1975 and in elections the following year the Communists received less than 15 percent of the vote.

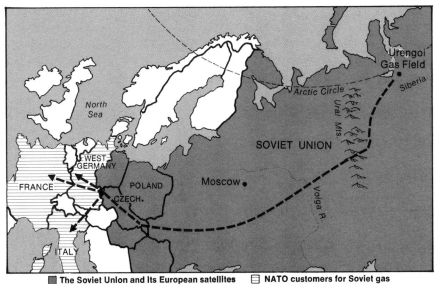

■ The Soviet Union and Its European satellites   ▤ NATO customers for Soviet gas

Soviet Gas Pipeline

(2) *Italy.* Following the 1976 parliamentary elections, the Christian Democrats formed a minority government; however, their ability to secure a parliamentary majority depended on the tacit cooperation of Italy's Communist party, which had the second largest bloc in parliament. The Communists indicated that they would accept this situation for the time being but that their goal was full membership in a coalition government.

In 1979 the Communists, having received no cabinet positions, caused the fall of the minority government. Thereafter Italy was governed by coalitions that excluded the Communists. (For details, check the Index.)

(3) *France.* In 1981, François Mitterrand was elected president and his Socialist party gained a strong majority in the National Assembly. Mitterrand, who took a hard line toward the Soviet Union, nevertheless accepted a cabinet that included four Communists.

The United States voiced grave concern over this development as setting an undesirable precedent for other West European countries. The Communists left the French government in a 1984 cabinet shakeup.

5. Reshaping NATO in the 1990's. Responding to the sudden collapse of Eastern Europe's Communist governments and the trend toward democracy throughout the region, NATO leaders reshaped the alliance.

a. Military Measures.

(1) *Reduction of Nuclear Weapons.* In 1991, as part of an overall reduction of nuclear forces, President Bush announced the withdrawal of all United States ground-based nuclear weapons from NATO positions. American nuclear-armed submarines remained available for Europe's defense.

(2) *Reduction of Armed Forces.* NATO announced cuts of 50 percent in its armed forces. Remaining forces were designed to respond to possible threats arising from instability in the formerly Communist-ruled nations.

(3) *Response to the Civil War in Bosnia.* NATO cooperated with the U.N. and the European Union in trying to bring the civil war in Bosnia to an end. In 1994, for the first time in its history, NATO engaged in military action, shooting down Bosnian Serb warplanes. In 1995 NATO planes bombed Serbian positions and forced a fragile cease-fire.

b. Political Measures: Relations With Central Europe. Many of Central Europe's new democracies wanted to join NATO, with several nations requesting formal guarantees of their security. Russia's government frowned on that idea. Hard-line Russian nationalists were even more outspoken in their opposition, describing an expanded NATO as a serious threat to Russian security.

As an alternative, NATO in 1994 offered a sort of partial membership to all former Soviet bloc and neutral nations in Europe, but NATO would not guarantee their security. While disappointed, several governments began to work out arrangements for joining the so-called "Partnership for Peace."

SOUTHEAST ASIA TREATY ORGANIZATION (SEATO)

1. **Defensive Military Alliance (1954).** Eight nations—the United States, Great Britain, France, Australia, New Zealand, Thailand, Pakistan, and the Philippines—established SEATO. Each member nation (a) agreed that armed aggression against any other member would "endanger its own peace and safety" and pledged to "meet the common danger in accordance with its constitutional processes"; (b) recognized that civil wars might involve foreign aggression; and (c) offered to aid, upon request, the Southeast Asian states of Cambodia, Laos, and South Vietnam.

2. **Weaknesses of SEATO.** (a) SEATO lacked a unified armed force and military command. (b) SEATO's main strength came from its non-Asian members. (c) Four important Southeast Asian nations—India, Burma, Ceylon (Sri Lanka), and Indonesia—refused to join SEATO. These nations sought to remain neutral in the cold war. (d) France refrained from active participation in SEATO. (e) Displeased by lack of SEATO support in its quarrels with India, Pakistan in 1972 withdrew from SEATO.

3. **End of SEATO (1976).** Following the Communist triumphs in Indo-China, SEATO was "phased out."

ADDITIONAL AMERICAN MILITARY ALLIANCES

Today the United States has military alliances with more than 40 nations. In addition to NATO, United States commitments include:

1. **The Rio Inter-American Defense Treaty (1947)** between the United States and the Latin American nations of the Organization of American States (OAS) provides for the common defense of the Western Hemisphere. (In 1982 Argentina appealed to the OAS for support in its dispute with Britain over the Falkland Islands. The OAS approved a resolution—with the United States and three Latin American nations abstaining—that affirmed Argentine sovereignty over the Falklands but also declared that Argentina must obey the U.N. Security Council resolution and withdraw its occupation forces from the Falklands. (For details, check the Index.)

2. **The ANZUS Pact (1951)** between Australia, New Zealand, and the United States provides that each nation (a) consider an attack upon one of the others as dangerous to its own safety, and (b) act to meet the common danger. (In 1984 New Zealand banned from its waters nuclear-powered and nuclear-carrying American warships. In response, the United States cut New Zealand out of ANZUS and suspended all military cooperation with New Zealand.)

3. Bilateral mutual defense treaties with Japan, the Philippines, and South Korea pledge the United States to consider an attack on any of these as a common danger and to assist the nation attacked.

Also, the United States maintains military bases in Spain.

The purpose of the U.S. system of military alliances, which provided for many strategic American bases in countries ringing the Communist world, was to deter the Communists from aggression.

COMMUNIST MILITARY ALLIANCES

1. **Chinese-Soviet Treaty (1950).** The Soviet Union and Communist China signed a 30-year treaty of "friendship, alliance, and mutual aid" providing for mutual military aid in case of attack. The two nations quarreled in the late 1950's, undercutting their military alliance. The treaty expired in 1980.

2. **Warsaw Pact (1955).** In response to West Germany's joining NATO in 1955, the Soviet Union and its East European satellites formed their own military alliance called the Warsaw Pact. The alliance had a unified military command under a Soviet general. Besides the Soviet Union, members were Bulgaria, Czechoslovakia, East Germany, Hungary, Poland, and Romania.

The sudden move toward democracy by Eastern European nations sent shudders through the Warsaw Pact in the early 1990's. The pact was formally ended in July 1991, and the Soviets began withdrawing troops from the former satellites.

MULTIPLE-CHOICE QUESTIONS

1. The term that best characterizes American foreign policy since World War II is (1) isolationist (2) bipartisan (3) economy-minded (4) appeasement.

2. Which is the *least* valid argument for isolation today? (1) the opportunity for investment at home (2) the protection afforded by the oceans (3) the domestic problems challenging the country (4) the danger of war in Europe.

3. A bipartisan foreign policy is one upon which there is agreement between the (1) House of Representatives and Senate (2) United States and Great Britain (3) President and Secretary of State (4) two major parties.

4. All of the following are characteristics of a democracy *except* (1) majority rule and respect for minority rights (2) existence of man for the state (3) responsible citizenship (4) government of, by, and for the people.

5. The Russian leaders claimed that the government of the Soviet Union was democratic because (1) elections were held and citizens had the right to vote (2) party patronage was unknown (3) all workers were members of the Communist party (4) each citizen shared equally in goods produced.

6. Which of the following was true of Russia under Soviet rule? (1) Workers had the right to strike. (2) Writers were free to criticize the government. (3) Agricultural shortages were eliminated. (4) Schools were provided for all children.

7. Which is a characteristic of both capitalism and Communism? (1) use of capital (2) a predominantly free-enterprise system (3) government ownership of the major industries (4) government planning of production.

8. Which was common to the United States and Soviet Russia? (1) freedom of speech (2) one-party government (3) collective bargaining to determine wages (4) expansion of productive capacity.

9. What was the aim of the United States policy of containment? (1) encouraging the people of Soviet Russia to revolt against Communism (2) overthrowing the governments of the satellite nations in Eastern Europe (3) encircling Soviet Russia with a belt of neutral nations (4) preventing the further spread of Communism.

10. Which of these was created to counteract Soviet propaganda? (1) Comintern (2) Voice of America (3) American Legion (4) Veterans of Foreign Wars.

11. From 1917 to 1941, relations between the United States and the Soviet Union were (1) generally friendly (2) friendly until 1933, then unfriendly (3) generally unfriendly (4) unfriendly until 1939, then friendly.

12. Which group was made up entirely of Soviet satellites? (1) Denmark, Poland, Turkey (2) Czechoslovakia, Greece, Austria; (3) Bulgaria, East Germany, Poland (4) Hungary, Israel, Romania.

13. Estonia, Latvia, and Lithuania are (1) islands taken by Russia from Japan (2) Russian satellite nations in the Balkans (3) neutralist nations (4) independent nations that were part of the Soviet Union.

14. Under both Czarist and Communist rule, Russia's policy toward Turkey has been influenced by Russia's desire to gain control of (1) the Red Sea (2) Gibraltar (3) the Suez Canal (4) the Dardanelles.

15. The Truman Doctrine was a (1) proposal for the peaceful use of atomic energy (2) program for general disarmament (3) policy of extending aid to nations threatened by Communism (4) policy of giving technical aid to underdeveloped nations.

16. One purpose of the Marshall Plan was to (1) promote political reforms in France (2) convert Germany into an agricultural nation (3) encourage the economic recovery of Western Europe (4) compel the Soviet Union to withdraw its troops from Eastern Europe.

17. Originally, the Marshall Plan was an offer made to (1) all European nations (2) all U.N. members (3) only English-speaking nations (4) only anti-Communist nations.

18. Which of these countries did *not* receive aid under the Marshall Plan? (1) West Germany (2) Italy (3) France (4) Czechoslovakia.

19. The most significant result of the Marshall Plan was that it (1) increased American control over the European economy (2) helped to restore the economy of Western Europe (3) aided refugees from Soviet Russia (4) discouraged Western European efforts toward economic integration.

20. The primary purpose of the Point Four Program was to help underdeveloped areas by (1) furnishing technical aid (2) providing food for starving people (3) spreading information concerning the American way of life (4) providing military aid to resist Communist aggression.

21. The Truman and Eisenhower Doctrines were most similar in that both were designed to (1) reduce tariff barriers (2) end the Korean War (3) resist Communist aggression (4) aid the same nations.

22. A basic purpose of the Peace Corps is to provide (1) jobs for unemployed American youths (2) scholarships for Americans to study in foreign countries (3) aid to people in underdeveloped areas (4) relief to Arab refugees in the Middle East.

23. The term "Inner Six" referred to (1) a trade and economic association in Western Europe (2) the Communist parties in Western Europe that have expressed independence of Moscow domination (3) a major power bloc in the United Nations (4) the original members of NATO.

24. The purpose of the Schuman Plan was to (1) pool the coal and steel resources of several Western European nations (2) bring West Germany into the North Atlantic Treaty Organization (3) organize a European army (4) promote the Point Four Program.

25. The Common Market is essentially a (1) military alliance (2) federal government (3) tariff union (4) communications corporation.

26. Britain's application for membership in the Common Market was vetoed by (1) Russia (2) France (3) West Germany (4) the United States.

27. A major reason for creating the North Atlantic Treaty Organization (NATO) was to (1) supervise the West German government (2) protect member nations against Communist aggression (3) distribute Point Four funds (4) regulate world trade.

28. Two nations included in the North Atlantic Treaty Organization are (1) Switzerland and West Germany (2) Belgium and Sweden (3) the Netherlands and Italy (4) Ireland and Canada.

29. In which respect is our participation in NATO significant? (1) It is our first peacetime military alliance with any European nation. (2) It marks a return to the foreign policy of George Washington. (3) It nullifies the power of Congress to appropriate money for the armed forces. (4) It violates the U.N. Charter.

30. Which country was *not* a member of the Southeast Asia Treaty Organization? (1) Australia (2) Thailand (3) India (4) the Philippines.

MODIFIED TRUE-FALSE QUESTIONS

1. The Truman Doctrine was intended to keep Russian influence out of Turkey and *Egypt*.

2. The Communists sought to keep democratic ideas from their people by means of a barrier known as the *Warsaw Pact*.

3. One reason why the United States refused to recognize the Soviet Union between 1917 and 1933 was that the Soviet Union supported *world revolution*.

4. Although still a member of the North Atlantic Pact, *Germany* has withdrawn its military forces from the NATO army.

5. A purpose of the Eisenhower Doctrine was to halt Communist aggression in *Eastern Asia*.

6. The Point Four Program of the United States closely parallels the United Nations program of *technical assistance*.

7. A NATO member having a common frontier with the former Soviet Union is *Turkey*.

8. The two nations, now both members of NATO, that have fought each other twice in this century are France and *Italy*.

9. The Peace Corps was originated by President *Truman*.

10. The European Communist country that first successfully resisted Russian domination was *Hungary*.

ESSAY QUESTIONS

1. During the past 50 years, the United States has moved from a policy of isolation to a policy of active leadership in world affairs. Discuss *three* historical events or movements that have led to this change of policy.

2. It is customary for Communist countries to attempt to disguise themselves as democracies. *(a)* Describe *three* democratic features of life in the United States that did *not* exist

in the Soviet Union. *(b)* Discuss *two* devices used by the Soviet Union to give the impression that it was democratic. *(c)* Discuss *two* differences in economic life between the United States and the Soviet Union.

3. *(a)* How would you characterize our relations with the Soviet Union (1) during World War II, and (2) after World War II? Give *two* facts to support your characterization of *each* period. *(b)* Discuss *two* reasons to account for the drastic change in relations that took place following 1945.

4. To win the cold war, the Western democracies estimated as correctly as possible their own strengths and weaknesses as well as those of the Soviet Union and its satellites. *(a)* Describe *one* strength *and one* weakness of the Western democracies. *(b)* Describe *one* strength *and one* weakness of the Soviet Union and its satellites.

5. *(a)* Give *two* reasons why the United States has extended military and economic aid to foreign nations since the end of World War II. *(b)* Name *two* American foreign aid programs. *(c)* Explain *one* criticism of American foreign aid. *(d)* Discuss *one* reason why the Communist bloc undertook its own foreign aid program.

Part 4. The United States Faces Problems Throughout the World

GERMANY

ALLIED DECISIONS REGARDING GERMANY (1945)

At the Yalta and Potsdam Conferences and in other agreements, the United States, Britain, and Russia made several decisions concerning Germany.

1. Territory. The eastern provinces were detached from Germany, with part occupied by Russia but most under Polish control (see map below). These territorial changes were meant to be temporary, pending a German peace treaty. Russia and Poland, however, considered the changes as permanent. In 1975 the Western powers assented to these boundaries by signing the Helsinki Pact. (Check the Index.)

2. Occupation Zones. The rest of Germany was divided into four zones, with each of the Big Four powers—Russia, Britain, the United States, and France—governing one zone. Berlin, lying 110 miles inside the Russian zone, was likewise divided into four sections, with each of the Big Four controlling one section. The three Western Allies were guaranteed access to Berlin by surface and air routes across the Russian zone. These divisions also were meant to be temporary, pending a formal peace treaty for Germany.

3. Economy. The German economy was to be directed toward agriculture and peaceful industries. War industries were barred. Certain German factories and industrial equipment were to be dismantled and removed, chiefly to the Soviet Union, as partial reparation.

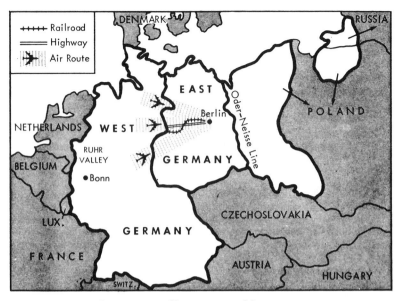

Germany Following World War II

The map shows the railroad, highway, and air routes guaranteed to the Western Allies for access across the Russian zone to Berlin.

4. Disarmament. Germany was to be disarmed so as to render her unable to wage aggressive warfare again.

5. Education. German schools were to work for the "development of democratic ideas." The Allies recognized that reeducation of the German people would be a long and difficult task.

6. Denazification. Nazism was to be wiped out completely. All Nazi organizations, including the Nazi party, Storm Troopers, and the Gestapo (secret police), were dissolved. Active Nazis were not to be allowed to hold public office or other positions of influence. War criminals were to be brought to trial.

WAR TRIALS

1. Nuremberg Trials. An *International Military Tribunal* met at Nuremberg (1945–1946) and tried Air Force Minister Hermann Goering and other top Nazi leaders. They were charged with crimes against humanity, violations of international law, and waging aggressive warfare. These trials, it was hoped, would serve to democratize Germany by exposing the evils of Nazism, would mark a step forward in international law, and would discourage future aggressors. The Tribunal found 19 of the 22 defendants guilty; it sentenced 12 to death and the others to prison.

2. In the American Zone. A special *United States Military Tribunal* held a series of trials for secondary Nazi leaders. *Alfred Krupp,* head of the Krupp munitions works, was sentenced to prison for exploiting slave labor and plundering Nazi-occupied countries. The United States later permitted West German *denazification courts* to try lesser Nazis. These courts were quite lenient, and many former Nazis regained positions of influence.

3. In the Russian Zone. At first, the Communists severely punished Nazi war criminals. After a short time, however, the Communists abandoned denazification trials and treated former Nazis leniently to gain their support.

THE WEST AND RUSSIA DISAGREE ON GERMANY

After World War II, the West and Russia came into conflict over Germany. Each side sought German support for itself. Western plans for German reunification that would swing Germany toward the West were rejected by Russia. Soviet plans for reunification that would bring Germany into the Communist camp were rejected by the West.

BERLIN BLOCKADE (1948–1949)

Under Stalin, Russia tried to drive the Western Allies out of Berlin by blockading the surface routes—roads, rails, and canals—between Berlin and the three Western zones of Germany. To thwart this *Berlin Blockade,* the Allies resorted to an *airlift.* For almost a year, the airlift supplied more than

Walt Partymiller, The Gazette and Daily, York, PA

Will we learn the lessons?

2 million West Berliners with food, medicine, and other necessities. The Soviets could halt the airlift by downing Allied planes but were unwilling to thus risk starting all-out war. They therefore abandoned the blockade.

From 1958 to 1961 the Soviets again threatened to drive the Western Allies from Berlin—in part to close a "showcase" of capitalism and democracy behind the Iron Curtain. (These threats were never implemented.)

DEVELOPMENTS IN WEST GERMANY

1. Establishment of the German Federal Republic. Unable to reach an agreement with Russia for German reunification, the three Western Allies in 1949 combined their zones to form the *Federal Republic of Germany* with its capital at *Bonn*. In 1955 West Germany was granted full sovereignty over domestic and foreign affairs (except for negotiations regarding German reunification and West Berlin) and was admitted to NATO.

West Germany's army, assigned to NATO, was limited to 12 divisions—a force of about 275,000. West Germany also was prohibited from making atomic, biological, or chemical weapons, guided missiles, or large warships.

2. Government of West Germany. The West German constitution provides for a democratic government with (*a*) a guarantee of civil liberties and free elections, (*b*) a two-house Parliament, and (*c*) a Chancellor responsible to the Bundestag, the popularly elected lower house of Parliament.

Germany's two major parties are the *Christian Democrats* and the *Social Democrats*. Although they differ on details, both parties support welfare state measures, NATO membership, and a pro-Western foreign policy.

From 1969 to 1982, the Social Democrats, in coalition with the minor Free Democratic party, controlled the government. The Chancellors, both Social Democrats, were first *Willy Brandt* and then *Helmut Schmidt*. They worked to improve relations with Communist East Europe, to strengthen West European unity, and to maintain cooperation with the United States.

In 1982, with the German economy in recession, Schmidt refused to make any drastic cutbacks in welfare spending. A number of Free Democratic deputies therefore abandoned the Schmidt coalition, causing its downfall, and transferred their support to the Christian Democrats. *Helmut Kohl* became Chancellor and pledged to improve the economy, to pursue good relations with Communist East Europe, and to seek friendship with the United States. In 1983 elections, the Kohl government retained control of the legislature.

In 1983 the Christian Democratic regime accepted the stationing of American medium-range missiles in West Germany. The Social Democrats, in a policy of reversal, voted to oppose such deployment.

DEVELOPMENTS IN EAST GERMANY

1. Establishment of the German Democratic Republic. Russia in 1949 transformed its zone into the *German Democratic Republic* with its capital at *East*

Berlin. This state was a Russian satellite occupied by Soviet troops. East Germany had an army of 100,000 troops and belonged to the Warsaw Pact.

2. Government of East Germany. A self-proclaimed "democratic republic," East Germany was in fact a typical Communist dictatorship with restrictions on civil liberties, a secret police, and only one political party. In 1953 East German riots against the satellite government were repressed by Soviet tanks and troops. Until the 1970's, the Western powers refused to recognize the East German regime.

For 25 years *Walter Ulbricht,* as head of the East German Communist party, exercised tight control over the country. In 1971 Ulbricht resigned because of ill health and old age, and was replaced by *Erich Honecker.*

COMPARISON OF THE TWO GERMANYS

1. Area. West Germany comprised 70 percent of the total area of postwar Germany as compared with 30 percent for East Germany.

2. Population. West Germany contained over 75 percent of the German people as compared with less than 25 percent for East Germany.

3. Industrialization. West Germany, the more industrial of the two Germanys, contained the industrial heart of Europe, the Ruhr Valley. East Germany also had industry but was more agricultural than West Germany.

4. Economic System. West Germany had a capitalist economy, typified by private enterprise, free labor unions, and limited government regulation of the economy. East Germany had a Communist economy, typified by government ownership of industry and collectivization of agriculture.

5. Economic Developments Since World War II. Aided by Marshall Plan funds, West Germany made a remarkable recovery from the devastation of World War II. Its cities, transportation system, and industry were all rebuilt. West Germany became the leading industrial nation of Western Europe with a high standard of living.

In contrast, East Germany made a far slower recovery. For years, its cities—notably East Berlin—were not rebuilt, and its people suffered shortages of food and consumer goods. Seeking a better life, many East Germans fled to West Germany, chiefly through Berlin. To stop this flow, the Communists in 1961 built a barbed-wire and concrete barrier, the *Berlin Wall.* Having thus halted the flight of skilled workers and also having relaxed economic controls, East Germany in the 1960's experienced considerable economic growth, but its living standard remained lower than that of West Germany.

STEPS TO REDUCE TENSIONS OVER BERLIN AND GERMANY (1970–1990)

1. West Germany Improves Relations With Communist East Europe (1970–1972). While affirming West Germany's strong adherence to the

Kuekes in The Cleveland Plain-Dealer

Maybe there is no solution.

Western world, Chancellor Willy Brandt moved in 1970 to "normalize" his country's relations with the Communist nations of Eastern Europe. Brandt traveled to Moscow and later to Warsaw, paying homage to the Soviet Unknown Soldier, the Polish Unknown Soldier, and the Jews who battled in the Warsaw Ghetto uprising—all victims of Nazi aggression in World War II. Brandt signed two separate treaties—with the Soviet Union and with Poland— by which (1) West Germany accepted the existing Soviet and Polish borders, including the *Oder-Neisse Line* as Poland's western boundary, thereby conceding sizable areas taken from prewar Germany (see map, page 574), and (2) the signatories renounced the use of force and agreed to strive for economic, scientific, and cultural cooperation. These treaties were hailed by Brandt as leading to a new era of peace for Europe, but they were opposed by many Germans for accepting the territorial losses to Poland and Russia. In 1972 the treaties secured a minimal approval in the Bundestag.

2. The Big Four Reach Another Berlin Agreement (1971). In 1971 the Big Four powers reached a new Berlin agreement *(a)* providing for unimpeded road and rail traffic, and continued commercial and cultural ties, between West Berlin and West Germany, *(b)* permitting personal and business visits by West Berliners to East Germany *(c)*, accepting West Germany's responsibility for, but limiting its political activity in, West Berlin, and *(d)* allowing Russia to open a consular office in West Berlin.

3. West Germany and East Germany "Normalize" Their Relations (1972). West Germany and East Germany signed a treaty that *(a)* confirmed the existence of two Germanys and established formal relations between them, *(b)* allowed additional visits by West Germans to relatives living in East Germany, *(c)* called for the two Germanys to cooperate in such areas as sports, environmental control, airlines, and technical knowledge, *(d)* proposed that both Germanys be admitted to the U.N. (which was done in 1973), and *(e)* left unanswered the question of German reunification.

GERMAN REUNIFICATION (1990)

1. East Germany's Collapse (1989–1990). Unable to stop a flood of East Germans fleeing through Hungary and Czechoslovakia, the East German Communist regime opened the Berlin Wall in the fall of 1989. Political turmoil forced the Communist leaders to grant free elections in March 1990. A new, non-Communist government signed a reunification agreement with West Germany, and East Germany went out of existence October 3, 1990.

2. Once Again: A Single Germany. For the first time in 45 years, a single German nation appeared on the map of Europe. Because of post-1945 territorial losses, it was the smallest unified German state in more than a century. Nonetheless, Germany had Europe's most powerful economy. Reunified Germany kept the democratic structure and the name of the German Federal Republic. In nationwide elections at the end of 1990, Helmut Kohl retained the position of chancellor, and a coalition of Christian Democrats and Free Democrats controlled the parliament. Plans were made to move the capital to its traditional site, Berlin.

3. Problems Facing United Germany. Among the problems facing reunified Germany were: *(a)* The economy of eastern Germany was in chaos, as state-run industries went bankrupt and millions of workers lost their jobs. The Kohl government pledged billions of marks in assistance. *(b)* Soviet troops remained at bases in eastern Germany. In exchange for West German economic help, the Soviets promised to withdraw their troops over four years. *(c)* Both Germans and non-Germans worried that hard times might spark a revival of the fanatic German nationalism that Hitler had exploited in the 1930's. Chancellor Kohl vowed that Germany would never again pose a threat to its neighbors.

MIDDLE EAST

LOCATION AND IMPORTANCE

The Middle East consists of northeastern Africa and southwestern Asia. The region's importance lies in its (1) *vital waterways*—the Suez Canal and the Dardanelles, (2) *valuable oil resources*—in Saudi Arabia, Kuwait, Iraq, and Iran, and (3) *strategic location*—at the crossroads of Europe, Asia, and Africa, and on the southern flank of Russia.

ISRAEL AND THE ARAB STATES

EMERGENCE OF ISRAEL

1. Jewish Claims to Palestine. *Theodor Herzl*, a journalist and Jewish intellectual, founded modern *Zionism*, the movement for a Jewish homeland in Palestine. Zionists claimed that the Jewish people (*a*) had lived in Palestine during ancient times, and (*b*) needed a refuge from anti-Semitic persecution. In 1917 Britain gave support to the Zionist movement by the *Balfour Declaration*, which viewed "with favor the establishment in Palestine of a national home for the Jewish people." To fulfill the Balfour Declaration, Britain in 1923 received the League of Nations mandate over Palestine.

By 1938 over 500,000 Jews had migrated to Palestine. They built modern cities, founded agricultural settlements, started industries, restored desert lands to fertility, reduced death from disease, and established schools.

2. Arab Opposition and a New British Policy. Opposition to Jewish immigration came from (*a*) Arab nationalists, who desired an Arab Palestine, (*b*) Arab ruling classes, who feared Western ideas of democracy, and (*c*) Arab peasants and nomads, who feared the loss of their traditional ways.

In 1939 just before the outbreak of World War II, Britain severely limited Jewish immigration to Palestine. By so appeasing the Arabs, the Zionists claimed, Britain was violating the Balfour Declaration.

During World War II, 6 million European Jews—men, women, and children—were savagely murdered by the Nazis. Of those who survived, many sought admission to Palestine. Britain, however, still kept the gates closed. Britain's policy was (*a*) defied by Palestinian Jews, who smuggled immigrants into the Holy Land, and (*b*) condemned by the United States. Britain rejected President Truman's requests to ease many restrictions.

3. Palestine and the U.N. In 1947 Britain turned the Palestine problem over to the U.N. General Assembly. It voted to (*a*) end the British mandate, (*b*) place Jerusalem under international control, and (*c*) partition Palestine into separate Arab and Jewish states.

Thereupon, in 1948 Israel proclaimed its independence under President *Chaim Weizmann* and Prime Minister *David Ben-Gurion*. The new Jewish

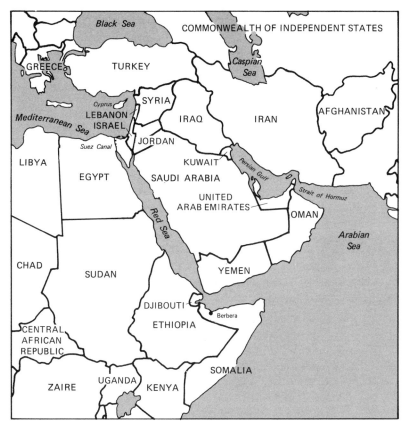

East Africa and the Middle East Today

state received immediate recognition from the United States. The Israeli republic is the Middle East's only modern democratic state.

4. Israel Maintains Its Existence

a. Israeli War for Independence (1948–1949). The Arab nations defied the U.N. decision for a Jewish state and attacked Israel. Despite their numerical superiority, the Arabs were driven back and lost some territory to the Israelis. In 1949 the Arab states accepted, as temporary, armistice agreements arranged by U.N. mediator *Ralph Bunche.*

(The Arab nations also defied the U.N. decision for a Palestinian Arab state. The areas proposed for such a state were seized—the Gaza Strip by Egypt and the land on the West Bank of the Jordan River by Jordan.)

b. Continued Arab Hostility (1949–1956). (1) The Arab League enforced an economic boycott against Israel and against Western companies doing business with Israel. (2) Under President Nasser, an Arab nationalist, Egypt barred Israeli ships from the Suez Canal. (3) Egyptian artillery on the Sinai Peninsula blockaded ships bound for Israel's southern port of Elath on the Gulf of Aqaba (see map, page 583). (4) Egypt allowed *fedayeen* (guerrilla) raids against Israeli border communities.

   c. Sinai Campaign (1956). Israel feared Egypt's military buildup that resulted chiefly from an arms deal in 1955 between Egypt and the Communist bloc. In 1956 Israel seized the initiative and invaded Egypt to wipe out fedayeen bases and end the Aqaba blockade. Israeli forces quickly scattered Nasser's armies and overran the Sinai Peninsula. (Britain and France also invaded Egypt to regain control of the Suez Canal. Check the Index.) The United Nations condemned the attacks, secured withdrawal of the invading forces, and stationed a *United Nations Emergency Force* *(UNEF)* in Egypt on the border with Israel and at the tip of the Sinai.

SURVEY OF ARAB NATIONALISM (SINCE 1945)

   1. **Roots.** Arab peoples became aware of their common cultural background: Arabic language, Moslem religion, and the Arab civilization of the Middle Ages.

   2. **Evidences of Arab Unity**

   a. Arab League. Founded in 1945, the Arab League seeks to unify Arab policy on world issues, especially Arab efforts to destroy Israel.

   b. Organization of Petroleum Exporting Countries (OPEC). Founded in 1960, OPEC groups six non-Arab and seven Arab states but is dominated by Arab nations like Saudi Arabia. OPEC's purpose is to increase its members' oil revenues. (For OPEC and the 1973 Arab-Israeli war, check the Index.)

   c. Palestine Liberation Organization (PLO). Because the PLO has been both a unifying and divisive force, it is discussed at greater length below.

   3. **Evidences of Arab Disunity.** The Arab nations reveal great diversity. (a) Libya, Syria, and Iraq are leftist, radical, and pro-Soviet, whereas Saudi Arabia, Egypt, Jordan, and Tunisia are more conservative and pro-Western. (b) Saudi Arabia, Jordan, Morocco, and Kuwait are monarchies headed by hereditary rulers; most other Arab nations are republics—often dictatorships or one-party states. Disputes often pit one Arab nation against another: (a) since 1963, Iraq and Syria have quarreled over rival versions of Arab nationalism. Syria supported non-Arab Iran against Iraq in the Persian Gulf War of 1980–1988. (b) Algeria and Morocco have had many disputes, most recently over Morocco's right to rule the Western Sahara. (c) Egypt and Libya became bitter enemies as Egypt tilted toward the United States, and Libya, under Colonel *Muammar al-Qaddafi,* became bitterly anti-American. (d) Syria and Jordan quarreled in the early 1980's, but relations improved after Jordan's King Hussein visited Syria in 1986. (e) In 1990, Iraq occupied oil-rich Kuwait and threatened Saudi Arabia.

PALESTINE LIBERATION ORGANIZATION (PLO)

1. **Background.** The Palestine Arab refugee problem arose out of the 1948–1949 war, when the Arab nations tried to destroy the newborn state of Israel. Mainly fearing for their safety, some 540,000 Arabs out of 700,000 in Israeli territory fled to neighboring Arab nations. After the war, Israel proposed that the refugee problem be part of an overall settlement involving boundaries and diplomatic recognition, but the Arab nations rejected the Israeli proposal.

The Arab nations did little to assimilate the refugees into their societies. Refugees often lived in squalid camps, dependent on international charity for the necessities of life. This environment gave rise to various guerrilla groups committed to Israel's destruction. In the mid-1960's, these groups formed an umbrella organization, the *Palestine Liberation Organization (PLO). Yasir Arafat,* leader of *Al Fatah,* the largest guerrilla group, became head of the PLO.

According to rough estimates, the Palestinian people number about 5 million, including 750,000 in Israel and 1.3 million in Israeli-occupied territories.

2. **Arab Support for the PLO.** In 1974 the Arab nations, meeting at Rabat, Morocco, unanimously declared the PLO to be the "sole legitimate representative of the Palestinian people" and called for the creation of a Palestinian state. Also in 1974, the Arab nations secured a U.N. General Assembly invitation for the PLO, as "representative of the Palestinian people," to take part in debate of the Palestine question. (Check the Index for Palestine Liberation Organization.)

3. **PLO as a Divisive Force in the Arab World.** The presence of Palestinian guerrillas has destabilized such Arab nations as Jordan and Lebanon.

Jordan's army drove the guerrillas out of Jordan in 1970–1971, but guerrilla organizers continued to find recruits among Jordan's many Palestinians.

Leftist Palestinian guerrillas took part in Lebanon's civil war, which began in 1975. At first they sided with leftist Lebanese Moslems in battling against rightist Lebanese Christians. Later, Palestinian guerrillas fought against the Lebanese Moslems who had formerly been their allies.

4. **Splits in the PLO.** In 1982, Israel invaded Lebanon and forced most PLO guerrillas to leave. (See page 591.) Syria helped chase out the rest in 1983. Factions within the PLO then divided into two camps. The largest faction, loyal to Yasir Arafat, spoke of seeking a negotiated solution to the Arab-Israeli conflict. A smaller faction, which included Marxist and pro-Syrian guerrilla groups, gave exclusive attention to military action.

5. **The PLO as a Palestinian "Government."** The PLO maintains what it calls a "parliament in exile," the *Palestine National Council,* made up of prominent Palestinians from many walks of life. The council holds its meetings periodically in friendly Arab countries, most recently Tunisia and Algeria. A smaller *executive council* contains representatives from various PLO factions and makes day-to-day decisions under Arafat's leadership. The PLO claims to represent Palestinians

who live in Israeli-occupied territory and in exile countries, and opinion polls suggest it has strong support from many Palestinians.

6. Palestine as an Independent "State" (Since 1988). In November 1988, Arafat and the Palestine National Council met in Algiers to proclaim the formation of an independent "state of Palestine" with its capital in Jerusalem. For the first time, Arafat signaled his acceptance of Israel's right to exist. He called for an international peace conference to resolve the Middle East conflict. He also proposed that a United Nations peacekeeping force be sent to oversee an Israeli withdrawal from "our occupied Palestinian land." Some 100 nations gave recognition of some sort to the new Palestinian "state."

In 1993, the PLO and Israel signed a preliminary agreement for the PLO to take over administration of the Gaza Strip and an area around the West Bank town of Jericho, which Israel had occupied since 1967. The agreement went into effect in 1994.

ARAB-ISRAELI WAR (1967)

1. Background. Egypt, Syria, and Jordan, in military alliance, moved their armies toward their borders with Israel. Nasser secured removal of the UNEF and closed the Gulf of Aqaba to Israeli shipping. Meanwhile, Israel called up its military reserves. Eventually war started.

2. The War. In a six-day war, the Israelis routed the Arab forces and seized (1) from Egypt—the Gaza Strip and the entire Sinai Peninsula westward to the Suez Canal and southward to Sharm el Sheikh, opening the Gulf of Aqaba to Israeli shipping; (2) from Jordan—all territory on the West Bank of the Jordan River, including the Old City of Jerusalem; and (3) from Syria—the Golan Heights.

U.N. Security Council resolutions helped end the fighting. Israel urged direct negotiations to achieve a permanent peace settlement, but Egypt and Syria spoke of another "round" of fighting.

ARAB HOSTILITY AND DIPLOMACY (1967–1973)

1. No War but No Peace. Arab guerrilla groups gave Israel no peace. They raided Israeli settlements and gunned Israeli commercial airplanes at airports in Europe. In 1972 Arab extremists employed Japanese leftists to massacre innocent civilians at the Tel Aviv airport; also Arab terrorists murdered 11 Israeli Olympic athletes at Munich. In response, Israel raided guerrilla bases in Syria and Lebanon. The main threat to Israel, however, was Egypt, whose leaders called for "fire and blood." Israel bested Egypt in artillery and airplane duels along the Suez Canal. Egypt became dependent upon Russia for military equipment and 20,000 military personnel, who manned missile sites and trained Egyptian forces.

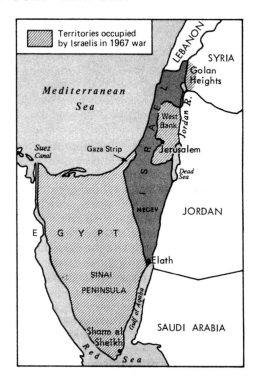

Israel and the
Bordering Arab States

2. Egypt Under Sadat. In 1970 Nasser died and his position was assumed by *Anwar al-Sadat*. This Egyptian President directed his nation's foreign policy away from dependence on the Soviet Union. In 1972 he ordered the 20,000 Soviet military personnel to leave Egypt. Although they left, the Soviet military equipment remained, and the Soviets continued to supply Egypt with military spare parts.

Sadat, however, was determined to regain Egyptian territory lost to Israel in the 1967 war—if necessary by a new war.

ARAB-ISRAELI WAR (1973)

1. Military Front. By attacking on Yom Kippur, the most holy day of the Jewish religion and devoted to prayer, the Syrians and Egyptians gained an initial surprise advantage. Syrian forces advanced on the Golan Heights, and Egyptian forces crossed the Suez Canal eastward into the Sinai desert. Hastily mobilized, Israeli forces slowly reversed the tide of battle. The Israelis lost many planes to Russian-built SAM antiaircraft missiles but eventually achieved air supremacy. They advanced against the Syrians on the Golan Heights and crossed the Suez Canal westward into Egypt proper, trapping a 20,000-man Egyptian force in the Sinai desert. Against this military background, the three warring nations accepted the U.N. cease-fire calls.

2. Arab Unity Moves

a. Military Matters. To aid Syria and Egypt, the other Arab states sent troops and planes and pledged economic support.

b. Oil Embargo. The Arab states—especially Saudi Arabia, Kuwait, the Arabian peninsula sheikdoms, Iraq, Libya, and Algeria—possess the world's major known oil fields and have supplied significant amounts of the oil needs of industrialized nations: the United States, West European countries, and Japan. Since 1960 Arab and other oil-producing countries have been joined in the *Organization of Petroleum Exporting Countries (OPEC)* coordinating efforts to increase their oil revenues. With the outbreak of the 1973 Arab-Israeli war, the Arab states seized the opportunity to further their economic goal and, at the same time, use oil as a political weapon. They raised oil prices fourfold, reduced shipments to most West European nations and Japan, and totally embargoed oil shipments to the United States. As the diplomatic price for easing their cutoffs, the Arab states demanded that the industrialized nations voice support for the Arab position in the Mideast. Japan and most West European nations did so.

After the U.N. achieved a cease-fire, American Secretary of State Kissinger negotiated an Israeli-Egyptian troop-separation agreement that restored Egyptian control of both sides of the Suez Canal. Thereafter most oil-producing Arab states lifted the embargo against the United States.

3. Superpower Involvement. After the outbreak of the 1973 war, the United States acted unsuccessfully to halt the hostilities. The Soviet Union, in contrast, acted to spur hostilities, voicing support for Egypt and Syria and urging the other Arab states to join in the struggle. As the war took a heavy toll of military equipment, the Soviets airlifted additional supplies to Egypt and Syria. The United States thereupon acted to resupply Israel.

After the Israelis gained the military advantage, the Soviet Union and the United States jointly sponsored a balanced U.N. resolution that achieved a Mideast cease-fire. A rumored Soviet plan to send Russian troops into the Mideast to bolster Egyptian forces led President Nixon to place the American military on a "precautionary alert." The danger of this possible confrontation was eased with the creation of the UNEF peacekeeping force—to serve as a buffer between the Israeli and Egyptian armies.

4. Observations: (*a*) Israel "won" the war militarily but in other ways "lost." With its small population, Israel suffered heavy casualties, although they were only one-tenth those inflicted on the Arabs. With its limited resources, Israel incurred heavy war costs. Israel finally was more isolated diplomatically than ever before. (*b*) Egypt experienced a tremendous upsurge of confidence as its armies demonstrated ability to master modern military equipment. (*c*) The United States increased its *leverage*—that is, its ability to influence Mideast affairs. While reaffirming its support for Israel's right to exist, the United States avoided an extreme partisan stand

and gained increased respect among moderate Arabs, especially Egypt. (*d*) The Soviet Union demonstrated its ability to influence Mideast affairs.

MIDDLE EAST DEVELOPMENTS (SINCE 1973)

LEBANON'S CIVIL WAR (1975–1990)

1. Background. Lebanon's deeply fragmented society fell into turmoil when civil war broke out in 1975. The free-for-all war pitted many rival militias against one another. The weak Lebanese army was only one faction among many.

Lebanese society had long been divided mainly along religious lines, and one or more militias represented each religious group—Maronite Christians, Sunni Moslems, Shiite Muslims, and Druses. Further complicating the picture were armed groups such as the PLO, backed by Palestinian refugees.

2. Syrian Intervention. Syria sent 15,000 troops into Lebanon in 1976 under an Arab League mandate to enforce a cease-fire. War rekindled in 1981 and caused massive destruction in the years that followed.

3. PLO Attacks and Israel's 1978 Invasion of Southern Lebanon. PLO commandos used southern Lebanon as a base for attacks inside Israel. In 1978 a PLO squad landed on the Israeli coast and killed 30 civilians on the beach, in buses, and elsewhere. In retaliation, Israeli troops occupied southern Lebanon for three months. They withdrew after organizing a Lebanese Christian militia to prevent Palestinians from reoccupying southern Lebanon.

4. Israel's 1982 Invasion. After the Lebanese civil war resumed in 1981, Lebanon's neighbors quickly became involved. Syrian troops battled on the side of Lebanese Muslims and Palestinians. Israeli armed forces bombed the Lebanese capital, Beirut, in 1981, and launched a full-scale invasion of Lebanon in 1982. The Israelis trapped several thousand PLO troops in Beirut and forced their evacuation to Tunisia and other Arab countries far from Israel's borders.

5. Suicide Bombings (1983). The United States joined France, Italy, and Britain in creating a multinational force to help the weak Lebanese government. Leftists and Muslims regarded the multinational force as supporting rightist Lebanese Christians. Suicide bombers drove trucks into United States and French military compounds in 1983, blowing up the trucks and killing 241 Marines and 58 French soldiers. In 1984 President Reagan withdrew United States forces.

6. Israeli Withdrawal (1985). Israel withdrew most of its forces in 1985, keeping a small "security zone" in southern Lebanon. The Israelis continued to arm a Lebanese Christian militia in southern Lebanon.

7. New Constitution (1989). The term of president *Amin Gemayel* expired in 1988 without agreement on a successor. After fighting flared up, Muslim and Christian members of Lebanon's parliament met in Taif (Saudi Arabia). In 1989 they approved a new constitution designed to increase the power of Lebanon's Muslim majority and end the civil war.

8. Shaky Peace (1990). Syrian troops assaulted the presidential palace in 1990 to remove a Christian general, *Michel Aoun*, who was a key holdout against the new constitution. A new "national unity" government re-established central authority and disarmed the rival militias. A shaky peace took hold. Syrian and Israeli troops remained on Lebanese soil, as did some PLO guerrillas.

ISRAELI-ARAB PEACE PROCESS

For years, efforts to put an end to Arab-Israeli hostility stumbled over two key problems: (1) the refusal of Palestinian leaders to recognize publicly Israel's right to exist as an independent nation, and (2) the refusal of Israeli leaders to recognize publicly the Palestinians' right to self-determination within a homeland of their own. The United States and Israel insisted that the Palestinians formally accept *U.N. Security Council Resolution 242*, adopted in 1967, calling for Arab recognition of Israel's existence and borders in exchange for Israeli withdrawal from land occupied in the 1967 war.

1. Geneva Peace Conference (December 1973). Israel, Egypt, and Jordan—but not Syria—sent delegates to a U.N.-backed peace conference in Geneva, Switzerland. The conference ended in failure after one day. Thereafter, on repeated trips between Middle Eastern capitals, Secretary of State Kissinger used "shuttle diplomacy" to persuade Israeli and Arab leaders to disengage their forces.

2. The Sadat Visit to Israel (1977). In a bold initiative, Egypt's President Sadat solicited an invitation from Israeli Prime Minister *Menachem Begin* and visited Israel in 1977, a year after ending Egypt's friendship treaty with the Soviet Union. Sadat thus became the first Arab leader ever to go to Israel, visiting a memorial to Holocaust victims and addressing Israel's parliament.

3. The Camp David (Maryland) Summit Conference (1978). At Camp David, Sadat and Begin met with President Carter and reached two agreements. One provided a framework for peace negotiations on the Israeli-occupied West Bank and Gaza Strip. The other dealt with Egypt's Sinai Peninsula. In return for Israeli withdrawal from Sinai within three years, Egypt agreed to (*a*) demilitarize much of the peninsula, (*b*) permit peacekeeping forces to be stationed there, (*c*) guarantee Israeli ships free passage through the Suez Canal and the Gulf of Aqaba, and (*d*) negotiate a peace treaty with Israel.

4. The Israeli-Egyptian Peace Treaty (1979). (*a*) Reaffirmed the Camp David agreement on the Sinai, (*b*) contained provisions for Israel to buy oil from the Sinai fields being returned to Egypt, and (*c*) provided for Israeli-Egyptian talks on Palestinian self-rule in the West Bank and Gaza Strip.

Also, the United States agreed to (*a*) extend economic and military aid and loans to both Israel and Egypt, (*b*) assist Israel in case of Egyptian violations of the peace treaty, (*c*) help meet Israel's oil needs for up to 15 years, and (*d*) take part in negotiations on Palestinian self-rule.

Reacting against the treaty, most Arab nations broke diplomatic relations with Egypt and the Arab League moved its headquarters out of Cairo.

5. Negotiations on Palestinian Autonomy. Talks began in 1979 among Egypt, Israel, and the United States, but Jordan and the Palestinians stayed away. Sharp disagreements surfaced at once. The United States urged compromise, criticizing new Jewish settlements on the West Bank as "harmful to the peace process."

6. The Syrian-Soviet Treaty (1980). Seeking support for his hard line against Israel, President Hafez al-Assad of Syria signed a twenty-year treaty of friendship with the Soviet Union. The Soviets provided the Syrians with powerful surface-to-air missiles, which the Syrians deployed in areas near the Israeli border and in Lebanon's Bekaa Valley.

7. Israeli Raid on Iraqi Reactor (1981). Israeli warplanes bombed and destroyed an Iraqi nuclear reactor being built with French aid. France and Iraq said the facility was for peaceful purposes; Israelis and some others said it might be used to produce nuclear bombs. The U.N. Security Council voted to "strongly condemn" Israel for the raid and urged Israel to open its own nuclear reactors to international inspection.

8. Assassination of Egypt's President Sadat (1981). Anwar al-Sadat was assassinated by four Egyptians who were later identified as belonging to a Muslim fundamentalist group critical of Sadat's policy of dealing with Israel.

Hosni Mubarak, a former air force commander trained in the Soviet Union, had been handpicked by Sadat as his Vice President and successor. As Egypt's new President, Mubarak continued the peace process. However, he was inclined to be more outspoken than Sadat in his criticisms of Israeli actions.

9. United States Sale of AWACS to Saudi Arabia (1981). After considerable debate, Congress agreed in 1981 to sell Saudi Arabia $8.5 billion of military equipment, including five Airborne Warning and Control System (AWACS) planes. Israel sharply criticized the sale, since Saudi Arabia is an Arab nation that supports the Arab cause. The Reagan administration argued that Saudi Arabia was an ally against Soviet penetration of the Middle East.

10. Israeli Annexation of the Golan Heights (1981). After capturing the Golan Heights from Syria in the 1967 war, Israel kept them under military rule. In late 1981, Israel formally annexed the strategic heights, which overlook Israeli towns and farms. The United States criticized the action as a violation of the Camp David accords, and the U.N. Security Council unanimously condemned the annexation as illegal.

11. Differences Among Israelis (1984–1990). Most Israelis supported the government's policy of keeping the occupied West Bank and refusing to negotiate with the PLO. However, a small Israeli peace movement called for greater flexibility.

When 1984 elections failed to produce a clear majority, Israel's two largest parties reached a power-sharing agreement. For two years, *Shimon Peres* of the left-wing Labor party served as prime minister and *Yitzhak Shamir*, leader of the right-wing Likud bloc, served as foreign minister. In 1986 the two men exchanged positions. Elections in 1988 produced another deadlock, and the two parties renewed their partnership with Shamir as prime minister from 1988 to 1990. While the two parties agreed on taking a hard line toward the PLO, they differed on many points. Thus, Israeli foreign policy was unsettled.

12. The Intifadah. In 1987 Palestinians living in lands under Israeli occupation began an uprising they called the *intifadah*. As strikes and violent demonstrations continued, Israeli repression intensified. The intifadah caused increasing polarization between Jews and Arabs in Israel and occupied lands.

13. American Talks With the PLO. In 1988 Yasir Arafat proposed a peace plan calling for two states—Israel and Palestine—to live peacefully side by side. He said he renounced terrorism and accepted Security Council Resolution 242, thus meeting American conditions for the opening of a "substantive" dialogue between the United States and the PLO. After years of ignoring the PLO, American representatives held informal talks with its representatives.

14. Concern About Weapons of Mass Destruction. The Persian Gulf War of 1991 drew attention to the threat of chemical and nuclear weapons in the Middle East. During Iraqi attacks, Israelis donned gas masks, because Iraq had threatened to use missiles carrying chemical warheads. As it turned out, the missiles all bore conventional explosives. Post-war inspections revealed that the Iraqis had been well on the way to building nuclear weapons. Israel itself is believed to have had nuclear-tipped missiles for many years.

15. Multilevel Peace Talks. After Iraq's defeat in the Persian Gulf War, the United States and the Soviet Union arranged a series of Middle East peace talks between Israel and its Arab neighbors.

a. Madrid (1991). While maintaining its refusal to deal directly with the PLO, Israel agreed to meet with other Palestinians and representatives of Arab nations in a three-day peace conference in Madrid, Spain, in November 1991. Among nations represented at the conference table were Jordan, Syria, Lebanon, Saudi Arabia, Egypt, and Israel.

b. Followup Conferences (After 1991). After the Madrid meeting, two-way peace talks continued in various locations between Israel and (1) neighboring Arab states and (2) the delegation of Palestinians.

16. Increased Israeli Flexibility. In June 1992, Israeli voters turned the hard-line Likud government out of office. The Labor party formed a coalition with a small religious party, and Labor's *Yitzhak Rabin* became prime minister. His government began to explore new options for progress in the peace negotiations. In January 1993 the Israeli parliament repealed a law that had banned contacts between Israelis and representatives of the PLO.

BREAKTHROUGHS TOWARD PEACE (1993-1995)

1. Israeli-PLO Accord. After months of secret peace talks in Norway between Israeli diplomats and representatives of the PLO, the two sides agreed to open formal diplomatic ties. The PLO accepted Israel's "right to exist in peace and security" and renounced "the use of terrorism and other acts of violence." In return, Israel recognized the PLO as "the representative of the Palestinian people."

In September 1993 the two sides signed a historic accord in Washington, D.C. A handshake encouraged by President Clinton between Israeli Prime Minister Rabin and PLO leader Yasir Arafat symbolized the dramatic turn in Israeli-Arab relations. U.S. and other world leaders hailed the agreement as a major breakthrough, and many Israelis and Palestinians rejoiced over the prospects for peace. However, some on both sides denounced the accord as a "sellout."

The accord, called *A Declaration of Principles on Palestinian Self-Rule*, left most issues to be decided in further negotiations. It provided for (*a*) the election of an interim governing council in most of Palestine to conduct affairs for five years while a permanent settlement was negotiated, (*b*) Israeli control over external security and foreign relations and Palestinian control over domestic affairs during the five-year period, (*c*) a staged Israeli withdrawal, beginning in the Gaza Strip and the West Bank town of Jericho, with a Palestinian police force taking charge of security there, and (*d*) further discussions on the return of Palestinian refugees.

In 1995 Israel and the PLO signed a second accord in which they agreed that Israel would give up its authority over the areas of the West Bank where most Palestinians lived but would retain control of Israeli settlements and military installations. The accord was denounced by Israeli West Bank settlers and by the militant religious right. In November Rabin was assassinated by a young

Israeli law student who was a militant religious extremist. Most Israelis mourned Rabin's death. Shimon Peres, who assumed the post of prime minister, said he would continue the process that Rabin had begun. Further talks between Israel and the PLO were scheduled for mid-1996.

2. Talks Between Israel and Neighboring States. (*a*) Soon after the Israeli-PLO accord, Israel and *Jordan* signed an agreement to seek "just, lasting, and comprehensive peace." The agreement set an agenda for further negotiations on issues such as boundaries, refugees, and the sharing of scarce water resources. In July 1994, King Hussein of Jordan and Prime Minister Rabin of Israel signed a treaty confirming the peace process. (*b*) Israel and *Syria* continued the talks they had begun at Madrid. Several militant Palestinian groups that oppose the Israeli-PLO accord have bases in Syria.

REVOLUTION AND WAR IN IRAN

1. Background. Iran is a major oil producer and a member of OPEC. Its people are mainly Persians and not Arabs. Most Iranians belong to the Shiite branch of Islam, which differs from the Sunni branch followed by most Arabs.

Iran was a monarchy ruled by a Shah. The last Shah, who ruled from 1941 to 1979, was *Mohammad Reza Pahlavi*. He ruled autocratically, employed secret police, and permitted no political opposition. The Shah, however, spurred economic and social modernization, including land reform, literacy, and women's rights. He followed a pro-Western foreign policy and maintained a "special relationship" with the United States.

2. Khomeini Seizes Control. By 1979 the Shah faced uncontrollable opposition by workers protesting low wages and inflation, by democratic and radical groups protesting autocratic rule, and by conservative religious groups protesting efforts to modernize the country. The Shah fled abroad, and Iran came under the control of *Ayatollah Ruhollah Khomeini*. This Islamic religious leader exercised dictatorial rule. He converted Iran into an Islamic republic based on the principles stated in the Koran, the holy book of Islam.

3. Americans Taken Hostage in Iran. Supporters of Khomeini despised the United States for having supported the Shah. Their anger increased when President Carter allowed the deposed Shah to enter the United States late in 1979 for cancer treatment. In Teheran, Iran's capital, young Islamic militants occupied the U.S. embassy in November 1979. They seized more than 50 Americans as hostages and demanded that the United States send the Shah to Iran for punishment. Iran's government supported the militants' actions.

The hostages remained in captivity for more than a year. Both the U.N. Security Council and the World Court backed the United States position that Iran must release the hostages without conditions. The United States imposed economic sanctions on Iran and sent a military mission to rescue the hostages. The attempt failed when three helicopters malfunctioned and two aircraft collided over the Iranian desert in April 1980.

After negotiations between the U.S. and Iranian governments, mediated by Algeria, Iran released the hostages in January 1981, on the day Ronald Reagan took office as President.

4. The Iran-Iraq War (1980–1988)

a. Background. Under the Shah, Iran had built up its military power and had secured Iraq's agreement to a 1975 treaty. This treaty established a boundary between the two nations providing for shared control of the *Shatt al-Arab* waterway at the northern tip of the Persian Gulf. Under Khomeini, Iran became militarily weak—its military leaders were purged, supplies from the United States were frozen, and Iranian society was chaotic.

b. The Stalemate. In 1980, President Saddam Hussein of Iraq canceled the "humiliating" 1975 treaty and attacked Iran. Iraqi forces penetrated some 30 miles into Iran. In 1982 the Iranians mounted a counteroffensive and drove the Iraqi forces back. A stalemate developed. To hamper oil sales on which both nations depended to finance the war, Iran and Iraq bombed oil tankers in the Persian Gulf.

c. United States Involvement. (*1*) The United States provided Iraq with intelligence information and other help in order to ward off an Iranian victory. (*2*) President Reagan sent warships to the Gulf in 1987 to escort Kuwaiti tankers. Because Kuwait supported Iraq, Iran had bombed Kuwaiti ships and damaged them with mines. American ships and planes attacked Iranian oil platforms and mine-laying boats when Iran continued to attack Kuwaiti tankers. (*3*) Thirty-seven United States sailors died when an Iraqi jet fired a missile at the U.S. frigate *Stark* in 1987. Iraqi leaders insisted the event was an accident. (*4*) In July 1988, the U.S. warship *Vincennes* shot down an Iranian civilian airliner over the Persian Gulf, killing 290 people. U.S. officials expressed "deep regret" but said the crew believed it was firing in self-defense.

d. Cease-fire (1988). The U.N. arranged a cease-fire in August 1988 that halted fighting. Casualties during the eight-year war exceeded one million people, of whom at least 365,000 died. Talks about a permanent peace bogged down at first in disputes over such issues as a prisoner exchange and reopening the Shatt al-Arab waterway. But Iran and Iraq resolved most of their differences shortly before the Persian Gulf War of 1991.

5. After Khomeini. Ayatollah Khomeini died in 1989, leaving Iran in the hands of a new spiritual leader, *Ali Khameini*, and a new president, *Ali Akbar Rafsanjani*. The new leaders promised to carry on the late ayatollah's policies, but they also made cautious moves to seek improved relations with the West.

TERRORISM AND ARMS DEALS: THE IRAN-CONTRA SCANDAL

After the Iran hostage crisis of 1979 to 1981, relations between the United States and Iran remained hostile. The United States continued its arms embargo, and its leaders accused Iran of supporting terrorist actions, including incidents in which pro-Iranian militants in Lebanon seized Americans as hostages. President Reagan urged United States allies to join in cutting off sales of arms to nations supporting terrorism. He said he would never negotiate with terrorists.

1. Controversy Over Secret Arms Sales. A storm of controversy arose following the revelation in November 1986 that President Reagan had secretly approved United States arms sales to Iran via Israel. Critics charged that the arms had been a "ransom" for hostages and that the President had violated his own policy against negotiating with terrorists. President Reagan argued that the arms deals had been part of a diplomatic move to win influence with moderates in the Iranian government and were not "ransom." Once the arms sales became public, President Reagan ordered them halted.

The arms sales had been handled by the *National Security Council* (NSC), a White House body that advises the President on security matters, and by the Central Intelligence Agency (CIA).

2. Controversy Over Secret Funds. A few weeks after the first revelations about arms sales, Attorney General *Edwin Meese III* announced the discovery that between $12 million and $30 million in Iranian payments for the arms had been secretly diverted to the Nicaraguan *contras* (United States-supported rebels fighting Nicaragua's leftist government). This news stirred an even bigger controversy. At the time of the alleged diversions, which took place earlier in 1986, the *Boland Amendment* barred either direct or indirect United States aid to the *contras*.

President Reagan said the NSC staff members responsible for the diversion of funds had resigned or been dismissed. The President added that he himself had neither known about nor approved the diversion of funds.

3. The Iran-Contra Investigations. The new revelations led to a flurry of investigations: (1) President Reagan appointed a three-member committee headed by former Senator John Tower. The report of the *Tower Commission* criticized the President for his detached "management style." (2) The Senate and the House set up special committees and held joint public hearings before a nationwide television audience. Key witnesses included *Rear Admiral John M. Poindexter*, head of the NSC in 1985–1986, and *Lieutenant Colonel Oliver L. North*, an assistant to Poindexter and his predecessors. The two men acknowledged their role in the fund diversions and asserted that they were carrying out policies they believed the President wanted. But Poindexter said he had not told the President. (3) At Meese's request, a federal court appointed an independent prosecutor to find out if federal laws had been broken.

President Reagan said he was "mad as a hornet" at not being told what his administration was doing. He pledged to cooperate fully with investigators in determining the facts.

Critics of the Reagan administration argued that (1) the arms deals with Iran had indeed begun as an exchange for hostages, (2) administration officials had repeatedly lied to Congress, and (3) decisions about foreign policy had been made in great confusion and in "arrogant disregard of the rule of law." Supporters of the Reagan administration argued that (1) although mistakes had been made, the administration had acted quickly to correct its mistakes, (2) members of Congress had exaggerated problems for partisan political purposes, and (3) secret help for the contras would not have been necessary if Congress had not wavered in its support for the contras' cause.

Congressional investigations concluded that the President had not known of the funds' diversion, but faulted him for failure to exercise proper authority over the activities of his subordinates.

4. The Iran-Contra Prosecutions. As independent prosecutor, *Lawrence E. Walsh*, won jury convictions against several figures in the Iran-contra case. However, appeals courts threw out the principal convictions. In his final report in 1994, Walsh asserted that President Reagan had a role in covering up the scandal but said he found "no credible evidence that President Reagan violated any criminal statute."

In 1989 a jury convicted Oliver North of obstructing Congress, destroying NSC documents, and accepting an illegal gift. Appeals courts threw out the conviction on grounds that the prosecution's case had been tainted by testimony North gave to Congress. (North and Poindexter had been given *grants of immunity*, so their testimony to Congress could not be used in court.) Poindexter too had his conviction overturned on appeal.

A number of lesser figures pleaded guilty to assorted charges. Most received fines and probation. Former Defense Secretary *Caspar Weinberger*, charged with lying to Congress, did not go to trial; President Bush pardoned him and five other Iran-contra figures on Christmas Eve, 1992.

THE PERSIAN GULF WAR (1991)

1. Iraq's Invasion of Kuwait (1990). Iraq and Kuwait quarreled over two issues: (*a*) Iraq's demand for changes in a border that divides a rich oil field, with most of the oil on the Kuwaiti side, and (*b*) Iraq's demand that Kuwait cancel loans made to Iraq during the Iran-Iraq War. After lengthy negotiations failed, Iraqi troops staged a lightning invasion of Kuwait in August 1990. Iraq declared that it was annexing Kuwait—incorporating it into Iraq.

2. Reaction. President Bush condemned the invasion as "naked aggression," comparing Iraq's President *Saddam Hussein* to Hitler and Iraq's surprise attack to Nazi Germany's *blitzkriegs* (see page 515). Leaders of the Soviet

Union and other nations, including most of Iraq's Middle Eastern neighbors, also condemned Iraq's aggression.

Warning that Iraqi troops were massing on the Kuwait–Saudi Arabia border, the United States won Saudi Arabia's permission to rush troops into that desert country. A coalition of nations that included the United States, Britain, France, Canada, Egypt, and Syria formed a multinational force that massed troops near Iraq's borders. Kuwait's monarch, the Emir *Sheik Jaber al-Ahmed al-Sabah*, who had fled into exile, requested help from the United Nations.

3. U.N. Sanctions. Free from the shackles of cold war quarrels, the United Nations responded quickly. (*a*) Less than a week after the invasion, the U.N. Security Council voted 13 to 0 to impose stiff trade sanctions against Iraq. The Soviet Union and China joined Western and Third World nations in backing the resolution. (*b*) Three weeks later, a similar Security Council majority adopted a resolution authorizing U.N. member nations to halt shipping to and from Iraq. Even before that, the United States navy had instituted a blockade of Iraqi oil exports to cut off Iraq's main source of income.

4. Operation Desert Storm. The trade embargo having failed to induce an immediate Iraqi withdrawal from Kuwait, the U.N. Security Council authorized the use of force to eject the Iraqis. On January 12, 1991, Congress voted to support military action against Iraq. Four days later, *Operation Desert Storm* began. Hundreds of U.S. and coalition planes and missiles struck targets in Kuwait and Iraq. They drove Iraqi planes from the skies, although Iraqi missiles did cause limited damage to Israel and Saudi Arabia. (Iraq's attacks on Israel were an unsuccessful attempt to split the coalition. Because of Arab hostility to Israel, the Israelis did not contribute forces to the coalition.)

In the United States and around the world, television viewers saw some of the air attacks on Baghdad live via satellite. Observers marveled at the instantaneous coverage in what was called "the first video war."

After more than a month of around-the-clock air attacks, United States and coalition ground forces smashed across the borders of Kuwait and Iraq. On February 27, 1991—six weeks after the first air strikes and only 100 hours after the ground war began—the U.S. and coalition forces achieved a complete victory over the Iraqi army. The American military commander, General *H. Norman Schwarzkopf*, returned home to a hero's welcome.

American authorities estimated that 100,000 Iraqi combatants and 343 coalition troops had died in the war. Casualties among Iraqi and Kuwaiti civilians numbered in the thousands.

5. The Aftermath

   a. Kuwait. Kuwait's emir returned from exile, promising limited measures to democratize his rule. Kuwait authorities expelled hundreds of thousands of Palestinians who had been living in Kuwait, accusing them of having sided with the Iraqi invaders. Oil well fires, reported to have been set deliberately by Iraqis during the war, burned for months, polluting the air over South-west Asia and delaying the resumption of Kuwaiti oil production.

b. Iraq. Saddam Hussein remained in power. Iraq was forced to pay reparation for war damages. U.N. and coalition peacekeeping forces entered Iraq, seeking to protect two Iraqi opposition groups—Kurds and Shiites—from reprisals by Hussein. The U.N. Security Council ordered Iraq to scrap its efforts to build weapons of mass destruction (nuclear, chemical, and biological). Because of damage to Iraq's economy, much of the population suffered from disease and hunger.

c. The Middle East. (1) While most United States troops pulled out quickly after the war, American leaders negotiated with Kuwait, Saudi Arabia, and other nations to forge an ongoing alliance to preserve Western access to the oil regions. (2) By jarring the status quo, the Persian Gulf War gave new impetus to the American push for Arab-Israeli peace talks.

FAR EAST

CHINA

NATIONALISTS LOSE CHINA TO THE COMMUNISTS (1949)

1. Nationalist Weaknesses. Following World War II the Chiang Kai-shek regime lost public support in China because it (*a*) was a thinly veiled dictatorship marked by corruption and inefficiency, (*b*) wasted a considerable portion of the American loans and military supplies, (*c*) failed to earn the soldiers' loyalty and prevent army desertions, and (*d*) ignored the peasants' desire for land and the workers' demand for better living conditions.

2. Communists Gain China. Chinese Communist armies, strengthened by equipment captured from the Japanese and supplies from the Soviet Union, defeated the Nationalists. In 1949 Communist armies drove Chiang Kai-shek to his only remaining stronghold, the island of Taiwan (Formosa). The Communists controlled mainland China, now with 1000 million (one billion) people.

At Peking (Beijing) the Communists proclaimed the *People's Republic of China* under Premier *Chou En-lai* (Zhou Enlai) and Communist party head *Mao Tse-tung* (Mao Zedong). (The spellings in parentheses conform to the Pinyin phonetic transcription system recently adopted officially by China.)

UNFRIENDLY RELATIONS BETWEEN COMMUNIST CHINA AND THE UNITED STATES (TO 1971)

1. Communist China's Policies. The Communists harshly treated American officials, missionaries, and businessmen caught in China during the civil war. The Communists directly intervened in the Korean War and fought

American troops. They sent military aid to the Communist forces in Vietnam. Communist China remained hostile toward the United States.

   2. America's Policies. In opposition to China, the United States (a) recognized the Nationalists on Taiwan as the legal government of China, (b) refused to recognize the Peking regime, (c) successfully opposed China's bid for admission to the U.N., (d) embargoed trade with Communist China, (e) fought to prevent a Communist takeover in South Vietnam, and (f) signed Mutual Defense Treaties to defend South Korea and Taiwan.

DISPUTE OVER TAIWAN (FORMOSA)

   The United States viewed Taiwan as a vital Pacific military base, the Nationalist army as a dependable anti-Communist force, and the Nationalist government as an ally. Consequently, the United States extended economic and military aid to Taiwan and vowed to defend Nationalist-held territory, as agreed in a Mutual Defense Treaty.

   Red China was determined to annex the island and destroy the Nationalist government. The Chinese Communists warned the United States that nothing will deter them from "liberating" Taiwan.

CHINESE-SOVIET SPLIT: IN THE OPEN BY 1963

   Despite their 1950 treaty of alliance, China and Russia gradually became hostile and by 1963 openly and bitterly disagreed as follows:

   1. Ideology. (a) *Russia.* Soviet leaders asserted that world Communism can be achieved through *peaceful coexistence.* They claimed that people, impressed by Soviet economic and scientific achievements, will turn to Communism. Meanwhile, Communist nations will subject the West to unremitting economic competition, propaganda, and subversion. However, Communists must make every effort to avoid nuclear war. A Communist paradise cannot be built upon millions of corpses. (b) *China.* Mao Tse-tung derided peaceful coexistence as a myth and held the view that war against capitalism is inevitable. If war does come, it will prove America to be a "paper tiger," will end capitalism, and will usher in a glorious Communist future.

   2. Russian Atomic Aid to China. (a) *Russia.* The Soviets trained Chinese atomic scientists, sent Russian technicians to China, and provided China with a reactor to produce nuclear materials. When the ideological conflict became acute, Russia terminated its aid. (b) *China.* Peking at first complained that Soviet aid was not enough and then deplored its termination.

   3. Chinese-Soviet Borders. (a) *Russia.* Soviet leaders contended that 19th-century treaties established the borders between Russia and China and must be respected. These treaties provided for Russian annexation of sizable territories, including the Amur River valley and the port of Vladivostok. (b) *China.* Chinese leaders argued that the treaties were imperialist-imposed and are not valid now. In 1969 Chinese and Russian forces clashed at several border points, most notably north of Vladivostok.

4. World Communist Leadership. (a) *Russia.* As the oldest and most advanced Communist nation, Russia claimed the leadership of the Communist bloc. Khrushchev conceded that there are many roads to Communism, including Tito's policies in Yugoslavia. The Soviets condemned Chinese appeals to nonwhite peoples as containing racial overtones. Russia retained the support of most Communist nations. (b) *China.* The most populous Communist nation, China claimed to be the true interpreter of Marxist-Leninist doctrine and the leader of the Communist world. The Chinese condemned the Yugoslavs as renegades. They also charged that Russia "sold out" the Communist movement in Latin America, Africa, and Asia.

CHINA DEVELOPS NUCLEAR WEAPONS: SINCE 1964

In 1964 China set off her first atomic bomb, in 1967 exploded a hydrogen bomb, and in 1970 sent up her first earth satellite, indicating sufficient thrust power to launch ICBM's. China's progress in developing nuclear weapons and missiles created a major new world problem. In particular, it caused concern in four nations—India and Japan, whose relations with China had been unfriendly; the Soviet Union, whose long border with China had been the scene of several armed clashes; and the United States, whose leaders considered the possibility of a Red Chinese missile attack.

RECENT DEVELOPMENTS

1. "Cultural Revolution" (1966–1969). (a) *Reasons.* Aged and ill, Mao Tse-tung wanted to assure that after his death China would continue his policies: (1) *within the country,* increased collectivization even over the opposition of the peasants, and (2) *in foreign affairs,* world revolution even at the risk of war. Mao did not want China to adopt "Soviet revisionism," by which he meant the use of profit as an economic incentive and the loss of revolutionary zeal in foreign affairs. Mao's opponents, holding important positions in the Communist party and the government, supported pay raises for workers and private garden plots for peasants, and considered Mao's views inappropriate for building the nation. (b) *Three Years of Turmoil.* Mao moved to crush his opponents by a "great proletarian cultural revolution." He mobilized millions of youths into *Red Guard* groups which denounced and terrorized the opposition. The cultural revolution shattered Chinese society, fragmented China's Communist party, and undermined production, education, and transportation.

2. Stability and a New Foreign Policy. By 1970 China returned to stability: the Red Guards were disbanded and order was restored by realistic and increasingly powerful army leaders; production recovered to the 1966 levels; and the government reflected control of moderate political leaders under Premier Chou En-lai. Thereupon China turned from preoccupation with internal matters to a more active foreign role, especially steps to improve Chinese-American relations.

China arranged a visit by an American table tennis team. Their visit, Premier Chou stated, "opened a new page in the relations of the Chinese and American people." President Nixon, who had made several overtures to "normalize" relations, was pleased by these Chinese responses and relaxed our trade embargo on exporting nonstrategic goods to China. Thereafter Chou En-lai invited President Nixon to visit China. Nixon accepted, expressing the hope that this "will become a journey for peace."

3. The Nixon Visit to China (1972). Accompanied by his national security adviser *Henry Kissinger,* President Nixon visited Communist China. Warmly received, Nixon spent a hectic week that included sightseeing, entertainment, banquets, a meeting with Mao Tse-tung, and numerous sessions with Chou En-lai. The visit concluded with the issuance of the Shanghai communiqué in which (a) the United States and China stated their differences regarding Vietnam, Korea, and Taiwan, (b) the United States agreed that Taiwan is part of China, urged peaceful settlement of the Taiwan issue by the Chinese themselves, and agreed ultimately to withdraw all American forces from Taiwan (but did not renounce its mutual defense pact with Taiwan), and (c) the United States and China agreed to peaceful coexistence and to improve and expand their contacts.

This visit, analysts believed, may signify the following: (a) *for China—* realization that the major threat to its national interests comes from the Soviet Union rather than the United States and (b) *for the United States—* less fear that China threatens American interests in Eastern Asia.

Following the Nixon visit, China and the United States encouraged reciprocal visits by scholars, doctors, musicians, and sports figures and also expanded trade. China placed large orders for American farm produce and bought some American jet airplanes.

4. Power Struggle Following the Deaths of China's Leaders (1976). With the death of Prime Minister Chou En-lai and, eight months later, of Chairman Mao Tse-tung, China experienced an open struggle for power between two Communist party factions labeled "radicals" and "moderates." The radicals favored strict adherence to Maoist theories of class warfare, no profit incentives, and "permanent revolution." The moderates stressed pragmatic goals of economic growth and political stability. The moderates attracted support of the industrial managers, government officials, and army leaders.

Hua Kuo-feng (Hua Guofeng), an active party and government figure, was named Prime Minister, and then Communist party chairman. He acted swiftly against four top radical leaders, the most notable one being Mao's widow, *Chiang Ching* (Jiang Qing). The radical leaders were purged from their party posts, placed under arrest, and charged with a plot to "usurp party and state power." Hua's action against the "gang of four" was acclaimed by huge demonstrations.

In foreign affairs, the new Chinese regime labeled the Soviet Union as a "peace swindler and most dangerous source of war today." Also, China indicated a strong desire to maintain and improve friendship with the United States.

5. Full Diplomatic Relations (1979). The United States and Communist China agreed to establish full diplomatic relations. For the United States, this agreement meant breaking diplomatic ties with Taiwan, withdrawing the American forces on that island, and giving the required one-year notice to end its mutual defense treaty with Taiwan. The United States, however, pledged to maintain cultural and economic ties with Taiwan, to sell Taiwan limited supplies of defensive arms, and to remain interested in the peaceful settlement of the Taiwan issue. For China, the agreement meant an implied promise—but no public statement—not to use force to take Taiwan.

Teng Hsiao-ping (Deng Xiaoping), the senior Deputy Prime Minister of China, had spurred the restoration of full diplomatic relations. A pragmatist and moderate, Teng wanted China to increase trade with and learn from the West so as to hasten China's modernization. Although twice purged during the Mao era, Teng became most influential in post-Maoist China.

President Carter hailed the new Sino-American relationship—economically as furthering trade and politically as "simple reality" that "contributes to the cause of peace." The Soviet Union, however, indicated its concern over this development as potentially dangerous to its interests. (In 1981, when the Reagan administration agreed to sell modern American weapons to China, the Soviets deplored the agreement as "highly dangerous for the cause of peace.")

6. Mao Downgraded: New Chinese Leaders. In 1981 the Chinese Communist party gave its official assessment of Mao Tse-tung. Stating that his contributions "far outweigh" his mistakes, the party called Mao a brilliant revolutionary but a blundering national leader. Mao was condemned for the Cultural Revolution that, the party said, "was responsible for the most severe setbacks and the heaviest losses suffered by the party, the state, and the people." In his later years, Mao was also blamed for being arrogant, for suppressing discussions, and for fostering his own personality cult.

Reflecting this statement of Chinese Communist views, the party made major changes in party and government leaders. *Hua Kuo-feng* was replaced as premier and as party chairman by two Teng supporters. *Chao Tzu-yang* (Zhao Ziyang) became premier, and Hu Yaobang (Pinyin spelling) became party general secretary. (The party chairman title was abolished as being too closely associated with Mao's personality cult.) Teng—now the most powerful man in China—thus arranged an orderly transfer of power to more youthful persons committed to his views.

7. China vs. Vietnam: Hostility Between Communist Nations (By 1979). Check the Index for Vietnam.

8. Sudden Crackdown. During the 1980's China's leaders permitted freer debate, and a movement for democratic reforms sprang up, gaining support even from the party-dominated press. In the spring of 1989, crowds surged through Beijing and other cities, and students staged a prolonged sit-in in the capital's Tiananmen Square. In June, calling the movement an "insurrection," Chinese leaders suddenly crushed the movement with soldiers and tanks. Hundreds died in the crackdown.

9. Recent Chinese Foreign Policies

a. Thaw in Chinese-Soviet Relations. After Mao's death in 1976, relations between the two Communist giants slowly improved. First there were low-level talks on border disputes. Then Soviet leader Mikhail S. Gorbachev said he was cutting troop strength in areas near the Chinese border. A further thaw came when Soviet troops pulled out of Afghanistan in 1989 (see page 620). Gorbachev flew to Beijing in May 1989 for the first Chinese-Soviet summit meeting in 30 years. The meeting led to a renewal of ties between the Soviet and Chinese Communist parties and to high-level talks about border disputes. In 1990, Chinese Prime Minister Li Peng visited the Soviet Union. American leaders expressed no alarm at the "normalization" of Soviet-Chinese ties, saying they welcomed any reduction in international tensions.

b. Relations with the United States. (1) China asked the United States to halt arms sales to Taiwan. The United States promised to reduce such sales. (2) For several months after the crushing of China's pro-democracy movement in 1989, President Bush suspended American loans and other assistance to China. By 1990 he had re-established normal ties. Some members of Congress said Bush had not acted strongly enough against China's suppression of human rights.

c. Agreements on Hong Kong and Macao. China made plans to take back two small territories on its southern coast. Britain's 90-year lease on Hong Kong expires in 1997, and in 1985 Britain agreed to return the territory when the lease expires. In 1987, Portugal agreed to turn Macao over to China in 1999.

JAPAN

TERRITORIAL LOSSES FOLLOWING WORLD WAR II

Following her surrender in 1945, Japan was stripped of her foreign territories. Japan lost Taiwan and Manchuria to China, and the Kuriles and the southern half of Sakhalin Island to Russia. The Ryukyu Islands, which contain Okinawa, were occupied by the United States. The Japanese-mandated Mariana, Marshall, and Caroline Islands in the Pacific were transferred to the United States as a U.N. trusteeship. Korea was divided into Russian and American zones pending independence (check the Index for Korea).

JAPAN UNDER AMERICAN OCCUPATION (1945–1952)

General Douglas MacArthur, serving as Supreme Allied Commander in Japan, proceeded as follows:

1. **New Constitution (1947).** Under MacArthur's direction, the Japanese people adopted a democratic constitution which (*a*) renounced the waging of war and the maintaining of offensive armed forces, (*b*) denied the Emperor's divine origin but retained him as a symbol of national unity, (*c*) contained a bill of rights guaranteeing civil liberties, including freedom of speech and press, separation of church and state (ending government support for Shintoism), equality under the law (including equal rights for women), and the right to a standard of wholesome living, and (*d*) provided for a cabinet responsible to an elected two-house legislature, called the *Diet*.

2. **Economic and Social Reforms.** MacArthur promoted actions by which Japan (*a*) dissolved the huge business monopolies, such as the *Mitsui* and *Mitsubishi*, which had controlled much of Japan's economic life, (*b*) encouraged free labor unions empowered with the right to strike, (*c*) provided farms for landless peasants, and (*d*) reformed education by removing ultranationalist teachers and textbooks and encouraging democratic learning.

3. **War Trials.** Japanese war leaders were tried before Allied courts on war crime charges: aggressive warfare and atrocities against prisoners. Some Japanese leaders were sentenced to prison; others were executed.

TREATY OF PEACE WITH JAPAN (1952)

Drawn up by the United States, the Japanese peace treaty was accepted by the major Allied nations except the Soviet Union. Russia refused to sign the treaty chiefly because it confirmed Japan's position as an ally of the United States. (In 1956 Russia signed a declaration of peace with Japan.) The 1952 treaty provided as follows:

1. **Territory.** Japan lost all its conquests but retained its four large home islands. (Japan consented to American administration of the Ryukyu Islands, including Okinawa, but retained the right to claim their return.)

2. **Reparations.** Japan was not required to pay reparations for war damages. However, Japan agreed to contribute goods and services to countries damaged by Japanese aggression in World War II.

3. **Defense.** Japan was recognized as an independent, sovereign nation possessing the right of military self-defense. In a separate pact, the United States and Japan agreed that American troops remain stationed in Japan.

AMERICAN FRIENDSHIP FOR JAPAN

1. **Reasons.** (*a*) Because of the reforms introduced in Japan during the American occupation, the United States considers Japan an Asian bulwark of democracy. (*b*) Japan's postwar government, democratically elected and controlled by the Liberal Democratic party, has been stable, pro-capitalist, pro-American, and anti-Communist. Among Japanese voters, Communist influence has been negligible. (*c*) Japan represents a counterbalance to the growth of Communist power in Asia. (*d*) Japan is a valuable ally because of its

industrial capacity, productive workers (drawn from a population of 117 million), and strategic location off the Asian continent.

2. Evidences. The United States (a) treated Japan generously in the peace treaty, (b) extended economic and military aid to Japan, (c) kept American forces in Japan for the defense of Japan and other free world nations in eastern Asia, (d) developed close commercial and cultural ties, and (e) in 1972 returned the Ryukyu Islands, including Okinawa, to Japan. (In contrast, the Soviet Union has refused to return four small northern islands seized at the end of World War II and repeatedly claimed by Japan.)

RECENT DEVELOPMENTS AND PROBLEMS

1. Limited Rearmament. In accordance with its constitution, Japan maintains only a small military force for "self-defense." These troops are insufficient to defend the nation. However, Japanese public opinion, strongly pacifist, remains unwilling to amend the constitution to permit more extensive rearmament. Meanwhile, the people are free of heavy military expenditures and depend on the United States to protect their homeland.

2. Economic Recovery. Under its free-enterprise economic system, postwar Japan achieved a remarkable economic growth rate. Industrial production had regained prewar levels by 1951 and has since then more than tripled. Japan ranks among the world's top manufacturers of automobiles, steel, synthetic fibers, electrical products, and cotton yarn; it is first in shipbuilding. Japan is the world's third greatest economic power and enjoys a standard of living approaching that of Western Europe. With limited farmland and mineral resources, however, Japan must "export or die."

3. Trade With the United States. Japan provides the second largest market for American exports and, in turn, finds the United States its best customer. Americans purchase Japanese autos, toys, cameras, radios, and television sets. American manufacturers protest this competition and request adequate tariff protection, complaining that Japanese wages are lower than those paid American workers. In recent years Japan has had a huge favorable balance of trade with the United States. In 1985 the Reagan administration ended restrictions on the import of Japanese autos but expected Japan to "open up" its home markets for American beef, citrus fruits, and cigarettes.

INDIA

BRIEF SURVEY

1. Independence and Government. In 1947 India received independence from Britain. *Jawaharlal Nehru*, India's independence leader, became Prime Minister and promoted a democratic government. In 1975 Prime Minister *Indira Gandhi*—Nehru's daughter—moved India away from democracy by declaring a "state of emergency," arresting political opponents, and instituting press censorship. In 1977 elections, Mrs. Gandhi and her Congress party were decisively defeated and for three years she was out of office.

In the 1980 elections, Mrs. Gandhi achieved a remarkable triumph as her faction of the Congress party won control of the legislature, and she again became India's Prime Minister.

2. Assassinations of Indira Gandhi and Rajiv Gandhi. Mrs. Gandhi aroused the wrath of the Sikh religious community by ordering the Indian army to suppress a Sikh extremist revolt for an independent state. Shortly afterward, 1984, Mrs. Gandhi was killed by two Sikh members of her bodyguard.

Rajiv Gandhi—son of Indira—became Prime Minister. He stirred passions by sending troops to help the Sri Lankan government combat a rebellion by Tamil separatists. A scandal in the government in 1989 caused Gandhi to lose control of parliament. During a campaign for reelection in 1991, Gandhi was assassinated, possibly by Indian Tamils.

3. Mixed Economy. To raise the low living standards of its 850 million people, India utilizes a "mixed economy" of private and public enterprise. To supplement the efforts of domestic entrepreneurs and foreign companies, the gov-

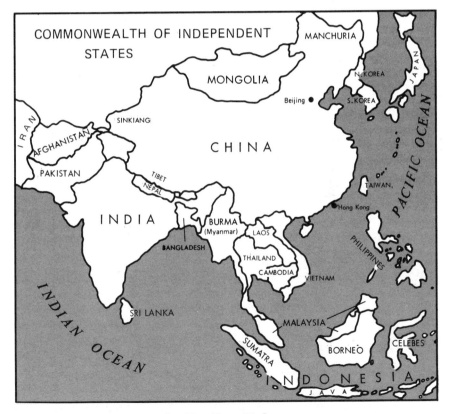

The Far East Today

ernment has undertaken *Five-Year Plans*: constructing irrigation projects, electric power plants, railroads, and steel mills; distributing land to the peasants; and fostering modern farming methods.

In 1984 *Bhopal* in central India suffered the worst industrial accident in history. From a factory owned by an American chemical company, poisonous fumes escaped, killing some 2500 persons and sickening many thousands more.

4. Foreign Policy of Neutrality. Nehru hoped to devote India's energies to domestic problems. Therefore, in the cold war, Nehru set a policy of nonalignment, or neutrality. Nehru's successors reaffirmed this policy.

COMMUNIST CHINESE AGGRESSION AFFECTS INDIA

Until 1959 Prime Minister Nehru expressed his fear of Western colonialism and his friendship for Communist China. Thereafter, Nehru's sympathy for China was severely shaken, if not destroyed, by Chinese actions in Tibet (India's northern neighbor) and on the Indian border.

1. Tibet. In 1959, after eight years of Chinese Communist occupation and rule, the Tibetan people revolted. The Chinese Communists (*a*) suppressed this revolt, taking many Tibetan lives, and (*b*) accused India of having aided the revolt, a charge that Nehru indignantly denied. Nehru condemned China's brutality in Tibet and granted asylum to thousands of Tibetan refugees, including that country's political and spiritual head, the *Dalai Lama*.

2. Indian Border. For many years China had disputed its boundary with India. In 1959, following the Tibetan revolt, Communist Chinese troops crossed India's northern frontier, attacked Indian border patrols, and occupied large areas of territory claimed by India. In 1962 the Chinese renewed their attack, overpowered Indian resistance, and occupied additional territory. Declaring that his country would resist Chinese aggression, Nehru requested and received military aid from Britain and the United States.

AMERICAN EFFORTS IN INDIA

The United States hopes that India will side with the free world because India (1) in Nehru's words, is "firmly wedded to the democratic way of life," (2) has been menaced by China, and (3) needs American aid to raise the living standards of its people. By 1971 India had received American economic aid worth billions of dollars.

During the 1959 India-China border dispute, President Eisenhower visited India and received a huge welcome. In 1962, when Chinese troops again attacked, President Kennedy airlifted weapons to India. In 1966 President Johnson authorized wheat shipments to prevent starvation in India.

In 1971, however, President Nixon condemned India for sending its troops into East Pakistan and forcibly gaining independence for Bangladesh.

RUSSIAN EFFORTS IN INDIA

Russia seeks to win India to the Soviet side or, at least, to keep it neutral in the cold war: (1) Russia granted loans for the development of India's heavy industry. (Russia's economic aid to India is far less, however, than that extended by the United States.) (2) In 1963, as the split between Russia and China widened, Soviet leaders voiced support for India in its border dispute with China. (3) In 1971 Russia signed a 20-year treaty of friendship with India; thereafter, as the Indian-Pakistani war started, Russia supported India by vetoing three Security Council resolutions for a cease-fire and withdrawal of Indian forces to their own soil. (Check the Index for "India, war with Pakistan.")

Russian efforts may have had some success. India's Prime Minister Indira Gandhi, while professing an evenhanded approach, had seemed to favor the Soviet Union. This policy, followed by subsequent prime ministers, was reassessed after the collapse of the Soviet Union in 1991.

KOREA

KOREA AFTER WORLD WAR II

In 1945 Korea (a colony of Japan since 1910) was divided at the 38th parallel: the North occupied by Russian troops, the South by American troops. Russia and the United States failed to agree regarding Korean reunification, and Russia defied U.N. attempts to unify the country by free elections. In North Korea, the Russians established a Communist government led by the Korean Workers Communist party head, *Kim Il-Sung*, and, in addition, equipped a powerful Korean army. In South Korea, the U.N.-supervised elections established an independent anti-Communist government headed by President *Syngman Rhee*.

COMMUNIST AGGRESSION AGAINST SOUTH KOREA (1950–1953)

In June, 1950, without warning, North Korean Communist forces crossed the 38th parallel and invaded South Korea. The U.N. Security Council, with Russia absent, promptly recommended that U.N. members furnish military assistance to South Korea. The U.N. army consisted chiefly of American and South Korean units, with contingents from 15 other anti-Communist nations. It was headed by General Douglas MacArthur.

At first, the U.N. forces retreated before the Communist assault. After reinforcements arrived, General MacArthur launched a counterattack that drove the North Korean armies back across the 38th parallel and deep into North Korea close to the Manchurian border. In November 1950, powerful Communist Chinese armies crossed into North Korea and attacked the U.N.

forces, inflicting heavy losses and compelling MacArthur to retreat. By the summer of 1951 the battle line had become stabilized near the 38th parallel.

Meanwhile, the U.N. General Assembly voted (with opposition only from the Soviet bloc) to declare Communist China guilty of aggression in Korea and to embargo the shipment of war goods to China.

MacARTHUR-TRUMAN CONTROVERSY

In 1951 President Truman, as commander in chief of the American armed forces, dismissed General MacArthur for insubordination. Truman charged that the General had repeatedly disregarded instructions to refrain from making foreign policy statements that criticized government policies.

The two men had disagreed sharply. MacArthur advocated carrying the war to China, especially Manchuria. He urged that the United States fight an all-out war to win complete victory over Communism in Asia. Truman feared that an invasion of Manchuria would lead to war with Russia. He held that the United States must fight a limited war in Asia so as not to leave Western Europe, the key to American security, defenseless.

TRUCE IN KOREA (1953)

Meeting mainly at *Panmunjom,* U.N. and Communist negotiators took two years to agree upon truce terms. The conference was long deadlocked regarding the return, or *repatriation,* of prisoners. The U.N. claimed that many of its prisoners did not want to return to Communist rule; the Communists insisted upon compulsory repatriation. Finally, the conference agreed that all prisoners be given freedom of choice. (Eventually, two of every five prisoners held by the U.N. refused to return to Communist rule.)

The truce (1) was hailed by the U.N. as a victory against aggression, (2) was criticized by the South Korean government for failing to unify the country under anti-Communist leadership, and (3) was greeted by most Americans with relief. The Korean struggle cost the United States $18 billion, 103,000 wounded, and 33,000 killed.

KOREAN DEVELOPMENTS SINCE THE TRUCE

1. **Continued American Interest.** In support of South Korea, the United States extended considerable economic and military aid, kept 39,000 troops there, and signed a bilateral Mutual Defense Pact. In turn, South Korea sent a fighting force to aid the Americans in South Vietnam.

In 1977 President Carter, while reaffirming America's commitment to defend South Korea, announced plans for a phased withdrawal by 1982 of 33,000 American ground troops from South Korea. These plans caused considerable anxiety among South Korean and Japanese leaders. In 1979, as President Carter became aware of the increased strength of North Korea's armed forces, he suspended the withdrawal of the American ground troops.

2. Governmental Changes in South Korea

a. Rhee Regime (1948–1960). In 1960 South Korea was swept by antigovernment riots protesting rigged elections, police terror, corruption, and autocratic rule. Syngman Rhee ended his 12-year presidency by resigning.

b. Park Regime (1961–1979). General *Park Chung Hee* seized power in 1961. He improved economic conditions and maintained a pro-American foreign policy. After imposing martial law in 1972, Park ruled by increasingly dictatorial methods. The head of Korea's Central Intelligence Agency assassinated Park in 1979.

c. Chun Regime (1980–1988). General *Chun Doo Hwan* seized control of the Seoul government. Pledging to wipe out corruption and to foster a "democracy suited to our political climate," Chun secured public approval of a new constitution containing such democratic features as guarantees of press freedom and habeas corpus, a ban on forced confessions, and a single seven-year presidential term. However, Chun continued martial law and repressed dissent.

Riots and unrest broke out as the 1987 presidential election approached. Chun favored an election by parliament, while opposition leaders called for direct election by the people. After weeks of disorder, Chun agreed to a direct election and eased repression. With opposition forces split, the ruling party's candidate, *Roh Tae Woo*, won the presidency with 36 percent of the vote.

d. Roh Regime (1987–1993). Under the Roh regime, South Korea continued its trend to greater democracy. Opposition parties won control of parliament in 1988 elections, leading to more than a year of political stalemate. In 1989 President Roh surprised the nation by announcing formation of a grand alliance between the ruling party and two of the three major opposition parties. The resulting *Democratic Liberal party* had a large legislative majority. A year later, the third big opposition party merged with a smaller group, creating the new *Democratic party*. Those changes brought greater stability to South Korean politics.

Under President Roh, South Korea opened diplomatic relations with the Soviet Union and China. Soviet President Gorbachev paid an unprecedented state visit to South Korea in 1991.

e. Kim Regime (1993–   ). *Kim Young Sam*, a long-time dissident who had spent many years under house arrest, joined the Democratic Liberal party in 1990 and won election as its presidential candidate in a three-way race in 1992. The first civilian president in three decades, Kim promised to bolster democracy by increasing the powers of provincial and local governments. Among his first acts was a sharp crackdown on corruption.

3. Recent Developments

a. Talks About Reunification. In the late 1980's, South Korea and North Korea began talks aimed at easing tensions and eventually reunifying the country. With 44 million people, rapidly industrializing South Korea has a per capita income of $6,200. North Korea, with a population of 22 million, has a per capita income less than one fourth that large.

In 1991, after North Korea dropped its objections, the two Koreas applied for and were granted membership in the United Nations.

b. American Moves. In 1990, with the cold war at an end, the United States began withdrawing some of the 43,000 troops it had stationed in South Korea. The following year the United States removed its nuclear weapons from South Korea.

c. North Korean Succession. Kim Il Sung, North Korea's leader for 46 years, died in 1994. His son, Kim Jong Il, assumed the Communist dictatorship.

d. Tensions Over North Korea's Nuclear Potential. Reports that North Korea might be on the verge of making an atomic bomb caused heightened tensions in the 1990's. The United Nations urged North Korea to permit full international inspection of its nuclear program, as required under the Nuclear Non-Proliferation Treaty of 1968, which North Korea had signed. North Korea said nuclear inspectors (who visited North Korea under the treaty's enforcement provisions) were exceeding their authority. It threatened to withdraw its adherence to the treaty. The United States suggested U.N. economic sanctions if North Korea refused to abide by the treaty.

On a visit to South Korea in July 1993, President Clinton warned that if North Korea ever developed and used an atomic bomb, "we would quickly and overwhelmingly retaliate." He added: "It would mean the end of their country as they know it." With tensions high, the United States offered Patriot missiles to help South Korea defend its capital against any North Korean attack.

NATIONS OF INDO-CHINA

INDO-CHINA UNDER FRENCH RULE

In the 19th century, France annexed Indo-China. This was an agricultural region in Southeast Asia with a predominantly Buddhist population. During World War II, while France was overrun by the Nazis, Indo-China was occupied by the Japanese. Indo-Chinese nationalists, opposed to both Japan and France, joined an independence movement called the *Vietminh*. Although this movement contained some non-Communist nationalists, it was controlled by Communists and led by Moscow-trained *Ho Chi Minh*.

COMMUNISTS SEEK CONTROL (1946–1954)

After the war, France promised partial independence to the three states of Indo-China: Laos, Cambodia, and Vietnam. The Vietminh rejected the

French offer and gained popular support by appealing to (1) *nationalism*, with promises to drive out the French completely, and (2) *land hunger*, with promises to distribute land to the peasants. For eight years, civil war raged in Indo-China. The Vietminh received military training and supplies from Red China. The French and their Indo-Chinese allies received military equipment from the United States. Finally, the tide of battle turned in favor of the Vietminh, who in 1954 won the crucial *Battle of Dien Bien Phu.*

GENEVA CONFERENCE: TRUCE FOR INDO-CHINA (1954)

Britain and the Soviet Union (as co-chairmen), the United States, Red China, France, and the states of Indo-China sent representatives to Geneva to negotiate a settlement. The Geneva Agreements, not signed by the United States or South Vietnam, provided as follows: (1) *Laos* and *Cambodia* were recognized as independent and were expected to observe neutrality in the cold war. (2) *Vietnam* was divided at the 17th parallel: the North under a Communist government in *Hanoi*, the South under a French-sponsored anti-Communist government in *Saigon*. The people in both the North and the South were to vote by mid-1956 for a single all-Vietnam government.

DEVELOPMENTS IN VIETNAM

1. **Communist North Vietnam.** Ho Chi Minh established a Communist dictatorship, increased the army's manpower, eliminated most private enterprise, and received considerable Russian and Chinese aid. The Communists sought control of South Vietnam.

2. **Anti-Communist South Vietnam.** The Saigon government became fully independent of France, was strongly anti-Communist, and rejected plans for all-Vietnam elections. It argued that honest elections were impossible in the Communist north. To undermine the Saigon government, the Communist Vietcong waged guerrilla warfare throughout the south—terrorizing villagers and killing government supporters—and established Vietcong control over large rural areas. Saigon requested American aid. This was first granted by President Eisenhower and later expanded by President Kennedy. American leaders feared that a Communist takeover in South Vietnam might cause the bordering nations in Southeast Asia to fall to the Communists like a row of "falling dominoes."

3. **Escalation of the War.** In 1964 a limited number of American troops and military advisers were in South Vietnam, and American naval units patrolled the international waters of the Gulf of Tonkin. When North Vietnamese torpedo boats attacked American destroyers in the gulf, President Johnson ordered an air strike against North Vietnam's naval bases. The President's action received almost unanimous support from Congress in its vote for the *Gulf of Tonkin Resolution.* (In 1970 Congress repealed this resolution.)

In 1965, after American bases in South Vietnam had been attacked by Communist forces, President Johnson ordered continuous air strikes against North Vietnamese military targets. The United States increased its forces in South Vietnam, eventually to over 500,000 individuals. Also, four SEATO members—Australia, New Zealand, the Philippines, and Thailand—augmented the South Vietnamese and American forces.

The Communist nations increased their support for the Vietcong and Hanoi. Moscow provided additional military equipment. Peking assigned service troops to maintain transportation in the North.

4. Debate in America Regarding Vietnam. American public opinion divided sharply regarding Vietnam. (a) The "hawks" argued for increased military action to halt aggression and contain Communist expansion in Asia. Many hawks demanded that we drastically step up military pressures on Hanoi. (b) The "doves" urged the United States to seek peace by reducing its military activities in Vietnam. They argued that America (1) had no vital interests in Vietnam, (2) was risking war with China, and (3) was supporting a Saigon government that commanded no loyalty among the people. (This government was dominated from 1967 to 1975 by the military leader who was elected as president, *Nguyen Van Thieu.*)

5. The Move to Peace Talks (1965–1968). President Johnson made several efforts to move the Vietnam conflict from the battlefield to the conference

Mansbridge, Punch (ROTHCO)

"Tell us again, old one, what peace was like."

table—all unsuccessful. In 1968 President Johnson again halted the bombing, this time of most of North Vietnam, and Hanoi agreed to peace negotiations. The two nations began talks in Paris. Later the peace talks were expanded to include the Saigon government and the Vietcong.

6. Nixon Administration and Vietnam (1969–1974)

a. Diplomatic Stalemate Continues. President Nixon sought a Vietnam settlement that would free American prisoners of war and enable the South Vietnamese people to decide their own future by honest, internationally supervised elections. Communist leaders demanded complete withdrawal of American forces and replacement of the "puppet" Thieu government by a pro-Communist regime. The Paris talks remained deadlocked.

b. Vietnamization. Nixon spurred *Vietnamization,* that is, shifting the burden of fighting the war to South Vietnamese forces. By late 1972 he had withdrawn over 500,000 personnel from Vietnam, leaving there only 27,000 American troops. American casualty lists grew much shorter.

c. The War Spills Over Into the Other Indo-Chinese States

(1) *Cambodia.* In 1970 a new, rightist-leaning regime took control. It reaffirmed Cambodia's neutrality and demanded the withdrawal of North Vietnamese and Vietcong forces from bases in Cambodia. Instead, the Communist forces attacked Cambodian towns. Thereupon, President Nixon ordered American forces to join with South Vietnamese troops in a limited "incursion" into Cambodia to destroy the Communist bases.

(2) *Laos.* In 1970 North Vietnamese and local Communist Pathet Lao forces overran much of southern Laos. In 1971 South Vietnamese forces with American air support began a limited "incursion" into southern Laos to disrupt enemy supply routes.

Both incursions aroused much controversy in the United States, again between the "hawks" and the "doves."

d. Secret Peace Talks. Since 1969 Washington and Hanoi had held, near Paris, a series of secret peace talks. The American negotiator was President Nixon's national security adviser, *Henry Kissinger;* the Hanoi negotiator was *Le Duc Tho.* In 1973 they reached an agreement.

7. The Paris Peace Agreement for Vietnam (1973)

a. Major Provisions

(1) *Military.* (a) The United States, North Vietnam, South Vietnam, and the Vietcong agree to a cease-fire. (b) The United States shall withdraw its remaining forces and dismantle its remaining military bases in South Vietnam. (c) Hanoi and the Vietcong shall return all American prisoners of war and provide the fullest accounting for persons "missing in action" (MIA). (d) All foreign troops shall be withdrawn from Laos and Cambodia. (e) No more troops and military supplies shall be introduced into South Vietnam.

(2) *Reunification.* (a) The reunification of Vietnam shall be achieved only by peaceful means. (b) Pending reunification, both North and South Vietnam shall respect the provisional demarcation line at the 17th parallel.

(3) *Political Arrangements for South Vietnam.* (a) Saigon and the Vietcong each shall retain the areas under its control at the time of the cease-fire. (b) The people of South Vietnam have a sacred right to decide their own political future through free and democratic elections.

b. Observations. (1) The agreement was a compromise, with neither side gaining all its objectives. The United States did *not* secure (a) the withdrawal of an estimated 145,000 Hanoi troops out of the South and back to the North and (b) a cease-fire for Laos and Cambodia. Hanoi did *not* secure (a) the overthrow of the Thieu regime in Saigon and (b) the establishment of a Communist-dominated government in the South. (2) The Vietnamese War cost the United States over an 11-year period $140 billion, more than 300,000 wounded, and 46,000 killed. It was one of the costliest and most divisive wars in American history.

COMMUNIST FORCES TRIUMPH IN INDO-CHINA (1975)

1. **Cambodia—(Kampuchea).** The rightist-leaning government faced increasing military pressure from Communist forces: some North Vietnamese units and the local *Khmer Rouge*. The government forces, despite a Congress-imposed cutoff of American air support, withstood the Communist insurgents for more than a year. In early 1975, however, the government forces collapsed; Communist troops took control of the entire country.

The Khmer Rouge executed Cambodian leaders who had opposed them, forcibly drove urban residents out of the major cities into rural areas, which caused many deaths, and on charges of spying, seized an American merchant vessel, the *Mayaguez*. When diplomatic efforts failed, President Ford ordered American forces to rescue the crew and vessel, which was done at a cost of almost 70 Americans killed and wounded.

2. **Laos.** The anti-Communist forces and the Communist Pathet Lao reached a cease-fire agreement and established a coalition government. In 1975, following the Communist victories in Cambodia and South Vietnam, the Communist Pathet Lao took full control of the government and country.

In 1976 reports out of Laos indicated that the Pathet Lao held 50,000 rightists and neutralists in harsh prison camps for punishment and "reeducation." Many inmates had died from lack of food and medicine.

3. **Vietnam.** (a) The United States withdrew its remaining military forces but continued to give limited economic and military aid to the Thieu regime. (b) North Vietnam, in violation of the Paris agreement, increased its forces in the South to an estimated 400,000 men. In 1975 the North Vietnamese and Vietcong mounted a major offensive and gained full control of the South.

It makes a nice shield.

Wright in the San Diego Union

During this final phase of the Vietnam War, the United States proceeded as follows: (1) President Ford pledged that American forces would not return to Vietnam. (2) The United States helped evacuate from their homeland thousands of South Vietnamese—many of whom had worked with the Americans and feared for their lives under Communist rule. Congress voted funds to assist some 120,000 Vietnamese refugees to come to the United States. (3) President Ford spoke out to reassure our allies who, viewing the downfall of the pro-American governments in Cambodia and South Vietnam, were concerned regarding the direction of American foreign policy and the credibility of American defense treaties. The President warned any potential enemies that "we will stand up to them" and affirmed that "no allies or time-tested friends of the United States should worry or fear that our commitments to them will not be honored."

In 1976 reports out of South Vietnam indicated that the Communists held between 100,000 and 300,000 persons in labor camps where brutal conditions caused many deaths. Also in 1976 the Communists proclaimed the official reunification of the country as the *Socialist Republic of Vietnam*.

REFUGEES FROM INDO-CHINA (SINCE 1975)

Following the Communist takeovers, more than 1 million people fled from the three Indo-Chinese states and became refugees. They were driven by varied motives: (1) The earliest refugees were those Indo-Chinese closely identified with the overthrown anti-Communist regimes, who feared for their lives under Communist rule. (2) The ethnic Chinese, many of families who had lived in Vietnam for generations, were pressured to leave by the Hanoi regime. The Chinese had been merchants and moneylenders—capitalist enterprises; they were considered of doubtful loyalty by Hanoi; and they were disliked by the Vietnamese. Many Chinese were compelled to pay large sums to the Hanoi regime before being permitted to depart. (3) Cambodians fled political instability and renewed warfare as Vietnamese troops invaded Cambodia to oust a pro-Chinese regime and install a government subservient to Hanoi. (4) Other refugees fled harsh Communist rule, forced evacuation from cities, and the lack of food, clothing, and other essentials.

Some refugees fled overland to Thailand and China; others fled by sea and became known as the *boat people.* Fewer than half the boat people were estimated to have survived their unsafe vessels, the hazards of the sea, and pirate attacks and to have reached land in the Philippines, Malaysia, Indonesia, and southern Thailand. The refugees were not welcomed—and in many cases were forcibly driven out—by the Southeast Asian nations. These nations insisted that they lacked the facilities and resources to care for the refugees and were unwilling to absorb the refugees into their societies.

Refugees in large numbers were accepted by the United States and in lesser numbers by other Western nations—notably Canada, Australia, and France. Some 250,000 ethnic Chinese found temporary safety in Hong Kong and southern China.

The plight of the refugees led to a 1979 U.N. conference at which (1) Hanoi promised to stem the flow of refugees, (2) the U.N. promised—with funds mainly from Western nations and Japan—to care for the refugees in transit camps, and (3) Western nations promised to accept additional refugees.

Vietnam meanwhile was viewed with grave mistrust by many Western powers, the Southeast Asian nations, and China.

VIETNAM VS. CHINA: HOSTILITY BETWEEN COMMUNIST NATIONS (BY 1979)

1. Reasons. By 1979 Vietnam had aroused the anger and hostility of Communist China. (*a*) Vietnam indicated its preference for the Soviet Union, which country China viewed as its major enemy. In 1978 Vietnam signed a 25-year friendship treaty with Russia, receiving pledges of economic aid and of "effective measures" in case of attack by a third party. Hanoi was cooperating with Moscow, so Peking believed, in encircling China with hostile states. (*b*) Vietnam moved to control all Indo-China. Whereas Laos yielded to Vietnamese dominance, Cambodia did not. Under *Pol Pot*, this Cambodian regime ruled with great brutality. It was pro-Chinese and received extensive Chinese military and economic aid. After a series of border skirmishes, Vietnam in late 1978 launched a full-scale invasion of Cambodia, overthrew the Pol Pot regime, and installed a puppet government under *Heng Samrin*, subservient to Hanoi. China resented the ousting of its ally and held that Moscow was using the Vietnamese in Asia as it had used the Cubans in Africa. (*c*) Vietnam harassed, exacted funds from, and expelled over 250,000 of its ethnic Chinese residents.

2. The Limited War (1979). After several border incidents, China announced that it would no longer tolerate "being pushed around" and would act to "teach Vietnam a lesson." Embarking upon a limited invasion, Chinese armies crossed the border into northern Vietnam and met strong resistance.

Russia warned China to withdraw "before it is too late" and speeded military equipment to Vietnam but itself undertook no military moves. At the U.N., Russia vetoed a Security Council resolution calling upon Vietnam to withdraw from Cambodia and upon China to withdraw from Vietnam. After four weeks of fighting, with heavy casualties on both sides, the Chinese withdrew their forces.

In 1983 Chinese and Vietnamese forces clashed in sporadic encounters.

EFFECTS OF THE VIETNAM WAR ON AMERICAN FOREIGN POLICY

1. The Nixon Doctrine (1969). President Nixon asserted that the United States would continue to play a major role in the Pacific but would seek to avoid involvement in another war like Vietnam. Consequently Nixon told our Asian friends that the United States would honor its treaty commitments, including military and economic aid, but would look to any Asian nation threatened by internal subversion or nonnuclear aggression to provide the manpower for its own defense. The *Nixon Doctrine*, said the President, was an American policy that could "be sustained over the long run."

2. War-Powers Resolution (1973). In ordering American forces into combat in Vietnam, three successive Presidents—Kennedy, Johnson, and Nixon—had used the Presidential power of commander in chief but had not secured a Congressional declaration of war. In 1973 Congress moved to limit Presidential war-making powers by enacting, over President Nixon's veto, the *War-Powers Resolution.* It provided that (*a*) if the President commits American troops to combat abroad, he must present his reasons to Congress within 48 hours, (*b*) if the President expects to keep American troops in

Valtman—ROTHCO

combat abroad for more than 60 days, he must secure Congressional approval, (c) if the President does not secure Congressional approval, he must terminate the military action, and (d) Congress can order withdrawal of American forces from abroad, before 60 days, by adopting a concurrent resolution not subject to a Presidential veto.

President Nixon condemned the resolution as "clearly unconstitutional" and declared that it would "seriously undermine this nation's ability to act decisively . . . in times of international crisis."

3. Other Effects. (a) *Thailand.* Now bordered by Communist Laos and Cambodia and fearful that these countries might aid local guerrilla bands, Thailand in 1975 moved to reduce the American presence. The Thai government requested the United States to close American bases and withdraw American forces on its soil. The United States so acted. (b) *Angola.* After Portugal withdrew in 1975, Angola experienced civil war between pro-Western and pro-Communist groups. When the United States Congress became aware that the Ford administration was sending covert (secret) aid to the pro-Western forces, Congress voted overwhelmingly to prohibit such aid. Congress feared that such aid could lead America to involvement in another Vietnam-type situation. (c) *El Salvador.* A number of Congress members opposed the Reagan policy of economic and military aid to the El Salvador government—battling leftist guerrillas—for fear of another Vietnam-type involvement.

AFGHANISTAN

1. Land and People. Located in central Asia, Afghanistan is a landlocked country of strategic importance. It is bordered on the north by the Soviet Union, on the west by Iran, on the south by Pakistan, and at its eastern tip by China (see map, page 605). Afghanistan is essentially an underdeveloped country.

The Afghan people, totaling 15 million, are devout Muslims. They belong to a number of different tribes and retain a strong sense of tribal identity and loyalty. They speak Persian or Persian-related languages.

2. Pro-Soviet Government (1978). By a 1978 revolution a pro-Marxist party seized control. It established an Afghan regime that signed a treaty of "friendship and cooperation" with the Soviet Union and accepted Soviet military and economic advisers. This pro-Soviet regime aroused strong opposition for being "godless" and anti-Islamic, subservient to the Soviet Union, and a threat to the traditional Afghan way of life. The Communist regime proved unable to suppress the rebellious Islamic tribal guerrilla bands, and by late 1979 government leaders were quarreling among themselves.

3. Soviet Invasion (1979–). The Soviet Union sided with one faction in Afghanistan's government, helping to install a new president, *Babrak Karmal,* in the capital, Kabul. Soviet troops poured into Afghanistan to try to crush the Islamic resistance. Many countries condemned the Soviet invasion. The United States accused the Soviets of "blatant military interference." China called the invasion a threat to its security. Third World nations also protested. The Soviet Union vetoed a U.N. Security Council resolution protesting the invasion. However, the U.N. General Assembly, by a vote of 104 to 18 (with 30 not voting), adopted a resolution deploring the intervention and calling for a withdrawal of all foreign troops. Year after year in the 1980's the Assembly passed new resolutions calling for Soviet withdrawal.

The war in Afghanistan was bitterly fought. Charges of torture and other atrocities were leveled against Soviet and Afghan government forces by the United States, by private groups such as Amnesty International, and by human rights reports at the United Nations. The Afghan government accused Muslim guerrillas of atrocities such as shooting down civilian airliners.

4. United States Help for the Islamic Resistance. The United States sent weapons to the Islamic resistance. Pakistan, Iran, and other nations did the same. The rebels' effectiveness was undermined, however, by quarrels among rival leaders. (In 1985 the seven main guerrilla groups joined in an alliance.)

a. The Carter Doctrine. In his 1980 State of the Union address, President Carter said the Soviet invasion of Afghanistan threatened the Persian Gulf region (see map, page 581), with its oil supplies essential to Western democracies. The President warned that any Soviet attempt "to gain control of the Persian Gulf region will be regarded as an assault" against the United States and "will be repelled by any means necessary, including military force." This warning became known as the *Carter Doctrine.*

The United States began to build up its naval presence in the Persian Gulf region and acquired bases in Somalia, Oman, and the Indian Ocean.

b. The Reagan Doctrine. In what became known as the *Reagan Doctrine,* President Reagan declared in 1986 that the United States would help "freedom fighters" in their efforts to overthrow oppressive, left-wing—especially Communist—regimes. The doctrine applied not only to the rebels in Afghanistan but also to guerrilla movements fighting against the governments of Nicaragua, Angola, and Cambodia.

After meeting with several Afghan rebel leaders in 1986, President Reagan ordered stepped-up aid to the Afghan resistance. The new aid included a type of shoulder-fired missile called the *Stinger* that proved very effective at shooting down Soviet and Afghan government aircraft.

5. Peace Talks. The Soviet Union eventually sent more than 110,000 troops to Afghanistan. By the late 1980's it had suffered more than 13,000 battle deaths. Thousands of government and rebel fighters and more than one million civilians had also died.

U.N.-sponsored negotiations began in Geneva, Switzerland, in 1985 between delegations from Afghanistan, the Soviet Union, and Pakistan. Pakistan was deeply involved because more than 2 million Afghans had fled across the border into Pakistan, and much of the aid to the resistance was funneled through Pakistan.

The talks led to the signing of agreements in 1988 by the Soviet Union, Afghanistan, the United States, and Pakistan. The Soviet Union pledged to withdraw its troops within nine months. The United States said it would stop supplying the Afghan rebels if the Soviet Union stopped arming the Afghan government now headed by President Najib.

6. After the Soviet Withdrawal (1989). Soviet troops completed their withdrawal in February 1989, but the war raged on. Finally, in 1992, Najib resigned, pushed out by rival party members. The rebels reached a shaky truce and backed Sibgatullah Mojadedi as the leader to put together a new anti-Communist government. Ethnic and religious differences remained unresolved.

LATIN AMERICA

GOOD NEIGHBOR POLICY AFTER WORLD WAR II

1. Rio Inter-American Defense Treaty. In 1947 the American nations signed the *Rio Treaty* providing that (*a*) an armed attack against any American state shall be considered an attack against all, and (*b*) the other American states shall assist the victim of attack. President Truman welcomed this expression of hemispheric solidarity.

2. Organization of American States (OAS). In 1948 at Bogota the American nations established the *Organization of American States*.

a. Purposes. The OAS Charter obligates the signatory nations to pursue the following: (1) cooperation in economic and social matters, (2) peaceful settlement of disputes, (3) nonintervention in the internal affairs of any state except to preserve hemispheric security, and (4) collective action against armed attack and against any threat to hemispheric peace.

b. Major Organs. (1) The *Inter-American Conference*, the supreme body, meets once every five years and determines general policy. (2) The *Council*, consisting of representatives of each member nation, is in permanent session as the executive body. (3) *Meetings of Consultation of Ministers of Foreign Affairs* are held as needed to consider urgent problems. (4) The *Inter-American Defense Board* coordinates hemispheric military defense. (5) The *Economic and Social Council*, the *Cultural Council*, and the *Council of Jurists* deal with special problems. (6) The *Pan-American Union* serves as the OAS secretariat.

c. Strengths. The OAS advances inter-American economic cooperation. It provides a forum for the American nations and makes possible hemispheric solidarity on international problems. Finally, by a two-thirds vote, the OAS may recommend action to protect its member nations.

d. Weaknesses. The OAS cannot be sure that its members will heed OAS recommendations. Further, the OAS operates on a limited budget and lacks a military force. Finally, many Latin American members resent the United States because of its economic wealth and military power, and complain that the United States dominates the OAS.

UNITED STATES NEGLECT OF LATIN AMERICA FOLLOWING WORLD WAR II

With the outbreak of the cold war, the United States concentrated its attention (1) upon Europe by such programs as the Truman Doctrine, the Marshall Plan, and NATO, and (2) upon the Far East by its defense of South Korea and its opposition to Communist China. Confident that the Good Neighbor Policy would assure solidarity in the Western Hemisphere, the United States tended to neglect Latin America and its major problems.

BASIC FACTORS UNDERLYING LATIN AMERICAN UNREST

1. Social Factors

a. Population Explosion. Now totaling over 445 million, the population of Latin America is growing faster than that of any other area except Africa. By surpassing the growth of Latin America's economy, its population explosion hinders efforts to raise living standards.

b. Population Divisions. The whites, a large minority, are chiefly descendants of Spanish colonists. (In Brazil, most whites are of Portuguese descent.) The whites also include recent immigrants, such as Italians and Germans. Generally, the whites constitute the upper and middle classes. Usually, they own the large estates and occupy high positions in the dominant Roman Catholic Church, in the armed forces, and in the government. The rest of the population consists of a large minority of *mestizos* (people of mixed white and Indian ancestry) and smaller groups of Indians and blacks. These peoples make up the lower classes of city workers and peasants. These divisions in Latin America's population add overtones of race and nationality to economic problems.

c. Illiteracy. While some Latin American countries have illiteracy rates of 60 percent and above, others have rates as low as 6 percent (Costa Rica). The 20th-century trend has been away from church control of education and toward free public schools. However, many children receive no education at all because they begin work at an early age, and because there are not enough schools. In more industrialized countries, such as Argentina, Uruguay, and Chile, illiteracy is low; in less developed lands, such as Bolivia, Guatemala, and Haiti, illiteracy is high.

2. Economic Factors

a. Poverty. Latin America is enmeshed in widespread poverty. The average income per person is very low, especially when compared to earnings of people in the United States. Great extremes exist between the rich and the poor. Two percent of the people possess 70 percent of the area's wealth. The Latin American masses are not content; they seek to escape poverty and want more of the material benefits of life. Their desire to advance economi-

Latin America—Annual Per Capita Income

cally, shared by peoples of most underdeveloped countries today, is called the "revolution of rising expectations."

   b. Agricultural Problems. Most Latin Americans earn their livelihood from agriculture. Yet only ten percent of the population owns 90 percent of the arable land, much of which is organized into large estates. The *peons*—peasants who work the estates—are practically serfs, many being heavily indebted to the landowner. Reformers have demanded that the large estates be broken up and distributed to the peasants as small family-size farms. In addition to land reform, other problems are primitive equipment, inadequate farming methods, and lack of fertilizer, irrigation, and electrification.

   c. One-Product Economies. The wealth of Latin America lies in its mineral resources and agricultural produce: tin in Bolivia; copper in Chile; oil in Venezuela; coffee in Brazil, Colombia, Costa Rica, and Guatemala; bananas in Ecuador, Honduras, and Panama. Latin America exports these minerals and foodstuffs, and imports manufactured goods. Its major trading partner is the United States. Most Latin American countries are plagued by economic instability. Any change in the world price of their major export affects their entire economy.

   d. Dependence on Foreign Investment. To develop its natural resources and industries, Latin America needs capital. However, the area lacks any significant middle class with funds to invest, and many wealthy Latin Americans, fearing revolution, have placed their capital in safe foreign banks. Consequently, Latin America looks for capital and technical know-how to

Rocky soil.
Hesse in the St. Louis Globe-Democrat

foreign, especially American, corporations. United States investments in Latin America total $33 billion.

3. Political Factors

a. Governmental Instability. Latin American nations have democratic constitutions providing for elected executives and legislatures. Nevertheless, dictators have often taken power in Latin American nations. Democratic traditions are weak, since (1) Spanish colonial rule was autocratic, (2) economic and political power are often in the hands of small elite, (3) the democratically minded middle class is weak, and (4) the masses are poorly educated. Early in the 1990's, for the first time, all members of the OAS had democratically elected governments. But military rule, dictatorship, and revolution remained a threat in many areas.

b. Doubts About Democracy. Latin Americans have had little experience with successful democratic government. Many consider the democratic system weak, corrupt, incapable of achieving basic reforms, and subject to manipulation by the wealthy.

COMMUNIST INFLUENCE IN LATIN AMERICA

To expand their influence among the discontented masses of Latin America, local Communist groups have demanded that the workers receive better wages and that the peasants be given their own land. They have stirred up nationalism against "Yankee imperialism" and have urged seizure of foreign-owned properties. The Communists have achieved some following among labor unions, college students, and intellectuals. These Latin Americans perhaps view communism as a reform movement rather than in terms of economic regimentation and political dictatorship.

The Communists have been encouraged by their (1) success under Castro in gaining control of Cuba, (2) use of Cuba to spread Communist influence into other Western Hemisphere countries—notably Nicaragua, El Salvador, and Grenada—and to stir up an independence movement in Puerto Rico, and (3) temporary ascendancy under Marxist-Leninist President Allende in Chile.

Despite poor economic conditions and Cuban efforts, the number of Communists in Latin America remains small. In the long run, however, some observers believe, Communism poses a serious threat.

FACTORS OPPOSING COMMUNIST INFLUENCE

(1) Latin American upper classes—landowners, businessmen, military leaders, and governmental officials—have feared the loss of their wealth and power. (2) Many Latin American governments have outlawed the Communist party and have no diplomatic relations with Communist Cuba. (3) The Roman Catholic Church has condemned communism as antireligious. (4) Many Latin Americans have strong cultural ties to Western nations,

especially the United States, France, and Spain. (5) Left-of-center non-Communist groups, determined to achieve reform without totalitarianism, have shown strength. An example is the Democratic Action party in Venezuela. (6) With interest in Latin America reawakened, the United States moved to improve relations and encourage reforms.

REAWAKENING OF AMERICAN INTEREST IN LATIN AMERICA

1. **Guatemala** (1951-1954). A leftist regime, with Communists holding a number of posts, ruled the country and carried out a land reform program. Many Americans feared that Guatemala was becoming a Communist bridgehead in the Western Hemisphere. In 1954 anti-Communist groups, reputedly with American assistance, revolted and ousted the leftist regime.

2. **Nixon Tour of South America** (1958). While he was on a goodwill tour, Vice President Richard Nixon received a hostile public reception. In Peru and Venezuela, Nixon faced jeers and assaults by rioting mobs. The incidents prompted the United States to reexamine and improve its policy toward Latin America. Nevertheless, in the next few years, the United States faced further problems in Cuba, Panama, and the Dominican Republic.

CUBA: FROM MILITARY DICTATORSHIP TO COMMUNISM

1. **Batista Dictatorship** (1952-1959). General *Fulgencio Batista* seized the Cuban government and set up a dictatorship. His regime was marked by corruption and terrorism. Beginning in 1956 Batista faced a rebellion led by *Fidel Castro*. Not then known as a Communist, Castro promised to restore democracy to Cuba. He gained support among students, peasants, businessmen, and professional people. Castro waged guerrilla warfare until Batista fled the country. In triumph, Castro entered Havana and proclaimed himself Premier.

2. **Castro Regime** (Since 1959)

   a. Denial of Democratic Rights. The Castro government adopted police state practices: suspending the writ of habeas corpus and other civil liberties, stifling press and radio criticism of Castro's policies, refusing to hold free elections, and trying Castro's opponents before military courts without legal safeguards. Over 500,000 Cubans, including many former Castro supporters, fled to the United States and other nations in the Western Hemisphere.

   b. Economic Changes. Castro decreed a drastic *Agrarian Reform Law,* expropriating land from large plantations (chiefly American-owned) for use by the landless peasants under a system of state-controlled cooperatives. Subsequently, Castro expropriated other properties owned by American corporations. In 1960 President Eisenhower responded by halting American imports of Cuban sugar and banning most American exports to Cuba. Its economy deteriorated, and Castro rationed gasoline, clothes, and food. Cuba required substantial Russian aid, now estimated at $8 million a day, to bolster its faltering economy.

c. Anti-American Attitude. Castro inflamed anti-American sentiment among the Cuban people. He claimed that the United States is imperialist, a supporter of counter-revolutionary forces, and the cause of Cuba's economic woes. Castro denounced the Rio Inter-American Defense Treaty. He challenged America's right to retain its Cuban naval base at Guantanamo Bay.

Several times the Castro regime went before the U.N. to charge the United States with economic aggression and intrigue against Cuba. After repeatedly denying such charges, President Eisenhower in 1961 broke diplomatic relations with Cuba, declaring that "there is a limit to what the United States in self-respect can endure."

d. Communist State. Castro granted key government positions to Communists. The government negotiated an economic pact with Russia, exchanging Cuban sugar for Russian manufactured goods, buying Russian machinery on credit, and securing Communist technicians. Castro also received Communist military equipment. Cuba extended recognition to Red China, becoming the first Western Hemisphere nation to do so. In 1961, for the first time, Castro publicly admitted being a "Marxist-Leninist." He announced plans to transform Cuba into a Communist state.

3. Bay of Pigs Invasion (1961). American-trained Cuban exiles launched a small-scale invasion of Cuba at the *Bay of Pigs.* Although easily crushed by Castro's military forces, the invasion sparked a bitter argument between Russia and the United States. Premier Khrushchev demanded that the United States halt its "aggression" against Cuba and warned that the Soviet Union would assist Castro. In reply, President Kennedy proclaimed American admiration for the Cuban invaders and warned Russia that the United States would "protect this hemisphere against external aggression."

4. Organization of American States and Cuba (1962). At *Punta del Este,* Uruguay, the 21 OAS nations conferred on the problem of Communist Cuba. By unanimous vote except for Cuba, the conference approved resolutions (a) declaring Communism incompatible with the principles of the inter-American system, (b) warning the peoples of the Western Hemisphere against Communist subversion, and (c) removing Castro's Cuba from the Inter-American Defense Board. By a two-thirds vote, the minimum required, the conference also excluded Cuba from all other OAS organs.

5. Soviet Missile Bases in Cuba (1962)

a. Crisis. President Kennedy disclosed that Russia secretly was bringing offensive bombers and missiles into Cuba and building Cuban missile bases

Alexander in The Philadelphia Evening Bulletin

Russian proverbs.

—a threat to the security of the Western Hemisphere. The President ordered a *quarantine* by American naval and air forces on shipments of offensive arms bound for Cuba. He demanded that Russia dismantle the Cuban missile bases and withdraw the bombers and missiles. Furthermore, the President warned that, if any nuclear missiles were launched from Cuba, America would reply with a full retaliatory blow against the Soviet Union. This firm stand by the United States won the support of our NATO and OAS allies.

At first, Russia called the American charges false and labeled the American quarantine "piracy." Then, after several suspenseful days, Khrushchev agreed to dismantle the missile bases and withdraw the offensive weapons. Kennedy agreed to lift the quarantine and pledged not to invade Cuba.

b. Reactions to the Settlement. (1) President Kennedy considered the settlement an honorable accord, not a victory. The President felt relieved that the Soviet offensive weapons were withdrawn in peace. However, the United States is aware that Cuba remains Communist, heavily armed with defensive weapons, and bolstered by Soviet military and technical personnel. (2) Premier Khrushchev called the settlement an example of his policy of peaceful coexistence. He claimed that the American pledge not to invade Cuba ended the need for the missile bases.

6. Communist Cuban Troops in Africa:

(a) *Angola.* In 1975 Cuba sent 15,000 troops to Angola, helping the pro-Soviet faction to gain control of the country. Over the years, the number of troops increased to about 50,000. Then, in 1988, Cuba agreed to withdraw its troops by mid-1991 as part of a settlement between Angola and South Africa to end the civil war in Angola.

(b) *Ethiopia.* In 1977, some Cuban troops in Africa moved to Ethiopia. They assisted the pro-Soviet regime in its war with Somali. Cuban troops were still in Ethiopia in 1991.

7. Soviet Combat Force in Cuba (1979). Check the Index for Cuba, Soviet force in.

PANAMA: SINCE 1964 (Check the Index.)

DOMINICAN REPUBLIC: FROM DICTATORSHIP TO FREE ELECTIONS

1. Trujillo Dictatorship (1930–1961).
General *Rafael Trujillo* seized control of the Dominican Republic, assumed dictatorial rule, suppressed civil liberties, and employed terrorism against his enemies. Trujillo used his power to become a partner in many Dominican business enterprises, thereby amassing a tremendous personal fortune. To improve the country, Trujillo built houses, hospitals, schools, and highways, and encouraged industry. In 1961 General Trujillo was assassinated by disgruntled military leaders, supposedly to avenge personal slights.

2. Political Unrest (1961–1965).
After Trujillo, the Dominican Republic was ruled by four provisional governments, and then by an elected government under left-of-center President *Juan Bosch.* After seven months, the military leaders deposed Bosch, charging him with being indifferent to what they felt was a Communist threat. They established an army-backed civilian junta. In 1965 rebel groups overthrew the junta and planned to reinstate ex-President Bosch. Thereupon, the military leaders who had opposed Bosch organized a counter-revolution. The result was civil war.

3. United States and OAS Intervention.
President Johnson sent American forces into the Dominican Republic—the first direct military intervention by the United States in Latin America in 30 years. Johnson's purposes were to protect American lives and to prevent a Communist takeover. Johnson asserted that "the American nations cannot, must not, and will not permit the establishment of another Communist government in the Western Hemisphere." This statement is sometimes referred to as the *Johnson Doctrine* or the *Johnson Corollary* to the Monroe Doctrine.

In response to a request by the United States, the OAS established an *Inter-American Peace Force*. Combining Latin American and United States troops, the OAS army put an end to the violence in the Dominican Republic.

4. Subsequent Developments. The Dominican Republic has held a number of presidential elections, considered to be relatively honest. The country suffers from high unemployment and lagging economic development.

HAITI: DICTATORSHIP TO DEMOCRACY

1. Duvalier Dictatorship (1957–1986). Haiti shares the island of Hispaniola with the Dominican Republic. After years of American intervention and control and a brief period of democracy in the 1940's, it suffered under the brutal dictatorship of the Duvalier family—*François Duvalier* from 1957 to 1971, then his son *Jean-Claude Duvalier* from 1971 to 1986. The two men used a security force called the *Tontons Macoutes* to maintain control through terror.

Many thousands of Haitians fled by boat to the United States and other countries, eager to escape both political repression and extreme poverty. Haiti had the lowest per capita income in the Western Hemisphere—$440 as of 1991.

2. Military Rule or Democracy? (Since 1986). After a popular uprising expelled Jean-Claude Duvalier, military leaders took control. A brief experiment with controlled elections ended when army leaders ousted an elected president in 1988 after he had been in office five months. Further efforts to institute democracy had the following consequences:

a. Election of Aristide. Observers from the U.N. and the OAS oversaw Haiti's first truly free elections in 1990. Voters gave a landslide victory to a leftist Roman Catholic priest, *Jean-Bertrand Aristide*, who promised to help Haiti's impoverished masses build a better future.

b. Military Rule Again. Military leaders overthrew Aristide in 1991 after he had been in office eight months. The United States, the U.N., and the OAS all demanded that Aristide be returned to office.

c. Trade Embargo and U.S. Involvement. The OAS, and later the U.N., instituted a trade embargo to put pressure on the military leaders. The embargo crippled the already weak Haitian economy, causing widespread suffering. Finally, in 1994, U.S. negotiators convinced the military leaders to leave the country. A force of 20,000 U.S. soldiers dismantled the repressive military controls and helped restore democratic government. Aristide returned to Haiti in triumph, promising democratic elections.

EFFORTS TO IMPROVE UNITED STATES-LATIN AMERICAN RELATIONS

1. Inter-American Development Bank. In 1959 the United States joined in founding the *Inter-American Development Bank*. The United States has provided considerable capital for this bank. Its purpose is to aid the development of Latin America by financing long-term development projects.

2. Information Activities. The United States Information Agency expanded its activities to correct the distorted picture of the United States held by many Latin Americans. Also, Congress voted funds for a student exchange program with Latin America.

3. Presidential Trips. Presidents Eisenhower, Kennedy, and Johnson all visited Latin American nations and received friendly welcomes.

4. Alliance for Progress. President Kennedy held that "those who make peaceful revolution impossible will make violent revolution inevitable." Accordingly, he proposed the *Alliance for Progress* to benefit the Latin American masses—not just the privileged few—and thereby eliminate conditions that breed Castro-type revolutions.

a. Plans. In 1961 the United States and the Latin American nations (Cuba excepted) adopted the following program: (1) *Aid.* The Alliance nations agreed to a 10-year $20-billion aid program for Latin America. Of this sum, the United States was to provide more than half, chiefly as long-term, low-interest loans; the rest was to come from international agencies, Western Europe, Japan, and private capital. (2) *Trade.* The Alliance nations agreed to seek to expand trade and to stabilize prices of Latin America's products, especially coffee and tin. (3) *Reform.* The Alliance nations agreed to improve conditions for the Latin American masses by social and economic reforms: providing free schools for all children, reducing adult illiteracy, eradicating malaria, building public housing, breaking up large estates and giving land to the peasants, and distributing the tax burden fairly.

The Alliance aroused opposition in Latin America from both extremes: left and right. The Communists feared that, if the Alliance improved conditions, they would be less likely to win the support of the masses. The privileged classes feared that, if the Alliance achieved its reforms, they would lose their estates and face heavy income taxes.

b. Mixed Record. The United States has sharply increased aid to Latin America. American funds have been used for distribution of food and for construction of schools, waterworks, power plants, housing, and highways. These efforts, however, have proved to be only a small step toward solving Latin America's massive problems.

On the other hand, (1) Latin America has not significantly attracted more private American capital, (2) most Latin American nations have postponed land reforms, (3) the prices of most Latin American exports have continued to fall, and (4) the GNP (output of goods and services) in Latin America has grown somewhat, but only slightly more than the region's population.

In the United States and Latin America, the record of the Alliance for Progress caused considerable disillusionment. Nevertheless, the Alliance received renewed pledges of Latin American support and of United States aid past 1971, the original terminal date.

CHILE: TROUBLED COUNTRY

1. **The Marxist-Leninist President (1970–1973).** *Salvador Allende Gossens,* supported by the Popular Unity coalition of Socialists, Communists, and other leftists, led in a three-man Presidential race, winning a popular plurality of 36 percent. He was named President by the Congress even though his supporters were a minority. The Congress upheld the Chilean tradition of selecting the first-place finisher.

With socialism as his goal, Allende moved to seize the large estates and distribute the land to peasant cooperatives, to nationalize banks and other businesses, to raise workers' wages while freezing prices, and to expropriate copper mines and other properties, chiefly owned by American companies. Allende promised to compensate the American companies for their nationalized properties but he added that Chile would deduct from such compensation undisclosed sums representing the "excess profits" of past years. Allende affirmed his belief in democracy and permitted non-Marxist parties and news media to exist, but acted to weaken his opponents through legal means. (In 1974 the United States Central Intelligence Agency revealed that, as authorized by the National Security Council, it had conducted covert or undercover activities in Chile, providing funds to keep alive political parties and news media threatened by the Allende government.)

In foreign affairs, Chile recognized Red China and resumed diplomatic relations with Castro's Cuba but also proclaimed a policy of cold war neutrality. Allende kept Chile in the OAS and promised to bar any foreign military bases in Chile that might threaten the United States.

By 1973 Allende was unable to govern Chile effectively and to end the economic chaos. He faced political problems: opposition from the parties controlling Congress and dissension among the parties in his Popular Unity coalition. Allende also faced economic problems. Chile suffered from shortages of foodstuffs and also from a severe inflation. The middle and upper classes, constituting half of Chile's population, opposed Allende's expropriation of large estates and nationalization of small businesses. The Allende government was challenged by a series of strikes and demonstrations by copper miners, truckers (mainly owners), small shopkeepers, doctors and other professionals, and city shoppers—all protesting shortages, inflation, and government economic policies.

2. **Military Rule (1973–1990).** In a swift military coup, marked by bloodshed and the death of Allende, army leaders overthrew the Allende government and replaced it with a conservative military junta headed by general *Augusto Pinochet Ugarte* as President. The military thus broke a 46-year-old Chilean tradition of nonintervention in political affairs, asserting a necessity to liberate Chile from a "Marxist yoke."

United States relations with Chile were strained during the late 1970's but improved in the 1980's. President Carter accused the Pinochet regime of murdering and torturing its opponents. President Reagan tended to be less critical, saying the regime had ended its human rights abuses. Reagan appreciated Pinochet's free-market economic policies and anti-Communist stance.

3. Return to Democracy. General Pinochet staged a plebiscite (yes-no vote) in 1980 that gave him an eight-year term as President. After losing a second plebiscite, the general permitted free elections. An elected government took over in 1990 under President *Patricio Aylwin,* a Christian Democrat supported by a broad coalition of centrists and leftist forces.

EL SALVADOR: CIVIL WAR AND INTERNATIONAL INVOLVEMENT

1. Background—The Christian Democratic Regime. El Salvador is a small, densely populated nation in Central America. The large landowners and military leaders are at the top of the economy, and peasants and urban workers are at the bottom. A succession of military regimes ruled El Salvador up to 1979. In that year, moderate army officers overthrew a right-wing military regime.

Efforts began to write a new constitution that would permit peaceful change and a better life for the poor. Moderates such as *José Napoleon Duarte,* a leader of the Christian Democratic party, played key roles. Under Duarte, the government nationalized banks and foreign trade. With United States support, Duarte's government began to distribute land to the landless.

2. Rightists, Leftists, and Centrists. The centrist Christian Democrats were opposed by both sides of the political spectrum. The extreme right used "death squads" to assassinate political opponents. The extreme left consisted of several guerrilla groups united in the *National Liberation Front* and dominated by Marxists. The guerrillas employed terror against government supporters and attacks against government forces, launching a civil war that would last for more than a decade. The United States provided military and civilian aid to El Salvador's government. American leaders accused the Soviet Union of funneling arms to the guerrillas through Cuba and Nicaragua.

3. War Without End? A series of leaders tried to reform the nation's social system and defeat the guerrillas, with little success on either front. In 1984 voters elected the moderate Duarte as president. In 1989 voters replaced him with a rightist, *Alfredo Cristiani,* a sharp critic of earlier land reforms.

El Salvador's civilian leaders had little success in controlling the military, and critics said that army death squads continued to operate. Warfare reached a new peak with a guerrilla attack on the capital city late in 1989. In 12 years of civil war, more than 70,000 people had died.

Peace talks between the government and the guerrillas began in Mexico City in 1989. With U.N. help, the two sides reached an agreement in 1991. They signed a peace treaty in 1992 and ended the war.

NICARAGUA: REVOLUTION AND FERMENT

1. The Somoza Regime (To 1979). The Somoza family for almost 50 years ruled Nicaragua as a military dictatorship. They manipulated elections, crushed political opposition, and employed terror against their enemies. The Somozas furthered economic growth by building roads, improving port facilities, and developing hydroelectric power. They invested in various business enterprises and amassed a vast family fortune. In foreign policy, the Somoza regime was strongly pro-United States and anti-Communist.

General *Anastasio Somoza Debayle*, who became president in 1967, felt the full force of opposition to dictatorial rule from workers, business leaders, students, professionals, Catholic clergy, and radical Marxists. The opposition was centered in the *Sandinista National Liberation Front*—named after reform leader *Augusto Sandino* who was reputedly killed in 1934 by Somoza orders. Although the Sandinista movement contained many moderates, it was dominated by leftist Marxist leaders. In the 1970's, Sandinista guerrillas, some trained in Cuba and armed with Cuban weapons, mounted attacks to topple the Somoza regime. Nicaragua experienced civil war.

2. The Sandinista Takeover. In 1979 Somoza fled. The Sandinistas named a five-member junta to govern the country. The new regime dissolved Congress, seized the Somoza estates and businesses, and pledged to rebuild Nicaragua.

3. The United States and the Sandinistas. The Sandinista government requested and received humanitarian assistance from the United States during the Carter administration. President Carter thought such help might strengthen moderate elements among the Sandinistas.

By 1982, officials of the Reagan administration believed that the Sandinistas were creating a Soviet-influenced, Marxist regime. The junta had postponed elections, suspended publication of an opposition newspaper, and built up the Nicaraguan military. President Reagan cut off aid to the Sandinistas.

The United States also provided covert aid, through the CIA, to anti-Sandinista guerrillas based in Honduras and Costa Rica. These guerrillas were generally called *contras*, for "counterrevolutionaries." President Reagan called them "freedom fighters" for opposing a Marxist government that ruled by military might.

In 1983, Congress approved $24 million in aid to the contras. It refused further aid the next year after hearing charges that the CIA had been involved in mining Nicaraguan harbors. Under the *Boland Amendment* of 1984, Congress forbade both direct and indirect aid to the rebels. Money and supplies continued to reach the contras from the United States and other countries, however, often coming through private sources that were encouraged and monitored by the Reagan administration.

In 1984, Nicaraguans elected a Sandinista, *Daniel Ortega Saavedra*, as president. Nicaraguan opposition leaders and the Reagan administration charged that the elections had been rigged in favor of the Sandinistas.

4. The Reagan Administration and the Contras. In 1985, President Reagan imposed a trade embargo on Nicaragua. He also secured from Congress $27 million in nonmilitary aid for the contras. But Congress turned down the President's request for military support and continued its ban on such aid.

Nicaragua brought charges of aggression against the United States in the World Court, a U.N. agency. The United States refused to recognize the court's jurisdiction. In 1986 the court ruled that the United States had committed acts of aggression against Nicaragua and had an obligation to pay for damages. The United States vetoed two U.N. Security Council resolutions urging it to obey the court, and officials said that they would ignore the court's ruling.

The United States stepped up aid to countries bordering Nicaragua. It built new airfields and other military facilities in the region and carried out joint maneuvers with Honduran forces. In 1986, after President Reagan warned that the United States faced "the reality of a Soviet military beachhead in Nicaragua," Congress approved both military and nonmilitary aid for the contras. The administration assigned the CIA to oversee contra activity.

In the months after the Congressional decision to aid the contras, major controversies erupted. Congress began investigations to determine (1) whether the CIA or other United States government agencies had aided the contras between 1984 and 1986, in violation of the Boland Amendment, (2) how profits from the secret sale of United States arms to Iran had been diverted to the contras (*see* page 596), and (3) whether individuals or groups among the contras had engaged in drug smuggling and other illegal activities. Eventually, Congress voted to cut off military aid and send only non-military supplies to the contras.

The contras themselves were an alliance of rival factions, ranging politically from moderate to ultraconservative. Under United States pressure, the contras united in 1986 to form the United Nicaraguan Opposition, or UNO.

5. Seeking a Negotiated Settlement in Central America. In August 1987 the presidents of Nicaragua, El Salvador, Guatemala, Honduras, and Costa Rica met in Guatemala and signed an agreement based on a plan by Costa Rican President Oscar Arias Sanchez. The *Arias Plan* called for cease-fires in Nicaragua and El Salvador, a cutoff of outside aid, talks between rival sides, and democratization. (For his achievement, Arias received the Nobel Peace Prize for 1987.)

The ultimate success of the Arias Plan in Nicaragua depended on the disbanding of the contras' army of 10,000 guerrillas and the holding of elections that both the Sandinistas and the contras would accept as democratic. The United States resisted efforts to demobilize the contras before free elections took place.

6. Sandinista Defeat (1990). In conformity with the Central American peace plan, Nicaragua held parliamentary elections in February 1990, inviting representatives of the United Nations, the Organization of American States, and other groups to judge the fairness of the balloting. The voters gave a landslide victory to a 14-party opposition coalition led by *Violeta Barrios de Chamorro.* She is the widow of Pedro Joaquin Chamorro, a newspaper publisher assassinated in the final years of the Somoza dictatorship. Among the reasons for Chamorro's victory were (a) the desperate state of Nicaragua's economy, which had shrunk by half during more than ten years of Sandinista rule and civil war; (b) complaints that the Sandinista government had violated civil rights; and (c) a widespread feeling that only an opposition victory would end the civil war. The United States government openly supplied funds to the Chamorro campaign.

After the elections, President Bush urged the contras to disband their forces and return to Nicaragua in peace. The United States offered millions of dollars in aid to the Chamorro government and said it would end its trade embargo.

Before turning over power, the Sandinistas approved an amnesty for all crimes committed by either side in the civil war. Sandinista leader Daniel Ortega vowed to return to power by peaceful political means.

THE AMERICAN-LED INVASION OF GRENADA (1983)

Grenada, an island nation in the eastern Caribbean, is the smallest country in the Western Hemisphere. Formerly a British possession, Grenada attained independence in 1974 as part of the Commonwealth. By a nonviolent coup in 1979, a leftist, friendly to Cuba, became prime minister. His regime enlisted the aid of Cuban workers, technicians, and soldiers to build a major airport. United States leaders criticized the project, arguing that the airport might be used by large Communist military jets. Grenadian leaders said the airport's purpose was to open Grenada to large-scale tourism.

In October 1983, the Grenadian regime was overthrown by hard-line Marxists who killed the prime minister and other leaders. A few days later, before dawn on October 25, 1983, about 7000 United States troops, together with a small Caribbean force, invaded Grenada. The United States asserted that the invasion (1) had been requested by a five-nation group called the Organization of Eastern Caribbean States, which considered the hard-line Marxists as aggressive and a threat to the region's stability, and (2) conformed to the OAS Charter permitting "collective action" against threats to "peace and security." The Reagan administration called the invading force a "rescue mission" and said its goals were to (1) protect some 1000 Americans on Grenada—mainly students at a medical school—and keep them from being seized as hostages, (2) restore order and democracy on Grenada, and (3) forestall Soviet-Cuban plans to use Grenada to "export terrorism and undermine democracy."

The invasion quickly succeeded, and most Grenadians seemed pleased. Elsewhere in the world, there was widespread criticism. Major NATO allies deplored the intervention. The U.N. General Assembly condemned it. A Security Council resolution "deeply deploring" the invasion was vetoed by the United States. Within the United States, many Americans hailed the invasion as a demonstration of United States resolve against communism. Others criticized it as unnecessary and morally wrong. Moderates backed by the United States took control of Grenada and organized elections in 1984 that put a centrist government in power. President Reagan visited the island in 1986, after the last United States troops had withdrawn, and received an enthusiastic welcome.

MULTIPLE-CHOICE QUESTIONS

1. Which came first in postwar Germany? (1) admission of West Germany to NATO (2) Berlin blockade (3) building of the Berlin Wall (4) Potsdam Conference.

2. Which was a result of both World War I and World War II? (1) All of Germany was placed under occupation by Allied armies. (2) The United States joined its allies in collecting reparations from Germany. (3) Germany was forced to give up all its African colonies. (4) Germany was forced to transfer territory to Poland.

3. After World War II the city of Berlin was located (1) within East Germany (2) within West Germany (3) on the border between East Germany and West Germany (4) on the border between East Germany and Poland.

4. The Soviets wanted to drive the Western powers from West Berlin because that city was (1) traditionally Communist (2) a valuable seaport (3) NATO military headquarters (4) a showcase of democracy and capitalism behind the Iron Curtain.

5. Western determination to remain in West Berlin was based upon (1) the failure of the airlift of 1948–1949 (2) the friendship given to the Western powers by Berliners throughout the 20th century (3) an effort to prevent the return of Nazism in West Berlin (4) the recognition that weakness there would encourage Soviet aggression.

6. The capital of West Germany was (1) Bonn (2) Berlin (3) Nuremberg (4) Munich.

7. America gave economic aid to West Germany after World War II to help (1) stop the spread of Communism (2) strengthen Germany against France (3) socialize German industry (4) raise the German standard of living above prewar levels.

8. Nazi leaders were charged at Nuremberg with (1) losing the war (2) destroying the German Republic (3) inventing missiles (4) committing crimes against humanity.

9. The Ruhr Valley, considered the industrial heart of Europe, is located in (1) East Germany (2) West Germany (3) France (4) Poland.

10. The most valuable resource of the Middle East is (1) iron (2) oil (3) tin (4) rubber.

11. Until the mid-1970's, which Middle East nation received substantial military aid from the Communist bloc? (1) Israel (2) Saudi Arabia (3) Egypt (4) Turkey.

12. The waterway that has been a trouble spot in the relations between Egypt and Israel is the (1) Mediterranean Sea (2) Dead Sea (3) Jordan River (4) Gulf of Aqaba.

13. In the Israeli-Egyptian War of 1956, the United States took a similar position to that of (1) France (2) Israel (3) Great Britain (4) Soviet Russia.

14. Which is a basic cause of unrest throughout Asia? (1) complete control by European powers (2) lack of important natural resources (3) labor shortage (4) low standard of living.

15. Where does the government of Nationalist China maintain its headquarters? (1) Peking (2) Taiwan (3) Hong Kong (4) Singapore.

16. Since the end of the Cultural Revolution, what has characterized China's foreign policy? (1) supporting Russia in the U.N. (2) improving relations with the United States (3) offering aid to SEATO (4) joining in an alliance with India.

17. What was a major point that created disunity between Maoist China and Soviet Russia? (1) Mao Tse-tung's rejection of Marxism (2) Russia's criticism of India (3) the downgrading of Lenin (4) the belief in the inevitability of war.

18. On which issue have the Soviet Union and Communist China agreed? (1) the ultimate triumph of Communism (2) the pooling of nuclear armaments (3) the validity of 19th-century treaties between Russia and China (4) the leadership of the Communist world.

19. One of the items below is a main topic and three are subtopics. Which item is the main topic? (1) military uses of nuclear energy (2) expansion of Communism in Southeast Asia (3) friction between the Soviet Union and the People's Republic of China (4) problems of international peace and security.

20. Our efforts to cultivate friendship with Japan were based chiefly upon (1) our desire to import Japanese products (2) our regret for having atom-bombed Hiroshima and Nagasaki (3) the influence of Japanese-American war veterans (4) our fear of further Communist expansion in the Far East.

21. In recent years, India (1) agreed to divide Kashmir with Pakistan (2) refused to recognize Communist China (3) joined SEATO (4) played the role of a neutral in world affairs.

22. Relations between India and Communist China were strained by (1) Communist China's refusal to provide nuclear weapons to India (2) India's efforts to spread Hinduism (3) Communist China's suppression of the Tibetan revolt (4) Communist China's alliance with Sri Lanka.

23. After World War II, United States troops occupied part of Korea because it had formerly been controlled by (1) Germany (2) China (3) Japan (4) Russia.

24. Which event in Korea occurred *first?* (1) North Korea's invasion of South Korea (2) the creation of the Republic of Korea (3) intervention of Chinese Communist troops in Korea (4) division of Korea at the 38th parallel.

25. In 1950, although Congress did not declare war, President Truman sent American troops into battle in Korea. The President's authority was based upon his position as (1) head of his political party (2) leader of the free world nations (3) commander in chief of the armed forces (4) interpreter of the Monroe Doctrine.

26. Which issue was the chief cause of delay in negotiating a truce in Korea? (1) the U.N. resolution calling Communist China an aggressor (2) the boundary line between North and South Korea (3) the exchange of war prisoners (4) the status of Taiwan.

27. Following the Korean truce (1) Korea was unified (2) Nationalist China obtained Korea (3) Communist influence in Korea was ended (4) Korea remained divided.

28. Which European country was directly involved in the civil war in Indo-China from 1946 to 1954? (1) Great Britain (2) France (3) Italy (4) the Netherlands.

29. Which nation in the Far East has achieved the greatest degree of industrial development? (1) Burma (2) India (3) China (4) Japan.

30. By joining the Organization of American States, the United States (1) achieved cooperation with Canada (2) abandoned the Good Neighbor Policy (3) achieved economic control over the Western Hemisphere (4) reaffirmed its rejection of the Roosevelt Corollary to the Monroe Doctrine.

31. The term "revolution of rising expectations" refers to the (1) desire of Communists to take over more of the world (2) desire of people in developing nations to raise their standards of living (3) demand of workers around the world for collective bargaining (4) hope of the United States to improve relations with China.

32. An important reason for the quarantine ordered by President Kennedy in the Cuban crisis of 1962 was to (1) protect refugees escaping from Cuba (2) protect the security of the United States (3) prevent a Cuban invasion of the Dominican Republic (4) prevent Communist China from shipping weapons to Cuba.

33. President Kennedy viewed the settlement of the 1962 missile base crisis over Cuba as (1) an American victory (2) a Russian victory (3) an honorable accord (4) proof of the value of the U.N.

34. A unique feature of the Alliance for Progress was the degree to which it required Latin American countries to (1) accept United States military bases (2) make trade concessions for products from the United States (3) agree to institute basic reform programs (4) repress local Communist movements.

35. Both President Franklin D. Roosevelt and President John F. Kennedy were very much concerned with (1) recognition of Communist China (2) relations with Latin America (3) the emerging nations of Africa (4) a treaty banning nuclear tests.

CHRONOLOGY QUESTIONS

(A) Harry S. Truman   (C) John F. Kennedy
(B) Dwight D. Eisenhower   (D) Lyndon B. Johnson

For each of the following events in American foreign affairs, select the *letter* of the President in whose administration the event took place.

1. American troops sent to aid Lebanon.
2. Airlift used to break Berlin blockade.
3. Hostile public reception given to Vice President on goodwill tour of South America.
4. Quarantine placed upon ships bound for Cuba with offensive weapons.
5. American troops sent into the Dominican Republic.
6. Requests made of Great Britain to ease restrictions on Jewish immigration into Palestine.
7. Air strikes ordered against North Vietnamese military targets.
8. Alliance for Progress inaugurated to improve conditions in Latin America.
9. Diplomatic relations broken with Cuba.
10. Air strikes against North Vietnam halted so as to spur peace talks.
11. Army general dismissed by commander in chief on grounds of insubordination.
12. Disagreement with Britain and France over their Suez invasion.

MAP QUESTIONS

For each country described below, write *both* (1) its name, and (2) the *letter* indicating its location on the map, or, if the country is *not* on the map, the letter *X*.

1. This Balkan country initiated the practice of national Communism. It received American aid designed to strengthen its independence of Russia.
2. This country received independence from Belgium and was beset by civil war. The U.N. sent troops to help restore order.
3. Located in the Far East, this nation was an enemy of the United States in World War II but is now its ally.
4. The U.N. General Assembly has condemned the policy of "apartheid" practiced by this country.
5. The United Nations sent an army which fought to keep this country from falling under Communist rule.
6. This divided country, whose former capital city was also divided, was the scene of several crises between the Communist world and the free world.
7. This populous nation, visited in 1972 by President Nixon, has challenged the leadership of Russia in the Communist world.
8. Formerly a territory of the United States, this nation became independent after World War II. It was a member of SEATO and aided the American military effort in Vietnam.
9. This West European country became a member of NATO in 1982 but previously had permitted the United States to maintain military bases on its soil.

10. This nation, formed from part of the French colony of Indo-China, is now independent and under Communist rule. It borders on the Gulf of Tonkin.

11. Fearing the possibility of a Communist seizure of power, President Johnson sent American troops into this Caribbean nation.

12. This Moslem nation, which received aid under the Truman Doctrine, controls the Dardanelles. It is a member of NATO.

13. Although a member of the British Commonwealth, this populous nation follows a foreign policy of neutrality. To improve economic conditions, it pursues a mixed economy of public and private enterprise.

14. This European nation, a strong ally of the United States, is a member of NATO and was a member of SEATO.

15. This nation, which nationalized the Suez Canal in 1956, claimed leadership of the Arab world. In 1979 it signed a peace treaty with Israel.

MODIFIED TRUE-FALSE QUESTIONS

1. The Inter-American Defense Treaty is also known as the *Bogota* Treaty.

2. OAS recommendations to the member nations regarding hemispheric defense require a *simple majority* vote.

3. The official language of Brazil is *Spanish*.

4. Latin Americans of mixed white and Indian ancestry are known as *mestizos*.

5. In the 19th century, schools in Latin America were chiefly under *state* control.

6. The chief mineral resource and export of Venezuela is *copper*.

7. The chief agricultural product and export of Brazil is *wheat*.

8. The *Paris* Agreements of 1954 provided for the division of Vietnam at the 17th parallel.

9. An Asian nation that supported the American effort in South Vietnam with troops was *South Korea*.

10. A term used to describe the increased pace of the war in Vietnam is *escalation*.

MATCHING QUESTIONS

For each office listed in column *A*, select the *letter* preceding the name of the person in column *B* who either once held or now holds that office.

Column A	*Column B*
1. Prime Minister of India	*a.* Helmut Kohl
2. President of Nationalist China	*b.* Menachem Begin
3. President of Egypt	*c.* Fidel Castro
4. Chancellor of West Germany	*d.* Chiang Kai-shek
5. President of South Korea	*e.* Ho Chi Minh
6. Chairman of Communist party of China	*f.* Nikita Khrushchev
7. President of North Vietnam	*g.* Chou En-lai
8. Prime Minister of Israel	*h.* Mao Tse-tung
9. United States negotiator of Vietnam peace agreement	*i.* Anwar al-Sadat
10. Premier of Cuba	*j.* Jawaharlal Nehru
	k. Chun Doo Hwan
	l. Rafael Trujillo
	m. Henry Kissinger

ESSAY QUESTIONS

1. The United States government has acted at times independently and at times jointly with other nations in regard to international problems originating in the following areas: (1) Latin America, (2) Far East, (3) Middle East, (4) Western Europe. (*a*) For *each* of these areas, discuss *one* specific instance of independent action by the United States government. (*b*) For each of these areas, discuss *one* specific instance in which the United States government has acted jointly with other nations. (*c*) Discuss *two* reasons why the United States has increasingly used joint action with other nations in attempting to solve international problems in the Cold War Era.

2. Write a brief essay about American foreign policy toward *either* Germany *or* Japan from 1930 to the present. Include in your answer the following topics: (*a*) *one* cause for ill feeling, during the period from 1930 to 1941, between the United States and the country you have selected, (*b*) a major aim of United States policy toward that country following World War II, and (*c*) *two* specific American attempts to carry out the aim given in your answer to part (*b*) .

3. "Who does not see, then, that the Pacific Ocean, its shores, its islands, and the vast regions beyond, will become the chief theater of events in the world's great hereafter?"—Senator William H. Seward (1852)

   Discuss *three* events or developments in Asia or the Pacific region since 1939 that indicate that Senator Seward was correct in his prediction that this region would become increasingly important in history.

4. To understand the problem of Vietnam, Americans should know the history of that country and of our involvement there. (*a*) Explain *two* reasons why the Communists in Vietnam were able to gain popular support against French rule. (*b*) State *two* agreements reached at the Geneva Conference of 1954 regarding Vietnam. (*c*) Explain *one* reason why either Soviet Russia or Communist China, supported the military effort of North Vietnam and the Vietcong in the South. (*d*) Trace the development of United States involvement in Vietnam

by describing *one* action of each of the following Presidents: (1) Eisenhower, (2) Kennedy, (3) Johnson. (*e*) Discuss *one* argument supporting *and one* argument opposing United States involvement in Vietnam.

5. The United States has faced serious problems in its relations with Latin America during recent years. (*a*) Describe *two* developments affecting the relations between Cuba and the United States since 1898. (*b*) Show how policies of the United States since 1900 toward *two* Latin American countries other than Cuba have been criticized by Latin America. (*c*) Describe *two* policies of the United States during the 20th century that have gained favor in Latin America.

Part 5. Scientific Developments Become a Matter of International Concern

NUCLEAR ENERGY

ISSUE OF INTERNATIONAL CONTROL

1. **Nuclear Energy: Greatest Means of Mass Destruction.** The single atom bomb (A-bomb) dropped on Hiroshima in 1945 contained about two pounds of uranium and had the explosive power of 20,000 pounds of TNT. It killed or injured 130,000 people and destroyed 60 percent of the city. Subsequently, scientists developed the *hydrogen bomb* (H-bomb), which can generate up to several thousand times the explosive power of the Hiroshima bomb. A single hydrogen bomb can wipe out all life within a 60- to 100-mile radius.

The destructiveness of nuclear weapons results from their explosive blast, tremendous heat, and radioactivity, which can contaminate whole areas. Widespread fear exists that a nuclear war could mean the end of civilization.

2. **Nations Possessing Nuclear Power.** The United States led the way in developing nuclear energy, exploding the first atomic bomb in 1945. Other nations followed: Russia in 1949, Great Britain in 1952, France in 1960, Communist China in 1964, and India in 1974. A number of other nations, scientists believe, possess the technical know-how to become nuclear powers.

Today the United States and Russia—the two superpowers—have more than enough nuclear weapons and delivery systems to cause incredible death and destruction.

3. **Failure to Achieve International Control**

a. Baruch Plan. In 1946 the *United Nations Atomic Energy Commission* was set up to prepare an effective system of international control of nuclear weapons. At that time the United States held a monopoly over such weapons. *Bernard Baruch*, America's representative to the Commission, proposed the following generous plan: The United States would destroy its atom bombs and share its technical know-how with the other nations of the world on condition (1) that an international authority insure the use of atomic energy for only peaceful purposes, and (2) that this international authority have the right of unlimited inspection and the power to punish violators without the restrictions of the Big Five veto in the U.N.

b. Russia Rejects the Baruch Plan. Russia violently criticized the Baruch Plan, especially the proposals (1) to eliminate the veto power, and (2) to provide unlimited inspection.

Instead, Russia proposed an international treaty to outlaw the atom bomb, but made no provision for effective enforcement. The United States therefore rejected the Russian proposal as unrealistic.

In the Security Council in 1948, Russia vetoed the Baruch Plan and brought the work of the United Nations Atomic Energy Commission to a halt. Unrestricted by international controls, Russia exploded her own atomic bomb in 1949, thereby ending the monopoly of the United States. Thereafter, both nations continued to develop nuclear weapons.

PEACEFUL USES OF ATOMIC ENERGY

Scientists have devised methods to control nuclear reactions and utilize the tremendous heat to change water into steam. In turn, steam can be used to propel boats and to generate electricity.

The United States possesses a fleet of atomic-powered surface ships and submarines, and a number of nuclear electric power plants. In many regions of the United States today, atomic power is competitive in cost with electricity generated by conventional fuels: natural gas, oil, and coal.

Also, atomic scientists have produced radioactive *isotopes*. These have significant uses (1) *in medicine*, to diagnose body ills, (2) *in agriculture*, to study plant growth and to preserve foods, and (3) *in industry*, to measure the flow of oil in pipelines and to uncover flaws in metal.

In the United States the *Atomic Energy Commission (AEC)* directed the development of nuclear energy. In 1974 the AEC was replaced: (1) The *Energy Research and Development Administration (ERDA)* was to spur research on nuclear energy and other energy supplies. In 1977 ERDA was abolished and its functions were transferred to the Department of Energy. (2) The *Nuclear Regulatory Commission (NRC)* was to regulate the use of nuclear materials.

HALTING NUCLEAR BOMB TESTS

In the mid-1950's the people of the world were becoming increasingly fearful of the rising level of radioactivity resulting from nuclear weapons testing. Their fears moved Russia, the United States, and Great Britain to seek agreement for halting nuclear tests. People also hoped that a test ban would be a first step toward nuclear disarmament. From 1958 to 1963 the three nuclear powers held a series of conferences at Geneva.

1. Conflicting Proposals for Halting Nuclear Tests. Russia proposed the immediate cessation of nuclear tests without any provision for enforcement. The Western powers rejected an unpoliced ban. Instead, they proposed a test ban coupled with a system of inspection and control. Western statesmen feared that Russia, as a dictatorship, could easily violate an unpoliced ban without the free world's knowledge. Russia vehemently rejected the Western proposal as a plot to establish, on Soviet territory, spy rings disguised as inspection stations.

In 1961 the United States offered a treaty to ban nuclear tests that could be detected without on-site inspection, but to exclude underground blasts, since these could be confused with earthquakes and could therefore not be detected from far away. The Russians rejected this proposal at first, but in 1963 Premier Khrushchev reversed Russia's position and indicated that the Soviet Union would accept a limited test ban.

2. Limited Nuclear Test Ban Treaty (1963)

a. Provisons. The Big Three powers (1) agreed not to conduct nuclear tests in the atmosphere, in space, and under water (these tests can be detected, by air-sampling and monitoring devices, without on-site inspection), (2) excluded underground tests from the ban but agreed to continue negotiations on this matter, (3) invited all other nations to sign the treaty, and (4) provided an escape clause permitting each signatory to withdraw from the test ban if it feels that the treaty jeopardizes its national interests.

b. France and Communist China Abstain. Although about one hundred nations joined the Big Three in signing this treaty, two key nations did not. (1) *France.* President de Gaulle insisted that France continue atmospheric testing and develop its own H-bomb. De Gaulle wanted to restore France to world prestige and end its dependence upon the nuclear strength of the United States. (2) *Communist China.* Chinese leaders denounced the treaty as an attempt by a few powers to monopolize nuclear weapons.

FURTHER EFFORTS TO HALT THE NUCLEAR ARMS RACE

1. Outlawing Nuclear Weapons in Outer Space. In 1966 the U.N. General Assembly approved a treaty on the peaceful uses of outer space. The treaty prohibited any nation from claiming sovereignty over the moon and forbade nations from placing weapons of mass destruction in outer space or on any heavenly body. In 1967 the treaty went into effect.

2. Outlawing the Spread of Nuclear Weapons. The *U.N. Disarmament Committee* met for 5 years to draft a treaty outlawing the spread, or *proliferation*, of nuclear weapons. The Committee believed that as more nations gain nuclear weapons, the more difficult it will be to prevent their accidental or deliberate use. In 1968 the United States and Russia agreed upon a draft treaty which provided that (a) nations without nuclear weapons agree not to develop such weapons and to accept an international system of inspection, (b) the nuclear powers assist the other nations in developing peaceful uses of atomic energy, and (c) the nuclear powers seek further agreements to halt the arms race.

The *Nuclear Non-Proliferation Treaty* was approved by the U.N. General Assembly. However, some nations without nuclear weapons, including Australia, India, Israel, Japan, and West Germany, expressed strong doubts. They were being asked to forego atomic weapons, which could be vital to national defense. To gain support for the treaty, the United States, Russia, and Britain each pledged to assist any signatory nation attacked by an aggressor using nuclear weapons. In 1970 the treaty went into effect.

Nuclear Proliferaton

a. Pakistan. In 1979 the United States ended its economic and military assistance to Pakistan after the Central Intelligence Agency reported that Pakistan secretly was building a plant to produce nuclear weapons. Pakistan denied the report but was unwilling to place its atomic facilities under international safeguards. In 1980, however, the Soviet invasion of Afghanistan placed Soviet troops at the Pakistani border. The United States therefore resumed aid to Pakistan. The United States explained that this aid was designed not against India but against the "serious threat" posed to Pakistan by Soviet troops in Afghanistan. The United States further warned Pakistan that the aid package would be terminated in the event of a Pakistani nuclear explosion. In 1982 the United States was informed by President Zia of Pakistan that his government did not seek to make nuclear weapons but wanted "nuclear technology" for peaceful purposes.

b. India. Having refused to sign the Nuclear Nonproliferation Treaty, India in 1974 exploded an underground nuclear device that it claimed was for peaceful purposes. India, however, rejected international safeguards for all its nuclear facilities and refused to rule out production of nuclear weapons.

In 1980 President Carter, citing a 1963 agreement, decided to ship India enriched uranium fuel. Although this fuel was meant for peaceful electric power production, it could be diverted to the making of atomic bombs. The President's decision was political, observers felt, intended to keep India from moving closer to the Soviet Union, but at the sacrifice of America's nonproliferation policy. With majority votes of both Houses of Congress needed to halt the uranium shipment, the House voted against the President but the Senate, by a two-vote margin, upheld the President's decision.

In 1982 India reached agreement with France to receive enriched nuclear fuel to be used "only for peaceful purposes" in the American-built *Tarapur* nuclear power plant near Bombay. India permits international inspection of the Tarapur plant but not of its other nuclear sites.

c. Other Third World Nations. Supposedly for peaceful purposes, other Third World nations have contracted with industrial powers for nuclear plants, fuel, and technology. They include Argentina and Brazil with West Germany and Iraq with France. (In 1981, fearing that the Iraqi facility was about to produce nuclear weapons for use against Israeli targets, Israel bombed and destroyed the Iraqi facility. For details, check the Index.)

3. Outlawing Nuclear Weapons on the Seabed. In 1970 the U.N. General Assembly overwhelmingly approved a treaty prohibiting any nation from placing nuclear weapons on the seabed outside its 12-mile limit. In 1972 this treaty, signed by almost one hundred nations, went into effect.

4. Strategic Arms Limitation Talks (SALT). Check the Index.

MISSILES

TYPES OF MISSILES

Since World War II both the United States and Russia have developed rocket-propelled missiles capable of delivering conventional or nuclear warheads. The smallest are tactical missiles that have a short range and carry warheads with a low yield. They can be used as battlefield artillery for close support of troops. The largest missiles are the *intermediate range ballistic missile (IRBM)* and the *intercontinental ballistic missile (ICBM)*. For defense, both nations have developed the *antiballistic missile (ABM)*.

1. Intermediate Range Ballistic Missile (IRBM). These missiles soar into space and then descend to earth, hitting a target up to 2500 miles away from the launching site. The United States has produced several types of IRBM's. Our main reliance is on the *Polaris* and on its newer version, the *Poseidon.* Both missiles can be launched from a surface ship or from a submarine.

Patrolling Norwegian and Mediterranean waters, American missile-carrying submarines are close enough to the Soviet Union to expose Russia's major military targets to IRBM attack. Russia also has IRBM's for use (*a*) from land-based sites against our European allies, and (*b*) from missile-carrying submarines in the North Atlantic against American targets.

2. Intercontinental Ballistic Missile (ICBM). These missiles soar into space, travel at a speed of up to 20,000 miles per hour, and descend to earth, hitting a target over 6000 miles away from the launching site. The earliest ICBM's carried a single warhead. More recent models are capable of carrying multiple warheads, with each warhead aimed at a different target. These are named *multiple individually targetable reentry vehicles (MIRV's).*

The ICBM has been called "the ultimate weapon" because its speed and its nuclear explosive power make any defense against it extremely difficult. The United States relies chiefly on the solid-fueled *Minuteman.* Russia has

ICBM's, which can be launched from sites in the Soviet Union against the United States. China is working to develop its own ICBM's.

3. Antiballistic Missile (ABM). These missiles are designed to destroy offensive missiles in space. When radar indicates that enemy missiles are en route, the ABM's are to be launched to explode in the path of the approaching missiles and destroy them by explosive force, heat, and radiation.

CONSIDERATIONS REGARDING ABM DEFENSE SYSTEMS

1. In Russia. By 1967 the Russians had begun installing an antiballistic missile system around Moscow. Western observers surmised that Russian ABM's were meant for defense against American as well as Chinese missiles.

2. American Plans. In 1969 the Nixon administration proposed the *Safeguard* ABM system. Its purpose was to protect not our cities, but our ICBM launching sites against any Soviet or Chinese initial attack, or *first strike*, so

© *1965 Herblock in The Washington Post*

"As nearly as we can translate, it says: 'We are agreed in principle on preventing the spread of nuclear weapons; however . . .' "

as to preserve our retaliatory, or *second-strike*, capacity. Nixon won narrow Congressional approval for two ABM sites.

TWO SALT I ACCORDS—SIGNED IN 1972

After almost three years of talks, American and Soviet negotiators completed two accords covering certain aspects of nuclear missiles systems. The accords, signed at the Moscow summit meeting by President Nixon and Communist party leader Brezhnev, provided as follows:

1. The Treaty on ABM's. The United States and the Soviet Union (*a*) agreed to protect by ABM defense systems only two sites each—the national capital and one ICBM launching site, (*b*) accepted a ceiling of 100 ABM launchers for each site, (*c*) pledged not to build nationwide ABM defense systems, and (*d*) provided that the treaty be of unlimited duration but allowed each nation, upon six months' notice, to withdraw from the treaty if "extraordinary events . . . have jeopardized its supreme interests." (In 1974 the number of ABM sites was reduced for each nation from two to one.)

Observations: This treaty (*a*) contained a withdrawal clause in apprehension of future Chinese developments and (*b*) reflected the belief that the United States and the Soviet Union both have the ability to absorb a "first strike" and to retaliate powerfully upon the other nation thereby making the outbreak of a nuclear war between them improbable. This treaty was overwhelmingly ratified by the United States Senate.

2. The Interim Agreement on Offensive Missiles. The United States and the Soviet Union "froze" at the current level their offensive-missile systems: (*a*) for the United States—1054 land-launched ICBM's and 656 submarine-launched missiles, and (*b*) for the Soviet Union—1618 land-launched ICBM's and 710 submarine-launched missiles.

Observations: This agreement (*a*) did *not* cover the number of warheads per missile, thereby giving the United States with its advanced MIRV technology the advantage of 5700 warheads as compared to 2500 for the Soviet Union, (*b*) did *not* cover the explosive power of each warhead, thereby giving the Soviet Union with its larger warheads a 3-to-1 lead in explosive power over the United States, (*c*) did *not* cover the number of long-range bombers capable of delivering nuclear bombs, thereby giving the United States a lead of 460 strategic bombers to 140 for the Soviet Union, (*d*) did *not* limit the construction of strategic bombers and did *not* prevent the replacement of existing missiles and submarines by more destructive models, and (*e*) did *not* provide for on-site inspection to prevent violations although both nations pledged not to interfere with other methods of inspection.

Supporters of the interim agreement pointed out that it (*a*) reflects the opinion that both nations are roughly equal in offensive missile power and (*b*) may encourage a feeling of friendship and arrest the arms race.

Critics of the interim agreement pointed out that it *(a)* will not reduce the current offensive missile arsenals, *(b)* will shift the arms race from competition in missile numbers to competition in technology and in areas not covered by its provisions, and therefore *(c)* will make highly improbable any significant reduction in arms defense spending.

● WESTERN BASES
■ PROBABLE SOVIET BASES

Western and Soviet Bases Facing the North Polar Region
(From the 1960's to the 1990's)

Strategic Launchers		U.S.	Soviet Union
	Land-based ICBM's	1,052	1,398
	Submarine-based missiles	576	989
	Long-range bombers	316	150
	Total Launchers	1,944	2,537
Nuclear Warheads		9,000	7,000
Total Explosive Power		2,968 megatons	5,111 megatons

Nuclear Strength of the Two Superpowers (1982)

THE SALT II TREATY—SIGNED IN 1979

The SALT II Treaty, signed at Vienna by President Carter and Soviet leader Brezhnev, was a highly technical 100-page document.

1. Provisions: (*a*) The United States and the Soviet Union each accepted, as of 1982, an overall ceiling of 2250 strategic nuclear-delivery vehicles. These included land-based intercontinental ballistic missiles (ICBM's), submarine-launched ballistic missiles (SLBM's), heavy bombers, and air-to-surface ballistic missiles (ASBM's) with a range of over 375 miles. Within the overall ceiling, the treaty imposed subceilings on these various missile types. It also set limits on the number of MIRV's, or warheads, per missile and the weight per missile. (*b*) The United States and the Soviet Union agreed to test and deploy no more than one new type of ICBM. (*c*) The treaty placed no limits on the *Backfire* bomber, which the Soviets insisted is an intermediate-range plane, but the Americans considered a strategic long-range bomber. (*d*) The treaty limited, until 1982, America's air- or sea-launched cruise missile to a maximum range of 375 miles. (The cruise missile is a low-flying, pilotless vehicle that can be guided to its target.) (*e*) The treaty did not provide for on-site inspection to verify compliance.

2. Arguments for the SALT II Treaty. (*a*) It would further the principle of equality in the superpowers' strategic missile arsenals. (*b*) It called for the Soviet Union to dismantle 10 percent of its strategic missile systems so as to conform to the 2250 ceiling. Also, by its other ceilings, the treaty would inhibit the growth of Soviet missile power. (*c*) In President Carter's words, the treaty would "lessen the danger of nuclear destruction while safeguarding our military security."

3. Arguments Against the SALT II Treaty. (*a*) Although the treaty would limit both nations equally on overall nuclear-delivery vehicles, the Soviets would have a major advantage in that their missiles are larger and more destructive than ours. (*b*) By limiting new-type ICBM's to only one, the treaty would severely handicap American efforts to deploy varied mobile missile systems. These were needed since the existing fixed, land-based *Minuteman* missiles were vulnerable to a surprise attack by increasingly accurate Soviet missiles. (*c*) By permitting limited modernization of existing weapons, the treaty would let the nuclear arms race continue.

4. Stalling of the Ratification Process. Like all treaties, SALT II required a two-thirds Senate vote for ratification.

a. To Quiet Senators' Fears: A Military Buildup. Many Senators feared that the treaty would confirm Soviet nuclear superiority. To quiet such fears, President Carter agreed to increase American military spending and to build the *MX mobile missile system.* This system would feature land-based missiles that could be moved about so as to disguise their exact location.

b. Complications in Cuba and Afghanistan. Reports in 1979 that a Soviet combat brigade had moved into Cuba caused an increase in opposition to the treaty. Then, with the Soviet invasion of Afghanistan in December 1979, President Carter requested the Senate to delay consideration of SALT II. While the President still held SALT II to be in the national interest, he declared that the Soviet invasion made ratification "inappropriate" for now.

The Carter administration—and the Reagan administration for a time—indicated that, as long as the Soviets honored the SALT II terms, the United States would do likewise, despite the lack of ratification.

SIDESTEPPING THE TREATIES

Both the Soviet Union and the United States found reason to sidestep various provisions of the 1970's arms accords: (*a*) In 1983, American satellites spotted a radar station at Krasnoyarsk, deep inside the Soviet Union. United States officials called it an early-warning radar that violated the 1972 ABM Treaty; Soviet officials insisted it was only for tracking space vehicles. In 1989 Soviet leaders admitted that the radar had been "an open violation" of the treaty and agreed to dismantle it. (*b*) Arguing that the Soviet Union had not fully complied with the SALT II Treaty, the United States broke the unratified treaty's limits in 1986 by deploying one more cruise missile than the treaty allowed. The Reagan administration said the United States "couldn't afford to reduce its future deterrent force structure" by dismantling any missile-carrying submarines, as would have been required in order to keep within treaty limits.

RECENT UNITED STATES ARMS POLICIES

1. Massive Buildup. President Reagan continued and expanded an arms buildup that began in the last years of the Carter administration: (*a*) President

Reagan sought funds for 100 long-range, multiple-warhead MX missiles, to be placed at fixed bases. Congress agreed to 50, and the first MX went into operation in 1986. In 1989 the Bush administration said it would turn the MX into a mobile missile by deploying all 50 MX's on special railroad trains by the end of 1994. (b) President Reagan revived the B-1 bomber program canceled by President Carter. The first of the fleet of 100 planes, known as B-1B's, went into operation in 1986. These planes replaced aging B-52's. (c) President Reagan expanded the *Stealth* program to build planes and missiles designed to be "invisible" to radar. (d) President Reagan revived production of chemical weapons, suspended in 1969. Congress approved a new generation of nerve gas weapons.

2. "Star Wars." Declaring a goal of making nuclear weapons "impotent and obsolete," President Reagan in 1983 announced a sweeping program of research into space-based defenses. He labeled his program the *Strategic Defense Initiative (SDI)*. Because of the program's emphasis on exotic techniques such as particle beams and orbiting mirrors, many people called it "Star Wars."

President Reagan described SDI as a system for destroying Soviet missiles soon after launching, before they had time to get close to their targets. The program depended heavily on technology that was still in the early stages of research. By providing "insured defense," Reagan said, SDI aimed "to make ballistic missiles obsolete."

Critics ridiculed the claim that SDI could act as an invisible shield against attack. They said the "nuclear astrodome" would never work.

In 1993, after spending $30 billion on the "Star Wars" system, the Defense Department concluded that the system was fatally flawed. The department renamed SDI and shifted its emphasis to ground-based defense systems, like the Patriot missile used in the Persian Gulf War of 1991.

RECENT TREATIES ON NUCLEAR WEAPONS

The Reagan administration deemphasized arms control talks at first. President Reagan argued that the United States had fallen behind the Soviet Union in military strength and should not negotiate from a position of weakness. But arms negotiations resumed in earnest in the late 1980's.

1. START Talks and INF Talks. American and Soviet negotiators met in Geneva, Switzerland, to discuss two types of nuclear arms. One set of meetings, called *Strategic Arms Reduction Talks (START)*, dealt with long-range missiles that would strike one of the two superpowers from the other's heartland. The second set of meetings, called the *Intermediate Nuclear Force (INF)* talks, dealt with medium-range missiles based mainly in Europe.

2. Interruption of Talks (1983–1984). In 1983, when the United States began to install cruise and Pershing missiles in Europe (see page 566), the Soviet Union broke off both sets of talks. In 1984, worried about American "Star

Wars" research, the Soviet Union proposed talks on preventing the militarization of space. New talks began on long-range and space-based weapons.

3. INF Treaty (1987). Meeting in Washington in 1987, President Reagan and Soviet leader Mikhail Gorbachev signed a treaty to abolish all nuclear missiles having a range of from 310 to 3,410 miles (500 to 5,500 kilometers). This *INF Treaty* was the first superpower arms pact since 1979 and the first ever to call for the actual abolition of existing nuclear weapons.

a. Provisions. (1) Both superpowers would dismantle all intermediate-range nuclear weapons in their arsenals. For the United States, this would mean abandoning the Pershing 2 and ground-launched cruise missiles it based in Europe during the early 1980's. For the Soviet Union, it would mean destroying *SS-4* and *SS-20* missiles based in Europe (against NATO) and in Asia (against China and Japan). (2) Verification procedures would include on-site inspections and procedures for the destruction of warheads and missiles.

b. Ratification (1988). The Senate ratified the INF Treaty by 93 to 5, and soon after the process of dismantling intermediate-range weapons began.

4. Conventional Forces in Europe Treaty (1990). Soviet and U.S. negotiators agreed in late 1990 to a treaty for vastly reducing their nonnuclear forces and conventional arms in Europe. Called the *Conventional Forces in Europe Treaty*, or *CFE Treaty*, it specified the number of tanks, armored vehicles, and artillery to be cut by both NATO and former Warsaw Pact countries.

5. START I (1991). The end of the cold war and the weakening of Soviet control over its republics contributed to a new breakthrough. At a summit conference in Moscow in July 1991, President Bush and President Gorbachev signed the first *Strategic Arms Reduction Treaty (START I)*.

The treaty provided for significant reductions in long-range nuclear missiles. The chief limits were for (*a*) strategic nuclear warheads—no more than 6,000 for each side, (*b*) strategic nuclear delivery systems (ICBM's)—no more than 1,600 for each side, and (*c*) sea-launched cruise missiles—no more than 880 for each side.

6. START II (1993). At Moscow in January 1993, 17 days before leaving office, President Bush signed with Russian President Boris Yeltsin the most sweeping arms-reduction treaty yet, called *START II.*

The treaty provided that, by the year 2003, (*a*) both nations must remove multiple warheads from long-range land-based missiles (MIRV's), (*b*) total nuclear warheads must be reduced to 3,000 for Russia and 3,500 for the United States, (*c*) the United States must reduce by half the number of warheads it has on submarine-launched missiles (where it previously had a large lead), and (*d*) Russians will be allowed to inspect the U.S. nuclear bomber fleet to verify the types and numbers of weapons being carried.

SATELLITES AND OTHER SPACE VEHICLES

RUSSIA'S SPUTNIK LAUNCHES THE SPACE AGE

The Soviet Union orbited the first artificial satellite, the 184-pound *Sputnik 1*, on October 4, 1957. Later in 1957 the Russians launched the 1120-pound *Sputnik 2*. Americans were shocked and frightened that the Soviets had taken the lead in space. The United States began a massive effort to overtake the Soviet Union. (1) Congress increased funds for missile and satellite research, development, and production. (2) Congress passed the *National Defense Education Act* (1958) to strengthen American defenses by improving education. (3) Congress established the *National Aeronautics and Space Administration (NASA)* to direct the nonmilitary aspects of space exploration. Both the Soviet Union and the United States have invested heavily in military uses of space. (Check the Index for "Strategic Defense Initiative.")

1. **Unmanned Flights.** (*a*) *Around the Earth.* Soviet satellites have mapped radiation belts, collected weather data, relayed communications, and conducted scientific experiments. In 1990 the Soviet Union carried its first commercial payload for an American company—an experiment to test protein crystals under conditions of weightlessness. Soviet authorities have contracted to launch private American satellites as well. (*b*) *To the Moon.* The *Luna 20* space vehicle brought back rocks from the moon in 1972. (*c*) *To the Planets.* The Soviets sent several spaceships to Mars and Venus. Some landed and sent back scientific data, such as surface temperatures.

2. **Manned Flights.** (*a*) *Firsts.* The Soviets achieved a number of space firsts. In 1961 *Vostok I* orbited the earth once, carrying the first cosmonaut, *Yuri Gagarin*. In 1963 *Valentina Tereshkova* became the first woman in space. In 1964 *Voskhod 1* became the first multipassenger space vehicle. In 1965 a cosmonaut left *Voskhod 2* to make the first space walk. The Soviets orbited *Salyut 1*, the first unmanned space station, in 1971 and later sent a three-man team there to perform scientific tasks. Soviet cosmonauts hold the endurance record in space—366 days in 1987 and 1988 aboard the space platform *Mir*, launched in 1986. (*b*) *Space Platform.* *Mir* is designed as a permanent manned orbiting laboratory. Vehicles from earth can dock at any of its six docking ports to unload passengers or equipment. (*c*) *Space Shuttle.* The Soviets lagged behind the United States in developing a space shuttle, a reusable vehicle for travel between earth and space. The *Buran* space shuttle made its first, unmanned trip of two orbits around the earth in 1988. It is designed to carry six or seven cosmonauts on space missions.

MAJOR AMERICAN EFFORTS IN SPACE

1. **Unmanned Flights.** (*a*) *Around the Earth.* The United States placed many satellites into orbit—the *Explorer* series to increase our scientific knowl-

edge of space; *Transit* satellites to assist airplane and ship pilots in navigation; *Telstar, Early Bird,* and *Intelsat,* all privately financed satellites, to build a global telecommunications system; and the *Tiros* series to gather weather data. (*b*) *To the Moon.* The United States sent a number of spacecraft to the moon; some landed on the moon's surface and sent back thousands of photographs. (*c*) *To the Planets.* The United States sent to Mars and Venus a number of *Mariner* spaceships that sent back pictures and scientific data. In 1973 *Pioneer 10* ended a 21-month journey to Jupiter and provided photographs of that outer planet. (Pioneer 10, carrying a pictorial plaque, later escaped from our solar system and traveled into the Milky Way—where it might be seen by other intelligent beings, if any exist.) In 1974 *Mariner 10* reached and photographed Mercury, the planet closest to our sun. In 1976 two *Viking* vehicles reached the vicinity of Mars and each placed a landing craft on that planet's surface. The Viking landers sent back photographs of the terrain, data regarding the atmosphere, and analyses of the Martian soil. In 1979, after a six-year trip, *Pioneer 11* swept past and sent back data about the rings, moons, and atmosphere of the planet Saturn. In 1980 *Voyager 1* flew by Saturn and revealed the existence of three previously unknown Saturn moons, making a total of fifteen. In 1981, after a four-year trip, *Voyager 2* sent back pictures and data as it flew by Saturn. The spacecraft sent back similar information about Uranus in 1986 and headed for a flyby of Neptune in 1989. It left the solar system after photographing Neptune on a passby in 1989.

2. Manned Flights. At first behind, the United States eventually caught up with and then surpassed the Soviets in the number and complexity of manned flights. In 1962 the United States sent *Friendship 7* to circle the earth three times with America's first orbiting astronaut, *John Glenn.* Thereafter, the United States orbited numerous multipassenger space vehicles. American astronauts practiced docking, or joining together, spacecraft in orbit, and then guiding a lunar module, or landing craft, to leave and return to the command ship.

In 1969, with the eleventh flight of the *Project Apollo* series, the United States achieved an historic first. While *Michael Collins* orbited the moon in the command ship *Columbia, Neil Armstrong* and *Edwin Aldrin* descended to the moon's surface in the lunar module *Eagle.* Armstrong, the first human to set foot on the moon, spoke the historic words "That's one small step for a man, one giant leap for mankind." The two astronauts gathered rock samples, set up scientific experiments, stationed a plaque saying, "We came in peace for all mankind," and then ascended to the command ship. The three men then returned safely to earth. Five subsequent Apollo flights repeated the moon-landing triumph.

In 1973 the United States placed into orbit its first space station, *Skylab.* Successive teams of American astronauts have lived in the space station, performing experiments and gathering data.

In 1981 NASA launched the first reusable winged *space shuttle,* the *Columbia.* A manned vehicle carrying two astronauts, it was placed into orbit, circled the earth 36 times, and glided to a safe landing in southern California. Because it could be reused for many trips, the space shuttle was less costly than previous single-use orbiting vehicles.

In 1983 a companion craft, the *Challenger* space shuttle, went into orbit. It released and then retrieved a satellite in space. This *Challenger* flight carried a crew of five, including the nation's first female astronaut, *Sally Ride*. Later that year, another space shuttle carried the nation's first black astronaut, *Stewart Bluford, Jr.*, into space.

3. Coping With the *Challenger* Tragedy. In 1986 the *Challenger* space shuttle exploded soon after takeoff, killing its seven crew members—including *Christa McAuliffe*, a schoolteacher who was to have been the first "ordinary" American in space. A Presidential investigating commission blamed the explosion on a faulty booster rocket. Critics argued that NASA had stressed frequent flights over safety in the shuttle program, and that the company that built the rocket should share in the blame for the tragedy. Shuttle flights were suspended for two years while preflight procedures were revised and the booster rocket was redesigned. The flights resumed in 1988.

JOINT U.S.-RUSSIAN SPACE PLANS

After the cold war, the United States and Russia joined forces in planning a permanent manned space station, to be called *Freedom*.

The concept of *Freedom* dates to 1984, when President Reagan directed NASA to develop such a station for earth orbit. The purpose: to (*a*) aid scientific experiments, (*b*) enhance knowledge of the universe, and (*c*) manufacture metals and medicines that can be produced only in a gravity-free environment.

In 1993 U.S. and Russian leaders signed an agreement to develop the space station together. The following year, for the first time, a Russian astronaut joined American astronauts for a mission aboard a U.S. space shuttle. In 1995 an American space shuttle rendezvoused with a Russian space station as a test run for future cooperative space ventures.

Part 6. Summary: Russian-American Relations Follow a Fluctuating Pattern

Since World War II, relations between Russia and the United States have varied from periods of great tension to periods of comparative calm.

1947–1953: PERIOD OF TENSION

While Stalin ruled, Russia pursued a "hard line" toward the free world, and the United States responded by its policy of containment. Evidences of tension were (1) Truman Doctrine (1947), (2) Berlin Blockade (1948–1949), (3) creation of NATO (1949), and (4) Korean War (1950–1953).

1954–1959: COMPARATIVE CALM

In the years after Stalin's death, Khrushchev espoused peaceful coexistence, and relations between Russia and the United States improved.

1. Summit Conference of 1955. President Eisenhower met at Geneva with the leaders of Great Britain, France, and Russia. They discussed East-West problems in a calm and friendly atmosphere but reached no settlements.

2. Scientific and Cultural Exchanges. In 1958 the United States and Russia inaugurated a scientific and cultural exchange program. Since then, reciprocal visits have been made by athletes, scholars, concert artists, orchestras, ballet groups, writers, and scientists.

3. Khrushchev's Visit to the United States. In 1959 Khrushchev visited the United States. The American people gave Khrushchev a friendly reception, and Khrushchev showed great interest in many facets of American life. He met with President Eisenhower, and the two men initiated plans for another summit conference.

1960–1962: ANOTHER PERIOD OF TENSION

1. U-2 Incident and the Summit Conference of 1960. Two weeks before a new summit conference was to be held in Paris, the Soviets shot down, deep inside Russian territory, an unarmed American U-2 reconnaissance plane. The Soviets, who maintained an extensive espionage system in the West, had known of such U-2 flights but had not previously protested against them. In Paris, Khrushchev accused America of aggression, vilified Eisenhower, and demanded an apology. Eisenhower denied the charge of aggression and refused to apologize. The summit meeting was dead.

2. Building of the Berlin Wall (1961). (Check the Index for "Berlin Wall.")

3. Cuban Missile Base Crisis (1962). (Check the Index for "Cuba, under Castro.")

1963–1968: COMPARATIVE CALM

Following the peaceful settlement of the Cuban crisis and the deepening of the Soviet-Chinese split, Russian-American relations improved.

1. Limited Nuclear Test Ban Treaty. In 1963 the United States and Russia agreed to a ban on all but underground nuclear tests. This was the first agreement to emerge from 18 years of East-West disarmament negotiations.

2. Hot Line. In 1963 Russia and the United States established a "hot line," or emergency communications link, between Washington and Moscow to reduce the risk of war by blunder or miscalculation.

3. Wheat Sale. With Russia suffering from a poor grain harvest in 1963, the United States sold substantial quantities of wheat to the Soviet Union.

4. Consular Treaty. In 1964 the United States and the Soviet Union negotiated their first bilateral treaty. It (*a*) permitted negotiations for establishing consulates outside of Washington and Moscow, (*b*) granted diplomatic immunity to consular officials, and (*c*) required that consular officials be informed of and granted access to any of their country's citizens placed under arrest. This treaty was ratified by both nations.

5. Nuclear Non-Proliferation Treaty. In 1968 the United States and Russia agreed upon a treaty to outlaw the spread of nuclear weapons.

1969 TO THE PRESENT: ALTERNATING PERIODS OF CALM OR TENSION— A SEARCH FOR DÉTENTE

American Presidents from Nixon onward and Soviet Communist party heads from Brezhnev onward all voiced support for moving American-Soviet relations into a new era of détente. Secretary of State Kissinger defined détente as the "process of managing relations with a potentially hostile country in order to preserve peace while maintaining our vital interests." A Soviet expert on foreign policy explained that détente "sets limits on what each side can do without risking war and gets officials concerned—Soviet and American—talking with each other."

SUCCESSES OF DÉTENTE

1. Four-Power Agreement on Berlin (1971). (Check the Index for "Berlin, new agreement on [1971].")

2. Nixon's Journey to Moscow (1972). Despite Soviet-American tensions over Vietnam, President Nixon journeyed to Moscow to a meeting with Communist leaders, especially party chief Brezhnev. Nixon received a restrained but correct welcome, and his time was occupied chiefly with businesslike negotiations. Nixon and the Soviet leaders signed a number of significant accords: (*a*) *on space*—to cooperate in 1975 in a joint Soviet-American docking and flight of manned spacecraft, (*b*) *on health*—to coordinate Soviet-American research on cancer, heart disease, and public health, (*c*) *on incidents at sea*—to set rules so that Soviet and American naval vessels operating near each other will avoid collisions, (*d*) *on environment and technology*—to cooperate in the study of pollution problems and in other scientific research, (*e*) *on trade*—to establish a joint commission to resolve trade problems so as to increase Soviet-American trade, and (*f*) *on nuclear arms*—to limit ABM sites and "freeze" current offensive-missile arsenals.

3. Strategic Arms Limitation Talks; Two SALT I Accords (1972). (Check the Index for "Strategic Arms Limitation Talks [SALT].")

4. Paris Peace Agreement for Vietnam (1973). (Check the Index for "Paris peace agreement [1973].")

5. Brezhnev's Visit to the United States. In 1973 Soviet Communist party chief Brezhnev visited the United States, projected a spirit of friendship, and spoke to the American people via television. He and President Nixon signed a number of accords: to make every effort to avoid a military confrontation, to expand air passenger service between the United States and the Soviet Union, to promote trade, to continue cultural and educational exchanges, and to cooperate in oceanography and agricultural research.

6. Helsinki Pact (1975). Leaders of the United States, Canada, and 33 European nations met at Helsinki, Finland, to conclude the *Conference on Security and Cooperation in Europe.* They signed a charter containing two major provisions:

a. Accepting as inviolate the post-World War II boundaries in Europe. By this provision the Western powers held that they were being realistic—acknowledging a situation they could not alter peaceably. Russia was jubilant because this provision formally recognized Soviet territorial gains in Europe, the division of Germany into two nations, and Soviet domination of Eastern Europe. This provision was hailed as a personal triumph for Soviet Communist party head Brezhnev.

b. Agreeing in principle to further human rights. By this provision the Soviet Union and the satellite Communist nations promised to ease the movement of individuals across frontiers, assist in the reunion of separated families, reduce restrictions on journalists, and increase East-West cultural and educational exchanges. Western observers wondered, however, whether these promises would be kept.

DISILLUSIONMENT ABOUT DÉTENTE

1. United States: (*a*) Members of Congress protested barriers to the emigration of Soviet Jews. In 1974 Congress approved a trade bill containing the *Jackson-Vanik Amendment,* which permitted trade benefits for the Soviets but only on condition that they allow emigrants to leave the Soviet Union without harassment. In the late 1970's and again in the late 1980's, the Soviet Union permitted as many as 50,000 Soviet Jews a year to emigrate. The United States nonetheless barred the Soviet Union from favorable trade treatment on grounds that it had not fully complied with provisions of the amendment. (*b*) President Carter and members of Congress criticized the Soviet Union for efforts to silence dissident intellectuals. Among the most prominent Soviet dissidents were *Alexander Solzhenitsyn,* author of *The Gulag Archipelago* and winner of the 1970 Nobel Prize for literature; *Andrei Sakharov,* an atomic scientist who won the 1975 Nobel Peace Prize; *Anatoly B. Shcharansky*; and *Yuri F. Orlov.*

2. Soviet Union: (*a*) Soviet trade experts protested that the United States, despite administration promises, was continuing to delay a comprehensive trade pact. The Soviets wanted substantial American credits and loans to help buy American machinery, technology, and grain and to develop Siberian oil and gas resources. (*b*) Soviet leaders objected to efforts by Congress to change Soviet policies regarding dissident intellectuals and minority groups.

3. Détente in Decline? With the 1979 Soviet invasion of Afghanistan and the Carter administration's responses—delaying consideration of the SALT II Treaty, restricting high-technology and grain exports to the Soviet Union, supplying the Afghan resistance, and boycotting the 1980 summer Olympic Games at Moscow—it seemed that the superpowers were abandoning détente. The Reagan administration adopted a hard line toward the Soviets in the early 1980's.

a. The Korean Airliner Incident (1983). In 1983 a Soviet fighter plane shot down a South Korean passenger jet that was illegally crossing Soviet territory in the Far East. All 269 passengers and crew members were killed. Western nations halted, for a time, all flights to and from the Soviet Union. The Soviets said they had shot down the plane because they believed the pilot had deliberately invaded Soviet airspace on a spying mission.

b. Disputes Over Spying. Each superpower accused the other of major spying operations in the 1980's. American investigators prosecuted a number of Americans on charges of spying for the Soviets. In a case that broke in 1985, authorities charged *John Walker,* his brother, his son, and a friend with running a Soviet spy ring. In 1987, the Reagan administration charged that Soviet agents had planted electronic listening devices in the walls of a new American embassy being built in Moscow. The Soviets responded by charging American bugging of the Soviet embassy in Washington.

c. World Trouble Spots. American and Soviet interests clashed in several parts of the world in the 1980's. In the *Middle East,* the Soviet Union sought a role in the Arab-Israeli peace process while the United States tried to exclude the Soviets. In the *Persian Gulf,* both superpowers sought to influence the outcome of the war between Iran and Iraq. In *Afghanistan,* the United States supplied missiles to Islamic guerrillas while Soviet troops backed the government. In *Indochina,* the Soviet Union supported Vietnam's occupation of Cambodia while the United States and China supported Cambodian resistance forces. In *Nicaragua,* the Soviets sent helicopters and other items to the Sandinista government while the United States backed contra forces seeking to overthrow the Sandinistas. In *Africa,* American and Soviet policies clashed in Ethiopia, Angola, Namibia (South-West Africa), and South Africa.

CHANGES IN THE COMMUNIST BLOC

In the second half of the 1980's, Soviet-American relations began to warm up again. The reform-minded Mikhail Gorbachev came to power in the Soviet Union in 1985 and began a sweeping reassessment of Soviet policies. Reforms championed by Gorbachev helped lead to the crumbling of Communist rule in much of Eastern Europe, beginning with dramatic suddenness in 1989.

1. "Perestroika" and "Glasnost." Gorbachev introduced to the Soviet Union a program of sweeping political and economic change that he called *perestroika,* or "restructuring." He also began permitting open dissent, calling for more *glasnost,* or "openness," in Soviet society.

    a. Domestic Soviet Reforms. Gorbachev's actions included: (1) efforts to revive the crippled Soviet economy by placing less stress on central planning; (2) permission for Soviet citizens to operate small private businesses; (3) revisions in theory and practice to separate the roles of the Communist party and the government; (4) revision of the constitution to end the Communist party's monopoly on power, opening the door to contested elections between rival political groups; (5) greater openness in the state-run press; and (6) new attacks on crimes of the Stalin era. But Gorbachev resisted efforts of the Baltic republics (*Lithuania, Latvia,* and *Estonia*) to achieve independence.

    b. Soviet Foreign Policy. In foreign policy, Gorbachev's actions included: (1) cuts in Soviet military spending and reductions in troop levels; (2) withdrawal of Soviet troops from Afghanistan; (3) new arms-control agreements with the United States; (4) improved relations with China; (5) repudiation of the Brezhnev Doctrine's claim of a Soviet right to intervene in other Communist countries; and (6) allowing democratic reforms in Eastern Europe.

2. Democratization of Eastern Europe. Responding to economic disasters and public unrest, several nations of Eastern Europe began reforms in the 1980's. During 1989 and 1990, Communist power suddenly crumbled in many countries of the region, and democratically-elected governments came to power. (For details, see pages 557–558.)

ENDING THE COLD WAR

Responding to Gorbachev's initiatives, President Reagan softened his hard-line policies, and President Bush too spoke of a new openness in Soviet-American relations. Smiles and summit meetings came into vogue again.

The changes in the Soviet Union and Eastern Europe led some Americans to conclude that the cold war had ended in a victory for democracy and free enterprise. Others warned, however, that the new situation was still shaky.

1. Reagan-Gorbachev Summit Conferences. Reagan and Gorbachev met on five occasions and made some significant decisions.

    a. Geneva Summit in 1985. The two leaders met for the first time in Geneva, Switzerland, in November 1985. Although the two spoke frankly about issues such as arms control and human rights, they reached no significant agreements.

    b. Reykjavik Meeting in 1986. After further talks between arms negotiators for the two sides, Reagan and Gorbachev met at Reykjavik, Iceland, in October

1986. Although both sides proposed sweeping cuts in long- and medium-range missiles, no agreement was reached. Stumbling blocks were: (1) American refusal to make any cuts in the "Star Wars" program and (2) Soviet insistence on putting all arms-control issues in one package.

c. Washington Summit in 1987. At Washington in December 1987, Reagan and Gorbachev signed the INF Treaty (see page 652 for details). In addition, the two leaders discussed the war in Afghanistan, "Star Wars" testing, and proposals for a new treaty to limit strategic (long-range) nuclear weapons. The mood was more optimistic than it had been at Reykjavik.

d. Moscow Summit in 1988. The two leaders signed the final documents ratifying the INF Treaty at Moscow in May and June 1988. They made no significant progress on the issue of limiting strategic weapons.

e. New York Meeting in 1988. When Gorbachev came to New York to address the United Nations in December 1988, he met President Reagan and Vice-President Bush for a two-hour luncheon at Governor's Island.

2. Modest Trade Gains. After farmers complained that they were losing sales, President Reagan allowed grain sales to the Soviet Union to resume. In 1983 the Soviets agreed to buy nine million tons of American grain a year for five years. At first they made few purchases, complaining that the price was too high. However, in 1987 the Reagan administration agreed to subsidize sales to the Soviet Union, as it subsidizes sales to other purchasers of American goods.

Overall trade between the superpowers has remained stable but modest for several years. The Soviet Union is one of the few countries with which the United States has a favorable trade balance: the Soviets buy more from us than we do from them. Because the United States has refused to grant "most-favored nation" treatment, importers must pay tariffs on Soviet goods that are as much as 10 times as high as tariffs on goods from other countries.

3. A Cultural "Thaw". Cultural exchanges in recent years have included visits to the United States by Soviet groups such as the Kirov Ballet and visits to the Soviet Union by rock singers such as Billy Joel. In 1987 the Soviet Union stopped jamming broadcasts of the Voice of America. In 1988 it stopped jamming broadcasts by the United States's Radio Free Europe and Radio Liberty.

4. Military Cutbacks. Besides opening up the Soviet Union to major reforms, Soviet President Gorbachev promised to cut back on Soviet armaments in Europe and to reduce Soviet troop strength by 500,000. One purpose appears to have been to enable Soviet planners to divert money from the military in order to build up the struggling Soviet economy. Some members of Congress urged corresponding moves by the United States, and the Bush administration began exploring possible reductions in United States military spending. The opening of the Berlin Wall and the democratization of Eastern Europe contributed to a growing feeling that the cold war was drawing to a close. Gorbachev proclaimed: "The cold war has ended, or is ending, not because there are victors and vanquished but because there is neither one nor the other."

5. Bush-Gorbachev Summit Conferences

a. The Malta Summit (1989). President Bush met the Soviet leader on a Soviet cruise ship off the Mediterranean island nation of Malta in December 1989. In an atmosphere of cordiality, the two leaders agreed to complete two new arms pacts (on strategic and conventional arms) during 1990. President Bush offered to reduce tariffs on Soviet goods and to support observer status for the Soviet Union in the world trading association, GATT.

b. The Washington Summit (1990). Presidents Bush and Gorbachev met again in May–June 1990 in Washington. They announced an agreement to reduce U.S. and Soviet arsenals of chemical weapons and ordered negotiators to conclude a treaty on drastic reductions in long-range nuclear weapons.

c. The Helsinki Summit (1990). The two leaders displayed a unified view on the Iraq-Kuwait crisis. The Soviet Union supported the United States' buildup in Saudi Arabia. In turn, the U.S. recognized that the USSR had an important role in the Middle East peace process.

6. Key Issues in Russian-American Relations. The collapse of the Soviet Union in late 1991 and its replacement by the Commonwealth of Independent States, headed by Russian President Boris Yeltsin, left a host of questions: *(a)* What could be done to keep nuclear weapons in steady hands? *(b)* How much economic aid should the United States offer to the new Commonwealth? *(c)* Is the new Commonwealth facing a danger of civil war? If so, what should the United States do about it?

The course of human events.
Shanks in the Buffalo Evening News

MULTIPLE-CHOICE QUESTIONS

1. The *least* important factor in explaining the destructiveness of nuclear weapons is their great (1) heat (2) radioactivity (3) blast (4) weight.

2. The Baruch Plan for international control of atomic energy did *not* propose (1) an international authority in which no nation would have the veto power (2) unlimited inspection (3) stockpiling of atomic bombs (4) sharing American atomic know-how with other nations.

3. The Baruch Plan never went into effect because of (1) the U.N.'s lack of interest in the problem (2) American opposition to international control (3) a Russian veto in the U.N. Security Council (4) Britain's refusal to cooperate.

4. Since World War II, the United States has *not* (1) developed atomic artillery (2) exploded hydrogen bombs (3) built nuclear submarines (4) used the atom bomb in Korea.

5. The chief factor that long blocked agreement between Russia and the United States on a nuclear test ban was the dispute regarding (1) admission of Red China to the test ban conference (2) the war in Vietnam (3) effective measures of inspection and control (4) the building of the Berlin Wall.

6. The limited nuclear test ban treaty permits testing (1) in the atmosphere (2) in space (3) below the ground (4) under water.

7. A leading European nation that refused to sign the limited nuclear test ban treaty was (1) Communist China (2) Czechoslovakia (3) France (4) Italy.

8. The "proliferation" of atomic weapons refers to their (1) spread to many nations (2) complexity (3) radiation (4) use to produce electricity.

9. The SALT I accords were signed by President (1) Nixon (2) Eisenhower (3) Carter (4) Ford.

10. In 1957 the first human-made satellite was placed into orbit around the earth by (1) a U.N. team of scientists (2) Russia (3) the United States (4) Great Britain.

11. Which is *not* the name of a Soviet space vehicle? (1) Sputnik (2) Vostok (3) Luna (4) Vladivostok.

12. Which term is *not* associated with the American space effort? (1) NASA (2) Project Apollo (3) falling dominoes (4) Cape Kennedy.

13. The Poseidon is (1) an atomic-powered submarine (2) the name of the project for the flight to the moon (3) an intercontinental ballistic missile (4) a missile capable of being fired from a submerged submarine.

14. Yuri Gagarin of the Soviet Union was the first man to (1) design a space vehicle (2) achieve a space flight (3) die on a space flight (4) take close-up photographs of the moon.

15. The first American astronaut to orbit the earth was (1) Alan Shepard (2) Virgil Grissom (3) John Glenn (4) John Young.

16. The chief object of Project Apollo was to (1) send space teams to the moon and back (2) gather data about Venus and Mars (3) establish a worldwide telecommunications system (4) improve the forecasting of weather.

17. The purpose of an antiballistic missile system is to increase the nation's (1) defensive strength (2) offensive power (3) scientific knowledge (4) ability to carry on nuclear testing below the ground.

18. The term "summit conference" refers to a meeting of the (1) heads of the world's leading nations (2) foreign ministers of the NATO powers (3) members of the U.N. Security Council (4) chiefs of staff of the United States Armed Forces.

19. The summit meeting of 1955 resulted in (1) the keeping of Red China out of the United Nations (2) the admission of East Germany to NATO (3) the barring of Americans from Russia (4) no significant solutions of East-West problems.

20. Which event immediately preceded the 1960 summit conference and led to its collapse? (1) a Russian nuclear test series (2) the Russian intervention in Hungary (3) the invasion by Cuban exiles at the Bay of Pigs (4) the downing of an American U-2 plane inside Russia.

21. Which event indicated a Soviet "hard line" toward the West? (1) establishing the "hot line" communications link (2) signing the limited nuclear test ban treaty (3) placing missiles in Cuba (4) differing with China regarding peaceful coexistence.

ESSAY QUESTIONS

1. While we continue to develop the peaceful uses of atomic energy, we must find a way to deal with the problem of more and more countries possessing nuclear weapons. (a) Mention *one* military development in nuclear energy since 1945 *and one* development of nuclear energy for a peaceful use. (b) Name *two* international agreements regarding nuclear energy and evaluate *each* as a means of reducing the possibility of nuclear warfare.

2. Science has taught us how to put the atom to work, but to make it work for good instead of evil is a problem in human relations. (a) Prove briefly that science has "put the atom to work." (b) Give *two* facts to show how the atom can "work for good instead of for evil." (c) Show why the major world problem today is not man's progress in science, but man's relationship to his fellow human beings.

3. Give *two* reasons for agreeing or disagreeing with *each* of the following statements: (a) It would have been better for humanity if nuclear energy had never been discovered. (b) The development of nuclear energy has increased the military security of the United States. (c) The INF Treaty was a major step toward world peace. (d) The space age will affect humanity as much as did the 16th-century age of discovery and exploration. (e) Now that the cold war is over, the United States can reduce its arsenal of nuclear weapons.

4. United States foreign policy since 1945 has had three specific goals: (a) the defense of the United States against attack, (b) the maintenance of world peace, (c) the promotion of economic and social welfare abroad. Discuss *two* specific means used by the United States in an effort to accomplish *each* of these goals.

INDEX